ISBN 978-1-5279-9162-0
PIBN 10982982

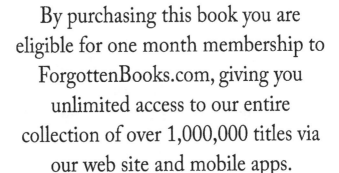

8 - 10 - 45

No. 10437

United States

Circuit Court of Appeals

For the Ninth Circuit.

RICHFIELD OIL CORPORATION, a corporation,

Petitioner,

vs.

NATIONAL LABOR RELATIONS BOARD,

Respondent.

Transcript of Record

Upon Petition for Review and for Enforcement of an Order of the National Labor Relations Board

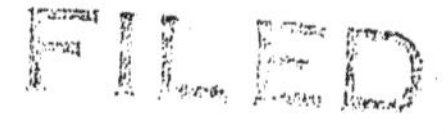

Rotary Colorprint, 590 Folsom St., San Francisco

No. 10437

United States
Circuit Court of Appeals
For the Ninth Circuit.

RICHFIELD OIL CORPORATION, a corporation,

Petitioner,

vs.

NATIONAL LABOR RELATIONS BOARD,

Respondent.

Transcript of Record

Upon Petition for Review and for Enforcement of an Order of the National Labor Relations Board

Rotary Colorprint, 590 Folsom St., San Francisco

INDEX

[Clerk's Note: When deemed likely to be of an important nature, errors or doubtful matters appearing in the original certified record are printed literally in italic; and, likewise, cancelled matter appearing in the original certified record is printed and cancelled herein accordingly. When possible, an omission from the text is indicated by printing in italic the two words between which the omission seems to occur.]

Page

Index Page

Index Page

Index **Page**

Index Page

Index Page

BOARD'S EXHIBIT NO. 1-A

United States of America
Before the National Labor Relations Board
21st Region

Case No. XXI C 2249

Date Filed 1/6/43

In the Matter of—

RICHFIELD OIL CORPORATION

and

PACIFIC DIST., SEAFARERS' INTL. ENGINE DIVISION, affil. Seafarers Intl. Union of North America, AFL

CHARGE

Pursuant to Section 10 (b) of the National Labor Relations Act, the undersigned hereby charges that Richfield Oil Corporation at Richfield Bldg., Los Angeles, Calif. employing approx. 60 in unit workers in operation of oil tankers has engaged in and is engaging in unfair labor practices within the meaning of Section 8 subsections (1) of said Act, in that since October 1942 the above named Corporation has refused and now refuses to grant passes to the undersigned labor organization, the duly authorized bargaining agent of all unlicensed personnel in the engine department of the Richfield Oil Corporation's Pacific Coast oil tankers, for the purpose of going on board in order to investigate and negotiate concerning grievances, said Corporation thereby interfering with, restraining and coercing its employees in the exercise of the rights guaranteed in Section 7 of the said Act. in violation of Section 8, subsection (1) of said Act.

The undersigned further charges that said unfair labor practices are unfair labor practices affecting commerce within the meaning of said Act.

Name and address of person or labor organization making the charge. (If made by a labor organization, give also the full name, local number and affiliation of organization, and name and official position of the person acting for the organization.)

PACIFIC DIST., SEAFARERS' INTL. ENGINE DIVISION, affil. Seafarers Intl. Union of No. America, AFL

By HARRY LUNDEBERG,
President
110 Market St.,
San Francisco, Calif.

Subscribed and sworn to before me this 6 day of January, 1943 At Los Angeles, California

E. J. EAGEN, Director
National Labor Relations Board
21st Region,
Los Angeles, Calif.

BOARD'S EXHIBIT NO. 1-B

United States of America
Before the National Labor Relations Board
21st Region

Case No. XXI C 2248
Date Filed 1/6/43

In the Matter of—

RICHFIELD OIL CORPORATION

and

PACIFIC DISTRICT, SEAFARERS' INTL. STEWARDS DIVISION, affil. Seafarers Intl. Union of North America, AFL

CHARGE

Pursuant to Section 10 (b) of the National Labor Relations Act, the undersigned hereby charges that Richfield Oil Corporation at Richfield Building, Los Angeles, California employing approx. 50 in unit workers in operation of oil tankers has engaged in and is engaging in unfair labor practices within the meaning of Section 8 subsections (1) of said Act, in that since October 1942 the above-named company has refused and now refuses to grant passes to the undersigned labor organization, the duly authorized bargaining agent of all unlicensed personnel in the stewards' department of the Richfield Oil Corporation's Pacific Coast oil tankers, for the purpose of going on board in order to investigate and negotiate concerning grievances, said Corporation thereby interfering with, restraining and coercing its employees in the exercise of the rights guaranteed in Section 7 of the said Act, in violation of Section 8, subsection (1) of said Act.

The undersigned further charges that said unfair labor practices are unfair labor practices affecting commerce within the meaning of said Act.

Name and address of person or labor organization making the charge. (If made by a labor organization, give also the full name, local number and affiliation of organization, and name and official position of the person acting for the organization.)

PACIFIC DISTRICT, SEAFARERS' INTL. STEWARDS DIV., affl. Seafarers Intl. Union of North America, AFL
By HARRY LUNDEBERG,
President
110 Market St.,
San Francisco, Calif.
Phone: Garfield 8225
5659

Subscribed and sworn to before me this 6 day of January, 1943 At Los Angeles, California

E. J. EAGEN, Director
National Labor Relations Board
21st Region,
Los Angeles, Calif.

BOARD'S EXHIBIT No. 1-C

United States of America
Before the National Labor Relations Board
Twenty-first Region

Case No. XXI C 2248

Date Filed 1/28/43

In the Matter of—

RICHFIELD OIL CORPORATION

and

SAILORS UNION OF THE PACIFIC, AFL

FIRST AMENDED CHARGE

Pursuant to Section 10 (*b*) of the National Labor Relations Act, the undersigned hereby charges that Richfield Oil Corporation at Richfield Building, Los Angeles, California employing approx. 50 in unit workers in operation of oil tankers has engaged in and is engaging in unfair labor practices within the meaning of Section 8 subsections (1) of said Act, in that since October, 1942 the above-named company has refused and now refuses to grant passes to the undersigned labor organization, the duly authorized bargaining agent of all unlicensed personnel in the deck department of the Richfield Oil Corporation's Pacific Coast oil tankers, for the purpose of going on board in order to investigate and negotiate concerning grievances, said Corporation thereby interfering with, restraining and coercing its employees in the exercise of the rights guaranteed in Section 7 of the said Act, in violation of Section 8, subsection (1) of said Act.

The undersigned further charges that said unfair labor practices are unfair labor practices affecting commerce within the meaning of said Act.

Name and address of person or labor organization making the charge. (If made by a labor organization, give also the full name, local number and affiliation of organization, and name and official position of the person acting for the organization.)

SAILORS UNION OF THE PACIFIC, AFL
By HARRY LUNDEBERG,
Secretary-Treasurer
110 Market St.,
San Francisco, Calif.
Phone GArfield 8225
5659

Subscribed and sworn to before me this 27th day of Jan., 1943 At San Francisco, Cal.

[Seal] MARIE H. TUTTLE
Notary Public in and for the City and County of San Francisco, State of California.

My Commission Expires Dec. 15, 1946

BOARD'S EXHIBIT NO. 1-D

United States of America

National Labor Relations Board

I, John E. Lawyer, Chief of the Order Section of the National Labor Relations Board, and official custodian of its records, do hereby certify that attached is a full, true, and complete copy of: Order Consolidating Cases In the Matter of Richfield Oil Corporation and Sailors Union of the Pacific, AFL Case No. XXI-C-2248. Richfield Oil Corporation and Pacific Dist. Seafarers' Intl. Engine Division, affil. Seafarers Intl. Union of North America, AFL Case No. XXI-C-2249.

In Witness Whereof, I have hereunto subscribed my name and caused the seal of the National Labor Relations Board to be affixed this 18th day of February A. D. 1943, at Washington, D. C.

(Seal) JOHN E. LAWYER

Chief, Order Section

United States of America
Before the National Labor Relations Board

Case No. XXI-C-2248

In the Matter of

RICHFIELD OIL CORPORATION

and

SAILORS UNION OF THE PACIFIC, AFL

Case No. XXI-C-2249

RICHFIELD OIL CORPORATION

and

PACIFIC DIST., SEAFARERS' INTL. ENGINE DIVISION, affil. Seafarers Intl. Union of North America, AFL

ORDER CONSOLIDATING CASES

A charge and amended charge, pursuant to Section 10 (b) of the Act, having been filed by Sailors Union of the Pacific, AFL, in Case No. XXI-C-2248, and a charge having been duly filed by Pacific District, Seafarers' International Engine Division, affiliated Seafarers International Union of No. America, AFL, in Case No. XXI-C-2249, and the Board having duly considered the matter, and deeming it necessary in order to effectuate the purposes of the National Labor Relations Act,

It Is Hereby Ordered, pursuant to Article II, Section 36 (b) of National Labor Relations Board

Rules and Regulations—Series 2, as amended, that these cases be, and they hereby are, consolidated.

Dated, Washington, D. C., February 17, 1943.

By direction of the Board:

[Seal] JOHN E. LAWYER
Chief, Order Section

BOARD'S EXHIBIT NO. 1-E

[Title of Board and Causes.]

COMPLAINT

It have been charged by Sailors Union of the Pacific, AFL, and by Pacific District, Seafarers' International Engine Division, affiliated with Seafarers' International Union of North America, AFL, that Richfield Oil Corporation, hereinafter called the Respondent, has engaged in, and is engaging in, certain unfair labor practices affecting commerce as set forth and defined in the National Labor Relations Act, 49 Stat. 449, hereinafter referred to as the Act, the National Labor Relations Board, by its Regional Director for its Twenty-first Region, designated as Agent of said National Labor Relations Board by its Rules and Regulations—Series 2, as amended, hereby issues its Complaint, and alleges the following:

1. The Respondent is, and at all times herein referred to has been, a corporation organized and existing under and by virtue of the laws of the State of Delaware, having its principal office at

Los Angeles, California. Respondent is engaged in the business of producing crude oil and natural gas, and manufacturing, selling and distributing petroleum products in the states of California, Washington, Oregon, Arizona, Nevada, Idaho and Utah.

2. Respondent, in the course and conduct of its business, as described above, causes, and has continuously caused, large quantities of materials and supplies to be purchased, obtained, shipped and transported in interstate and foreign commerce from and through various states of the United States, and from and through foreign countries.

3. Respondent, in the course and conduct of its business, as described above, causes, and has continuously caused, large quantities of its products to be sold, shipped and transported in interstate and foreign commerce into and through various states of the United States and into and through foreign countries.

4. (a) Sailors Union of the Pacific, a division of Seafarers' International Union of North America, affiliated with the American Federation of Labor, hereinafter called Sailors Union, is a labor organization within the meaning of Section 2, Subsection (5) of the Act.

(b) Seafarers' International Engine Division, a division of Seafarers' International Union of North America, affiliated with the American Federation of Labor, hereinafter called Seafarers Engine Division, is a labor organization within the meaning of Section 2, subsection (5) of the Act.

5. (a) Sailors Union is, and has been at all times herein mentioned, the exclusive representative for the purpose of collective bargaining with the Respondent, of all unlicensed personnel in the deck department of the Respondent's Pacific Coast oil tankers.

(b) Seafarers' Engine Division has been at all times herein mentioned the exclusive representative for the purpose of collective bargaining with the Respondent, of all unlicensed personnel in the engine department of the Respondent's Pacific Coast oil tankers.

6. The Respondent while engaged in the course and conduct of its business, as set out above, on or about October 1942, did refuse, and at all times since that date has refused, to permit duly authorized representatives of Sailors Union, and duly authorized representatives of Seafarers Engine Division to go aboard the Respondent's Pacific Coast oil tankers, and at all times herein mentioned has prevented such representatives from going aboard said vessels.

7. The Respondent, by the acts set forth in paragraph 6 above has interfered with, coerced and restrained, and is interfering with, coercing and restraining its employees in the exercise of rights guaranteed in Section 7 of the Act, and has thereby engaged in, and is thereby engaging in, unfair labor practices within the meaning of Section 8, subsection (1) of the Act.

8. The aforesaid acts of the Respondent set forth in paragraph 6 above constitute unfair labor

practices within the meaning of Section 8, subsection (1), and Section 2, subsections (6) and (7) of the Act.

9. The aforesaid acts of the Respondent, as set forth in paragraph 6 above, occurring in connection with the business operations of the Respondent as described herein above, have a close, intimate and substantial relation to trade, traffic and commerce among the several states and between the states of the United States and foreign countries, and tend to lead to labor disputes, burdening and obstructing commerce and the free flow of commerce.

Wherefore, the National Labor Relations Board on this 19th day of February 1943, issues its Complaint against Richfield Oil Corporation, Respondent herein.

[Seal] E. J. EAGEN

Regional Director National Labor Relations Board
808 Post Office and Court House
Los Angeles, California.

BOARD'S EXHIBIT No. 1-F

[Title of Board and Causes.]

NOTICE OF HEARING

Please Take Notice that on the 4th day of March, 1943, at 10:30 A. M. in Room 808, U. S. Post office and Court House, Los Angeles, California, a hearing will be conducted before a duly designated Trial Examiner of the National Labor Relations Board on the allegations set forth in the Complaint attached hereto, at which time and place you will have the right to appear in person, or otherwise, and give testimony.

A copy of the Charges upon which the Complaint is based is attached hereto.

You are further notified that you have the right to file with the Regional Director for the Twenty-first Region, with offices at 808 U. S. Post Office and Court House, Los Angeles, California, acting in this matter as agent of the National Labor Board, an answer to the said Complaint, within ten (10) days from the service thereof.

Please Take Notice that duplicates of all exhibits which are offered in evidence will be required unless, pursuant to request or motion, the Trial Examiner in the exercise of his discretion and for good cause shown, directs that a given exhibit need not be duplicated.

In Witness Whereof the National Labor Relations Board has caused this, its Complaint and Notice of Hearing, to be signed by the Regional

Director for the Twenty-first Region on this 19th day of February, 1943.

[Seal] ELWYN J. EAGEN
Director
National Labor Relations Board 21st Region,
Los Angeles, California

BOARD'S EXHIBIT NO. 1-G

[Title of Board and Causes.]

AFFIDAVIT AS TO SERVICE

State of California
County of Los Angeles—ss.

I, Lee Smedley being duly sworn, depose and say that I am an employee of the National Labor Relations Board, in the 21st Region at Los Angeles, Cal.; on the 19th day of February, 1943, I served by postpaid registered mail, bearing Government frank, a copy of Complaint, Notice of Hearing and Charges to the following named persons, addressed to them at the following addresses:

Pacific Dist., Seafarers' Intl. Engine Division affil. Seafarers Intl. Union of No. America, AFL
110 Market St.
San Francisco
California

Richfield Oil Corporation
Richfield Building
Los Angeles, California

Sailors Union of the Pacific, AFL
110 Market St.
San Francisco, California

LEE SMEDLEY

Subscribed and sworn to before me this 19th day of February, 1943

MARION ANDERSON
Designated Agent, N.L.R.B.

BOARD'S EXHIBIT NO. 1-H

REGISTERED RECEIPTS OF COMPLAINT, NOTICE OF HEARING AND CHARGES

[Printer's Note: Boards Exhibit No. 1-H consists of three registered mail receipts and three return cards. Registered mail receipt No. 384808, dated Los Angeles, Calif., Feb. 19, 1943. Return card receipt for Registered mail No. 384808 is addressed to National Labor Relations Board, Los Angeles, Calif., and is signed by Richfield Oil Corp. by B. J. Sanders. Date of delivery, Feb. 22, 1943, Registered mail receipt No. 384809, dated Los Angeles, Calif., Feb. 19, 1943. Return card receipt for Registered mail No. 384809 is addressed to National Labor Relations Board, Los Angeles, Calif., and is signed by S.I.U., by T. O. Skinner. Date of delivery, 2-23, 1943. Registered mail receipt No. 384810, dated

Los Angeles, Calif., Feb. 19, 1943. Return card receipt for Registered mail No. 384810 is addressed to National Labor Relations Board, Los Angeles, Calif., and is signed by S.U.P., by T. O. Skinner. Date of delivery, 2-23, 1943.]

BOARD'S EXHIBIT No. 1-I

[Title of Board and Causes.]

ANSWER

Comes now Respondent Richfield Oil Corporation and for answer to the complaint herein in the above causes, admits, denies and alleges as follows:

I.

Admits the allegations contained in paragraph numbered 1 of the complaint.

II.

Admits the allegations contained in paragraph numbered 2 of the complaint.

III.

Admits the allegations contained in paragraph numbered 3 of the complaint.

IV.

Admits the allegations contained in paragraphs numbered 4 (a) and 4 (b) of the complaint.

V.

Admits the allegations contained in paragraphs numbered 5 (a) and 5 (b) of the complaint.

VI.

Admits the allegations contained in paragraph numbered 6 of the complaint.

VII.

Denies each, every and all of the allegations contained in paragraph numbered 7 and in this connection specifically denies that Respondent has interfered with, coerced, and restrained, and is interfering with, coercing and restraining its employees in the exercise of rights guaranteed in Section 7 of the National Labor Relations Act, or other rights or at all, and further, specifically denies that Respondent's acts as alleged in paragraph 6 of the complaint constitute an unfair labor practice within the meaning of Section 8, Subsection (1) of the National Labor Relations Act, or otherwise, or at all.

VIII.

Denies each, every and all of the allegations contained in paragraph numbered 8 of the complaint, and in this connection Respondent specifically denies that any of its acts as set forth in paragraph 6 of the complaint constitute unfair labor practices within the meaning of Section 8, Subsection (1), and Section 2, Subsections (6) and (7) of the National Labor Relations Act, or otherise, or at all.

IX.

Admits that Respondent's acts as set forth in paragraph 6 of the complaint occurred in connection with the business operations of Respondent and that such acts have a close and intimate relation to trade, traffic, and commerce among the several states and between the states of the United States and foreign countries, and except as herein expressly admitted, denies each, every and all of the allegations contained in paragraph numbered 9 of the complaint.

As a further and affirmative answer to the complaint herein, Respondent alleges:

I.

That shortly after the declaration of war by the United States against Germany, Italy and Japan, Respondent resolved to cancel all existing passes to its ships as soon as existing contracts with Unions, including the Sailors' Union of the Pacific, would permit, and resolved further to refuse during the remainder of the period of the war to issue passes to any person or persons not in its employ; that such cancellation of passes was effected on or about the 15th day of February 1942 and that since that date Respondent has adhered to the policy of refusing passes to any and all persons indiscriminately.

II.

That on or about the 20th day of February, 1942, Respondent was notified by the Regional Director of the National Labor Relations Board for the Twenty-First Region, in case No. XXI-C-2001 that the National Maritime Union of America had filed a charge pursuant to Section 10(c) of the National Labor Relations Act alleging that this Respondent was engaging in unfair labor practices within the meaning of Section 8, Subsection (1) of the Act, by refusing permission to officers of said Union to visit vessels of this respondent and to talk with members of its Union on said vessels; that upon Respondent's showing that it had adopted a policy of not granting any passes to anyone for the period of the war, the Regional Director refused to issue a complaint and upon appeal, the National Labor Relations Board upheld him in so refusing.

III.

That Respondent's policy of refusing to grant passes to any one was adopted for the sole purpose of promoting the war effort by safeguarding, not only the tank vessels, cargoes, and terminal facilities, but also safeguarding the lives of officers and men employed upon such vessels; that the establishing and carrying out of such policy is not an unfair labor practice within the meaning of Section 8 of the National Labor Relations Act, but on the contrary, is a reasonable exercise of the prudent judgment of Respondent in the conduct of its business and in its capacity as Agent of the War Shipping Administration.

IV.

That this Respondent is informed and believes and therefore alleges that if it were to issue passes to representatives of the complaining Unions, it would be an unfair labor practice to refuse similar passes to other labor representatives requesting the same, and Respondent would be required to issue passes indiscriminately to all labor representatives requesting the same, thereby increasing the number of persons having access to the vessels and port facilities, resulting in multiplying the possibilities of acts inimicable to the war effort and security of the personnel, the vessels, cargoes, and shore installations.

V.

That to require this Respondent to issue passes would subject Respondent's vessels, their personnel and cargoes, and the port facilities to grave, unreasonable and wholly unnecessary hazards because of:

(1) Negligent acts of pass holders likely to result in

(a) Fires and explosions;

(b) Personal injuries and death;

(c) Damage to or loss of vessels, cargoes and port facilities.

(2) Increased hazards of tank ship loading and unloading of highly inflammable cargoes.

(3) Lessening of efficiency of men on watch aboard through distraction from their duties, possibly resulting in——

(a) Admixture of products;

(b) Breaking of lines;

(c) Spilling inflammable products.

(4) Facilitating the acquisition of information valuable to the enemy, such as:
   (a) Vessel armament;
   (b) Courses, destinations, routes;
   (c) Cargoes;
   (d) Ports of Call;
   (e) Escort vessels, convoys, etc.

(5) Facilitating sabotage, such as tampering with armament, machinery and equipment, and similar acts.

(6) Lessening the efficiency of the port watch against sabotage and the approach of unauthorized persons and craft to the vessel and port facilities, through distraction from their duties.

VI.

That to require this Respondent to issue passes would violate war time security and safety rules of the Captain of the Port, Los Angeles-Long Beach Harbor area, by giving access to Terminal facilities and vessels to persons whose presence is unnecessary.

VII.

That to require this Respondent to issue passes would result in violation of Security Orders of the War Shipping Administration which require the strictest secrecy as to armament, courses, departures, destinations, cargoes, escort vessels, convoys, and the like, and which require that "visitors to piers and vessels should be limited to cases of absolute necessity."

VIII.

That to require this Respondent to issue passes would violate the General Orders of the War Shipping Administration which require the utmost dispatch in the handling of the vessels and their cargoes.

IX.

That to require this Respondent to issue passes would constitute a violation of the Statement of Policy agreed upon between the War Shipping Administration and various Unions, including the complaining Unions herein, which prohibits "crews' mass meetings, and crews' committee meetings, and other similar meetings aboard ship.".

X.

That Respondent is informed and believes and therefore alleges that the issuing of passes could only result in organization efforts, not only by the complaining Unions, but by rival Unions, leading to jurisdictional disputes and interference with the handling of the vessel and the vessel's business with the utmost dispatch, as required by orders of the War Shipping Administration.

XI.

That tank vessels under the present war conditions constitute one of the most precious assets of our Nation and their protection demands the utmost diligence and care, and further, outweighs any mere inconvenience to individuals whether they be representatives of organized labor or representatives of the vessel owners.

XII.

That Respondent is not operating its vessels merely as an owner in peace time but, on the contrary, is operating said vessels as Agent for and under the direction of the United States Government, acting by and through the War Shipping Administration; that the operation of said vessels under present exigencies, in fact, constitutes emergency operations, making it imperative to handle cargoes with the utmost dispatch, thereby greatly increasing the everyday hazards of loading and discharging and other port activities, making it necessary to take not only ordinary precautions but to take extraordinary precautions to safeguard the vessels, their invaluable personnel, the cargoes, and shore facilities.

XIII.

That precautionary measures which under ordinary peace time conditions would be considered strict and technical, become commonplace and imperative under war time conditions.

Wherefore, this Respondent prays that the complaint issued herein be dismissed.

[Seal] RICHFIELD OIL CORPORATION,
Respondent herein,
By CLEVE B. BONNER,
Its Secretary.
DAVID GUNTERT,
Attorney for Respondent.

State of California
County of Los Angeles—ss.

Cleve B. Bonner being first duly sworn, deposes and says: That he is an officer, to wit, secretary of Richfield Oil Corporation, Respondent herein; that he has read the foregoing Answer and knows the contents thereof; that the same is true of his own knowledge except as to matters which are therein stated on information and belief and that as to those matters he believes the same to be true.

CLEVE B. BONNER.

Subscribed and sworn to before me this 1st day of March, 1943.

[Seal] CHAS. A. ROOT,
Notary Public in and for said County and State.
My Commission Expires Mar. 29, 1944.

[Title of Board and Causes.]

Messrs. Charles M. Ryan and Thomas C. Moore, for the Board.

Mr. David Guntert of Los Angeles, California, for the Respondent.

Mr. Harry Lundeberg of San Francisco, California, for the Unions.

INTERMEDIATE REPORT.

Statement of the Case.

Upon an amended charge duly filed by Sailors Union of the Pacific, affiliated with the American

Federation of Labor, and upon a charge duly filed by the Pacific District, Seafarers' International Engine Division, affiliated Seafarers' International Union of North America, affiliated with the American Federation of Labor, herein called the Unions, the National Labor Relations Board herein called the Board, by the Regional Director for the Twenty-first Region (Los Angeles, California,) issued its consolidated complaint[1] dated February 19, 1943, against the Richfield Oil Corporation, herein called the respondent, alleging that the respondent had engaged in and was engaging in unfair labor practices within the meaning of Section 8 (1) and Section 2 (6) and (7) of the National Labor Relations Act, 49 Stat. 449, herein called the Act.

With respect to the unfair labor practices, the consolidated complaint, as further amended at the hearing, alleged in substance that the respondent on or about October 1942, and at all times thereafter refused to permit the duly authorized representatives of the Unions to go aboard the respondent's Pacific Coast oil tankers, thereby interfering with, restraining, and coercing its employees in the exercise of the rights guaranteed in Section 7 of the Act.

Copies of the complaint, accompanied by notice of hearing were duly served upon the respondent and the charging Unions.

---

(1) The Board on February 17, 1943, pursuant to Article II, Section 36 (b) of the Rules and Regulations, as amended, ordered the consolidation of the cases herein.

In its answer the respondent admitted refusing passes to the duly authorized representatives of the Unions but denied the alleged unfair labor practices and interposed several affirmative defenses to the allegations of unfair labor practices.

Pusurant to notice, a hearing was held on March 4, and 5, 1943, at Los Angeles, California, before James C. Batten, the undersigned Trial Examiner duly designated by the Chief Trial Examiner. The Board and the respondent were represented by counsel and the Unions by their representative. All parties participated in the hearing and were afforded full opportunity to be heard, to examine and cross-examine witnesses, and to introduce evidence bearing on the issues. During the course of the hearing, the Board's motion to amend the consolidated complaint was granted without objection on the part of the respondent.[2] At the conclusion of the hearing, the Board moved to conform the pleadings to the proof as to minor details. The motion was granted without objection.

At the conclusion of the hearing counsel for the Board and the respondent and the Unions' representative argued orally. The undersigned advised all parties that they might file briefs provided such briefs were submitted within 5 days from the close of the hearing. Briefs were filed by the Board and respondent and the Unions.

---

(2) The motion to amend referred to paragraph 5 (b) of the complaint, by inserting after the words "Seafarers' Engine Division" the words "is and."

From the entire record thus made and from the undersigned's observation of the witnesses, the undersigned makes in addition to the above, the following:

FINDINGS OF FACT.

I. The business of the respondent.

Richfield Oil Corporation is a Deleware corporation, authorized to do business in the State of California, with its principal place of business at Los Angeles, California. The respondent operates ocean-going oil tankers which transport its petroleum products between the various ports of the Pacific Coast and certain unidentified off-shore ports. The respondent's oil tankers are now under time charter with the War Shipping Administration, it acting as an agent of the Administration in the operation of the tankers:[3] The respondent admits that it is engaged in commerce within the meaning of the Act. The undersigned finds that the Richfield Oil Corporation is engaged in the operation of its oil tankers in traffic, transportation, and commerce among the several States on the Pacific Coast and certain unidentified off-shore ports, and that its employees thereon are directly engaged in such traffic, transportation, and commerce.

---

(3) This war-time arrangement does not affect the respondent's control over the hire and tenure of its seamen or their conditions of employment. The respondent operates its tankers as usual, except for certain security restrictions promulgated by governmental agencies.

II. The organizations involved.

Sailors Union of the Pacific, a division of Seafaring International Union of North America, is a labor organization affiliated with the American Federation of Labor. It admits to its membership the unlicensed personnel employed in the deck department on the respondent's oil tankers.

Seafarers' International Engine Division, a division of Seafarers' International Union of North America, is a labor organization affiliated with the American Federation of Labor. It admits to its membership the unlicensed personnel employed in the engine department on the respondent's oil tankers.

III. Unfair labor practices.

A. The issue and the contentions of the parties.

The complaint alleges and the respondent admits that the Unions are and have been at all times material herein, the exclusive representatives of the unlicensed deck and engine personnel on board the respondent's tankers and that the Unions were refused by the respondent passes for the purpose of access by their duly authorized representatives to go aboard the tankers. The sole question in the case is whether, as the complaint alleges, such refusal to grant access by the respondent interfered with, restrained, and coerced, and is interfering with, restraining, and coercing the respondent's unlicensed deck and engine personnel in their exercise of the rights guaranteed in Section 7 of the Act, thereby violating Section 8 (1) of the Act.

The Board contends under the circumstances of

the operations of the respondent, hereinafter related, a denial of passes to the Union's duly authorized representatives interferes with the right of the unlicensed deck and engine personnel to bargain collectively through representatives of their own choosing and to engage in concerted activities for their mutual aid and protection.

The Unions contend that since September 23, 1942, the date upon which the Unions were certified as the collective bargaining representatives for the unlicensed deck and engine personnel on respondent's tankers, they have sought passes for their representatives through direct negotiations, for the purpose of settling grievances on board the tankers. The Unions state that the refusal of access to respondent's tankers, denies to the unlicensed deck and engine personnel, who are unable to adequately adjust grievances, the right to have their own chosen representatives negotiate adjustments for them.

The respondent asserts that the denial of passes to its tankers, on a non-discriminatory basis, is not interference within the meaning of Section 8 (1) of the Act; that on December 7, 1941, as a precautionary measure to protect its tankers and personnel from unnecessary hazards, all passes to board its tankers were cancelled except those of the Unions and that upon the expiration of contracts with the Unions, the passes of the Union's representatives were cancelled; that to require the respondent to issue passes to the Union's representatives would violate the war security and safety regulations of the "Captain of the Port," Los Angeles,

Long Beach Harbor, the Security Orders of the "War Shipping Administration," and the Statement of Policy agreed upon between the "War Shipping Administration" and various unions, including the Unions herein, which prohibits "crews' mass meetings, crews' committee meetings, and other similar meetings aboard ship"; and finally that to require the respondent to grant passes to the representatives of the Unions here involved would force it to grant passes to representatives of all unions desirious of coming on board its tankers, in order to avoid charges of discrimination.[4]

B. Interference with the exercise of the rights guaranteed in Section 7 of the Act.

1. The necessity for the right of access[5]

In the exercise of the rights guaranteed in Section 7, the Act provides that "Employees shall have

---

(4) The respondent's contention that the Regional Director's (Twenty-first) refusal, on February 20, 1942, to issue a complaint, upon a charge by the National Maritime Union, that respondent had denied passes for representatives is a bar to the present proceeding, is without merit, either upon the theory of estoppel or res judicata. It is noted that the National Maritime Union was not the duly authorized representative of the respondent's unlicensed seamen.

(5) The term "access" in the shipping industry means the boarding of vessels by union representatives, in order to ascertain whether or not seamen on board have grievances, to determine the validity of the alleged grievances, and to settle those possible of settlement with the proper officials on board the vessels.

the right to . . . bargain collectively through representatives of their own choosing, for the purpose of collective bargaining. . . .'' Since it is obvious that grievances concern "conditions of work'' within the meaning of Section 9 (a) of the Act, they are proper subjects for collective bargaining. It follows that Section 7 guaranteed employees the right to bargain collectively concerning grievances. The Unions herein are the collective bargaining representatives of all the unlicensed deck and engine personnel employed on the respondent's tankers.'[6] Therefore any interference by the respondent with the employees' rights to bargain collectively concerning grievances through their duly designated representatives, the Unions, is proscribed by Section 8(1) of the Act.

In order to determine whether or not denial of passes to the representatives of the Unions for the purpose of obtaining access to respondent's tankers to confer with the unlicensed deck and engine personnel thereon, interferes with the rights of these employees to bargain collectively through their duly chosen representatives concerning grievances, it is essential to give consideration to the operations of the respondent's tankers and to the collective bargaining procedure in dealing with grievances in the tanker and shipping industry.

---

(6) The Sailors Union of the Pacific and the Seafarers' International Union were certified by the Board on September 23, 1942, as the exclusive representatives, respectively, of the unlicensed deck and unlicensed engine personnel on respondent's tankers.

The respondent operates six ocean-going tankers which ply between Pacific Coast ports, including Seattle, Washington, Portland, Oregon, San Francisco, California, and the Los Angeles, California area (Long Beach, Wilmington, San Pedro and Terminal Island) and off-shore and foreign ports. The loading and discharging terminals in the Pacific Coast ports are in most instances located in the bay areas some distances from the shipping districts, requiring a round trip of from 1 hour to 3 hours to the Unions' office. Coast-wise trips require several days each way, and off-shore and foreign trips require substantially longer periods. Respondent's tankers spend approximately 30 hours discharging cargo and approximately 14 hours in loading a cargo.[7] The usual tanker crew on respondent's vessels comprises 38 men, 27 of them unlicensed personnel distributed as follows: 11 in the deck department, 9 in the engine department, and 8 in the steward's department. "Watches" are maintained for certain seamen while the tankers are in port, while certain other seamen work on miscellaneous jobs such as loading stores, painting and minor repairs. Watches are 4 hour shifts with 8 hours off duty between shifts. Approximately 1/3 of the unlicensed deck and engine personnel, except-

(7) "Port time" as distinguished from discharging and loading time is calculated from the moment the tanker arrives in the harbor until it leaves the harbor; it does not indicate the elapsed time spent at the dock or *or* discharging or loading a cargo. On occasion tankers without docking discharge and load cargoes, either into lighters or from submarine outlets.

ing wipers in the engine room, are on duty at all times. The seamen working on the miscellaneous jobs work at irregular hours depending upon the "extra" work to be performed; the steward's hours of work in port, is determined largely by the number of seamen who eat their meals on the tankers. Stewards may enjoy shore leave only after meals have been served; unlicensed deck and engine personnel, who stand watch cannot be absent from the tanker more than 8 hours, including the time required by them to prepare for their departure and return and they cannot all leave the tanker simultaneously since their watches terminate at different times; those of the seamen who are working on miscellaneous jobs, because of the short time the tankers are at dock, cannot leave the tanker until their work is completed.[8] Although some of the tanker personnel have families and homes in various ports, while employed on the tankers their homes are actually on the vessels, for it is on board that they eat, sleep, and work. Moreover, even those who have homes can only visit them when the tankers happen to arrive in those ports in which the homes are located, and then only during the time normally allotted by the regular schedules of the tankers. The respondent employs approximately 165 unlicensed

(8) At times the respondent employs "work parties" to perform the miscellaneous jobs on the tankers but when as now under war time conditions extra men are not available, the Captain delegates a part of the crew to perform this work.

seamen and as is usual in the shipping industry, there is a large turnover among this personnel.

The union representative in the shipping industry on the Pacific Coast who has access to vessels is known as a "patrolman."[9] When the vessel "docks" the patrolman boards the vessel in order to ascertain whether or not the crew on board have grievances. Is so the patrolman investigates and determines the validity of the alleged grievances and then proceeds to settle those possible of settlement with the master, mate, or the proper official on board the vessel. The patrolmen are experienced seamen and negotiators, whose jurisdiction includes all of the tankers which arrive in the port in which they are on duty.[10] The patrolman functions as follows: He boards the vessel immediately after it is moored to the dock, proceeds to the crews' quarters and confers with the ship's delegate representing the department, (deck, engine, and steward) who relates to the patrolman the various grievances, if any, concerning food, living conditions, or overtime pay which have arisen during the voyage.[11] The patrol-

(9) In some ports known as a "shore delegate."

(10) The record shows that patrolmen are assigned to certain ports and where the performance of a patrolman's duty requires more than one in a port, each is assigned to handle all the vessels of certain companies thus limiting access to one patrolman.

(11) Grievances usually involve one or more of these basic conditions of work. The record indicates that approximately 90 per cent of the grievances reported are disposed of on board the vessel after access by the patrolman in conference with

man then interviews the allegedly aggrieved seaman and decides whether the grievance is meritorious, using as a guide his long experience and intimate knowledge of the nature of seaman's grievances, their attitude toward such grievances and the problems of the shipping industry. In most instances before deciding the merits of the grievances, the patrolman interviews others interested in its adjustment, including the master or other official aboard. If he decides it is a valid grievance the patrolman then attempts settlement with the master or proper official aboard the vessel. If these negotiations fail, the patrolman refers the grievance to the Union Port Committee on shore, who proceed to discuss the grievance with the respondent's shore officials. It is apparent that under this collective bargaining procedure providing for the prompt adjustment of grievances, which necessitates access, the seamen have complete opportunity to confer with their duly designated representatives who are well equipped by training and experience[12] to assess their grievances, and who are specialized negotiators.[13]

---

the proper officials, who have the requisite authority to settle them. The balance of the grievances which are of a major nature are referred to the Union Port Committee, and such grievances constitute as a rule matters affecting the general standards to be applied to the crew as a whole.

(12) Patrolmen must have had, before selection to their positions, 3 years actual sea service.

(13) The refusal to issue passes to the Unions' representatives prevents the most effective sort of

By Section 7 of the Act, "employees shall have the right to self-organization, to form, join, or assist labor organizations . . . for the purpose of . . . mutual aid or protection." Interference, restraint or coercion in the exercise of their rights is also proscribed by Section 8 (1) of the Act. The rights

---

collective action by the seamen. See N.L.R.B. v. Cities Service Oil Co., 122 F. (2d) 149 (C.C.A. 2) where the Second Circuit, per Augustus N. Hand, J., said:

Ships, and particularly these oil tankers, which ordinarily remain in port for a day only, afford less oportunity for investigation of labor conditions than do factories where the employees go home every afternoon and have the evenings at their disposal. There is no cessation of work at the end of each day for seamen on a tanker. A large number of them are on watch, others are loading or discharging cargo; their hours for work and shore leave are different and, in the short time the vessel is in port, it is impossible for Union representatives to assemble the unlicensed personnel either on shore or on shipboard to discuss grievances or investigate conditions. Therefore, the Union must have the members of the crew readily accessible in order to work to any real advantage. Moreover, the complaints frequently relate to conditions on and even of the vessel itself.

It may be true that many, or even most, grievances are settled on the ship by the ship's committee without the intervention of the Union, but one of the prime objects of the Union is to afford the seamen advisors and negotiators who are not continually under the eye of the master and inclined through fear of untoward consequences to defer to his demands. Its advice as to major differences would naturally be needed and in many cases it cannot advise the personnel wisely without visiting the ship and seeing the conditions under which work is done and of which criticism is made.

thus guaranteed to employees against impairment by the employer include full freedom to the employees, upon request, to receive aid, advice and information from their chosen representatives. The issue, presented by the "mutual aid or protection" clause of the Act, is whether the respondent's denial of passes to the chosen representatives of the unlicensed deck and engine personnel, for the purpose of obtaining access to its tankers, under the circumstances of this case, interfered with, restrained, and coerced these employees in the exercise of their rights to obtain the aid of their chosen representatives.

It is unnecessary here to again state the details, hereinbefore related, which make ineffective collective bargaining through chosen representatives, where there is a denial of the right of access, except to note that substantially all of the factors making prohibitive effective bargaining procedure also prevent the unlicensed deck and engine personnel on respondent's tankers from participation in the exercise of their rights to "mutual aid or protection" through representatives chosen by them. Moreover, the denial of access, interferes with the aid and protection the seamen receive through burial and insurance benefits, of special importance during the war, an incident to their membership in the Unions, because of their inability to visit the Union's headquarters to pay current dues.[14]

---

(14) The collection of dues and the distribution of the Unions' newspaper has been and now is considered by the Pacific Coast Shippers, who grant access, a proper form of aid to be given by the

The respondent by not permitting access to the Union's representatives to aid the unlicensed deck and engine personnel at their request, is exercising, "domination and control" over the efforts of these seamen to engage in "mutual aid and protection" thereby infringing upon Section 8 (1) of the Act. To hold otherwise would be, in effect, to exempt the respondent's tankers from the prohibitions of the Act. But Congress did not exclude the respondent's tankers from the operation of the Act, by implication or otherwise. Congress has declared that "the policy of the United States" shall be to remove obstructions to the free flow of commerce "by protecting the exercise by workers of full freedom of association, self-organization and designation of representatives of their own choosing, for the purpose of mutual aid or protection."

The undersigned finds that the denial of right of access to respondent's tankers, by the chosen representatives of the unlicensed deck and engine personnel prevents these seamen from exercising their rights to collective bargaining and to other mutual aid or protection.[15]

---

representatives of the Unions. The respondent's contention that such representatives should not solicit seamen for membership in the Unions is well taken and such practice if persisted in should be grounds for the revocation of the passes of these representatives who engage in such activities.

(15) While the respondent does not clearly assert that other methods, than access, are available to the unlicensed deck and engine personnel to exercise their rights under Section 7, the record suggests the possibility of the seamen visiting union headquarters or of conferring with their represen-

2. Respondent's position—relation of the War to the exercise of the rights guaranteed in Section 7.

The respondent does not in fact, contend that

---

tatives on shore where reports would be made of the grievances. The Court is the Cities Service Case, referring to alternative grievance procedures stated:

Respondents suggest that the so-called ship's committee consisting of three members of the crew chosen by the seamen can present complaints to the ship's officers and if the grievances are not settled thus, can report in person or mail statements to the Union of matters in dispute which the Union may then take up with the respondent's shore officials. But negotiations conducted in such a way would be slow and the men would lack the advantage of having their bargaining agent promptly acquainted with grievances by the seamen themselves and ready at once to negotiate with the shore officials. Moreover, so far as possible the men themselves should have the privilege of airing their individual complaints to their representatives, just as do employees whose work is on land. The suggestion that the Union representatives can be stationed on the dock, there investigate complaints by meeting members of the crew as they come off the ship and after thus learning the facts from seamen can then bargain with respondents' shore officials, is subject to the objection that the dock is manifestly no place for an adequate discussion of labor grievances. Even if, despite the inconvenience, the men were able to visit Union headquarters for such discussion of their grievances, they would not have the presence and backing of experienced bargaining representatives when presenting their claims to the ships' officers. Nor under such restrictions can there be adequate discussion by the delegate with the ships' officers of matters requiring explanation. See N.L.R.B. v. Cities Service Oil Co., 122 F (2d) 149. (C.C.A. 2).

under peace time conditions it would be justified in refusing passes to the duly authorized representatives of its unlicensed deck and engine personnel for the purpose of access to its tankers, but asserts in its answer that the policy of refusing to grant passes to anyone was adopted for the sole purpose of promoting the War effort, by reducing the "grave, unreasonable and wholly unnecessary hazards" incident to non-employees boarding the tankers, and by complying with the war time security orders, rules, and regulations of "Captain of the Port," the "War Shipping Administration" and a "Statement of Policy" issued by the "War Shipping Administration."

Although the respondent considers that the presence of the duly authorized representatives of the unlicensed desk and engine personnel, would increase the hazards to which the tankers are normally exposed, it has not seen fit to exclude laundry agents, extra work parties, not members of the crew and in most instances "picked up", and several employees of the respondent whose presence on the tankers are not essential. In fact the record does not indicate that any individuals formerly permitted access have been denied that right except the Unions' representatives. At the present it is the almost universal practice of the shipping industry on the West Coast to grant access to the duly authorized representatives of their seamen, whether or not such right is provided for in collective bargaining contracts. Access during the War has been granted to representatives to board all types of vessels, including oil tankers, and ships whose entire cargoes, include explosives and war supplies, as well as troops. Frequently the officials of Shipping companies and the military or naval authorities have requested representatives of the seamen to board vessels in order that grievances might be promptly adjusted. Thus, under war time conditions it appears that access is necessary. The respondent is practically alone in its fear of increased hazards from the presence of seamen's representatives on board vessels.[16]

The contention of the respondent that to grant access to the duly authorized representatives of the seamen would violate the war time security, orders, rules or regulations of the "Captain of the Port" (Coast Guard), the "War Shipping Administration" or any other Governmental agency is without merit. Of utmost significance is the fact that the Navy and the Coast Guard have provided the representatives of the respondent's unlicensed deck and engine personnel with the proper identification and

---

(16) The Union's representatives who board tankers are men who are thoroughly familiar with conditions prevailing on such vessels, and with safety precautions which must be taken; more so it would appear, than others who are permitted to board the tankers All docks, terminals, and vessels are now guarded by military or naval personnel. This security measure insures to the respondent the protection needed, by any increased hazards due to the War.

authority to enter restricted areas and to board tankers and vessels, including respondent's tankers, providing respondent issues its passes to the representatives. The War Shipping Administration in a "Statement of Policy" agreed to by the Unions, has stabilized for the duration, collective bargaining contracts which contain provisions for passes for authorized representatives of seamen, thus affording access.[17]

The undersigned does not believe that these contentions of the respondent are valid reasons for denying access.[18]

---

(17) The respondent's allegation in its answer that the "visitors to piers and vessels should be limited to cases of absolute necessity," (Security Orders of the War Shipping Administration) and the prohibition of crews' mass meetings, crews' committee meetings, and other similar meetings aboard ships" (Statement of Policy, War Shipping Administration) does not refer to the duly authorized representatives of unlicensed deck and engine personnel, having access to transact business in conformity with the provisions of the Act. The respondent's admission that no official of any governmental agency has so interpreted these provisions and practices of the shipping industry on the Pacific Coast, would indicate that there is no basis for such position.

(18) The undersigned has given consideration to the various war-time safety laws and the duties and obligations of the Master on respondent's tankers and finds that neither the laws nor the duties of the Master in any way are at variance with the rights of the unlicensed deck and engine personnel to exercise their privileges under the Act.

C. Concluding Findings.

In conclusion, the undersigned finds that respondent's unlicensed deck and engine personnel are in port for a short time with very little time ashore; that tanker terminals are usually located in port areas inaccessible to union headquarters; that collective bargaining procedures for the settlement of grievances, which do not involve access are in a practical sense unworkable, and do not afford the respondent's unlicensed deck and engine personnel the opportunity to bargain collectively concerning their grievances; that the refusal of respondent to issue passes to the duly authorized representatives of its unlicensed deck and engine personnel for the purpose of access, prevents these seamen from receiving aid, advice, and information through their duly chosen representatives; that procedure which involves access, for these purposes is prevalent today, and has long been in use in the West Coast shipping industry; that with access these representatives may investigate the nature of, assess the value of, and properly present grievances on behalf of these seamen and give to them the aid, advice and information essential for mutual protection; that without access, the respondent's unlicensed deck and engine personnel would be denied the benefits of essential rights, conferred upon them by the Act, providing for collective bargaining and other mutual aid through their duly chosen representatives.

It is plain from these findings and from the entire record, and the undersigned finds that the respondent by refusing to grant passes to the duly designated representatives of its unlicensed deck and engine personnel in order that such representatives might confer with and aid such personnel on board respondent's tankers, has interfered with, restrained, and coerced, and by continuing such refusal is interfering with, restraining, and coercing its unlicensed deck and engine personnel in the exercise of the rights guaranteed them in Section 7 of the Act, and is thereby violating Section 8(1) of the Act.

IV. The effect of the unfair labor practices upon commerce.

The activities of the respondent set forth in Section III above, occurring in connection with the operations of the respondent described in Section I above, have a close, intimate, and substantial relation to trade, traffic, and commerce among the several States, and tend to lead to labor disputes burdening and obstructing commerce and the free flow of commerce.

V. The remedy.

Since it has been found that the respondent has engaged in certain unfair labor practices, the undersigned will recommend that it cease and desist therefrom and take certain affirmative action designed to effectuate the policies of the Act.

The undersigned having found that the respondent has interfered with, restrained and coerced its unlicensed deck and engine personnel in the exercise of the right guaranteed in Section 7 by refusing to issue passes to its oil tankers to representatives of the Sailors Union of the Pacific and the Seafarers' International Union of North America, the duly designated collective bargaining representatives of the respondent's unlicensed deck and engine personnel in order to make effective the guarantees of Section 7 of the Act, and thereby to minimize strife which burdens and obstructs commerce, and thus effectuate the policies of the Act, the undersigned will recommend that the respondent issue passes to the unlicensed deck and engine personnels' duly designated representatives of the Sailors Union of the Pacific and the Seafarers' International Union of North America, in order that they may board the respondent's oil tankers and confer with and aid the unlicensed deck and engine personnel thereon.

The respondent contends that if it grants passes to the Unions herein involved, it will also have to grant passes to all unions who demand such passes, to board is vessels, in order to avoid accusations of discrimination. Since the instant case does not involve any union jurisdictional problem and the question of discrimination is not now before the undersigned for decision, he does not decide it.

Upon the basis of the foregoing findings of fact and upon the entire record in this proceeding, the undersigned makes the following:

CONCLUSIONS OF LAW

1. Sailors Union of the Pacific, a division of Seafarers' International Union of North America is a

labor organization within the meaning of Section 2 (5) of the Act.

2. Seafarers' International Engine Division, a division of Seafarers' International Union of North America, is a labor organization within the meaning of Section 2 (5) of the Act.

3. By interfering with, restraining and coercing its employees in the exercise of the rights guaranteed in Section 7 of the Act, the respondent has engaged in and is engaging in unfair labor practices within the meaning of Section 8 (1) of the Act.

4. The aforesaid unfair labor practices are unfair labor practices affecting commerce within the meaning of Section 2 (6) and (7) of the Act.

RECOMMENDATIONS

Upon the basis of the foregoing findings of fact and conclusions of law, the undersigned recommends that the respondent, Richfield Oil Corporation, and its officers, agents, successors, and assigns, shall:

1. Cease and desist from:

(a) Refusing to grant passes to representatives of the Sailors Union of the Pacific, a division of Seafarers' International Union of North America and Seafarers' International Engine Division, a division of Seafarer's International Union of North America, in order that such representatives may go aboard the respondent's vessels and confer with and aid the unlicensed deck and engine personnel thereon;

(b) Engaging in like or related acts or conduct interfering with, restraining or coercing its employees in the exercise of the right of self-organization, to form, join, or assist labor organizations, to bargain collectively through representatives of their own choosing and to engage in concerted activities for the purpose of collective bargaining or other mutual aid or protection as guaranteed in Section 7 of the Act.

2. Take the following affirmative action which will effectuate the policies of the Act:

(a) Grant passes to the duly authorized representatives of the Sailors Union of the Pacific a division of Seafarers' International Union of North America and Seafarers' International Engine Division, a division of Seafarers' International Union of North America, to go aboard its vessels to confer with and aid the unlicensed deck and engine personnel;

(b) Post immediately in conspicuous places on its vessels for a period of at least sixty (60) consecutive days from the date of posting notices to the unlicensed deck and engine personnel, stating: (1) that the respondent will not engage in the conduct from which it is ordered to cease and desist in paragraph 1 (a) and (b); (2) that the respondent will take the affirmative action set forth in paragraph 2 (a) hereof;

(c) Notify the Regional Director for the Twenty-first Region in writing within ten (10) days from the receipt of the Intermediate Report what steps the respondent has taken to comply herewith.

It is further recommended that unless on or before ten (10) days from the receipt of this Intermediate Report the respondent notifies said Regional Director in writing that it will comply with the foregoing recommendations, the National Labor Relations Board issue an order requiring the respondent to take the action aforesaid.

As provided in Section 33 of Article II of the Rules and Regulations of the National Labor Relations Board, Series 2—as amended, effective October 28, 1942—any party may within fifteen (15) days from the date of the entry of the order transferring the case to the Board, pursuant to Section 32 of Article II of said Rules and Regulations, file with the Board, Shoreham Building, Washington, D. C., an original and four copies of a statement in writing setting forth such exceptions to the Intermediate Report or to any other part of the record or proceeding (including rulings upon all motions or objections) as he relies upon, together with the original and four copies of a brief in support thereof. As further provided in said Section 33, should any party desire permission to argue orally before the Board, request therefor must be made in writing to the Board within ten (10) days from the date of the order transferring the case to the Board.

Dated: March 27, 1943.

JAMES C. BATTEN,
Trial Examiner.

[Title of Board and Causes.]

ORDER TRANSFERRING CASE TO THE NATIONAL LABOR RELATIONS BOARD

A hearing in the above-entitled cases having been held before a duly designated Trial Examiner and the Intermediate Report of the said Trial Examiner, a copy of which is annexed hereto, having been filed with the Board in Washington,

It Is Hereby Ordered, pursuant to Article II, Section 32, of National Labor Relations Board Rules and Regulations—Series 2, as amended, that Case No. XXI—C-2248 be, and it hereby is, transferred to and continued before the Board as Case No. C-2568, and that Case No. XXI—C-2249 be, and it hereby is, transferred to and continued before the Board as Case No. C-2569.

Dated, Washington, D. C., March 31, 1943.

By direction of the Board:

[Seal] JOHN H. LAWYER
Chief, Order Section

[Title of Board and Causes.]

EXCEPTIONS TO INTERMEDIATE REPORT

The respondent Richfield Oil Corporation hereby excepts to the Intermediate Report of James C. Batten, Trial Examiner, dated March 27, 1943, in the following particulars:

1. To so much of the Finding of Fact numbered I (footnote 3) which finds—"The respondent operates its tankers as usual,".

2. To Findings of Fact numbered III A, paragraph 1 thereof, appearing on page 1, lines 23-33, inclusive, to the extent that said Findings of Fact do not confine "exclusive representatives of the unlicensed deck and engine personnel on board the respondent's tankers" to matters of collective bargaining; and to the extent that "The sole question in the case" is not confined strictly to a matter of law.

3. To so much of the Findings of Fact numbered III A, paragraph 3 thereof appearing on page 3, which sets forth the contention of the unions that they have sought passes from respondent "for the purpose of settling grievances on board the tankers. The unions state that the refusal of access to respondent's tankers denies to the unlicensed deck and engine personnel, who are unable to adequately adjust grievances, the right to have their own chosen representatives negotiate adjustments for them."

4. To the Findings of Fact numbered III A, paragraph 4 thereof, appearing on pages 3 and 4, to the extent that such Findings of Fact do not completely state respondent's contentions.

5. To the Findings of Fact contained in footnote 4 on page 4 under Findings of Fact numbered III A and to each and every part thereof.

6. To the Findings of Fact contained in foot-

note 5 on page 4 under Findings of Fact numbered III B(1) and to each and every part thereof.

7. To the Findings of Fact contained in paragraphs 1 and 2 under Findings of Fact III B (1) in lines 15-37, inclusive, on page 4, and to each and every part thereof.

8. To so much of the third paragraph of Findings of Fact numbered III B(1) which finds that:

> "the loading and discharging terminals in the Pacific Coast ports are in most instances located in the bay areas some distances from the shipping districts, requiring a round trip of from one hour to three hours to the unions' office."

and to so much thereof as finds that:

> "Stewards may enjoy shore leave only after meals have been served; unlicensed deck and engine personnel, who stand watch, cannot be absent from the tanker for more than eight hours, including the time required by them to prepare for their departure and return, and they cannot all leave the tanker simultaneously since their watches terminate at different times."

9. To so much of the Findings of Fact numbered III B (1) as is contained in the fourth paragraph appearing on page 5, lines 35-45, inclusive, and on page 6, lines 1-19, inclusive, and to each and every part thereof.

10. To Findings of Fact contained in footnote 10, appearing on page 5, under Findings of Fact numbered III B (1) and to each and every part

11. To Findings of Fact contained in footnote 11, appearing on page 6, under Findings of Fact numbered III B (1) and to each and every part thereof.

12. To Findings of Fact contained in footnote 13, appearing on page 6, under Findings of Fact numbered III B (1), and to each and every part thereof.

13. To Findings of Fact contained in paragraph 5 under Findings of Fact numbered III B (1), appearing on page 7, lines 1-14, inclusive, and to each and every part thereof.

14. To Findings of Fact contained in paragraph 6 under Findings of Fact numbered III B (1), appearing on page 7, lines 16-27, inclusive, and to each and every part thereof.

15. To Findings of Fact contained in footnote 14, appearing on page 7, under Findings of Fact numbered III B (1), and to each and every part thereof.

16. To Findings of Fact contained in footnote 15, appearing on pages 7 and 8, under Findings of Fact numbered III B (1), and to each and every part thereof.

17. To Findings of Fact contained in paragraph 7 under Findings of Fact numbered III B (1), appearing on page 7, lines 29-40, inclusive, and each and every part thereof.

18. To Findings of Fact contained in paragraph 8 under Findings of Fact numbered III B (1), appearing on page 7, lines 41-45, inclusive, and each and every part thereof.

19. To so much of paragraph 1 on page 8 under Findings of Fact numbered III B (2) which finds that:

> "The Respondent does not in fact, contend that under peace time conditions it would be justified in refusing passes to the duly authorized representatives of its unlicensed deck and engine personnel for the purpose of access to its tankers,"

20. To Findings of Fact contained in paragraph 2 under Findings of Fact numbered III B (2), appearing on page 8, lines 16-33, inclusive, and on page 9, lines 1-3, inclusive, and each and every part thereof.

21. To Findings of Fact contained in footnote 16, appearing on page 9, under Findings of Fact numbered III B (2), and to each and every part thereof.

22. To Findings of Fact contained in paragraph 3 under Findings of Fact numbered III B (2), appearing on page 9, lines 5-17, inclusive, and to each and every part thereof.

23. To Findings of Fact contained in footnote 17, appearing on page 9, under Findings of Fact numbered III B (2), and to each and every part thereof.

24. To Findings of Fact contained in paragraph 4 under Findings of Fact numbered III B (2) appearing on page 10, lines 19-20, inclusive, reading:

"The undersigned does not believe that these

contentions of the respondent are valid reasons for denying access."

25. To Findings of Fact contained in footnote 18, appearing on page 9, under Findings of Fact numbered III B (2), and to each and every part thereof.

26. To Findings of Fact contained in the first paragraph under Findings of Fact numbered III C appearing on page 9, lines 24-34, inclusive, and on page 10, lines 1-8, inclusive, and each and every part thereof.

27. To Findings of Fact contained in second paragraph under Findings of Fact numbered III C appearing on page 10, lines 10-17, inclusive, and to each and every part thereof.

28. To Findings of Fact contained in Findings of Fact numbered IV appearing on page 10, and to each and every part thereof.

29. To Findings of Fact contained in Findings of Fact numbered V, paragraph 1 thereof, appearing on page 10, and to each and every part thereof.

30. To Findings of Fact contained in Findings of Fact numbered V, paragraph 2 thereof, appearing on page 10, and to each and every part thereof.

31. To so much of the Finding of Fact contained in paragraph 3 of Finding of Fact numbered V on page 10, which finds that:

> "Since the instant case does not involve any union jurisdictional problem and the question of discrimination is not now before the undersigned for decision, he does not decide it."

32. To Conclusions of Law numbered 3 and 4 appearing on page 11, and to each and every part thereof.

33. To Recommendations numbered 1(a), 1(b), 2(a), 2(b), 2(c), and the additional Recommendation contained in lines 52-57, inclusive, on page 11 of the Intermediate Report and to each and every part thereof.

The following exception is taken to rulings of the Trial Examiner upon objections appearing in the record:

1. At page 90 of the record, to the overruling of respondent's objection to testimony concerning passes.

And for general exceptions, respondent states:

1. That the Trial Examiner was prejudiced, and offers in proof thereof the Intermediate Report as compared with the record.

2. That the Board has no jurisdiction over the subject matter of the complaint upon the several grounds set forth in respondent's brief filed herewith.

3. That respondent renews each and every of its objections stated in its answer appearing in the oral argument of respondent's counsel at pages 183-187, inclusive, of the record and set forth in its brief filed with the Trial Examiner.

Wherefore respondent respectfully prays that the complaint against it be dismissed and for such other and further relief as may be just and proper.

Dated at Los Angeles, California, this 9th day of April, 1943.

RICHFIELD OIL CORPORATION
By DAVID GUNTERT
Its Attorney

EXCEPTIONS TO INTERMEDIATE REPORT; GROUNDS OF OBJECTIONS

Respondent's exceptions to the Intermediate Report filed concurrently herewith are based primarily on the following general propositions:

A. The recommendations of the Trial Examiner are improper for the reason that the subject matter of the complaint is outside the jurisdiction of the Board and an order of the Board putting them into effect would be invalid.

B. The recommendations of the Trial Examiner are an attempt through "quasi-judicial legislation" to broaden the power of the National Labor Relations Board so that the Board may write terms and conditions of employment into the contract between this respondent and its employees.

C. The recommendations of the Trial Examiner are improper because they are based on a part only of the N.L.R.B. vs. Cities Service Oil Co. case, 122 Fed. (2d) 149, and directly in conflict with the remaining portion thereof. If any portion of that case is controlling, the remaining portions thereof are also controlling and to the extent that the recommendations are in conflict therewith, they are contrary to law.

D. The recommendations of the Trial Examiner are improper because his findings of fact and conclusions of law, as well as his recommendations, are not based on substantial evidence.

E. If recommendation 1(a) were valid and proper, which we deny, recommendation 1(b) is not proper because it exceeds the power of the Board and is contrary to law.

F. Recommendation 2(a) is improper because it is an order of the Board directing respondent to do acts which the respondent is not required to do by the National Labor Relations Act, or otherwise.

G. Recommendation 2(b) is improper because it would require respondent to admit violations of the National Labor Relations Act of which the respondent is not guilty.

At a stated term, to wit, The October Term 1942, of the United States Circuit Court of Appeals for the Ninth Circuit, held in the Court Room thereof, in the City and County of San Francisco, in the State of California, on Monday the second day of August in the year of our Lord one thousand nine hundred and forty-three.

Present:

Honorable Curtis D. Wilbur, Senior Circuit Judge, Presiding,

Honorable William Denman, Circuit Judge,

Honorable Albert Lee Stephens, Circuit Judge.

No. 10437

RICHFIELD OIL CORPORATION,

Petitioner,

vs.

NATIONAL LABOR RELATIONS BOARD,

Respondent.

ORDER DENYING MOTION TO AMEND DESIGNATION AND GRANTING MOTION TO AMEND CERTIFICATION

Ordered (1) motion of respondent, filed July 20, 1943, to strike parts of petitioner's designation and (2) motion of petitioner filed July 21, 1943, to require Board to amend its certification of proceedings before the Board, argued by Mr. John Jennings, Regional Attorney, National Labor Relations Board, counsel for respondent, and by Mr. David Guntert, counsel for petitioner, and submitted to the Court for consideration and decision.

Upon consideration thereof, It Is Ordered that the grounds of the exceptions contained in respondent Richfield Oil Corporation's brief in support of exceptions to the Intermediate Report, dated April 9, 1943 be, and hereby are made a part of the certified transcript of record.

It Is Further Ordered that the motion of respondent National Labor Relations Board to strike parts of petitioner's designation be, and hereby is denied except that the portion of such designation as follows: "before the Regional Director of the Twenty-first Region" appearing in lines 21 and 22 of page 7 of such designation, be, and hereby is stricken.

United States of America
Before the National Labor Relations Board

Case No. C-2568

In the Matter of

RICHFIELD OIL CORPORATION

and

SAILORS UNION OF THE PACIFIC, A.F.L.

Case No. C-2569

In the Matter of

RICHFIELD OIL CORPORATION

and

PACIFIC DIST. SEAFARERS' INTL. ENGINE DIVISION, affil. SEAFARERS' INTERNATIONAL UNION OF NORTH AMERICA, A.F.L.

DECISION AND ORDER

On March 27, 1943, the Trial Examiner issued his Intermediate Report in the above-entitled proceeding, finding that the respondent, Richfield Oil Corporation, had engaged in and was engaging in certain unfair labor practices and recommending that it cease and desist therefrom and take certain affirmative action as set out in the copy of the Intermediate Report attached hereto. Thereafter, the respondent filed exceptions to the Intermediate Report with a brief in support thereof. The Board has considered the rulings of the Trial Examiner at the hearing and finds that no prejudicial error was committed. The rulings are hereby affirmed.

The Board has considered the Intermediate Report, the exceptions and brief, and the entire record in the case and hereby adopts the findings, conclusions, and recommendations of the Trial Examiner except as hereinafter modified:

1. The Trial Examiner has referred to the prevailing practice under which unions having access to vessels collect dues and distribute the organizations' trade papers to their members. We find that it is necessary to the mutual aid and protection of union members that they be enabled thereby to pay their union dues and receive their union trade papers on board the respondent's vessels, and that these activities are included within the necessary and appropriate scope of concerted activities as an incident to which we shall order passes to be issued. We emphasize in this connection, however, that we do not intend to require the respondent to permit the passes to be used for the solicitation of membership.

2. We shall order the respondent to issue passes to the Unions for the purposes of collective bargaining, for the discussion and presentation of grievances, and for other mutual aid and protection of the employees represented by the Unions, including the collection of dues and distribution of trade papers to union members, and providing that the respondent is not required to issue passes for the solicitation of membership. Upon consideration of the various wartime security laws and regulations

applicable to the instant case, and which the Trial Examiner also has considered, we find that our order, as described, does not require any conduct which is in derogation of such laws and regulations, of which would endanger the safety of the respondent's vessels or adversely affect discipline on board these vessels.[1]

ORDER

Upon the entire record in the case, and pursuant to Section 10 (c) of the National Labor Relations Act, the National Labor Relations Board hereby orders that the respondent, Richfield Oil Corporation, Los Angeles, California, and it officers, agents, successors, and assigns, shall:

1. Cease and desist from:

(a) Refusing to grant passes to representatives of the Sailors Union of the Pacific, a division of Seafarers' International Union of North America, and Seafarers' International Engine Division, a division of Seafarers' International Union of North America, in order that such representatives may go aboard the respondent's vessels for the purposes of collective bargaining, for the discussion and presentation of grievances, and for other mutual aid and protection of the employees represented by these Unions, including the collection of dues and distribution of trade papers to union members, provided, however, that the respondent is not required to issue passes for the solicitation of membership;

---

[1]See Matter of The Texas Company, Marine Division and National Maritime Union, Port Arthur Branch, 42 N.L.R.B. 593, 604-607.

(b) Engaging in like or related acts or conduct interfering with, restraining, or coercing its employees in the exercise of the right of self-organization, to form, join, or assist labor organizations, to bargain collectively through representatives of their own choosing, and to engage in concerted activities for the purposes of collective bargaining or other mutual aid or protection as guaranteed in Section 7 of the Act.

2. Take the following affirmative action which will effectuate the policies of the Act:

(a) Grant passes to the duly authorized representatives of the Sailors Union of the Pacific, a division of Seafarers' International Union of North America, and Seafarers' International Engine Division, a division of Seafarers' International Union of North America, to go aboard its vessels for the purposes of collective bargaining, for the discussion and presentation of grievances, and for other mutual aid and protection of the employees represented by the Unions, including the collection of dues and distribution of trade papers to union members, provided, however, that the respondent is not required to issue passes for the solicitation of membership;

(b) Post immediately in conspicuous places on its vessels, for a period of at least sixty (60) consecutive days from the date of posting, notices to the unlicensed deck and engine personnel, stating: (1) that the respondent will not engage in the conduct from which it is ordered to cease and desist in paragraphs 1 (a) and (b); (2) that the respondent will take the affirmative action set forth in paragraph 2 (a) hereof;

(c) Notify the Regional Director for the Twenty-first Region in writing within ten (10) days from the date of this Order what steps the respondent has taken to comply herewith.

Signed at Washington, D. C., this 8 day of May 1943.

HARRY A. MILLIS
Chairman
GERARD D. REILLY
Member
JOHN M. HOUSTON
Member

(Seal) NATIONAL LABOR RELATIONS BOARD

[Printer's Note: Copy of Intermediate Report, attached to Decision and Order, is an exact duplicate of the Intermediate Report, set out in full at pages 24 to 48, Incl., of this printed record.]

[Title of Board and Causes.]

AFFIDAVIT AS TO SERVICE

District of Columbia—ss:

I, Jack McCaleb being first duly sworn, on oath saith that I am one of the employees of the National Labor Relations Board, in the office of said

Board in Washington, D. C.; that on the 8th day of May, 1943, I mailed postpaid, bearing Government frank, by registered mail, a copy of the Decision and Order [and Intermediate Report] to the following named persons, addressed to them at the following addresses:

Sailors Union of the Pacific; Seafarers Intl. Engine Division
Att: Harry Lundeberg
110 Market St.
San Francisco, California

Harry Lundeberg
59 Clay St.
San Francisco, California

Richfield Oil Corporation
Richfield Building
Los Angeles, California

David Guntert
555 South Flower St.
Los Angeles, California

/s/ JACK McCALEB

Subscribed and sworn to before me this 8th day of May 1943

(Seal) KATHRYN B. HARRELL
Notary Public, D. C. My commission expires March 1, 1947.

In the United States Circuit Court of Appeals
In and for the Ninth Circuit

No. 10437

RICHFIELD OIL CORPORATION,
a corporation,

Petitioner,

vs.

NATIONAL LABOR RELATIONS BOARD,
Respondent.

PETITION FOR REVIEW OF DECISION OF NATIONAL LABOR RELATIONS BOARD

To the Honorable, the Judges of the United States Circuit Court of Appeals for the Ninth Circuit.

Comes Now, Richfield Oil Corporation, a corporation, organized and existing under and by virtue of the laws of the State of Delaware, and believing itself to be aggrieved by a certain decision and order issued on the 8th day of May, 1943, by the National Labor Relations Board (hereinafter sometimes referred to as the "Board"), in the Consolidated proceeding entitled "In the Matter of Richfield Oil Corporation and Sailors' Union of the Pacific," Case No. C-2568 (XXI-C-2248) and "In the Matter of Richfield Oil Corporation and Pacific Dist. Seafarers' Intl. Engine Division, affil. Seafarers' International Union of North America, A.F.L." Case No. C-2569 (XXI-C-2249), files its petition pursuant to the provisions of Section 10 of the Act of Congress of July 5, 1935 (Chapter 372, 49 Stat. 453, 29 USCA 151-166) known and cited as the National Labor Relations Act, repesctfully asking this Honorable Court to review and set aside said order, and in support of its petition respectfully represents—

I.

JURISDICTION

1. That petitioner is, and at all times herein mentioned was, a corporation organized and existing under and by virtue of the laws of the State of Delaware, having its home office and principal place of business in the city of Los Angeles, State of California. Petitioner owns and operates, and at all times herein mentioned has owned and operated, six tank steamships, hereinafter referred to as "tankers", in interstate and foreign commerce.

2. That respondent is a public body known as the National Labor Relations Board, created pursuant to the Act of Congress of July 5, 1935, (Chapter 372, 49 Stat. 453, 29 USCA 151-166), hereinafter referred to as the National Labor Relations Act, or the "Act"; that said Board has an office and a Regional Director at Los Angeles, California, within the Ninth Circuit and within the jurisdiction of this Court.

3. That as will hereinafter more fully appear, the so-called unfair labor practices in which it is alleged in this proceeding that the petitioner has

been engaged, all occurred at or near Los Angeles, California, within the Ninth Circuit and within the jurisdiction of this Court.

4. That by reason of the matters alleged in paragraphs 1, 2 and 3 hereof, this Court has jurisdiction of this petition by virtue of section 10 (f) of the National Labor Relations Act, 49 USCA Section 160 (f).

II.

STATEMENT OF PROCEEDINGS

1. Filing of Charges.

That on January 6, 1943, one Harry Lundeberg, acting for and on behalf of the Pacific District Seafarers' International Engine Division, affil. Seafarers' International Union of North America, A.F.L. (hereinafter sometimes referred to as the "Seafarers' Union"), filed with the regional director of the National Labor Relations Board at Los Angeles, California, (Case No. XXI-C-2249) charges to the effect that petitioner had engaged in, and was engaging in, unfair labor practices within the meaning of the Act concerning petitioner's unlicensed Engine Department personnel.

That on January 28, 1943, one Harry Lundeberg, acting for and on behalf of the Sailors' Union of the Pacific, A.F.L. (sometimes hereinafter referred to as "Sailors' Union") filed with the regional director of the National Labor Relations Board at Los Angeles, California, (Case No. XXI-C-2248) amended charges, to the effect that petitioner had engaged in, and was engaging in, unfair labor practices within the meaning of the Act concerning petitioner's unlicensed Deck Department personnel.

That on February 17, 1943, the Board, pursuant to Article II, Section 36 (b) of the Board's rules and regulations, as amended, ordered the consolidation of the above cases.

2. Complaint and Its Contents.

That thereafter and on February 19, 1943, the National Labor Relations Board, acting by and through its regional director for its Twenty-first Region issued a consolidated complaint (hereinafter referred to as the "complaint"), in substance alleging:

(a) That petitioner was a corporation engaged in producing, manufacturing, selling and distributing petroleum products and natural gas in the states of California, Washington, Oregon, Arizona, Nevada, and Idaho, and that petitioner in the course of said business, transported large quantities of petroleum products in interstate and foreign commerce via petitioner's tankers.

(b) That the Seafarers' Union and the Sailors' Union (hereinafter sometimes referred to jointly as the "complaining unions") were labor organizations within the meaning of Section 2, subsection (5) of the Act.

(c) That the complaining unions were the exclusive representatives for petitioner's unlicensed Deck Department personnel and unlicensed Engine Department personnel for the purpose of collective bargaining.

(d) That petitioner, since October 1942, refused to permit duly authorized representatives of the complaining unions to go aboard petitioner's tankers and that by such refusal, petitioner was interfering with, coercing and restraining its employees in the exercise of rights guaranteed by Section 7 of the Act and was thereby engaging in unfair labor practices affecting commerce within the meaning of Section 8, subsection (1) of the Act and Section 2, subsections (6) and (7) of the Act.

That concurrently with the issuance of said complaint, the Board, acting by and through its Regional Director for its Twenty-first Region, issued a notice of hearing, which said notice and the said complaint were served upon petitioner on February 22, 1943.

3. Answer and its Contents.

That thereafter and within the time prescribed for filing an answer, petitioner filed its answer admitting that it was a corporation engaged in interstate and foreign commerce, admitting that it had refused to grant passes to the complaining unions, but denying that such refusal was an unfair labor practice within the meaning of the Act, or otherwise. The petitioner's answer affirmatively alleged:

"As a Further and Affirmative Answer to the Complaint Herein, Respondent Alleges:

I.

"That shortly after the declaration of war by the United States against Germany, Italy and

Japan, Respondent resolved to cancel all existing passes to its ships as soon as existing contracts with Unions, including the Sailors' Union of the Pacific, would permit, and resolved further to refuse during the remainder of the period of the war to issue passes to any person or persons not in its employ; that such cancellation of passes was effected on or about the 15th day of February 1942 and that since that date Respondent has adhered to the policy of refusing passes to any and all persons indiscriminately.

II.

"That on or about the 20th day of February, 1942, Respondent was notified by the Regional Director of the National Labor Relations Board for the Twenty-First Region, in case No. XXI-C-2001 that the National Maritime Union of America had filed a charge pursuant to Section 10(c) of the National Labor Relations Act alleging that this Respondent was engaging in unfair labor practices within the meaning of Section 8, Subsection (1) of the Act, by refusing permission to officers of said Union to visit vessels of this Respondent and to talk with members of its Union on said vesels; that upon Respondent's showing that it had adopted a policy of not granting any passes to anyone for the period of the war, the Regional Director refused to issue a complaint and upon appeal, the National Labor Relations Board upheld him in so refusing.

III.

"That Respondent's policy of refusing to grant passes to any one was adopted for the sole purpose of promoting the war effort by safeguarding, not only the tank vessels, cargoes, and terminal facilities, but also safeguarding the lives of officers and men employed upon such vessels; that the establishing and carrying out of such policy is not an unfair labor practice within the meaning of Section 8 of the National Labor Relations Act, but on the contrary, is a reasonable exercise of the prudent judgment of Respondent in the conduct of its business and in its capacity as Agent of the War Shipping Administration.

IV.

"That this Respondent is informed and believes and therefore alleges that if it were to issue passes to representatives of the complaining Unions, it would be an unfair labor practice to refuse similar passes to other labor representatives requesting the same, and Respondent would be required to issue passes indiscriminately to all labor representatives requesting the same, thereby increasing the number of persons having access to the vessels and port facilities, resulting in multiplying the possibilities of acts inimicable to the war effort and security of the personnel, the vessels, cargoes, and shore installations.

V.

"That to require this Respondent to issue passes would subject Respondent's vessels, their personnel and cargoes, and the port facilities to grave, unreasonable and wholly unnecessary hazards because of:

(1) Negligent acts of pass holders likely to result in

(a) Fires and explosions;

(b) Personal injuries and death;

(c) Damage to or loss of vessels, cargoes and port facilities.

"(2) Increased hazards of tank ship loading and unloading of highly inflammable cargoes.

"(3) Lessening of efficiency of men on watch aboard through distraction from their duties, possibly resulting in—

(a) Admixture of products;

(b) Breaking of lines;

(c) Spilling inflammable products.

"(4) Facilitating the acquisition of information valuable to the enemy, such as:

(a) Vessel armament;

(b) Courses, destinations, routes;

(c) Cargoes;

(d) Ports of Call;

(e) Escort vessels, convoys, etc.

"(5) Facilitating sabotage, such as tampering with armament, machinery and equipment, and similar acts.

"(6) Lessening the efficiency of the port watch against sabotage and the approach of unauthorized persons and craft to the vessel and port facilities, through distraction from their duties.

VI.

"That to require this Respondent to issue passes would violate war time security and safety rules of the Captain of the Port, Los Angeles-Long Beach Harbor area, by giving access to Terminal facilities and vessels to persons whose presence is unnecessary.

VII.

"That to require this Respondent to issue passes would result in violation of Security Orders of the War Shipping Administration which require the strictest secrecy as to armament, courses, departures, destinations, cargoes, escort vessels, convoys, and the like, and which require that 'visitors to piers and vessels should be limited to cases of absolute necessity.'

VIII.

"That to require this Respondent to issue passes would violate the General Orders of the War Shipping Administration which require the utmost dispatch in the handling of the vessels and their cargoes.

IX.

"That to require this Respondent to issue passes would constitute a violation of the Statement of Policy agreed upon between the War Shipping Administration and various Unions, including the complaining Unions herein, which prohibits 'crews' mass meetings, crews' committee meetings, and other similar meetings aboard ship.'

X.

"That Respondent is informed and believes and therefore alleges that the issuing of passes could only result in organization efforts, not only by the complaining Unions, but by rival Unions, leading to jurisdictional disputes and interference with the handling of the vessel and the vessel's business with the utmost dispatch, as required by orders of the War Shipping Administration.

XI.

"That tank vessels under the present war conditions constitute one of the most precious assets of our Nation and their protection demands the utmost diligence and care, and further, outweighs any more inconvenience to individuals whether they be representatives of organized labor or representatives of the vessel owners.

XII.

"That Respondent is not operating its vessels merely as an owner in peace time but, on the contrary, is operating said vessels as Agent for and under the direction of the United States Government, acting by and through the War Shipping Administration; that the operation of said vessels under present exigencies, in fact, constitutes emergency operations, making it imperative to handle cargoes with the utmost dispatch, thereby greatly increasing the every-day hazards of loading and discharging and other port activities, making it necessary to take not only ordinary precautions but to take exraordinary precautions to safeguard the vessels, their invaluable personnel, the cargoes, and shore facilities.

XIII.

"That precautionary measures which under ordinary peace time conditions would be considered strict and technical, become commonplace and imperative under war time conditions."

4. Proceedings Before the Trial Examiner.

That pursuant to said notice of hearing, said complaint came on for hearing at 10:30 a. m. on March 4, 1943, before James C. Batten, agent of the Board, designated by the Board as Trial Examiner for said hearing, and said hearing was held by said Trial Examiner on March 4th and 5th, 1943; that the Board appeared by its attorneys and offered evidence in support of the charges of the complaint, and the petitioner appeared by its attorney and offered evidence in refutation of such charges; that at the conclusion of said hearing, at the request of the Trial Examiner oral argument was had on behalf of the Board, on behalf of the complaining unions, and on behalf of the petitioner, and at the request of the Trial Examiner, briefs were filed on behalf of the Board, the complaining unions, and the petitioner.

That on March 27, 1943, James C. Batten filed his Intermediate Report in which he made Findings of Fact and Conclusions of Law that petitioner, by refusing to grant passes to representatives of the complaining unions so that they could board petitioner's tankers, was interfering with, coercing and restraining its employees in the exercise of rights guaranteed by Section 7 of the Act and therefore petitioner was engaging in unfair labor practices affecting commerce within the meaning of Section 8, subsection (1), and Section 2, subsections (6) and (7) of the Act. Upon such Findings of Fact and Conclusions of Law the Trial Examiner made the following recommendaions:

Recommendations

"Upon the basis of the foregoing findings of fact and conclusions of law, the undersigned recommends that the respondent, Richfield Oil Corporation, and its officers, agents, successors, and assigns, shall:

1. Cease and desist from:

(a) Refusing to grant passes to representatives of the Sailors Union of the Pacific a division of Seafarers' International Union of North America and Seafarers' International Engine Division, a division of Seafarers' International Union of North America, in order that such representatives may go aboard the respondent's vessels and confer with and aid the unlicensed deck and engine personnel thereon;

(b) Engaging in like or related acts or conduct in interfering with, restraining or coercing its employees in the exercise of the right of self-organization, to form, join, or assist labor organizations, to bargain collectively through representatives of their own choosing and to engage in concerted activities for the purpose of collective bargaining or other mutual aid or protection as guaranteed in Section 7 of the Act.

2. Take the following affirmative action which will effectuate the policies of the Act.

(a) Grant passes to the duly authorized representatives of the Sailors Union of the Pacific a division of seafarers' International Union of North America and Seafarers' International Engine Division, a division of Seafarers' International Union of North America, to go aboard its vessels to confer with and aid the unlicensed deck and engine personnel;

(b) Post immediately in conspicuous places on its vessels for a period of at least sixty (60) consecutive days from the date of posting notices to the unlicensed deck and engine personnel, stating: (1) that the respondent will not engage in the conduct from which it is ordered to cease and desist in paragraph 1 (a) and (b); (2) that the respondent will take the affirmative action set forth in paragraph 2 (a) hereof;

(c) Notify the Regional Director for the Twenty-first Region in writing within ten (10) days from the receipt of the Intermediate Report what steps the respondent has taken to comply herewith.

"It is further recommended that unless on or before ten (10) days from the receipt of this Intermediate Report the respondent notifies said Regional Director in writing that it will comply with the foregoing recommendations, the National Labor Relations Board issue an order requiring the respondent to take the action aforesaid."

A true copy of the Intermediate Report is attached hereto, marked Petitioner's Exhibit "A" and by this reference made a part hereof.

5. Proceedings before the Board.

That on March 31, 1943, John E. Lawyer, chief of the Order Section of the National Labor Relations Board, entered the following Order:

"It is hereby ordered, pursuant to Article II, Section 32, of National Labor Relations Board Rules and Regulations—Series 2, as amended, that Case No. XXI-C-2248 be, and it hereby is, transferred to and continued before the Board as Case No. C-2568, and that Case No. XXI-C-2249, be, and it hereby is, transferred to and continued before the Board as Case No. C-2569."

That copy of such Intermediate Report and said Order were received by petitioner on April 2, 1943; that thereafter petitioner duly served on the Board an original and four copies of its Exceptions to the Intermediate Report, and an original and four copies of a Brief in support thereof, as required by Article II, Section 32 of the Rules and Regulations of the National Labor Relations Board, Series 2, as amended, effective October 28, 1942, and notified the Regional Director in writing of such action.

6. Decision and Order of the Board.

That thereafter on May 8, 1943, the Board entered its Decision and Order, which Decision and Order were received by petitioner on May 11, 1943. That in said Order the Board stated that it had reviewed the rulings of the Trial Examiner, found no prejudicial error, and affirmed said rulings; that the Board had considered the Intermediate Report, the Exceptions and Brief, and the entire record and that the Board adopted the Findings, Conclusions and Recommendations of the Trial Examiner, except as follows:

"1. The Trial Examiner has referred to the prevailing practice under which unions having access to vessels collect dues and distribute the organizations' trade papers to their members. We find that it is necessary to the mutual aid and protection of union members that they be enabled thereby to pay their union dues and receive their union trade papers on board the respondent's vessels, and that these activities are included within the necessary and appropriate scope of concerted activities as an incident to which we shall order passes to be issued. We emphasize in this connection, however, that we do not intend to require the respondent to permit the passes to be used for the solicitation of membership.

"2. We shall order the respondent to issue passes to the Unions for the purposes of collective bargaining, for the discussion and presentation of grievances, and for other mutual aid and protection of the employees represented by the Unions, including the collection of dues and distribution of trade papers to union members, and providing that the respondent is not required to issue passes for the solicitation of membership. Upon consideration of the various wartime security laws and regulations applicable to the instant case, and which the Trial Examiner also has considered, we find that our order, as described, does not require any conduct which is in derogation of such laws and regulations, or which would endanger the safety of the respondent's vessels or adversely affect discipline on board these vessels. (See Matter of The Texas Company, Marine Division and National Maritime Union, Port Arthur Branch, 42 N.L.R.B. 593, 604-607)." That said Order of the Board required petitioner to:

"1. Cease and desist from:

(a) Refusing to grant passes to representatives of the Sailors Union of the Pacific, a division of Seafarers' International Union of North America, and Seafarers' International Engine Division, a division of Seafarers' International Union of North America, in order that such representatives may go aboard the respondent's vessels for the purposes of collective bargaining, for the discussion and presentation of grievances, and for other mutual aid and protection of the employees represented by these Unions, including the collection of dues and distribution of trade papers to union members, provided, however, that the respondent is not required to issue passes for the solicitation of membership;

"(b) Engaging in like or related acts or conduct interfering with, restraining, or coercing its employees in the exercise of the right of self-organization, to form, join, or assist labor organizations, to bargain collectively through representatives of their own choosing, and to engage in concerted activities for the purposes of collective bargaining or other mutual aid or protection as guaranteed in Section 7 of the Act.

"2. Take the following affirmative action which will effectuate the policies of the Act:

(a) Grant passes to the duly authorized representatives of the Sailors Union of the Pacific, a division of Seafarers' International Union of North America, and Seafarers' International Engine Division, a division of Seafarers' International Union of North America, to go aboard its vessels for the purposes of collective bargaining, for the discussion and presentation of grievances, and for other mutual aid and protection of the employees represented by the Unions, including the collection of dues and distribution of trade papers to union members, provided, however, that the respondent is not required to issue passes for the solicitation of membership;

"(b) Post immediately in conspicuous places on its vessels, for a period of at least sixty (60) consecutive days from the date of postping, notices to the unlicensed deck and engine personnel, stating: (1) that the respondent will not engage in the conduct from which it is ordered to cease and desist in paragraphs 1 (a) and (b); (2) that the respondent will take the affirmative action set forth in paragraph 2 (a) hereof;

"(c) Notify the Regional Director for the Twenty-first Region in writing within ten (10) days from the date of this Order what steps the respondent has taken to comply herewith."

A true copy of said Decision and Order is attached hereto, marked Petitioner's Exhibit "B" and by this reference made a part hereof.

7. Petitioner's Reasons for Non-Compliance.

That upon receipt of the Decision and Order aforesaid petitioner considered the same carefully and within the said ten day period filed with the Regional Director of the Board at Los Angeles, California, a statement in writing setting forth the following reasons for non-compliance:

(a) The subject matter of the complaint is beyond the jurisdiction and power of the Board and therefore its Order is invalid.

(b) The Board's Findings of Fact as to unfair labor practices, upon which the Board's Decision and Order are predicated, are not supported by adequate or substantial evidence and the evidence affords no reasonable basis therefor.

(c) There is no legal basis for the conclusions of Law upon which the Board's Order is predicated.

(d) The Board's Conclusions are contrary to law and even if they were not, the Board's Order based thereon is too broad.

(e) To comply with the Order of the Board, petitioner would be required to publicly admit in effect that it had committed acts which are unfair labor practices under the National Labor Relations Act, when, in fact, the acts alleged in the complaint are not unfair labor practices.

(f) To comply with the Order of the Board, petitioner would be required to publicly admit in effect the commission of acts in violation of the Act when, in fact, such acts were neither committed nor even mentioned in the complaint.

III.

SPECIFICATIONS OF ERRORS RELIED UPON

The Board's Order is erroneous and beyond the power and jurisdiction of the Board and in contravention of the National Labor Relations Act and of the Constitution of the United States and void, and of no effect, and should be annulled and set aside by this Honorable Court for the following reasons which are hereby assigned as errors:

1. The Board's Findings of Fact as to unfair labor practices on the part of petitioner are not supported by adequate or substantial evidence.

2. The evidence affords no reasonable basis for the conclusions of the Board as embraced in its Findings of Fact and Conclusions of Law, that there were unfair labor practices on the part of petitioner.

3. It was error for the Board to make Conclusions of Law upon which its Order was based that this petitioner has engaged in and is engaging in unfair labor practices within the meaning of Section 8 (1) of the Act affecting commerce within the meaning of Section 2 (6) and (7) of the Act by interfering with, restraining and coercing its employees in the exercise of the rights guaranteed in Section 7 of the Act, because

(a) Section 7 of the Act does not require the inclusion in a collective bargaining agreement of any particular term or condition of employment.

(b) Whether or not passes should be issued to representatives of the complaining unions is a term or condition of employment to be included in or excluded from a contract between the employer and its employees, depending upon agreement, and therefore it is properly the subject matter of collective bargaining, and upon failure of agreement concerning the inclusion or exclusion thereof, will constitute a dispute subject to settlement under the procedure established by the President's Executive Order No. 9017 of January 12, 1942.

(c) The procedure to be followed in settling grievances and in collecting dues upon the vessels is also properly the subject matter of collective bargaining and upon failure of agreement, will constitute disputes subject to settlement under the procedure established by said Executive Order No. 9017.

(d) Section 7 of the Act does not guarantee to the complaining unions a particular mode or method of grievance procedure and dues collecting procedure to be determined by them and ordered by the Board upon the failure of the employer to agree, nor does it guarantee to the complaining unions free access to petitioner's vessels during wartime conditions for the purpose of transacting union business.

4. The Board's Order goes beyond the Board's power and jurisdiction under the Act and contravenes the constitution of the United States by denying due process of law to petitioner, because

(a) The subject matter of the complaint is outside the jurisdiction and power of the Board and is a matter of collective bargaining between the employer and employees.

(b) The Board by its Order is prescribing terms and conditions of employment by establishing grievance procedure and dues collecting procedure and substituting its judgment for the judgment of the employer in these matters, thereby destroying petitioner's right to bargain with the representatives of its employees.

(c) The Board by its Order is enlarging its jurisdiction and overruling and setting aside decisions of the courts of the United States in that it has adopted as controlling a portion of the decision in NLRB vs. The Cities Service Oil Company, 122 Fed. (2d) 149, C.C.A. 2, and overruled and set aside the remaining portion of said decision.

(d) The Board by its Order is overruling and annulling decisions of the courts of the United States by ordering petitioner to cease and desist from doing acts not alleged in the complaint or even intimated in the evidence contrary to the law laid down by the several courts of the United States.

(e) The Board by its Order is exceeding the limits of its authority as established by the Act and the decisions of the several courts of the United States by ordering this petitioner to publicly admit the commission of acts prohibited by the National Labor Relations Act when, in fact, petitioner was not guilty thereof and no such charge was made in the complaint and no evidence was introduced to show the same or from which they could be inferred.

5. It was error for the Board to base its Findings of Fact, upon which the Decision and Order of the Board are predicated, upon only a part of the evidence and totally disregard and put aside all other undisputed evidence.

6. The Board was in error in issuing its Order based on Findings of Fact and Conclusions of Law that the failure to issue passes to representatives of the complaining unions constitutes an unfair labor practice within the meaning of the National Labor Relations Act.

7. The sole issue before the Board was the question of whether or not as a matter of law the refusal of petitioner to issue passes to representatives of the complaining unions interfered with, coerced and restrained petitioner's employees in the exercise of their right to self organization, to form, join or assist labor organizations, to bargain collectively through representatives of their own choosing, and to engage in concerted activities for the purpose of collective bargaining, or other mutual aid or protection, and the Board has failed to apply the governing principles of law.

8. The Board erred in concluding, as embraced in its Findings of Fact, that because the collective bargaining agreements with other shipowners contained provisions for issuing passes, that passes to union representatives are necessary to the enjoyment

by employees of the benefits of Section 7 of the Act, and that the refusal by petitioner to issue passes constituted interference, coercion, and restraint upon its employees in the exercise of such rights, and, therefore, an unfair labor practice within the meaning of Section 8 (1) of the Act.

9. The Board erred in concluding, as embraced in its Findings of Fact, that the petitioner by not issuing passes to representatives of the complaining unions was exercising "domination and control" over the efforts of its employees to engage in "mutual aid and protection."

10. It was error for the Board to rely upon NLRB vs. The Cities Service Company, supra, for the proposition that passes were necessary to the enjoyment by employees of their rights under Section 7 of the Act because, even if the holding in the Cities Service case on that point were correct, it is no longer effective because Executive Order No. 9017 of January 12, 1942, set up a procedure under which the dispute between an employer and the representatives of its employees concerning the issuance of passes will be determined on its merits by the National War Labor Board. There can no longer be any reason for holding that the refusal to issue passes without discrimination is an unfair labor practice.

IV.

PRAYER

Wherefore, your petitioner, Richfield Oil Corporation, petitions this Honorable Court for a review of the aforementioned Order of the National Labor Relations Board issued on May 8, 1943, and respectfully prays:

1. That the Board may be required in conformity with law to certify for filing in this court a transcript of the entire record in the aforementioned proceedings, including pleadings and testimony upon which said Order was entered and including the Intermediate Report, Exceptions thereto with supporting brief, and the Decision and Order of the Board.

2. That if it is desired that additional testimony be taken, that request should be made herein.

3. That the proceedings before the Trial Examiner and the Board as set forth in said transcript be reviewed by this Honorable Court and that said Order be set aside, vacated and annulled, and that the respondent be ordered to dismiss its complaint against petitioner.

4. That this Honorable Court exercise its jurisdiction over the parties and the subject matter of this petition and restrain the Board from enforcing its said Decision and Order pending a final determination of this petition.

5. That this Honorable Court exercise its jurisdiction over the parties and the subject matter of this petition and grant to the petitioner such other and further relief in the premises as the rights and equities in the cause may require.

Dated this 14th day of May, 1943.

RICHFIELD OIL CORPORATION

By A. M. KELLEY
Its Vice President

DAVID GUNTERT
Attorney for Petitioner

State of California
County of Los Angeles—ss.

A. M. Kelley, being first duly sworn on oath, deposes and says that he is an officer, to wit, Vice President of Richfield Oil Corporation, that he has read the foregoing Petition subscribed by him on behalf of said corporation, and has knowledge of the contents thereof, and further, on oath says that the statements made in said Petition are true to the best of his knowledge and belief and that the reason that this vertification is not made by Richfield Oil Corporation in person is that the said Richfield Oil Corporation is a corporation, and that this verification is made on its behalf by its authority.

A. M. KELLEY

Subscribed and sworn to before me this 14 day of May, 1943

[Seal] R. A. HARBAUGH
Notary Public in and for said County and State.
My Commission Expires Mar. 5, 1947

[Endorsed]: Filed May 17, 1943. Paul P. O'Brien, Clerk.

[Printer's Note: Petitioner's Exhibit "A," a true copy of the Intermediate Report, is an exact duplicate of the Intermediate Report set out in full at pages 24 to 48, incl., of this printed Record. Petitioner's Exhibit B, a true copy of the Decision and Order, is an exact duplicate of the Decision and Order set out at pages 59 to 63, incl., of this printed record.]

[Title of Circuit Court of Appeals and Cause.]

ANSWER OF THE NATIONAL LABOR RELATIONS BOARD TO PETITION FOR REVIEW OF ITS ORDER AND REQUEST FOR ENFORCEMENT OF SAID ORDER

To the Honorable, the Judges of the United States Circuit Court of Appeals for the Ninth Circuit:

Comes now the National Labor Relations Board, herein called the Board, and pursuant to the National Labor Relations Act (49 Stat. 449, c. 372, 29 U.S.C., Sec. 151, et seq.), hereinafter called the Act, files this answer to the petition to review and set aside an order issued by the Board against the Richfield Oil Corporation, petitioner herein, and the Board's request for enforcement of its said order.

(1) The Board admits the allegations contained in Section I of the Petition for Review.

(2) Answering the allegations contained in Section II, of the Petition for Review, the Board prays reference to the certified transcript of the record, filed herein, of the proceedings heretofore

had herein, for a full and exact statement of the pleadings, evidence, findings of fact, conclusions of law, and order of the Board, and all other proceedings had in this matter.

(3) Answering the allegations contained in Section III of the Petition for Review, the Board denies each and every allegation therein contained.

(4) Further answering, the Board avers that the proceedings had before it, the findings of fact, conclusions of law, and order of the Board, were and are in all respects valid and proper under the Act.

Wherefore, having answered each and every allegation contained in the Petition for Review, the Board respectfully prays this Honorable Court that said petition be denied insofar as it prays that the Board's order be set aside and that petitioner shall have other and further relief.

Further answering, the Board, pursuant to Section 10 (e) and (f) of the Act, respectfully requests this Honorable Court for the enforcement of its order, issued against petitioner on May 8, 1943, in the consolidated proceeding designated on the records of the Board as Cases Nos. C-2568 and C-2569, entitled "In the Matter of Richfield Oil Corporation and Sailors Union of the Pacific, A.F.L., and in the Matter of Richfield Oil Corporation and Pacific Dist. Seafarers' Int. Engine Division, affiliated with the Seafarers' International Union of North America, A.F.L."

In support of this request for enforcement of its order, the Board respectfully shows:

(a) Petitioner, a Delaware corporation, has its principal place of business in Los Angeles, California, within this judicial circuit. This Court has jurisdiction of the Petition for Revew herein and of this request for enforcement by virtue of Section 10 (e) and (f) of the Act.

(b) Upon proceedings had in said matter, as more fully shown by the entire record thereof, certified by the Board and filed with this Court herein, to which reference is hereby made, and including without limitation a complaint, answer, hearing for the purpose of taking testimony and receiving other evidence, Trial Examiner's report and exceptions filed thereto, as more fully shown by the certified record filed herewith, the Board on May 8, 1943, duly stated its findings of fact and conclusions of law, and issued its order directed to petitioner, its officers, agents, successors, and assigns.

The aforesaid order provides as follows:

ORDER

> Upon the entire record in the case, and pursuant to Section 10 (c) of the National Labor Relations Act, the National Labor Relations Board hereby orders that the respondent, Richfield Oil Corporation, Los Angeles, California, and its officers, agents, successors, and assigns, shall:
>
> 1. Cease and desist from:
>
> (a) Refusing to grant passes to representatives of the Sailors Union of the Pacific, a

division of Seafarers' International Union of North America, and Seafarers' International Engine Division, a division of Seafarers' International Union of North America, in order that such representatives may go aboard the respondent's vessels for the purposes of collective bargaining, for the discussion and presentation of grievances, and for other mutual aid and protection of the employees represented by these Unions, including the collection of dues and distribution of trade papers to union members, provided, however, that the respondent is not required to issue passes for the solicitation of membership;

(b) Engaging in like or related acts or conduct interfering with, restraining, or coercing its employees in the exercise of the right of self-organization, to form, join, or assist labor organizations, to bargain collectively through representatives of their own choosing, and to engage in concerted activities for the purposes of collective bargaining or other mutual aid or protection as guaranteed in Section 7 of the Act.

2. Take the following affirmative action which will effectuate the policies of the Act.

(a) Grant passes to the duly authorized representatives of the Sailors Union of the Pacific, a division of Seafarers' International Union of North America, and Seafarers' International Engine Division, a division of Seafarers' International Union of North America, to go aboard its vessels for the purposes of collective bargaining, for the discussion and presentation of grievances, and for other mutual aid and protection of the employees represented by the Unions, including the collection of dues and distribution of trade papers to union members, provided, however, that the respondent is not required to issue passes for the solicitation of membership;

(b) Post immediately in conspicuous places on its vessels, for a period of at least sixty (60) consecutive days from the date of posting, notices to the unlicensed deck and engine personnel, stating: (1) that the respondent will not engage in the conduct from which it is ordered to cease and desist in paragraphs 1 (a) and (b); (2) that the respondent will take the affirmative action set forth in paragraph 2 (a) hereof;

(c) Notify the Regional Director for the Twenty-first Region in writing within ten (10) days from the date of this Order what steps the respondent has taken to comply herewith.

(c) On May 8, 1943, the Board's Decision and Order was duly served upon petitioner and all other parties.

(d) Pursuant to Section 10 (e) and (f) of the Act, the Board has certified and filed with this Court a transcript of the entire record in the proceeding.

Wherefore, the Board prays this Honorable Court

that it cause notice of the filing of this answer and request for enforcement, and the filing of the certified transcript of the entire record in said proceeding, to be served upon petitioner, and that this Court take jurisdiction of the proceedings and of the questions to be determined therein, and make and enter upon the pleadings, evidence, and proceedings set forth in the entire record of said proceeding, and upon the order made thereupon, set forth hereinabove, a decree denying the petition to review and set aside, and enforcing in whole said order of the Board, issued on May 8, 1943, and requiring petitioner and its officers, agents, successors, and assigns to comply therewith.

NATIONAL LABOR RELATIONS BOARD
By ERNEST A. GROSS
Associate General Counsel.

Dated at Washington, D. C., this 5th day of June 1943.

District of Columbia—ss.

Ernest A. Gross, being first duly sworn, states that he is Associate General Counsel of the National Labor Relations Board, and that he is authorized to and does make this verification on behalf of said Board; that he has read the foregoing answer and has knowledge of the contents thereof; and that the statements made therein are true to the best of his knowledge, information, and belief.

ERNEST A. GROSS
Associate General Counsel

Subscribed and sworn to before me this 5th day of June 1943.

[Seal] JOHN E. LAWYER
Notary Public, District of Columbia
My Commission Expires August 31, 1944.

Before the National Labor Relations Board
Twenty-First Region

Case No. XXI-C-2248

In the Matter of

RICHFIELD OIL CORPORATION

and

SAILORS UNION OF THE PACIFIC, A. F. L.

Case No. XXI-C-2249

In the Matter of

RICHFIELD OIL CORPORATION

and

PACIFIC DIST., SEAFARERS' INTL. ENGINE DIVISION, affiliated with Seafarers International Union of North America, A. F. L.

Room 808, United States Post Office
and Court House Building,
Spring, Temple and Main Streets,
Los Angeles, California,

Thursday, March 4, 1943.

The above-entitled matter came on for hearing, pursuant to notice, at 10:00 o'clock a. m.

Before:

James C. Batten,
Trial Examiner.

Appearances:

Charles M. Ryan and
Thomas C. Moore,
Attorneys for the National Labor Relations Board. [1*]

David Guntert,
555 South Flower Street, Los Angeles, California, appearing for Richfield Oil Corporation.

Harry Lundberg,
59 Clay Street, San Francisco, California, appearing on behalf of Sailors Union of the Pacific and Seafarers International Union of North America, A. F. L. [2]

PROCEEDINGS

Trial Examiner Batten: The hearing will come to order. In hearings I usually follow the practice of asking the Board's attorney to introduce first what is known as Board's Exhibit 1, Board's Exhibit 1 being the pleadings, the formal papers, affidavits of service, and so forth.

I also want to request the attorneys that if they have any written motions or later in the proceeding if there are any further pleadings, I want them all made a part of Board's Exhibit 1, 1-A, 1-B, 1-C, and so forth.

* Page numbering appearing at top of page of original Reporter's Transcript.

Now, I do that so that counsel at any later stage in the proceedings will find all formal papers in one exhibit. Then you don't have to be looking through the file to find the formal papers.

Of course, by filing all of the formal papers in Board's Exhibit 1, that, of course, is without prejudice in any way because it happens to be the union pleading or a motion by the Respondent's answer or any other written motions or pleadings.

Now, is there any objection to proceeding in that manner?

Mr. Guntert: No objection.

Mr. Moore: No objection.

The Court: If there is no objection, then, I will ask Board's counsel to have marked and offered Board's Exhibit 1.

Mr. Guntert: Mr. Examiner, I assume that includes our answer? [4]

Trial Examiner Batten: That's right. As soon as they are marked, they will be submitted to you to look over.

Mr. Moore: I offer at this time for identification Board's Exhibit 1, consisting of the formal papers upon which this proceeding rests.

As Board's Exhibit 1-A, the original charge filed in case No. XXI*I*-C-2249.

Trial Examiner Batten: Now, I don't think it is necessary to read into the record what all those exhibits are. If you will just have them marked, they speak for themselves.

Mr. Moore: Very well. I will ask the reporter, then, to mark these formal documents as Board's

Exhibit 1, subdivided A, B, C, starting at the back of the file as it is now composed.

I offer Board's Exhibit 1-A through 1-I to counsel for their examination.

(The documents referred to were marked for identification as Board's Exhibits 1-A to 1-I, inclusive.)

Mr. Moore: I offer Board's Exhibits 1-A through 1-I in evidence.

Trial Examiner Batten: Is there any objection?

Mr. Guntert: No objection.

Trial Examiner Batten: If not, Board's Exhibits 1-A to 1-I will be received. [5]

(The documents heretofore marked for identification as Board's Exhibits 1-A to 1-I, inclusive, were received in evidence.)

[Printer's Note: Board's Exhibits Nos. 1-A to 1-I, inclusive are set out in full at pages 1 to 24 of this printed record.]

Mr. Moore: May I ask at this time, will the Respondent stipulate that due notice of this proceeding was received?

Mr. Guntert: We will so stipulate.

Mr. Moore: Thank you.

Trial Examiner Batten: And I presume the union agrees to that stipulation?

Mr. Lundeberg: Yes.

Mr. Guntert: We will also stipulate that due notice and answer was received in time.

Mr. Moore: Yes, so stipulated.

Trial Examiner Batten: It is customary at these

hearings for the Trial Examiner to make a few remarks. I presume you have all been present at these proceedings and are probably familiar with what a Trial Examiner usually states. You are all familiar with the fact that this is a hearing before the National Labor Relations Board in the matter of the Richfield Oil Corporation and the Sailors Union of the Pacific, A. F. of L., being Case No. XXI-C-2248, consolidated with the matter of Richfield Oil Corporation and Pacific District Seafarers Engine Division, affiliated with the Seafarers International Union of North America, A. F. of L., being Case No. XXI-C-2249.

Now, as you are familiar with the fact, of course, that [6] the reporter that is now taking this proceeding is the official reporter of the Board and the record which is furnished by that reporter is the official record and the only record which may be used in this proceeding or any proceeding hereafter. During the course of the proceeding you may desire to make corrections in the record. If you do, you will draw up your suggestions for changes or corrections in the record in the form of a stipulation and have other counsel sign it. When it has been signed by all counsel and representatives, you will present the stipulation to the Trial Examiner and I will dispose of the matter. If you should draw a stipulation and there are parts that you agree to and parts that you cannot agree to, you will indicate on the stipulation those parts which you agree to and the parts which you cannot agree to, stating why you cannot, and then present the matter to the Trial Examiner.

Now, you will follow that same proceeding if you desire to correct the record up to the time that the case is transferred to the Board; and if it is after the hearing, you will forward the necessary papers to the Trial Examiner, attention Chief Trial Examiner, in Washington, D. C. If, after the case is transferred to the Board, you desire to make corrections in the record, you will draw it up in the form of a motion for correction of the transcript; and, if possible, secure a stipulation from the parties which you will attach thereto. [7] If you cannot agree, the Board then as a usual practice notifies the parties of the motion to correct, and you will have an opportunity to express your views in the matter.

If there are any oral motions—and this applies in the case of objections—I will appreciate it if you will first state your motion or your objection, followed by the reasons. Then if you care to argue the matter, will you please state that fact so that I may know when you begin your argument with respect to a motion or objection.

I want to say this: that there is no such thing as "off the record" in hearings which I conduct. So don't ask for it. In other words, you are either on the record or you are not, as far as this proceeding is concerned.

You will be allowed an automatic exception to all adverse rulings. So you do not need to take exceptions. I doubt whether it will occur in this hearing, but it does at times. Sometimes counsel or a representative is in doubt as to whether or not a ruling is adverse. If you are, I may be of some assistance to you in that. I don't think it is necessary for me to say anything about hearsay testimony or leading questions or whose witness this is. I might say a word or two:

I think there was a time when there was a hearsay rule. The exceptions have grown to the point where I don't think that even in court there is any longer such rule, except as it would [8] apply in this hearing. In other words, I have no objection to hearsay testimony, except that it must be such type of hearsay testimony which, of course, enables the opposing party to know what it's about and make some preparation to rebut such testimony.

In other words, it must identify people or places or time. Rumors and things of that sort I don't think are properly admissible. As to leading questions, I have never objected to them if it is on a matter that is not particularly in dispute. I mean, if it is the date of a meeting, the number of people who attended or something of that sort, why, don't let's waste time on that. But when it comes to the point of telling the Examiner and the Board what was said to the parties and what was done, I then permit the witnesses to testify.

Now, it doesn't make any difference to me whether the witness on the stand is a witness who was put on by the Board or someone else. It is not your witness or my witness. We are here to get all the facts upon which the Examiner and the Board may act.

At any time in a proceeding which I conduct, if it becomes obvious that a witness becomes adverse, even though you put the witness on, you may proceed in the matter of cross examination if the witness becomes really adverse.

If you will file with the Examiner any further written [9] motions or written pleadings, you will furnish them, please, with an original and four copies in order that I may see that the proper parties receive copies to file them. You undoubtedly are all familiar with the fact that you are entitled to orally argue this matter at the close of the testimony before the Examiner.

Again I want to say that that is on the record.

You are also entitled to file a brief at the close of the hearing with the Examiner.

Now, I want to say this: whether you desire to orally argue the matter or file a brief, I may decide that I want you to, either upon all of the issues or upon some particular point that has arisen in the hearing.

I want to say this: that if you do want to file a brief or if I require a brief, it will be a very, very short time. In other words, to use the more or less stock phrase, during the present emergency, of course these hearings are important and no extended time will be given to any of the parties for the purpose of filing a brief.

Now, I think that covers my opening statement. Are there any questions concerning it?

(No response.)

If not, are there any motions by any of the parties at this time?

(No response.) [10]

If there are no motions, then Board's counsel may proceed.

Mr. Moore: I beg your pardon. There is one motion I would like to make. That is to correct a typographical error in the complaint. I direct your attention to page 2, paragraph 5, subdivision (b) where the first line reads "Seafarers Engine Division has been at all times herein mentioned. . . ."

I move to amend the complaint by inserting in that line before the word "has" the words "is and."

Trial Examiner Batten: It will then read "is and has been at all times"?

Mr. Moore: Yes.

Trial Examiner Batten: Is there any objection to such amendment?

Mr. Guntert: No objection.

Trial Examiner Batten: If not, the amendment will be allowed.

Mr. Moore. In the ordinary course we would now present evidence on the question of jurisdiction of the Board; in other words, some facts as to the business of the company.

Respondent's counsel has very considerately prepared a statement, but I have suggested that we defer that until during the recess when we can go over it together and get it in final form.

Trial Examiner Batten: of course, I presume any form will be agreeable, won't it? I mean, I have hastily looked [11] over the pleadings. I understand Respondent doesn't question jurisdiction, do they?

Mr. Guntert: That is correct, Mr. Examiner.

Trial Examiner Batten: And commerce. So why is there any necessity of postponing it?

Mr. Moore: Because in the statement that has been prepared I have looked over it and in my opinion it needs a few additional facts.

Mr. Guntert: I am prepared to make those, Mr. Examiner.

Trial Examiner Batten: If you are, it seems to me you ought to go ahead. In fact, if there are any facts in it at all, it ought to be sufficient. Then there is no question of jurisdiction.

Mr. Moore: All right. We will go ahead with it that way.

Trial Examiner Batten: Let's proceed with the matter of jurisdiction and get it out of the way.

Mr. Guntert: Well, the Respondent Richfield Oil Corporation has admitted all allegations on the question of jurisdiction.

Trial Examiner Batten: And Respondent admits that it is engaged in commerce within the meaning of the Act, is that correct?

Mr. Guntert: We have. And the only allegation that we have denied is the allegation that what we have done as alleged is an unfair labor practice. That is the only issue. The [12] Richfield Oil Corporation is a Deleware Corporation. It is authorized to do business in the State of California, has its principal place of business at Los Angeles, California. It owns six tank ships. It is an integrated oil company. It engages in the production, refining, transportation and marketing of petroleum products.

The tank vessels are used to transport petroleum

products between the ports of the states of Oregon, Washington and California, and also offshore.

The Richfield Oil Corporation's tankers are now under time charter with the War Shipping Administration and the Richfield Oil Corporation is acting as an agent of the War Shipping Administration in the operation of those tankers.

Any products that are now being carried for Richfield are carried under voyage charters between the War Shipping Administration and the owner and Richfield as charterer.

Do you know of anything else to add?

Mr. Moore: I am prepared to stipulate to the facts as stated by Mr. Guntert, beginning, I believe, where you stated that the Respondent is a Deleware Corporation and ending just before you began speaking of the manner in which they are now chartering to the War Shipping Administration. I have no knowledge of that, and I don't object to it, of course. I have no knowledge of it, and I don't believe it is material so far as the Board's jurisdiction is concerned. [13]

Mr. Guntert: Perhaps not.

Trial Examiner Batten: Of course, up to that point you stipulate and agree with the statement which counsel has made?

Mr. Moore: That's right.

Trial Examiner Batten: Is that your position?

Mr. Guntert: I would prefer it to remain as a statement for the record.

Trial Examiner Batten: Is that satisfactory?

Mr. Guntert: Yes.

Trial Examiner Batten: I am asking the union

if that is agreeable, stipulating and agreeing up to the point where counsel started to talk about the War Shipping Administration?

Mr. Lundeberg: That's all right.

Trial Examiner Batten: And the balance you want to remain as your statement?

Mr. Guntert. That's right.

Trial Examiner Batten: Now, are there any additional facts that you want in that connection?

Mr. Moore: I should like to get an idea of the approximate volume of the company's business or the approximate volume of oil handled by the tankers, some idea of what magnitude the operation has.

Mr. Guntert: I could state that the Richfield Oil Corporation's business is in excess of 20 per cent—the gross [14] business is in excess of 20 per cent of the petroleum business on the west coast.

Mr. Moore: I will stipulate to that.

Trial Examiner Batten: Any further facts?

(No response.)

Well, that apparently is satisfactory, so far as the matter of commerce is concerned.

We will proceed.

Mr. Moore: I should like to ask Mr. Wilder to take the stand.

WALDO HAMMOND WILDER

called as a witness by and on behalf of the National Labor Relations Board, having been first duly sworn, was examined and testified as follows:

Direct Examination

Q. (By Mr. Moore). Will you state your full name, please? A. Waldo Hammond Wilder.

Q. By whom are you employed?

A. Richfield Oil Corporation.

Q. In what capacity? A. Port captain.

Q. Where are you stationed?

A. 1400 West 7th Street, Long Beach, California.

Q. By "port captain" does that mean that your authority is restricted to the Los Angeles area? [15]

A. Not necessarily, no, sir.

Q. In your capacity as port captain, what are your duties?

A. The dispatch of the vessels, inspection and maintenance of crew and certain supplies.

Q. Where do those operations take place?

A. Anywhere on this coast where the vessels operate and touch.

Q. Do you operate in various ports along the west coast? A. Yes.

Q. How many tankers does the Richfield Oil Corporation operate at the present time?

A. We own and operate six ocean-going tankers.

Q. Between what points do these tankers operate?

A. Pacific Coastwise and other places.

Q. Ports on the Pacific Coast? A. Yes.

(Testimony of Waldo Hammond Wilder.)

Q. And also foreign ports or ports off the mainland? A. Yes.

Q. Speaking generally, how long do voyages take?

A. I wouldn't care to answer that question without advice.

Mr. Guntert: I don't see where it is material, Mr. Examiner. There is only one issue here.

The Witness: I am not allowed to divulge that information. It's national secrecy.

Trial Examiner Batten: Do you mean how long does the average voyage [16] take?

Mr. Moore: Yes.

Trial Examiner Batten: Well, is there any objection to giving us an average time?

The Witness: I can't say that, sir.

Trial Examiner Batten: Considering your coastwise and otherwise?

The Witness: No, sir, I can't say that. I am instructed not to by the Government.

Trial Examiner Batten: Well, with due respect to what the Government has instructed you, I certainly see no reason why you shouldn't give us an average.

Mr. Moore: Mr. Examiner, I will withdraw the question.

Q. (By Mr. Moore.) Under ordinary circumstances, are the tankers that Richfield operates at sea for periods of several days or more?

Q. I would say several days. I am not limiting the number of days, not stating the number of days.

(Testimony of Waldo Hammond Wilder.)

Q. I understand that.

A. Several can be any number.

Q. Would you state what ports on the Pacific Coast the vessels visit?

A. I would say they are liable to visit any port on the Pacific Coast.

Q. What ports in your experience have they visited in the past? [17]

A. I don't feel that I am allowed to even say that, sir. I am under instructions by the Navy Department not to name ports or places or the names of vessels.

Trial Examiner Batten: I think it is sufficient to say that all of the ports——

The Witness: It would be any coastwise port.

Trial Examiner Batten: Any coastwise port from time to time covered in your business transactions?

The Witness: Yes.

Mr. Moore: Well, we may be able to get along with information as general as that. We will try.

I will attempt to ask these question in such a way that they won't elicit proscribed information.

Trial Examiner Batten: Well, let's proceed. As the witness thinks he may answer, he may do so. And if he thinks he shouldn't he may refuse. Then I will express my opinion.

Q. (By Mr. Moore) When tankers operated by the company visit Seattle, where do they dock?

A. You mean the terminals?

(Testimony of Waldo Hammond Wilder.)

Q. Yes.

A. They are liable to dock at any petroleum terminal up there.

Q. Can you state the one at which they have in the past docked?

A. Well, they have docked at Richfield. They have docked at others. [18]

Q. Where is the Richfield dock there, with reference to the town of Seattle?

A. It's in the west waterway.

Q. Where is that with reference to Seattle?

A. It's west of the city.

Q. About how far?

A. Of the city proper. Pardon?

Q. About how far?

A. I should say about five-eighths of a mile by airline, and it might be 2 to 2½ miles to the nearest part of the mainland of the city.

Q. You mean you have to cross water to get from that dock to the mainland to the city?

A. You go over a bridge, yes, sir.

Q. At Portland at what docks have the ships come in?

A. It's the same. They go to all docks there.

Q. And does Richfield——

A. Not each trip, not each trip. I can't say what docks they do. Sometimes when I dispatch them I don't know which dock they will go to.

Q. Does Richfield have a dock there?

A. Yes.

Q. And where is that dock located?

(Testimony of Waldo Hammond Wilder.)

A. That is at Linton.

Q. Where is Linton with reference to the City of Portland? [19]

A. It is about six miles north of the city proper. It's part of the city.

Trial Examiner Batten: Is this for the purpose of commerce?

Mr. Moore: No. It is for the purpose of showing how these seamen——

Trial Examiner Batten: I was going to say if it is for that purpose, I don't think it is necessary. If it is for some other purpose, go ahead.

Mr. Moore: Oh, it is.

Trial Examiner Batten: Proceed.

Mr. Moore: I am not going to introduce anything further on commerce.

Q. (By Mr. Moore) Now, in the San Francisco bay area where do Richfield ships go there?

A. Our terminal is at Point Richmond.

Q. Point Richmond?

A. They make other terminals, though.

Q. What other terminals?

A. Our main one is Point Orient, our terminal in San Francisco.

Q. Where is Point Orient?

A. That is near the north end of the bay proper, of San Francisco bay on the east side.

Q. Is it near Vallejo?

A. No, it is not near Vallejo. That is the San Pablo bay you are speaking of. It's near Richmond which would be the [20] nearest town.

(Testimony of Waldo Hammond Wilder.)

Q. Do your ships visit Oleum? A. Yes.

Q. Do they stop at Avon?

A. They do, yes, sir.

Q. Do they put in at Oakland ever?

A. I haven't known them to put in at Oakland for some time. We had a terminal, but it's not in use.

Q. Does the Richfield Company have a dock in the San Francisco Bay area? A. Yes.

Q. Is it in use at this time? A. Yes.

Q. Where is that located?

A. Point Richmond.

Q. In the Los Angeles area where do Richfield tankers dock?

A. Oh, they dock at all the terminals, sometimes two terminals on one voyage.

Our principal terminals are in Long Beach.

Q. Where else do they dock?

A. They might dock in Wilmington or in San Pedro or Terminal Island.

Q. Does Richfield own a dock in this rea, the Los Angeles area?

A. They own two terminals in Long Beach and one that is not used [21] in San Pedro.

Q. How long is a tanker ordinarily in port when it is loading?

A. Various times. Loading operations could be anywhere from 12 to 24, 36 or 48 hours. There is no limit.

Q. Can you say what the average time for loading a tanker would be?

(Testimony of Waldo Hammond Wilder.)

A. That is difficult to answer now. It depends upon what the Government allows us, accumulation on the shore tanks and the terminals.

Q. Well, under present——

A. Sometimes it's a thousand barrels an hour and sometimes it could be up to 12 or 15 thousand barrels an hour.

Q. Yes. Well, can you say what the average time that is required is right now?

A. Well, we had a tanker in one particular time where it was supposed to load about six thousand barrels an hour, but it only loaded about four thousand barrels an hour. It depends on the size of the tanker, what her capacity is.

Q. It depends also on the type of cargo it is taking on? A. Very true, yes, sir.

Q. Well, can you say what the average time is that is required to load one of them, your best estimate, I mean?

A. Well, it would generally run about 12 to 15 hours. That's average. [22]

Q. Now, that is from the time loading operations start until it's ready to go, is it?

A. That's loading operations.

Q. Well, now, how long would the ship be in the port all together?

A. Well, if she was loading 12 hours, I should say she would be 16 hours, something like that.

Q. If it came into port empty——

A. There are factors there, sir, that I can't

(Testimony of Waldo Hammond Wilder.)

answer on that. It's military and naval secrecy involved.

Q. How long ordinarily does it take to unload a tanker?

A. That is a difficult question also, as any tanker man would also admit. It depends on how far you pump and what pressure you are working against, the height that the product is in a shore tank that you are pumping into. Sometimes it will range anywhere in our vessels from six thousand an hour down to 500 an hour. It's rather difficult to answer.

Q. In your experience in west coast ports here will you give us your best estimate as to the average length of time it takes to unload——

A. Discharge a cargo?

Q. Pardon me?

A. To discharge a cargo, one commodity?

Q. To unload a tanker.

A. Well, that's rather involved, too, because some of them [23] carry many products, several products; and some of them only carry one. And it varies from trip to trip. I should say anywhere from 20 to 48 hours under present conditions.

Q. The tankers unload always at a dock, do they?

A. Not necessarily, no sir. Unload?

Q. Yes. A. They unload at a dock?

Q. Always unload at a dock, never moored offshore?

(Testimony of Waldo Hammond Wilder.)

A. Yes, but they haven't had that occasion for some years.

Q. Is the same true of loading?

A. No, sir. We have outside ports for loading more than they do discharging.

Q. You load from what? A lighter, or how do you do it? A. Submarine pipe line.

Q. That would be in a bay area but not attached to the shore——

A. Not necessarily in a bay area. Some are in open roadsteds, some in bays.

Q. Well, is most of your loading done at a dock? A. Yes, sir.

Q. Will you describe briefly the crew that is used on the tankers that Richfield operate?

A. The civilian crews are 36 to 40.

Q. How many unlicensed personnel would that include?

A. That would include about 27 or 28 or more.

Q. How would those be divided between deck, engine and [24] steward's department?

A. Well, the average one of our ships would carry ten men in the deck department, unlicensed and 8 to 9 men in the engine department unlicensed and 8 men in the steward's department unlicensed.

Q. Now, while the tankers are in port what duties do the unlicensed deck personnel perform?

A. Principally the loading operations.

Q. Loading or unloading?

A. Yes. Tanktop watch, we call it, hose watch.

(Testimony of Waldo Hammond Wilder.)

Q. In your operations do you ever go into a port and unload and then reload? A. Yes.

Q. Here on the west coast? A. Yes, sir.

Q. Does that happen most of the time?

A. No, not most of the time.

Q. Does it happen infrequently?

A. Well, it happens frequently.

Q. You were saying what the deck department does while the ship is in port. Will you continue with that?

A. Well, there might be small amounts of stores they will take aboard while in port. If she is in port any extent or length of time and the watches are broken, they might paint.

Q. Under ordinary circumstances, I think your estimate of the [25] average loading was 12 to 15 hours? A. Something like that.

Q. Will you state how many of the unlicensed personnel in the deck department are aboard during those operations?

A. There is sufficient to move the vessel at all times, if necessary, in an inflammable or gaseous condition as required by the safety rules of the Board.

Q. How many would that be?

A. That would be at least one watch.

Q. One-third of the normal crew?

A. Yes, sir.

Q. What requirements are you under with regard to the engine department, if any?

A. One watch would take care of that also.

(Testimony of Waldo Hammond Wilder.)

Q. So that when the vessel is in port is it true to say that one-third of the deck and engine department personnel must be aboard at all times?

A. Not necessarily on the engine department. Your wipers wouldn't be on duty at night time. We favor the less aboard the ship the safer she is, insofar as she has enough to be removed from the harbor in an emergency.

Q. You mean by that you ask part of the crew to leave the ship?

A. No, we don't ask them to. If they wish to, they may go.

Trial Examiner Batten: Generally speaking, as a protective [26] measure it would require one-third of the crew?

The Witness: Not the total crew, no, sir. The steward's department wouldn't come into it at all.

Trial Examiner Batten: And it would only be one-third of what department? The unlicensed personnel?

The Witness: Well, one-third of the deck department, one-third of the engine department, roughly speaking, with the exception of the wipers.

Trial Examiner Batten: I don't mean to break it down any further. It would be approximately one-third of the engine department and one-third of the deck department?

The Witness: Approximately one-third, yes, sir.

Q. (By Mr. Moore) Do you take on stores in all ports every time you dock?

A. Not all. We generally buy small stores to

(Testimony of Waldo Hammond Wilder.)

replenish, like perishables, and the like of that, sometimes in the north. But we store heavily in the southern end. That is where the home office is, where the purchasing department is.

Q. When you take on stores who does that loading and storing of that material?

A. It's just small incidentals. We might request some of the crew and pay them overtime for it if they are off duty. Otherwise, when a work party is available, we hire a work party just for that purpose.

Q. What is a "work party"? [27]

A. Well, we try to get seamen. In fact, we have been getting seamen to do it, men acquainted with vessels.

Q. How do they go about loading that?

A. Well, some of it is done over the gangway and certain packages that we wish to take over the gangway, it's done that way. Otherwise, it's taken on a sling, on possibly the ship's gear or dock gear derricks.

Q. Do the outside work parties come aboard to store the material in the vessel?

A. Yes, sir, they come aboard.

Q. Where those outside work parties are not available does the captain delegate a part of the crew to do that work? A. Yes.

Q. And is that in addition to the men who are on watch? Or do the men on watch do that work?

A. No. The men on a tanktop watch, they don't do it. The men on watch in the engine room, they

(Testimony of Waldo Hammond Wilder.)

don't come up and get anything. That would be men off watch. That very infrequently happens.

Q. Would it be unlicensed personnel of the deck department?

A. Yes, mostly. Sometimes is would be some of the unlicensed engine department which might possibly go up and pick up one piece, or something like that, that they wouldn't want the deck department to handle. That is very infrequent, though.

Q. Is there any day work in addition to ordinary watches [28] aboard ship?

A. Not unless the watches are broken.

Mr. Guntert: Mr. Examiner, I can't see the materiality of this. I don't want to be objecting——

Mr. Moore: I will be glad to say what the materiality is.

Trial Examiner Batten: You may proceed until you get to the point where I can tell the purpose of it.

Q. (By Mr. Moore) When a tanker is in port what opportunities do the unlicensed deck and engine personnel have to go ashore?

A. They are off watch and sometimes we get men who are acquainted with the vessels to come aboard and relieve them when they are available.

Q. How often is that done?

A. I can't say offhand. If it's night sometimes we will have them—the fact of the matter is sometimes the men don't come back for their watches, and we are forced to get men to keep from shutting down and delaying the war activity.

Q. Is it true, then, to say that a seaman in the

(Testimony of Waldo Hammond Wilder.)

unlicensed deck or engine department can go ashore whenever he is not on watch? A. Yes, sir.

Q. You would have to qualify that, wouldn't you, by saying unless there is other work for them to do such as loading [29] stores? A. Yes.

Q. Sometimes we request them to remain and load stores. We pay overtime under that condition.

Q. Is it necessary for a man to get permission to go ashore?

A. Not if he is off watch, unless the officer in charge at the time would request them to remain for such specific duty or job that he had in mind. Otherwise they would go.

Q. How are the watches arranged? During what hours do the men stand watches in the deck and engine department?

A. Well, they range in two sets of four hours a day, four on and eight off, it's commonly called.

Q. That would be eight hour's work split into two shifts during a 24-hour period? A. Yes.

Q. That is true for the deck and engine department? A. Yes.

Q. Do the unlicensed personnel live aboard the ship men they are in port? A. They may.

Q. Facilities are furnished so that they may?

A. Yes. Certain times we don't feed aboard when we are handling explosive cargoes, dangerous cargoes. Then they are given meal money.

Q. Do the unlicensed personnel generally live aboard the ship? [30] By "live aboard" I mean eat and sleep there?

(Testimony of Waldo Hammond Wilder.)

A. Yes, sir. That is the general practice.

Q. Will you describe just briefly how your tanker personnel sign on and off, how they are employed by the company and how they end their employment, if they do?

A. Well, when they first come aboard they sign shipping articles describing the nature of the trade insofar as we are allowed to give it under these war time conditions. And when they resign or are discharged, why, they just sign a release.

Q. Are those shipping articles for a stated period of employment?

A. On coastwise generally not to exceed three calendar months or six calendar months or—we allow the master to set that particular time.

Q. Is that the language? Not to exceed that period? A. Yes.

Q. How are the men paid? How and when are the men paid?

A. In coastwise trade we pay them every 30 days, but we allow them to withdraw on their wages practically as often as they want to, generally at each port, sometimes two and three times in one day. We don't object to that.

Q. When they ask for an advance do they go to the captain or do they go to a shore representative? A. They go to the captain. [31]

Q. That is aboard the ship? A. Yes, sir.

Q. Has your experience been that the turnover is large or small in the tanker industry as it affects Richfield?

(Testimony of Waldo Hammond Wilder.)

A. Well, quite large, I should say, since the great expansion of shipbuilding and launching, much more than the normal times because we have been paying bonuses and one thing and another.

Mr. Moore: No further questions.

Trial Examiner Batten: Does the union have any questions of this witness?

Mr. Lundeberg: No.

Trial Examiner Batten: Mr. Guntert?

Mr. Guntert: There are one or two points that I would like to clear there.

Cross Examination

Q. (By Mr. Guntert) Captain, in your designating the time required for the vessel to load or discharge, you were speaking only of the actual pumping operations, were you not?

A. Yes, sir.

Q. It is a fact the vessel may be in port a good deal longer than that? A. Oh, yes, yes.

Q. You speak of handling stores. You say members of the deck department off duty. If you had some stores to handle, [32] they would be asked to handle them? A. Yes, sir.

Q. And if they did, they would get overtime; is that correct? A. Yes, sir.

Mr. Guntert: That is all.

Trial Examiner Batten: Any further questions?

Redirect Examination

Q. (By Mr. Moore)) The captain has the authority to order them to load the stores, has he not?

(Testimony of Waldo Hammond Wilder.)

A. Oh, I presume he has, as long as they are on the shipping articles they are subject to his orders, his legal orders.

Q. Can you say what the average in port time of your tankers is?

A. Well, I would have to take the abstract and add them all up and divide them by the number of trips, they vary so much. We had a ship recently that was in port about 56 hours. I expected she would be in port about 32 hours.

It's hard to say, particularly under the conditions of the war.

Q. Well, can you estimate how long your ships are tied at a dock on the average?

Trial Examiner Batten: I think you testified, did you not, the average was 15 hours?

The Witness: I should say something like that. It's pretty difficult to say what dock they go to, what terminal [33] they go to. In fact, we load at one terminal. We load one commodity at one particular terminal and another commodity at the other. They are handled differently, and, in the —under the Government setup we are not allowed to get the cargoes down to the terminals, except under certain conditions; and I never know when that will be until the last moment. It's secret. We have to get permission from the Government.

It is a very difficult question to answer. I would have to figure to get that.

Q. What you call the time in port is different from the time at a dock, is it not?

(Testimony of Waldo Hammond Wilder.)

A. Oh, yes. That is different, yes.

Q. The time in port is judged from the time the ship enters the port until it leaves that port, is it not? A. That's right.

Q. And the time in dock is generally shorter than that?

A. Well, that necessarily is shorter than that. If the vessel comes right to a dock and goes right out again, that is one situation. She might go out to anchor, and that's another situation. The reasons why she goes out to anchor I am not at liberty to answer here.

Mr. Moore: That is all.

Trial Examiner Batten: Any further questions?

(No response.) [34]

If not, that is all.

The Witness: Pardon?

Trial Examiner Batten: That is all.

(Witness excused.)

Trial Examiner Batten: I think we will recess for about ten minutes.

(Brief recess.)

Trial Examiner Batten: Let us proceed, gentlemen.

Mr. Moore: Mr. Wilder, would you mind taking the stand again for a few minutes?

WALDO HAMMOND WILDER

called as a witness by and on behalf of the National Labor Relations Board, having been previously duly sworn, resumed the stand and testified further as follows:

Redirect Examination (Resumed)

Q. (By Mr. Moore) I wanted to ask you, Mr. Wilder, while the tanker is in port, who is in charge of the crew?

A. The senior deck officer aboard or deck officer on duty.

Mr. Moore: That is all.

Recross Examination

Q. (By Mr. Guntert) Captain, you a few moments ago testified about the time that the sailors have in port. What is the actual thing that happens when the vessel come in? Do these men stay aboard? Or do they go ashore?

A. Well, they just pile off. Those that are not on watch do, [35] if I might use that expression.

Q. Do you have to encourage them to leave?

A. No. They are gone anyway. Sometimes I have difficulty in keeping them there until they get their mail.

Q. Do these men have homes ashore?

A. Sometimes, you know, I have to think of several things on mail these days because quite a number of the draft communications go to them; and I want to see that they get them. Sometimes I have difficulty getting them to them before they are gone.

(Testimony of Waldo Hammond Wilder.)

Q. Do many men have homes in the area?

A. I should say the greater number of them have homes in the south.

Q. They are privileged, however, to come back to the ship for their meals, if they wish, or to sleep? A. Oh, yes, yes.

Q. And those meals are free? It is a part of them——

. That is a part of their remuneration, yes.

Q. You mentioned the ships sometimes going to anchor. That is within the port. Will you distinguish between the time the vessel is in dock at any port? Are the men permitted to go ashore if the vessel is not actually docked and is lying outside at anchor?

A. Yes, generally, unless we get naval orders otherwise. And that is very, very rare. I fact, I haven't been ordered [36] to hold them aboard.

Q. Now, you have stated that these men go ashore as soon as they get in port if they are off watch; and you have also stated that you would prefer that they did.

Now, can you give us your reasons for your preference?

A. Well, I always figured under these conditions the fewer there are aboard the safer, down to the number that is required by the authorities.

Q. Are you familiar with the policy of Richfield with respect to the issuance of passes in order to go on board ship? A. Yes, sir.

Q. What is that policy?

A. There isn't any passes.

(Testimony of Waldo Hammond Wilder.)

Q. You do not issue passes? A. No, sir.

Q. And the reason for that?

A. The safety of the crew and the surrounding property, the terminals, the vessels.

Q. Is it your opinion that every additional man that is aboard ship increases the hazards?

A. Yes, sir. That is my——

Mr. Moore: Objected to.

Mr. Guntert: I will reframe the question, Mr. Examiner.

Q. (By Mr. Guntert) If passes are issued to representatives of the labor unions, what is your opinion as to the result of [37] that?

Mr. Moore: Objected to.

Trial Examiner Batten: What is the basis of the objection?

Mr. Moore: That it is immaterial. It calls for a conclusion of the witness.

Trial Examiner Batten: Well, of course, I think a man who is a port captain or a business agent of a union should be permitted to express an opinion or a conclusion. That is, I have always felt that anyone in authority, in a responsible position, whether a member of the union or a part of the company organization, should be permitted to express opinions and conclusions.

You may answer.

The Witness: What was the question?

Trial Examiner Batten: Read the question, please.

(Question read.)

(Testimony of Waldo Hammond Wilder.)

The Witness: I don't understand the "labor unions."

Q. (By Mr. Guntert) Organizations?

A. Well, when passes are issued to one organization, I presume they would have to be issued to all organizations. Otherwise we would have trouble. Then we would have trouble.

Q. And what would be the result of issuing passes to all these representatives, then?

A. Well, we would have inter-union trouble.

Q. Would that increase the number of men that go on board ship? [38]

Q. Would that increase the hazards aboard ship?

A. As I said, the fewer men aboard the ship the safer I think she is.

Q. In your opinion is the loading and discharging of petroleum products a hazardous operation?

A. It is, yes, sir.

Q. You stated that the more people aboard the greater the possibility of accidents and disaster?

A. That's right.

Q. Can you give some specific hazards attending this operation at which you state would be increased by having many people coming aboard?

A. Well, the loading officer or the mate or loading officer, or whoever it is has charge of the vessel at the time, the more aboard the vessel the more his attention is taken from the loading or discharging operations. We have armament aboard

(Testimony of Waldo Hammond Wilder.)

those ships. Certainly a loading officer can't be responsible for a number of people coming aboard. The armament might be tampered with. It might become known what it was.

We have directives against allowing anybody aboard the ship, unless there is urgent necessity of their being aboard ship. If the loading officer's attention is detracted——

Q. Would one coming aboard the vessel have an opportunity of acquiring information which would be of value to the enemy?

A. I should say yes, sir. He can certainly see what the armament [39] is. He would know what vessel he is aboard, what vessel is in port. We have removed and been required to remove all identification of the vessel. Even the names on the life boats are painted off, the names of the vessels are taken off. If they are metal, they have been taken off. If they have been painted on, they are painted off.

Q. Could the party coming aboard have an opportunity of learning the courses and convoy information and escort vessels?

A. I should say yes, by conversation, having accessibility to the crew they could.

Q. How could, for example, courses and positions and movements of vessels be ascertained?

A. Well, it wouldn't take a man very long to find out the names of the headlands along this coast, islands, how far they passed off. He could cer-

(Testimony of Waldo Hammond Wilder.)

tainly establish routes, what islands they went between, if any. That would establish routes.

Q. Would this issuing of passes facilitiate sabotage?

Mr. Ryan: We object to this. In the first place, we object on the ground that the witness is being led, and furthermore, on the ground that he isn't necessarily qualified to express opinions in that respect.

Trial Examiner Batten: Well, I think the questions are quite leading, particularly with a man who ought to know all these matters without any leading. I think it would be pre- [40] ferable to have the witness tell us what these different factors are, what he believes increases, if it does, the difficulties.

Mr. Guntert: I don't know just what your procedure is about introducing documents or introducing documentary evidence.

Trial Examiner Batten: With exhibits first have the reporter mark them for identification. Then when you have identified the exhibit, and so forth, you may then offer them or you may examine the witness after they have been marked for identification.

Mr. Guntert: I would like to have these marked for identification.

Trial Examiner Batten: That will be Respondent's Exhibit 1. How many do you have there?

Mr. Guntert: There are two. I have some more. I have two at this time.

(Testimony of Waldo Hammond Wilder.)

(The documents referred to were marked for identification as Respondent's Exhibits 1 and 2.)

Mr. Guntert: What was the ruling on that question, Mr. Examiner?

Trial Examiner Batten: Well, I suggested to you that I thought your questions were leading. I would suggest that you have the witness tell us as to the factors which increase the hazards. When his knowledge has been exhausted, I would say then, of course, you may proceed with rather leading quest- [41] tions. But let's have the witness tell us what he knows first. I think your questions are leading.

Are there any others that you recall that increase the hazards, any other factors?

The Witness: Well, I have stated that the more aboard the vessel, why, the more the officer in charge, his attention is detracted from his duties. And if people come aboard the vessel, any person aboard the vessel is under the control of the loading officer or the officer on duty. If he is loading a vessel, he can't watch visitors aboard the vessel, if he is paying attention to his duties.

As I have said, we have armament aboard that is supposed to be secret, and a person coming aboard certainly knows what that armament is that we have got aboard and can take that information ashore with him.

It could be very easily done to sabotage any of

(Testimony of Waldo Hammond Wilder.)

these pieces of ordinance. All ship owners have been warned against the possibility of sabotage, such as these pencil bombs or fire paper, as it is commonly called, and the identification of the vessel, coming aboard, being allowed access to the ship, it would take them very long to find out how much she is loaded, about what time she would be finished loading; therefore, approximately what time she would be ready to depart. He has the name of the vessel from learning it when he comes aboard, and there is certain cargoes that tankers load that [42] identify the port to which they are bound.

Q. (By Mr. Guntert) You stated that persons coming aboard distract the officer on watch. What about the men that are actually doing the work?

A. Their attention would also be detracted.

Q. Captain, is Richfield in its tanker operations under any particular body of federal regulations, under these wartime conditions?

A. Yes, sir. They work under the directives and rules and regulations as laid down by the War Shipping Administration, also under the safety rules as laid down by the captain of the port, the United States Coast Guard.

Q. I am handing you what has been marked for identification as Respondent's Exhibits 1 and 2 and ask you what they are?

Mr. Ryan: Mr. Examiner, I might say that it is the practice in this area to show exhibits to

(Testimony of Waldo Hammond Wilder.)

counsel before they are shown to a witness. We have not yet seen those .

(Brief pause in proceedings.)

Mr. Guntert: Has everybody had an opportunity now to examine this, to identify this?

Trial Examiner Batten: I think you may proceed.

Q. (By Mr. Guntert) Captain, I hand you what have been marked Respondent's Exhibits 1 and 2 and ask you what they are?

A. This No. 1 is the Security Order No. 1 of the War Shipping Administration. [43]

Q. Is Richfield obligated to abide by those orders? A. Yes, sir.

Q. What is the principal purpose of that Order No. 1?

Mr. Moore: I will object to that.

Trial Examiner Batten: Well, I think that is objectionable. I presume anybody reading that could tell that, could they not?

Mr. Guntert: I will ask it in this way: I wanted to call attention to a particular portion of that order.

Mr. Moore: Unless he has some knowledge outside of what it states——

Trial Examiner Batten: I think the question should be re-stated.

Q. (By Mr. Guntert) Captain, is there any particular part of that order which in your opinion directly is pertinent to the issue here, the

(Testimony of Waldo Hammond Wilder.)

question which we have been discussing here, the security of the vessels, the men and the cargoes?

A. Well, the third paragraph——

Trial Examiner Batten: Will you speak more loudly, Captain? I can't hear you.

The Witness: The third paragraph reads:

> "All agents are directed to comply with such security orders and to take all other reasonable precautions to accomplish the objectives of such orders. Failure to comply with such orders on the part of any agents will constitute cause for relocation of such agency." [44]

Q. (By Guntert) In establishing the policy of not issuing passes to anyone not in the employ of the company, is that in your opinion carrying out the provisions of this order?

A. I should say it was.

Trial Examiner Batten: Well, now, tell us how you can construe this to include passes.

The Witness: Well, I have in mind what I have already stated, that the more people that are aboard the ship, the more danger there is.

Trial Examiner Batten: Is there any other reason that you have?

The Witness: No, sir.

Trial Examiner Batten: What is it?

The Witness: No, sir.

Trial Examiner Batten: Is that the only reason?

The Witness: That is the main reason, yes, sir, that is on this particular exhibit.

(Testimony of Waldo Hammond Wilder.)

Q. (By Mr. Guntert) Calling your attention now to Security Order No. 2, I would like to call particular attention to paragraph 10. Can you tell us what that provides? A. Paragraph 10:

> "Visitors: Visitors to piers and vessels should be limited to cases of absolute necessity."

Q. In your opinion is it absolutely necessary that union representatives go aboard ship in order to meet with their [45] membership.

Mr. Moore: Objected to.

Trial Examiner Batten: Will you read that question?

(Question read.)

Trial Examiner Batten: Well, I don't think this man is qualified to answer that question.

Mr. Guntert: I asked him his opinion. I think he is qualified, Mr. Examiner.

Trial Examiner Batten: I don't think the witness is qualified. This says "visitors." You want to ask him whether visitors should be permitted to go on the piers and on the vessels. I think perhaps he can express an opinion. The question is whether union agents are visitors. I don't know. I don't think this witness is qualified to say whether a union official——

Mr. Guntert: I withdraw the question.

I would like to offer these in evidence as Respondent's Exhibits 1 and 2.

(Testimony of Waldo Hammond Wilder.)

Trial Examiner Batten: If there is no objection, they will be received.

(The documents heretofore marked for identification as Respondent's Exhibits 1 and 2 were received in evidence.)

RESPONDENT'S EXHIBIT NO. 1

War Shipping Administration
Washington

Security Order No. 1

To All Agents of the War Shipping Administration:

Is is extremely important that information relating to ship movements and communications be properly protected and that any laxness in the manner in which such information is handled by those to whom it is given in the course of shipping operations be eliminated. Any disclosure of such information is highly detrimental to the conduct of the war by the United States and the United Nations. The methods of handling such information must be further improved immediately.

In order to accomplish these objectives, the Administrator has designated J. C. Cutler, Director, Division of Security and Communications, as Security Officer for the War Shipping Administration. The Security Officer will issue "Security Orders" from time to time with the approval of the Administrator.

All agents are directed to comply with such Se-

(Testimony of Waldo Hammond Wilder.)

curity Orders, and to take all other reasonable precautions to accomplish the objectives of such Orders. Failure to comply with such Orders on the part of any agent shall constitute cause for the revocation of such agency.

This Order shall be effective as of October 26th, 1942.

By Direction of the Administrator
(Sgd.) W. C PEET, Jr.
Secretary

October 24, 1942.

RESPONDENT'S EXHIBIT No. 2

War Shipping Administration
Washington

Security Order No. 2

To All Agents of the War Shipping Administration:

The following rules and instructions are hereby promulgated and shall be observed by all agents in the operation of vessels:

1. Appointment of Security Officers

Each agent shall appoint promptly a responsible person, preferably an official, from his organization as Security Officer, and shall report the name of such officer, together with his employment record giving full information bearing upon such person's security qualifications, including place of birth, former employment, etc. to the Security Offifficer of the War Shipping Administration on or before No-

(Testimony of Waldo Hammond Wilder.)

vember 2nd, 1942. Such Security Officer for each agent shall be directed by the agent to cooperate with the Security Officer of the War Shipping Administration in carrying out all orders and other instructions received from the War Shipping Administration, and to cooperate in all other respects in the maintenance of absolute security of information.

2. Education of Personnel Regarding Security

The Security Officer for each agent shall be authorized and directed by such agent to take such measures as may be appropriate to inform adequately all employees, officers, and agents of such agent of the scope and purpose of the Security Orders and appropriate means for their enforcement, and shall generally be charged with the responsibility of educating the staff of the agent as to the need for security of such information.

3. Employment of Personnel

All agents of the War Shipping Administration are directed to review the personal history and other pertinent factors with respect to each administrative officer or employee employed by such agent, particularly those newly employed within the last eighteen months. No additional administrative personnel shall be employed by any agent without careful advance scrutiny as to each such employee's history and background and other pertinent qualifications and without careful check of all references and past employment.

(Testimony of Waldo Hammond Wilder.)

4. Security of Secret Documents

Agents of the War Shipping Administration are required to maintain maximum security of documents which would be of assistance to the enemy. Such documents include stowage plans, ships' manifests, cargo work sheets, bills of lading and any document containing informaiion regarding the routing of ships, the current and forward position of ships, convoy information, marine and war risk casualties. The circulation of all such documents should be restricted to officials who must have such information in connection with the day-to-day operation of vessels. When not in use, such documents should be kept in a safe place under combination lock, if possible; if not, then under lock and key and such documents shall not be retained in the agents' general files.

5. Nou-Disclosure of Information

Loose talk must be curbed at once, and all officers and employees of agents are required to refrain from disclosing, verbally or in writing, information regarding the following matters, except where absolutely necessary:

(a) The sailing or arrival date of any vessel. Whenever practicable references to sailing dates should be made indefinite so as to place the date within an indefinite peried of not less than a week's time, such as "expected arrive 1st part October" or "due mid-October" or "expected sail end October."

(Testimony of Waldo Hammond Wilder.)

(b) The route which any vessel is to follow. Since routing instructions are furnished by the Navy and constitute the most vital single item of information in connection with vessel operations, the utmost care must be taken to make certain that this information is not made available by the Master to anyone (including the owner and agents) except a properly constituted Naval authority.

(c) Information as to destination of vessel.

(d) Any other vital military information such as armament-defensive or offensive weapons or installations, escort vessels, convoy or assembly ports, etc.

(e) Marine and war risk casualties involving information as to routes or positions of ships.

6. Shippers and Consignees

Arrivals from and sailing for particular destinations must never be announced in the press, in advertisements, nor in any manner whatsoever except to the extent absolutely necessary for the purposes of efficient operation of the vessel and in such instances such information shall be discreetly disseminated to the very limited extent consistent with the necessities presented. Detailed instructions regarding shipping documents such as bills of lading, dock receipts, etc., will be furnished at later date by separate order.

7. Ordering Supplies and Services

In ordering bunkers, stores, supplies and other

(Testimony of Waldo Hammond Wilder.)

material, also pilots, tug boats, repairmen, surveyors, lighters, etc., care should be taken not to disclose the sailing or arrival date or the destination of the vessel, and purchases must be restricted to sources deemed to be reliable.

8. Position Reports

Daily or periodic position charts, bulletins, or reports and the dissemination of them must be restricted to absolute necessity. Pierboards or signs, including gangway signs, indicating the names, destinations, or sailing dates of vessels should also be eliminated entirely.

9. Shoreside and Seagoing Personnel

Crew's Articles should be drawn so as not to disclose the nature, duration, or area of the intended voyage. Crews should be impressed with the necessity for secrecy for themselves and their families. Further instructions as to labor relations security will be covered by separate Order.

10. Visitors

Visitors to piers and vessels should be limited to cases of absolute necessity.

11. Communications

All communications that cannot be handled by registered mail regarding confidential and secret matters directed to the War Shipping Administration or other agencies having teletype connections should be handled by teletype as first choice, and by telephone as second preference, or telegram as third

(Testimony of Waldo Hammond Wilder.)
choice, and then only in cases of emergency. All communications containing secret information as defined in Paragraph 5, a to e inclusive, sent to War Shipping Administration by registered mail shall be addressed to an individual. Such communications sent by registered mail (ordinary mail shall not be used) shall be sent in a regular envelope with an inner envelope marked "Secret" and addressed to the person or section for whom it is intended.

12. Manifests, Stowage Plans, Bills of Lading

Whenever practicable, Consignees' mail, manifests, stowage plans, bills of lading and all other documents transmitted to the port of destination in connection with discharge of the vessel should go forward on the vessel itself in a locked, weighted and perforated box, and should not be transmitted so as to arrive prior to the date of vessel arrival.

13. Cables and Foreign Communications

All foreign communications should be handled in conformity with the Administrator's letter dated June 1st, 1942.

14. Cooperation with Other Agencies

Every agent will be required to extend the utmost cooperation with Army, Navy, State Department, Post Office Department, Federal Bureau of Investigation and all other governmental agencies concerned with the problem of security of shipping information.

15. Circulation of Security Orders

Copies of every Security Order shall be distrib-

(Testimony of Waldo Hammond Wilder.)

uted to every administrative official and employee of the agent.

16. Effective Date

This Order shall be effective as of October 26th, 1942.

By Direction of the Administrator

(Sgd.) W. C. PEET, Jr.
Secretary

October 24, 1942.

Trial Examiner Batten: Mr. Guntert, you are going to pass over to some other directive now, are you? [46]

Mr. Guntert: Yes.

Trial Examiner Batten: Do you have any objection if I ask the witness a question?

Mr. Guntert: There is just one other question on that same point.

Trial Examiner Batten: Then you may proceed.

Mr. Guntert: I skipped over it before I got into this matter.

Q. (By Mr. Guntert) That was the question, as to the time the men leaving the ship when it gets into port, Captain, in your opinion, what percentage of the time that a vessel is in port do the men that are not on watch spend aboard ship? What would you say would be the average time?

A. Very little, very little.

Q. In other words, practically all the time that they are not on watch when the ship is in port they are ashore; is that your statement?

(Testimony of Waldo Hammond Wilder.)

A. Yes, sir. That is my experience.

Mr. Guntert: That is all I wanted to ask on that, Mr. Examiner.

Trial Examiner Batten: I wanted to ask you with respect to Respondent's Exhibits 1 and 2. I notice in Respondent's Exhibit 1 that Mr. Cutler was appointed as director. Now, has any person connected with the War Shipping Administration advised you, either verbally or in writing, that either of these [47] orders was intended or is applicable to the class of people that we are considering in this hearing? Or is that your personal interpretation of it?

The Witness: The question is whether any member of the War Shipping Administration stated that to me?

Trial Examiner Batten: That's right.

The Witness: No, sir, they have not.

Trial Examiner Batten: In other words, is that yours or your company's interpretation of this security order? I mean, to comply with it it would be necessary to refuse passes, is that right ?

The Witness: Yes, sir.

Mr. Guntert: Were you through, Mr. Examiner?

Trial Examiner Batten: Yes, I am through.

Q. (By Mr. Guntert) Captain, has the War Shipping Administration, or any federal office that you know of, advised that those orders do not include representatives of organizations such as labor unions? A. No, sir.

Trial Examiner Batten: Of course, it has always

(Testimony of Waldo Hammond Wilder.)

been the customary practice to issue those passes, hasn't it, up to the time that you issued this instruction on the basis of these orders?

The Witness: I don't know of a pass being issued by my company since before the war, just about the time of the war. [48]

Trial Examiner Batten: Is there any reason, Mr. Wilder, that you discontinued issuing passes before you received these orders?

The Witness: I was at sea until midsummer, sir. What transpired previous to my taking this shore position I do not know, sir.

Trial Examiner Batten: These are October, 1942.

The Witness: I became port captain in October, 1942.

Trial Examiner Batten: What date?

The Witness: October 8th, as I recall.

Trial Examiner Batten: And when you took charge had the order already been issued revoking passes?

The Witness: I had received orders from the manager of the Marine Department that all passes had been revoked; that they were not issuing any passes.

Trial Examiner Batten: So prior to the issuance of Security Order No. 1 and 2, Respondent's Exhibits 1 and 2, you had already revoked passes?

The Witness: I hadn't revoked passes, no, sir.

Trial Examiner Batten: The company had?

The Witness: The company had. Taking the

(Testimony of Waldo Hammond Wilder.)

word of the Marine manager, they had, yes, sir, prior to my acceptance of this position.

Mr. Gunter: Is that all, Mr. Examiner?

Trial Examiner Batten: Yes. [49]

Q. (By Mr. Guntert) Captain, speaking of passes, do you know to whom passes were issued?

A. Well, in years gone by all those passes were issued to slop chest venders.

Mr. Guntert: Mr. Examiner, I don't know whether the captain is very familiar with that or not, but for the record I would like to say that the Richfield has never issued any passes to any representatives of any organizations, except pursuant to contracts.

May I have Respondent's Exhibits 3 and 4 marked for identification.

(The documents referred to were marked for identification as Respondent's Exhibits 3 and 4.)

Q. (By Mr. Guntert) Captain, I am handing you what have been marked for identification as Respondent's Exhibits 3 and 4 and ask you what they are.

A. No. 3: "Regulations for Tank Vessels within the Los Angeles-Long Beach defensive sea area."

No. 4: "War regulations for protection of waterfront petroleum terminals, Los Angeles and Long Beach harbors, prepared by the Captain of the Port, Los Angeles."

Q. Is Richfield required to conform with these regulations? A. Yes, sir.

(Testimony of Waldo Hammond Wilder.)

Q. Calling your attention to Respondent's Exhibit 3, which is a photostatic copy of the front cover, and pages 3 and 4, [50] I call your attention to the regulation which has a check mark indicated opposite. Would you tell us what that regulation is?

A. No. 7: "No person shall be admitted to a tank ship except upon establishing a reasonable necessity therefor. He shall be required to exhibit a badge or card."

Q. And on the next page there is another part checked?

A. "Identification is not a pass or license to go on board. Anyone who is present on board the vessel or the dock that appears inimicable to the war effort shall be excluded from the premises, despite possession of a valid identification."

Mr. Guntert: I would like to offer into evidence Respondent's Exhibit No. 3.

Trial Examiner Batten: Well, I don't know. This is apparently just a part of an order. Do you have the complete order?

Mr. Guntert: I have the complete order. That is the only regulation that was pertinent to this.

Trial Examiner Batten: I will not receive this, then, until counsel and the others have had an opportunity to look through the complete order, in case they have any objections to the receipt of a portion. In other words, you have selected a part. They may have other parts they desire to select.

Mr. Guntert: I am willing to put the whole order in, but I think it is not necessary. [51]

(Testimony of Waldo Hammond Wilder.)

Trial Examiner Batten: I will reserve decision on it until such time as counsel advise me they have looked over the entire order. That means, of course, that you may proceed to use it for purposes of examination.

Mr. Moore: I don't believe the record shows anything more than that these are regulations. I doesn't show now by whom they are issued.

Mr. Guntert: The captain testified they are issued by the Port Captain of the Long Beach-Los Angeles harbor area.

The Witness: The United States Coast Guard. It's a Government agency. It's the United States Coast Guard which is a part of the United States Navy.

Q. (By Mr. Guntert) Captain, I am handing you what is marked for identification as Respondent's Exhibit 4 and call your attention to the regulation with the check on it. Can you tell us what that is?

A. ". . . prevent access of persons to terminals who do not exhibit the authorized credentials and who do not have necessity for entering."

Mr. Guntert: I would like to offer that.

Trial Examiner Batten: I will reserve decision.

Mr. Guntert: This is the other one.

Trial Examiner Batten: This is not complete, is it?

Mr. Guntert: It is the same as the other. They are the pertinent portions of these regulations. [52]

(Testimony of Waldo Hammond Wilder.)

Trial Examiner Batten: You mean they are what you think are the pertinent portions. Do you have the complete order?

Mr. Guntert: The complete order is here, and counsel is examining it.

Trial Examiner Batten: Counsel may examine them, and you will advise me after lunch whether you have any objections to the introduction of the part of the regulations.

Incidentally, did you men decide on the hours that you want to meet?

Mr. Guntert: Well, it will only take us just a very short time to complete our side of this.

Trial Examiner Batten: Well, of course, we won't finish before lunch, everybody, I presume.

Mr. Guntert: This is as good a stopping place now as any.

Trial Examiner Batten: I would suggest this: What do you want to do? Take an hour for lunch? Or do you want to take an hour and a half?

Mr. Lundeberg: I think an hour is good.

Trial Examiner Batten: What is that?

Mr. Lundeberg: I think an hour would be good.

Trial Examiner Batten: Is that agreeable, Mr. Guntert?

Mr. Guntert: Yes.

Trial Examiner Batten: Is that agreeable, counsel?

Mr. Moore: That is agreeable, yes.

Trial Examiner Batten: Suppose we reconvene

at 1:15. [53] That will be an hour and five minutes. Is there any objection?

(No response.)

(Thereupon, at 12:10 o'clock p. m., a recess was taken until 1:15 o'clock p. m. of the same day.) [54]

Afternoon Session

(The hearing was resumed at 1:20 o'clock p.m.)

Trial Examiner Batten: We will proceed. Will you resume the stand, Mr. Wilder, please?

WALDO HAMMOND WILDER,

resumed the stand as a witness by and on behalf of the National Labor Relations Board, having been previously duly sworn, and was examined and testified further as follows:

Mr. Moore: I believe now, Mr. Examiner, that a ruling can be made on Respondent's Exhibits 3 and 4. We will have no objection to the introduction of photostats, provided that we may read a very little additional material appearing in these regulations into the record.

Trial Examiner Batten: Is that satisfactory to you, Mr. Lundeberg?

Mr. Lundeberg: That's all right.

Trial Examiner Batten: Well, then, Exhibits 3 and 4 will be received. You may at the proper time read such portions into the record as you care to.

(Thereupon the documents heretofore marked

(Testimony of Waldo Hammond Wilder.)

for identification as Respondents' Exhibits 3 and 4, and received in evidence.)

RESPONDENT'S EXHIBIT No. 3

REGULATIONS FOR TANK VESSELS WITHIN THE LOS ANGELES-LONG BEACH DEFENSIVE SEA AREA

(Cut of Naval Insignia)

Prepared by
the
Captain of the Port
Los Angeles, California
Eleventh Naval District

(2) The fire hydrant, fire hose and valve nearest to his post,

(3) The vessel's own general alarm control nearest to his post,

(4) The city fire alarm box on shore nearest to his post,

(5) The available telephone nearest to his post.

(e) Guards on tankships will be instructed as to their duties. They will be limited to men of satisfactory vision, hearing and vigor. They will be responsible to resourcefully safeguard the premises from jeopardies that become apparent, though not ordered in their specific task. One of the guards on duty shall be designated as the chief guard.

(f) Guards will halt and challenge persons before they approach within striking distance. During the night when there is a military, naval, cus-

(Testimony of Waldo Hammond Wilder.)

toms or other guard within hail, such guards shall be called upon to stand alert while the ship's guard examines the identification and credentials of a stranger. The photograph and personal description of strangers shall be carefully compared for resemblance.

Acceptable Identification

7. No person shall be admitted to a tankship except upon establishing a reasonable necessity therefor. He shall be required to exhibit a badge or card having

(a) A photograph of, and resembling, that person,

(b) That person's brief personal description, and

(c) That person's finger print.

(The badge or card must have been issued by a creditable organization that has filed the finger prints with the Federal Bureau of Investigation.)

(d) The badge or card must have been issued by a creditable organization known to require reasonable proof of the person's stated citizenship.

8. Identification cards or badges issued by the Coast Guard and other naval and military forces, seaman's certificates, valid passports, war industry employer's cards and other credentials of like character which include (a), (b), (c) and (d) as above are acceptable. Less authentic identification is not satisfactory to the Captain of the Port. Persons not exhibiting satisfactory identification shall be refused admittance to tankships.

9. Guards shall beware of glib persons propos-

(Testimony of Waldo Hammond Wilder.)

ing to gain admittance by presentation of identification not meeting the requirements.

—3—

10. Military, naval, federal, police and fire fighting forces may, when properly uniformed, be passed aboard as the occasion requires, when identified as such.

11. An identification is not a pass or license to go on board. Anyone whose presence on board the vessel or the dock appears inimical to the war effort, shall be excluded from the premises, despite possession of valid identification.

Enemy Aliens

12. No enemy alien will be permitted to tankships or waterfront premises to which tankships are moored, unless in possession of an especial permit issued by the Captain of the Port, subsequent to 25 June, 1942.

Boiler Fires

13. Tankships loading or discharging inflammables shall extinguish furnace fires unless the master and chief engineer submit a signed statement that the ships vapor venting and compartmentation is such that it will be safer under the circumstances to maintain steam pressure than to extinguish the boiler fires. Due regard shall be taken as to scotch as compared to express-type boilers and the need for fire fighting facilities for which the ship's own power plant is required. When there is a reasonable doubt the fires will be extinguished, the master will

(Testimony of Waldo Hammond Wilder.)

be responsible then to see that all compartments on, facing, open and adjacent to parts of the loading dock are at all times kept tightly closed off from apertures leading to the furnaces. Before the transfer of inflammables to or from vessels with boiler fires, the terminal superintendent shall certify on the statement submitted by the master and chief engineer that loading of the vessel under the conditions existing will be permissable at the terminal for that time. The aforesaid certificates will be prepared in triplicate, one of which will be retained on board for exhibition to inspecting officers. The statement of the master and chief engineer will not be delegated to subordinate officers and they are cautioned to prepare the certifications before departing from the vessel.

14. Tankships are NOT required to keep steam for getting under way on short notice when by maintaining boiler fires the vessel would be jeopardized while laden with inflamables.

Galley Fires

15. Galley fires shall be extinguished before the transfer of grades A, B and C, nor shall galley fires be lighted until it is ascertained after the loading or discharging that vapor conditions are not a hazard. While tankships are at bulk loading docks the galley doors and air ports facing the deck on the side to which hoses are attached, shall be closed.

—4—

(Testimony of Waldo Hammond Wilder.)

RESPONDENT'S EXHIBIT No. 4

WAR REGULATIONS
FOR
PROTECTION OF WATERFRONT
PETROLEUM TERMINALS
LOS ANGELES-LONG BEACH HARBORS

(Cut of Naval Insignia)

Prepared by the
Captain of the Port
Los Angeles, California
Eleventh Naval District

War Regulations
for
Protection of Waterfront Petroleum Terminals
Los Angeles-Long Beach Harbors

General

1. Owners, agents, operators and lessees of waterfront oil terminals are requested to safeguard their premises in order to protect the storage and facilitate the transfer of petroleum products to the armed forces and the industries of the United States. The purposes of the following regulations are to:

(a) Prevent access of persons to the terminals who do not exhibit the authorized credentials and who do not have necessity for entering.

(b) Light and fence the terminals so efficiently that malicious persons will not venture attempts to break in or to enter by stealth.

(Testimony of Waldo Hammond Wilder.)

(c) Illuminate the terminals so that night operations may be conducted without mishap and for the detection of persons attempting to molest the terminal, or vessels at the docks.

(d) Select and train competent men for the operation of the terminal facilities and for the guarding of the premises.

(e) Fix the responsibility for the loading of tankships and tank barges, so that persons, facilities and vessels will not be needlessly jeopardized.

(f) Minimize the accumulation of waterfront oil storagè in order to decrease the danger to persons, vessels and harbor facilities, resultant from enemy attack.

—1—

Mr. Moore: I shall do that now, and I shall ask counsel for the respondent to observe this while I read it. I am reading now from Respondent's Exhibit 4, page 4, Section 18, which reads as follows: [55]

"Militarized guards shall be provided at all times to prevent undetected entry to the property at any point, to supervise and control entry at gates and to exclude unauthorized persons."

Section 20 reads as follows:

"(a) Main gate guards shall (1) prevent entry of unauthorized persons or vehicles, (2) check articles and materials entering gate, (3) check and

(Testimony of Waldo Hammond Wilder.)
list authorized visitors into and out of terminal." Reading from the same exhibit, page 6, item 25:

"Guards shall admit only persons exhibiting a pass or identification as follows: (a) a photograph of and resembling that persons, (b) that person's brief personal description, (c) that person's fingerprints."

Under that in parenthesis:

"The badge or card must have been issued by a creditable organization that has filed the fingerprints with the Federal Bureau of Investigation."

Still under Section 25:

"(d) The badge or card must have been issued by a creditable organization known to require reasonable proof of the person's stated citizenship."

Section 26 reads as follows:

"Identification cards or badges issued by the [56] Coast Guard and other Naval and Military Forces, seamen's certificates, valid passports, war industry employers' cards and other credentials of like character, which include (a), (b), (c) and (d) of Article XXV are acceptable. Less authentic identification is not satisfactory to the Captain of the Port. Persons not exhibiting satisfactory identification shall be refused admittance to vessels or waterfront facilities."

Mr. Guntert: I have no objection to that going in at all.

Trial Examiner Batten: Any objection, Mr. Lundeberg?

Mr. Lundeberg: No.

(Testimony of Waldo Hammond Wilder.)

Mr. Guntert: I want to point out, however, that in dealing with entry into terminals. That is the regulation with respect to terminals. The other one is respecting vessels.

Mr. Moore: That is all.

Trial Examiner Batten: How about Respondent's Exhibits 1 and 2?

Mr. Moore: With respect to the foundation?

Trial Examiner Batten: Those were complete, I guess.

The Reporter: They were received.

Trial Examiner Batten: They were received?

The Reporter: Yes, sir.

Trial Examiner Batten: Well, that takes care of the matter [57] up to the present time.

Were you through, Mr. Guntert?

Mr. Guntert: Yes.

Redirect Examination

By Mr. Moore:

Q. Mr. Wilder, when a tanker comes into port who, not a member of its crew, goes aboard the vessel ordinarily?

A. Myself for one, possibly one of the terminal representatives to talk with the loading officer with respect to the cargo, the port steward, that is, the Richfield Oil Corporation port steward, and the Richfield Oil Corporation port engineer; possibly the manager of the marine department of the Richfield Oil Corporation, if he so happens to be there at the time.

(Testimony of Waldo Hammond Wilder.)

Q. And anyone else?

A. No, sir. Well, there is the guards.

Q. What guards?

A. The guards that you mentioned a moment ago.

Q. By whom—— A. Militarized guards.

Q. Beg pardon? A. Militarized guards.

Trial Examiner Batten: Do they remain on the vessel as long as it is in port?

The Witness: Yes, they or the relief. [58]

Q. (By Mr. Moore): Does anyone else go aboard regularly? A. No, not regularly.

Q. Does anyone else ever go aboard?

A. I mentioned work parties here a while ago in connection with taking stores. There is one that not regularly goes aboard. He is in connection with the control of vermin, vermin extraction.

Trial Examiner Batten: Is he an employee of Richfield or some company employed by them?

The Witness: He is contracted for.

Q. (By Mr. Moore): He is what?

A. Contracted for.

Q. What does he do aboard?

A. Examines to see if there are vermin on there, and he takes measures to combat the vermin if there are any.

Q. The company contracts with him to do that?

A. Yes, sir.

Q. Is that all that he does? A. Yes, sir.

(Testimony of Waldo Hammond Wilder.)

Q. Does anyone else ever go aboard the ships, the tankers, rather?

A. Not without permission, as I recall.

Q. Does anyone else ever go aboard with permission?

A. There is a possibility of a laundry serviceman taking personal property of the crew aboard. The ship's laundry is [59] left on the dock, however. If he has to collect money from one of the crew, if he is aboard, why, and the crew man is on duty, he might take it to him. Otherwise, why, it's held until the next trip.

Q. What authority does he have to go aboard the ship?

A. He gets my permission. I delegate the chief officer or the loading officer that it will be permissible for him to go aboard for that particular purpose only.

Q. Now, is there anyone else to whom you give permission to go aboard the ship?

A. Not that I recall.

Q. Is it ever necessary to send messages from the company's office to the ship?

A. That message would be called aboard.

Q. Will you explain that?

A. You asked if there is anybody else like messages sent to the ship, what kind of a message?

Q. Messengers, I say. A. No, sir.

Q. No messengers go between the company offices and ship? A. No, sir.

Q. Is that because you have telephone service?

(Testimony of Waldo Hammond Wilder.)

A. We have telephone service on the docks.

Q. All the docks? A. Yes, sir. [60]

That is, I am speaking of our terminals. I can't say telephone service on all docks because I don't know all docks.

Q. When you say that there is telephone service to the dock, you mean that the telephone is on the dock or that it connects with the ship?

A. No. It's on the dock.

Q. Do the ship's officers go out on the dock to answer telephone calls?

A. Not when they are on duty. They are not supposed to leave their duty. There are several kinds of telephones. I would like to ask what telephone you are referring to. There is a company telephone, and there is a public telephone which is out of the gate. The man is sent out to the gate.

Q. In the event that you as a representative of the company are at the dock and want to get in touch with someone on the ship, how do you do it?

A. I would give one of the dockmen the message to deliver it to him, and he would call it aboard, the foreman of the dock.

Q. And the man with the message would go aboard to deliver the message?

A. I said he would call aboard. It's only a matter of speaking up.

Q. Oh, I see. You mean that he would relay the message by voice?

(Testimony of Waldo Hammond Wilder.)

A. I very seldom ever send for information such as that. [61]

Q. Is there ever any delivery of telegrams aboard the vessel?

A. They are received on the dock, not on the vessel.

Q. And who conveys them or takes them on the vessel?

A. If the telegram comes before the ship has arrived and I happen to be there, I take them aboard or the steward or the port engineer would take them aboard, or they would be given to one of the armed guards to take aboard.

Trial Examiner Batten: How about insurance companies? Do they ever have representatives who check the boats or go aboard?

The Witness: No, sir. They don't allow any solicitation.

Trial Examiner Batten: I don't mean solicitation. Do you carry your own insurance on your boats?

The Witness: Oh, the insurance on the vessel?

Trial Examiner Batten: Yes, on the vessel.

The Witness: In that case if there was a survey, there would be a special arrangement made. That would be out of necessity.

Trial Examiner Batten: My point is, doesn't your policy with the insurance company provide that their representatives have a right, under certain conditions, to go aboard the boat and make inspections?

The Witness: I have not seen anything on that,

(Testimony of Waldo Hammond Wilder.)

sir, since the war started. I presume they do have something that they [62] have a right to inspect the vessel. I haven't seen it, though.

Trial Examiner Batten: Well, of course, if the insurance company requested you——

Mr. Guntert: I think I can clarify that for you, Mr. Examiner, if you would care for me to.

Trial Examiner Batten: Yes.

Mr. Guntert: We carry insurance on our vessels, and we have the steamboat inspections, and that is the basis of determining the condition of the vessel. If she has a casualty, then surveyors are brought in. They are regular established, recognized firms of men who have knowledge of vessels and who form a survey party. They go aboard or take one of the vessels in dry dock, and the inspector is usually with the Master.

Trial Examiner Batten: They make a survey and a report, is that it?

Mr. Guntert: They make a written report.

The Witness: May I add something to that? I get the idea of the question now. I didn't comprehend it at first.

At such times the vessels are gas-free on those surveys. They are safe, in so far as danger from petroleum is concerned.

Trial Examiner Batten: Well, you mean under those circumstances the surveyor would go aboard? [63]

The Witness: Not regularly, no, sir.

(Testimony of Waldo Hammond Wilder.)

Trial Examiner Batten: No, I don't mean regularly.

The Witness: On an emergency.

Trial Examiner Batten: In other words, there is nothing prohibiting them from going on at a time, if the situation warrants it, is there, if you give them permission?

The Witness: No. No, sir.

Mr. Guntert: They would ordinarily never go aboard without specific request to come aboard by the Master to make a survey.

The Witness: Yes, that is true.

Mr. Guntert: In other words, it is not like a fire insurance company or a casualty insurance company on shore installations.

The Witness: We have what they call periodical surveys, other than in the case of disaster and such as that.

Some of the Government inspection is on periodical surveys. When you mentioned persons coming aboard I didn't presume that you included the United States Navy Officials or the Army officials in uniform.

Q. (By Mr. Moore): Referring to Respondent's Exhibit 3, Regulations for Tank Vessels, do you know when those were promulgated?

A. They were promulgated previous to my acceptance of the position as port captain. Some of the directives of the [64] War Shipping Administration have come along since.

Mr. Guntert: I think it can be stipulated that

(Testimony of Waldo Hammond Wilder.)

these regulations are now in effect. They are dated in June of 1942.

Mr. Moore: May it be stipulated that they are dated June 22, 1942, or, rather June 28, 1942?

Mr. Guntert: And that they are presently in effect?

Mr. Moore: Yes.

Trial Examiner Batten: Is that stipulated and agreed, Mr. Lundeberg?

Mr. Lundeberg: Yes.

Trial Examiner Batten: Mr. Guntert?

Mr. Guntert: Yes.

Trial Examiner Batten: Mr. Moore?

Mr. Moore: So stipulated, and that the war regulations for protection of waterfront petroleum terminals, Respondent's Exhibit 4, with respect to that exhibit may it be stipulated that they were approved and promulgated September 4, 1942?

Mr. Guntert: Yes.

Trial Examiner Batten: Is that agreeable to you, Mr. Lundeberg?

Mr. Lundeberg: That is agreeable.

Trial Examiner Batten: Mr. Guntert?

Mr. Guntert: Yes.

Trial Examiner Batten: Mr. Moore? [65]

Mr. Moore: So stipulated.

Q. (By Mr. Moore): Mr. Wilder, you say that some times after the ships have finished their business at a dock, they anchor out in the Bay and then the men are at liberty to go ashore then. Is that true?

(Testimony of Waldo Hammond Wilder.)

A. Providing there is sufficient time to go ashore previous to departure.

Q. Do you know at the time you anchor how much time they are going to have?

A. Generally, yes, sir, providing orders don't interfere or the Navy doesn't change the orders. I don't always know, though, sir.

Q. Do you tell the unlicensed personnel when the sailing time is?

A. No, sir. They are told when to be aboard.

Q. They are told when to be aboard?

A. When to be aboard.

Q. Watches continue while you are at anchor, while the tanker is at anchor?

A. Yes, sir, so far as I know. I am not aboard when she is at anchor out there. If I should go aboard, it would be only for a moment or two.

Q. While the tankers are in port, is it ever necessary to do any repair work on them?

A. *Then* they are in port? [66]

Q. In port, yes.

A. Yes. That is where they would have repair work done.

Q. Is it ever necessary to do any work on them?

A. Why, certainly it is necessary to do work in port.

Q. In doing that work do you use the crew to do it? Or do you bring in men from the outside?

A. For repair work?

Q. Yes.

A. We bring in men from the outside, from

(Testimony of Waldo Hammond Wilder.)

shipyards. We generally go to a shipyard. For that matter, any repairs are very limited, as allowed by the authorities during the war for tankers.

Q. Is minor repairing done at the dock?

A. Non-metal repairs might be done. Any metal repairs would not be done at the dock.

Q. Do any repairmen come at the dock to make minor repairs? A. Yes, sir.

Mr. Moore: That is all, I believe.

Trial Examiner Batten: Is that repair work done under contract? I mean, you have certain companies that you have arrangements with?

The Witness: No, sir.

Trial Examiner Batten: Or do you just call anyone you can get?

The Witness: Oh, no. It's always shipyards or some [67] organization who repairs ships.

Trial Examiner Batten: I understand that. What I meant was, for instance, we will say in Long Beach you have a boat in. Is there some particular company, shipyard company, you always use?

The Witness: We find out which one would do the job at the time, sir. The way things are now you can't be choosey.

Trial Examiner Batten: Whoever can give you the emergency service, is that right?

The Witness: Yes, providing their work has been satisfactory. We don't take anybody.

Trial Examiner Batten: I understand that. They would have to satisfy you.

(Testimony of Waldo Hammond Wilder.)

The Witness: All employees have to pass the requirements of the Coast Guard and the Government as to identification, such as mentioned in one of those exhibits; and they wear a badge and they are required to show their identification before they are allowed on the ship.

Trial Examiner Batten: I assume no one, including yourself, is allowed without identification?

The Witness: No, sir. Mine is on here (indicating) when I am around the terminal at all.

Mr. Guntert: There is one question, if you are through, Mr. Examiner. [68]

Recross Examination

Q. (By Mr. Guntert) With reference to men going aboard from the shipyards for repair work, I believe you testified the vessel was gas free. Would you explain that and tell us if that makes the vessel more safe than when she is not gas free?

A. Well, any petroleum product, unless it's a solid product, such as coke, is highly inflammable if it is heated, and explosive also. It generates gas. Well, if a ship is going into the shipyard, the ship is put into condition where there is no petroleum products aboard, that is, where the work will be done, other than the ship's bunkers, the fuel oil.

Q. Then the danger of fire and explosion from such things as smoking, and things like that, would not be as great in a shipyard as at the dock?

A. No, sir. Before the work is commenced the ship is inspected by a certified chemist, and

(Testimony of Waldo Hammond Wilder.)

all compartments where cargo would be carried or had been carried or will be carried are inspected and a label placed, certifying that it is safe before any work is done in that surrounding section of the vessel.

Mr. Guntert: That is all.

Redirect Examination

Q. (By Mr. Moore) Mr. Wilder, is it your opinion that you are prohibited by the rules of the War Shipping Administration [69] to grant passes to duly accredited union representatives?

A. I don't say we are prohibited. I don't know. I haven't seen anything. I don't say we are prohibited from issuing passes.

I testified this morning I was against passes, anyway. I didn't want people on the ships. I didn't want to have to identify people.

Trial Examiner Batten: Just a moment. That isn't the question. The question to you is whether any of these regulations would prohibit you from issuing to a properly accredited representative of the union a pass to go on the boat.

The Witness: I have no authority to issue passes, sir.

Trial Examiner Batten: That, of course, is not the answer. The question is whether it is the position of your company, we will say, that these regulations prevent the issuance of a pass to a duly accredited representative of a union to go on the boat?

(Testimony of Waldo Hammond Wilder.)

The Witness: I have been informed by the manager of the marine department of my corporation that they will issue no passes for safety reasons.

Trial Examiner Batten: Well, did he ever tell you that these regulations prevent the issuance of a pass to an accredited labor representative?

The Witness: No, sir, I don't think he did. [70]

Trial Examiner Batten: Did any government representative ever tell you that?

The Witness: No, sir.

Trial Examiner Batten: A representative of the Army, the Navy, the Coast Guard, the War Shipping Administration or any other department?

The Witness: In one particular instance there was orders issued that no passes be honored on a vessel that I commanded. That vessel was then under the United States Army.

Trial Examiner Batten: Well, I am asking you what is the situation now. Did any government representative tell you that you should not issue passes to accredited representatives of the union?

The Witness: No, sir.

Trial Examiner Batten: That is solely, as far as you know, an instruction of the manager of the marine department?

The Witness: As far as I am concerned, yes, sir, other than that case I quoted.

Trial Examiner Batten: Is the manager of the marine department going to be here?

Mr. Guntert: No.

(Testimony of Waldo Hammond Wilder.)

Trial Examiner Batten: Well, if he is not, I shall have to issue a subpoena for him. Do you want me to do that? Or can you arrange for him to be here?

Mr. Guntert: I think I can clarify that, Mr. Examiner. [71]

Trial Examiner Batten: I don't want you to clarify it. I want the man here that issued the order.

Mr. Guntert: I will stipulate to this: that we have never received instructions from any governmental organization, that is, any governmental branch that we were prohibited from issuing passes, nor have we been told that we could issue passes, nor have we been told that we could not issue passes to labor representatives or anyone else. I will stipulate to that much. Will that answer your purpose?

Trial Examiner Batten: Well, I don't know.

Mr. Moore: May I ask that the proposed stipulation be read?

(The record was read.)

Mr. Moore: That stipulation is acceptable.

Trial Examiner Batten: Mr. Lundeberg?

Mr. Lundeberg: Acceptable.

Trial Examiner Batten: It is not to me, however. I think the marine manager that issued this order is the man that ought to be here to testify.

My question to you was whether you would have him appear here today or tomorrow, or whether

(Testimony of Waldo Hammond Wilder.)

I shall issue a subpoena for him. That's my question.

Mr. Guntert: Whatever the Examiner wants. But I don't see the necessity of it.

Trial Examiner Batten: Well, perhaps you don't. I think [72] that in a case of this kind—after all, I have to make the first decision. I have to write a report here.

Now, I don't like to write a report ever unless the people who are concerned testify. I have had cases involving some question concerning labor organizations, and I just won't do it unless the labor representative who is responsible is available.

It may be that nothing may be accomplished by the examination of the marine manager, or whatever his name is. But I feel to have a complete record, Mr. Guntert, he should be.

Now, I have some questions I would like to ask him, and I don't think it will take very long. If you can have him here in the morning, that is perfectly satisfactory.

Mr. Guntert: I will have to communicate with him to find out.

Trial Examiner Batten: Well, you communicate with him when we have our next recess, and you can let me know. Any further questions of this witness?

Mr. Moore: No questions.

Mr. Ryan: Mr. Examiner, as I understand it, this marine man that you are just referring to

(Testimony of Waldo Hammond Wilder.)

now is an employee of the company and not an employee of any government agency?

Trial Examiner Batten: That's right. He is an employee of the company, is he not? [73]

Mr. Guntert: Yes, sir. He is the manager of the marine department.

Trial Examiner Batten: He is the manager of the marine department. In other words, he is the boss of the marine department, is that true?

Mr. Guntert: That is correct.

I guess that is all, Mr. Wilder.

Mr. Lundeberg: These oil companies are also agents for the War Shipping Administration. In other words, the marine manager, if he comes in here, he is an agent directly from the War Shipping Administration.

Trial Examiner Batten: Well, Mr. Wilder, he is on the payroll of the Richfield Oil Company, is he not? I don't care who he is an agent of.

Mr. Lundeberg: I mean the marine manager, Mr. Examiner, which he referred to a little while ago.

Trial Examiner Batten: Yes. But he is *he* paid, as I understand it—as Mr. Wilder has just said—by the company.

Mr. Lundeberg: And the Government pays him. Mr. Wilder is paid indirectly by the United States Government.

Trial Examiner Batten: I think we all are. I think during the present emergency there are very

(Testimony of Waldo Hammond Wilder.)

few people that aren't paid either directly or indirectly by the Government.

Mr. Guntert: I don't think that is a correct statement, Mr. Lundeberg. [74]

Mr. Lundeberg: It is, indeed.

Trial Examiner Batten: I don't care, if he is the man who issues the orders. I don't care who he works for or who pays him.

Mr. Lundeberg: I would like to see him myself.

Mr. Moore: Mr. Guntert, may it be stipulated that all shipping companies on the Coast are controlled by the War Shipping Administration in the same manner that Richfield Oil Corporation is?

Mr. Guntert: No, because I don't think that is correct. I don't see that that would be material here.

Trial Examiner Batten: Well, of course, I don't know. But my understanding is that there isn't a shipping company operating that isn't under the control and administration of the War Shipping Administration.

Mr. Guntert: That is almost correct. There are some that are not, or at least some of their vessels are not. But as far as the tankers are concerned, I am sure that that is so.

Trial Examiner Batten: Well, are you willing to stipulate and agree that all the companies who operate tankers are now in a similar position as your company so far as the War Shipping Administration is concerned?

Mr. Guntert: I don't know that they are. I

(Testimony of Waldo Hammond Wilder.)

know some of them have different types of contracts. [75]

Mr. Moore: I propose that in order to shorten time. But we can have testimony on it.

Trial Examiner Batten: All right. That is all, Mr. Wilder.

(Witness excused.)

Mr. Moore: I will call Mr. Lundeberg.

HARRY E. LUNDEBERG,

called as a witness by and on behalf of the National Labor Relations Board, having been first duly sworn, was examined and testified as follows:

Direct Examination

Q. (By Mr. Moore) Will you give your full name, please? A. Harry Lundeberg.

Q. What is your employment, Mr. Lundeberg?

A. I am the secretary-treasurer of the Sailors Union of the Pacific, which is the executive office, and I am the president of the Seafarers International Union of North America, which is an organization of seamen, fishermen and fish cannery workers on the Atlantic, the Gulf, the Great Lakes and Pacific Coast, affiliated with the American Federation of Labor.

Q. How long have you held the office of secretary-treasurer of the Sailors Union of the Pacific?

A. Since January, 1936.

(Testimony of Harry E. Lundeberg.)

Q. How long have you held the position of president of the Seafarers International Union of North America? [76]

A. Since October, 1938.

Q. Beg pardon? A. Since October, 1938.

Q. Prior to becoming secretary-treasurer of the Sailors Union of the Pacific, what experience had you had; what business had you been in?

A. I have been a sailor all my life. I have been sailing since I was 14 years old, sailing on decks, able bodied seaman, as a boatswain, as a mate in sailing ships, second mate in steamers. I have a license from the United States Government, second mate's license for steam, and I have sailed as boatswain in some of the biggest ships on the Coast, and able bodied seaman for 20 years.

Q. Where have you had that experience?

A. I sailed along the Pacific Coast from 1923 to 1934. Prior to that I sailed out of England, out of Australia, out of New York, out of South America and under various nationalities and flags.

Q. Have you sailed on different kinds of ships?

A. I have sailed on all kinds of ships: steamers, tankers, sailing vessels, schooners, square rigged ships, passenger vessels.

Q. In your present capacity as officer of the two unions, you have mentioned—I will withdraw that.

Is the Seafarers International Union, Engine Division, [77] affiliated with the organization of which you are president?

(Testimony of Harry E. Lundeberg.)

A. Yes. That is the Pacific District Division of the Seafarers International Union.

Q. Now, in your capacity as an official of these two labor organizations, what generally are the duties that you perform?

A. I negotiate agreements. I appear before various government bureaus, such as the Maritime Commission, the War Shipping Administration. I appear once in a while before Congressional Committees dealing with seamen's legislation, and I settle disputes which arise under various agreements. I appear before Port Committees consisting of labor representatives and unions and shipowners ou behalf of our organization, and I am on the banking committee of the union, a trustee, and so forth.

Q. Now, what procedure does the Sailors Union of the Pacific and Seafarers International, Engine Division, follow in negotiating collective bargaining contracts?

A. We elect a committee from each port on the Coast which meet with the operators, and I am acting as the chairman of the negotiating committee. These committees elect——

Q. How long have you done that?

A. I have done that since 1935. Prior to taking office I was elected on various committees while I was a sailor.

Q. Has it been your experience that shipowners generally deal as an association, or do they deal individually? [78]

(Testimony of Harry E. Lundeberg.)

A. Our experience in the dry cargo vessels and the passenger vessels is that the shipowners deal as an association. In our dealings with the oil tanker companies, in 1938 we dealt with them as a body. In other words, they have what they call the "Tanker Fleet Association" on this Coast, composed of operators of tankers. And in the previous negotiations with these people, in 1938 we met with a representative from Richfield, General Petroleum, Hillcone Steamship Company, and Tidewater Associated Oil. That is what they call the small tanker operators on this Coast. There is only one more, which is the Standard Oil Company of California.

Q. Now, is it your procedure to enter into and sign written agreements with companies operating ocean-going vessels?

A. Yes. We attempt to negotiate agreements, and then after it is referred back to the membership for approval or disapproval. Then if it is approved, then we sign it, sign agreements for yearly periods. However, we recently signed an agreement with an oil tanker company on this Coast, the Tidewater Associated Oil, for a two-year period; and besides the month of May, 1942, we signed, together with Admiral Land, the Chairman of the War Shipping Administration, a stipulation which will freeze our agreements for the duration of the war. In other words, we will keep the same agreements as we have already

(Testimony of Harry E. Lundeberg.)

negotiated for the duration of the war [79] without any changes in them.

Q. Now, after you have negotiated a contract with a company or an association of companies, is it ever necessary or has it ever been necessary in your experience to adjust any differences or grievances arising under that contract?

A. Oh, yes. That is an every-day occurrence. As a matter of fact, every agreement we negotiate has the stipulation in the agreement dealing with labor relations, what we call "port committees", machinery set up to handle disputes arising under the various clauses of the agreement.

Q. Is the settling of those grievances that arise under a contract an important part of your duties?

A. A very important part of the duties.

Q. Will you state what procedure the Sailors Union of the Pacific and the Seafarers International, Engine Division, have set up to handle those grievances?

A. Well, when the crew on board a vessel or an individual member have any dispute dealing with the agreement he works under, he usually brings that into port. It isn't taken up on the voyage, except, for instance, if there is a question about food, then they might ask the skipper or complain to the skipper if it's too bad. Otherwise they wait until they get into port. Then they call one of the union representatives, one of their elected delegates down, and turn the dispute over to him. He then takes it up with the [80] master

(Testimony of Harry E. Lundeberg.)

of the vessel or the chief mate or the chief engineer, whoever it may be. If they can't settle the dispute between themselves to the satisfaction of everybody, then it is turned over to the shore representative. The big shipowners, they have what they call the "port committee". We call upon them to have a meeting to deal with the subject. But first we go through the channel of settling it aboard the vessel, because there may be various reasons. There may be such a thing as the quarters being rotten, and the ship maybe needs a fumigation; the mattresses might be old and they want to renew the mattresses. The food might be rotten. It is our duty to check up to see if their complaint is legitimate or not, and we don't back up a beef except its legitimate.

Q. In carrying out that procedure has it been customary for a representative of those unions to board the vessels? A. Yes, we board——

Q. Where the grievance arises?

A. We have passes to board 470 ships on the Pacific Coast under agreements with the various ship owners. The only ones we have not passes with is the Richfield, the General Petroleum and the Standard Oil. All other vessels on this Coast, we have passes, incuding two oil tanker companies: the Tidewater Associated Oil Company, which we recently signed an agreement with on November 18, 1942, granting us passes, and with the Hillcone Steamship Company which granted [81] us passes

(Testimony of Harry E. Lundeberg.)

to all our representatives on a coastwise scale in January, 1943.

These particular companies—we won an election and were certified by the National Labor Relations Board later than we were with Richfield Oil Company.

Q. These passes that you speak of: are they good only for the home port of the company involved?

A. No. We have passes for every port of the Pacific Coast where these vessels stop. In other words, we have passes at Seattle, Honolulu, San Pedro, Portland, Oregon, San Francisco; in the case of one oil company, the Hillcone Steamship Company, we also have passes to board their vessels in Port Arthur in Texas and also Tampa, Florida, due to the fact that one or two of the vessels is running *stead* out of those ports.

Q. Now, returning to the grievance procedure, what is the title of the representative of the union who boards the ship?

A. In the Sailors Union we call them "patrolmen." Other unions possibly would call them "business agents." I don't know where the expression "patrolmen" comes from, except maybe they patrol all the vessels in the harbors. They have had that name since the organization was started in 1885.

Q. Is he also sometimes called a "shore delegate"?

(Testimony of Harry E. Lundeberg.)

A. Sailors don't call him that. They call them "patrolmen," [82] but that's exactly what they are: shore delegates.

Q. Have you ever been a patrolman?

A. Yes. I was a patrolman in the Port of Seattle for a period of nine months.

Q. Did you board ships in the course of your duties?

A. I boarded every ship that came into the Port of Seattle, including tankers.

Q. Would you state just the various steps that you took upon boarding a ship and thereafter?

A. Whenever I came aboard a ship I boarded a ship upon arrival of the ship and went to the ship's delegate and asked him whether there was any trouble aboard the ship or——

Q. Who is the ship's delegate?

A. The ship's delegate is one of the crew members appointed by the union to protect the men aboard the ship and also to see that the agreements are lived up to. In other words, he is there for the protection of both the company and the men. No chiseling is done from either side.

Q. All right.

A. Then he gives me his dispute. Maybe, for instance, the ship has been in some other port and the men have been working overtime. Then the mate says he doesn't want to pay that particular overtime. Well, according to our agreement, that man might be entitled to it. So the delegate, he turns it over to me. I take it up with the mate

(Testimony of Harry E. Lundeberg.)

or the skipper [83] and argue the question of that overtime dispute from another port. In most cases we are able to settle it there. If we can't settle it there, then we have to take it up with the company's representative.

Q. When you say "there" you mean where? On the ship?

A. On board the ship, yes, sir. That is *where handle* most of our disputes. Then there may be such other question arise such as about food, which has been a very frequent trouble, and living quarters and sanitary conditions. Well, then, I am in the capacity as a patrolman or delegate, and I check on the food; I check on the quarters. I might look at the mattresses and see if they are rotten, and so forth, as the complaints say; and if they are, I take it up with the skipper and tell him "We want that changed because that is a violation of the agreement." And in most cases we are able to settle it that way.

Q. While you are on the ship? A. Yes.

Q. When the ship's delegates calls to your attention a condition that he believes constitutes a grievance, what do you do by way of investigating his statement?

A. I check directly myself. Say, for instance, if he complains about the food or the quarters or the utilities, for instance, some of these companies, including the Richfield Oil, instead of giving the men crockery ware to eat from they [84] give them in some instance tinware which is not sani-

(Testimony of Harry E. Lundeberg.)

tary and unhealthy. And in a case like that I want to see for myself if some of these men aboard the ship don't pull a fast one.

We don't argue a dispute, except it's legitimate.

Q. Has it been your experience that grievances, complaints may be made by crew members that are not justified?

A. Oh, yes. There is several times somebody has made a complaint that is not justified, and after investigating the complaint and whoever is the shore delegate, say, "Well, it's not legitimate. It's no complaint. We won't do anything about it."

Then, of course, the shore delegates, due to the fact that the vessel may not be in port long, the shore delegate is also authorized to collect the union dues.

It's very important that a man keeps his dues paid for his own benefit because should the ship go out and the man was not in good standing with the union and the ship should founder, then he wouldn't be entitled to a shipwreck benefit. Or should he die or be killed, then his relatives wouldn't be able to get his burial benefit if he was not in good standing. So these seamen lots of times haven't got time to get up to the hall. So we have got to handle that directly so every union representative, shore representative, is an authorized dues collector at the same time. [85]

Q. The unions you represent do provide the benefits that you have been speaking of?

A. Yes.

(Testimony of Harry E. Lundeberg.)

Q. Has it been your experience that collection of dues on board the ship is the most feasible way to get dues collected?

A. Oh, yes. The men insist that you take it aboard the ship because they are paid off. Usually when they get into harbor they are paid off. They get paid for the voyage, and so forth. They want to pay up their union dues. As a matter of fact, they call in to the hall time and again and say "Come down and collect some dues. We are in bad standing and want to get straightened out before we leave."

Q. Do the Sailors Union of the Pacific and the Seafarers International Engine Division have regular meetings of their membership?

A. They have meetings every Monday night, and of course, in a coastwise scale, in every port where we maintain a union office.

Q. Where do you maintain union offices?

A. We maintain union offices on the Pacific Coast in the ports of Honolulu, San Pedro, San Francisco, Portland, Oregon, Seattle, Washington, and Vancouver, British Columbia. And we also have, of course, on the Atlantic and the Gulf, the Atlantic and Gulf divisions. They are located in every [86] major port on the Atlantic Coast and they hold the same meetings.

Q. Your headquarters are where, Mr. Lundeberg? A. Headquarters in San Francisco.

Q. Is that where your office is?

A. That's right, yes, sir.

(Testimony of Harry E. Lundeberg.)

Q. Are you familiar with the places where Richfield Oil tankers dock in the San Francisco Bay area? A. Yes, I am.

Q. At what address in San Francisco is your headquarters? A. 59 Clay Street.

Q. Do you have any other office in the San Francisco Bay area?

A. We have one at Richmond, Point Richmond at Richmond proper in the Labor Council over there.

Q. How far from your office in San Francisco is Point Orient? A. Approximately 22 miles.

Q. Have you ever traveled to Point Orient from your office? A. Lots of times, yes, sir.

Q. How long would it take you?

A. It all depends. If you have your own car you can make it in about 45 minutes. Of course, you can't do it now with the 35 mile speed limit. But if you are going to depend on the best facilities, then it may take you about two to three hours on the one way, because you have got to wait. [87]

Q. Have you traveled to Oleum? A. Yes.

Q. How long would it take you to go from your headquarters to there?

A. Approximately the same amount of time.

Q. Would the same be true of Avon?

A. No. Going up to Avon it would take me about an hour. It's about 40 miles from San Francisco.

Q. In your car, you mean? A. Yes.

Q. And by public transportation how long?

(Testimony of Harry E. Lundeberg.)

A. I would say if you are lucky and you can get a train, the train only goes during certain times of the day. You can go down in an hour on the train if you happen to catch the train. Otherwise, it would take you about four hours to wait.

Q. With reference to these membership meetings that you have, is it possible for tanker personnel, unlicensed tanker personnel, to attend those meetings regularly?

A. Should they be lucky and be in town, in port on a Monday night, they could. But that doesn't happen that way very often. And those men, they are only in port for a limited period from 16 to 24 hours, and they are laying away from the cities. It takes them some time to get in and out, and naturally they want to go home and see their people if they [88] have any, or they want to go to a show because they only get a few hours. So it's very hard for them to——

Q. Now, you have described at some length the procedure for adjusting grievances where the union has passes to board ship. Has the union established any procedure for dealing with grievances where it is unable to board the ships of which it represents employees?

A. No, we haven't established anything like that.

Q. Why not?

A. Because you can't handle a grievance today without being on board a ship, going on board a ship. I haven't heard or seen a case yet with no steamship company. As a matter of fact, the com-

(Testimony of Harry E. Lundeberg.)

pany themselves insist that we go on board the ship and check up.

Q. Has that happened in your experience?

A. It happens every day. The port captain of the big steamship companies on this coast call our representatives up, call me up. As late as a week ago the marine manager who operates the biggest oil tanker in the Pacific Coast, the tanker Quebec, Mr. Ames of the Hillcone Steamship Company, called me up and insisted I go on board the ship and take a look at the vessel and to see if there was any complaints or anything. He wanted to get it settled because the vessel was due. He was proud of his ship and wanted to show us. That is the biggest oil tanker in the Pacific Coast, [89] recently put in order. As a matter of fact, it is owned by the United States Government but operated by Hillcone Steamship Company for them.

Q. Mr. Lundeberg, will you give some of the reasons, based upon your experience, why it would not be possible to adjust grievances without having access to the ship?

Mr. Guntert: I am going to object to that, Mr. Trial Examiner. I have been rather patient and have been interested in listening to this. But I object to this whole line. I don't see its materiality. The particular question is assuming that it is not possible to adjust grievances. As a matter of fact, grievances have been settled with our company not aboard ship.

(Testimony of Harry E. Lundeberg.)

Trial Examiner Batten: Well, of course, the question to the witness is why it isn't possible to adjust them without boarding ship. I think it is a proper question. I think this man ought to know whether it is or is not possible.

Now, what weight would be given to his testimony is another question. I think your objection goes to the weight that would be given to it and not to the admissibility of it.

You may tell us.

The Witness: The reasons that you can't adjust disputes without going aboard a ship is (1) the men aboard the ship, if they have a dispute they want it settled before the ship and the only way you can do it and settle it is right on the [90] job; and (2) if a dispute is going to be handled, you will have to check up on the dispute properly; (3) if one of the men aboard the ship takes it up himself and complains to the company without the backing of the union delegate, they will usually fire him because they class him as a disrupter and agitator. After all, the master aboard the ship, he is the law aboard the vessel. A seaman is naturally reluctant to go up and to take it upon himself to argue with the skipper while he is on the ship's payroll because if he should stress his argument too much and the skipper wouldn't like it, and the company wouldn't like it, they would just fire him; that's all. They will find some reason to get rid of him.

We have numerous examples of that. That is one reason why they insist upon having their own

(Testimony of Harry E. Lundeberg.)
spokesmen come down, the spokesmen they elect. They are all seamen themselves, all men who handle disputes are seamen. They can't hold office in our union unless they have had three years sailing experience.

Q. (By Mr. Moore) Mr. Lundeberg, do you have with you a copy of the constitution of your organization?

A. No, I haven't got it with me here. But I can bring it up here. I can bring it up from the San Pedro branch. I will have it up here for you.

Trial Examiner Batten: Well, is that for the purpose of [91] proving they are a labor organization?

Mr. Moore: No.

Trial Examiner Batten: Or for other reasons?

Mr. Moore: To show the qualifications of patrolmen. I think that I will just ask Mr. Lundeberg what they are. He knows.

Q. (By Mr. Moore) What are the qualifications of a patrolman, Mr. Lundeberg?

A. The qualifications for a patrolman in our union and any official: first of all, they must be citizens; secondly, they must be bona fide seamen with three years government discharge to prove so that they have sailed for three years.

Q. Do they receive any training in addition to that?

A. That's my job, to train the new men in labor relations, explain the agreement to me, and so forth.

(Testimony of Harry E. Lundeberg.)

Q. Do those men work directly under your supervision?

A. On a coastwise scale, yes, they do.

Mr. Moore: Will you mark this Board's Exhibit 2, for identification, please?

(Thereupon the document referred to was marked as Board's Exhibit No. 2, for identification.)

BOARD'S EXHIBIT No. 2—Rejected

AGREEMENT

Between

SAILORS' UNION OF THE PACIFIC

And

STEAMSHIP COMPANIES

In the
Intercoastal And Offshore Trade
And the Alaska Lines

Dated: November 4, 1941

Geertz Printing Co. (Label) San Francisco

This Agreement, entered into this 4th day of November, 1941, between the Sailors' Union of the Pacific, hereinafter referred to as the "Union," and

Admiral Oriental Line.
American-Hawaiian Steamship Company.
American Mail Line.
American President Lines, Ltd.

(Testimony of Harry E. Lundeberg.)

Board's Exhibit No. 2—Rejected—(Continued)

Alaska Steamship Company.

Alaska Transportation Company.

Coastwise Pacific Far East Line.

W. R. Grace & Co. (as Agents for Grace Line, Inc. Pacific Coast West Coast Mexican Central American Panama Service of Grace Line, Inc.) and (Pacific Coast South American Service of Grace Line, Inc.)

Luckenback Gulf Steamship Company, Inc.

Matson Navigation Company.

The Oceanic Steamship Company.

Pope and Talbot, Inc.
(McCormick Steamship Company Division)
(All services except Steam Schooner Trade).

Northland Transportation Company.

Pacific Lighterage Corporation.

Pacific Republics Line
(Moore-McCormack Lines, Inc.)

Santa Ana Steamship Company.

States Steamship Company.

Pacific-Atlanta Steamship Company (Quaker Line).

Sudden & Christenson
(Arrow Line-Intercoastal Service).

Shepard Steamship Company.

The Union Sulphur Company, Inc.

Weyerhaeuser Steamship Company.

hereinafter referred to as the "Employers,"

(Testimony of Harry E. Lundeberg.)

Board's Exhibit No. 2—Rejected—(Continued)

Witnesseth, As Follows:

General Rules

Section 1. The Employers agree to recognize the Sailors' Union of the Pacific as the representative for the purpose of collective bargaining for their unlicensed personnel.

Section 2. The Employers agree to give preference in employment to members of the Sailors' Union of the Pacific, and to secure their unlicensed deck personnel through the offices of the Union.

Section 3. The Sailors' Union of the Pacific agrees to (3*) furnish capable, competent, and satisfactory employees.

Section 4. The Sailors' Union of the Pacific does not claim jurisdiction over Cadets, when such are required to be carried on mail contract vessels.

Section 5. The Union agrees that the Employers shall have the right, in their discretion, to reject men furnished who are considered unsuitable and unsatisfactory. In case any person is rejected, the Union agrees to furnish a prompt replacement. When any person is rejected, the employer shall furnish a statement in writing to the Union stating the reason for the rejection. If the Union feels that any rejection has been unjust and has worked a hardship on the person, the Union shall without delay take the matter up with that particular employer and attempt to secure an adjustment.

---

* Page numbering appearing at foot of page of Original Printed Agreement.

(Testimony of Harry E. Lundeberg.)

Board's Exhibit No. 2—Rejected—(Continued)

Section 6. If a satisfactory adjustment cannot be secured with the Employer, the Union shall thereupon refer the matter to the Port Committee, and the Port Committee shall then hear the case and may order any adjustment that the circumstances in its judgment may warrant.

Section 7. The Employers agree not to discriminate against any man for legitimate Union activity.

Section 8. The Employers agree to recognize one employee on each vessel, designated by the Union, to act as the delegate and representative of the Union, whose duty shall be to see that the members of the Union on that vessel observe the agreement, and at the same time that the rights and interests of such members under this agreement are protected.

Section 9. The Sailors' Union of the Pacific recognizes that at times replacements must be secured at ports where there are no branches of the Union, and the Union therefore agrees not to discriminate against such replacements when vessels arrive at ports where regular branches of the Union are maintained. The Employers, however, shall make every reasonable effort to secure the services of members of the Union, and the delegate of the Union shall assist in this respect.

Section 10. Members who are in good standing with the Union may remain continuously in employment on the same vessel provided the Employers and the members desire such employment to continue.

(Testimony of Harry E. Lundeberg.)

Board's Exhibit No. 2—Rejected—(Continued)

Section 11. A Port Committee shall be established at the Port of San Francisco. The Committee shall consist of (4) six members; three to be appointed by the Union and three by the Employers.

(a) The duties of the Port Committee shall be to investigate and adjudicate all grievances and disputes which may arise between any of the parties and to take the necessary steps to secure compliance with this agreement, and to prevent violations. At the request of either party the Port Committee shall meet within twenty-four (24) hours.

(b) The Employers and the Union shall appoint representatives at Seattle, Portland, and San Pedro to hear and adjudicate disputes arising at such ports, but no decision involving a basic interpretation of this agreement shall become effective unless approved by the Port Committee at San Francisco. In the event the representatives at any of such ports fail to agree on any matter it shall be referred to the Port Committee at San Francisco for decision.

(c) In the event the Port Committee at San Francisco fails to agree on any matter, it shall be referred to a referee whose decision shall be rendered promptly in writing and shall be final and binding.

(d) Referees shall be appointed by a Board of four persons not directly connected with either party, two of whom shall be named by the Union

(Testimony of Harry E. Lundeberg.)

Board's Exhibit No. 2—Rejected—(Continued)

and the other two by the Employers. Appointments shall be in writing, signed by any three members of the Board. If three members of the board are unable to agree within three (3) days, Sundays and holidays not included, then the Senior Circuit Judge of the Federal Bench, or the Senior District Judge of the Federal Bench in San Francisco will be added to the Board to break the deadlock. Each party shall have three challenges which must be exercised within twenty-four (24) hours after appointment; after a referee is challenged new appointments shall be made until challenges are waived or exhausted. The expenses of any referee shall be borne equally by the Union and the Employers. When it becomes necessary to appoint a referee the Board of four (4) persons referred to herein, shall be named within three (3) days time, Sundays and holidays not included.

Section 12. There shall be no strikes, lockouts, or stoppages of work during the period of this agreement for any cause.

Section 13. (a) Members of the Deck Department shall perform the necessary and customary duties of that department; each member of the Deck Department shall perform only the recognized and customary duties of his (5) particular rating. Any work necessary for the safety of the vessel, passengers, crew or cargo, or for the saving of other vessels in jeopardy and the lives therein, or when in port or at sea in the performance of

(Testimony of Harry E. Lundeberg.)

Board's Exhibit No. 2—Rejected—(Continued)

fire, lifeboat or other drills, shall be performed at any time, and such work shall not be considered overtime.

(b) When lifeboat or other drills are held on Saturday afternoons, Sundays or holidays, preparation for such drills, such as stretching fire hoses, hoisting or swinging boats out, shall not be done prior to signal for such drills, and after drill is over, all hands shall stand by until boats and gear are properly secured, without payment of overtime.

Section 14. The members of the Union will comply with all lawful orders of superior officers and with all company rules not inconsistent with this agreement.

Section 15. The Union shall not interfere with the performance of work outside of the general scope of this agreement, provided such work is customary in the particular trade, and is arranged for with the employees by the employers on mutually satisfactory terms and conditions; nor shall the Union or its members interfere with the performance of any work by other employees; provided it is customary in particular trades to employ other employees to perform such work.

Section 16. Employers shall only be required to comply with the law and regulations of the Bureau of Marine Inspection and Navigation in all matters relating to manning, quarters, and equipment, construction and arrangement of the ship.

(Testimony of Harry E. Lundeberg.)

Board's Exhibit No. 2—Rejected—(Continued)

(Upon request any vessel subject to the provisions of this agreement shall be inspected by a joint committee representing the Union and the Employers and when checked and passed by the committee, their decision shall be final.)

Section 17. This agreement is binding with respect to ships operating in the particular service appearing after the signature of the steamship companies parties to the agreement respectively, and if no particular service is specified, to all ships operated by them.

Section 18. This agreement governs only the relations between steamship companies and the Union, and the wages, hours, and working conditions for unlicensed deck department personnel of the steamship companies.

Section 19. Any crew member engaged and discharged at United States Pacific Coast or Island ports of the Pacific on account of lay-up of a ship, who has been employed (6) fifteen days or less, shall be given immediate first-class transportation and subsistence to the port of engagement; or if transportation and berth are not provided, a sum equal to the current tariff rate for fare and berth plus subsistence at the rate of $3 per day. If a crew member is entitled to transportation under the foregoing provision and neither rail nor bus facilities are available, he shall receive transportation on company vessels with meals and berth equivalent to crew's quarters.

(Testimony of Harry E. Lundeberg.)

Board's Exhibit No. 2—Rejected—(Continued)

(b) Any crew member discharged at any port except as provided in subdivision (a) of this Section because vessel is withdrawn from service for any cause except shipwreck, he shall receive not less than first class transportation and berth plus subsistence at the rate of $3 per day and wages to the home port or port of engagement. When bus or rail service are not available, transportation with meals and berth equivalent to crew's quarters and wages will be provided.

(c) No transportation shall be allowed should a man be discharged by mutual consent before the termination of the articles.

(d) Members paid off under Section 19 (a) or 19 (b) shall be entitled, at their option, to the following cash equivalent:

Los Angeles—San Francisco	$ 21.00
Los Angeles—Portland	48.50
Los Angeles—Seattle	55.00
San Francisco—Portland	31.00
San Francisco—Seattle	38.00
Portland—Seattle	18.00
Coast Ports—Atlantic Ports	125.00
Coast Ports—Gulf Ports	92.50

(e) Members hired in Honolulu and paid off under Section 19 (a) and 19 (b) shall be entitled at their option to the following cash equivalent:

If paid off in West Coast ports	$ 40.00
If paid off in East Coast ports	125.00

(Testimony of Harry E. Lundeberg.)

Board's Exhibit No. 2—Rejected—(Continued)

Section 20. The Employers shall furnish safe gear and working equipment and safe working conditions when in any harbor or roadstead.

Section 21. Any vessel going into war zones, areas rendered unsafe by virtue of hostilities, shall be subject to special negotiations with regard to increase of wages or bonus or other special benefits. (7)

The Union agrees that no sailings shall be delayed because of failure to reach a prompt agreement, but that, if it becomes necessary, the prescribed steps for adjustment of the dispute shall be followed subsequent to the vessel's departure.

Section 22. This agreement shall be binding upon the respective parties for the period of October 1, 1941 to and including September 30, 1942, and shall be considered as renewed from year to year thereafter between the respective parties hereto, unless either party hereto shall give written notice to the other of its desire to amend or terminate the same. Any such notice shall be given at least thirty (30) days prior to the expiration date and after notice has been given specific proposals must then be submitted and negotiations commenced within ten days. If such shall not be given, the agreement shall be deemed to be renewed for the succeeding year.

The wages set forth in this agreement with the emergency increases specified herein shall be subject to review semi-annually hereafter from the

(Testimony of Harry E. Lundeberg.)

Board's Exhibit No. 2—Rejected—(Continued)

effective date of this agreement at the request of either party.

Wages

Section 1. The classification and minimum rates of wages of the deck department is attached hereto.

(a) In vessels of 10,000 to 15,000 gross tons, basic wages of Chief Boatswain and Carpenter shall be not less than $105 per month.

(b) In vessels of 15,001 to 20,000 gross tons, basic wages of Chief Boatswain and Carpenter shall be not less than $110 per month.

(c) In vessels where Boatswain's mates are carried, the basic wages shall be $92.50 per month.

(d) Members of the crew who are required to wear uniforms, such as Quartermasters and Night Watchmen on passenger ships; and where special uniforms, blue, white caps and extreme cleanliness are demanded, and where uniforms are not furnished by the Company, shall be paid wages at a rate of not less than $10 per month more than the regular able seamen.

(e) The ship's Carpenter will furnish his own tools and shall be paid $7.50 additional per month.

Working Rules

Section 1. The regular overtime rate shall be 85 cents per hour. (8)

Section 2. In port, the hours of labor shall be eight (8) hours between 8 a.m. and 5 p.m. and all work performed in port after 5 p.m. and before 8 a.m. shall be paid for at the regular overtime rate.

(Testimony of Harry E. Lundeberg.)

Board's Exhibit No. 2—Rejected—(Continued)

Section 3. (a) When vessel is in port and watches are broken and men are called back to work after 6 p.m. and before 8 a.m., or on Saturday afternoons, Sundays and holidays for the purpose of shifting ship in inland waters a minimum of two (2) hours' overtime shall be paid for each call, except when men are knocked off for a period of one hour or less, in which case time shall be continuous.

(b) When sea watches are set, crew members shall be required to report on board and be availabel for duty not less than one hour before time posted on sailing board.

If the vessel's departure is delayed and the delay is due to the loading or discharging of cargo, the new time of departure shall immediately be posted on the board and if such delay exceeds one (1) hour the watch below may be dismissed and shall receive one (1) hour's overtime for such reporting. This section includes the watch on deck on Saturday afternoons, Sundays and holidays.

Section 4. In port, Quartermasters shall be required to stand gangway watches and Night Watchmen and Stationmen their regular night watches between the hours of 5 p.m. and 8 a.m. without payment of overtime (except on Saturday afternoons, Sundays and holidays).

Stationmen's duties shall consist of the following: Sounding bilges, care of deck lights, relieve Quartermasters, and stand wheel watch. (When

(Testimony of Harry E. Lundeberg.)

Board's Exhibit No. 2—Rejected—(Continued)

Stationmen are required to rig up or handle cargo lights between the hours of 5 p.m. and 8 a.m. Saturday afternoons, Sundays, or holidays, they shall be paid overtime for such work performed.)

Watchmen shall be required to make their regular round of the key stations and punch the clocks.

Section 5. In port, work on Saturday afternoons, Sundays, and holidays shall constitute overtime except as follows:

(a) Work preparatory to anchoring or leaving anchorage, mooring or unmooring to or from buoy, buoys or piers.

(b) Except as otherwise provided in this agreement, the regular duties of the watch on deck on days of arrival or days of departure shall not constitute overtime.

(c) If watch on deck are required to break out mooring (9) lines on Saturday afternoons, Sundays or holidays, when such days are days of arrival, such time shall be overtime.

Section 6. Work performed at sea in excess of eight (8) hours between midnight and midnight of each day, except work done for the safety of passengers, cargo, ship or crew, shall be paid for at the regular overtime rate.

Section 7. (a) If cargo *if* not properly secured before going to sea and the watch below is required to secure such cargo, they shall be paid overtime for such work performed.

(Testimony of Harry E. Lundeberg.)

Board's Exhibit No. 2—Rejected—(Continued)

If the watch on deck is required to perform such work after 5 p.m. or before 8 a.m., Saturday afternoons, Sundays, and holidays, they shall be paid overtime for such work performed.

(b) On vessels arriving in port the watch on deck may be required to handle cargo gear including hoisting booms, stripping tarpaulins, etc., without payment of overtime between the hours of 8 a.m. and 5 p.m., but shall be paid at the overtime rate when required to take off hatches or hatch beams prior to anchoring or mooring of the vessel.

Work on Passenger Vessels at Sea

Section 1. No work except for the safe navigation of the vessel shall be performed at sea after 5 p.m. and before 8 a.m., and on Saturday afternoons, Sundays, and holidays except as listed below:

The watch on deck between the hours of 5 p.m. and 8 a.m. shall be required to perform the following work without payment of overtime on passenger vessels:

(a) Cleaning paint work;

(b) Barberizing;

(c) Washing or sweeping down decks;

(d) Washing windows;

(e) Polishing brass;

(f) Wiping rails.

If the watch on deck between the hours of 5 p.m. and 8 a.m., Saturday afternoons, Sundays, or

(Testimony of Harry E. Lundeberg.)

Board's Exhibit No. 2—Rejected—(Continued)

holidays are required to wash or paint masts, high ventilators, and king posts or are required to wash or barberize boat covers or awnings, they shall be paid overtime for such work performed.

Section 2. On Saturday afternoons, Sundays and holidays at sea, the crew shall be required to do the necessary work for the safe navigation of the vessel. (10)

If the watch on deck Saturday afternoons, Sundays, or holidays are required to wash down, they shall be paid overtime for such work performed. However, the watch on deck may be required to sweep down during such hours without payment of overtime.

Work on Freighters at Sea

Section 1. No work except for the safe navigation of the vessel is to be done after 5 p.m. and before 8 a.m. Sanitary work shall be done between 6 a.m. and 8 a.m. without payment of overtime.

Sanitary work under this section shall mean cleaning wheel house and chart rooms, cleaning windows and mopping out wheel house, washing down bridge decks and cleaning Sailors' quarters and washrooms.

Only necessary sanitary work shall be done on Sundays and holidays.

Section 2. When members of the deck crew are required to clean tanks which have been used for the purpose of transporting fluid cargo, such as Fuel Oil, Molasses, Cocoanut Oil, etc., they shall

(Testimony of Harry E. Lundeberg.)

Board's Exhibit No. 2—Rejected—(Continued)

receive as extra compensation for performing such work 85c per hour during straight time hours and $1.15 per hour during overtime hours. Company shall furnish boiler suits for this operation.

Section 3. Molasses: When washing tanks after discharging Molasses, the Boatswain and six men will be used and two tanks will be cleaned simultaneously.

Section 4. Fuel Oil: When washing tanks after discharging of Fuel Oil, Boatswain and six men will be used cleaning one tank at a time and using hose not in excess of 2½ inches, two men in the tank at one time.

Section 5· When Sailors are required to go on the dock to sling up hose and lowering same to dock between 8 A. M. and 5 P. M. no overtime to be paid.

Section 6. When Sailors are required to go on dock to handle, and-or connect or disconnect hose between 8 a.m. and 5 p.m., overtime to be paid.

Section 7. When men are required to clean bilges they shall be paid $1.05 per hour during straight and overtime hours.

Section 8. (a) Members of the deck crew shall be required to clean and sweep cargo holds on their watch on deck without payment of overtime for such work.

(b) When required to clean holds where Potash, Soda (11) Ash, Sulphur, or Ore in bulk have been carried, the men performing such work shall be

(Testimony of Harry E. Lundeberg.)

Board's Exhibit No. 2—Rejected—(Continued)

paid 85 cents per hour straight time and $1.15 per hour overtime.

When a consignment of Cement in sacks of 25,000 or more has been carried on a particular voyage, and members of the Deck Department are required to clean the compartments in which such Cement has been carried, they shall be paid 85 cents per hour straight time and $1.15 per hour overtime for such work performed on such voyage.

(c) When crew is required to lay dunnage they shall be paid at the overtime rate for such work performed.

Section 9. (a) In all ports, members of the Deck Department may be required to chip, scale, prime and paint the vessel oversides; either in port or at sea; members of the Deck Department may be required to chip, scale, prime or paint messrooms, lockers, storerooms, inside alleyways or inside work, cargo spaces, deck houses, etc. Overtime shall be paid when Sailors are required, either in port or at sea to chip, scale, prime or paint enclosed alleyways amidships or paralleling crew's quarters, messrooms, pantry or laundry and all forecastles, lavatories, washrooms, lockers and storerooms which are not used by the Deck Department.

(b) In ports where the company employs a regular shore gang for the purpose of performing this work, this practice shall not be interfered with.

(Testimony of Harry E. Lundeberg.)

Board's Exhibit No. 2—Rejected—(Continued)

Section 10. When members of the deck crew are required to work dynamite or handle explosives, they shall be paid $1.45 per hour for such work.

Section 11. In outports, where there are no regular longshoremen, members of the crew may be required to drive winches or handle cargo and for such work they shall be paid at the rate of $1.05 per hour straight and overtime.

Section 12. Crew shall be paid overtime when handling mail.

Section 13. (a) On vessels not carrying a Carpenter, a competent member of the unlicensed deck department may be required to do this work and when required to use Carpenter's tools he shall be paid at the rate of 85 cents per hour during straight time and $1.15 per hour during overtime hours. (12)

(b) Members of the crew actually engaged in handling Carpenter's tools assisting the Carpenter shall be compensated at the rate of 25 cents per hour.

(c) Carpenter shall shore up cargo and do carpenter work aboard the vessel.

(d) Carpenters shall be required to stand by the windlass when mooring or unmooring or anchoring.

(e) In port, when Carpenters are required to take soundings after 5 p.m. and before 8 a.m., Saturday afternoons, Sundays and holidays, they shall be paid overtime for such work performed.

Section 14. When members of the crew are re-

(Testimony of Harry E. Lundeberg.)

Board's Exhibit No. 2—Rejected—(Continued)

quired to use spray guns they shall be paid 25 cents during straight time hours for all outside work, and for any inside work done in an enclosed compartment they shall be paid 85 cents per hour during straight time hours and $1.15 per hour for overtime hours.

Section 15. The watch on deck may be required to handle hatches, strongbacks, tarpaulins, tank covers, during straight time hours (8 a.m. to 5 p.m. week days, 8 a.m. to 12 noon Saturdays) without payment of overtime.

Section 16. When Sailors are required to clean Steering Engine or Steering Engine Bed, they shall be paid overtime for such work performed. However, Sailors may be required to clean Steering Engine Room and grease Tiller Chains in their watch on deck during straight time hours without payment of overtime.

Ships' Stores

Section 17. (a) Sailors may be required to handle deck stores both on the dock and on board ship during regular hours without payment of overtime.

Regular working hours are defined to mean—8 a.m. to 12 noon, 1 p.m. to 5 p.m. week days; and 8 a.m. to 12 noon Saturdays.

(b) When Sailors are required to handle Stewards' or Engine Room stores, both on dock and aboard ship, they shall be paid overtime at the regular overtime rate.

(Testimony of Harry E. Lundeberg.)

Board's Exhibit No. 2—Rejected—(Continued)

(c) Daily supplies of fresh provisions such as milk, bread, and vegetables shall be brought on board by Sailors when required to do so without payment of overtime.

(d) Ships' officers shall determine the number of Sailors to be used in handling ships' stores. (13)

(e) The company reserves the right at any time to use shore gangs to handle ships' stores.

Section 18. Watchmen shall be required to stand an eight hour watch any time between midnight and midnight, without payment of overtime and shall receive one night off a week. This section refers to "Watchman's duties at sea."

Section 19. If ship does not carry a regular Watchman and a member of the deck department is required to act as Watchman in port, he shall be paid overtime for such time worked between the hours of 5 p.m. and 8 a.m., Saturday afternoons, Sundays and holidays.

Section 20. (a) Where actual overtime worked is less than one hour, payment for one hour will be allowed. Where overtime exceeds one hour, payment will be allowed for actual time worked but not less than half-hour periods.

(b) Time starts when men are called if they report for work within fifteen minutes. If they do not report within fifteen minutes time is to start from the time of reporting for duty and time shall count from the time men are turned to until they are released, including time of standing by.

(Testimony of Harry E. Lundeberg.)

Board's Exhibit No. 2—Rejected—(Continued)

If men are knocked off for a period of one hour or less, time shall be continuous.

Section 21. When working overtime, the Deck Delegate shall compare time with the officer in charge of the work as soon as practicable after work ceases.

Watches

Section 1. (a) Sea watches shall be set not later than noon on the day of departure except when the vessel sails before noon, in which event sea watches shall be set not later than the departure of the ship for sea. The setting of sea watches earlier than provided herein shall be optional with the Master.

Section 2. When a vessel arrives from sea, watches must be maintained until 12 noon on such day of arrival. If arrival occurs after 12 noon, watches shall be broken when the vessel is moored at the loading or discharging berth.

Section 3. The calendar day is from midnight to midnight. If watches are set prior to the day of departure, any work performed by the members of the Deck Department from 5 p.m. to 12 midnight the day prior to day of departure is overtime.

Section 4. When the watch below is called out to work (14) they shall be paid overtime for work performed during their watch below.

Section 5. Quartermasters standing regular

(Testimony of Harry E. Lundeberg.)

Board's Exhibit No. 2—Rejected—(Continued)

gangway watch and stationmen standing their regular watches on Saturday afternoon, Sundays, or holidays shall be paid overtime for such watches.

Section 6. The day the vessel arrives from sea to a port of call shall be considered the day of arrival and subsequent moves from that port occurring in inland waters, bays, rivers, and sounds shall be considered as moving ship.

Section 7. The following moves are exempt from the above section:

Puget Sound: All moves from American ports to British Columbia ports or vice versa.

Chesapeake Bay: Norfolk to Baltimore or vice versa.

New York Area: New York to Albany or vice versa. New York to Bridgeport or vice versa.

River Platte: Montevideo or Buenos Aires to Rosario or points above or vice versa.

Moves from Baltimore through the Chesapeake and Delaware Canal to Wilmington, Camden or Philadelphia or vice versa shall be considered a move of the ship and for such work after 5 p.m. and before 8 a.m., or Saturday afternoons, Sundays or holidays, shall be paid for at the overtime rate.

Section 8. On Freighters not less than a full watch shall be used on inland waters when ship is being moved.

Section 9. The day of departure shall be the day the vessel leaves for sea from the port from which

(Testimony of Harry E. Lundeberg.)

Board's Exhibit No. 2—Rejected—(Continued)

the vessel is cleared and sea watches shall be set and maintained from that port.

Section 10. Rigging up or securing cargo gear shall be done by the watch on deck between the hours of 8 a.m. and 5 p.m. week days and 8 a.m. and 12 noon Saturdays without payment of overtime. Overtime shall be paid for such work when done in hours other than those stated.

Section 11. The Sailors shall while at sea be divided into three watches, which shall be kept on duty successively for the performance of ordinary work incident to the sailing and management of the vessel.

Section 12. If the Boatswain or Carpenter are required to stand watches due to the shortage of men, they shall receive (15) overtime for all watches stood on Saturday afternoons, Sundays and holidays.

Holidays

The following holidays shall be observed as legal holidays in addition to Sundays:

New Year's Day, Lincoln's Birthday, Washington's Birthday, Memorial Day, Independence Day, Labor Day, Armistice Day, Thanksgiving Day, and Christmas.

When any of the above holidays fall on Sunday, they shall be observed on the following Monday.

When in West Coast ports of the United States, the unlicensed Deck Department personnel shall

(Testimony of Harry E. Lundeberg.)

Board's Exhibit No. 2—Rejected—(Continued)

be granted any additional holidays granted by the employers to the longshoremen in such ports.

Meals

Section 1. (a) Breakfast time shall be between 7:30 a.m. and 8 a.m.

(b) If the breakfast time is postponed beyond 8 a.m., overtime shall be paid until breakfast is given.

Section 2. (a) The crew shall have one unbroken hour for dinner while lying in any port or roadstead and no work shall be performed during such hours. The dinner hour shall be from 12 noon to 1 p.m., but may be varied not to exceed one hour either way to perform work as it is hereinafter specified:

(a) Work that is necessary for the safety of the vessel, her passengers, cargo, and crew;

(b) Landing of passengers, baggage and mail;

(c) Moving vessel;

(d) Departure of vessel.

If members of the crew are not given one full hour for dinner they shall be paid one hour's overtime in lieu thereof.

Section 3. Supper time shall be at 5 p.m., but may be postponed not to exceed one hour. One hour shall be allowed for supper but at no time shall the supper hour be advanced.

If the crew has less than one hour for supper and are required to turn to after 5 p.m. and before

(Testimony of Harry E. Lundeberg.)

Board's Exhibit No. 2—Rejected—(Continued)

6 p.m. they shall be paid one hours' overtime in lieu thereof.

Members of the crew shall be given at least a half-hour for breakfast, dinner or supper; if members of the crew are given less than one hour for either breakfast, dinner or supper, (16) they shall be paid one hour's overtime in addition to actual time worked.

Section 4. If members of the crew work four or more hours between the hours of 6 p.m. and 3 a.m. they shall be served a hot lunch at midnight. This meal to be served either before or after working periods.

Section 5. In port, not more than fifteen minutes shall be allowed for coffee at 10 a.m. and 3 p.m., or at convenient times near these hours.

Section 6. When board is not furnished the crew shall receive 75 cents for breakfast, 75 cents for dinner, and 75 cents for supper and when compelled to sleep on shore on account of repairing, cleaning or fumigating the sleeping quarters, they shall receive one dollar and fifty cents ($1.50) per night for rent.

Section 7. (a) All dishes shall be crockery-ware.

(b) Mattress and pillow with cover, white sheets and sufficient blankets, towels and soap and matches shall be furnished to men on request; they to be responsible for the safekeeping of the same. Bed linen and towels to be changed weekly. When

(Testimony of Harry E. Lundeberg.)

Board's Exhibit No. 2—Rejected—(Continued)

linen is not changed weekly each member of the crew shall be compensated by payment of $2 for each week that linen is not changed.

Section 8. When men are hired for regular ship standby work in port and neither board nor lodging is furnished, the rate of pay shall be $7.20 per day of eight hours. Men shall be paid a minimum of four hours at the straight time rate.

When men work under this stand-by clause, the overtime rate shall be time and one half.

Straight time hours shall be 8 a.m. to 12 noon, 1 p.m. to 5 p.m. week days; and from 8 a.m. to 12 noon Saturdays.

Section 9. When men are hired in port to shift ship to lay up requiring them to remain aboard at night, board and lodging shall be provided.

The straight time hours shall be from 8 a.m. to 12 noon and from 1 p.m. to 5 p.m. week days and from 8 a.m. to 12 noon Saturdays.

The straight time rate of pay for such work shall be 90 cents per hour. The overtime rate shall be $1.35 per hour.

There shall be a minimum guarantee of $8 plus one hour's traveling time for the shift.

Necessary transportation to or from the vessel shall be furnished by the vessel. (17)

Transportation

Men who are employed fifteen days or less and are laid off are to receive first class transportation

(Testimony of Harry E. Lundeberg.)

Board's Exhibit No. 2—Rejected—(Continued)

and subsistence back to the port of engagement and at no time shall the company keep men on articles who would be entitled to transportation when the rest of the crew are signed off.

This section shall not apply to replacements for crew members removed by the Union, unless otherwise agreed upon.

Alaska Run

The following applies to vessels engaged in the Alaska Trade:

A. Sections 1 to 22, inclusive, of the "General Rules" shall apply.

B. In addition, the following rules and Working Rules and no others to apply.

Section 1. The classification and rates of wages to be as follows:

Wage Scale Attached

Section 2. On passenger vessels where seamen are assigned to duties as Quartermasters and when required to wear uniform and exercise care as to appearance for which they shall be paid $10 per month above Able Seamen's rate. This does not apply to relief men.

The ship's Carpenter will furnish his own tools and shall be paid $7.50 additional per month.

Section 3. (a) Rate of overtime shall be 85 cents per hour. When actual overtime worked is less than one hour, one (1) hour shall be paid.

When overtime exceeds one hour, payment will

(Testimony of Harry E. Lundeberg.)

Board's Exhibit No. 2—Rejected—(Continued)

be allowed on actual time worked, but not less than one-half (½) hour periods.

(b) Continuous time will be paid men who are knocked off for two hours or less when they are working on overtime.

Continuous time clause to be interpreted as follows:

A. When members of the Deck Department are working either ship's overtime or cargo time and are knocked off for periods or two hours or less and are again required to turn to on ship's overtime or cargo time, their pay shall be continuous. (18)

B. When members of the Deck Department are working either ship's overtime or cargo time and are knocked off and subsequently turned to on watch time the continuous two-hour clause shall not apply.

C. When members of the Deck Department are shifted from "Watch Work" to "Ship's Overtime" or from "Watch Work" to "Cargo Time" (Section 3 (b) (continuous time clause) shall not apply.

D. When men on either ships overtime or on cargo time have been working beyond the even hour or half hour, and are dismissed, the time below to commence at the next quarter-hour period, regardless of time to which paid. Time on deck commences when men are called to turn to, provided they report for work within fifteen minutes.

(Testimony of Harry E. Lundeberg.)

Board's Exhibit No. 2—Rejected—(Continued)

Example 1: Knocked off at 2:40 p.m.
Paid to 3 p.m.
Time below starts at 2:45 p.m.
Continuous time broken after 4:45 p.m.

Example 2: Knocked off at 2:10 p.m.
Paid to 2:30 p.m.
Time below starts at 2:15 p.m.
Continuous time broken after 4:15 p.m.

Example 3: Knocked off at 2:50 p.m.
Paid to 3 p.m.
Time below starts at 3 p.m.
Continuous time broken after 5 p.m.

Example 4: Knocked off at 3 p.m.
Paid to 3 p.m.
Time below starts at 3 p.m.
Continuous time broken after 5 p.m.

In connection with the foregoing examples, it is understood between both sides in cases where continuous time is broken that leeway of about two to five minutes will be allowed to avoid any possibility of misunderstanding or disputes as to the correct time.

Section 4. (a) Except at home port of Seattle, Sailors will load and discharge cargo as and when directed, for which they shall be paid $1.05 per hour, day or night time, on or off watch, for any number of hours that may be worked.

(Testimony of Harry E. Lundeberg.)

Board's Exhibit No. 2—Rejected—(Continued)

(b) Cargo work shall include handling, loading and discharging all kinds and types of cargo, mail, baggage, and express; and shall include raising, lowering and securing gear; taking off and putting on hatches and strongbacks, (19) cleaning tanks and laying dunnage to receive cargo, and work in connection with bulk cargo oils as defined in Section 4 (c).

(c) When required to handle oil hose and (or) move pumps or stand by hose, tanks or pumps in connection with pumping fish oil, such Sailors as directed by deck officer in charge to perform this work shall be paid the cargo rate.

Clarification—Section 4 (c)

When Sailors are not engaged in working cargo in Alaskan ports and revenue cargo bulk oil is being pumped aboard or ashore, not to exceed three men shall be required to stand by, shift hose or perform any other work required in connection with such operation for which they shall be paid overtime at the cargo rate of $1.05 per hour for time actually worked, but not less than one hour.

In home port when pumping fish oil into tank cars, members of the Deck Department not to exceed four men including a Winchdriver, shall, when required, perform such work for which they shall be paid the cargo rate.

Unless directed by the Deck Officer in charge Sailors will not stand by or participate in the work of bunkering fuel, pumping oil from ship to ship,

(Testimony of Harry E. Lundeberg.)

Board's Exhibit No. 2—Rejected—(Continued)

tanker or barge, or pumping fish oil into regular storage tanks.

(d) Two hours minimum to be paid any time cargo work is performed. Sailors shall, when turned to on cargo, work the full two hours either on cargo or ship's work, but shall be paid the cargo rate. When requested to work two full hours, Sailor or Sailors refusing to work full two hours shall only be paid for actual time worked, but not less than one hour. Two hour minimum shall be pyramided when men go to meals and continue to work thereafter. If men are turned to for less than one hour before meals, it shall count as one hour in computing the two-hour minimum. Cargo work in excess of two hours shall be computed in half-hour periods.

(e) When required by Master at gangplank, Quartermasters will be paid the cargo rate without penalties, while cargo is being worked by Sailors. If no cargo is being worked by Sailors, Quartermaster will stand regular watch at gangplank or other designated location without payment of overtime. Same rule applicable to crew member relieving Quartermaster. The company, at its discretion, may or may not require Quartermaster at the gangplank and can require Quartermaster to work cargo. (20)

(f) Regular Quartermaster on watch to be paid at the cargo rate when members of the Deck Department are turned to coming into port to raise gear, take off hatches, strong backs, etc.; and when leaving port, and members of the Deck Department

(Testimony of Harry E. Lundeberg.)

Board's Exhibit No. 2—Rejected—(Continued)

are engaged in securing gear, placing strongbacks, hatches, etc., or securing cargo. The foregoing clause does not apply when men are turned to on ship's work.

(g) While vessel is working cargo, Sailors will not be knocked off cargo work to avoid paying cargo rate unless mutually agreeable to deck officer in charge and the Sailors; provided, however, that this shall not apply when in the judgment of the master it is necessary to knock off cargo work for the watch taking vessel to sea. It is understood that this shall not be used by the Master or chief officer in charge of the work for the purpose of discrimination. Any Sailor who refuses or fails to do work assigned in connection with cargo when such work is being performed, shall not be paid.

(h) When leaving or approaching home port and necessary to raise, lower or secure gear preparatory to loading or discharging cargo, Sailors so employed shall be paid a minimum of one hour at the cargo rate. If such work takes more than one hour, two-hour minimum shall apply.

When Sailors are required to handle hatches, strongbacks, express, baggage or mail, or perform stationmen's duties, two-hour minimum shall apply. When this work is done in addition to raising, lowering or securing gear, only two-hour minimum shall apply unless it requires more than two hours, then actual time shall be paid.

This rule is not intended to apply to customary Sailors' work in connection with hatches, gear,

(Testimony of Harry E. Lundeberg.)

Board's Exhibit No. 2—Rejected—(Continued)

booms, strongbacks (unless such work is done preparatory to loading or discharging cargo), while shifting around harbor or for the safe navigation of the vessel.

Home port is considered all ports in Puget Sound area south of the Canadian Boundary Line.

(i) This section covers all members of the unlicensed Deck Department regardless of what work performed in connection with cargo.

(j) Where bona fide longshoremen are not available, Sailors shall have preference ahead of other members of the ship's crew to sling-up work at one hatch only. Winchdrivers, with one gear working, will alternate between winches and (21) hatchtending. When two gears are working and gangs are made up from ship's crews, Sailors shall have preference of hatch-tending at the second hatch.

(k) Members of the Deck Department will not be required to handle gear, strongbacks, hatches, etc., while vessel is under way in heavy weather or at night without proper lighting facilities. Every effort will be made to avoid delay to ship as long as such safety precautions are observed.

(l) When members of the Deck Department other than regular ship's winchdrivers are required to drive winches for the purpose of handling cargo, they shall be paid at the rate of $1.55 per hour straight or overtime on or off watch. This section

(Testimony of Harry E. Lundeberg.)

Board's Exhibit No. 2—Rejected—(Continued)

shall not apply in cases where the regular winch-driver may be relieved for short periods.

(m) Handling Mail, Baggage, and (or) Express on Regular Passenger Vessels While Under Way:

There shall be no less than the following members of the unlicensed Deck Department personnel paid and (or) employed at the cargo rate of $1.05 per hour, with the understanding that the work is to be rotated among Winchdrivers and Hold Men as equally as possible:

One Boatswain supervising the work;

Regular Quartermaster on watch;

Winchdriver—not less than one Winchdriver to a hatch, standing by;

A.B.'s—As required, but not less than four men to a hatch.

Section 5. (a) Twenty-five cents (25c) per hour extra, shall be paid to each man, either daytime or night time, engaged in loading and discharging the following commodities:

Gypsum; cement; plaster; lime; creosoted lumber; soda ash; hay; sulphur; green and creosoted piling; all animal and fish fertilizer; decalite and sealite in sacks; phosphates; nitrates, bulk and sack; bulk salt; bulk grain; flue dust; coal; (sack, bulk); hides, tallow; manure, meals and other offensive material used as fertilizer; scrap metal cargoes; (bulk and mixed including bales, excluding rails); dynamite; dynamite caps; gun powder; blasting powder; bulk coke; empty cement sacks; ground redwood bark;

(Testimony of Harry E. Lundeberg.)

Board's Exhibit No. 2—Rejected—(Continued)

rock glass; sack or bulk ore. For cleaning tanks in which bulk oils have previously been carried (company shall furnish boiler suits for this operation); and for all shoveling. For Sailors actually handling cargo inside cold-storage boxes, or refrigerators, where freezing temperature is maintained. Includes Sailor assigned to (22) duties of Stationman. Does not include coolroom boxes.

There shall be no extra payment for less than one-half hour's work for this kind of work.

(b) Sailors will clean and sweep cargo holds as and when directed. For cleaning holds where penalty cargo has been carried a penalty of 25c per hour shall be paid each man either daytime or night time engaged in cleaning that portion of the holds affected by the penalty cargo. There shall be no extra payment for less than one-half hour's work for this kind of work.

(c) If men are required to act as sling-tenders or hook-on men on board lighters in the Bering Sea, they shall be paid twenty-five (25c) per hour in addition to the cargo rate ($1.05).

(d) When vessels are loading or discharging cargo and such cargo is required to be either slung up for discharging or stowed by hand while loading not less than 8 men shall be employed in the hatch.

Section 6. (a) The Sailors shall, while at sea, be divided into watches, as required by law, which shall be kept on duty successively for the performance

(Testimony of Harry E. Lundeberg.)

Board's Exhibit No. 2—Rejected—(Continued)

of ordinary work incident to the sailing and management of the vessel.

(b) Work performed at sea in excess of eight (8) hours between midnight and midnight of each day except work done for the safety of passengers, cargo, ship or crew shall be paid for at the regular overtime rate.

(c) No work except for the safe navigation of the vessel and sanitary work between the hours of 6:00 a.m. and 8:00 a.m. shall be performed at sea after 5:00 p.m. and before 8:00 a.m. and on Saturday afternoons, Sundays and holidays without the payment of overtime.

(d) Sanitary work between the hours of 6 a.m. and 8 a.m. shall include the following: cleaning wheel house and chart room, windows, cleaning and mopping out wheel house.

Section 7. If cargo is not properly secured before going to sea and the watch below is required to secure such cargo they shall be paid overtime for such work performed.

If the watch on deck is required to perform such work after 5 p.m. or before 8 a.m., Saturday afternoons, Sundays and holidays, they shall be paid overtime for such work performed.

Section 8. (a) In home port, eight (8) hours shall (23) constitute a day's work from 8 a.m. to 12 noon and 1 p.m. to 5 p.m. week days and 8 a.m. to 12 noon Saturdays.

(b) The hours for day men, winchdrivers, deck

(Testimony of Harry E. Lundeberg.)

Board's Exhibit No. 2—Rejected—(Continued)

boys and boatswain when on day work at sea shall be 8 a.m. to 12 noon and 1 p.m. to 5 p.m. week days and 8 a.m. to 12 noon Saturdays.

(c) Time worked in port, at port anchorages and roadsteads (defined as places where cargo or passengers are customarily loaded or discharged) on Saturday afternoons, Sundays and legal holidays and all work in home port beyond the regular working hours on week days, as defined in Section 8 (a), shall be paid for at the regular overtime rate, except such work as is necessary for the immediate safety of the vessel, her passengers, cargo or crew.

Section 9. (a) Departure. On days of departure from home port all watches shall be set not later than 12 noon.

If vessel leaves before noon, watches shall be set not later than one hour before departure.

(b) Arrival. On days of arrival in home port, watches must be maintained until noon or later, but crews shall be required to work eight hours on such days without payment of overtime. When watch below is called out to work they shall be paid overtime for work performed during their watch below.

When vessel arrives after noon, watches shall be maintained until vessel is safely moored at loading or discharging berth.

Section 10. (a) When vessel is in home port and watches are broken and men are called back to work after 6 p.m. and before 8 a.m. or on Saturday afternoons, Sundays and holidays for the purpose of

(Testimony of Harry E. Lundeberg.)

Board's Exhibit No. 2—Rejected—(Continued)

shifting ship in inland waters a minimum of two (2) hours' overtime shall be paid for each call, except when men are knocked off for a period of two hours or less in which case time shall be continuous.

(b) Where men are ordered back to shift vessel in home port at 1:00 a.m. or later and before 6:00 a.m. they shall be entitled to a minimum of three (3) hours.

(c) When sea watches are set, crew members shall be required to report on board, and be available for duty not less than one hour before time posted on sailing board.

If the vessel's departure is delayed and the delay is due to the loading or discharging of cargo, the new time of departure (24) shall immediately be posted on the board and if such delay exceeds one (1) hour the watch below may be dismissed and shall receive one (1) hour's overtime for such reporting. This section shall apply to the watch on deck on Saturday afternoons, Sundays and holidays.

Section 11. (a) The crew shall have one unbroken hour for dinner while laying in any port or roadstead and no work shall be performed during such hour. Dinner hour shall be from 12 noon to 1 p.m., but may be varied not to exceed one (1) hour either way to perform work as it is hereinafter specified: (a) work that is necessary for the safety of the vessel, her passengers, cargo and crew; (b) landing of passengers, baggage and mail; (c) moving vessel; (d) departure of vessel. Breakfast time shall

(Testimony of Harry E. Lundeberg.)

Board's Exhibit No. 2—Rejected—(Continued)

be between 7 a.m. and 8 a.m., supper time shall be at 5 p.m., but may be postponed not to exceed one (1) hour. One (1) hour shall be allowed for supper. If crew works overtime men shall be provided with hot lunch at 12 midnight. One (1) hour to be allowed for such meal. Lunch referred to in this section provided at midnight if vessel is working shall be a "hot lunch."

(b) When men off watch are called at 6 a.m. for breakfast, and eat breakfast between 6 a.m. and 7 a.m. and turn to immediately thereafter they shall be paid one hour overtime, for the time between 6 a.m. and 7 a.m.

(c) If the dinner hour or supper hour is postponed one hour for the purpose of working cargo, the men shall be allowed one hour at the cargo rate.

The following interpretations of the several meal hour provisions in the Agreement have been agreed upon:

1. Where crew eats between 11:00 p.m. and 12:00 midnight and works through on cargo, breakfast hour shall be between 6:00 a.m. and 7:00 a.m. Under this example crew has privilege of knocking off at 5:00 a.m. to await breakfast hour at 6:00 a.m. without penalty, or to work through to 6:00 a.m. and be paid for breakfast hour 6:00 a.m. to 7:00 a.m.

2. If cargo work is finished at 12:00 midnight and crew has worked on cargo two and one-half

(Testimony of Harry E. Lundeberg.)

Board's Exhibit No. 2—Rejected—(Continued)

hours or more, crew shall be entitled to hot meal at time knocked off.

3. Where crew is turned to on cargo work at 1:00 a.m. or prior to 3:00 a.m. and work through on cargo, breakfast hour shall be between 6:00 a.m. and 7:00 a.m. without penalty. If crew requested to eat between 7:00 (25) a.m. and 8:00 a.m., they shall be entitled to one hour's penalty.

4. Where crew is turned to on cargo work at 3:00 a.m. or later and work through on cargo, breakfast hour shall be between 7:00 a.m. and 8:00 a.m. If crew are requested to eat between 6:00 a.m. and 7:00 a.m. they shall be entitled to one hour's penalty.

5. Breakfast hour 7:00 a.m. to 8:00 a.m. If required to eat between 6:00 a.m. and 7:00 a.m. for 7:00 a.m. start on cargo work crew entitled to penalty hour.

6. Dinner hour 12:00 noon to 1:00 p.m.:
   (a) Knocked off cargo work—12:20 p.m.
   Paid to—12:30 p. m.
   Meal hour—12:30 p.m. to 1:30 p.m., for which paid.
   Paid to—1:00 p.m.
   (b) Knocked off cargo work—12:50 p.m.
   Meal hour—1:00 p.m. to 2:00 p.m., for which paid.

(Testimony of Harry E. Lundeberg.)

Board's Exhibit No. 2—Rejected—(Continued)

(c) Knocked off cargo work—1:00 p.m.
Paid to—1:00 p.m.
Meal hour—1:00 p.m. to 2:00 p.m., for which paid.

7. Supper hour, 5:00 p.m. to 6:00 p.m.:

(a) Knocked off cargo work at 5:15 p.m.
Paid to—5:30 p.m.
Meal hour—5:30 to 6:30 p.m., for which paid.

(b) Knocked off cargo work—5:45 p.m.
Paid to—6:00 p.m.
Meal hour—6:00 p.m. to 7:00 p.m., for which paid.

(c) Knocked off cargo work—6:00 p.m.
Paid to—6:00 p.m.
Meal hour—6:00 p.m. to 7:00 p.m., for which paid.

8. 12:00 midnight to 1:00 a.m., if entitled to meal hour under Section 2, above:

(a) Knocked off cargo work—12:20 a.m.
Paid to—12:30 a.m.
Meal hour—12:30 a.m. to 1:30 a.m., for which paid.

(b) Knocked off cargo work—12:50 a.m.
Paid to—1:00 a.m. (26)
Meal hour—1:00 a.m. to 2:00 a.m., for which paid.

(c) Knocked off cargo work—1:00 a.m.
Paid to—1:00 a.m.

(Testimony of Harry E. Lundeberg.)

Board's Exhibit No. 2—Rejected—(Continued)

Meal hour—1:00 a.m. to 2:00 a.m., for which paid.

9. 11:00 p.m. to 12:00 midnight, if entitled to meal hour under five hour spread account having worked through on cargo from 6:00 p.m.:

(a) Knocked off cargo work—11:15 p.m.
Paid to—11:30 p.m.
Meal hour—11:30 p.m. to 12:30 a.m., for which paid.

(b) Knocked off cargo work—11:45 p.m.
Paid to—12:00 midnight.
Meal hour—12:00 midnight to 1:00 a.m., for which paid.

(c) Knocked off cargo work—12:00 midnight.
Paid to—12:00 midnight.
Meal hour—12:00 midnight to 1:00 a.m., for which paid.

10. Where meal hour is advanced to 11:00 a.m. and-or 11:00 p.m. to commence working cargo at 12 noon or 12 midnight, and crew off watch are paid one hour's overtime for the advanced meal hour, watch on deck shall be entitled to similar payment.

Under no other circumstances shall the watch on deck be entitled to penalty meal hour.

Section 12. At no time shall more than five hours elapse between meals and one unbroken hour shall be allowed for dinner and supper.

(Testimony of Harry E. Lundeberg.)

Board's Exhibit No. 2—Rejected—(Continued)

Section 13. When working overtime later than 8:00 p.m., coffee and lunch shall be served at 9:00 p.m. and fifteen minutes shall be allowed for this lunch. Fifteen minutes shall be allowed for coffee at 3:00 a.m. if crew works all night.

Coffee time during the day shall be at 1:00 a.m. and 3:00 p.m. approximately. Not more than four men are to go for coffee at one time. When crew is split not more than two men shall go from each gang.

Section 14. When vessels are in commission and the men are on articles or port payroll and sleeping accommodations and (or) subsistence are not furnished, a cash allowance (27) of one dollar and fifty cents ($1.50) per night for lodging and seventy-five cents (75c) per meal shall be allowed each member of the crew.

Section 15. In port when crew is sleeping on board, heat and lights to be furnished.

Section 16. (a) All dishes shall be crockery ware.

(b) Mattress and pillow with cover, white sheets and sufficient blankets, towels, soap and matches shall be furnished to men on request, they to be responsible for the safekeeping of the same. Bed linen and towels to be changed weekly. When linen is not changed weekly each member of the crew shall be compensated by payment of $2.00 for each week that linen is not changed.

(Testimony of Harry E. Lundeberg.)

Board's Exhibit No. 2—Rejected—(Continued)

Section 17. Forecastles and messrooms shall be sealed and properly heated so as to be suitable for the northern run.

Section 18. The following holidays shall be observed as legal holidays:

New Year's Day	Labor Day
Lincoln's Birthday	Armistice Day
Washington's Birthday	Thanksgiving Day
Memorial Day	Christmas
Independence Day	

When these holidays fall on Sunday, the following Monday shall be observed.

When in West Coast ports of the United States, the unlicensed Deck Department personnel shall be granted any additional holidays granted by the employers to the longshoremen in such ports.

Section 19. When mate calls Sailors off watch to turn to on ship's work or cargo work, overtime or cargo rate starts when men are called, provided they report for work within fiteen (15) minutes. If they do not report within fifteen (15) minutes, time is to start from the time they report for duty.

Section 20. Where a vessel is in port, port anchorage or roadstead over twenty-four hours, operators reserve the right to break watches.

Section 21. Stand-by Work In Port.

When men are hired for stand-by work in port and neither board nor lodging is furnished, the rate of pay shall be $7.20 per day of eight hours. Men shall be paid a minimum of four hours. (28)

(Testimony of Harry E. Lundeberg.)

Board's Exhibit No. 2—Rejected—(Continued)

Stand-by hours in port shall be 8:00 a.m. to 12.00 noon and 1:00 p.m. to 5:00 p.m. weeks days and 8:00 a.m. to 12:00 noon Saturdays.

Overtime to be paid at the rate of $1.35 per hour.

Section 22. Deck boys promoted at sea to take care of emergency shall be paid rate to which promoted.

Day men required to stand navigating watch to receive overtime for all watches stood on Saturday afternoons, Sundays and holidays.

Section 23. When a vessel is laid up the crew will be entitled to a full day's pay, plus three (3) meals. However, if the crew are laid off and are not paid off the same day they will be entitled to their room money in addition.

Section 24. Deck Watchmen on passenger vessels shall receive one day off per week.

Section 25. Except as to single pieces, the weight of slingloads while cargo is being loaded or discharged by ship's crew shall not exceed 2100 lbs.

Section 26. Where men are required to stand by the windless to moor, unmoor or drop the anchor, winch drivers shall do this work.

Section 27. It is agreed that changes in existing practices or interpretations of this agreement are to be made only as herein provided and neither party will otherwise issue instructions which will affect such changes unless mutually agreed upon.

(Testimony of Harry E. Lundeberg.)

Board's Exhibit No. 2—Rejected—(Continued)

Section 28. If members of the deck department are required to clean or paint closed passageways midships, messroom and midships toilets, galleys, storerooms, they shall be paid at the regular overtime rate. Sailors shall not be required to clean steering engine or steering engine bed.

Section 29. When vessel arrives in Seattle from Alaska and is kept in commission and is regularly scheduled (company's published schedule) to return to Alaska within seven (7) days from arrival, Sailors shall continue in the service of the vessel, on sea pay, during said period.

Section 30. When there is a difference of opinion resulting in a dispute between the employer and Union over the interpretation of any provision of this agreement, past or present practices under the agreement, or any other reason that causes a dispute, it is definitely agreed that the Employer, the Union and its membership are to observe and abide by the Port Committee machinery set up and provided for (29) under the General Rules of this agreement. If the Port Committee machinery does not settle the dispute prior to the scheduled sailing of a vessel involved in the dispute, it is agreed that neither the Union nor its membership shall directly or indirectly prevent the sailing of the vessel on schedule.

Section 31. In no event shall there be any pyramiding or duplication of overtime or cargo rate under this agreement.

(Testimony of Harry E. Lundeberg.)

Board's Exhibit No. 2—Rejected—(Continued)

Section 32. Seattle, Washington, is the home port under this agreement. Home port for any feeder vessels operating in Alaska shall be mutually agreed upon.

Section 33. Add Boatswain to crew of SS SUTHERLAND, and SS DELLWOOD. The MARY D will also be required to carry a Boatswain when operated by the Alaska Steamship Company.

Section 34. When sacked ore, requiring no stowage by hand, is dumped four men shall be employed in the hold.

Section 35. When crew member fails to stand his regular watch or fulfill his recognized obligations due to drunkenness, making it necessary for other crew members to perform his work, said crew members shall be compensated for additional work performed by the crew member or member failing to or being unable to report on account of drunkenness.

In Witness Whereof, the parties hereto have executed this agreement on the day and year first therein written.

SAILORS' UNION OF THE PACIFIC

(sgd) HARRY LUNDEBERG,

(Testimony of Harry E. Lundeberg.)

Board's Exhibit No. 2—Rejected—(Continued)

PACIFIC AMERICAN SHIP-OWNERS ASSOCIATION

(sgd) J. B. BRYAN,
President.

Acting on behalf of the aforementioned Steamship Lines. (30)

MEMORANDUM OF RATES OF PAY

Deck Department
Pacific American Shipowners Association
and
Sailors' Union of the Pacific

BASE WAGE—EMERGENCY WAGE—OVERTIME WAGE

(Under Agreement dated November 4, 1941)

Rating	Basic Wages 10-1-41	War Emergency Increase 2-10-41	Total Wage 10-1-41
Boatswain*	$95.00	$17.50	$112.50
Carpenter*	95.00	17.50	112.50
Boatswain's Mate	92.50	17.50	110.00
Carpenter's Mate	90.00	17.50	107.50
Storekeeper	87.50	17.50	105.00
Quartermaster	87.50	17.50	105.00
Able Seamen	82.50	17.50	100.00
Watchmen	82.50	17.50	100.00
Ordinary Seamen	65.00	17.50	82.50
Deck Boy	60.00	17.50	77.50

* Vessels of 10,000 to 15,000 gross tons, wages shall be not less than $105.00 plus $17.50 War Emergency Increase. 15,001 to 20,000 gross tons, wages shall be not less than $110.00 plus $17.50 War Emergency Increase.

(Testimony of Harry E. Lundeberg.)

Board's Exhibit No. 2—Rejected—(Continued)

Ship's Carpenter will furnish his own tools and shall be paid $7.50 additional per month.

Overtime Rate............$ .85 per hour

Stand-by Rate

Off-shore, Intercoastal
and Alaska Trades......$7.20 per day
$1.35 per hour overtime

SS PERMANENTE, SS PHILLIP and SS WAIMEA,

Matson Navigation Company
(When operated as Cement Carrier)

Rating	Basic Wages 10-1-41	War Emergency Increase 2-10-41	Total Wage 10-1-41
Boatswain	$110.00	$17.50	$127.50
Able Seamen	95.00	17.50	112.50
Ordinary Seamen	77.50	17.50	95.00

(31)

Overtime Rate ....$ .90 per hour

Special Rate for—

(a) Cleaning Cement holds
8 a.m. and 5 p.m.............................$ .90 per hour
5 p.m. and 8 a.m.,
Saturday afternoons
and Sundays ....$1.15 per hour

(b) Handling cargo equipment in connection with loading and unloading Cement ....$1.05 per hour

(Testimony of Harry E. Lundeberg.)

Board's Exhibit No. 2—Rejected—(Continued)

TANKER MAKAWELI

WAGES

Rating	No.	Basic rate	War emergency increase	Total amount per month on articles
Boatswain	1	$110.00	$17.50	$127.50
Able seamen	6	95.00 ea.	17.50 ea.	112.50 ea.
Ordinary seamen	3	75.00 ea.	17.50 ea.	92.50 ea.

Overtime Rate ....$ .90 per hour

WORKING RULES THAT APPLY TO TANKER SS MAKAWELI

1. LOADING AND DISCHARGING OIL—There shall be not less than one able-bodied seaman on deck at all times while loading or discharging oil or molasses with one hose. If more than one hose is used during discharge and loading, one additional sailor shall be used for each additional hose.

2. Sailors shall, at all times, handle oil hoses within the ship's rail while at oil berth. When handled between 8 a. m. and 5 p. m. no overtime is to be paid.

3. WASHING TANKS—When washing tanks after discharge of molasses, the boatswain and six men will be used and two tanks will be cleaned simultaneously. When washing tanks after discharging of fuel oil, Boatswain and six men will be used cleaning one tank at a time, using 2½" hose and two men in the tank at one time.

(Testimony of Harry E. Lundeberg.)

Board's Exhibit No. 2—Rejected—(Continued)

4. WASHING TANKS — BUTTERWORTH SYSTEM. No overtime shall be paid the watch on deck during regular working hours if not required to enter tanks. When one Butterworth machine is used, two men and a boatswain shall be used. When operating two machines simultaneously, three men and a boatswain shall be employed. (32)
5. When cleaning tanks during overtime hours, the rate shall be 90 cents per hour per man working on deck and $1.15 per hour per man working in the tanks.
6. When sailors are required to go on dock to sling up hose and lowering same to dock between 8 a. m. and 5 p. m., no overtime to be paid.
7. When sailors are required to go on dock to handle and/or connect or disconnect hose between 8 a. m. and 5 p. m., overtime to be paid.

VESSELS ENGAGED IN THE ALASKA TRADE

Rating	Basic Wages 10-1-41	War Emergency Increase 2-10-41	Total Wage 10-1-41
Boatswain	$102.50	$10.00	$112.50
Carpenter	102.50	10.00	112.50
Winchdriver	100.00	10.00	110.00
Quartermaster	95.00	10.00	105.00
(When required to wear uniform)	100.00	10.00	110.00
Able Seamen	90.00	10.00	100.00
Watchman	90.0	10.00	100.00
Ordinary Seamen	72.50	10.00	82.50
Deck Boy	62.50	10.00	72.50

(Testimony of Harry E. Lundeberg.)

Board's Exhibit No. 2—Rejected—(Continued)

OVERTIME RATE

Ship's Work	$ .85 per hour
Cargo Work	$1.05 per hour (any time work)
	.25 per hour addltional to Hook-on men on board Freighters in the Bering Sea.
	.25 per hour additional when handling certain commodities referred to as Penalty Cargoes (Section 5 (a).

SECURITY WATCHES AMERICAN AND FOREIGN PORTS

MEMORANDUM OF AGREEMENT

Between

PACIFIC AMERICAN SHIPOWNERS ASSOCIATION

and

SAILORS' UNION OF THE PACIFIC

This Memorandum of Agreement dated.................., 1942, between the Pacific American Shipowners Association, hereinafter called the "Association" and the Sailors' Union of the Pacific, hereinafter called the "Union". (33)

WITNESSETH:

The Memorandum of Agreement between the parties dated June 16, 1942, is hereby cancelled and the

(Testimony of Harry E. Lundeberg.)

Board's Exhibit No. 2—Rejected—(Continued)

provisions set forth in this Supplementary Agreement shall govern in lieu thereof and shall be binding upon the respective parties upon the same terms and conditions as set forth in Section 22 of the General Agreement between the parties dated November 4, 1941.

The following rules shall govern respecting overtime payments to members of the Sailors' Union of the Pacific required to remain aboard vessels in port (whether domestic or foreign) between the hours of 5 P. M. and 8 A. M. week days and on Saturday afternoons, Sundays and Holidays for the purposes of vessel security or for the standing of safety watches required by Federal authorities.

1. When it is required that a member of the Unlicensed Deck Department be aboard at night (5 P. M. to 8 A. M.) week days, he shall receive $6.00 per night. If called upon to do work, overtime according to agreement shall be paid for the period worked in addition to the $6.00. If the crew is required to work during such hours between 5 P. M. and 8 A. M. the total compensation for one night shall not exceed the equivalent of 15 hours' overtime.

The foregoing provision does not apply to crew members required to stand their regular watches as provided in Section 4, Working Rules—

> "Section 4. In port, quartermasters shall be required to stand gangway watches and night

(Testimony of Harry E. Lundeberg.)

Board's Exhibit No. 2—Rejected—(Continued)

watchmen and stationmen their regular night watches between the hours of 5 P. M. and 8 A. M. without payment of overtime (except on Saturday afternoons, Sundays and holidays)."

2. Overtime shall be paid to all Unlicensed Deck Crew members for all hours during which they are required to remain aboard the vessel by Federal authorities (in United States ports or United States controlled ports) or by foreign government authorities in other ports for purposes of vessel security or for the standing of safety watches from Saturday noon until 8 A. M. Monday morning and on holidays except, however, no overtime shall be paid to crew members when required to remain aboard only because of orders in regulations of authorities in U. S. ports or U. S. controlled ports or by foreign government authorities in other ports preventing shore leave.

3. When the vessel is loaded and ready for sea, and is held at anchor or at the dock awaiting naval or military orders to sail in convoy, sea watches shall be set upon notification to the (34) Master by the proper Federal authorities that the vessel is to proceed to sea. Overtime shall be paid for all such time on sea watches after 5 P. M. and before 8 A. M. week days in excess of 24 hours before actual sailing time. However, the 24 hours to be subject to being extended for an additional time if the vessel is held by Federal authorities. Overtime

(Testimony of Harry E. Lundeberg.)

Board's Exhibit No. 2—Rejected—(Continued)

shall be payable for any work performed on such sea watches while the vessel is in port on Saturday afternoons, Sundays and Holidays.

Upon approval of the War Shipping Administration this Supplementary Agreement shall become effective on all vessels upon the date of execution thereof.

PACIFIC AMERICAN SHIP-OWNERS ASSOCIATION,
J. B. BRYAN,
President.
SAILORS' UNION OF THE PACIFIC,
HARRY LUNDEBERG,
Secretary-Treasurer.

CLARIFICATION

No. 1........Security Watches in the U. S. Continental ports, Island and Canal ports are payable in full at eighty-five cents per hour, from December 7th, 1941, to February 6th, 1942.

From February 6th, 1942, security watches in American ports, Island ports and Canal Zone ports are payable as per the agreement above.

Payment for security watches in foreign ports is payable from.., as per the agreement above.

No. 2........While on Security Watches it is understood that no work shall be done.

You are to be aboard the vessel, subject to call;

(Testimony of Harry E. Lundeberg.)

Board's Exhibit No. 2—Rejected—(Continued)

if you are required to be on deck, overtime is payable right through.

If you are called upon to do any work for a couple of hours or more, that is payable at the overtime rate in addition to your $6.00.

If you are called upon to work from 5 P. M. to 8 A. M. in the morning, you are only entitled to straight overtime.

If you are required to be aboard on Saturday afternoon, Sundays or holidays for the purpose of security watches, you get paid overtime straight through. You are not required to

If the entire crew is required to stay abroad for military reasons or otherwise and are denied shore leave, then only the ones assigned to the security watch are entitled to pay.

work. (35)

. . . If while standing security watch you are called upon to do emergency work, no overtime is payable for such work.

This has been concurred in by the membership and O.K.'d by Shipowners. It becomes effective as soon as the War Shipping Administration okehs same.

When you are on security watches on Saturday afternoon and Sunday you are paid straight overtime from 12 noon Saturday until 8 A. M. Monday morning.

When you stand security watches on a straight holiday, such as Armistice Day, Labor Day or any

(Testimony of Harry E. Lundeberg.)

Board's Exhibit No. 2—Rejected—(Continued)

other holiday, you receive straight overtime from twelve midnight until 12 midnight on that day.

From 5 P. M. up until midnight of the holiday, you receive $3.00.

From 12 midnight until 12 midnight on the holiday you receive 85c per hour.

From midnight until 8 A. M. in the morning the following day, you receive $3.00.

The Agreement between the Sailors' Union of the Pacific and Matson Navigation Company provides for the following wage rates:

1. Painters (hull) and for men performing general work, One Dollar and Five Cents ($1.05) per hour for straight time work.

2. Chipping (pneumatic tools), One Dollar and Fifteen Cents ($1.15) per hour for straight time work.

3. Painters (spraying), One Dollar and Fifteen Cents ($1.15) per hour for straight time work.

4. Riggers in rigging loft, One Dollar and Twenty-Five Cents ($1.25) per hour for straight time work.

5. "Leading men," supervising all classes of work, One Dollar and Twenty Cents ($1.20) per hour for straight time work.

6. When me are required to clean holds of cement for the first time after each carriage of bulk cement in these compartments of the S.S. Wai-

(Testimony of Harry E. Lundeberg.)

Board's Exhibit No. 2—Rejected—(Continued)

mea, also when men are required to clean holds of other ships of the fleet for the first time after each carriage of chrome ore, the rate of pay will be 25 cents per hour above the base rate for shore gang labor.

MATSON NAVIGATION COMPANY,

By: ....

(36)

SAILORS' UNION
OF THE PACIFIC

59 Clay Street San Francisco

Phones:
EXbrook 2228
(Dispatcher: EXbrook 2229)

Branches

Richmond, California
Phone Richmond 2599

Seattle, Washington
86 Seneca Street Phone Elliott 6752

Portland, Oregon
111 W. Burnside St. Phone Beacon 4336

San Pedro, California
206 W. 6th Street Phone San Pedro 2491

Honolulu
16 Merchant Street Phone 3599

New York City
105 Broad St. Phone Bowling Green 9-9530

Vancouver, British Columbia
Phone Pacific 7824

(Testimony of Harry E. Lundeberg.)

Mr. Guntert: I want to object to the introduction of this.

Trial Examiner Batten: Of course, it hasn't been offered yet.

Q. (By Mr. Moore) I show you a booklet marked Board's [92] Exhibit 2 for identification and ask you if you can tell me what it is?

A. This is the agreement between the Sailors Union of the Pacific——

Mr. Guntert: I object to the introduction of this or any testimony in connection with it.

Trial Examiner Batten: It hasn't been introduced, Mr. Guntert.

Mr. Guntert: I am objecting to this line of questioning.

Trial Examiner Batten: I know. But, Mr. Guntert, how could an attorney possibly introduce the document, at least until the witness tells you what it is?

Mr. Guntert: Go ahead.

Trial Examiner Batten: In other words, the witness has a perfect right to identify a document.

The Witness: It's an agreement between the Sailors Union of the Pacific and the Pacific American Shipowners Association, covering wages, working rules and conditions, deck personnel on the Pacific Coast.

Q. (By Mr. Moore): Are the companies listed on page 3 members of the Pacific American Shipowners Association?

A. Yes, they are all members.

(Testimony of Harry E. Lundeberg.)

Q. Is this contract now in force and effect?

Mr. Guntert: I object, because I think if counsel wants to go into this now, knowing that I am going to object—— [93]

Trial Examiner Batten: Of course, this question is not for the purpose of identifying the document, is it, that you are now asking?

Mr. Moore: No, it's to show the document is not something in the past, but that it is a current document.

Trial Examiner Batten: Well, of course, I think it is a proper question. In other words, if it isn't in force and effect, then there is no use of bothering with it.

Mr. Moore: That's right.

Trial Examiner Batten: You may answer.

The Witness: It's in effect for the duration of the war, and it is underwritten by Admiral Land of the War Shipping Administration.

Mr. Guntert: I think that is going pretty far afield.

Trial Examiner Batten: Just a minute. If you have an objection, Mr. Guntert, you may state it.

Mr. Guntert: I do object to the answer. The witness has gone far beyond the question. They know I am going to object to it, and they are trying to get in everything they can.

Trial Examiner Batten: The only question, Mr. Guntert, thus far is: "Is it in effect?"

Mr. Guntert: And the answer was "Yes."

(Testimony of Harry E. Lundeberg.)

Trial Examiner Batten: But no witness ever has to say "yes" or "no." I have had lawyers say, "Answer 'yes' or 'no'." [94] I always say "You don't have to answer 'yes' or 'no.' "

That is a lawyer's way frequently of tying a witness up. No witness ever has to say "yes" or "no."

The question was: Was this in effect? The witness aid, "Yes, for the duration of the war, in agreement with the War Shipping Administration." Is that right?

The Witness: That's right.

Trial Examiner Batten: It seems to me that is entirely proper.

Mr. Moore: I offer Board's Exhibit 2 for identification in evidence.

Mr. Guntert: I object to the introduction of this document on the ground it is immaterial. It has no bearing whatsoever on the controversy here. What these unions have done with some 25 or 30 or 10 or 15 other companies with whom they have agreements has no bearing on whether or not it is an unfair labor practice for Richfield to adopt the policy that it did. This contract has no bearing whatever. In fact, the unions have been aboard many ships on the coast, many hundreds of them, as Mr. Lundeberg said.

It has no bearing on this issue at all. I think, Mr. Examiner, that we have gone far afield from the issues here; and I seriously object to the introduction of this agreement. It has no bearing whatsoever on this case.

(Testimony of Harry E. Lundeberg.)

Trial Examiner Batten: What is the purpose of the [95] document?

Mr. Moore: The purpose of offering this contract and two others which I shall presently offer is to show that it is the general practice followed almost 100 per cent on this coast to grant access to union representatives for the purpose of permitting them to contact their members, not to show that Richfield should follow that practice as a matter of moral obligation, but simply to show that for a long period heretofore it has been considered necessary for shore delegates to board ships in order to properly settle grievances, considered not only by the men themselves but by the companies that they deal with.

Mr. Guntert: Well, as a matter of fact, Mr. Examiner, we have had an agreement in effect in the past with these very same unions in which they were given access to our ships. But we don't have those contracts now. Only recently negotiations were going on for a new contract. And the only question before you now is whether or not we are engaged in unfair labor practices by refusing to issue passes to these men. And we have explained that our reason is for safety purposes in the interest of the world war going on now. And we have said why we thought that was so.

We think it is the exercise of due diligence that is required of us. And the fact that these security orders came out, we think simply confirms the wisdom of our policy. [96]

(Testimony of Harry E. Lundeberg.)

Trial Examiner Batten: Just at that point, Mr. Guntert, the question arises. If other companies, all these other companies, have continued the practice and on the basis of the same orders, then apparently it is a question of what interpretation you put upon it.

Now, that is one of the things I will have to determine, I presume, whether or not in the light of these instructions and orders you are justified in placing any such interpretation upon it.

Now, certainly, at least to that extent, I think they are material.

Mr. Guntert: Well, to this extent: that these contracts were in effect some time prior to the security orders, as you yourself indicated.

Trial Examiner Batten: Yes.

Mr. Guntert: And the contracts which we have had with these unions have been terminated. There certainly is no reason for drawing an inference or for introducing a contract to draw an inference because under certain contracts certain rights were given and agreed upon.

Trial Examiner Batten: Well, I think it is more important because you don't have a contract than it would be if you did have.

Mr. Guntert: That is a matter——

Trial Examiner Batten: Now, I'll tell you why because I [97] want you to understand it. I think there is no question about this organization having a majority. You aren't questioning that?

Mr. Guntert: No. They have been certified.

(Testimony of Harry E. Lundeberg.)

Trial Examiner Batten: Well, if that is the case, then, they are the exclusive representatives of the employees, whether you have any contract or whether you don't. It seems to me these employees are entitled to certain rights and privileges, the right of representation under the Wagner Act.

Now, the fact that you don't have a contract appears to me to make the problem more important than if you did have. I mean by that not that it is an unfair labor practice. Don't misunderstand me. I think it is more important that it be determined where there is not a contract than where there is a contract, not only from your standpoint but from the standpoint of all the companies.

In other words, this is an issue, and I think you will agree with me—and I think Mr. Lundeberg will—that this is almost entirely a legal question that needs determination.

Now, if it does, we ought to have all of the facts we can get. I, for one, wouldn't want to attempt to decide this issue, Mr. Guntert, without all the information.

Mr. Moore: Mr. Examiner, before you rule on this exhibit let me advise you that it doesn't have any written provision [98] providing for passes. The two which I propose to introduce do have.

Trial Examiner Batten: What is the purpose of offering this, then?

Mr. Moore: To show that the companies bound by the agreement, Board's Exhibit 2 for identification, have freely granted passes.

(Testimony of Harry E. Lundeberg.)

Trial Examiner Batten: Of course, if they have freely granted passes, it isn't on the basis of a contract, is it?

Mr. Moore: No, it is not. But they have a contract in addition to passes. The matter of passes is taken up separately and apart.

Trial Examiner Batten: Then why encumber the record with this?

Mr. Moore: For one thing it identifies the companies involved, and I want to ask what types of ships they operate.

Trial Examiner Batten: Well, of course, if the only purpose of it is to identify the companies on the first page——

Mr. Moore: It does more than that. It differentiates between that type of treatment on the question of passes and the type of treatment that is given in the cases of where it is permissible.

Trial Examiner Batten: If it is not in the contract, it is a verbal arrangement, even though the contract is in existence. You don't need the contract to determine that. [99] I don't suppose Mr. Guntert will dispute the fact that this contract is in existence.

Mr. Guntert: Of course not.

Trial Examiner Batten: In existence with these named companies. So why do you need the contract?

Mr. Moore: Very well.

Trial Examiner Batten: Mr. Guntert, why do you need it, then?

(Testimony of Harry E. Lundeberg.)

Mr. Guntert: I don't want it. I am objecting to it.

Trial Examiner Batten: I mean Mr. Moore.

Mr. Moore: It isn't essential.

Trial Examiner Batten: Well, then, let's don't encumber the record. I understood that there was a provision in here providing for passes.

The Witness: Your Honor, they send us passes every year.

Trial Examiner Batten: Well, I know. But the contract doesn't show that, Mr. Lundeberg. I am talking about a contract that is several pages long, and Mr. Guntert admits that there is a contract in existence with all these named companies, and he said a moment ago they operate several hundred ships.

I will refuse the offer.

Mr. Moore: May I ask, Mr. Examiner, if this will be classed as a rejected exhibit?

Trial Examiner Batten: That's right. [100]

Q. (By Mr. Moore): Will you refer to Board's Exhibit 2 for identification, Mr. Lundeberg, and state what steamship companies specifically are members of the Pacific American Shipowners Association?

A. The Admiral Oriental Line, the American-Hawaiian Steamship Company, the American Mail Line, the American President Lines, Ltd., Alaska Steamship Company, Alaska Transportation Company, W. R. Grace & Co., Matson Navigation Company, The Oceanic Steamship Company, Pope and

(Testimony of Harry E. Lundeberg.)

Talbot, Inc., Northland Transportation Company, Pacific Lighterage Corporation, Pacific Republic Line, Santa Ana Steamship Company, States Steamship Company, Pacific-Atlantic Steamship Company, Sudden & Christensen, Shepard Steamship Company, The Union Sulphur Company, Inc.

Trial Examiner Batten: Let's see. Did you mention Coastwise Pacific Far East Line?

The Witness: No. I think I skipped that.

Trial Examiner Batten: I think you skipped that.

The Witness: Pacific Far East Lines.

Q. (By Mr. Moore): The unions you represent are under a collective bargaining contract with the Association representing the companies you have just named? A. Yes.

Q Is the contract now in force and effect?

A. That is in force and effect. [101]

Q. Does it, to your knowledge, contain any provision relating to passes to permit union representatives to board ships?

Mr. Guntert: I object to the question, all this line of questioning, on what is in these other contracts. It has no bearing whatever on this issue, Mr. Examiner. I don't want to continue to be objecting, but I think we are far afield of the issues, as I said before.

Trial Examiner Batten: Well, of course, I will have to disagree with you because I think the practice on the coast is material to the issues here.

You may tell us, Mr. Lundeberg.

(Testimony of Harry E. Lundeberg.)

Mr. Moore: Do you want the question read?

The Witness: No, I remember the question. There is no provision in that agreement which gives us passes.

Q. (By Mr. Moore): I will ask you whether or not representatives of the unions you represent have passes to board vessels operated by the companies represented by Pacific American Shipowners Association? A. Yes, we do.

Q. Are those passes good in all ports on the Pacific Coast?

A. They are issued in every port on the Pacific Coast, yes, sir, good in every port. I have one here.

Q. How do you obtain those passes, Mr. Lundeberg?

A. The company sends them to us every year, and it's good [102] until revoked by the companies. I have one I will show you.

We don't even ask for them. They sent them to us.

Q. Can you tell me, Mr. Lundeberg, what types of vessels the companies belonging to this Association operate?

A. What types of vessels? That is passenger vessels and dry cargo vessels, all these types of ships now, of course, carrying war materials. Some of them is carrying troops and ammunition, and so forth.

Q. Have you observed war materials being loaded into these ships?

(Testimony of Harry E. Lundeberg.)

A. I can't help it. When you go on board these ships you can't miss seeing it.

Trial Examiner Batten: Well, of course, that isn't the question whether you can't help you. The question is, Did you see them loading these materials?

The Witness: Yes, I have seen them loading all kinds of war materials, torpedoes, light aircraft and so forth crated up, and thousands of troops. Some of these vessels here pack as high as 5000 troops. They are all manned by our crews, and we board all of them.

Q. (By Mr. Moore): Have you been aboard such ships while they were being loaded?

A. Yes, sir. I have been aboard while they are being loaded, and just prior to their leaving port. We are called on board by the companies and sometimes called on board by the [103] Navy to see that everything is all right.

Mr. Moore: May I ask that this document be marked as Board's Exhibit 3 for identification?

(Thereupon the document referred to was marked as Board's Exhibit No. 3 for identification.)

Mr. Moore: And that this document be marked as Board's Exhibit 4 for identification?

(Thereupon the document referred to was marked as Board's Exhibit No. 4 for identifition.)

(Testimony of Harry E. Lundeberg.)

Q. (By Mr. Moore): Mr. Lundeberg, I show you a document marked Board's Exhibit 3 for identification and ask you if you can tell me what it is.

A. It's an agreement between the Sailors Union of the Pacific and the Shipowners Association of the Pacific Coast.

Q. Is that agreement now in force and effect?

A. That is in force and effect, yes, sir.

Q. Referring to page 15 of the document, are the companies named there members of the Shipowners Association of the Pacific Coast?

A. Yes, sir.

Mr. Moore: I offer Board's Exhibit 3 for identification in evidence and call attention particularly to page 12, clause 3.

Mr. Guntert: And I object to the introduction of that on the same grounds stated, Mr. Examiner, and on the [104] additional ground that these are quite evidently dry cargo vessels having conditions entirely different from tank vessels.

Trial Examiner Batten: Well, of course, I will rule upon this one on the basis that it indicates the union's authorized representatives have permits to board the ships, which means that I shall overrule the objection and receive the exhibit.

(Thereupon the document heretofore marked for identification as Board's Exhibit 3, was received in evidence.)

(Testimony of Harry E. Lundeberg.)

BOARD'S EXHIBIT No. 3

THIS AGREEMENT, made and entered into the 27th day of October, 1941, by the Sailors' Union of the Pacific, party of the first part, hereinafter known as the Union, and Shipowners' Association of the Pacific Coast, (on behalf of its members here listed, covering their vessels operating in the Steam Schooner trade) party of the second part, hereinafter known as the shipowners, shall be binding on the parties for the period to and including September 30, 1942, and shall be renewed from year to year thereafter unless either party shall give written noice to the other at least thirty (30) days prior to such expiration date, of a desire to amend or terminate this agreement, and the parties shall meet within five (5) days to begin negotiations. If during the thirty-day period the parties fail to agree with reference to such amendments, this agreement shall terminate at the expiration date, provided, however, that parties may by mutual written agreement extend this agreement for a specified period beyond such expiration date for the continuance of negotiations.

Wages:

1. Able Bodied Seamen.........$107.50 } Effective 12:01 A.M.
   Winchdrivers .... 117.50 } Oct. 16, 1941
2. The overtime rate shall be $1.10 per hour.

Day Work:

1. When hired by the day, rate of pay shall be $7.50 for eight (8) hours' work between eight A. M. and five P. M., and $1.35 per hour for all work in

(Testimony of Harry E. Lundeberg.)

Board's Exhibit No. 3—(Continued)

excess of eight hours, effective 12:01 A. M. October 28, 1941. A minimum of one full day's pay is guaranteed for the first day's work and nothing less than one-half days thereafter.

Penalty Cargo:

1. Crew shall load and discharge cargo at the basic rates of pay specified in this agreement, provided that twenty-five (25) cents per hour extra shall be paid to each man, either daytime or night time, engaged in loading or discharging the following commodities:

All animal and fish fertilizers,
Bulk salt and bulk coke,
Bulk grain,
Building bulkheads,
Carboys of Acid,
Creosoted Lumber,
Cement,
Cleaning holds after penalty cargoes,
Coal (bulk and sacks),
Decalite and Sealite in sacks,
Empty cement sacks,
Flue dust,
Green and creosoted piling; gypsum and ground redwood bark,
Hay,
Hides,
Live Stock,
Lime,

(Testimony of Harry E. Lundeberg.)

Board's Exhibit No. 3—(Continued)

Meals, and other offensive materials used as fertilizers,
Manures,
Nitrates (bags or bulk)
Ore (bulk and sack)
Plaster,
Poultry,
Phosphates,
Soda Ash,
Sulphur,
Silicate of Soda,
Scrap metal cargoes (bulk and mixed, including bales, excluding rails)
Tallow,
Rock glass,
Working lumber in tanks where oil fluid cargoes have been carried
Also for all shoveling. (2*)

There shall be no extra pay for less than one-half hour's work for this kind of freight.

Penalty rates do not apply to ship's stores.

2. All explosives, such as Dynamite caps, gun powder, blasting powder and munitions to be worked at overtime pay during straight time hours and when working overtime, twenty-five cents an hour in addition to the overtime rate shall be paid.

Damaged Cargo:

1. If a cargo of a vessel, either in whole or in part,

* Page numbering appearing at foot of page of original Printed Agreement.

(Testimony of Harry E. Lundeberg.)

Board's Exhibit No. 3—(Continued)

is badly damaged by fire, collision, springing a leak or stranding, the wages for handling that part of the cargo only which is in a badly damaged or offensive condition, shall be $1.40 per hour during straight or overtime periods.

2. Two dollars and ten cents ($2.10) per hour shall be paid when fire is present or cargo is smouldering in the hatch which is being worked.

3. When sailors are required to clean deep tanks in which bulk oils have been previously carried, the overtime rate of pay for straight time and the overtime rate, plus twenty-five cents per hour for overtime, shall be paid. Boiler suits shall be provided by the shipowners.

4. When actual overtime worked is less than one hour, one hour shall be paid.

5. Where overtime worked exceeds one hour, payment shall be made for actual time worked, but not less than one-half hour periods.

6. Cleaning bilges shall be overtime at any time.

Working Rules:

1. The working day in port shall be eight hours between the hours of eight A. M. and five P. M. and all work outside of these hours shall be paid for at the regular overtime rate.

2. All work in port on Sundays, holidays and beyond the regular working hours on week days shall be paid for at the prescribed overtime rates. (3)

(Testimony of Harry E. Lundeberg.)

Board's Exhibit No. 3—(Continued)

2 (a). Effective 12:01 A. M. Oct. 28, 1941 all work in port on Saturday afternoon, between the hours of 1:00 P. M. and 5:00 P. M., shall be paid for at overtime rate. There shall be no pyramiding or duplication of overtime account Saturday afternoon work in port falling on arrival or departure day.

3. Any work, necessary in fact for the safety of the vessel, passengers, cargo or crew shall be performed at any time without extra compensation. All cargo, cargo gear and hatches shall be properly secured before leaving sheltered waters.

4. Moving vessel, when crew is on day work in any river, harbors, bays, or sounds after five P. M. and before eight A. M. and on Sundays and holidays, shall be paid for at the overtime rate to the members of the crew that are engaged in moving the vessel.

5. When vessel is moving, crew shall not be required to handle hatches or strong backs.

6. In port when members of the crew not on watch are called after six P. M. and before five A. M. and there is not a continuity of work (meal hours do not break "continuity of work") to work cargo, to move vessel, raise or lower cargo booms, open or close hatches, they shall be paid a minimum of two hours overtime, provided they turn to fifteen minutes after being called. Any man not turning to within 15

(Testimony of Harry E. Lundeberg.)

Board's Exhibit No. 3—(Continued)

minutes after being called shall be paid only for the time actually worked.

7. When members of the crew, not on watch, are called on or after five A. M. to work cargo, to move vessel, raise or lower cargo booms, or open or close hatches, they shall be paid at overtime rate from the time they are called until eight A. M., provided that they turn to fifteen minutes after being called. Any man not turning to within fifteen minutes after being called, shall be paid overtime from the time he reports on the job until eight A. M.

8. When members of the crew, not on watch, are called to moor or unmoor vessel coming from or going to sea, they shall be paid a minimum of one hour.

9. When working on overtime and crew is knocked off for (4) two hours or less, overtime shall be paid straight through. This means exactly two hours or less of actual work.

10. Overtime work performed during any 24 hour period of time shall be at single rate of overtime.

EXCEPTION: After 16 or more consecutive hours of work, meal hours included, if men are knocked off and then called again for any work before expiration of 24 hours from the beginning of the 16 or more hour period, they shall receive no overtime for time knocked off, but shall receive overtime at double rate, with two hour minimum, for work, performed from time called until given 8 hours below.

(Testimony of Harry E. Lundeberg.)

Board's Exhibit No. 3—(Continued)

The term "8 hours below" includes time off for meals.

After working 16 or more consecutive hours, meal hours included, if men are knocked off and are not called again for work before the end of the 24 hour period, their 8 hours below shall start at the time they were knocked off and they shall not be called out again until the 8 hours below are completed. Exception: Men may be called after the expiration of the 24 hour period for purpose of taking vessel to sea or shifting or moving, in which case overtime at double rate, with two hour minimum, shall be paid for work performed from time called until given 8 hours below.

If work is continuous for 24 consecutive hours, including meals, the overtime worked therein shall be paid for at single rate. Men shall be given 8 hours below at end of the 24 hour period, unless vessel proceeds to sea, in which event men that stand watches shall be paid double overtime for watches or any part thereof actually stood until the 8 hours below is given.

When crew works cargo and one watch, or men comprising same, completes 24 consecutive hours of work, meals included, before the other two watches, or men comprising same, and crew continues to work cargo, the first-mentioned watch shall continue working beyond their 24 hour period at double overtime rate until the rest of the watches (or men) have com-

(Testimony of Harry E. Lundeberg.)

Board's Exhibit No. 3—(Continued)

pleted their 24 hour period, or until cargo work ceases.

During any period when men are on their 8 hours below, work may be continued in any or all hatches by (5) longshoremen and no claim for lodging money shall be made.

11. Where actual overtime worked is less than one hour, one hour shall be paid.

12. Where overtime worked exceeds one hour, payment shall be made for actual time worked but not less than half-hour periods.

13. When working overtime, the crews' delegate shall compare time with the officer in charge of the work as soon as knocking off.

14. The unlicensed deck crew shall not be required to work on the dock, except in ports where there are no longshoremen, or in ports where longshoremen are not available or where longshoremen refuse to work with sailors. If sailors are required to work on the dock, they shall do so at the direction of the Officer in charge, and they shall be paid for the work so performed at the prevailing longshoremen's scale for such work.

15. When the crew is working on lighters or barges, they shall be paid the prevailing longshore scale for such work.

16. On ships that carry only one winchdriver, he shall be paid $142.50 per month.

(Testimony of Harry E. Lundeberg.)

Board's Exhibit No. 3—(Continued)

17. On ships that carry package lumber, piling, etc. and where sailors crew are split and where winchdrivers normally work one man per gear, such as the Coos Bay boats, the Baxter boats, etc., the winchdrivers shall be paid at the rate of $142.50 per month.

18. On ships where winchdrivers normally work together on cargo and lumber (aside from ships carrying package loads and piling such as the Coos Bay boats and the Baxter boats, etc.) and they are split for any reason, they shall receive $1.10 per hour for all work between 8:00 A. M. and 5:00 P. M. on week days and $1.35 per hour for all work between 5:00 P. M. and 8:00 A. M. and on Sundays and holidays.
The hourly rates set forth in this rule include the 25c per hour for penalty cargo. (6)

19. When three men are not available on any watch, the winchdriver shall fill the vacancy at the overtime rate of pay, plus his regular wages on Sundays and holidays. On week days the winchdriver shall be paid his regular wages plus the regular wages of the missing man for watches stood. Any work on week days in excess of the watch time shall be at the regular overtime rate.

20. A full watch shall be used when shifting ships.

21. At all times members of the deck department not engaged in working cargo shall receive the same penalty and overtime as those members actually en-

(Testimony of Harry E. Lundeberg.)

Board's Exhibit No. 3—(Continued)

gaged in working cargo. No unnecessary ship's work will be done after 5:00 P. M. and before 8:00 A. M.

22. Crews may be split to handle package lumber, piling, etc.

23. Crews may be split in two hatches when ships work bulk ore, flue dust and/or bulk salt in two hatches simultaneously.

24. Longshoremen may relieve sailors' hatch during noon hour if necessary.

25. Sailors are to take ship's stores aboard without the payment of overtime between the hours of 8:00 A. M. and 5:00 P. M. on week days providing the stores are placed as close as possible to the gangway.

Watches:

1. When a vessel arrives from sea, watches may be broken when vessel is properly moored at loading or discharging berth, but when vessel arrives between midnight and eight A. M. four (4) hours' time is to be allowed for any part of a watch that is actually stood in computing the eight (8) hours' work on the day of arrival. However, men are to stand the full watch when required by the officer in charge.

2. Sea watches shall be set when the vessel leaves for sea; but not later than 4:00 P. M. on day of departure.

3. Any work performed by sailors in excess of eight

(Testimony of Harry E. Lundeberg.)

Board's Exhibit No. 3—(Continued)

hours, on days of arrival and days of departure, shall be (7) considered overtime. The calendar day on arrival and departure shall be reckoned from midnight to midnight. The work day in port "after arrival or before departure" (arrival and departure as explained in Rule 5) shall be from 8:00 A. M. to 5 P. M. and any time worked in port outside of these hours is overtime. No overtime paid for time at sea prior to arrival but each man's time on watch at sea to be added to the time he works in port in computing the eight hours' work day. All cargo work performed by the watch on deck prior to 8:00 A. M. on day of arrival shall be paid for at the overtime rate.

4. When crew is on watch and watch either at sea or in port, any men called from a watch below shall be paid overtime for the time worked on their watch below.

5. The day the vessel arrives from sea to a port of call shall be considered arrival, and any subsequent moves from that port occurring in inland waters, bays, and sounds, shall be considered as moving ship. The day of departure shall be the day the vessel leaves directly for sea, and sea watches shall be set and maintained from that port.

Moves between British Columbia ports and American ports (or vice-versa) over one hundred and twenty miles, shall be considered as going to or arriving from sea, but after arrival at first American

(Testimony of Harry E. Lundeberg.)

Board's Exhibit No. 3—(Continued)

or British Columbia loading or discharging port, preceding paragraph shall govern.

6. On sailing day when watches are set and are then broken before sailing the same day any part of a watch stood shall constitute a full watch.

7. Sailors while at sea shall be divided into watches as prescribed by law, in no cases consisting of less than three (3) watches of three (3) men each. Exception: The master shall determine how many men are required on an anchor watch.

When vessel arrives and/or sails on Sundays or holidays, watches are to be broken and set in accordance with regular rules for watches. All work performed in port on Sundays or holidays is to be overtime and all work in excess of eight (8) hours on Sundays or holidays, when same are days of arrival and days of departure, including sea watches, is overtime. (8)

When watches and cargo or ship's work equal 8 hours on Sundays or holidays, overtime shall be paid for all time worked or watches stood in excess of the combined 8 hours.

Example:	12 to 4 Watch	4 to 8 Watch	8 to 12 Watch
Vessel arrives at 1:00 P.M.	5 hours	4 hours	4 hours
Works Cargo to 5:00 P.M.	4 "	4 "	4 "
Supper, 5 P.M. to 6 P.M.	0 "	0 "	0 "
Resumed cargo work, 6 P.M. to 9 P.M.	3 "	3 "	3 "
Vessel went to sea 9 P.M.	0 "	0 "	3 "
Total	12 "	11 "	14 "

(Testimony of Harry E. Lundeberg.)

Board's Exhibit No. 3—(Continued)

All work in port is overtime; all work in excess of 8 hours including watch time is overtime.

9. No overtime payable to watch on sailing day when eating from 5:00 P. M. to 6:00 P. M.

Holidays:

The following shall be observed as holidays in port: New Year's Day, Lincoln's Birthday, Washington's Birthday, Decoration Day, Independence Day, Labor Day, Armistice Day, Thanksgiving Day, Christmas Day, and all holidays observed by the longshoremen in the port where the vessel may be shall be observed by the deck department.

Crews Quarters:

1. Clean white linen, which shall include both face and bath towels, two sheets and a pillow slip, sufficient blankets and spreads, shall be issued to each man upon joining the vessel, and linen and towels shall be changed once each week. Each man is responsible for same. $2.00 will be allowed for each week linen is not changed.

2. Soap and matches shall be furnished each week.

3. Each member of the crew shall be provided with a suitable locker and sufficient space for his gear.

4. Each vessel shall be furnished with a messrom or messrooms for the accommodation of the crew, such mess- (9) rooms to be in each case so constructed as to afford sitting room for all when it is prac-

(Testimony of Harry E. Lundeberg.)

Board's Exhibit No. 3—(Continued)

tical and available to do so, and to be so situated as to afford full protection from the weather and from heat and odor arising from the vessel's engine room, fire-room and hold.

5. Heat to be furnished.

6. Electricity to be furnished where plug-in facilities are available.

Meals:

1. Breakfast shall be from seven-thirty A. M. to eight A. M.

When men are called for breakfast before regular hour they shall receive overtime from the time called until eight A. M.

If breakfast is postponed until eight A. M., one-half hour shall be allowed for eating for which one-half hour's overtime shall be paid.

2. Dinner is to be one unbroken hour between 11:00 A. M. and 1:00 P. M., commencing at 11:00 A. M., 11:30 A. M. or 12:00 Noon. Supper is to be one unbroken hour between 5:00 P. M. and 6:00 P. M. However, on sailing day or when moving vessel, Section 6 or Section 7 shall apply. At no time is more than five hours of work to be permitted to elapse between meals.

3. When moving ship, men actually engaged in moving vessel during dinner hour shall, in lieu of unbroken hour, receive an hour's overtime and at

(Testimony of Harry E. Lundeberg.)

Board's Exhibit No. 3—(Continued)

least an unbroken hour for noon meal either before or after moving vessel.

4. Supper on sailing day may be postponed two hours if cargo can be finished by 7:00 P. M., in which event double overtime shall be allowed for one hour from 6:00 P. M. to 7:00 P. M.

5. If vessel moves before 5:00 P. M. and move is completed before 5:30 P. M., actual overtime rate shall be paid up to 5:30 P. M. If move is completed later than 5:30 P. M., one and one-half hour's overtime shall be paid (10)

6. Supper hour may be postponed to 6:00 P. M. to move vessel in which event time and one-half of the overtime rate of pay to be paid to men actually engaged in this operation.

7. If ship is working cargo to midnight supper hour may be postponed to 6:00 P. M.

8. When working overtime later than 8:00 P. M., coffee and lunch shall be served at 9:00 P. M. and 3:00 A. M. and fifteen minutes shall be allowed for these lunches. Coffee time during the day shall be at 10:00 A. M. and 3:00 P. M., approximately. Not more than four men are to go for coffee at one time. When crew is split not more than two men shall go from each gang.

9. If crew works cargo as late as 11 P. M., a hot

(Testimony of Harry E. Lundeberg.)

Board's Exhibit No. 3—(Continued)

meal shall be served at 11:00 P. M. and one hour shall be allowed for this meal.

10. If crews are required to work between the hot meal period of 11:00 P. M. to 12 midnight, double overtime rate shall be paid.

11. On Sundays and Holidays when crews are not working, besides the usual hot breakfast, a hot dinner shall be served and a cold supper shall be set upon notice given not later than Saturday supper, that not less than four members of unlicensed deck or engine departments will be present for dinner.

12. When no cooking is done on board for any reason and the crew have to eat ashore, seventy-five cents (75c) shall be allowed for breakfast, seventy-five cents (75c) for dinner, and seventy-five cents (75c) for supper. If crew is compelled to sleep ashore, they shall be allowed one dollar and fifty cents ($1.50) per night room rent.

13. If a vessel is laid up and it resumes operations and men are ordered to report for work and turn to not later than 9:00 A. M. or 1:00 P. M., they shall be served a meal before turning to, or allowed a specified equivalent in cash. (11)

Conditions of Employment:

1. The members of the Sailors' Union of the Pacific shall be given preference of employment, and the parties agree that the Sailors' Union of the Pacific shall furnish unlicensed deck personnel as re-

(Testimony of Harry E. Lundeberg.)

Board's Exhibit No. 3—(Continued)

quired by the Companies, now signatory to this agreement.

2. There shall be no discrimination against any men for union activity.

3. Authorized representatives of the Union shall be allowed to visit members of the Union aboard ship at any time.

4. No man shall be required to work under unsafe conditions.

5. There shall be no stoppages of work as long as the covenants of this agreement are performed.

6 (a) When ships are laid up any man who has been employed for fifteen days or less shall be given immediate first-class transportation and subsistence back to the port of engagement. First-class transportation shall include railroad ticket and berth. Subsistence shall be at the rate of $3.00 per day.

(b) Men that are entitled to transportation shall not be kept by the ship longer than the balance of the crew for the purpose of avoiding the payment of transportation.

(c) Men that receive transportation shall not return to the same ship within ten days.

(d) Men paid off under paragraph (a) above shall be entitled, at their option, to the following cash equivalent:

(Testimony of Harry E. Lundeberg.)

Board's Exhibit No. 3—(Continued)

Los Angles to San Francisco	$21.00
" to Portland	48.50
" to Seattle	55.00
" to Eureka	33.00
San Francisco to Portland	31.00
" to Seattle	38.00
" to Eureka	12.00
Portland to Seattle	10.00

(12)

7. In case of shipwreck or disaster, necessitating the abandonment of the ship, the crew shall be paid all wages due as well as subsistence and transportation back to the port of engagement.

General:

1. This is a complete new agreement. All previous agreements and clarifications thereof are hereby cancelled.

2. No clarification of or change in this agreement shall be effective or issued by either party unless dated, numbered and signed by both parties.

3. It is agreed that any changes in this agreement that are mutually agreeable to both parties may be made and incorporated in the agreement at any time during the life of this agreement.

4. The companies signatory to this agreement agree to carry insurance providing maximum payments for any individual member of the crew in the sum of $75.00 against loss of clothing, personal effects, etc., in case of shipwreck or disaster, as covered by Policy No. 246, Hartford Fire Insurance Company of Hartford, Conn.

(Testimony of Harry E. Lundeberg.)

Board's Exhibit No. 3—(Continued)

5. The basic wage rates and overtime rates of pay set forth in said agreement shall be subject to review at the request of either party on the 30th day of March, 1941, and at the expiration of each six-months period thereafter.

Port Committees and Labor Relations:

A "Port Committee" shall be set up in each of the following ports: San Francisco, Seattle, Portland and San Pedro.

Each Port Committee shall be composed of an equal number of members appointed by and representing each party to this agrement, but shall not exceed three members from either party. Each party shall have an equal number of votes.

The duty of each Port Committee shall be to hear and adjudicate any dispute relative to the interpretation or (13) performance of this agreement which may arise between the parties to this agreement, at that Committee's particular port.

If any Port Committee becomes deadlocked, that Port Committee shall immediately refer the matter to the San Francisco Port Committee for decision, who shall within 24 hours meet and adjust the dispute. Failing to adjust the dispute within 48 hours or if the San Francisco Port Committee becomes deadlocked, then the dispute shall immediately be referred to the Conciliation Service of the Department of Labor of the U. S. Government for mediation and conciliation, who shall make further effort

(Testimony of Harry E. Lundeberg.)

Board's Exhibit No. 3—(Continued)

to adjust the dispute, and if they fail within 48 hours, then the Director of Conciliation and/or Secretary of Labor shall appoint a referee to hear and decide the issue. His decision shall be in writing and shall be final and binding on all parties to this agreement.

It is further understood and agreed that the conditions existing at the time the dispute arose shall prevail until a decision is handed down by either the Port Committee of San Francisco, the Conciliation Service of the U. S. Department of Labor, or finally the referee, as this agreement provides.

The decision of any port committee shall be in writing and shall be binding upon both parties until such decision is revoked or changed by the Port Committee of San Francisco.

The day and year first hereinabove written.

SAILORS' UNION OF THE PACIFIC
By HARRY LUNDEBERG
Secretary-Treas.

SHIPOWNERS' ASSOCIATION OF THE PACIFIC COAST,
By R. W. MYERS
President (14)

(Testimony of Harry E. Lundeberg.)

Board's Exhibit No. 3—(Continued)

Members of the Shipowners' Association
of the Pacific Coast

Baxter & Co., J. H.
Burns Steamship Co.
Chamberlin & Co., W. R.
Coastal Steamship Co.
Coastwise Steamship & Barge Co., Inc.
Consolidated-Olympic Line
Coos Bay Lumber Co.
Dorothy Philips Steamship Co.
Freeman & Co., S. S.
Gorman Steamship Co.
Griffiths & Sons, James
Griffith Steamship Co.
Hammond Lumber Company
Hammond Shipping Co., Ltd.
Hanify Co., J. R.
Hart-Wood Lumber Co.
Hobbs, Wall & Co.
Johnson Lumber Co., A. B.
Kingsley Company of California
Lawrence-Philips Steamship Co.
Linderman, Fred
Moore Steamship Co.
Olson & Co., Oliver J.
Owens-Parks Lumber Co.
P. L. Transportation Co.
Pope & Talbot, Inc.
McCormick Steamship Co. Division

(Testimony of Harry E. Lundeberg.)

Board's Exhibit No. 3—(Continued)

Port Orford Lumber Co.
Ramselius, Capt. J.
Schafer Bros. Steamship Lines
Sierra Steamship Corporation
Solano Steamship Co.
Sudden & Christenson
Wheeler-Hallock Co.
Wood Lumber Co., E. K. (15)

Sailors' Union of the Pacific

59 Clay St. San Francisco

Phones: EXbrook 2228 (Dispatcher: EXbrook 2229)

Branches

Seattle....Phone Elliott 6752....86 Seneca Street
Portland..Phone Beacon 4336..111 W. Burnside
San Pedro..Phone San Pedro 2491..206 W. 6th St.

Q. (By Mr. Moore) I show you, Mr. Lundeberg, a document marked Board's Exhibit 4 for identification and ask you if you can tell me what that is?

A. That is an agreement between the Sailors Union of the Pacific and the Pacific District Seafarers International Union, Engine Division, Pacific District Seafarers Union, Stewards Division, and the Tidewater Associated Oil Company.

Q. Is that agreement now in force and effect?

A. That is in force and effect, yes sir.

(Testimony of Harry E. Lundeberg.)

Q. What type of vessels does Tidewater Associated Oil Company operate?

A. Oil tankers the same as Richfield.

Mr. Moore: I offer Board's Exhibit 4 for identification in evidence and call attention particularly to page 4, Section 10 thereof. [105]

Mr. Guntert: Same objection, Mr. Examiner.

Trial Examiner Batten: Well, of course, it's not quite the same. These are tankers. It's the same, except for the fact that they are tankers, is that it?

Mr. Guntert: That's right.

Trial Examiner Batten: I will make the same ruling, and overrule the objection and receive the exhibit.

(The document referred to was received in evidence and marked Board's Exhibit No. 4.)

(Testimony of Harry E. Lundeberg.)

BOARD'S EXHIBIT No. 4

AGREEMENT
Between
Sailors Union of the Pacific
Pacific District, Seafarers' International
Engine Division
Pacific District, Seafarers' International
Stewards Division
Affiliated with the
Seafarers International Union
of North America
A. F. of L.
and
Tidewater Associated Oil Company
(Associated Division)
November 18th, 1942
(Deepwater Agreement)

Geertz Printing Co. (Label) San Francisco

Agreement

Articles of Agreement between Tide Water Associated Oil Company (Associated Division), hereinafter referred to as Company, and Sailors' Union of the Pacific, affiliated with the Seafarers' International Union of North America, A. F. of L., acting on behalf of the employees of the Company described in Article I hereof, hereinafter referred to as Union.

This agreement, entered into this 18th day of November, 1942, between the Sailors' Union of the Pacific, affiliated with the Seafarers International

(Testimony of Harry E. Lundeberg.)

Board's Exhibit No. 4—(Continued)

Union of North America, A. F. of L., hereinafter referred to as the Union and the Tide Water Associated Oil Company (Associated Division), hereinafter referred to as the Company.

Witnesseth As Follows:

Article I

General Rules

Section 1. This agreement shall apply to employees of the Company for whom the Sailors' Union of the Pacific, affiliated with the Seafarers International Union of North America, A. F. of L., was certified as the exclusive bargaining representative in and by that certain "Decision and Certification of Representatives" signed by the National Labor Relations Board at Washington, D. C., on March 22, 1942, namely:

The unlicensed deck personnel on tankers operated out of Pacific Coast ports by Company.

This agreement governs only the relations between the Company and the Union, and the wages, hours and working conditions for unlicensed deck personnel on tankers operated out of Pacific Coast ports by Company.

Section 2. Preferential Hiring: The Company agrees to give preference in employment to members of the Sailors' Union of the Pacific, affiliated with Seafarers International Union of North America, A. F. of L., when members of the Union are available, provided, however, that this shall not require the discharge of any employee of the

(Testimony of Harry E. Lundeberg.)

Board's Exhibit No. 4—(Continued)

Company, who may not be a member of Union, whether or not such employee is absent on account of leave of absence, illness, accident or vacation. (1)

In the event Union fails to furnish capable, competent and physically fit person, or persons are not furnished with sufficient promptness to avoid delay in any scheduled sailing, the Company is at liberty to hire persons from any source available and persons so hired may be continued in employment upon the Company's vessels without regard to Union affiliation.

It is further understood and agreed that Union will not discriminiate against persons so employed.

Section 3. Union Delegates Aboard Ship: Company agrees to recognize one employee designated by the Union on each vessel to act as a delegate and representative of the Union.

Section 4. Grievance Procedure: For the purpose of adjusting complaints and grievances any employee shall endeavor to adjust the matter either in person or through the Union delegate according to the following procedure:

a. The employee's complaint shall be presented to the Captain or his delegated representative. If a satisfactory adjustment is not reached immediate notification shall be given to the Captain or his delegated representative of intent to carry the grievance to the second step of the grievance procedure; then,

b. The complaint, in writing with full explanation and argument, shall be then presented to the

(Testimony of Harry E. Lundeberg.)

Board's Exhibit No. 4—(Continued)

Company's shore representative and representatives of the Union; if satisfaction shall not be had thereby within twenty-four hours after presentation; then

c. The matter shall be referred to an arbitration committee consisting of one member chosen by the Union, one member appointed by the Company and a third member selected by these two; then

d. If Union and Company representatives cannot agree on selection of a third member within twenty-four hours, the third member shall be selected by the presiding judge of the Ninth Circuit Court of Appeals. The decision of this committee shall be final and binding.

Section 5. Strikes and Lockout: There shall be no strikes, lockouts or stoppages of work during the life of this agreement. (2*)

Section 6. (a) Emergency Duties and Drills. All employees represented by the Union shall perform only the customary duties of their department. Any work necessary for the safety of the vessel, passengers, crew or cargo or for the saving of other vessels in jeopardy and the lives therein, or when in port or at sea in the performance of fire, lifeboat or other drills, shall be performed at any time, and such work shall not be considered overtime.

(b) When lifeboat or other drills are held on Saturday afternoons, Sundays or holidays, preparations for such drills, such as stretching fire hoses,

* Page numbering appearing at foot of page of Original Agreement.

(Testimony of Harry E. Lundeberg.)

Board's Exhibit No. 4—(Continued)

hoisting or swinging boats out, shall not be done prior to signal for such drills and after drill is over, all hands shall stand by until boats and gear are properly secured; such work shall not be considered overtime.

Section 7. Orders and Rules: All employees represented by this Union will comply with all lawful orders of superior officers and with all Company rules not inconsistent with this agreement.

Section 8. Transportation: (a) When ships are sold or laid up, employees shall be given immediate first-class transportation, wages and subsistence back to the port of engagement. First-class transportation shall include railroad ticket and berth.

Subsistence shall be at the rate of $3.00 per day, except when traveling by water. Nothing herein shall be construed as preventing the Company from providing transportation in their own vessels; provided that no such employee shall be required to travel on the Company's own vessels unless covered by war risk insurance and bonuses as established by the Maritime War Emergency Board, and then in effect.

(b) Men that are entitled to transportation shall not be kept by the ship longer than the balance of the crew for the purpose of avoiding the payment of transportation.

(c) In case of shipwreck or disaster, necessitating the abondonment of ship, the crew shall be paid all wages as well as subsistence and transportation

(Testimony of Harry E. Lundeberg.)

Board's Exhibit No. 4—(Continued)

back to the port of engagement.

Section 9. Working Equipment: The Company agrees to furnish safe working gear and equipment.

(3)

Section 10. Passes: Company shall distribute passes to authorized representatives of the Union who may board Company's vessels in ports for the purpose of transacting Union business. The Union agrees that it will comply with all rules and regulations at the place of entry. Such passes will be issued only while insurance satisfactory to the Company is held by the Union.

The Union agrees that its representatives shall in no way interfere with or retard vessel operations. Any pass issued is subject to revocation.

Section 11. Overtime: (a) Overtime shall commence at the time any employee shall be called to report for work outside of his regular schedule, provided such employee reports for duty within 15 minutes. Otherwise overtime shall commence at the actual time such employee reports for duty, and such overtime shall continue until the employee is released.

(b) When overtime is worked less than one hour overtime for one full hour shall be paid. Where the overtime work exceeds one hour the overtime work thereafter shall be paid for in one-half hour periods, a fractional part of such period to count as one-half hour.

When an employee in his watch below is called

(Testimony of Harry E. Lundeberg.)

Board's Exhibit No. 4—(Continued)

to work overtime and is released for two hours or less and is again called to work overtime, the overtime shall be continuous from the time he is first called.

(c) After overtime has been worked, the senior officer of the department concerned will present to each employee who has worked overtime a slip stating hours of overtime and nature of work performed. An overtime book will be kept to conform with individual slips, for settlement of overtime.

(d) Overtime shall not be worked without authority of the Captain or his delegated authority.

(e) Time customarily required for relieving watches shall not constitute overtime.

Section 12. Changing Day Men to Watch Duty, etc.:

(a) At sea when day men are switched to sea watches, they shall receive overtime for all watches stood on Saturday afternoons, Sundays and holidays for the duration of the voyage.

(b) When an employee is promoted or assumes duties of a higher classification aboard ship, he shall be paid the wage of such higher clasification.

(4)

Section 13. Vacations:

The vacation policy of the Company issued and dated November 3, 1942, shall govern herein as if fully set forth, except that during and as long as this agreement shall remain in force and effect, pro-

(Testimony of Harry E. Lundeberg.)

Board's Exhibit No. 4—(Continued)

visions thereof that employees actively engaged in the service of the Company, upon completion of one year of continuous service shall be eligible for one week's vacation with pay and after having been in the continuous service of this Company for two years or more, shall be eligible for two week's annual vacation with pay, shall not be subject to cancellation by Company.

Section 14. Authority of Officers:

Nothing in this agreement is intended to and shall not be construed to limit in any way the authority of the master or other officers or lessen the obedience of any member of the crew to any lawful order.

Section 15. Additional Employees Hired by the Day:

(a) When additional employees are hired by the day in port on temporary work, and do not eat or sleep aboard ship, the wages for such work shall be $7.20 per day including 80 cents per day temporary emergency increase.

The hours of work shall be between 8:00 a. m. and 12:00 noon, and 1.00 p. m. and 5:00 p. m. Any work performed outside of these hours or on Saturday afternoons, Sundays, or holidays, shall be paid for at the rate of time and one-half or $1.35 per hour.

(b) Any man employed for the above standby work shall receive not less than one-half days' pay

(Testimony of Harry E. Lundeberg.)

Board's Exhibit No. 4—(Continued)

and such half-days' work shall not exceed four hours.

Section 16. Transportation to and from Ship:

When a vessel is lying at anchor in a safe harbor for more than 24 hours, the Company shall provide launch service twice daily from ship to shore and shore to ship when available. This shall not apply to open roadstead loading and discharging ports nor shall it apply to a vessel being detained by direction of Governmental authorities.

Arrangements between unlicensed personnel for shore leave shall be in accordance with Section 17.

Section 17. Relieving for Time Ashore:

With approval of the head of the department, employees may arrange to relieve each other in port in order to secure time ashore. Any such arrangements are to be without overtime penalty to the Company. (5)

Section 18. Port time:

(a) Port time shall commence when the vessel is properly secured at a dock or when moored in a harbor for the purpose of loading or discharging cargo or from pipelines, lighters, barges or other vessels, except as otherwise provided in this agreement.

(b) Port time shall cease when all dock lines are let go or anchors hove up to proceed to sea or when shifting to another berth when such shifting requires more than five hours, except as otherwise provided in this agreement.

(Testimony of Harry E. Lundeberg.)

Board's Exhibit No. 4—(Continued)

(c) In open roadstead loading and discharging ports, vessels will be considered moored when hose is lifted from the sea and unmoored when hose is returned to the sea.

(d) Detention of a vessel in a harbor due to awaiting berth for less than 24 hours, or by reason of fog or other impediments to navigation, awaiting tides, or by Governmental direction, shall not constitute port time.

(e) When the vessel is under port time, sea watches may be continued at the option of the master.

Section 19. Holidays:

The employer agrees to recognize the following holidays:

New Year's Day, Lincoln's Birthday, Washington's Birthday, Memorial Day, Independence Day, Armistice Day, Labor Day, Thanksgiving Day, Christmas Day.

In the event any of the above-named holidays falls on a Sunday, the Monday following shall be observed as such holiday.

Section 20. Equipment:

The following items shall be supplied to the unlicensed personnel employed on board vessels of the Company:

1. A suitable number of clean blankets.
2. Cots while in tropics.
3. Bedding consisting of spread, two white

(Testimony of Harry E. Lundeberg.)

Board's Exhibit No. 4—(Continued)

sheets, and one white pillow slip, which shall be changed weekly, and

4. One face and one bath towel, which shall be changed twice weekly; face soap, laundry soap, lava soap, and safety matches issued when required.

After signing for original issue of linen to secure next issue, piece for piece must be returned.

Blankets and cots must be returned before paying off.

Suitable mattresses and pillows shall be suppied, but excelsior or straw shall be considered unsuitable.

All dishes provided for use of the unlicensed personnel shall be of crockery. (6)

Section 21. Messrooms:

Each vessel shall be furnished with a messroom or messrooms for the accommodation of the crew. Such messrooms to be in each case so constructed as to afford sitting space for all when it is practicable to do so.

Section 22. Ventilation:

All quarters assigned to the unlicensed personnel and all messrooms provided for their use shall be adequately screened and ventilated, and a sufficient number of fans or other apparatus to secure such ventilation shall be provided.

Section 23. Lockers:

One locker shall be provided for each employee so that he shall have one locker of full length, wherever space permits, with sufficient space to stow

(Testimony of Harry E. Lundeberg.)

Board's Exhibit No. 4—(Continued)

a reasonable amount of gear and personal effects.

Section 24. Refrigerators:

The Company will undertake to install a refrigerator on each of its vessels for night lunches, which refrigerator will be available to the unlicensed personnel.

Section 25. Washrooms:

Adequate washrooms and lavatories shall be made available for the unlicensed personnel; washrooms to be equipped with a sufficient number of shower baths which shall be adequately equipped with hot and cold water whenever practicable.

Section 26. Crews Quarters:

All quarters assigned for the use of the unlicensed personnel are to be kept free from vermin in so far as possible. This is to be accomplished through the use of exterminating facilities provided by the Company, or fumigating the quarters with gas when necessary. When forecastles are painted, men must be furnished other sleeping quarters until the paint is dry.

Section 27: Coffee Time:

15 minutes shall be allowed for coffee, at 10:00 a. m. and 3:00 p. m., or at convenient times near these hours. (7)

Section 28. Meal Hours:

The meal hours for the unlicensed personnel employed in the deck department shall be as follows:

Breakfast: 7:30 a. m. to 8:30 a. m.
Dinner: 11:30 a. m. to 12:30 p. m.
Supper: 5:00 p. m. to 6:00 p. m.

(Testimony of Harry E. Lundeberg.)

Board's Exhibit No. 4—(Continued)

(a) These hours may be varied, but such variations shall not exceed one hour either way, provided that one unbroken hour shall be allowed at all times for dinner and supper when vessel is in port.

At such times as watches are broken, if one unbroken hour is not given, the man involved shall receive one hour overtime in lieu thereof.

(b) On sailing day the lunch hour for any man on the 12:00 o'clock noon to 4:00 p. m. watch, whose watch has been broken, shall be from 11:00 a. m. to 12:00 noon.

(c) When any employee is called to work before breakfast, and work continues after 7:30 a. m., a full hour shall be allowed for breakfast. If breakfast is not served until after 8:00 a. m. overtime shall continue stright through until breakfast is served.

Section 29. Milk, Fruit, and Vegetables:

Fresh milk, fruit, and vegetables when in season, if available, will be furnished at each United States port in such quantities as can be kept without spoiling.

Section 30. Room and Meal Allowances:

When room or board are not furnished aboard ship, employees are to receive the following allowances:

(a) In lieu of room, a base allowance of $1.50 plus a temporary emergency allowance of fifty cents or a total of $2.00 per night.

(Testimony of Harry E. Lundeberg.)

Board's Exhibit No. 4—(Continued)

(b) In lieu of breakfast, 75 cents.

(c) In lieu of dinner, 75 cents.

(d) In lieu of supper, 75 cents.

Section 31. Midnight Meal:

Any employee working overtime continuously between the hours of 6:00 p. m. and 9:00 p. m. shall be allowed 15 minutes for coffee and lunch at 9:00 p. m. If work continues until 12:00 midnight, he shall be served with a hot meal. If work continues after 12:00 midnight, he shall be allowed one hour for such meal and be paid for such hour.

Members of the stewards' department shall not be called upon to prepare or serve coffee and lunch, but shall prepare the hot meal at midnight. (8)

Article II

Wages and Working Rules

Deck Department

Section 1. Classification and Rates of Wages:

The classifications and rates of wages of the deck department shall be as follows:

	Basic Wage	Total Temporary Emergency Wages	Total Wages
Boatswain	$105.00	$17.50	$122.50
Able Seaman	90.00	17.50	107.50
Ordinary Seamen	70.00	17.50	87.50

Section 2. Overtime:

The regular overtime rate in the deck departmen shall be 80 cents an hour base rate plus 5 cents an hour emergency increase or a total of 85 cents per hour.

(Testimony of Harry E. Lundeberg.)

Board's Exhibit No. 4—(Continued)

Article III

Deck Department Working Rules

Section 1. Day Workers:

The hours of work for day workers shall be 8 hours per day week days, except Saturdays, from 8:00 a.m. to 5:00 p.m., with an hour off for dinner; and from 8:00 a.m. to 12:00 noon on Saturdays.

Section 2. Work in Port:

(a) When watches are broken, the hours of labor shall be 8 hours, between the hours of 8:00 a.m. and 5:00 p.m. week days; Saturdays 8:00 a.m. to 12:00 noon.

All work performed after 5:00 p.m. and before 8:00 a.m. and on Saturday afternoons, Sundays and holidays, shall be paid for at the regular overtime rate except as otherwise provided in this agreement.

(b) When a vessel is in port and employees off watch are required to report back to the vessel for the purpose of moving or hauling ship, a minimum of 2 hours' overtime shall be paid for each call, except when men are knocked off, for a period of 2 hours or less, in which case overtime shall be continuous.

Section 3. Work at Sea:

(a) All work in excess of 8 hours between midnight and midnight of each day shall be paid for at the regular overtime rate, except as provided in Article I, Section 6(a) and (b).

(Testimony of Harry E. Lundeberg.)

Board's Exhibit No. 4—(Continued)

(b) No work except for the safe navigation of the vessel is to be done after 5:00 p.m. and before 8:00 a.m. Sanitary work shall be done between 6:00 a.m. and 8:00 a.m. without the payment of overtime. Sanitary work under this section shall mean cleaning the wheel house and chart room, cleaning windows and mopping out wheel house. (9)

Section 4. Tank and Bilge Cleaning:

When employees are required to enter and clean tanks or bilges, the watch on duty shall be paid overtime for this work at the regular overtime rate.

Employees off watch shall be paid for this work at the base rate of $1.00 per hour plus 10 cents per hour temparary emergency increase or a total of $1.10 per hour.

If watches are broken, regular overtime shall be paid for such work performed between the hours of 8:00 a.m. and 5:00 p.m. on week days, except Saturday afternoons. $1.10 per hour, including 10 cents per hour temporary increase shall be paid for this work between the hours of 5:00 p.m. and 8:00 a.m. and on Saturday afternoons, Sundays, and holidays.

Sea boots and oilskins shall be furnished by the Company for employees working in tanks.

Section 5. Chipping, Painting, etc.:

(a) Employees in the deck department shall, in port, chip, scale, paint and wash paint on ship's sides, deck and superstructure, their own quarters,

(Testimony of Harry E. Lundeberg.)

Board's Exhibit No. 4—(Continued)

lavatories, washrooms, and all open passageways and spaces. At sea the same work shall be performed except painting over ship's sides.

Overtime shall be paid for all such work performed between the hours of 5:00 p.m. and 8:00 a.m.

(b) Overtime shall be paid when unlicensed personnel of the deck department are required either in port or at sea to chip, soogey, scale, prime or paint galleys, storerooms, pantries, salons or living quarters which are not part of the unlicensed deck department quarters and forecastles, lavatories, and washrooms, which are not used by the unlicensed deck department.

Section 6. Dropping or Heaving Up Anchor:

The boatswain when available shall be required to stand by the windlass at all times when dropping or heaving up anchor.

Section 7. Cleaning Steering Engine:

When unlicensed deck personnel are required to clean steering engine or steering bed, they shall be paid overtime for such work performed. However, sailors may be required to grease tiller chains in their watch on deck during straight time hours without the payment of overtime. (10)

Section 8. Spray Painting:

Employees when actually engaged in spray painting in enclosed spaces shall be paid overtime at the rates established for tank cleaning, but no overtime shall be paid for outside spray painting ex-

(Testimony of Harry E. Lundeberg.)

Board's Exhibit No. 4—(Continued)

cept when performed beyond their regular working hours.

Section 9. Ship's Stores:

Employees of the deck department shall handle deck and steward stores on dock and ship, and heavy engine department stores requiring use of gear. When such work is performed between the hours of 5:00 p.m. and 8:00 a.m., it shall be paid for at the regular overtime rate.

Section 10. Watches:

(a) When watches are broken, they shall be set not later than 12:00 noon on sailing day. When vessel sails before noon, watches shall be set when vessel is clear of the dock.

(b) When a vessel docks between 12:00 midnight and 8:00 a.m. and sea watches are broken, any part of a watch between midnight and 8:00 a.m. shall constitute a complete watch. This shall not apply to anchor or gangway watches.

(c) In port when watches are not broken, employees in the deck department shall stand anchor and gangway watches between the hours of 5:00 p.m. and 8:00 a.m. without payment of overtime, except that on Saturday afternoons, Sundays and holidays, overtime shall be paid for such work unless otherwise provided in this agreement.

Employees standing these watches shall assist the officer on watch in attending mooring lines, gangway lines and gangway lights.

(d) When anchor or gangway watches are nec-

(Testimony of Harry E. Lundeberg.)

Board's Exhibit No. 4—(Continued)

essary they shall be maintained from arrival to departure.

(e) When the watch below is called out to work they shall be paid overtime for the work performed during their watch below.

Section 11. Arrival Time:

The date the vessel arrives from sea at a port of call shall be considered the date of arrival.

Section 12. Departure Time:

The day of departure shall be the day the vessel leaves for sea from the port from which the vessel is cleared; sea watches shall be set and maintained from the port. (11)

Section 13. Watches at Sea:

Unlicensed personnel of the deck department shall, while at sea, be divided into three watches which shall be kept on duty successively for the performance of work incident to the sailing and management of the vessel.

Section 14. Washing Down:

When members of the deck department are required to wash down after 5:00 p.m. and before 8:00 a.m. and on Saturday afternoons, Sundays and holidays, they shall be paid overtime except as provided in Article III, Section 3(b).

Section 15. Docking and Undocking:

(a) When men off watch are called on to assist in docking or undocking they shall be paid for such work at the regular overtime rate.

(Testimony of Harry E. Lundeberg.)

Board's Exhibit No. 4—(Continued)

(b) Time required for undocking shall, excepting for employees on watch, constitute overtime for all employees so engaged. On Saturday afternoons, Sundays and holidays, all unlicensed personnel employed in undocking, including those on watch, shall receive overtime for such work.

(c) The practice of putting sailors ashore to the dock to handle lines when docking or undocking, is to be avoided as far as possible. However, if no other means for handling lines are available and sailors are put on the dock to catch the lines or let them go, the sailors actually going on the dock are to receive $1.00 each in each case. This is to be in addition to the overtime if they are working on overtime at that particular time.

Section 16. Cleaning Quarters:

One employee on duty shall be assigned daily to clean the quarters, washrooms and toilets of the unlicensed personnel in the deck department. This work shall be performed between the hours of 8:00 a.m. and 12:00 noon, if possible.

Section 17. Cleanliness of Quarters:

The unlicensed personnel of the deck department shall keep their respective living quarters clean and tidy at all times. However, this shall not be construed to mean the daily cleaning by the ordinary seamen each morning.

Section 18. Garbage:

When members of the deck department are re-

(Testimony of Harry E. Lundeberg.)

Board's Exhibit No. 4—(Continued)

quired to handle or dump garbage, they shall be paid at the regular overtime rate. (12)

Section 19. Helmsman:

Any seaman covered by this agreement assigned to regular wheelsman's duties shall not be relieved for soogeying, chipping, painting, shining brass and cleaning work during the regular wheel watch.

Section 20. Watches in Port:

Watches shall be set at 12:00 noon on Saturdays, Sundays and holidays when such days are days of departure, as per the agreement, and all watches stood on Saturday afternoon, Sundays, or holidays, shall be paid for at the regular overtime rate, up until the ship departs for sea. However, the men on watch shall be required to remain on board the vessel.

Section 21. Division of Overtime:

Overtime work will be assigned as equally as possible among the members of the deck crew.

This agreement made and entered into the 18th day of November 1942, by the Seafarers International Union of North America for the Engine Division and for the Stewards Division, and Sailors Union of the Pacific, affiliated with the Seafarer's International Union of North America, Deck Department, A. F. L., hereinabove known as the Union, and Tide Water Associated Oil Company (Associated Division), hereinabove known as the Company, shall be binding on the parties for the period of two years, and be deemed renewed

(Testimony of Harry E. Lundeberg.)

Board's Exhibit No. 4—(Continued)

from year to year thereafter unless either party shall give written notice to the other at least thirty (30) days prior to such expiration date of a desire to terminate this agreement, or to negotiate for amendments to this agreement, in which case the parties shall meet within five (5) days to begin negotiations.

If during the thirty (30) day period of negotiations the parties fail to agree then this agreement shall terminate at the expiration date; provided, however, that the parties may by mutual written agreement extend this agreement for a specific period beyond such expiration date for the continuance of negotiations.

(Signed) HARRY LUNDEBERG,

President Seafarer's International Union of North America; Secretary-Treasurer Sailors Union of the Pacific, affiliated with the A. F. of L.

(Signed) H. B. HANEY,

Tide Water Associated Oil Company (Associated Division). (13)

Article II

Wages and Working Rules

Engine Department

Section 1. Classifications and Rates of Wages:

The classifications and rates of wages in the Engine Department shall be as follows:

(Testimony of Harry E. Lundeberg.)

Board's Exhibit No. 4—(Continued)

	Basic Wage	Total Temporary Emergency Wages	Total Wages
Pumpman	$120.00	$18.00	$138.00
Oiler	95.00	17.50	112.50
Fireman	90.00	17.50	107.50
Wiper	77.50	20.00	97.50

Section 2. Overtime:

Regular overtime rate is 80 cents an hour base rate plus 5 cents an hour emergency increase, or a total of 85 cents per hour.

Article III

Working Rules

Section 1. Work in Port:

(a) The hours of work for day workers shall be 8 hours per day weekdays between 8:00 a.m. and 5:00 p.m., with one hour for dinner; and from 8:00 a.m. to 12:00 noon on Saturdays.

(b) When watches are broken, the hours of labor shall be eight, between the hours of 8:00 a.m. and 5:00 p.m. weekdays and between 8:00 a.m. and 12:00 noon Saturdays.

All work performed after 5:00 p.m. and before 8:00 a.m. Saturday afternoons, Sundays and holidays shall be piad for at the regular overtime rate except as otherwise provided in this agreement.

Section 2. Work at Sea:

(a) All work in excess of 8 hours between midnight an midnight of each day shall be paid for at the regular overtime rate, except as otherwise provided in this agreement.

(b) Work performed between the hours of 5:00

(Testimony of Harry E. Lundeberg.)

Board's Exhibit No. 4—(Continued)

p.m. and 8:00 a.m. except for the necessary safe operation and navigation of the vessel shall be paid for at the overtime rate. (14)

Section 3. Tank Cleaning:

When employees are required to enter and clean tanks, bilges and engine room or fire room tank tops, the watch on duty shall be paid overtime for this work at the regular overtime rate. Employees off watch shall be paid for this work at the base rate of $1 per hour plus 10 cents per hour temporary emergency increase, or a total of $1.10 per hour.

If watches are broken, regular overtime shall be paid for such work performed between the hours of 8:00 a.m. and 5:00 p.m. on weekdays except Saturday afternoons. $1.10 per hour, including 10 cents per hour temporary emergency increase shall be paid for this work between the hours of 5:00 p.m. and 8:00 a.m. and on Saturday afternoons, Sundays and holidays.

Sea boots and oilskins shall be furnished by the Company for employees working in tanks.

Section 4. Ships Stores:

Employees of the Engine Department shall handle engine room stores on dock and ship, except that heavy stores that require the use of gear shall be handled by the deck department.

Section 5. Watches:

(a) When watches are broken, they shall be set not later than noon on sailing day.

(Testimony of Harry E. Lundeberg.)

Board's Exhibit No. 4—(Continued)

(b) When a vessel docks between 12:00 midnight and 8:00 a.m. and sea watches are broken, any part of a watch between midnight and 8:00 a.m. shall constitute a complete watch.

(c) In port employees in the Engine Department shall stand their regular watches between the hours of 5:00 p.m. and 8:00 a.m. without the payment of overtime, except that on Saturday afternoons, Sundays and holidays, overtime shall be paid for such work unless otherwise provided in this agreement.

Section 6. Time of arrival:

The day a vessel arrives at a port from sea shall be considered the date of arrival.

Section 7. Cleaning Quarters:

One wiper on duty shall be assigned daily to clean the quarters, washrooms and toilets of the unlicensed personnel in the Engine Department. This work shall be performed between the hours of 8:00 a.m. and 12:00 noon if possible. (15)

Section 8. Cleanliness of Quarters:

Employees of the Engine Department shall keep their respective living quarters clean and tidy at all times. This shall be in addition to the daily cleaning by a wiper.

Section 9. Division of Overtime Work:

Overtime work shall be assigned to the different ratings of the Engine Department employees as equally as practicable.

(Testimony of Harry E. Lundeberg.)

Board's Exhibit No. 4—(Continued)

Section 10. Arrivals and Departures:

When a vessel arrives in port on Saturday afternoons, Sunday or holidays, overtime for men on watch shall be begun when "Finished with engine" bell is rung.

When a vessel departs for sea on Saturday afternoons, Sundays or holidays, overtime for men on watch shall be paid until the "Ahead" or "Astern" bell is rung.

Section 11. Working Spaces:

No member of the unlicensed personnel of the Engine Department other than the pumpman or wiper, or if carried, the machinist or utility man, shall be required to work outside of the engine room without payment of overtime. Engine space to consist of fire room, engine room, ice machine room, tool shop and shaft-alley, and steering engine room. For the purposes of routine watch duties, the engine room spaces shall consist of fire room, engine room, ice machine room, steering engine room and shaft-alley. However, they may enter engine room storage space for the purpose of securing equipment with which to work.

Section 12. Pumpman—Duties at Sea:

A pumpman's duties at sea shall consist of handling cargo and tank equipment and all work necessary for the operation and maintenance of cargo pumps, deck auxiliaries, general cargo lines, room heating system and all deck machinery. He shall not be required to do any work that is not consid-

(Testimony of Harry E. Lundeberg.)

Board's Exhibit No. 4—(Continued)

ered his regular duties such as chip, scale, paint, polish brass, and so forth. He shall not be required to do any work in the engine room except his regular duties such as steam lines, cargo lines, etc. If at any time the pumpman is required to enter the tanks to make repairs, he shall be paid at the overtime rate.

The hours of a pumpman at sea shall be from 8:00 a.m. to 12:00 noon and 1:00 p.m. to 5:00 p.m. weekdays and from 8:00 a.m. to 12:00 noon on Saturdays. All work performed after 5:00 p.m. and before 8:00 a.m. and on Saturday afternoons, Sundays and holidays, shall be paid for at the regular overtime rate except as otherwise provided in this agreement. (16)

Section 13. Pumpman—Duties in Port:

While vessel is discharging cargo, a pumpman's hours of work shall be any eight consecutive hours in 24. If vessel is not discharging cargo, the hours of work shall be the same as at sea.

Section 14. Duties of Oilers on Sea Watches:

(a) Oilers on sea watches shall perform routine duties, oil main engine (if reciprocating), watch temperatures and oil circulation (if turbine), oil auxiliaries, steering engine, and ice machine. They shall pump bilges and tend water where gauges and checks are in the engine room and no water tenders are carried.

(b) Oilers shall do no cleaning or station work but they shall be required to leave safe working

(Testimony of Harry E. Lundeberg.)

Board's Exhibit No. 4—(Continued)

conditions for their relief, keeping the spaces around the main engine and auxiliaries clean of oil before going off watch.

(c) Oilers shall not be required to do any cleaning of boilers, painting, cleaning of paint, polishing work, wire brushing, chipping or scaling.

Section 15. Oilers—Duties in Port:

(a) Oilers in port shall perform routine duties and assist engineers in maintenance and repair work.

They shall not be required to do any boiler cleaning, painting, cleaning paint, polishing work, wire brushing, chipping or scaling, except cleaning piston rods, connecting rods, and link gear of main engine.

(b) Only such maintenance and repair work as is necessary and practicable shall be performed between the hours of 5:00 p.m. and 8:00 a.m.

(c) When watches are broken, oilers hours are to be those of day workers.

Section 16. Firemen—Duties at Sea:

(a) Firemen shall perform routine duties, keep burners, drip pans, and fuel oil strainers clean on all watches, punch carbon, keep steam, watch oil pressures and temperatures and shall tend water when gauges are in fire room. They shall not be requested to leave the confines of the fire room to oil auxiliaries or do any work not directly connected with steaming of boilers

(b) Firemen on watch may be assigned stations

(Testimony of Harry E. Lundeberg.)

Board's Exhibit No. 4—(Continued)

to keep clean. Each man to have a station equal in area below the lower grating and not below the floor plates or behind the boilers. On vessels having irregular gratings, 10 feet from the floor plates shall be considered the fireman's limit. (17)

(c) Blowing tubes shall not be a part of a fireman's recognized sea duty on ships where tubes are blown by hand or on any ship that has only one fireman on watch without a water tender on watch; provided, however, that the fireman on watch may be required to assist in blowing tubes to the extent of helping to open and close breeching doors, and turning steam on or off. Where automatic soot blowers are used, firemen shall handle valves connecting with same.

Section 17. Fireman—Duties in Port:

(a) When watches are not broken their duties shall be the same as at sea. When watches are broken, their hours of employment shall be the same as day workers. They shall assist in general repair and maintenance work, general cleaning, polishing and painting work as directed by the officer in charge.

(b) They shall wash down steam drums of water tube boilers or water side of Scotch boilers.

(c) When required to do any cleaning of boilers and fire boxes other than the above, they shall be paid overtime.

Section 18. Wipers—Duties at Sea and in Port:

(Testimony of Harry E. Lundeberg.)

Board's Exhibit No. 4—(Continued)

(a) The hours of employment shall be those of day workers.

(b) Wipers shall do general cleaning, scaling, painting and polishing work in the engine department, including pump rooms, handle engine room stores as provided in Section 4 of this Article, and any work in connection with taking on fresh water and fuel oil.

(c) Wipers shall do general maintenance and repair work as directed and supervised by the officer in charge.

(d) In all cases after blowing tubes by hand, the wiper must be released from duty to clean and wash up at least one hour before 5:00 p.m. on weekdays and 11:30 a.m. on Saturdays.

(e) Wipers shall be required to paint and clean fidley behind and on top of boiler spaces. This work shall not be done while vessel is in tropics.

(f) Wipers shall wash down fire room and engine room tank tops but shall be paid overtime when required to clean tank tops or bilges by hand. Cleaning bilge strainers and cleaning away sticks or rags shall be regarded as part of the wiper's usual duties and be done without payment of overtime.

(g) Wipers shall be paid overtime when required to clean inside the boilers. They shall, however, wash boilers with hose, haul up refuse and help clean fire room without payment of overtime.

(18)

(Testimony of Harry E. Lundeberg.)

Board's Exhibit No. 4—(Continued)

Article II

Wages and Working Rules

Stewards' Department

Section 1. Classifications and Rates of Wages:

The classification and rates of wages in the Steward's Department shall be as follows:

	Basic Wage	Total Temporary Emergency Wages	Total Wages
Steward-Cook	$165.00	$25.00	$190.00
Cook	120.00	23.75	143.75
Junior Cook	100.00	15.00	115.00
Messman	75.00	12.50	87.50
Messboy	70.00	12.50	82.50

Section 2. Overtime:

The regular overtime rate in the Stewards' Department shall be 80 cents an hour base rate plus 5 cents an hour emergency increase or a total of 85 cents per hour.

Article III

Working Rules

Section 1. Head of Stewards' Department:

The steward-cook shall be recognized as head of the Stewards' Department and shall direct the work of the employees in that department. His immediate superior is the captain of the vessel.

Section 2. Working Hours:

(a) The hours of labor at sea and on board shall be 8 hours in a spread of 12 hours.

(b) In port the regular overtime rate shall be paid for work performed on Saturday afternoons, Sundays and holidays.

(Testimony of Harry E. Lundeberg.)

Board's Exhibit No. 4—(Continued)

(c) A sufficient number of Stewards' Department personnel shall be employed on Saturday afternoons, Sundays and holidays, for the preparation and serving of meals to crew members who eat aboard ship on those days.

Section 3. Routine Duties:

The regular routine laid out below shall be carried out within the regular working hours as specified, and it shall be the duty of the Stewards' Department to organize their work so that it is accomplished.

Routine duties for members of the Stewards' Department shall be to prepare and serve regular meals, to clean and maintain the quarters of the licensed personnel, all dining rooms, messrooms, washrooms, galley, pantry and storerooms; to chip, scrape, paint and wash paint. (19)

However, if the cooks are required to do chipping, scraping, painting, or washing paint, those actually engaged in this work shall be paid for such work at the regular overtime rate.

Section 4. Ship's Stores:

Employees in the Stewards' Department shall not be required to handle stores from dock to ship or ship to dock, except quantities of perishables such as milk, bread, fruit, vegetables, etc.

Stewards' stores shall be distributed to meat, chill, and storerooms by the Deck Department and be stowed by Stewards' Department employees.

(Testimony of Harry E. Lundeberg.)

Board's Exhibit No. 4—(Continued)

Section 5. Cleaning Ice Box and Chill Room:

When employees on duty are required to wash down and clean ice box and/or chill room, they shall be paid at the regular overtime rate for such work.

Employees shall be paid at the rate of $1.10 per hour, consisting of $1.00 per hour base rate plus 10 cents per hour temporary emergency increase, for all such work performed during other than regular working hours or on Saturday afternoons, Sundays, and holidays while in port.

Section 6. Meal Service Outside of Dining Rooms and Messrooms:

When any member of the Stewards' Department is required to serve meals outside of the messroom, he shall receive one hour overtime for such service, regardless of the number of men served. The members of the Stewards' Department shall not be required to enter the fire room or engine room.

Neither shall they ordinarily be required to go up on the bridge for the purpose of serving coffee or meals, except when the master or pilot are required to be on the bridge in the performance of regular duties, and for such service no overtime shall be paid.

Members of the Stewards' Department shall not be required to serve meals on the deck except when necessity demands and the galley and messroom functions have been moved on to the deck.

In such case meals will be served on the decks

(Testimony of Harry E. Lundeberg.)

Board's Exhibit No. 4—(Continued)

not only to the master but to the pilot and to the entire personnel, if so required, without overtime.

When sick or injured officers or crew members are unable to go to eating places for their meals, members of the Stewards' Department will serve meals to them without overtime. (20)

Section 7. Extra Meals:

(a) When extra meals are served to other than regular members of the crew signed on articles, passengers and/or pilots, when carried, overtime shall be paid to not exceeding four members of the Stewards' Department at the rate of one hour for every four meals prepared and served.

(b) The amount of extra meals served shall be totaled and computed in accordance with paragraph (a) of this section and at the end of each voyage.

(c) When members of the Stewards' Department are required to serve late meals due to the failure of officers eating within the prescribed time, the members of the Stewards' Department actually engaged in preparing and serving the meals shall be given one hour overtime.

(d) No extra meals are to be served without the authority of the master or officer in charge of the vessel.

(e) When extra personnel is carried in the Stewards' Department for the purpose of serving naval personnel, meals served to such personnel shall not be considered extra meals.

(f) Service of meals to pilots in the messroom

(Testimony of Harry E. Lundeberg.)

Board's Exhibit No. 4—(Continued)

shall not be considered as service of extra meals.

Section 8. Night Lunches:

(a) Employees in the Stewards' Department shall be required to prepare night lunches for officers and crew.

(b) Employees in the Stewards' Department (not exceeding two) actually engaged in preparing and serving the midnight meal shall be paid for three hours at the regular overtime rate.

Section 9. Meal Hours Delayed:

When meal hours are delayed on account of crew being occupied and unable to eat at their regular meal hours, all necessary members of the Stewards' Department will be paid at the regular overtime rate for the time delayed.

Section 10. Bread Supply:

In all parts of the United States bread shall be supplied from shore if available.

Section 11. Employment of Steward-Cook:

The Union agrees that the Company may employ its Steward-Cook from any source it sees fit and without regard to Union affiliation. (21)

Stewards Division

This agreement made and entered into this 18th day of November, 1942, by the Seafarers International Union of North America for the Engine Division and for the Stewards Division, and Sailors Union of the Pacific, affiliated with the Seafarer's International Union of North America, Deck Department, A. F. of L., hereinabove known as the

(Testimony of Harry E. Lundeberg.)

Board's Exhibit No. 4—(Continued)

(Associated Division), hereinabove known as the Company, shall be binding on the parties for the period of two years, and be deemed renewed from year to year thereafter unless either party shall give written notice to the other at least thirty (30) days prior to such expiration date of a desire to terminate this agreement, or to negotiate for amendments to this agreement, in which case the parties shall meet within five (5) days to begin negotiations.

If during the thirty (30) day period of negotiations the parties fail to agree then this agreement shall terminate at the expiration date; provided, however, that the parties may by mutual written agreement extend this agreement for a specific period beyond such expiration date for the continuance of negotiations.

(Signed) HARRY LUNDEBERG,

President Seafarer's International Union of North America; Secretary-Treasurer Sailors Union of the Pacific, affiliated with the A. F. of L.

(Signed) H. B. HANEY,

Tide Water Associated Oil Company (Associated Division). (22)

(Testimony of Harry E. Lundeberg.)

Board's Exhibit No. 4—(Continued)

INDEX

GENERAL RULES

(Applies to Deck, Engine and Stewards Departments)

(Testimony of Harry E. Lundeberg.)

Board's Exhibit No. 4—(Continued)

DECK DEPARTMENT

Wages and Working Rules

(24)

ENGINE DEPARTMENT

Wages and Working Rules

(Testimony of Harry E. Lundeberg.)

Board's Exhibit No. 4—(Continued)

(25)

STEWARDS DEPARTMENT

Wages and Working Rules

(26)

Trial Examiner Batten: We will recess until 3:00 o'clock.

(Brief recess.)

Trial Examiner Batten: Let us proceed.

Q. (By Mr. Moore): Referring, Mr. Lundeberg, to Board's Exhibit 3, will you state what types

(Testimony of Harry E. Lundeberg.)

of vessels are operated by the companies who are members of the shipowners Association of the Pacific Coast?

A. These people operate what you call coastwise vessels, lumber schooners and freighters. During peacetime they usually run up and down the coast. At the present time most of them is run out to the Islands to the Hawaiian Islands or up to Alaska for the Army or the Navy.

Q. Do you know what types of cargoes they carry now?

A. They carry war material for the armed forces.

Q. What types specifically have you observed being located on ships operated by those companies? [106]

A. Ammunition, torpedoes, supplies, food to the various Army bases in the Pacific.

Q. Has any governmental agency taken any steps, to your knowledge, to stabilize labor relations in the shipping industry on the Pacific Coast?

A. Yes.

Q. I will ask you if any steps, to your knowledge, have been taken with reference to the contract which is in evidence as Board's Exhibit 3 by any government agency?

A. The War Shipping Administration, Admiral Land, called us all together in Washington——

Q. By "us" whom do you mean?

A. All the union representatives. (Continuing): ——called us into Washington, D. C., in the month

(Testimony of Harry E. Lundeberg.)

of April, last year, 1942, and we had a meeting there which was presided over by Admiral Land. And then he told us, he said, "We have a war on. Now we want to get everything running smooth. We want to stabilize these agreements so we will have no trouble."

So various solutions were offered, and we offered this solution that Admiral Land guarantee us our existing agreements for the duration of the war, with all clauses in them as is. In other words, we voluntarily froze the agreements for the duration of the war. He agreed to that, and then he issued a directive which guaranteed us our collective bargaining, including this here, for the duration of the war. [107]

Q. By "this" you mean Board's Exhibit 3?

A. Yes.

Mr. Guntert: Mr. Examiner, I move that be stricken. If we have any directive, I think we should see it. It's a conclusion of this witness as to whether or not Admiral Land guaranteed anything.

Trial Examiner Batten: Do you have a copy of that directive, Mr. Lundeberg?

Mr. Lundeberg: I have a copy in San Francisco signed by Admiral Land and signed by ourselves. I can get it down here.

Trial Examiner Batten: When can you get it?

The Witness: I will have to call San Francisco and have them send it down. It is called a "Statement of principle."

(Testimony of Harry E. Lundeberg.)

Trial Examiner Batten: Will you try and have it down hereby tomorrow?

The Witness: Well, I will get ahold of San Francisco right now and call them up and have them send it air mail.

Trial Examiner Batten: You mean right now? Or do you want to go ahead?

The Witness: If there is no objection—go out and call San Francisco and reverse the charges (addressing Mr. Gries.) Ask them to send down the statement of principles.

Trial Examiner Batten: You have more than one copy of it?

The Witness: Yes. [108]

Trial Examiner Batten: Well, you had better send down about three or four copies if you have several.

Mr. Moore: Just a moment, before you do that. May I ask whether Respondent doesn't have a copy of the same thing?

Mr. Guntert: That was in the general orders and directives sent out by the War Shipping Administration?

The Witness: It is called the "Statement of Principles," governing the labor relations of the merchant marine, signed by Admiral Land.

Mr. Guntert: As I understand it from your testimony, that applies to contracts in existence?

The Witness: Yes.

Mr. Guntert: I object to it being brought down because it has no bearing on this case at all.

(Testimony of Harry E. Lundeberg.)

Trial Examiner Batten: I wouldn't pass on it without seeing it.

Mr. Guntert: I want to urge again that we are so far afield from the issue. Here we are talking about contracts between members of other companies, numbers of other organizations, which have no bearing here at all.

Trial Examiner Batten: Mr. Guntert, I think they do have a bearing. I think they are material to a determination of this issue. I mean, after all you can't determine the case of the Richfield Oil Company in a vacuum.

Now, it is true that your company has a right to issue [109] any order it wants. The Wagner Act doesn't tell you you can't issue an order. But it is just the same as with a discharge of a man. You can fire a man because he has red hair, black hair or no hair. But the only issue here is whether or not it is an 8(1) violation for your company to refuse to issue passes to representatives of the union.

That is the issue. You base it upon the fact that it is a safety provision.

Now, when we decide the issue I shall have to decide how much merit there is in your decision to put it upon that basis, whether the motive for issuing it is proper or not.

Now, I think to do that I have to have all the information I can get. I think the Board should have it. How much weight will be given to it I don't know. But I think it is relevant.

Mr. Moore: I will state that my purpose in

(Testimony of Harry E. Lundeberg.)

bringing up this action of Admiral Land has a bearing on the interpretation which Respondent says it has placed upon orders eminating from that agency.

Now, obviously, if an agreement containing a provision for passes were approved for the duration of the war, that may not be a statement that passes must be granted. But it certainly negatives any positive belief on Admiral Land's part that passes are improper.

Trial Examiner Batten: Well, we will get them down here. I am not receiving them now. When they are here and marked [110] and offered, then I shall pass upon them.

We will proceed.

Q. (By Mr. Moore): Mr. Lundeberg, do you have any identification card or badge issued by the Coast Guard or other naval or military force?

A. This is issued by the 12th Naval District, Commandant La France, and admits me to any pier or any ship where the Navy has anything to do with it, which covers pretty near all the ships on the coastwise scale now.

Mr. Moore: May the record show that the witness is referring to a card in a metal container which he removed from his belt?

Mr. Guntert: May I see that, counsel?

Mr. Moore: Yes.

Trial Examiner Batten: Mr. Lundeberg, do your patrolmen in these various ports have those also?

The Witness: Yes.

(Testimony of Harry E. Lundeberg.)

Mr. Ryan: He has another pass, too.

The Witness: That is the federal fingerprint card.

Q. (By Mr. Moore): You have also produced another card, Mr. Lundeberg, a card which bears your picture. Will you state what that is?

A. This is what is required by the United States Coast Guard for me to get on the waterfront in the various Pacific Coast ports. If I haven't got that, I can't get near the waterfront. [111]

Q. Do other representatives of your union, namely, patrolmen, have such identification cards?

A. Every one of them has the same thing.

Mr. Guntert: I call attention to the fact that this says this is not a pass. There is nothing on here——

Trial Examiner Batten: Well, of course, no one contends, I don't think, Mr. Guntert, that it is a pass.

Mr. Guntert: Well, this line of testimony would seem to indicate that. He said it would permit him to go on any pier.

Trial Examiner Batten: No, I don't think so.

Q. (By Mr. Moore): I will ask you, Mr. Lundeberg, these identification cards that you produce do not entitle you to go on board ships, do they?

A. If you haven't got one of those when you go on board one of the ships, usually most of the ships got a Navy man on the gangway and if he doesn't see this he won't let me aboard.

(Testimony of Harry E. Lundeberg.)

Trial Examiner Batten: Even if you have a pass?

The Witness: That's right. They want me to back it up with these.

Trial Examiner Batten: You have both of these, the metal button with the picture, the card with your fingerprint and picture and a pass?

The Witness: That's right.

Trial Examiner Batten: You need all three of those?

The Witness: Yes. [112]

Trial Examiner Batten: In order to get on a boat?

The Witness: Yes.

Trial Examiner Batten: Now, do you need all three of *us* to go on the dock or the pier?

The Witness: Yes. Most of the time we need all three of them because there is always a naval guard on the docks now, and for us to get on the waterfront we pass the armed guards, and you show them this and this. He doesn't ask for the pass to the ship. When you go on board at the various docks, then you must show this again, and this, and also the company pass. And then when you go on board of a ship you show the regular pass, and in most of the ships they have a Navy man, especially those ships that pack troops, and so forth, and supplies. They have Navy guards on every one of those ships. That's what they are interested in.

(Testimony of Harry E. Lundeberg.)

Trial Examiner Batten: The one with the metal picture in it?

The Witness: Yes. And I might state that before we get a pass like that it takes about three weeks of investigation by the F. B. I. and the Naval Intelligence.

Mr. Moore: I will offer this in evidence as Board's Exhibit 5 and request permission to substitute a photostatic copy of the metal pass which the witness has produced which is inscribed "12th Naval District, San Francisco, No. 1539."

The Witness: Well, I can't let you have that. I am [113] going to hang onto that myself.

Q. (By Mr. Moore): Can you have a photostat made?

A. Yes. But I am not supposed to let anybody else have that.

Trial Examiner Batten: Can't you take it somewhere and have it photostated and stay there while they photostat it, Mr. Lundeberg?

The Witness: Yes, I can do that.

Trial Examiner Batten: And have the other one photostated also.

Mr. Moore: Yes. I offer now as Board's——

Trial Examiner Batten: I won't receive them now. When he gets the photostats, bring them in here and see whether they are proper reproductions.

Mr. Ryan: Mr. Examiner, I might say that inasmuch as there is important matter on both sides that he have both sides photostated.

(Testimony of Harry E. Lundeberg.)

Trial Examiner Batten: You have both sides photostated, and we will want two copies for the record.

The Witness: Yes.

Trial Examiner Batten: I will determine at the time the photostats are presented whether they are proper reproductions and whether they are material and whether they should be received.

Q. (By Mr. Moore): Well, you testified, Mr. Lundeberg, with reference to the practice among shipping companies on the Pacific [114] Coast in the matter of granting passes to unions representing their employees for collective bargaining.

Are you familiar with the practice in that respect that is followed on the Gulf and Atlantic Coasts? A. Yes, sir.

Q. What is the practice there?

A. The practice prevails the same on the Atlantic and Gulf Coasts as on the Pacific Coast, and all shipping companies which we have been recognized by and have agreements with, we also have passes from them.

Trial Examiner Batten: Do you have passes on any of the companies that operate tankers in the Gulf and Atlantic Coasts?

The Witness: We have passes from the Hillcone, which is a Pacific Coast Company but which has a vessel or two operating out of the Gulf, and we have been granted passes to all of our representatives down there. But we have no contract with any Atlantic and Gulf tanker company.

(Testimony of Harry E. Lundeberg.)

Q. (By Mr. Moore): Mr. Lundeberg, has Richfield Oil Corporation ever issued passes to representatives of the unions you represent?

A. Yes. They granted us passes here in 1938 for the Port of San Pedro only.

Q. You mean by that that you do not have passes for their ships in other ports?

A. No. [115]

Q. And for how long did you continue to use passes of the Richfield Oil Corporation?

A. Of the Richfield Oil Corporation? They cancelled our passes on February 15th, 1942. They also cancelled our agreement.

Q. Since February 15, 1942, have you personally carried on any negotiations or correspondence with Richfield Oil Corporation with reference to obtaining other passes?

A. Yes, verbally and written.

Mr. Moore: May I have this document, consisting of two typewritten pages, marked Board's Exhibit 5 for identification?

Trial Examiner Batten: Yes. I would mark that 5. Then when we get the photostats they can be numbered at the time.

(The document referred to was marked for identification as Board's Exhibit No. 5.)

Q. (By Mr. Moore): Mr. Lundeberg, I show you a document consisting of two pages marked Board's Exhibit 5 for identification and ask you if you will identify it, if you can?

A. Yes. This is a letter from Mr. Jones who is

(Testimony of Harry E. Lundeberg.)

tion, a letter to me sent on January 18th, denying us passes.

Q. Was this letter received at your office?

A. It was received at the office in San Francisco.

Q. That is, the office of the unions you represent?

A. Yes. [116]

Mr. Moore: I offer Board's Exhibit 5 for identification in evidence.

Trial Examiner Batten: Have you shown it to the attorneys?

Mr. Moore: I have shown them a copy.

Trial Examiner Batten: Do you have any copies of this?

Mr. Moore: Yes, sir.

Trial Examiner Batten: Mr. Guntert, do you have any objection to this letter?

Mr. Guntert: No, sir.

Trial Examiner Batten: If there is no objection, it will be received.

(The document heretofore marked for identification as Board's Exhibit No. 5 was received in evidence.)

(Testimony of Harry E. Lundeberg.)

BOARD'S EXHIBIT No. 5

RICHFIELD OIL CORPORATION

Richfield Building, Los Angeles, California
January 18, 1943.

Office of the
President
Mr. Harry Lundeberg
Secretary-Treasurer, Sailors Union of Pacific
President, Seafarers International Union
Headquarters: 402-404 Lumbermen's Building
San Francisco, California

Dear Sir:

I am replying to your letter of January 7, 1943, with which you enclosed a copy of the agreement dated November 18, 1942 between the labor organizations which you represent and Tidewater Associated Oil Company (Associated Division), and in which you offer Richfield Oil Corporation the same kind of agreement "contingent upon acceptance" by us "of that agreement as a whole, including the preferential employment clause".

I understand from Mr. P. C. Lamb, Manager of our Marine Department, that he has had numerous meetings with you, that you and he are in substantial agreement as to most of the matters pertaining to working conditions which you have discussed, but that the negotiations have been protracted because of your insistence on a preferential hiring clause and a provision for passes for your representatives

(Testimony of Harry E. Lundeberg.)

to our ships. Mr. Lamb has now referred to me these two controversial questions.

Richfield Oil Corporation will not voluntarily grant a preferential hiring clause because we are opposed to it as a matter of fundamental principle. We consider it monopolistic, undemocratic and un-American to abandon the freedoms involved, freedom on our part to hire the ablest men available, and freedom on the part of the men who seek employment on our ships to belong or not to belong to a labor organization as they may choose.

With the advent of war we resolved to eliminate as soon as possible all passes to our ships. You will recall that we at that time had an agreement with the Sailors Union of Pacific which contained a provision for passes, but when the agreement expired by its terms February 15, 1942 we did not renew it because of that provision. Upon termination of that agreement we were in a position to cancel and did cancel passes issued pursuant to an agreement we had with Marine Engineers Beneficial Association No. 79, Inc. We also allowed to terminate on March 31, 1942 an agreement with Pacific Coast Marine Firemen, Oilers, Water Tenders, and Wipers' Association, which provided for passes.

On February 20, 1942 we were informed by the Regional Director of the National Labor Relations Board that National Maritime Union of America had filed a charge against us alleging that we en-

(Testimony of Harry E. Lundeberg.)

gaged in unfair labor practices in refusing passes to representatives of that Union. Upon our showing that we had adopted a policy of not granting any to passes/anybody for the period of the war, the Regional Director refused to issue a complaint, and upon appeal, the National Labor Relations Board upheld him in so refusing. You, of course, are familiar with the principle that if passes are granted even to certified bargaining agents, they must also be granted to any and all other labor organizations requesting them. This would result in many people visiting our ships whenever they are in port.

The reasons why this Corporation does not want visitors on its ships, either representatives of labor organizations or anybody else, are almost self-evident. Inherent dangers and hazards exist on a tank ship loaded with, loading, or unloading highly inflamable products. The slightest bit of carelessness can result in disaster. The more people there are on board, the greater are the possibilities that some act of negligence or carelessness may occur. Tank ships are precious beyond any measure in this war, and all risks to them should be kept to an irreducible minimum. Furthermore, the critical tanker shortage demands that there be the least possible delay in loading and unloading of ships and that all operations be kept at maximum efficiency to minimize the loss of tanker time. When our ships are in port the men not on watch are not required to be, and should not be, on board. The men who are

(Testimony of Harry E. Lundeberg.)

on watch are busy in the performance of their duties and should not be distracted therefrom by visitors, particularly in times of all-out war effort.

Mr. Lamb is quite willing to sit down with you at any time and reduce to a formal contract all of the matters upon which you have already reached an agreement, and such other matters upon which you may agree. He tells me that the wages provided for in the agreement with Tidewater Associated are substantially what we are paying now, and that the "general rules" (except the provisions as to preferential hiring and as to passes) and the "working rules" as applied to the Deck and Engine Department, contained in the Tidewater Associated Agreement are approximately what we will be willing to agree to. Therefore, there should be very little difficulty in reducing the agreement to writing.

Yours very truly,

CHAS. S. JONES.

Mr. Moore: No further questions.

Trial Examiner Batten: Mr. Guntert?

Mr. Guntert: No cross examination.

Trial Examiner Batten: That is all, Mr. Lundeberg.

The Witness: Thank you.

(Witness excused.)

Mr. Guntert: There is a matter I would like to take up now, unless counsel has something more.

Mr. Moore: Go right ahead.

Mr. Guntert: Pending Mr. Lamb's arrival. [117]

Trial Examiner Batten: Do you have any further witnesses?

Mr. Moore: Yes. I intend to call Mr. William Gries. He is out of the room right now, I think, telephoning.

Mr. Lundeberg: I will go and get him.

Mr. Guntert: What I have here might save some time.

Trial Examiner Batten: All right.

Mr. Guntert: In our answer we alleged that on or about February 20th we, the Richfield Oil Corporation, received a communication from the Regional Director announcing the complaint, and we answered that; and the Regional Director declined to issue the complaint and he was sustained by the Board.

I would like to introduce as an exhibit copies of that exchange of communications.

Trial Examiner Batten: Will you have them marked, Mr. Guntert?

Mr. Guntert: Yes. Let's see. The next number, I believe, is 5, is it not, for the Respondent?

(The documents referred to were marked for identification as Respondent's Exhibits 5-A to 5-E for identification.)

Mr. Guntert: Could we have about a five minute recess?

Trial Examiner Batten: Let's dispose of this matter first, Mr. Guntert.

Mr. Moore: Have Respondent's Exhibits 5-A, et cetera, been [118] offered in evidence?

Mr. Guntert: They haven't, but I now offer them.

Mr. Moore: I will object to them upon the ground that this material is not material to the case at issue, for this reason, among others:

It is not shown that the National Maritime Union of America is the exclusive bargaining agent of any employees of the company. The case is in no way analogous to the present one for that reason.

Further, a refusal to issue a complaint by the Regional Director is not a finding of the Board that no unfair labor practices have occurred. The Board has issued its complaint in this matter on a stated set of facts, and the Board will depend on the evidence in this case rather than some other case.

Trial Examiner Batten: Well, I think they ought to be in the record. I think they are a part of the history of this case.

Mr. Guntert: It's the identical situation.

Trial Examiner Batten: When I say "this case" I don't mean this particular numbered case. I presume we might say, as is so frequently said, this might be background.

Mr. Moore: Then I will further object to the foundation. As I understand it, there is none here.

I would like to know what the foundation is before the ruling is made. [119]

Trial Examiner Batten: Well, what foundation?

Mr. Moore: Well, we have certain documents here with the numbers 5-A through E on them, but that's all we have.

Trial Examiner Batten: Well, what foundation do you want? Do you want Mr. Guntert to prove that this is Mr. Walsh's letter and that these letters are contained in the files of the Labor Board? Is that what you want?

Mr. Moore: No, no. I want him to prove how they happened to have these. What I mean, Mr. Examiner, is that I don't believe these things should be permitted to speak for themselves just the way they appear here. They have no meaning. They don't state the controversy.

Trial Examiner Batten: Well, don't you think that is Mr. Guntert's responsibility and not yours?

Mr. Moore: That is exactly what I say.

Trial Examiner Batten: If they don't properly stated the situation and don't show anything, then Mr. Guntert is the one that will have to assume the responsibility for that, isn't he?

Mr. Moore: That is one way to look at it, Mr. Examiner. But, on the other hand, something that is not identified in any way can't be used by the Board and would be encumbering the record.

Trial Examiner Batten: We will have a recess while you go in the Board's files and bring them out here and check against [120] the Board's file. If you don't find anything like this in the Board's file, then I will take the proper steps.

So we will recess now until 25 minutes of 4:00.

(Brief recess.)

Trial Examiner Batten: We will proceed. Have you checked up those letters, Mr. Moore? If you haven't, let me know what you find after you have checked them.

Mr. Moore: I want to ask counsel if it may be stipulated that the National Maritime Union was not a certified bargining agent for any of the employees of the Richfield Oil Corporation?

Mr. Guntert: I don't know whether they were representing anyone, but I am sure that they were not certified. Am I correct in that, Mr. Lamb?

Mr. P. C. Lamb: The National Maritime Union was certified at one time, I think about 1929. But the question as to whether any employees were still employed during the past few years is very doubtful.

Trial Examiner Batten: Well, of course, they were not certified, were they?

Mr. Lamb: They were certified.

Trial Examiner Batten: Well, I mean in 1942.

Mr. Lamb: No. This was in 1929.

Trial Examiner Batten: Well, is that satisfactory, Mr. Moore? [121]

Mr. Lundeberg: Mr. Examiner, the National Maritime Union never came into existence before 1937. They weren't in effect.

Trial Examiner Batten: Well, let's don't get into that. What we are trying to do, Mr. Lundeberg—just a moment—is to agree here that in 1942 they were not certified. And, as I understand it, you are all agreed that in 1942 they were not.

Mr. Lamb: That's right.

Mr. Moore: That is agreeable.

Trial Examiner Batten: Is that agreed, Mr. Guntert?

Mr. Guntert: So stipulated.

Trial Examiner Batten: Mr. Lundeberg?

Mr. Lundeberg: That's right.

Mr. Moore: Now, may it be stipulated that in October, 1942, and subsequent thereto the Sailors Union of the Pacific had been certified by the National Labor Relations Board as the exclusive collective bargaining representative of the company's unlicensed personnel in the deck department?

Mr. Guntert: That is the allegation which we have admitted.

Trial Examiner Batten: You have admitted it?

Mr. Moore: That is not the allegation that is admitted.

Trial Examiner Batten: Well, whether it is or not, I presume that is a fact, Mr. Guntert?

Mr. Guntert: Yes, they are certified, I understand. [122]

Trial Examiner Batten: Yes. And, Mr. Lundeberg, is that correct?

Mr. Lundeberg: That is correct.

Mr. Moore: And may it be further stipulated that the Seafarers International Engine Division was certified by the Regional Director prior to October, 1942, after an election among the employees, as the exclusive collective bargaining representative of unlicensed personnel in the company's engine department?

Mr. Guntert: So stipulated. It was prior to October, 1942.

Mr. Moore: Yes.

Trial Examiner Batten: Is that agreeable to you, Mr. Lundeberg?

Mr. Lundeberg: Yes.

Mr. Moore: Then I will withdraw my objection to Respondent's Exhibit 5.

Trial Examiner Batten: I think it was previously received. But if there is any doubt about it, I will receive it again.

(The document heretofore marked for identification as Respondent's Exhibits 5-A to 5-E, inclusive, were received in evidence.)

RESPONDENT'S EXHIBIT No. 5-A

(Copy)

National Labor Relations Board
Twenty-First Region
U. S. Post Office and Courthouse
Los Angeles, California

In reply refer to:
Case No. XXI-C-2001
Richfield Oil Corporation

May 25, 1942

Richfield Oil Corporation
Richfield Building
Los Angeles, California
Attention—Mr. R. W. Ragland

Gentlemen:

An appeal was taken from the Regional Director's refusal to issue complaint in the above matter.

The Board has considered the appeal and has sustained the Regional Director's decision in the matter.

Very truly yours,
(signed) WM. R. WALSH
WILLIAM R. WALSH
Director

MA

RESPONDENT'S EXHIBIT No. 5-B

(Copy)

National Labor Relations Board Letterhead
In reply refer to:
Case No. XXI-C-2001
Richfield Oil Corporation

March 20, 1942

National Maritime Union of America
57 Post Street
San Francisco, California
Attention—Mr. Benjamin Dreyfus

Gentlemen:

The above captioned case, charging a violation of Section 8, subsection (1) of the National Labor Relations Act, has been carefully investigated and considered.

Further proceedings do not seem warranted, and I am, therefore, refusing to issue complaint in this matter.

Pursuant to the National Labor Relations Board Rules and Regulations, Series 2, as amended, Article II, Section 9, you may obtain a review of this action by filing a request therefor with the National Labor Relations Board in Washington, D. C., and by filing a copy of such request with me. This request shall contain a complete statement setting forth the facts and reasons upon which the request is based.

Very truly yours
(signed) WILLIAM R. WALSH
Director

WRW:MA
cc: National Labor Relations Board
Washington, D. C.
Richfield Oil Corporation
Richfield Bldg., Los Angeles

RESPONDENT'S EXHIBIT No. 5-C

(Copy)

National Labor Relations Board Letterhead

March 13, 1942

In reply refer to:
Richfield Oil Corp.
XXI-C-2001

Richfield Oil Corporation
Richfield Building
Los Angeles, California
Attention—Mr. R. W. Ragland

Gentlemen:

This will acknowledge receipt of your letter of March 12, 1942 in regard to the above case.

It is my understanding that the company will

issue no passes to any organization enabling any organization to send representatives aboard any of the company's tankers for the remainder of the war period. A recommendation for disposition of the charge is being made on this basis.

We appreciate the cooperation of the corporation in assisting in the tentative settlement of the charge and your personal assistance in supplying the information requested.

Very truly yours,
(signed) ROGER G. McGUIRE
Field Examiner

RESPONDENT'S EXHIBIT No. 5-D

(Copy)

March 12, 1942

National Labor Relations Board
Twenty-First Region
U. S. Post Office and Courthouse
Los Angeles, California.

Attention: Mr. Roger G. McGuire,
Field Examiner
Your Docket: Richfield Oil Corporation
XXI-C-2001

Gentlemen:

We are replying to Director Walsh's letter of February 20, 1942 informing us that National Maritime Union of America has filed a charge pursuant to Section 10 (c) of the National Labor Relations

Act, alleging that this Corporation is engaged in unfair labor practices within the meaning of Section 8, subsection (1) of the Act, in that:

> "The aforesaid company did, on or about July 16, 1941, and at various times thereafter, refuse permission to officers of this Union to visit the vessels of the company, and to talk with the members of this union on these vessels.
>
> "Said company has, to the knowledge of the National Maritime Union of America, issued passes to other labor organizations, and gave permission to visit its boat to officers and members of other organizations; and the aforesaid company's failure to give such permission and passes to officers of the National Maritime Union of America constitutes an unfair labor practice, and violates the rights and privileges accorded to employees under Section 7, and Section 8, sub-section (1), of the National Labor Relations Act."

We are without knowledge or information sufficient to form a belief as to whether any person employed on or about July 16, 1941 or thereafter is a member of the National Maritime Union of America and we, therefore, deny that we refused permission to officers of that union to talk with members of that union on our ships.

We admit that we refused permission to officers of the National Maritime Union of America to go aboard our ships, but we deny that such refusal violated any provision of the National Labor Relations Act.

We further deny that the issuance of passes by us to other labor organizations constituted a discrimination against the National Maritime Union of America, since (a) the passes we have issued to other labor organizations have been issued pursuant to provisions of agreements between the Corporation and such other labor organizations, made after certification of such labor organizations as bargaining agents by the National Labor Relations Board, and (b) we have never issued passes to any labor organization except pursuant to an agreement made after certification by the National Labor Relations Board.

In connection with cases XXI-R-1569, XXI-R-1570 and XXI-R-1571, we have previously furnished you copies of the following agreements between this Corporation and labor organizations:

(1) Agreement dated February 15, 1939 with Sailors' Union of the Pacific.

(2) Agreement dated September 1, 1938 with Marine Engineers Beneficial Association No. 79, Inc.

(3) Agreement dated April 1, 1939 with Pacific Coast Marine Firemen, Oilers, Water Tenders and Wipers' Association.

These agreements were made with the respective labor organizations after their certificaton by the National Labor Relations Board.

Each of the agreements provided that the Corporation would issue passes to representatives of the union to board ships for the purpose of transacting union business with union members or for visiting union members.

In the early Summer of 1941 (prior to July 16, 1941) a large number of American Flag tankships were drafted by the United States Maritime Commission for the so-called "shuttle service" in the interest of national defense. It immediately became evident that there was a shortage of tanker tonnage in relation to requirements for national defense, and that such shortage would become more and more serious. At that time, this Corporation determined not only that it would not issue more passes to its ships, but that it would cancel all then existing passes as soon as it could do so without violation of agreements with labor organizations.

The agreement with the Sailors' Union of the Pacific, mentioned above, was terminated February 15, 1942 and all passes issued pursuant thereto were immediately cancelled.

The Corporation was then in a position to cancel, and did cancel, passes issued pursuant to the agreement with Marine Engineers Beneficial Association No. 79, Inc., mentioned above.

Under the provisions of the agreement with Pacific Coast Marine Firemen, Oilers, Water Tenders and Wipers' Association, above mentioned, such agreement could be terminated by either party on March 31, 1942, and this Corporation has notified said labor organization of the termination of such agreement on said date, unless prior thereto the agreement is amended by the deletion therefrom of the provisions under which the Corporation is required to issue passes.

The reasons why the Corporation does not want visitors on its ships, either representatives of labor organizations or anybody else, are almost self-evident. Inherent dangers and hazards exist on a tankship loaded with, loading, or unloading highly inflammable products. The slightest bit of carelessness can result in disaster. The more people there are on board, the greater are the possibilities that some act of negligence or carelessness may occur. Tankships are precious beyond any measure of price in this war, and all risks to them should be kept to an irreducible minimum.

Furthermore, the critical tanker shortage demands that there be the least possible delay in the loading and unloading of ships and that all operations be kept at maximum efficiency to minimize the loss of tanker time. When our ships are in port the men not on watch are not required to be, and should not be, aboard. The men who are on watch are busy in the performance of their duties, and should not be distracted therefrom by visitors, particularly in times of "all out" war effort.

In addition to the foregoing considerations, we have been enjoined by the Navy to use the utmost attainable degree of secrecy as to the arrivals, departures, and movements of our ships. Although visitors to a ship may keep secret anything they may learn as to arrivals and departures, the fact that they are habitual visitors to ships and that their movements may be watched would constitute an additional difficulty in limiting knowledge of the arrivals and departures of our ships as narrowly as possible.

We have been, and are, mindful of the principle that if we issue passes to the representatives of any labor organization, with which we have no contract providing for passes, it would seem to follow that we would have to issue passes to any and all organizations (which we would have to determine, at our own risk and peril, to be or not to be bona fide labor organizations) claiming the right to visit an alleged member of the organization aboard our ships. We respectfully submit that for at least the duration of the war such a principle may contain elements of hazard and danger that can be avoided and, therefore, should be avoided.

Very truly yours,

RICHFIELD OIL CORPORATION

By ....

Assistant to the President

RWR:F

RESPONDENT'S EXHIBIT No. 5-E

(Copy)

Letterhead of
National Labor Relations Board
Twenty-First Region
U. S. Post Office and Courthouse
Los Angeles, California

February 20, 1942

In reply refer to:
Richfield Oil Corporation
XXI-C-2001

Richfield Oil Corporation
333 Montgomery Street,
San Francisco, California.

Gentlemen:

This is to inform you National Maritime Union of America has filed a charge pursuant to Section 10 (c) of the National Labor Relations Act, alleging that Richfield Oil Corporation is engaged in unfair labor practices within the meaning of Section 8, subsection (1) of the Act, in that:

> "The aforesaid company did, on or about July 16, 1941, and at various times thereafter, refuse permission to officers of this union to visit the vessels of the company, and to talk with the members of this union on these vessels.
>
> "Said company has, to the knowledge of the National Maritime Union of America, issued passes to other labor organizations, and gave permission to visit its boats to officers and members of other organizations; and the afore-

said company's failure to give such permission and passes to officers of the National Maritime Union of America constitutes an unfair labor practice, and violates the rights and privileges accorded to employees, under Section 7, and Section 8, sub-section (1), of the National Labor Relations Act."

It appears there is sufficient interstate commerce information in other files, making it unnecessary for a request at this time. Will you please state the company's version with regard to the allegations cited above.

For your information, the case has been assigned to Roger G. McGuire, Field Examiner in this office, who can be reached at Room 808, U. S. Postoffice and Courthouse, Los Angeles, or by telephone at Madison 7411, Extension 647.

Yours very truly,
(signed) WILLIAM R. WALSH
W. R. WALSH
Director

RGM/aj

Trial Examiner Batten: You may proceed.

Mr. Moore: I offer as Board's Exhibit 6 a copy of a letter written by Mr. E. J. Eagen, director of the 21st Region [123] of the National Labor Relations Board on January 6, 1943, to Richfield Oil Corporation.

Trial Examiner Batten: Do you have a duplicate of that?

Mr. Moore: I will furnish copies.

Trial Examiner Batten: All right. Is there any objection to the receipt of this document?

Mr. Guntert: No, Mr. Examiner. But isn't that already a part of this file? It was a letter notifying us of the complaint.

Trial Examiner Batten: Well, of course, it may be a part of the Board's file, but it isn't, I don't think, a part of this case record, Mr. Guntert, unless it is received here. In other words, as you perhaps know, the Examiner nor the Board uses the files in the determination of the issues in these cases. In other words, it's only the evidence which is introduced at the hearing.

If there is no objection, Board's Exhibit 6 will be received.

(The document referred to was received in evidence and marked Board's Exhibit No. 6.)

BOARD'S EXHIBIT No. 6

(Copy)

In reply refer to:
Case Nos. XXI-C-2248
XXI-C-2249
Richfield Oil Corporation

January 6, 1943

Richfield Oil Corporation
Richfield Building
Los Angeles, California

Gentlemen:

Please be advised that charges have been filed by Pacific District, Seafarers' International, Stewards Division, AFL, and Pacific District, Seafarers' International, Engine Division, AFL, alleging that your Company has since October 1942 refused to grant passes to such labor organizations, who have been duly selected by the unlicensed personnel in the stewards' and engine departments of your Company's Pacific Coast oil tankers, and that your Company has thereby engaged in an unfair labor practice within the meaning of Section 8, subsection (1) of the National Labor Relations Act.

Will you please advise us whether a request has been made for passes. If so, by whom the request was made, when, and what reply was made in each instance by the Company representative. Please also state the Company's position relative to granting passes to duly authorized bargaining agents for the purpose of investigating and handling grievances and other similar matters.

As you undoubtedly know, the Board and the Courts have held that bargaining agents are entitled to such passes.

Appreciating your cooperation and a prompt reply,

Very truly yours,
E. J. EAGEN
Director

EJE:MA

Trial Examiner Batten: You will furnish copies of that, Mr. Moore?

Mr. Moore: Yes, I will.

Mr. Guntert: I would like to introduce the answer to the letter that has just been introduced, if there is no objection. [124]

Mr. Moore: No objection.

Trial Examiner Batten: That will be Respondent's 6. What date is that, Mr. Guntert?

Mr. Guntert: A letter dated January 14th, 1943, from Mr. Ragland, assistant to the president of Richfield Oil Corporation, in answer to this letter. It also encloses a copy of the letter dated March 12, 1942, which is referred to in the letter.

Trial Examiner Batten: Well, if there is no objection, it will be received. Will it be agreeable to the parties, when copies are furnished, that this original may be withdrawn so it may be placed back in the file?

Mr. Moore: That is agreeable.

(The document referred to was received in evidence and marked Respondent's Exhibit No. 6.)

unfair labor practices within the meaning of Section 8, subsection (1) of the Act, in that:

> "The aforesaid company did, on or about July 16, 1941, and at various times thereafter, refuse permission to officers of this Union to visit the vessels of the company, and to talk with the members of this union on these vessels.
>
> "Said company has, to the knowledge of the National Maritime Union of America, issued passes to other labor organizations, and gave permission to visit its boat to officers and members of other organizations; and the aforesaid company's failure to give such permission and passes to officers of the National Maritime Union of America constitutes an unfair labor practice, and violates the rights and privileges accorded to employees under Section 7, and Section 8, sub-section (1), of the National Labor Relations Act."

We are without knowledge or information sufficient to form a belief as to whether any person employed on or about July 16, 1941 or thereafter is a member of the National Maritime Union of America and we, therefore, deny that we refused permission to officers of that union to talk with members of that union on our ships.

We admit that we refused permission to officers of the National Maritime Union of America to go aboard our ships, but we deny that such refusal violated any provision of the National Labor Relations Act.

We further deny that the issuance of passes by us to other labor organizations constituted a discrimination against the National Maritime Union of America, since (a) the passes we have issued to other labor organizations have been issued pursuant to provisions of agreements between the Corporation and such other labor organizations, made after certification of such labor organizations as bargaining agents by the National Labor Relations Board, and (b) we have never issued passes to any labor organization except pursuant to an agreement made after certification by the National Labor Relations Board.

In connection with cases XXI-R-1569, XXI-R-1570 and XXI-R-1571, we have previously furnished you copies of the following agreements between this Corporation and labor organizations:

(1) Agreement dated February 15, 1939 with Sailors' Union of the Pacific.

(2) Agreement dated September 1, 1938 with Marine Engineers Beneficial Association No. 79, Inc.

(3) Agreement dated April 1, 1939 with Pacific Coast Marine Firemen, Oilers, Water Tenders and Wipers' Association.

These agreements were made with the respective labor organizations after their certification by the National Labor Relations Board.

Each of the agreements provided that the Corporation would issue passes to representatives of the union to board ships for the purpose of transacting union business with union members or for visiting union members.

In the early Summer of 1941 (prior to July 16, 1941) a large number of American Flag tankships were drafted by the United States Maritime Commission for the so-called "shuttle service" in the interest of national defense. It immediately became evident that there was a shortage of tanker tonnage in relation to requirements for national defense, and that such shortage would become more and more serious. At that time, this Corporation determined not only that it would not issue more passes to its ships, but that it would cancel all then existing passes as soon as it could do so without violation of agreements with labor organizations.

The agreement with the Sailors' Union of the Pacific, mentioned above, was terminated February 15, 1942 and all passes issued pursuant thereto were immediately cancelled.

The Corporation was then in a position to cancel, and did cancel, passes issued pursuant to the agreement with Marine Engineers Beneficial Association No. 79, Inc., mentioned above.

Under the provisions of the agreement with Pacific Coast Marine Firemen, Oilers, Water Tenders and Wipers' Association, above mentioned, such agreement could be terminated by either party on March 31, 1942, and this Corporation has notified said labor organization of the termination of such agreement on said date, unless prior thereto the agreement is amended by the deletion therefrom of the provisions under which the Corporation is required to issue passes.

The reasons why the Corporation does not want visitors on its ships, either representatives of labor organizations or anybody else, are almost self-evident. Inherent dangers and hazards exist on a tankship loaded with, loading, or unloading highly inflammable products. The slightest bit of carelessness can result in disaster. The more people there are on board, the greater are the possibilities that some act of negligence or carelessness may occur. Tankships are precious beyond any measure of price in this war, and all risks to them should be kept to an irreducible minimum.

Furthermore, the critical tanker shortage demands that there be the least possible delay in the loading and unloading of ships and that all operations be kept at maximum efficiency to minimize the loss of tanker time. When our ships are in port the men not on watch are not required to be, and should not be, aboard. The men who are on watch are busy in the performance of their duties, and should not be distracted therefrom by visitors, particularly in times of "all out" war effort.

In addition to the foregoing considerations, we have been enjoined by the Navy to use the utmost attainable degree of secrecy as to the arrivals, departures, and movements of our ships. Although visitors to a ship may keep secret anything they may learn as to arrivals and departures, the fact that they are habitual visitors to ships and that their movements may be watched would constitute an additional difficulty in limiting knowledge of the arrivals and departures of our ships as narrowly as possible.

We have been, and are, mindful of the principle that if we issue passes to the representatives of any labor organization, with which we have no contract providing for passes, it would seem to follow that we would have to issue passes to any and all organizations (which we would have to determine, at our own risk and peril, to be or not to be bona fide labor organizations) claiming the right to visit an alleged member of the organization aboard our ships. We respectfully submit that for at least the duration of the war such a principle may contain elements of hazard and danger that can be avoided and, therefore, should be avoided.

Very truly yours,

RICHFIELD OIL CORPORATION

By /s/ R. W. RAGLAND

Assistant to the President

RWR:F

Trial Examiner Batten: Who will furnish copies of this letter?

Mr. Moore: I can do that.

Trial Examiner Batten: All right. We will proceed.

Mr. Moore: Mr. Gries, will you take the stand, please?

WILLIAM GRIES

called as a witness by and on behalf of the National Labor Relations Board, having been first duly sworn, was examined and testified as follows: [125]

Direct Examination

Q. (By Mr. Moore) Will you state your full name, please.

A. William Gries, G-r-i-e-s.

Q. What is your occupation, Mr. Gries?

A. Basically I am a seaman. But now I am organizer for the Sailors Union of the Pacific and representative for the Seafarers International, Pacific District.

Q. How do you prononce your name?

A. "Grise."

Q. "Grise?" A. That's right.

Q. How long have you been occupied in your present position?

A. Approximately 9 months.

Q. What title do you have?

A. Organizer of the Sailors Union of the Pacific. I am representative for the Seafarers International Union, Pacific District.

Q. Does that include the Seafarers International Engine Division?

A. That includes both divisions, engine and stewards.

Q. Where are you stationed, Mr. Gries?

A. The office is at 206½ West 6th Street, San Pedro.

Q. Are you familiar with the places where Rich-

(Testimony of William Gries.)

field Oil Corporation tankers dock in the Los Angeles area? A. Yes, sir. [126]

Q. Will you state where that is?

A. The Richfield docks have two in Long Beach. One is on 7th Street and one is on, I guess it is, 8th Street. One is known as the "Rio Grande dock," and one is called the "Richfield dock."

Q. Just a little louder, please.

A. One is on 8th Street, the Rio Grande dock on 8th Street, and the Richfield dock is on 7th Street. That is in Long Beach.

Q. Do you have occasion to go from the union office to that location? A. I do, yes, sir.

Q. How far is it?

A. Well, I couldn't state the mileage. I guess it's about 7 or 8 miles over there.

Q. And have you——

Trial Examiner Batten: To which dock? Both docks?

The Witness: Well, it's a difference of one street.

Trial Examiner Batten: I see.

Q. (By Mr. Moore) Have you had occasion to go over there by public transportation?

A. Yes, I have, for a long time.

Q. How long did it take you?

A. Well, it takes you about half an hour to 40 minutes from the time you get on the car to get over there. There [127] is only the red car running over there, but if you miss the car you may have to wait around for another 40 minutes for a car to come.

(Testimony of William Gries.)

Q. Do you have any duties in connection with your occupation that cause you to settle grievances among seamen?

A. That's what my business is.

Q. Will you state how you have done that in the past?

A. Well, I can give you a specific instance. Here Mr. Richards who is agent for the Waterman Steamship Company, recently had a ship here, rather, down in San Diego the ship was, and he called me. There was some dispute between the mate and the captain and the crew in regards to a security watch agreement we have whereby the men have to stay on watch at night, stay aboard at night under this Coast Guard regulation, requiring a certain number of men to be on board to move the ship. And they couldn't seem to get it straight. And I had to go down on board the ship and got the mate together and the skipper and the gang and explained the whole thing to them so they all understood it, see. That is one instance.

Another instance, up at Port Hueneme, the port captain, Captain Odean, of the Alcoa Steamship, he called me from Port Hueneme. They were paying the crew off, and there was some question of overtime involved in the steward's department and the black gang. The port captain claimed that the men [128] didn't have the overtime coming, and I went up there and went on board and talked to the men, and they claimed they had it coming and I seen what work they had done; and I believed that it was com-

(Testimony of William Gries.)

ing and I argued it out with the port captain and the chief engineer. We settled it. They paid it. They paid the overtime.

That's an every day occurrence. Right here now in San Pedro there is a dispute. I don't know whether you would call it a dispute. The War Shipping Administration or the Navy, or somebody, can't seem to get it straight. We have a directive from San Francisco stating what quarters are going to be allocated to the unlicensed personnel of the ship, and the Navy wants to put more men on the ship and they want to take over some of the quarters that have been assigned to the crew.

Well, we have to stand pat on what we have got. Otherwise, they will take over the whole ship. The men are entitled to certain quarters on the ship, and we have got to see that they get it.

Q. How has that affected your own work? What have you done in connection with that?

A. I have gone down and talked to the crew. I have talked to the skipper, the agent of the company and to the representative of the War Shipping Administration in San Pedro who is in charge of quarters and repairs and things. [129]

Q. Did you go aboard that ship?

A. I had to go aboard. I had to go aboard and see what the layout was, what rooms they had assigned to different men. Sometimes they put sailors in the firemen's forecastle in the messmen's forecastle because they don't know when the ships come out. I guess they are a bunch of land lovers

(Testimony of William Gries.)

and don't know anything about how ships are run, how the crews should be laid out.

Another thing, they are marked in the shipyard under an old plan, see, under the original plans.

The crew's quarters are marked and are marked wrong. And when they come aboard the ship the mate and the skipper assign guys to different quarters, and later they find out they have to be shifted. And we try to keep the steward's department in one corner of the ship and the black gang on the other side and the sailors on the other side so each department is together, see.

Q. Do you perform the duties of a patrolman in your occupation?

A. Yes, sir, I do.

Q. Do you wait, Mr. Gries, until you are called before you board a ship on which you represent employees?

A. Not necessarily. Lots of time I have information that ships are coming in. I know when they are coming in, or I am called generally by the agent or the port captain, see. [130]

Q. By whom?

A. The agent of the company or the port captain?

Q. Or the port captain?

A. To come down and straighten out the dispute.

Q. Have you followed the practice of going down and boarding ship, whether you knew of a specific grievance or not. A. All the time.

(Testimony of William Gries.)

Q. What do you do after you board the ship in a case of that character?

A. Well, I generally go to the ship's delegate and ask him what is going on.

Q. Where? A. And what's the trouble.

Q. Where do you look for him?

A. Back in the forecastles.

Q. Is that the crew's quarters?

A. I make it a practice generally of going aboard, if I can, around what they call "coffee time." You see, they have coffee time in the morning or coffee time in the afternoon. Or I go aboard in the afternoon, noontime. And I don't interfere with their work and I take up the dispute then with the men.

When I hear a story all around from the ship's delegate, I generally take him up to the mate or the skipper and argue it out with him. [131]

Q. Has it ever occurred that you needed to interview a man who was on watch at the time?

A. Yes. Sometimes the dispute involves the man that is on watch. In that case we send out a release, one of the men in the crew. If it's an A. B. involved in it, we send an A. B. out to relieve him while he comes in and discusses the situation. If it is an ordinary, we send out an ordinary. If it is a man below, a fireman, a fireman goes down and relieves him and takes on his duties while he gets straightened out.

Q. Has any ship's officer ever objected to that procedure, in your experience?

A. No, sir, none of them ever objected to it.

(Testimony of William Gries.)

Q. Do you do anything else other than what you have mentioned while you are aboard ship?

A. Yes. I collect dues. The men want their dues paid up, and things like that. I collect the dues for them. In fact, there's lots of times when I go on board the ship just for that purpose. I mean, the men call up and say, "Come on down here. I have got to pay some dues. I haven't got time to go down to the hall."

I go down there and collect dues, and any time you get down there to collect dues, why, they have always got something to show you, the mess room isn't right, or the chow isn't right, or maybe the toilets aren't clean and they need to be repainted, [132] or the forecastles are kind of dirty. They want to have them painted, or something like that. I always take care of that while I am right there.

Q. Is there anything else now that you recall that you do while aboard ship?

A. That is all my duties are.

Q. Do you distribute anything to the men?

A. Yes, our trade paper, the West Coast Sailor.

Q. What is that?

A. It is news of the seamen, of our union, the union paper.

Q. Do you make a regular practice of distributing that?

A. Yes. The men ask for it. They want it just the same as you want your daily paper. They want their West Coast Sailor every time they can get it.

(Testimony of William Gries.)

Q. How long, ordinarily, are you aboard ship, having specific reference now to tankers?

A. Well, to do my business, generally an hour, an hour and a half, two hours. And if there is any dispute, if there is a dispute it might be longer, see. Or maybe there's some of the gang that is missing. The agent will call me up and the ship is ready to go. I will come down there and check up with the boys and see if I can find out where he lives to get ahold of him.

Well, the time varies according to what is going on.

Q. You mentioned the agent. To whom do you refer as the agent? [133]

A. Well, the agent in this case on the tanker was Mr. Reeves, of the Associated Oil Company.

Trial Examiner Batten: You mean the representative of the company when you say "agent"?

The Witness: Yes, sir, the agent. That's right. He is called the agent in San Pedro with the Associated Oil Company.

Q. (By Mr. Moore). Mr. Gries, have you had any sailing experience aboard tankers?

A. Yes, sir. I sailed about 12 years altogether. I have got about four and a half of that time on tankers.

Q. How long ago was that?

A. Well, I just come off a tanker before I come on this job. From last October, 1941, until June, 1942, I was with the Union Oil Company and the Standard Oil Company on tankers exclusively.

(Testimony of William Gries.)

Q. Was that experience out of west coast ports?

A. Yes, for the Standard Oil Company of California and the Union Oil of California. I also sailed with Associated Oil Company out of California on their tankers and a couple of them back East.

Q. Do you recall any specific grievance among employees, unlicensed employees, aboard Richfield Oil Corporation tankers that has occurred since October, 1942? A. Well, yes.

Trial Examiner Batten: Well, now, just a moment. I don't [134] know that we want to go into this question of grievances against the Richfield Oil Company. What bearing would that have, particularly upon this issue?

Mr. Moore: To show the futility of attempts to settle those grievances by the procedure that was available.

Trial Examiner Batten: Well, if you want the witness to relate a specific instance of an attempt to adjust that matter——

Mr. Moore: That's what I was asking about.

Trial Examiner Batten: You may tell us.

The Witness: Well, it happened on one ship a couple of months ago. It didn't happen here in San Pedro, but it was referred to me in the office here. The port captain was here, and that's that one I had to go and see.

Mr. Moore: Just a moment. I can't quite hear you.

The Witness: The incident happened up in San

(Testimony of William Gries.)

Francisco. But the story was referred to me down here.

Q. (By Mr. Moore). By whom?

A. By the men that were involved. They were fired off the ship, see. And they came down here and told me the story, so that I could go to Richfield and see what could be done about it.

Q. What was the nature of that?

A. The case was that they had rotten chow on the ship, and a bunch of mess gear, as Mr. Lundeberg said before, was [135] all tin cans made up into eating utensils, you know.

Mr. Guntert: Mr. Examiner, I object to that.

Trial Examiner Batten: I don't think we are interested in going into the details of that.

The Witness: I see.

Trial Examiner Batten: The only purpose of the testimony, as I understand it, is to show the difficulty in attempting to adjust it off the ship. So you don't need to give us all the details.

The Witness: We took it up with the port captain out here.

Trial Examiner Batten: Just a moment.

Mr. Guntert: If this is a question of men being fired off the ship, they certainly wouldn't be on the ship to settle the dispute.

Trial Examiner Batten: Of course, the witness may tell us his effort to adjust the difficulty. But I don't care about all the details of what it was. I don't think that is material.

(Testimony of William Gries.)

The Witness: Well, I spoke to the port captain about it.

Q. (By Mr. Moore): Meaning whom, Mr. Gries? Mr. Wilder?

A. Captain Wilder, in one of our meetings we were negotiating.

Mr. Guntert: Could we have the date, please?

The Witness: *She* said it wasn't so. And that adjustment had been made. However, when I talked to some of the gang later on—I was on the ship again—they said there was the same thing going on. The captain told me that that condition [136] doesn't exist on the ship, see. I have to go there to see it. I saw some of the gear that the guys brought off and showed me.

Trial Examiner Batten: You mean you were not able to go on the ship?

The Witness: That's right.

Trial Examiner Batten: And verify the fact as to whether or not the men were telling you the truth?

The Witness: That's right.

Trial Examiner Batten: Is that right?

The Witness: That's right, sir.

Trial Examiner Batten: In other words, you had to rely upon the information the men gave you and upon the information that Captain Wilder gave you?

The Witness: Yes, sir.

(Testimony of William Gries.)

Trial Examiner Batten: But you were never able to see for yourself the situation? Is that what you mean?

The Witness: That's right, sir.

Mr. Guntert: Would you give me the date of that occurrence you were speaking of? Not the exact date but the approximate time?

The Witness: I would say it was around the middle of December.

Trial Examiner Batten: '42?

The Witness: Yes, sir, around the middle of December. [137]

Q. (By Mr. Moore). In your experience, Mr. Gries, about what percentage of the grievances that come up have been settled on the ship by you?

A. Oh, 90 per cent.

Q. How is that?

A. I would say 90 per cent or better.

Q. And with reference to the other 10 per cent, how are they handled?

A. Well, it was a case of having to take it up with the company, and the company had to go back to their board of directors to get the O. K. on it, or something, see. It was more or less something new that came up on the ship where the crew was too short, see, and they decided to put another man on the ship in lieu of paying the crew, that is, on their overtime. That was a matter that had to be taken up by the company to get other men on the ship.

(Testimony of William Gries.)

However, it's a beef that comes up quite often now.

Trial Examiner Batten: Well, you said "90 per cent." Do you mean by that that 90 per cent of these grievances or beefs you can settle between the skipper and the mate and the men?

The Witness: Yes, sir, right there.

Trial Examiner Batten: On the boat?

The Witness: That's right. It is mostly a matter of interpretation of the agreement. The mate interprets it one [138] way and the men interpret it another way. Some of the mates don't seem to use any intelligence. They interpret it their own style, not the style that has been worked all the time. And they suddenly get an idea that it should be worked this way, and I go down and tell them why it should be worked the other way. And he argues with me why he wants it changed. But I say, "Take it up with the ship owners. This is the way it should be worked."

We go to see the skipper, and the skipper says, "If that's the way it's supposed to be, that's the way it's supposed to be." It is clear in his own mind. And the mates and the skippers, they rely an awful lot on the patrolmen, see, who come down there to straighten out them kind of disputes. They figure he knows his business. That's what they do. They know what the score is without fooling around about it. He knows his navigation. I know my business.

Q. (By Mr. Moore). Mr. Gries, have you ever

(Testimony of William Gries.)

requested Richfield Oil Corporation to issue passes to the unions you represent for the purpose of boarding their tankers?

A. Yes, sir, I have, on numerous occasions.

Q. When was the first such occasion?

A. It was the first week in October. That was the first meeting I had with Mr. Lamb.

Q. Of what year?

A. 1942. Then I was out of town. We got about three meetings [139] in November, and at each meeting I made it a point to ask for passes. There were three more meetings in December, and finally here around the first week in January Mr. Lundeberg requested passes for us.

Q. When was the last occasion on which you requested passes?

A. The exact date I am not sure of. It was around the 4th or 5th or 6th, something like that, of January of this year.

Q. Who was present on that occasion?

A. Oh, I wasn't there myself. But Mr. Lundeberg was there. He asked Mr. Lamb, I guess.

Q. Has any representative of Richfield Oil Corporation ever told you that they would issue passes to your union, subject to any stated conditions?

A. Yes. Mr. Lamb promised me that as long as we went along with negotiations with our contract and he can show the board of directors that we were making progress and were acting in good faith and were negotiating, he felt that at the end

(Testimony of William Gries.)

of that time he might give us a pass. However, he didn't say that they definitely would.

Q. I believe you misunderstood my question. My question is this: Did the company ever offer to give you passes subject to certain stated conditions?

A. No, sir. Voluntarily you mean?

Q. Yes.

Trial Examiner Batten: In other words, did the company ever agree to give you passes if you agreed to do *something* [140]

The Witness: Oh, no, sir.

Mr. Moore: All right. No further questions.

Trial Examiner Batten: Mr. Guntert?

Mr. Guntert: Just one question.

Cross Examination

Q. (By Mr. Guntert) In the process of your duties as a patrolman, does that afford an opportunity of negotiating with seamen for membership in your union? A. Do I?

Q. Yes. A. Yes, I do.

Q. You do that on board ship?

A. No, not on board ship.

Trial Examiner Batten: The question was: Does it afford you an opportunity, not whether you do it, but whether does it give you an opportunity to do that?

The Witness: The men on board the ship are already organized.

Trial Examiner Batten: Well, supposing there were some men on the ship that were not mem-

(Testimony of William Gries.)

bers of the union and you had a pass to go on, the question is: Does the fact that you have a pass to go on the ship give you a chance, if you want to take the chance, of soliciting membership?

The Witness: Certainly. I have the opportunity.

Q. (By Mr. Guntert) Do you take advantage of the opportunity? [141]

A. No, I never have had to.

Q. You never have?

A. I never have had that opportunity.

Q. You have been talking about ships where you have passes, and I am speaking about ships where you have passes, too. Supposing you are on board ship with a pass; you are there collecting dues and taking care of the business. Do you not also take care of getting new members?

A. No.

Q. You never do? A. No.

Mr. Guntert: That is all.

Mr. Lundeberg: May I ask a question?

Trial Examiner Batten: Yes.

Q. (By Mr. Lundeberg) When you go on board a ship where you have passes, you already have an agreement with most of them and some of them you don't have, isn't it a fact, and that all hands is already organized in your union?

A. Those men already belong to the union, that's right.

Q. Would you waste any time in soliciting new members? A. No.

(Testimony of William Gries.)

Q. Doesn't the organization you represent take the members in in the office, not aboard the ship?

A. That's right.

Q. In other words, if they join the union, if they didn't [142] belong to the union, then they had to come up to the office to join the union and go through a certain procedure?

A. That's right.

Q. Don't they have to fill out an application blank in it? A. That's right.

Q. In the union office? A. That's right.

Mr. Lundeberg: That's all.

Trial Examiner Batten: Mr. Moore?

Mr. Moore: No questions.

Trial Examiner Batten: Mr. Guntert?

Mr. Guntert: No questions.

Trial Examiner Batten: That's all.

(Witness excused.) [143]

Mr. Moore: Now, with the exception of the two exhibits, the photostats which we expect to offer and perhaps some further evidence on the question of that statement of principles that Mr. Lundeberg has asked for, the Board's case is concluded.

Trial Examiner Batten: If that is the case, then, Mr. Guntert, do you have any witnesses that you want to offer, except Mr. Land, whom I requested you to bring down?

Mr. Guntert: I think not. But I would like to speak to the captain.

Trial Examiner Batten: Well, do you want to recess a few minutes?

Mr. Guntert: No, just one word.

(Brief pause in proceedings.)

Mr. Guntert: That is all I have.

Trial Examiner Batten: Well, then, Mr. Lundeberg, do you have something further?

Mr. Lundeberg: Yes. I would like to bring the fact to the Examiner here that Judge Hand, of the Circuit Court of Appeals——

Trial Examiner Batten: You mean in New York, the Second Circuit?

Mr. Lundeberg: Yes. He handed down the decision in July 25, 1941.

Trial Examiner Batten: What is the name of the case, Mr. [144] Lundeberg?

Mr. Lundeberg: Just a minute and I will find it here.

National Labor Relations Board vs. City Service Oil Company, National Maritime Union of North America, Intervenor, No. 340, Circuit Court of Appeals, Second Circuit, July 25, 1941.

He handed down the decision granting the passes to that particular union.

Trial Examiner Batten: Well, you may do that, Mr. Lundeberg, when the testimony is all in. If you want to make any further statement on it, I will ask any of you if you care to make a statement at that time.

Mr. Lundeberg: O.K.

Trial Examiner Batten: But I would prefer to

finish up the testimony first before we get into any argument you may have on it.

Well, if there is nothing further, then, except Mr. Lamb, I believe I requested you to have Mr. Lamb come down. Mr. Lamb, will you be sworn, please?

P. C. LAMB,

called as a witness by the Trial Examiner, having been first duly sworn, was examined and testified as follows:

Trial Examiner Batten: Now, I presume in view of the fact that I called Mr. Lamb I probably should start. However, would any of you prefer to start? [145]

Mr. Guntert: You may start.

Direct Examination

Q. (By Trial Examiner Batten) I asked Mr. Guntert to have you come down, Mr. Lamb, because Captain Wilder stated that you were the man or, I believe, Mr. Guntert or perhaps both, that you were the individual of the company who in the first instance issued the instruction or order or whatever it was, abolishing passes. Is that correct?

A. Well, the orders that Captain Wilder received, that is correct. I issued the orders to him.

Q. Now, how about prior to the time that Captain Wilder—as I understand it, Captain Wilder came here in October? A. Yes.

(Testimony of P. C. Lamb.)

Q. Now, weren't there some orders issued prior to that time? A. I don't know.

Q. At the time that the contract expired, or something, from that time on you have not issued any passes; have you? A. No.

Q. Well, now, was it your action at that time that discontinued passes?

A. The passes were discontinued. I may be a little hazy on dates. I haven't referred to the dates for some time. But it was about the time that the National Maritime Union filed a complaint with the Board of Unfair Labor Practice for our refusal to give them passes. [146]

Q. Well, at that time, whatever the time was, were you the official of the company who issued those instructions?

A. Well, I was manager of the marine department that issued those instructions to my department.

Q. Yes.

A. Captain Wilder is a part of that department.

Q. That's right. But he wasn't there then, was he? Captain Wilder?

A. No. Prior to that there was a vacancy in the position of port captain, but we had an organization.

Q. You had someone acting? A. Yes.

Q. And it was then that you as manager of the marine department decided that it was not advisable to hereafter issue passes, is that correct?

(Testimony of P. C. Lamb.)

A. Well, I wouldn't say that it was me. It was the company policy.

Q. The company policy?

A. The policy is not determined by me.

Q. And you, of course, the company having determined that, passed it on to those under your supervision? A. Put it in effect, yes.

Q. Is that correct? A. That is correct.

Q. Now, when you instructed Captain Wilder about it when he [147] took over the position, what did you tell him, if you recall?

A. Well, I think Captain Wilder, before he took over the position, was pretty familiar with that policy, having been master of one of our ships.

Q. Well, let's assume that he knew all about it. What did you tell him at the time he took over the job, if you told him anything?

A. I did tell him that after he took over the job and several times discussed the policy and the matter of issuing passes and that the company's policy was not to issue passes to anyone.

Q. To anyone?

A. Yes, to go aboard the ships.

Q. Now, were you in on the conference that helped determine the policy of the company to not issue passes?

A. Well, I would say that I discussed it with the executives of the company.

Q. Well, now, the policy to discontinue passes, if I understand it, and if I state it incorrectly, will you tell me, please—that policy was estab-

(Testimony of P. C. Lamb.)

lished before the issuance of any instructions? For instance, here is Security Order No. 1 of the War Shipping Administration, issued October 24, '42, and here is Order No. 2 issued on the same date. Now, the policy of the company to not issue passes, of course, was formulated prior to that time; is that correct? [148]

A. I would say it was about that time. We had a contract with the Sailors Union of the Pacific that expired February 15th, as I recall. Is that correct?

Mr. Guntert: That is the correct date, yes, sir.

The Witness: And up to that time we had passes outstanding to representatives of the Sailors Union of the Pacific and to other unions, the Marine Engineers Beneficial Association; and when this policy was determined those passes were cancelled and there were not other passes issued after that.

Q. (By Trial Examiner Batten) Well, now, in a letter of the company dated March 12, '42—I will show you the letter which is Respondent's Exhibit 5-D. You had already determined as a company policy on March 12, 1942 that you would not issue passes, had you not?

A. That is correct.

Q. Well, then, it is correct to say that several months prior to October the policy of the company had already been determined?

A. That is true.

Q. Is that right?

(Testimony of P. C. Lamb.)

A. That is correct. This is subsequent to that.

Q. Yes. A. To the date of the policy.

Q. Now, there is in evidence here Respondent's Exhibits 3 [149] and 4 being regulations for tank vessels and protection of waterfront petroleum terminals issued by the captain of the port, and it has been stipulated and agreed both of these were issued, as I recall it—when?

Mr. Guntert: In June, I believe.

Mr. Moore: June or September. I don't remember which.

Trial Examiner Batten: One was issued in June, '42, and one was issued in September, '42.

Q. (By Trial Examiner Batten) Now, would it be correct to say that the policy of the company not to give passes was established prior to June, '42? A. Yes, I would say it was.

Q. Well, then, would it be correct, Mr. Lamb, to say that the issuance of these regulations and instructions had nothing to do with the establishment of your policy to refuse passes to your vessels?

A. You have reference to the captain of the port regulations now?

Q. That's right.

A. I am not sure of the date. Mr. Moore said June. My impression was that these were issued in about January.

Q. Your lawyer agreed that those were issued in June or after. So my question to you is: Would it be correct to say that those had nothing to do

(Testimony of P. C. Lamb.)

with the determination of the company's policy not to issue passes? [150]

A. Not those particular orders.

Q. In other words, they couldn't have, could they? A. No.

Q. Because they were issued subsequent?

A. But there may have been conditions that this order was attempting to deal with that had been taken into consideration.

Q. Let's assume that the condition did exist. The fact still remains that you couldn't have used these instructions or orders as the basis of determining your policy?

A. No, not if they were issued in June.

Q. Because they weren't issued?

A. That is correct.

Q. Now, can you tell me, Mr. Lamb, why the company determined upon that policy? What was the reason for it?

A. Well, the reason I would say was primarily because of the war conditions, and I think the other reasons were probably contributing reasons, the demands that were made for passes by other unions that we had no contracts with and the threatening increase of that policy—or, not policy—but increase in the number of passes that would be outstanding.

Q. Well, had you had demands from other unions? A. Yes.

Q. For passes?

A. Requests for passes. [151]

Q. Requests for them? A. Yes.

(Testimony of P. C. Lamb.)

Q. As to other organizations, for instance, have they requested passes?

A. Well, the National Maritime Union had requested passes repeatedly, and the Masters, Mates and Pilots Association had requested passes. I remember those two distinctly. I think the Cooks and Stewards Union had requested passes.

Q. Now, during the time that you issued passes, when you had a contract you issued passes; did you?

A. To these unions that we had a contract with, an agreement.

Q. Yes. Now, during that time when you issued these passes under the contract, did you have any trouble with other unions insisting upon having passes?

A. Yes. We had requests intermittently all the time.

Q. I would presume you had requests. But did you have any particular difficulty with those requests? Did it cause you any trouble particularly?

A. Well, we had one of the requests that I believe was answered here in your Labor Board in a citation of unfair labor practice.

Q. But outside of that did you have any trouble?

A. Only the requests, the repetition of it.

Q. In other words, you wouldn't say that the fact that some union wrote you a letter requesting it, that that was trouble [152] particularly, would you?

A. No, I wouldn't call that trouble. We had telephone calls and we had visits from them; and,

(Testimony of P. C. Lamb.)

of course, it took a little time. But I wouldn't care to classify it as trouble really.

Q. Well, now, can you tell me any other reasons, Mr. Lamb, why the company determined upon this policy, if there were any?

A. I would say that in my judgment the primary objection to passes generally is a matter of safety and a matter of hazards.

Q. In other words, you think that is the important factor in the policy?

A. I think that is in normal times.

Q. Either normal or war times?

A. That hazard is aggravated in war times.

Q. Would you say, Mr. Lamb, the fact that some representative of a laundry comes down to deliver laundry and goes on your boat is less of a hazard than, we will say, a union official that has been approved by the Navy and the F.B.I.?

A. I certainly would not.

Q. In other words, certainly one wouldn't be any more obnoxious than the other, would they?

A. They certainly would not. I would say they could be termed equally, depending upon the period of time they spent [153] on the ship.

Q. That's right. So you would say, then, that this policy is based primarily upon the judgment of the company that for the safety of the vessel and to reduce the hazard you determined to discontinue passes, is that right?

A. That's right.

Trial Examiner Batten: I have no further questions. Mr. Moore, do you have any questions?

Mr. Moore: Just a moment, please.

Mr. Guntert: For the record, Mr. Examiner, I want to be sure that it was clear on one point. You were discussing the effect upon the determination of this company's policy by these orders which came out after the policy was established. We do not contend in any way that the policy was established by reason of those orders.

Our position is that those orders simply confirm the wisdom of that policy.

Trial Examiner Batten: Well, I understand that. In other words, you take the position that the company, having determined this policy, that the company's good judgment has since been verified by these governmental agencies; is that it?

Mr. Guntert: That is correct.

Trial Examiner Batten: Mr. Moore?

Q. (By Mr. Moore): I might ask one question. Do you know when the policy was first discussed among the company, the [154] policy against issuing passes, among the officials of the company?

A. No, I don't think I could answer very definitely, Mr. Moore, because it has been under discussion for years and it's always been predicated on the safety of the ship. We had, for instance, before we had even passes to any unions, before we had any contract with the Sailors Union of the Pacific—you spoke of laundry men boarding the vessel. We at one time gave passes in limited quantities to people of that description, cleaners who would come

(Testimony of P. C. Lamb.)

aboard to get the seamen's clothes for cleaning purposes. If we issued one, why, there was another one that felt that he was entitled to a pass.

We had that problem and that question of issuing passes before we had any union agreements.

Trial Examiner Batten: You probably had that on the first boat that you ever had, didn't you?

The Witness: Yes, before we had any requests from the unions for a pass. So it would be hard to say when that was discussed.

Trial Examiner Batten: Mr. Gunter, do you have any questions?

Mr. Gunter: No.

Trial Examiner Batten: Mr. Lundeberg?

Mr. Lundeberg: Yes. [155]

Q. (By Mr. Lundeberg): I would like to ask Mr. Lamb if he recalls how long since he had any requests from other unions to get passes from him?

A. I don't think we have had any requests since the N.M.U. filed their unfair labor practices charge.

Q. And that is over a year ago, isn't it?

A. Yes, I think so.

Mr. Guntert: That was in May, 1942.

Mr. Lundeberg: It was before May, 1942.

Trial Examiner Batten: The witness has said it was over a year ago.

Mr. Lundeberg: All right.

Q. (By Mr. Lundeberg): Do you recall around about the 16th of September that the Sailors Union of the Pacific and the Seafarers International En-

(Testimony of P. C. Lamb.)

gine Division was certified by this Board here as the collective bargaining agreement agency?

A. Yes, I know that.

Q. You have a copy of that?

A. I don't recall the date, but I know that certification was made.

Q. And we have called on you repeatedly to try to get passes? A. That is true.

Q. Has any other union tried to?

A. I don't recall any other requests we have had since that [156] certification.

Mr. Lundeberg: That's all.

Mr. Guntert: That's all.

Mr. Moore: That is all.

Trial Examiner Batten: That is all, Mr. Lamb, thank you.

(Witness excused.)

Trial Examiner Batten: Is there anything further, outside of the answers which will be brought in in the morning, I presume, Mr. Lundeberg?

Mr. Lundeberg: Why, I expect to have them here.

Trial Examiner Batten: By 10:00 o'clock?

Mr. Lundeberg: Yes. If there is no delay in the flights up and down the coast, they should be here.

Trial Examiner Batten: I presume we may adjourn until 10:00 o'clock in the morning. Let me ask you this——

Mr. Guntert: Pardon me, sir. May Mr. Lamb be excused?

Trial Examiner Batten: Yes.

May I ask you this: Do you men intend to take up some time in the oral argument in this matter?

Mr. Guntert: I had not planned to make any oral argument. I did plan on asking you to permit me to file a short brief.

Trial Examiner Batten: Let's see. How about you, Mr. Moore?

Mr. Moore: Unless you desire oral argument, I don't believe that I shall argue at all. [157]

Trial Examiner Batten: I don't know as I want oral argument, but I do want you all to do this much, and I wouldn't call it argument: I want you to each tell me why you think—you—why you think this is an unfair labor practice in your own words. In other words, you probably in your own mind have some sort of theory or idea about this. I want you to tell it to me.

Now, Mr. Guntert, you, in working up this matter, have come to the conclusion that it is not; and you have come to that conclusion because of certain things which you can tell me probably in five or ten minutes.

Now, Mr. Lundeberg, you, having worked at this business some probably have some ideas as to what you think about it. So you be prepared to take five or ten minutes and tell me what you think about it in the record.

Now, as to the briefs: Mr. Guntert, you have expressed the opinion that you want to file a brief. Mr. Moore, do you?

Mr. Moore: No, I don't believe that it will be necessary.

Trial Examiner Batten: Whether you want to or not, I might tell you that I expect one.

Mr. Moore: If you do that, sir, I will be happy to submit one.

Trial Examiner Batten: Let me tell what I mean about briefs. You don't have to follow my suggestions, but I will appreciate it if you do. I don't want a brief that [158] is made up of titles, subtitles, sub-sub-titles until there is no substance to the brief; it's just a lot of titles.

I would much prefer that you just sit down—and you don't even have to have the record, particularly—and dictate to a stenographer why you think I should decide that this is an unfair labor practice and you, Mr. Guntert, tell me your thoughts, mental processes, why you think it is not.

Do you see what I mean?

Now, I will read the record from cover to cover and the testimony. And you make the brief in any way you please. If you want to cite cases, if you want to go into the legal aspects of this, which I think are quite important in this case, you may do so.

Now, Mr. Lundeberg, if you want to do the same thing, I will be glad to have the same from you. You are not going to have much time, however, to do it.

Mr. Lundeberg: I already got my two pages.

Trial Examiner Batten: All right. It's along the same lines you suggested.

All right. You may hand it in here, then, when we finish and tell me about it tomorrow.

Mr. Lundeberg: All right.

Trial Examiner Batten: I would say five days

from the close of the hearing. In other words, tomorrow I will set the date. [159]

We will adjourn until 10:00 o'clock in the morning.

(Thereupon, at 4:32 o'clock p.m., Thursday, March 4, 1943, an adjournment was taken until 10:00 o'clock a.m., Friday, March 5, 1943.) [160]

Room 808, United States Post Office and Court House Building, Spring, Temple and Main Streets, Los Angeles, California, Friday, March 5, 1943.

The above entitled matter came on for hearing, pursuant to adjournment, at 10:00 o'clock a.m. [161]

PROCEEDINGS

Trial Examiner Batten: I think we will proceed. Mr. Lundeberg, do you have that copy of the directive you spoke of yesterday?

Mr. Lundeberg: Yes.

Mr. Moore: I have it here. I will ask that it be marked for identification as exhibit for the Board, next in order.

(The document referred was marked for identification as Board's Exhibit No. 7.)

Mr. Moore: May we introduce this by stipulation? It is a statement of policy, mimeographed by the War Shipping Administration and sent out by that administration to interested parties.

Mr. Guntert: Yes, if you will introduce that with it, the questions and answers. We received a copy of that and I checked it, and this was attached to it.

Mr. Moore: Referring to Board's Exhibit 7?

Mr. Guntert: Yes.

Mr. Moore: May we introduce this Board's Exhibit 7 for identification in evidence, then, with the understanding that that will also be included?

Mr. Guntert: Yes.

Mr. Moore: I offer Board's Exhibit 7 for identification, in evidence, then.

Trial Examiner Batten: There is no objection to it being [164] received? Do you have a duplicate of this?

Mr. Moore: No, sir.

Mr. Guntert: Last night I had a photostatic copy made.

Trial Examiner Batten: Did you?

Mr. Guntert: And if you care to use it——

Trial Examiner Batten: Why don't you have the photostat marked, then?

Mr. Lundeberg: Why don't you put them in together? They came out together?

Trial Examiner Batten: Do you have two copies of that we could use?

Mr. Guntert: Yes.

Trial Examiner Batten: If there is something else that goes with it it would be well to have them together.

Mr. Moore: Yes. May I withdraw the Board's Exhibit 7 that was introduced and have another document marked in its stead?

Trial Examiner Batten: Yes, have it marked the same number.

Mr. Moore: Board's Exhibit 7, yes. Probably we should mark it Board's Exhibit 7-A.

Trial Examiner Batten: And 7-B.

Mr. Moore: Yes, and the other document can be marked Board's Exhibit 7-B.

Trial Examiner Batten: Any objection to Board's Exhibits 7-A and 7-B being received in evidence? If not, they will [165] be received.

(The documents referred to were marked Board's Exhibits 7-A and 7-B and were received in evidence.)

BOARD'S EXHIBIT No. 7-A

(Pacific Coast Seamen, Firemen, and Cooks and Stewards—May 4, 1942.)

STATEMENT OF POLICY

I. Existing Collective Bargaining Agreements to Stand.

Article 3 (d) of the Service Agreement signed between Agents and the War Shipping Administration under which Agents handle vessels owned by or bareboat chartered to the War Shipping Administration shall remain in force and effect. This article reads as follows:

"(d) The General Agent shall procure the Master of the vessels operated hereunder, subject to the approval of the United States. The Master shall be an agent and employee of the United States, and shall have and exercise full

> control, responsibility and authority with respect to the navigation and management of the vessel. The General Agent shall procure and make available to the Master for engagement by him the officers and men required by him to fill the complement of the vessel. Such officers and men shall be procured by the General Agent through the usual channels and in accordance with the customary practices of commercial operators and upon the terms and conditions prevailing in the particular service or services in which the vessels are to be operated from time to time. The officers and members of the crew shall be subject only to the orders of the Master. All such persons shall be paid in the customary manner with funds provided by the United States hereunder."

The intention of this clause is that the General Agent will procure and make available to the Master for engagement by the Master, officers and men through the channels which the Agent has heretofore used for his own merchant ships. If the General Agent has contracts with unions and those contracts require for example preference of employment or use of union hiring halls, the Agent would be required to procure men in accordance with the contracts.

II. Wages and Working Conditions

Inasmuch as base wages, emergency wages, overtime rates, bonuses, war risk compensation, repatriation and allotment conditions have been generally equalized in East Coast, West Coast and Gulf

Collective Bargaining Agreements,, which agreements have established equitable practices and standards in manning the American Merchant Marine now necessary to furtherance of the war effort, it is therefore agreed that the existing Collective Bargaining Agreements be frozen for the duration of the war.

III. Discipline.

The conditions aboard ship, including common hazard and peril, in wartime require the highest standard of order and discipline. To accomplish this purpose, the unions agree to cooperate fully with the War Shipping Administration, as follows:

(1) Maintenance of the authority of the Master and of discipline including strict and prompt enforcement of laws relating to conduct aboard ship.

(2) Elimination of crews' mass meetings, crews' committees and other similar meetings or groups aboard ship. However, one man in each department will be recognized as the spokesman for that department, but all disputes shall be settled only upon termination of the voyage in port where shipping articles are closed.

(3) It is understood that all disputes will be settled through the regular machinery now in existence under the collective bargaining agreements between the unions and the steamship operators.

(4) Without waiving the right to strike, the unions hereby give firm assurance and guaran-

tee that the exercise of this right will be absolutely withheld for the duration of the war.

IV. Duration.

This Statement of Policy will remain in effect as long as the War Shipping Administration has jurisdiction of vessels of the American Merchant Marine.

(Sgd.) E. S. LAND,
(Sgd.) EDWARD MACAULEY,
For the War Shipping Administration.
(Sgd.) HARRY LUNDEBERG,
Secretary-Treasurer S. U. P., President S. I. U.
(Sgd.) JOHN HAWK,
Secretary-Treasurer Atlantic & Gulf District Seafarer's International Union.
(Sgd.) V. J. MALONE,
Secretary, Pacific Coast Marine Firemen, Oilers, Watertenders & Wipers Assn.
(Sgd.) JAMES W. BURKE,
Secretary, Marine Cooks & Stewards Assn.

Dated May 4, 1942
Washington, D. C.

BOARD'S EXHIBIT No. 7-B

War Shipping Administration
Washington

December 28, 1942

Operations Regulation No. 1
Supplement No. 5
Pertaining to
Vessels Owned by or Under Charter to
the War Shipping Administration

Subject: Policy With Respect to Seagoing Personnel—Clarification of Statement dated May 4, 1942.

The Statement of Policy dated May 4, 1942, signed by the Pacific Coast Marine Firemen, Oilers, Watertenders and Wipers Association, Marine Cooks and Stewards' Association, and the War Shipping Administration, has been clarified by the following answer given by Edward Macauley, Deputy Administrator, War Shipping Administration, to the question asked by the aforenamed Associations:

Question: With regard to the Statement of Policy, we would appreciate a letter of clarification in line with our discussions during negotiations on the Statement of Policy to the effect that the prohibition of mass meetings, etc., on ships is not intended to apply to ordinary "coffee sessions" in messrooms, or in fo'c'sles, but does apply to any stop-work meetings or mass meetings which are dangerous or inimical to the movement of the vessel.

Answer: As paragraph (1) in Section III under the heading "Discipline" indicates, it is considered sound policy under war conditions that the authority of the Master be strictly maintained. Paragraph 3 contemplates that no meetings be permitted aboard ship "where they tend in any way to interfere with the ship's operation"; and of this the Master must be the judge. If there may be some Masters who will abuse their discretion in this regard, it is thought better in view of war conditions to remedy abuses ashore rather than to have arguments and disputes aboard ship whether a given meeting "interferes with the ship's operation." Should any such abuses develop, the War Shipping Administration will remedy them.

All General Agents are instructed to follow this policy.

(Sgd.) J. E. CUSHING,
J. E. Cushing,
Assistant Deputy Administrator for Ship Operations.

Trial Examiner Batten: Anything further?

What is the status of those photostats, Mr. Moore, on that?

Mr. Moore: They will be ready in about five or

ten minutes, and I have left word to have them sent up here immediately.

Trial Examiner Batten: Well, do you want to recess five or ten minutes before you make the statements? Do you want to proceed with that?

Mr. Moore: I would prefer to recess.

Trial Examiner Batten: And you, Mr. Guntert?

Mr. Guntert: I have no choice.

Trial Examiner Batten: One minute before you go. My records do not indicate that Board's Exhibit 4 was offered and received. In case there is any question about it, it is the agreement of the Unions with the Tidewater Associated Oil. Do you attorneys have any notes to indicate whether it was offered or received? My recollection is that it was.

Mr. Moore: I believe it was, sir.

Trial Examiner Batten: In order to clarify the record Board's Exhibit 4 will be received, subject, of course, to the same objection which Respondent made as to the introduction of Board's Exhibit 3, in case there is any question about it, [166] and I will make the same ruling with regard to it.

(A brief recess was taken.)

Trial Examiner Batten: Are you ready to proceed?

Mr. Moore: I will ask that this photostat be marked Board's exhibit for identification next in order.

(The document referred to was marked as Board's Exhibit No. 8 for identification.)

Mr. Moore: And I will ask that this photostat,

which is attached to a sheet of paper for convenience be marked Board's Exhibit 9 for identification.

(The document referred to was marked as Board's Exhibit No. 9 for identification.)

Mr. Moore: Mr. Lundeberg, will you take the stand, please?

HARRY E. LUNDEBERG

called as a witness by and on behalf of the National Labor Relations Board, having been first duly sworn, was examined and testified as follows:

Direct Examination

Q. (By Mr. Moore) Mr. Lundeberg, I show you Board's Exhibit 8 for identification, and ask you if you can tell me what that photostat is a copy of?

A. That is a copy of the United States Coast Guard identification card, which gives me admission——

Mr. Guntert: I object to that last statement, I think that is self evident. [167]

Trial Examiner Batten: Of course he testified yesterday what it was for. The only question now is what is this.

Mr. Moore: I want to identify it.

Trial Examiner Batten: Is this the same card that you testified to yesterday which was issued to you by the Coast Guard, which has your finger-

(Testimony of Harry E. Lundeberg.)

print and picture on? And which was issued to you by the Coast Guard, is that right?

The Witness: Yes.

Mr. Moore: I will offer that exhibit in evidence.

Trial Examiner Batten: Is there any objection?

Mr. Guntert: No objection.

Trial Examiner Batten: It will be received.

(The document referred to heretofore marked Board's Exhibit No. 8 was received in evidence.)

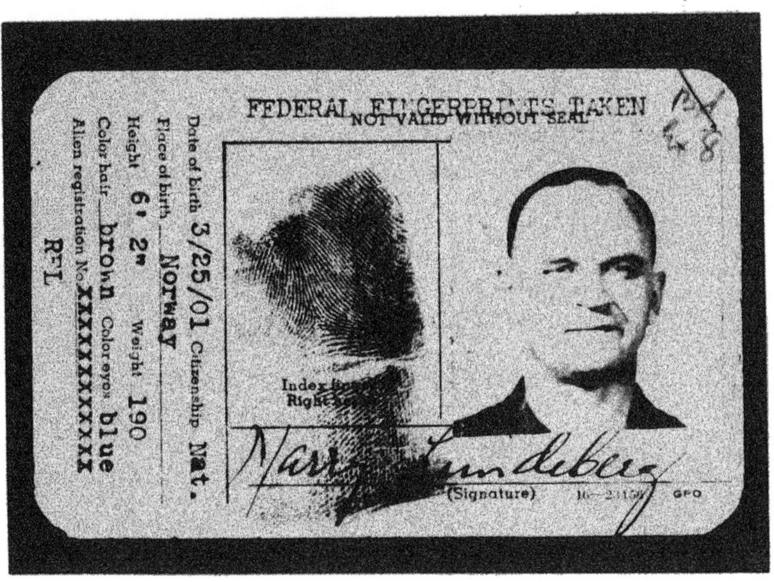

FEDERAL FINGERPRINTS TAKEN
NOT VALID WITHOUT SEAL

Date of birth 3/25/01 Citizenship Nat.
Place of birth Norway
Height 6' 2" Weight 190
Color hair brown Color eyes blue
Alien registration No. XXXXXXXXXXX
R-L

Index finger
Right hand

Harry Lundeberg
(Signature) 16—23150 GPO

NATIONAL LABOR RELATIONS BOARD

XXI-C-2248
CASE NO. 2249 BOARD PETITIONER RESPONDENT **EXHIBIT NO.** 8

IN THE MATTER OF Richfield Oil

3-4-43 WITNESS

ETHEL E. FISHER, OFFICIAL REPORTER

BY Dodge

(Testimony of Harry E. Lundeberg.)

Q. (By Mr. Moore) And I show you Board's Exhibit 9 for identification, and ask you if that is a photostat of the pass issued by the Navy Department, concerning which you testified yesterday?

A. That is right.

Trial Examiner Batten: I object to it being called a pass, it is a badge issued by the Navy District Officer, is that correct, Mr. Lundeberg?

A. Issued by the Commandant of the 12th Navy District of San Francisco, which is a pass, which takes me into any place——

Trial Examiner Batten: Whatever it is, so far as the [168] Navy is concerned, it permits you to go any place you want to go, is that it?

A. That is right.

Mr. Moore: I offer Board's Exhibit 9 in evidence.

Trial Examiner Batten: No objection?

It will be received.

(The document heretofore marked as Board's Exhibit No. 9 was received in evidence.)

NATIONAL LABOR RELATIONS BOARD

CASE NO. XXI-C-2248 2249 { BOARD PETITIONER RESPONDENT } EXHIBIT NO. 9

IN THE MATTER OF Richfield Oil

DATE 3-5-43 WITNESS

ETHEL E. FISHER, OFFICIAL REPORTER

BY Dodge

(Testimony of Harry E. Lundeberg.)

Trial Examiner Batten: Does that finish this?

Mr. Moore: I want to ask a few questions on an exhibit that was introduced this morning.

Q. (By Mr. Moore) Mr. Lundeberg, I will show you Board's Exhibit 7-B and direct your attention to the paragraph labelled "Answer." Will you look that over and familiarize yourself with it?

A. Yes.

Q. That paragraph refers to a meeting aboard ship and in quotation marks says "where they don't in any way cause interference with the ship's operation."

Do you know of any such meetings that were ever held on board ships on the Pacific Coast?

A. Yes, they held meetings here prior to this statement of policy when the contracts were frozen for the duration of the war. Prior to that some meetings were held by some unions once a week and it was definitely understood when we were back [169] in Washington that we ourselves went on record as being opposed to having meetings at sea, and we cancelled that. As a matter of fact, our own union never did go for meetings at sea, but there were other unions in the sea, other departments, who believed in meetings at sea—affiliations, and we relinquished that when we were back in Washington, D. C.; we never had any trouble about that.

Q. How recently in point of time have such meetings of the crews at sea been held?

A. In our organization we have no record of

(Testimony of Harry E. Lundeberg.)

that at all, because it is against the policy of the union.

Q. Are you familiar with the practice in that regard that has been followed by other unions?

A. Yes, some other unions.

Q. What type——

Trial Examiner Batten: How long did they discontinue, that is the question.

The Witness: They discontinued that May 4th.

Q. (By Mr. Moore) Of what year?

A. May 4th.

Q. May 4th, what date—what year? Oh, May 4th is the date on the statement of policy, as you understand? A. That is right.

Q. What type of meetings are you referring to that were held at sea? [170]

A. Well, these unions that held meetings that were supposed to hold the meetings to hear their grievances, and so forth, and open up any subjects which might pertain to the welfare of the crew. However, in some instances they develop into political rallies. That is one of the reasons we never did go for it.

Q. Were they meetings of union membership, or were they meetings with the officers of the ship?

A. No, it was meetings between—by the members on board the ship.

Q. Not meetings with the officers?

A. No officers at all. They kept the whole bunch together in certain departments, mainly amongst the steward department and especially on passen-

(Testimony of Harry E. Lundeberg.)

ger vessels, they used to have these meetings which didn't do anybody any good at no time, just put us on the spot, I think.

Q. To your knowledge are all shipping operators on the coast now under the jurisdiction of the War Shipping Administration?

A. To my knowledge all ships are—all deep water ships are—all shore vessels, all tankers, are, and all schooners except perhaps 12 lumber schooners which run between San Pedro, California, and Coos Bay, Oregon. All other American registered vessels was taken over on April 20, 1942, by an executive order of President Roosevelt.

Mr. Moore: No further questions. [171]

Trial Examiner Batten: That is all, Mr. Lundeberg.

Mr. Guntert: Are all these exhibits introduced in evidence?

Trial Examiner Batten: Yes, they have all been received. That is all, Mr. Lundeberg. Well, I think we are now ready to proceed with the statement I asked you to make on this matter. Mr. Moore, are you now ready to proceed?

Mr. Moore: Yes, sir.

Trial Examiner Batten: I would suggest that you do not go too fast.

Mr. Moore: The question to be decided in this case is a comparatively simple one. The facts are that the employees of the Richfield Oil Corporation through agents that they have selected, have requested their employer the right to have their representatives come aboard the ship, and assist them, and act for them in settling grievances that arise, and that their request, made through their authorized agents, has been unconditionally refused by the company. There is very little dispute on this subject. The question should be decided whether this refusal constitutes a violation of Section 8, subsection 1 of the National Labor Relations Act. In other words, does the refusal interfere with, restrain and coerce employees in their right to self-organization and to collective bargaining through agents of their own choosing.

In order to decide the question we will have to examine the collective bargaining processes. One phase of the process [172] is the negotiation of contracts, the overall contracts, and the evidence here shows that they are generally negotiated between a union and a large number of employees, so that the contracts are limited in the amount of specific detail that they can cover.

Now, of course, those contracts are negotiated on behalf of the union by agents selected by the employees, and generally there is no occasion for the employees to take any active part in that. There is another phase of the collective bargaining procedure which is, according to the testimony here, extremely important, and that is the settlement of grievances. Grievances concern conditions under which seamen must work, and they are therefore subjects of collective bargaining under the Act.

And these grievances that arise may arise through differences of interpreting contracts, or through some adverse condition, or some supposed adverse condition, that arises despite the existence of a contract.

The grievances that arise affect the individual seamen very directly, and it certainly is not a sufficient answer to him to say, "You have a contract." If there is a condition that he believes is inimical to his working conditions he wants that particular problem settled, and he wants it settled sensibly—in time.

We should also explore the methods that are available to the [173] seamen for the settlement of their grievances that arise. It may be said, and there has been some indication here, that seamen might go ashore, and they might go to their union officers and contact their elective representatives, and tell them what the grievance is, and let them handle it from there on.

The evidence shows, however, that *the cause* of the locations of the union officers, for one thing, that in many instances this can't be done. It is too much of a trip in the limited time that the seaman has ashore, to go to union headquarters, and to spend the time that would be necessary there in explaining his grievance, and in remaining there until all questions that the union representatives might have have been answered.

Then, too, as soon as the agent, the employee's agent, the employee of the union learns what the grievance is in the union office, if he is not permitted to go aboard the ship, there is only about one thing he can do, and that is to telephone the shore representative of the company. I think it is fair to say that if he did that, the shore representative would not know anything about the grievance. He would say he would have to investigate it, and he would probably contact the union representative later on. Investigation might take a day, and then he might call back and say the seaman is all wrong. The condition doesn't exist, he might say, everything is [174] fine, and everything going along as it should be. Of course, by that time the ship will be out of the harbor and the union representative would have no come back, he wouldn't know, he hadn't been aboard the ship, and he hadn't seen for himself—he is dealing with hearsay, and he just can't put up a forceful argument on hearsay.

There is one other consideration in this matter of asking seamen to leave the ship and go to union headquarters, and that is that minor grievances of seamen in all probability simply wouldn't be settled that way. The reason for that is not hard to find. A man may be working at sea, with a grievance which is not too bad, but which makes him dissatisfied. Nevertheless, when he comes to port he has perhaps eight hours during which he has to clean up, eat his meals, and go ashore to do whatever he may want to do. Now, it would take a seaman with a very peculiar twist of his mind, I think, to spend that entire leave out, as he probably would have to do, in getting that minor grievance settled up. It is very likely that he would go ahead and just depend on working under the grievance, or he might quit the ship rather than take the time and go through the trouble that is necessary to get the argument settled.

Mr. Wilder testified that the turnover on these tankers was large, and he was not asked the reasons for it, but it may very well be that that is a reason; I think it is fair to [175] say it has a bearing on the question, at any rate.

And despite all that there is testimony here by Mr. Lundeberg, who I think is as competent as any man on the west coast to express an opinion on the matter, that that system just won't work. And I will say that business agents, being human beings, would probably be the first to recognize that the system would work if it were effective, because if they could do their work efficiently and well, and represent their men, who are paying them, properly, by sitting in their offices waiting for business to come to them, I think they would do that. But they have had time to find out that that is not the practice, and the testimony is that it won't work.

It has been said also that seamen when they come to shore when the ship docks, might contact their union representative on the dock. That the union representative might come to the dock and remain outside on the dock and see the men as they come off the ship. That also has some very serious drawbacks. The men don't all get off at once. At least a third of them, and if there is any extra work to do, more, have to stay on the ship at all times. The union representative would have to interview the men singly if a grievance came to his attention. He would not be able to interview other seamen to see whether or not it was well founded. He would not be able to inspect the ship, and when finally he did come around to negotiating with the shore representatives out of the company, [176] he would run into the same difficulties that he would where the seamen contacted him in the office. He would be told purely from hearsay. His aggrieved seaman would have had to return to the ship and possibly the ship would have been gone and the grievance would be carried over until the next trip in.

I spoke of the port Captain, or shore representative of the company, who, if the business agent would have happened to contact in a situation like that, would have to make an inspection or an investigation before he could discuss the grievance—naturally, he would have to. The seaman, knowing that the company sent a man aboard to inspect the conditions would be very dissatisfied if he did not have the same privilege at having a man inspect the ship in his behalf, if in the final outcome the grievance were not settled.

Now, this dissatisfaction may be of no concern to the Respondent. However, it is one of the reasons why seamen have united and formed and joined unions in order to gain the advantage of the cooperative actions.

There is one other possible way in which an aggrieved seaman might possibly have a grievance adjusted. The union might appoint a ship delegate —as a matter of fact, they ordinarily do. I think the average ship appoints a ship's delegate, and it might be argued that the ship's delegate is perfectly capable of taking up grievances of the crew with [177] the officers and settling such of those as can be settled. I believe the answer to that can be found largely in the nature of the seamen's relation to their master or a captain. The captain aboard a ship at sea, and very largely in port, is the law. There is no dispute with that, and it should be—discipline should be strict. The point is to expect a man who has been subject to that strict discipline for long periods to become more normal and to cross an imaginary line which bounds the port, to become then an independent and forceful and collective bargaining agent, is just expecting results that are not in human nature.

The testimony here shows that the seamen want and they need an experienced collective bargaining agent who is *not the* employ of the ship owner and who is experienced in the ways of collective bargaining. And the employees have chosen and selected men just like that. They request that their representatives have sea experience—a substantial amount of it. And their representatives are trained in the process of collective bargaining.

The method of adjusting grievances as shown by the evidence here that is used almost 100 per cent on this coast, and is used on the Gulf and the east coast also, involves the boarding of the vessels by a patrolman or a shore delegate of the particular union which represents the men aboard the ship. Upon boarding the ship the patrolman may go to the [178] crews' quarters and talk to the men, and see if there are any grievances. He distributes newspapers to them so they may know what others with whom they have joined a union membership are doing—if he receives grievances, that is, if he receives from employees whom he represents allegations that there are adverse working conditions on the ship, he can go and inspect the ship, and with his wide knowledge of conditions as they should be, can recognize whether or not the conditions complained of are really adverse, or simply an unjustified complaint. He can also interview fellow seamen. He gets the story not only from one, but from all of the seamen who are involved in the particular instance. There is no interference with the operation of the ship, as the evidence shows here.

One patrolman testified, Mr. Gries, and he stated that if it became necessary to talk to a man about a grievance, who was on duty at the time, another man who is not on duty was sent to relieve that man and to take his work over while the discussions were on, and he further stated that there has never been any complaint by any ship owner about that procedure so far as he knows.

The testimony further showed that about 90 per cent of the grievances that are settled are settled aboard the ship by the patrolman on his visit to the ship, and if it were otherwise I think it is fair to say that probably 90 per cent [179] of the grievances that arise would never be settled, and the 10 per cent that were settled by the shore method would be slowly and very unsatisfactorily settled.

I believe that is enough as to the actual operation of the grievances procedure.

The necessity for this boarding of ships by patrolmen elected by the employees on those ships, I think, is very clearly reflected in the practice here on the Pacific Coast to grant access to those patrolmen. The testimony shows that it is almost a universal practice on this coast to grant access to these union representatives. Only two or three small companies do not grant access; all the others do, and have for a considerable period. And it is not only done, the evidence shows as a matter of collective bargaining contracts, passes also are granted by a substantial number of operators using contracts containing no provisions in themselves for passes. And these operators who duly grant passes to the union operator are on all types of ships, carry all types of cargo, and in the present war emergency, who carry the high explosive supplies for the armed forces, supplies that have to get through expeditiously, and supplies that are very dangerous, very subject to explosion in case of any carelessness.

Now, if this practice on the Pacific Coast is standard practice—and on the Gulf and the Atlantic Coast too, for that [180] matter—should we not conclude here that as a matter of moral obligation the Richfield Oil Corporation ought to go along with the majority? It was not for that purpose at all. It was simply to show what, over a period of years, the employees, the seamen in the industry, have considered necessary as a part of their collective bargaining procedure, and what the ship operators have recognized that they are entitled to, that is necessary for their exercise of their right to collective bargaining.

I will mention briefly the reason, or some of the reasons, at least, which have come out herein for the companies not granting these passes for union representatives——

Trial Examiner Batten: You have now taken about 20 minutes—I suggested 5 or 10, I think.

Mr. Moore: I haven't been looking at the clock. It has taken longer than I intended it to.

Trial Examiner Batten: But, of course, I don't want to stop you.

Mr. Moore: Well, the main reason that the company has expressed—at least in testimony, for not granting these passes, is that hazards are thereby increased, but despite that you have had instances of laundrymen going on board ship; they have permitted work parties aboard, and various officials of the company also board the ship quite regularly. Now, I don't propose to accuse the officials of the company of being [181] potential sabotage men, but nevertheless I think they will admit that they are just as subject to being careless at times as anyone else, and the evidence also shows that Richfield trembles, practically alone, in the face of this danger. No one else has mentioned it.

They also introduce evidence that a prior case has been decided in their favor. In the first place, I think the evidence shows that the case is not in point, that it was not a case in which there was a certified collective bargaining agent involved, as there was in this case, and in the second place the evidence on which the case turned is not here. And further I think that their position, depending upon this previous case, is somewhat inconsistent with their further assertion that if they are compelled to grant passes to the complaining unions here, they will have to grant passes to anyone who says he is a union organizer. Their policy with reference to not granting passes was established before the case ever came before the Regional Office, and they have not changed their policy. They have done nothing by way of reliance on that decision, so I don't believe they could argue that the Board has estopped itself from proceeding in this case.

I have nothing further to say. In conclusion I will simply say that employees have shown by universal practice on this coast that they unite to get the specific benefits involved in this action, and I think that the denial of those [182] rights to them is a violation of Section A, Subsection 1, of the Act.

Trial Examiner Batten: Mr. Guntert.

Mr. Guntert: There are several predominant circumstances which must be given full consideration: first, we are at war; second, there is a critical tanker shortage, and there is a critical shortage of competent seaman. The best way to combat these shortages is to prevent further loss and the best way to prevent loss is to prevent the hazards to which they are exposed, and it is incumbent upon all of us to do all in our power to bring those hazards to an irreducible minimum.

The loading and discharging of petroleum products is, under the most favorable of peacetime conditions, a hazardous operation requiring the utmost attention to the job at hand and the strictest observation of safety rules. In war time those hazards are greatly increased, and in addition there are the hazards of sabotage and destruction from enemy action made possible or facilitated by the leading out of information as to cargoes, departures, arrivals, courses, escort vessels, convoys, armament, names of vessels, and the like.

These hazards are increased in direct ratio to the number of persons having access to vessels—the more persons going aboard, the greater the likelihood of careless acts, distraction, sabotage, or leaking out of information valuable to the enemy. Therefore the presence of persons aboard ship must be [183] limited to those whose presence aboard is absolutely necessary. What reasons may be deemed to be absolutely necessary, is a matter which must be judged in the light of war conditions and the hazards incident to the handling of highly inflammable petroleum products in bulk on board ship.

In its solemn judgment, with a full realization of its responsibility to the Nation, and the seamen as well, this Respondent considers the issuance of passes to any one not in its employ, a real and highly unnecessary hazard, and accordingly took steps to eliminate that hazard, and the evidence shows that the policy of denying, for the duration of the war, any and all requests for ship passes, was put into effect as the then existing contracts with labor organizations would permit. The evidence further shows that this policy was motivated by security and safety reasons, namely, to bring to an irreducible minimum the exposure of vessels and personnel and cargoes to unnecessary and unreasonable hazards.

As a result of this policy, a complaint was filed before the Director of this Region by the National Maritime Union but upon the showing of this Respondent that it carried out that policy without discrimination, he declined to issue a complaint and upon appeal to the National Labor Relations Board the Regional Director was sustained, this decision being handed down in May of 1942. [184]

The complaint herein raises the identical issue and alleges that this same policy constitutes an unfair labor practice, and so the issue here, as at that time in the other case, is whether this Respondent's refusal, without discrimination, to give access to its tank vessels during the remaining period of the war, is an unfair labor practice.

The evidence in support of the complaint does no more than establish that the complaining unions want passes to facilitate the handling of their union business and including the collection of dues. Admittedly it is more convenient and effective for delegates and union representatives to be on hand to catch the sailors before they can get ashore on leave. It is claimed that it is necessary to go aboard ship to settle grievances. Experience, however, has shown that if a sailor really has a grievance, he will find his way to the union hall readily enough and when called to the attention of the employer the matter can be and usually is readily settled. With the great turn-over in ship personnel, it is almost self-evident that the principal concern of the union is the retention of membership and the collection of dues, rather than grievances.

A large part of the testimony of the union representatives constituted an interesting though wholly immaterial recitation of practices by the complaining unions under existing contracts with dry cargo ship operators. Presumably this was [185] for the purpose of attempting to show that these union representatives had access to hundreds of ships and that a fortiori the access should be given to respondent's ships, just as freely. There can be no comparison and the fallacy of such reasoning should be apparent. What acts would be reasonable and prudent practice on board dry cargo vessels might be the grossest of negligence on board a tanker.

Practically all of the evidence in support of the complaint may be summed up by saying that because these unions under their various contracts, the great majority of which are with dry cargo ship operators, permit them free access to such vessels and greatly facilitate the handling of the union's business including the collection of dues, they should have free access to the vessels of this respondent; and therefore the policy of this respondent is an unfair labor practice even though not one scintilla of evidence indicates any discriminatory treatment nor anti-labor act or motive.

On the contrary, the evidence shows that not only is respondent's policy sound, but is commendable, especially in time of war and its wisdom is confirmed by the Security Orders of the War Shipping Administration.

This is a matter of extreme importance, not only to this respondent, but to the Nation at large in the prosecution of this war, and we are weighing, on the one hand, the [186] hazards to extremely valuable tank vessels, their personnel and cargoes, and on the other, the mere inconvenience of representatives of the complaining unions in the conduct of their business. It is submitted that if there be any doubt whatsoever, the same should be resolved in favor of safeguarding the safety of these critical tankers and the lives of our seamen. One vessel saved is worth a thousand times the inconvenience experienced by the complaining unions. One life saved is worth a thousand times the dues that union patrolmen can collect, for the duration of the war. The time to save these vessels and lives is not after a casualty, but before disaster strikes, and the most efficient way to prevent loss is to prevent exposure to hazards.

It is for these reasons that the complaint herein should be dismissed.

Trial Examiner Batten: Anything further?

Mr. Lundeberg: Well, Mr. Examiner, I haven't

got any of this written up in all that shape. I will have to talk straight to you and give you my arguments the way I see them.

After listening to the company's representatives the attorney here, why we shouldn't have the passes to board vessels our reasons are: No. 1, the Wagner Act protects us. The law of the land states specifically that we are entitled to same. Furthermore, Judge Hand on July 25, 1941, Judge Augustus M. Hand, of the United States Circuit Court of Appeals, [187] of the Second Circuit, case of National Labor Relations Board, petitioner, vs. City Service Oil Company and Pure Oil Company and the Texas Company—Judge Hand gave a decision in this case. And in this decision by Judge Hand he upheld the Wagner Act, and ordered all companies to issue passes to the union involved. That is one of our reasons.

The other reason why the union should have passes to contact the members aboard the ship is that grievances can only be settled properly by direct contact in checking up all conditions on the vessel, and the seamen themselves, if they take up the grievance directly with the captain on board of a ship are subject to be fired and we have hundreds of cases on the Pacific Coast, or any other coast, where if a union man takes up a grievance and insists upon his rights then he is subject to be fired, and it has been done time and again. So the only protection a union seaman has is to call upon his own chosen representatives who are also seamen, and can act freely. These men can act freely because the company can't fire them.

Now, from the practical experience anyone who knows steamboating and knows shipping knows well that if you want to adjust a dispute involving a seaman and a ship you have to be on the ground and check up what is going on and see for yourself. And that has been accepted by all the ship operators on the Pacific Coast with the exception of three oil [188] companies on the Pacific Coast.

We have been granted passes and have had them for a number of years prior to the war, during the war, and at the present time, by all the major steamship companies on the Pacific Coast who carry as valuable and dangerous cargo as any oil tanker company does. When I say valuable, I say the ship carries 5,000 soldiers, and that is more important and valuable than 60 and 70 thousand barrels of black oil. And when a ship is loaded with the hold full of torpedoes for submarine stations in the South Pacific, and the union representatives can go aboard the ship, I say that is as important and as dangerous as any cargo of gasoline and oil.

Now, the statement of the company that they should be an exception because they are oil tankers, that doesn't hold water. Due to the fact that our organization was certified by the National Labor Relations Board as a collective bargaining agency for another oil company on the Pacific Coast, namely the Hillcone Steamship Company. We were certified in this particular company one month after we were certified for Richfield, and this company granted us passes to our representatives in every port on the Pacific Coast, and also on portions of the Gulf Coast where the vessel contacts.

Furthermore, in another election we won last year in the Tidewater Associated Oil Company, which is also a Pacific Coast tanker company, we have also received passes for our represen- [189] tatives on a coastwise scale in every port. They carried the same kind of freight as the Richfield Oil Company, namely, black oil, gasoline and fluid cargo. There is nothing mysterious about that regardless of what the company's representative wants to make an impression about.

Another question was brought up by the company's representative dealing with the possibility of sabotage and that union representatives could convey vital information regarding movements of vessels. Of course, I don't know if the company expects us to take that seriously, or whether it is a little propaganda. Anyone who is familiar with the operations of vessels today knows that no one knows where a vessel is destined for, when they leave any shore in any waters of the United States. The only one who knows that is the convoy or the naval commander in the respective ports, and the skipper on board the vessel does not know where. He leaves before he gets the sea route from the Navy Commander. So how can a union representative find it out?

Another statement made by the company's witness, Captain Wilder, that if a union representative came aboard and found out what kind of cargo the vessel was loading, he then might determine where the ship was going to, and thus implicating that he might sabotage the war effort by conveying the information that so and so vessel was bound for so and so place because he had seen that black oil went into the hold of the [190] vessel, or gasoline. That argument is so childish, we won't even answer it. Because black oil and gasoline goes to every port, from the Pacific Coast through the South Pacific waters—it goes all over the world. Now, the statement of Captain Wilder and the eminent attorney for the company to the effect that they don't want anyone, outsiders, to get aboard a vessel in port doesn't hold water for another reason. Captain Wilder stated on the stand here that they engage work parties. The work parties they engage they work in some of these tankers in port, and they are not by any stretch of the imagination employees, steady employees of the company. They are people picked up for a day or two's work. They might work for the company once in the year. They might be, a seaman who is on the beach waiting for a ship, or they may be anyone who is open on the labor market for a job. There is laundry agents coming aboard the ships, collecting laundry, delivering laundry. There is tailors coming aboard the ships peddling their wares with the approval of the company. Now, those people are not employees of the companies by any stretch of the imagination.

So because of that sabotage and endangering the war efforts in our opinion, is not a fact.

We further want to prove that the War Shipping Administrator, the very man who is in charge of all American ships, Admiral Land, and who, by the way, is in charge of these various companies at the present time, he is in absolute agreement with [191] keeping prevailing practices of labor relation conditions, and so forth, upheld for the duration of the war. They know that we have passes to go aboard the ships. They underwrote an agreement which guaranteed us our collective bargaining agreements for the duration of the war, and in those agreements there was a clause giving the union representatives their rights to contact, to board any vessels.

Now, we feel that the labor union has as much interest in the war effort as any company or any employer, barring none, and we feel that the labor unions have done their share in arguing it every day towards winning the war, and we have so been told time and again by various governmental authorities. And when you look at the casualty list of merchant seamen, and see how many has been killed during this war, I believe that is the answer, it answers it well enough.

The representative of the Richfield Company states that there is a terrific turnover in the shipping industry—in the hiring of men. Sure, there is a terrific turnover in all these companies, the three of them on the Pacific Coast who have no union agreement, and who have no protection for the men. And if anyone took it upon themselves to check up on the turnover in Richfield, they will probably find they have about 50 per cent more turn-over than the union agreement ships on the coast here. And the reason for that is because they deny the right to the seamen to get shipping agreements and have their [192] representative deal for their grievances for them.

Now, our organization ships handles approximately 1800 to 2000 seamen every month on the Pacific Coast. They are shipped out from our union halls, and ship aboard the ships, and all these ships carry supplies to the armed forces, and yet had it not been for the unions being in existence with well established machinery to handle the labor problems the American Merchant Marine after the war started would have been in a sad shape to talk, for the reason that there is no agency established capable of handling the shipping problem so far as seamen are concerned outside of unions. Which has also been acknowledged by Admiral Land.

Now, when a company comes in who has six tank vessels and starts to wave the flag and say that their policy is the only policy, and that they have the only right solutions for the labor problem, and when their policy differs entirely from about 500 American ships on the Pacific Coast, we wonder if they are here in good faith. As a matter of fact, we know they are not. This company has given us a constant headache for years, together with the Standard Oil of California. They have

a break up the unions, and this is one of their ways of doing it.

We hope that we will receive the passes so that we can protect these men aboard the ships, and that is about all we have got to say, your Honor. [193]

Trial Examiner Batten: Well, now, I think you all understand you have five days in which to file the memorandum brief; that is, five days after today, and those may be sent to the Trial Examiner, attention of the Chief Trial Examiner, in Washington, D. C.

Mr. Moore: You do not want them here?

Trial Examiner Batten: No, because I don't know that I will be here—in other words, if they are postmarked by midnight five days after today that will be sufficient.

Mr. Moore: Thursday?

Trial Examiner Batten: Now, as I said I don't want to be formalized too much, but what I am interested in is the substance of the thing, and not the titles, and so forth.

Mr. Moore: May I have that address again?

Trial Examiner Batten: You just send it to the National Labor Relations Board, Washington, D. C., attention of the Chief Trial Examiner. Addressed to me, James C. Batten, Trial Examiner, care of the Chief Trial Examiner.

Well, I don't believe there is anything further. Mr. Lundeberg, do you intend to present a memoranda of some sort?

Mr. Lundeberg: I had a little one here, and

then I think so far as I am concerned that is all we are going to present.

Trial Examiner Batten: Of course, if you now have it you may give it to me. And you have more than one copy? [194]

Mr. Lundeberg: Yes.

Trial Examiner Batten: I want more than one because I have to see they are placed in the files. If you give me two then I can give the other counsel one. I want to say this: I am not going to follow the practice of exchanging briefs—there is no reason—first one opens and then the other replies, and so on—I am not going to follow that practice here.

Mr. Moore: Before we close, I would like to move to conform the printing to the proof informal matters, such as dates or names.

Trial Examiner Batten: Is there any objection to that, Mr. Guntert? As to the minor details, typographical errors, dates—— It is not for the purpose of enlarging upon the issues, or changing the issues in any way. That will apply only to the printing—if there is no objection the motion will be allowed.

If there is nothing further the hearing is closed.

Mr. Moore: Mr. Examiner, how many copies should be sent?

Trial Examiner Batten: I would say at least two, preferably three. Two is enough, but three is better. I will see that they are placed in the various files.

(Whereupon, at 12:05 o'clock p.m. Friday, March 5, 1943, the hearing in the above-entitled matter was closed.) [195]

In the United States Circuit Court of Appeals
For the Ninth Circuit

RICHFIELD OIL CORPORATION,
Petitioner,

vs.

NATIONAL LABOR RELATIONS BOARD,
Respondent.

CERTIFICATE OF THE NATIONAL LABOR RELATIONS BOARD

The National Labor Relations Board, by its Chief of the Order Section, duly authorized by Section 1 of Article VI, Rules and Regulations of the National Labor Relations Board—Series 2, as amended, hereby certifies that the documents annexed hereto constitute a full and accurate transcript of the entire record in a consolidated proceeding had before said Board entitled, "In the Matter of Richfield Oil Corporation and Sailors Union of the Pacific, A.F.L., and In the Matter of Richfield Oil Corporation and Pacific Dist. Seafarers' Intl. Engine Division, affil. Seafarers' International Union of North America, A.F.L.," the same being Cases Nos. C-2568 and 2569, before said Board, such transcript including the pleadings, testimony and evidence upon which the order of the Board in said proceeding was entered, and including also the findings and order of the Board.

Fully enumerated, said documents attached hereto are as follows:

(1) Stenographic transcript of testimony held before James C. Batten, Trial Examiner for the National Labor Relations Board, on March 4 and 5, 1943, together with all exhibits introduced in evidence.

(2) Copy of Trial Examiner Batten's Intermediate Report, dated March 27, 1943.

(3) Copy of order transferring case to the National Labor Relations Board, dated March 31, 1943.

(4) Copy of petitioner's exceptions to the Intermediate Report, dated April 9, 1943.

(5) Copy of Decision and Order issued by the National Labor Relations Board, May 8, 1943, with Intermediate Report annexed, together with affidavit of service thereof.

In Testimony Whereof the Chief of the Order Section of the National Labor Relations Board, being thereunto duly authorized as aforesaid, has hereunto set his hand and affixed the seal of the National Labor Relations Board in the city of Washington, District of Columbia, this 5th day of June 1943.

[Seal] JOHN E. LAWYER
Chief, Order Section
National Labor Relations
Board

[Endorsed]: No. 10437. United States Circuit Court of Appeals for the Ninth Circuit. Richfield Oil Corporation, a corporation, Petitioner, vs. National Labor Relations Board, Respondent. Transcript of Record. Upon Petition for Review and for Enforcement of an Order of the National Labor Relations Board.

Filed June 10, 1943.

PAUL P. O'BRIEN,
Clerk of the United States Circuit Court of Appeals for the Ninth Circuit.

In the United States Circuit Court of Appeals
In and for the Ninth Circuit

No. 10437

RICHFIELD OIL CORPORATION, a corporation,
Petitioner,

vs.

NATIONAL LABOR RELATIONS BOARD,
Respondent.

PETITIONER'S STATEMENT OF THE POINTS UPON WHICH PETITIONER INTENDS TO RELY AND DESIGNATION OF PARTS OF THE RECORD PURSUANT TO RULE 19

STATEMENT OF POINTS

Richfield Oil Corporation, petitioner herein, hereby states the points upon which it intends to rely in its petition for review:

1. The National Labor Relations Board erred, as a matter of law, by not finding and concluding that the subject matter of the complaint was outside of and beyond its jurisdiction and power.

2. The National Labor Relations Board erred, as a matter of law, in not finding and concluding that the question of whether or not passes should be issued is a matter about which there should be collective bargaining between the employer and the representatives of its employees.

3. The National Labor Relations Board erred, as a matter of law, in ascribing to unions certified as collective bargaining representatives, functions and duties neither conferred nor required by the National Labor Relations Act.

4. The National Labor Relations Board erred, as a matter of law, by injecting itself into the collective bargaining procedure between your petitioner and its employees, thereby assuming functions neither required nor permitted by the National Labor Relations Act.

5. The National Labor Relations Board erred, as a matter of law, by substituting its judgment for the judgment of the employer concerning the terms and conditions of a contract between the employer and its employees, contrary to the intent and purpose of the National Labor Relations Act.

6. The National Labor Relations Board erred, as a matter of law, in finding and concluding that petitioner's refusal to grant passes without discrimination interfered with, restrained, and coerced its employees in the exercise of rights guaranteed

by Section 7 of the National Labor Relations Act and therefore constituted a violation of Section 8 (1) of said Act.

7. The National Labor Relations Board erred, as a matter of law, in finding and concluding that your petitioner:

> "by not permitting access to the Unions' representatives to aid the unlicensed deck and engine personnel at their request, is exercising, 'domination and control' over the efforts of these seamen to engage in 'mutual aid and protection' thereby infringing upon Section 8 (1) of the Act."

8. The National Labor Relations Board erred, as a matter of law, in finding and concluding that:

> "the denial of right of access to respondent's tankers, by the chosen representatives of the unlicensed deck and engine personnel prevents these seamen from exercising their rights to collective bargaining and to other mutual aid or protection."

9. The National Labor Relations Board erred, as a matter of law, in finding and concluding that:

> "the refusal of respondent to issue passes to the duly authorized representatives of its unlicensed deck and engine personnel for the purpose of access, prevents these seamen from receiving aid, advice, and information through their duly chosen representatives;"

10. The National Labor Relations Board erred, as a matter of law, in finding and concluding that:

> "The term 'access' in the shipping industry means the boarding of vessels by union representatives, in order to ascertain whether or not seamen on board have grievances, to determine the validity of the alleged grievances, and to settle those possible of settlement with the proper officials on board the vessels."

11. The National Labor Relations Board erred, as a matter of law, in finding and concluding that "access" is necessary under war time conditions, or otherwise.

12. The National Labor Relations Board erred, as a matter of law, in basing its findings and conclusions upon an assumption that "access" is guaranteed by the National Labor Relations Act for the purpose of settling grievances, collecting dues, distributing papers, or for any other purpose.

13. There is no substantial evidence in the record to support the National Labor Relation Board's findings and conclusions that your petitioner, by refusing to accede to the demands of the complaining unions for passes, or by any other means, interfered with, restrained and coerced its employees in the exercise of any or all of the rights guaranteed by Section 7 of the National Labor Relations Act, and therefore engaged in unfair labor practices within the meaning of Section 8 (1) of said Act.

14. There is no substantial evidence in the record to support the National Labor Relation Board's findings and conclusions that the conten-

tions of your petitioner were without merit and were not valid reasons for denying "access", but on the contrary, the uncontradicted evidence clearly shows that your petitioner had valid and impelling reasons for refusing to issue passes.

15. The National Labor Relations Board erred, as a matter of law, in finding and concluding that the passes demanded by the unions are necessary for the purpose of settling grievances, collecting dues, distributing trade papers, or for any other purpose.

16. There is no substantial evidence in the record to support the National Labor Relations Board's findings and conclusions that passes are necessary for the purpose of settling grievances, collecting dues, distributing trade papers and for other purposes.

17. The National Labor Relations Board erred, as a matter of law, in finding and concluding that the complaining unions were the exclusive representatives of your petitioner's employees without limiting such finding as to exclusive representation to the purposes for which such representatives were chosen, namley, collective bargaining.

18. The National Labor Relations Board erred in appraising the weight of evidence upon the issue of whether passes should be granted in the light of its mistaken belief that the National Labor Relations Act requires your petitioner to agree to any particular term or condition of employment demanded by the collective bargaining representatives of its employees.

19. The National Labor Relations Board erred in appraising the weight of evidence upon the issue of whether passes should be granted in the light of its mistaken belief that the National Labor Relations Act grants to collective bargaining representatives unrestricted access to your petitioner's vessels without its consent and against its wishes.

20. The National Labor Relations Board erred in appraising the weight of evidence upon the issue of whether passes should be granted in the light of its mistaken belief that the National Labor Relations Act delegates to unions certified as collective bargaining representatives of your petitioner's employees, duties and functions in addition to and beyond that of collective bargaining agencies.

21. The National Labor Relations Board erred, as a matter of law, in directing your petitioner to cease and desist and to take affirmative action as specified in the Board's Decision and Order and to post notices to such effect.

22. Even if the National Labor Relations Board had power to direct your petitioner to cease and desist from refusing to grant passes, the Board erred, as a matter of law, in directing the issuance of passes without any limitations or restrictions.

23. Even if the National Labor Relations Board had jurisdiction and power to order your petitioner to cease and desist from refusing to grant passes, the Board erred, as a matter of law, in directing petitioner to cease and desist as specified in paragraph 1 (b) of the Board's Order.

24. Even if the National Labor Relations Board

had jurisdiction and power to order your petitioner to cease and desist from refusing to grant passes, the Board erred, as a matter of law, in directing petitioner to take affirmative action as specified in paragraph 2 (a) of the Board's Order.

25. The National Labor Relations Board erred as a matter of law, in concluding that all or any part of the decision in NLRB vs. Cities Service Oil Co., 122 F. (2d) 149, (C.C.A. 2) is controlling herein.

DESIGNATION OF PARTS OF THE RECORD

Petitioner hereby designates the parts of the record which it deems necessary for the consideration of the aforesaid points, as follows:

The entire record of the proceedings before the Trial Examiner, and before the National Labor Relations Board, including the brief of respondent filed in support of its exceptions to the Intermediate Report.

Dated: June 19, 1943.

Respectfully submitted
DAVID GUNTERT
Attorney for Petitioner

[Endorsed]: Filed June 23, 1943. Paul P. O'Brien, Clerk.

TOPICAL INDEX.

TABLE OF AUTHORITIES CITED.

CASES. PAGE

PAGE

PAGE

INDEX TO APPENDIX.

No. 10437

IN THE

United States Circuit Court of Appeals

FOR THE NINTH CIRCUIT

Richfield Oil Corporation,

Petitioner,

vs.

National Labor Relations Board,

Respondent.

BRIEF FOR THE RICHFIELD OIL CORPORATION, PETITIONER.

Jurisdiction.

This case is before the court upon petition of Richfield Oil Corporation, a Delaware corporation, pursuant to Section 10 (f) of the Act of Congress of July 5, 1935 (49 Stat. 449, c-362 – 29 USC 151 *et seq.*) known and cited as the National Labor Relations Act, (hereinafter referred to as the "Act"), to review and set aside an order issued by the National Labor Relations Board (hereinafter referred to as the "Board") under Section 10 (c) of the Act.

The jurisdiction of the court is based on Section 10 (f) of the Act, which provides that any person aggrieved by a final order of the Board may obtain a review thereof in any Circuit Court of Appeals of the United States in the circuit wherein the unfair labor practice was alleged to have been engaged in, or wherein said person resides or transacts business.

Your petitioner is aggrieved by a final order of the Board issued on May 8, 1943 [R. 61-63]. Your petitioner is, and at all times mentioned in said petition has been, a corporation organized and existing under and by virtue of the laws of the State of Delaware, having its home office and principal place of business in the City of Los Angeles, State of California [R. 9; R. 16; R. 27] within the jurisdiction of this court, and it is alleged in the Board's complaint that your petitioner has engaged in an unfair labor practice within the State of California and within the jurisdiction of this court [R. 11; R. 66-67].

Statement of the Case.

The Questions to Be Decided.

This court is being asked in this case to decide whether the Act gives to the Board the power and jurisdiction to deprive an employer of the right (if not the duty) to bargain collectively with the chosen representatives of its employees concerning wages, hours and working conditions affecting such employees by:

1. Injecting itself into the negotiations being carried on in good faith by such employer and the collective bargaining representatives of its employees;

2. Substituting its judgment for that of the employer;

3. Ordering the inclusion in the contract being negotiated of specific provisions, and

4. Enforcing compliance with its will by issuing a blanket injunction against violating any of the provisions of the Act.

The principal reason asserted by the Board for issuing its order is to give union representatives "access" to your petitioner's vessels for the purpose of "collective bargaining" on board such vessels—all this before there is a contract and when there is no one on board your petitioner's vessels who has authority to engage in collective bargaining on behalf of your petitioner.

This court is also being asked in this case to decide whether the Board can, by its own *quasi*-judicial fiat, amend the Act so that the Act will confer upon the complaining unions new and novel rights and privileges neither conferred nor permitted under the Act as enacted by Congress and interpreted by the courts.

Circumstances Immediately Preceding Board Action.

Your petitioner was bargaining with the Sailors' Union of the Pacific and Seafarers' International Union of North American (hereinafter referred to as "complaining unions") for the purpose of entering into a written contract covering wages, hours and working conditions of the unlicensed deck department and unlicensed engine department personnel employed by your petitioner on its tank vessels. These negotiations had progressed steadily and satisfactorily to the point where but two important provisions in the contract remained unsettled, namely, the provision concerning a closed shop (the so-called "preferential hiring" clause) and a provision concerning the issuance of passes to union representatives.

The parties could not agree concerning these two points and thus a dispute existed which should have been settled by having them certified to the National War Labor Board pursuant to the procedure established by the President's Executive Order 9017 of January 12, 1942.

The Proceedings Before the Board.

At this stage of the collective bargaining and while negotiations were still going on, the complaining unions filed charges under the Act and the Board issued its complaint alleging that your petitioner's refusal to issue passes constituted a violation of Section 8 (1) of the Act. On this bare issue ,namely, whether the failure of your petitioner to agree to the inclusion in the contract then being negotiated of a provision concerning the issuance of passes to representatives of the complaining unions so that they could go on board your petitioner's vessels was an unfair labor practice, a very brief hearing was held and the Board made findings and conclusions which not only went far beyond and outside of the issue raised by the complaint, but which in fact were not supported by substantial evidence. (A summary of the oral testimony appears herein as Part A in the Appendix. A summary of the exhibits introduced appears herein as Part B of the Appendix.) Upon such findings and conclusions the Board entered an all-inclusive order which was not only a blanket injunction against violating the Act but required the issuance of passes without restriction as to number or safeguards of any kind and went still further and ordered your petitioner to publicly admit violations of virtually every provision of the Act, when only a single violation was charged and no violation was proved. (Full text of the Board's order appears herein as Part C of the Appendix.)

Specification of Errors.

[NOTE: The errors herein specified are contained in Specification of Errors in our Petition for Review [R. 83-87] but have been rearranged here to present them, as nearly as possible, in the order in which argument will be presented.

We will indicate the number of each specification appearing in the Petition for Review, as well as the page in the Record where the same appear.]

The petitioner contends that the National Labor Relations Board erred in the following respects:

1. The Board Erred in Not Finding and Concluding That the Subject Matter of the Complaint Was Outside of and Beyond the Jurisdiction and Power of the Board [Spec. 4, R. 84-86, Point I of Argument].

In this connection the Board erred specifically:

(a) In failing to find and conclude that the question of whether passes should be issued is a matter to be determined by collective bargaining [Spec. 4(a) – R. 85], or, should collective bargaining fail, to be determined under the provisions of Executive Order 9017, of January 12, 1942 [Spec. 3(b) and Spec. 3(c) – R. 84];

(b) In issuing an order which provides specific terms and conditions of employment [Spec. 3(a) – R. 83; Spec. 3(d) –R. 84; and Spec. 4(b) – R. 85];

(c) In ascribing to representatives of unions that have been certified as collective bargaining representatives, duties and functions neither conferred nor permitted by the Act [Spec. 7, R. 86];

(d) In substituting its judgment for the judgment of the employer concerning matters about which there should be collective bargaining between the employer and the bargaining representatives of its employees [Spec. 4(b) – R. 85].

2. Even if the Board Did Have Jurisdiction Over and Power to Consider the Subject Matter of the Complaint Under Some Circumstances, the Board Erred in Not Applying Applicable Principles of Law to the Facts in This Case [Spec. 7, R. 86; Points I and IV of Argument].

In this connection the Board erred specifically:

(a) In going beyond the power and jurisdiction conferred upon it by the Act as interpreted by the several courts of the United States [Spec. 4(c), 4(d) and 4(e), R. 85; Spec. 10, R. 87];

(b) In finding and concluding that the failure to issue passes to union representatives is an unfair labor practice, within the meaning of the Act [Spec. 6, R. 86];

(c) In finding and concluding that your petitioner by not issuing passes was exercising "domination and control" over the efforts of its employees to engage in "mutual aid and protection" [Spec. 9, R. 87];

(d) In finding and concluding that because other ship owners have granted passes to union representatives that passes are necessary to the enjoyment by employees of benefits conferred upon employees under Section 7 of the Act, and that your petitioner's refusal to issue passes interferes with, restrains and coerces employees in the exercise of such rights [Spec. 8, R. 86].

3. Even if the Board Were Acting Within Its Power and Jurisdiction, and Even if Its Findings and Conclusions Were Supported by Substantial Evidence, the Board's Order Is, Nevertheless, Too Broad, and Therefore Invalid (Point II of Argument).

In this connection the Board erred specifically:

(a) By issuing an order as contained in paragraphs 1 (a) and 2 (a) of the Board's Order [R. 61] without any limitation whatsoever as to the number of passes to be issued, and without affording the employer any protection whatsoever as to the manner of use [Spec. 4(c) and 4(d), R. 85; Spec. 7, R. 86];

(b) By issuing an order as contained in paragraph 1(b) of the Board's Order [R. 62] which, in effect, is a blanket injunction against violating the Act [Spec. 4(d) and 4(e), R. 85];

(c) By issuing an order as contained in paragraph 2(b) of the Board's Order [R. 62] which, in effect, requires your petitioner to publicly admit the commission of violations of the Act of which it was never charged, and concerning which no evidence was introduced to show such violations, or from which such violations could be inferred [Spec. 4(d), 4(e), R. 85].

4. Even if the Board Did Have Jurisdiction Under Certain Circumstances and Had Properly Applied Governing Principles of Law in All Other Respects, the Board, Nevertheless, Erred in That Its Findings and Conclusions, Upon Which the Board's Order Is Predicated, Are Not Supported by Substantial Evidence, and the Evidence Affords No Reasonable Basis Therefor [Spec. 1 and 2, R. 83; Spec. 5, R. 86; Point III of Argument].

SUMMARY OF ARGUMENT.

POINT I.

The Subject Matter of the Complaint Is Outside of and Beyond the Jurisdiction of the Board.

Your petitioner contends that the question of whether or not passes should be issued for the purpose of settling grievances, collecting dues, distributing papers, or for any other reason, or for no reason at all, is solely a question involving terms and conditions of employment to be included or excluded from the contract as the parties may agree. This question, therefore, is a matter about which there should be collective bargaining, and in the event the parties cannot agree and a dispute results, such dispute should be settled pursuant to the provisions of Executive Order 9017, of January 12, 1942 (which is just exactly what happened in this case.)

There has been no charge or proof of a failure to bargain collectively in good faith; of any discrimination whatsoever; or of any improper motive or intent. The *only* charge is that your petitioner refused to issue passes and that it, therefore, was guilty of an unfair labor practice. The sole issue, therefore, is whether it is a violation of the Act for your petitioner in the course of collective bargaining to resist the demands of the complaining unions that a certain clause be included in the contract then being negotiated.

It is your petitioner's contention that the Act does not require any particular term or condition of employment; that the Act does not require your petitioner to agree to any particular term or condition of employment demanded by the complaining unions, so long as it bargains in good faith concerning the same; that the Board cannot inject itself into the collective bargaining procedure and substitute its judgment for the judgment of the employer concerning the terms and conditions of employment; that the Board cannot destroy your petitioner's right and duty to bargain collectively as required by the Act; that Section 9(a) of the Act does not give selected representatives the exclusive right to settle grievances for employees or the exclusive right to determine how grievances will be settled.

That as will more fully appear in a complete discussion of this point, the Board is ascribing novel functions and duties to unions certified as collective bargaining representatives, which functions and duties are neither conferred nor permitted by the Act.

Your petitioner also contends that in other respects the Board has failed to apply the principles of law which are controlling in this case.

POINT II.

The Board's Order Is Too Broad, and Therefore Contrary to Law.

It is your petitioner's contention that, assuming the Board in all other respects had issued a valid order, and that it had power and jurisdiction to order your petitioner to cease and desist from refusing to issue passes, its order is, nevertheless, invalid because it is so broad and unlimitetd in its scope that it is, in fact, a blanket injunction against violating the Act.

In addition to the foregoing, it is our contention that paragraph 2(b) of the order is invalid because it requires your petitioner to publicly admit violations of the Act of which it was neither charged nor proven guilty. As we have previously pointed out, there is a sole and single issue which is, in fact, a question of law. No other charges were made, and no proof was introduced to prove any other acts, or from which any other acts could be inferred.

POINT III.

The Findings, Conclusions and Order of the Board Are Not Supported by Substantial Evidence.

We contend that the Board's Order is invalid because it is not supported by substantial evidence, and moreover, there is nothing in the evidence providing a reasonable basis for the Board's Order.

We contend that the refusal to issue passes is not an unfair labor practice simply because the unions want the passes to facilitate their business and because union representatives have concluded that grievances cannot be adequately settled without passes. The Board suggests that the only way shown in which grievances can be settled is through the use of passes and indicates that the burden is upon the employer to point out another way [Footnote 15, R. 38]. Apparently the Board is unaware of the reservation in Section 9(a) of the Act, which not only reserves to employees the right to take up grievances directly with the employer but places a duty upon the employer to provide an adequate means of handling grievances. See the opinion of this court in *NLRB v. North American Avia-*

tion, Inc., Case No. 10313, June 24, 1943, 136 Fed. (2d) 898. The Board quite evidently completely disregards the complete and speedy grievance procedure contained in Board's Exhibits 2 (rejected), 3 and 4, which do not contemplate the use of passes.

We think the motive and purpose of the employer in refusing to issue passes is controlling on the question of whether the refusal is an unfair labor practice. Of course, if the intent and purpose of the employer in refusing to issue passes was to interfere with, restrain and coerce its employees in the exercise of rights guaranteed to them under the Act, and its refusal actually did interefere with, restrain and coerce the employees in some right conferred by the Act, the Board would have the power to order the employer to cease and desist from refusing to issue passes just as the Board could order the employer to cease and desist from discriminating against employees for union affiliation, or order the employer to reinstate an employee discharged from union activity, *but in this case there has been no charge or proof of any such intent or purpose.* On the contrary, the only evidence on the point is that the employer adopted the policy of refusing to issue passes to better safeguard its vessels, their crews and cargoes under wartime conditions [Testimony of Mr. Wilder, R. 127, 135, 171; Testimony of Mr. Lamb, R. 386, 390]. The employer introduced documentary evidence to show the reasonableness of such policy [WSA Security Order No. 1, R. 137; WSA Security Order No. 2, R. 138; Wartime Tanker Regulations, R. 152; Wartime Terminal Regulations, R. 156; see also Board's Exhibit No. 7-A, R. 398; and Board's Exhibit No. 7-B, R. 402].

Under the circumstances, we contend that the employer is free to adopt this policy just as the employer would be free to discharge a man "because he has red hair, black hair, or no hair" [to adopt the language of the Trial Examiner, R. 327] without violating the Act unless such policy or discharge results from the employer's intent and purpose to interfere with, restrain and coerce its employees.

POINT IV.

The Cities Service Case, 122 Fed. (2d) 149, C. C. A. 2, Relied Upon Heavily by the Board, Is Not Controlling.

It will be noted that throughout the Intermediate Report the Trial Examiner has continuously referred to the *Cities Service* case; in fact, he has quoted at length therefrom. It is also apparent from the Intermediate Report that the Trial Examiner has made a studied effort to have his findings of fact and conclusions of law in most respects identical with those in the *Cities Service* case.

We contend that the *Cities Service* case was incorrectly decided, and further, that even if there were some merit in that decision at the time it was rendered, the basis therefor no longer exists and, if there is any question about its controlling, the same should be overruled.

ARGUMENT.

POINT I.

The Subject Matter of the Complaint Is Outside of and Beyond the Power and Jurisdiction of the Board.

As to the Subject Matter of the Complaint.

The pleadings frame the issue and the issue thus framed must control the result in a proceeding. The complaint alleges [R. 11] and your petitioner admits [R. 17] that it has refused to accede to the demands of the complaining unions for passes to permit union representatives to go aboard your petitioner's vessels. The complaint alleges [R. 11] but your petitioner denies [R. 17] that such refusal interferes with, restrains and coerces your petitioner's employees in the exercise of rights guaranteed by Section 7 of the Act.

No other charge is contained in the complaint. Therefore, no other issue exists. Under the circumstances there is no question of any discrimination on the part of your petitioner. There is no question as to whether or not your petitioner had been bargaining in good faith. If there were any such question, the evidence clearly shows [Board's Exhibit 5, R. 335-338] that your petitioner had been bargaining in good faith. There is no question of the motive or intent on the part of your petitioner in refusing to issue passes. Indeed, if there were any such question, the evidence clearly shows [R. 127, 151, 153] that your petitioner's refusal was for the sole purpose of better safeguarding its vessels, their crews and cargoes in furtherance of the war effort, which certainly could not be considered an unfair labor practice.

At the time charges were filed, your petitoner was negotiating a contract with the complaining unions through the procedure established by the Act, namely, through collective bargaining. The negotiations had progressed steadily and satisfactorily and to the point where but two principal issues remained unsettled, namely, the question of whether the contract should contain a closed shop provision and whether or not the contract should contain a pass provision. The parties could not agree upon this and a dispute resulted subject to being settled through the procedure established by the President's Executive Order 9017 of January 12, 1942.

It is obvious, therefore, that the subject matter of the complaint is but a single issue, namely, whether as a matter of law your petitioner's refusal to accede to the union's demand that the contract provide for the issuance of passes interferes with, restrains and coerces your petitioner's employees in the exercise of rights guaranteed them in section 7 of the Act, *when such refusal is without discrimination, and it is neither charged nor even attempted to be proved that there was any anti-labor purpose or motive behind the refusal or that your petitioner had not at all times carried on negotiations in good faith.*

As to the Power and Jurisdiction of the Board.

The power and jurisdiction conferred upon the Board and invoked in this case is found in Section 10 (a) of the Act which provides that "The Board is empowered, * * * to prevent any person from engaging in any unfair labor practice (listed in Section 8) * * *." [See Part D of Appendix for complete text of Sections 7, 8, 9 and 10.] The remaining subsections of Section 10 provide the mechanics or procedure for carrying out the Board's power and are not pertinent here except that it should be noted that under subsection (c) the Board is required to dismiss a complaint where it is found that an unfair labor practice was not committed.

The bare allegation in the complaint is that your petitioner's refusal to issue passes interferes with, restrains and coerces its employees "in the exercise of rights guaranteed in Section 7." Admittedly, if your petitioner was performing an act (which it ordinarily would have the right to do) with the intent and purpose of interfering with, restraining and coercing its employees in some right which *they* possess under the Act, the Board would have jurisdiction and power to prevent it, but the complaint does not charge any such intent or purpose.

It is important, therefore, that we determine just what are the requirements of the Act to see what duties it imposes upon the employer and to see just what rights have been conferred upon the employees and the complaining unions by the Act.

As to the Requirements of the Act.

The Act does not require that your petitioner issue passes against its better judgment or its wishes for it is well settled that the Act does not compel an agreement between the employer and the bargaining agents of its employes concerning any particular term or condition of employment. Indeed, it does not compel any agreement whatsoever. See *NLRB v. Jones & Laughlin Steel Corporation,* 301 U. S. 1, 57 S. Ct. 615, 81 L. ed. 893, 108 A. L.

R. 1352 (1937), wherein the Court stated, beginning on page 45:

> "The Act does not compel agreements between employers and employees. It does not compel any agreement whatever. It does not prevent the employer 'from refusing to make a collective contract and hiring individuals on whatever terms' the employer 'may by unilateral action determine' * * *. The Act does not interfere with the normal exercise of the right of the employer to select its employees or to discharge them. The employer may not, under cover of that right, intimidate or coerce its employees with respect to their self-organization and representation, and, on the other hand the Board is not entitled to make its authority a pretext for interference with the right of discharge when that right is exercised for other reasons than such intimidation and coercion * * *."

This court in its decision in *NLRB v. Union Pacific Stages, Inc.*, 99 Fed. (2d) 153 (C. C. A. 9), 1938, followed the above quoted section in the *Jones & Laughlin Steel Corporation* case.

See also:

NLRB v. Biles Coleman Lumber Co., C. C. A. 9, 98 Fed. (2d) 18, 22;

NLRB v. P. Lorillard Co., C. C. A. 6, 117 Fed. (2d) 921, 923, 924;

NLRB v. Boss Mfg. Co., C. C. A. 7, 118 Fed. (2d) 187, 189.

The Board is a public agency created to administer the Act and it is not a tribunal created for the purpose of enforcing claimed private rights by means of administrative remedies, and the unlawful labor practices against which the Board may issue a cease and desist order under the Act are strictly limited to those enumerated in Section 8 of the Act.

See:

Amalgamated Utility Workers v. Consolidated Edison Co., 309 U. S. 261; 84 L. ed. 738; 60 S. Ct. Rep. 561;

Phelps Dodge Corp. v. NLRB, 313 U. S. 177; 85 L. ed. 1271; 61 S. Ct. 845; 133 A. L. R. 1217.

Now it is well settled that an employer may hire or discharge an employee for any reason not proscribed by Section 8 of the Act.*NLRB v. Jones & Laughlin Steel Corporation, supra.* Even the Trial Examiner agrees with that proposition for he stated [R. 327] that: "you can fire a man because he has red hair, black hair, or no hair." The only question is whether the hiring or discharging was for a reason or purpose proscribed by the Act. This same principle applies equally to other terms or conditons of employment and it has been expressly so held. (*Singer Mfg. Co. v. NLRB,* 119 Fed. (2d) 131 (C. C. A. 7) Mar. 21, 1941 (Cert. den. 313 U. S. 595); 85 L. ed. 1549; 61 S. Ct. 1119; rehearing denied 314 U. S. 708; 86 L. ed. 565; 62 S. Ct. 55.)

In the *Singer Mfg. Co.* case, *supra,* at page 136, the court held that the refusal of the employer to agree to Article III (concerning hours), Article V and Article VI (concerning grievances, strikes and lockouts), and Article VII (concerning the term of the agreement), as well as other provisions, was not in violation of the Act because the employer did not agree to them, but the employer had violated the Act because he had failed to bargain in good faith concerning them. On page 138, the court said:

> "Obviously petitioner was not bound to accept any particular provision. *The only question is as to whether its resistance was bona fide*" (Emphasis ours.)

See also:

Cupples Co. Mfgs. v. NLRB, 106 Fed. (2d) 100 (C. C. A. 8) (1939);

American Smelting & Ref. Co. v. NLRB, 126 Fed. (2d) 680 (C. C. A. 8), Mar. 12, 1942.

In the case now before this court, the complaining unions and the petitioner had reached substantial agreement concerning hours of work, grievance procedure, payment of overtime in port, payment of overtime for handling lines on the dock, the amount and quality of table service and bed linen which petitioner was to furnish its employees, and many other matters. The parties had not agreed on two matters, namely, the question of passes and the question of a closed shop. The complaining unions were not content to permit settlement of these two disputes through the procedure set up under the President's Executive Order 9017, but, while negotiations were still in progress, filed charges with the Board alleging that your petitioner's refusal to issue passes was an unfair labor practice. Upon such charges the Board issued its complaint *but did not allege any failure to bargain or in any way raise the question of whether your petitioner's resistance was bona fide.*

The complaint was on the theory that the bare refusal in and of itself was an unfair labor practice. As was clearly stated in the *Singer* case, your petitioner had a perfect right to resist the inclusion in the contract of a pass provision and the only question should have been whether your petitioner's resistance was *bona fide*. That question is not raised by the complaint and the Board made no attempt to prove that point.

Indeed, the only evidence on the point sustains your petitioner's contentions and is specifically to the effect that the sole reason for refusing to issue passes was to better safeguard the vessels, their crews and cargoes under wartime conditions.

By its action in this case, the Board has injected itself into the collective bargaining procedure; it has substituted its judgment for that of your petitioner, and is granting to union representatives "access" to your petitioner's vessels for the purpose of "collective bargaining" on board such vessels when the contract was being negotiated ashore and when there is no one on board such vessels who has authority to negotiate on behalf of your petitioner. The Board is holding that the Act confers upon bargaining agents the right and privilege of deciding how grievances shall be settled, how, in fact, and where "collective bargaining" shall be conducted, and what terms and conditions of employment your petitioner must agree to. Moreover, the Board is lending itself and its processes to the complaining unions for the purpose of enforcing these claimed private rights by means of administrative remedies. These things the courts will not permit the Board to do.

Amalgamated Utility Workers v. Consolidated Edison Co., supra;

N. L. R. B. v. Jones & Laughlin Steel Corporation, supra;

N. L. R. B. v. Union Pacific States, supra;

Singer Mfg. Co. v. NLRB, supra.

As to the Rights Conferred by the Act.

So that there may be no doubt that this pass issue is a dispute over a term or condition of employment and not an unfair labor practice, let us examine carefully the rights guaranteed under section 7 which reads as follows:

> "Sec. 7. Employees shall have the right to self-organization, to form, join, or assist labor organizations, to bargain collectively through representatives of their own choosing, and to engage in concerted activities, for the purpose of collective bargaining or other mutual aid or protection."

These rights are divided into three general categories—first, the employees have the right "to self-organization, to form, joint, or assist labor organizations." Clearly, the rights falling in this category are not involved in the action now before the Court. The employees have joined the complaining unions, the complaining unions have been certified as collective bargaining agencies, and your petitioner has been negotiating with them in good faith. Furthermore, the Board has expressly held in its decision and order that passes need not be issued for the purpose of solicitation of membership, and the Board has not ordered the issuance of passes on the theory of any assistance to the labor organizations.

Second, employees have the right "to bargain collectively through representatives of their own choosing." In relation to the employees' rights in this category, the complaining unions have been certified as bargaining agencies, and your petitioner has been bargaining in good faith with the complaining unions.

The bargaining agent's first duty is to negotiate an agreement with the employer on behalf of the employee and *until that is done, it has no other duty and it has no other functions conferred by the Act.* Until an agreement is reached, there are no "grievances" but only matters about which there shall be collective bargaining. Obviously, passes cannot be of any assistance for the purpose of collective bargaining as such, for it is plain common sense that they do not need passes to negotiate an agreement for there is no one on board the ships who has authority to negotiate an agreement. It may be true that after the agreement is reached, the bargaining agent may have some other duties or functions, but only if and to the extent that they are provided for in the agreement.

The Board's order ascribes duties and functions to the unions beyond that of bargaining for an agreement (even before the agreement is reached) and is clearly erroneous for the Act does not delegate to unions the exclusive right to settle grievances or the right to dictate the grievance procedure. Quite to the contrary, the Act expressly reserves to the *employees* the right to settle grievances directly with the employer. This Court in its decision in *NLRB v. Union Pacific Stages, Inc., supra,* at page 164, in rejecting the union attorney's view that the employer was deprived of the right of settling grievances directly with employees, held:

> "Section 9(a) of the Act, 29 U. S. C. A. Sec. 159(a), contains the proviso that 'any individual employee or a group of employees shall have the right at any time to present grievances to their employer.' Thus the Act does not inhibit adjustment of individual grievances directly between employee and employer *and such procedure is entirely consistent with collective bargaining in matters affecting employees as a class."* (Emphasis ours.)

The foregoing expressions of this court find support in *NLRB v. Jones & Laughlin Steel Corporation, supra.*

In the case now before the Court, the Board used the same reasoning that was condemned by this Court in *National Labor Relations Board v. North American Aviation, Inc.*, Case No. 10313, June 24, 1943, 136 Fed. (2d) 898. In the *North American* case the Board held that the furnishing by the employer of a means of settling grievances directly with employees was interfering with the *rights and duties of* union representatives as collective bargaining agents, reasoning that "collective bargaining" is not complete upon the execution of the contract negotiated, but continues in the form of bargaining concerning grievances under the contract. The Board also reasons that if an employer "bargains" directly with an employee concerning a grievance, such action by the employer is a refusal to bargain with the chosen bargaining representatives of the employees and therefore an unfair labor practice.

In this case the Board is ascribing the same *rights and duties* to the union representatives, reasoning that "collective bargaining" agents have the right and duty under the Act to bargain concerning settlement of individual grievances because grievances normally concern terms and conditions of employment and these bargaining agents are the exclusive bargaining agents concerning terms and conditions of employment. This reasoning closely parallels the reasoning of the Board in the *North American* case, but it is more objectionable because it does not stop there, for the Board in this case reasons that the unions have the exclusive right to say what procedure will be followed in settling individual grievances and holds that any resistance by the employer to the demands of the unions concerning such procedure during collective bargaining concerning an over-all contract, constitutes a violation of the Act.

We submit that in both cases the Board has totally disregarded the usual connotation of "collective bargaining" as well as the fundamental difference between bargaining collectively concerning the terms and conditions of work as affecting all employees in an appropriate unit and the presentation and settlement of individual grievances under the contract arrived at by collective bargaining, which is really not collective bargaining at all.

The usual and accepted meaning of "collective bargaining" as set out in Webster's Dictionary is as follows:

> "Negotiation for the settlement of the terms (for example, as to wages) of a labor contract between an employer or group of employers on one side and an organized body of workers on the other."

Webster's Dictionary defines a "grievance" as:

> "The cause of uneasiness and complaint; the wrong done and suffered."

and defines the word "present" as follows:

> "'Present' means 'to lay before a judge, magistrate, or governing body for action or consideration; submit, as a petitioner, remonstrance, etc., for a decision or settlement to the proper authorities.'"

The fundamental purpose of the Act is to promote industrial peace. To hold that the unions have the exclusive right to determine how grievances shall be settled or the right to insist that they alone settle grievances for employees would not promote industrial peace, but would be clearly contrary to the intent of Congress (see section 9(a) of the Act) as well as contrary to the decision of the Supreme Court of the United States and of this Court to which we have just referred, for such a holding would destroy the employer's right and duty to bargain and would destroy the *employees'* rights protected by this Court in the *North American* case, *supra.*

Our view finds support in the National War Labor Board decision on March 23, 1943, in *Art Metal Const. Co. and International Federation of Technical Engineers, Architects and Draftsmen Union Local No. 64 AFL,* Case No. 395 (3/23/43), wherein the National War Labor Board stated:

> "The union demanded that employees be permitted to take up grievances in the first instance only through union representatives, since, it claimed, employees inexperienced in collective bargaining might agree to things counter to their own interest.
>
> *"The unions demand is denied not only because of its doubtful propriety under the National Labor Relations Act but because it believed that, if the individuals concerned can resolve complaints between themselves, the summoning of another person only complicates the issue."* (Italics ours.)

We contend that the poistion which we have asserted herein is entirely consistent with the right "to bargain collectively through representatives of their own choosing" and that it is not an unfair labor practice.

Third, employees have the right to "engage in concerted activities, for the purpose of collective bargaining and other mutual aid and protection." This category of rights belongs to employees as among and between themselves without interference by anyone, even by labor organizations or the Board. If a labor organization has any functions at all in respect of the rights of employees under this category, it is a function that must necessarily be derived from the agreement arrived at through collective bargaining. The Board's order in this case, therefore, directs the issuance of passes for purposes entirely outside the scope of collective bargaining and outside the scope of any agreement arrived at by collective bargaining. By its order, under the circumstances, the Board is dictating terms or conditions of employment, and, as we have seen, the Board does not have the power or jurisdiction to do that.

The purpose of Section 7 of the Act is to enable employees to organize, to enhance their position in collective bargaining concerning terms and conditions of employment, and to engage in concerted activities for their mutual aid and protection, and to further collective bargaining. Thus, employees may assert any demands, rights or privileges which they deem appropriate in the course of their collective bargaining and to use their collective strength to that end. It does not guarantee them specific terms or conditions of employment. It does not guarantee them any particular rate of wage or any particular right of privilege incident to their employment, and it certainly does not grant to the Board or the complaining unions the right to determine by unilateral action what terms and conditions of employment your petitioner must agree to.

It follows therefore that the subject matter of the complaint is a dispute (not involving any discrimination or anti-union activity or motive, and not involving a refusal to bargain in good faith) over which the Board has no power or jurisdiction, and being the only issue before the Board, its order is invalid and should be set aside.

POINT II.

The Board's Order Is Too Broad, and Therefore Contrary to Law.

Assuming for the purpose of argument that the Board has the power and jurisdiction to order your petitioner to cease and desist from refusing to issue passes, its order is, nevertheless, invalid for the following reasons:

1. Board's Order numbered 1 [(a) and (b)] is too broad and, in fact, amounts to a blanket injunction against violating the Act.

There have been many cases on the question of whether, after finding a specific violation of the Act and entering a cease and desist order concerning that particular violation, the Board may also enter an order to cease and desist from violating the Act generally. The rule on this question was definitely established in *National Labor Relations Board v. Express Publishing Co.,* 312 U. S. 426; 85 L. Ed. 930; 61 Sup. Ct. Rep. 693, 1941, wherein the court laid down the general principles recited in its headnotes as follows:

Headnote 4.

> "An employer's violation of the provisions of the National Labor Relations Act in one respect does not justify the making of a blanket order restraining the employer from violating the statute in any manner whatsoever, where other unlawful practices are not found to have been pursued or to be related to the proven unlawful conduct."

Headnote 5.

> "A cease and desist order of the National Labor Relations Board which, when judicially construed, the

courts may be called upon to enforce by contempt proceedings, must, like the injunction order of the court, state with reasonable specificity the acts which the employer is to do or refrain from doing."

Headnote 6.

"While a Federal court has broad power to restrain acts which are of the same type or class as unlawful acts which the court has found to have been committed or whose commission in the future, unless enjoined, may fairly be anticipated from the defendant's conduct in the past, the mere fact that a court has found that a defendant has committed an act in violation of a statute does not justify an injunction broadly to obey the statute and thus subject the defendant to contempt proceedings if he shall at any time in the future commit some new violation unlike and unrelated to that with which he was originally charged."

Following the *Express Publishing Co.* case, *supra,* two supplemental rules were developed in the cases, the first to the effect that where there has been persistent attempts by the employer by varying methods to interfere with the rights of self-organization, collective bargaining, etc., the Board is justified in following its primary cease and desist order with an order against other like or related acts.

American Enka Corporation v. N. L. R. B., 119 Fed. (2d) 60; C. C. A. 4 (Apr. 7, 1941);

N. L. R. B. v. Entwistle Mfg. Co., 120 Fed. (2d) 532; C. C. A. 4th (June 10, 1941);

N. L. R. B. v. Reynolds Wire Co., 121 Fed. (2d) 627; C. C. A. 7th (June 12, 1941);

F. W. Woolworth Co. v. N. L. R. B., 121 Fed. (2d) 658; C. C. A. (2d) (July 2, 1941);

Sperry Gyroscope Co., Inc. v. National Labor Relations Board, 129 Fed. (2d) 922; C. C. A. (2d) (July 3, 1942);

National Labor Relations Board v. Bradley Lumber Co., 128 Fed. (2d) 768; C. C. A 8th (June 26, 1942);

Rapid Roller Co. v. National Labor Relations Board, 126 Fed. (2d) 452; C. C. A. 7th (Feb. 2, 1942);

National Labor Relations Board v. Aintree Corporation, 132 Fed. (2d) 469; C. C. A. 7th (Nov. 12, 1942);

National Labor Relations Board v. Baldwin Locomotive Works, 128 Fed. (2d) 39; C. C. A. 3rd (March 23, 1942).

Clearly, under the facts of this case, this principle is inapplicable.

The second principle, and the one controlling in this case, is that where the Board finds only an isolated violation of the Act there is no justification whatsoever and it would be improper to issue an order to cease and desist from violating the Act generally or cease and desist from engaging in like or related unlawful acts for the reason that the order of the Board, like an injunction of the court, must state with reasonable certainty the acts which the respondent is to do or refrain from doing.

Aluminum Ore Co. v. National Labor Relations Board, 131 Fed. (2d) 485 (C. C. A. 7);

Press Co., Inc. v. N. L. R. B., 118 Fed. (2d) 937, U. S. Ct. of Appeals for Dist. of Col. (Dec. 9, 1940);

N. L. R. B. v. West Texas Utilities Co., 119 Fed. (2d) 683; C. C. A. 5th (May 2, 1941);

Warehouseman's Union, Local 117, etc. v. N. L. R. B., 121 Fed. (2d) 84, U. S. Ct. of Appeals for Dist. of Columbia (May 5, 1941);

N. L. R. B. v. Continental Oil Co., 121 Fed. (2d) 120; C. C. A. 10th (June 23, 1941);

N. L. R. B. v. Calumet Steel Division of Borg-Warner Corporation, 121 Fed. (2d) 366, C. C. A. 7th (June 12, 1941);

N. L. R. B. v. Grower-Shipper Vegetable Ass'n of Central California, et al., 122 Fed. (2d) 368; C. C. A. 9th (July 21, 1941);

Wilson & Co., Inc. v. N.L .R. B., 123 Fed. (2d) 411; C. C. A. 8th (Nov. 29, 1941);

N. L. R. B. v. Burry Biscuit Corporation, 123 Fed. 540, C. C. A. 7th (Nov. 26, 1941);

N. L. R. B. v. Swift & Co., 129 Fed. (2d) 222, C. C. A. Eighth Circuit (July 10, 1942);

N. L. R. B. v. Cleveland-Cliffs Iron Co., 133 Fed. (2d) 295, C. C. A. 6th, Feb. 11, 1943;

Canyon Corporation v. N. L. R. B., 128 Fed. (2d) 953, C. C. A. 8th, June 30, 1942;

American Smelting & Refining Co. v. N. L. R. B., 126 Fed. (2d) 680; C. C. A. 8th, Mar. 12, 1942;

National Labor Relations Board v. Mason Mfg. Co., 126 Fed. (2d) 810, C. C. A. 9th, Feb. 13, 1942.

It will be noted that the Circuit Court for the Ninth Circuit in *National Labor Relations Board v. Mason Mfg. Co.*, 126 Fed. (2d) 810, C. C. A. 9th Circuit has recognized the above principle and went further to declare that there should be great care exercised in entering general cease and desist decree, broader than warranted by the evidence, the court citing the *Express Publishing Company* case, and holding on page 814:

> "The court believes it should exercise great care in entering general cease and desist decrees in such cases as these whereby a single mistaken act on the part of the employer would, on the face of the decree, transfer from the experience, skill and knowledge of the Board future claims of violations of the Act affecting some entirely different labor organization, in an entirely different way, and place their determination in contempt proceedings in the more restricted area of evidence of court procedure."

In this case where there is but a sole issue (in fact, that issue is solely a question of law) and where there has been neither a charge nor any proof that your petitioner did anything but refuse to issue passes, it follows that the provisions of paragraph numbered 1 (b) of the Board's Order are invalid.

2. Order numbered 2 (a) requiring your petitioner to take affirmative action is unlimited in scope.

The evidence shows that the issuance of passes will substantially increase the hazards on board ship. Yet no limitations whatsoever as to the number or use have been included and accordingly not one single safeguard is given. In its decision the Board has totally disregarded the existing law which would require that your petitioner grant passes to other unions demanding them.

In re South Atlantic SS. Co. v. NLRB, 116 F. (2d) 480, C. C. A. 5, 1941;

In re Waterman SS. Co., 309 U. S. 206, 226; 84 L. Ed. 704, 60 Sup. Ct. 493;

In re American-West African Lines, 6 L. R. R. 119,

Moreover, the pass provision in the Associated Oil Company's contract [Board Exhibit 4, R. 285] contains a number of safeguards for the protection of the employer, all of which have been totally disregarded by the Board in its order.

3. Board's Order numbered 2 (b) is invalid because it would require your petitioner to publicly admit of violations of the Act. This Order of the Board would require your petitioner to post notices in conspicuous places on its vessels for a period of at least sixty consecutive days, such notices to state that your petitioner will cease and desist from failure to issue passes *and from engaging in like or related acts or from interfering with or restraining or coercing its employees in the exercise of the right of self-organization, to form, join, and assist labor organizations, to bargain collectively through representatives of their own choosing and to engage in concerted activities for collective bargaining or other mutual aid or protection as guaranteed in Section 7 of the Act.*

We submit that such a posting is outrageous under the facts of this case for it is a public admission that your petitioner has committed all of the acts recited when as a matter of fact the charge covers but an isolated act, which in no way violates the Act. The requiring of such a public announcement is contrary to law.

NLRB v. Eagle Mfg. Co., 99 F. (2d) 930 (C. C. A. 4, Nov. 10, 1938);

NLRB v. A. S. Abell Co., 97 F. (2d) 951 (C. C. A. 4, July 14, 1938);

Virginia Ferry Corp v. NLRB, 101 F. (2d) 103 (C. C. A. 4).

POINT III.

The Findings, Conclusions and Order of the Board Are Not Supported by Substantial Evidence.

THE REQUIREMENTS OF THE ACT.

It is now well settled that "the statute, in providing that 'the findings of the Board as to the facts, if supported by evidence, shall be conclusive' means supported by substantial evidence" [Sec. 10 (e) and (f) of the Act— See Part D of Appendix for complete text.] *Consolidated Edison Co. v. NLRB,* 305 U. S. 197; 83 L. Ed. 126; 59 S. Ct. 206 (1938). In that case the Supreme Court at page 229 said:

> "Substantial evidence is more than a mere scintilla. It means such relevant evidence as a reasonable mind might accept as adequate to support a conclusion."

It is equally well settled that the Court will not enforce a Board's order unless such order is based upon substantial evidence.

> *Washington, Virginia & Maryland Coach Co. v. NLRB.,* 301 U. S. 142; 81 L. Ed. 965, 57 S. Ct. 648;
>
> *NLRB v. Bell Oil & Gas Co.,* 91 Fed. (2d) 509; C. C. A. 5 (1937);
>
> *Appalachian Electric Power Co. v. NLRB,* 93 Fed. (2d) 985; C. C. A. 4 (1938);
>
> *NLRB v. Sheboygan Chair Co.,* 125 Fed. (2d) 436; C. C. A. 7 (1942).

See also:

> *NLRB v. Virginia E. & P. Co.,* 314 U. S. 469; 86 L. Ed. 348; 62 S. Ct. 344,

wherein it was held that the court is not required to accept findings that are not free from doubt.

Nor will a court enforce a Board's order when the Trial Examiner has based his statements of fact and conclusions of law on certain portions of the evidence and totally disregarded other material and relevant evidence, particularly where the same is uncontroverted. *NLRB v. Sheboygan Chair Co., supra.*

See also *Peninsular & Occidental S. S. Co. v. NLRB,* 98 Fed. (2d) 411; C. C. A. 5 (1938); Cert. den. 305 U. S. 653; 83 L. Ed. 423; 59 S. Ct. 248, wherein it was held that the Board has wide discretion in administering the Act, but in doing so it must deal fairly with both parties to the controversy; *it is its duty to decide the case before it on all the evidence; and it is not at liberty to rely upon part of the evidence in support of its findings and put aside all other undisputed evidence.* (Emphasis ours.)

Now it is true that Congress intended that the administrative and *quasi*-judicial proceedings before the Board should not be hampered by technical rules so that the mere admission of matter which would be deemed incompetent in judicial proceedings would not invalidate the administrative order. [Sec. 10 (b) of the Act—See Part D of Appendix for complete text.] However, this assurance of a desirable flexibility in the administrative procedure does not go so far as to justify orders without a basis in evidence having rational probative force.

Consoldated Edison Co. v. NLRB, supra.

Since there is nothing in the Act indicating an intention to nullify the rules of evidence prevailing in courts of law or equity, they are controlling in a proceeding in the Circuit Court of Appeals to review and set aside an order of the National Labor Relations Board.

On petition for rehearing in the *Bell Oil & Gas Co.* case (98 Fed. (2d) 870, C. C. A. 5 (1938)), the Court said at page 871:

> "We held in this case that the rules of evidence prevailing in courts of law and equity were not aboliished by the National Labor Relations Act, 29 U. S. C. A. Sec. 151 *et seq.* We adhere to this ruling, notwithstanding the provision that, in proceedings before the Board, such rules shall not be controlling. . . . The fact that incompetent evidence is heard does not invalidate an order of the Board, provided the findings upon which the order is based *are supported by competent, relevant, and material evidence.* * * *
>
> "The provision in paragraph (b), section 10, 29 U. S. C. A. Sec. 160 (b) with reference to the rules of evidence prevailing in courts of law and equity not being controlling, *means that it is not error for the Board to hear incompetent evidence. It does not mean that a finding of fact may rest solely upon such evidence. Whether there be any competent evidence to support the findings of the Board is a question of law;* whether it is sufficient is a question of fact. The decision of the Board upon a question of law is not conclusive in this court.
>
> "In one instance, in the case under review, the sole evidence to support an essential finding of the Board was the incompetent evidence quoted in our opinion. In the others, there was no substantial evidence to support essential findings. Therefore, as a matter of law, the order was deemed invalid." (Emphasis ours.)

See also *NLRB v. Lion Shoe Co.,* 1st C. C. A. 1938, 97 Fed. (2d) 448, where it was held that though the Board was not bound by the usual rules of evidence, this did not change the principle requiring reasonable deductions from evidence.

Upon petition to the Circuit Court of Appeals and the filing therein of a transcript of the entire record, the entire nature of the proceeding is changed and becomes wholly judicial and there is nothing in the Act to indicate that the Circuit Court of Appeals should consider irrelevant, immaterial or incompetent evidence in its determination of the question whether the Board's order is supported by substantial evidence, *and irrelevant, immaterial or incompetent or hearsay and non-expert opinion evidence may not be used in the Circuit Court of Appeals as a basis to support the findings of the Board* upon which an order which is sought to be enforced, rests. *NLRB v. Bell Oil & Gas Co., supra.* (Emphasis ours.)

In *NLRB v. Union Pacific Stages, Inc.*, 99 Fed (2d) 153 (C. C. A. 9, 1938, this court at page 177 said:

> "It is suggested that this court should accept the findings of the Board; that contradictions, inconsistencies, and erroneous inferences are immune from criticism or attack by Section 10 (e) of the Act, 49 Stat. 453, 29 U. S. C. A. Sec. 160 (e), which provides that 'the findings of the Board, as to the facts, if supported by evidence, shall be conclusive.' But the courts have not construed this language as compelling the acceptance of findings *arrived at by accepting part of the evidence and totally disregarding other convincing evidence.*
>
> " 'We are bound by the Board's findings of fact as to matters within its jurisdiction, where the findings are supported by substantial evidence; but we are not bound by findings which are not so supported. 29 U. S. C. A. Sec. 160 (e) (f); Washington, Virginia & Maryland Coach Co. v. NLRB, 301 U. S. 142, 57 S. Ct. 648, 650, 81 L. Ed. 965. * * *

Substantial evidence is evidence furnishing a substantial basis of fact from which the fact in issue can reasonably be inferred; *and the test is not satisfied by evidence which merely creates a suspicion or which amounts to no more than a scintilla or which gives equal support to inconsistent inferences. Cf.* Pennsylvania R. Co. v. Chamberlain, 288 U. S. 333, 339-343, 53 S. Ct. 391, 393, 394, 77 L. Ed. 819.' Appalachian Electric Power Co. v. National Labor Relations Board, 4 Cir., 93 F. 2d. 985, 989.

" 'Substantial evidence' means more than a mere scintilla. It is of substantial and relevant consequence and excludes vague, uncertain, or irrelevant matter. It implies a quality of proof which induces conviction and makes an impression on reason. It means that the one weighing the evidence takes into consideration all the facts presented to him and all reasonable inferences, deductions and conclusions to be drawn therefrom and, considering them in their entirety and relation to each other, arrives at a fixed conviction.

" '*The rule of substantial evidence is one of fundamental importance and is the dividing line between law and arbitrary power.* Testimony is the raw material out of which we construct truth and, unless all of it is weighed in its totality, errors will result and great injustices be wrought.' National Labor Relations Board v. Thompson Products, Inc., 6 Cir., 97 F. 2d 13, 15." (Emphasis ours.)

The foregoing authorities definitely establish, and we think the rule unquestionably is that the Board is not bound by technical rules of evidence in ascertaining the true facts concerning an issue raised by the pleadings; and that in its consideration of the case it is not error for the

Board to hear incompetent, irrelevant evidence or hearsay evidence. But it is error to base its findings upon such evidence *for the Board's order must be supported by substantial evidence.*

We submit that this is a question of substantive law, for the reason that the Board's order is invalid as a matter of law, unless it is so supported, and the Court on review will be guided by the rules of evidence in determining whether the Board's order is supported by substantial evidence.

THE EVIDENCE DOES NOT MEET THE REQUIREMENTS OF THE ACT.

We will now show wherein the essential findings of the Board are not supported by substantial evidence. For orderly analysis, these are presented in the order in which they appear in the Intermediate Report, and we will give page and line references to the Intermediate Report, page in the printed record, the exceptions, and the page where such exceptions appear in the printed record.

1. *Footnote 3, Page 2 of the Intermediate Report* [R. 27], *Exception 1.* [*R. 50.*]

Counsel's Opening Statement [R. 106]; Statement of witness Wilder [R. 133]; Respondent's Exhibit 1 [R. 137]; Respondent's Exhibit 2 [R. 138]; Respondent's Exhibit 3 [R. 153]; and Respondent's Exhibit 4 [R. 156, all show that your petitioner's tankers are not being operated as usual. Even if it were not for this evidence, which is directly contrary to the finding, we think the court would take judicial notice that the operation of the petitoner's tankers is now completely regulated in aid of the war effort.

2. *Finding 3-A, Lines 23-33, Page 3 of Intermediate Report [R. 28]— to the Extent That This Finding Does Not Confine "Exclusive Representation" to Matters of "Collective Bargaining" as Such and to the Extent That "the Sole Question in This Case" Is Not Confined Strictly to a Matter of Law. [Exception 2, R. 50.]*

Paragraph 5 of the Complaint alleges that the complaining unions are the exclusive representatives *for the purpose of collective bargaining.* [R. 10.] This was admitted in the answer. [R. 17.] There is nothing further in the record on this point but the Board did not so limit the finding and, in fact (as more fully appears under Point I) ascribes duties and functions to collective bargaining agents outside of and beyond collective bargaining. This is an essential finding under the Board's theory and it is without any foundation whatsoever. As to the remaining portion of this exception, the finding should be limited strictly to a question of law, for there is no charge in the complaint nor any evidence to show or from which it may be inferred that the employer had any intent or purpose prohibited by the Act when it refused to issue passes. The bare issue, therefore, must necessarily be solely a question of law as to whether the refusal is in and of itself a violation of the Act.

3. *Footnote 4, Page 4 of Intermediate Report [R. 30], Exception 5. [R. 50.]*

Here the Board found that the National Martime Union was not the duly authorized representative of your petitioner's unlicensed seamen when that organization filed charges against your petitioner on February 24, 1942, for refusal to issue passes to them. On that finding, the Board concludes that your petitioner's contention that the prior decision of the Board should bar the proceedings in this case, is without merit either on the theory of estoppel or *res judicata.*

All of the evidence in the record bearing on the charge of the National Maritime Union and the Board's refusal to issue a complaint because your petitioner was not discriminating concerning passes is contained in Respondent's Exhibits 5-A to 5-E, inclusive [R. 344-354]. This action by the Board is really a conclusion of law that Respondent's Exhibits 5-A to 5-E, inclusive, are without merit for any purpose in this proceeding because the National Maritime Union was not the duly authorized representative of the unlicensed seamen. In this way it has actually excluded evidence which has great probative value by showing that your petitioner's conduct, which the Board now finds to be an unfair labor practice, has previously been approved by the Board.

This finding presupposes that the Act makes it an unfair labor practice to refuse "access" to a certified union when such refusal to a union represnting employees before election of certified representatives is not an unfair labor practice.

4. *Footnote 5 on Page 4 of the Intermediate Report* [*R. 30*], *Exception 6* [*R. 50, 51*].

There is no evidence in the record to show that the word "access" has any meaning in the shipping industry, let alone the definition conceived by the Board.

5. *Lines 15-27, on Page 4 of the Intermediate Report [R. 30-31], Exception 7 [R. 51].*

This entire paragraph is really not a finding but it is a conclusion of the Board arrived at by confused reasoning without basis whatsoever in the record. This erroneous conclusion is the foundation of the Board's theory of this case. We do not find fault with the quoted portions of the Act but the error lies in their application. The Board concludes that because the Act guarantees the right to bargain collectively concerning terms and conditions of work, that the Act also guarantees to collective bargaining representatives the exclusive right to settle grievances because grievances concern terms and conditions of work. Having made this erroneous conclusion, it takes the next step and concludes that *any disagreement by the employer with the demands of the certified union concerning the manner or method of settling grievances is a violation of the Act.*

This is the same theory advanced by the Board in *NLRB v. North American Aviation, Inc.,* Case No. 10313, June 24, 1943, 136 Fed. (2d) 898, wherein this court properly held that the duties and functions of collective bargaining agents are not so broad. We contend that the first duty of collective bargaining agents is to negotiate a contract. When the contract is completed it will determine how grievances shall be settled and it will determine what additional functions, if any, are conferred upon collective bargaining representatives.

The conclusion that a refusal to grant passes is a refusal to bargain is not within the single issue raised by the pleadings and it has no basis whatsoever in the record, for your petitioner has been in good faith bargaining with the collective bargaining agents. [See Board's Exhibit 5; R. 335.]

6. *Lines 29-36, Page 4 of the Intermediate Report* [*R. 31*], *Exception 7* [*R. 51*].

This is really another conclusion by the Board based on the assumption that collective bargaining agents have the absolute right, conferred by the Act, to settle any and all grievances. This conclusion is erroneous because it is the Act itself, as construed by the courts, that will determine whether your petitioner is guilty of an unfair labor practice—this whole question is a question of law. What is customarily done in another industry and, in fact, by another employer, has no bearing upon your petitioner's conduct. The conduct of the many dry cargo operators and the one tanker company (Tide Water Associated Oil Company) holding written contracts with the unions, is governed by their individual and respective contract arrangements arrived at through collective bargaining processes. If those contracts confer any duties and functions on the complaining unions in addition to the negotiation of an overall contract, those duties and functions must necessarily arise from contract, all of which is wholly immaterial to the issues in this case.

However, if the Board is correct and it is necessary to look to the contracts between the unions and the other operators to determine whether your petitioner is violating the Act, the only possible conclusion would be that your petitioner was not violating the Act. We have set forth in the Appendix a summary of the grievance procedure provisions contained in Board's Exhibits 2 (rejected), and 3, and the complete text of the grievance procedure in Board's Exhibit 4 [See Part B, pp. 9 to 12 of Appendix]. All of these grievance procedures are identical in that not one of them provides for "access". On the contrary, those contracts which provide for the issuance of passes specifically specify that passes are for the purpose of transacting union business or for visiting members. During contract negotiations, the complaining unions and your petitioner agreed upon the grievance procedure set forth in the Associated Oil Company contract [Board's Exhibit 4 — see Part B, p. 11 of Appendix]. That grievance procedure does not contemplate the presence of shore representatives of the unions and accordingly the evidence shows clearly that there is no need to issue passes.

7. *Lines 38-43 on Page 4, and Lines 1-32 on Page 5 of the Intermediate Report* [*R. 32 and 33*] *Exception No. 8* [*R. 51*].

To the extent that this section of the Intermediate Report refers to stewards, it has no basis whatsoever in the record, and if it did it would be immaterial, for the stewards are not involved in this proceeding and the unions are not representatives of the stewards.

8. *The 4th Paragraph Under* B(*1*) *of the Intermediate Report Appearing on Lines 35-45, Inclusive, on Page 5, and Lines 1-19, Inclusive on Page 6 of the Intermediate Report* [*R. 34-35*]; *Exception 9* [*R. 51*].

This finding of fact is immaterial to the issues in this case and therefore not supported by substantial evidence.

9. *Footnote 10 Page 5 of the Intermediate Report* [*R. 34*], *Exception 10* [*R. 51*].

There is no evidence in the record that so-called "access" is confined to any one person in any one port. This finding not only is without basis but it is misleading and tends to throw an improper light on your petitioner's position on the question of issuing passes. The record shows that there are two complaining unions [Board's Exhibit 1-A, R. 1; Board's Exhibit 1-B, R. 3; Board's Exhibit 1-C, R. 5]; and paragraph 5 of the complaint [R. 11]. Each of the complaining unions has demanded at least one pass for each principal port on the Pacific Coast. In addition, the law requires your petitioner to issue passes to all other unions that might demand them if your petitioner issues passes to the complaining unions. See *In re Waterman Steamship Company,* 309 U. S. 206, 226; 84 L. Ed. 704, 60 Sup. Ct. 493; *In re So. Atlantic Steamship Co. v. NLRB,* 116 F. (2d) 480, C. C. A. 5, 1941; *In re American-West African Lines,* 6 L. R. R. 119.

We want to emphasize the length to which the Board has gone in the *American-West African Lines* case just cited. In that case the Board ordered the employer to issue passes to a rival union when the employer had a valid closed shop contract with another union. If the rival union with its passes were able to secure a member among the seamen of that employer, the employer under its contract would have been required to discharge the seaman, but the Board held that the employer could not discriminate on the question of passes.

These cases were cited to the Board, and the employer urged throughout the proceedings that one of its principal objections to the issuance of passes to the complaining unions was that it would be required to issue them to all other unions demanding the same; otherwise, the employer would be guilty of an unfair labor practice, thus permitting many persons to go on board your petitioner's vessels, thereby greatly increasing the hazards to which such vessels are exposed. Therefore, this finding or statement by the Board is misleading to the point of being prejudicial and there is nothing in the record which will support it.

10. *Footnote 11 Page 11, of the Intermediate Report* [*R. 34*], *Exception No. 11* [*R. 52*].

There is no evidence whatsoever in the record that 90% of the grievances reported are disposed of on board by shore representatives of the union. The only evidence concerning the 90% figure was the statement of witness Gries [R. 376] to the effect that *he* has settled 90% of the disputes referred *to him* on board.

11. *Footnote 13, Page 6 of the Intermediate Report* [*R. 35-36*], *Exception 12* [*R. 52*].

This is an immaterial conclusion of the Board and an attempt to conform the findings in this case to the findings in the *Cities Service* case, which we have shown under Point IV hereof to be erroneous. It is immaterial, primarily for the reason that it is outside the scope of the single issue raised by the pleadings.

12. *Lines 1 to 14, Page 7 of the Intermediate Report [R. 36-37], Exception No. 13 [R. 52].*

There is no charge in the complaint and no evidence that your petitioner interfered with the right of self-organization, to form, join, or assist a labor organization. The evidence is clearly directly to the contrary for the record shows that the complaining unions are certified as bargaining agents and that at the time charges were filed, your petitioner was bargaining in good faith with such agents for the purpose of entering into a written contract.

13. *Lines 16 to 27, page 7, Intermediate Report [R. 37], Exception 14 [R. 52].*

We have shown that there is no evidence to support the finding or conclusion that your petitioner's conduct interfered with collective bargaining. This finding is a repetition which brings in "mutual aid and protection" and is clearly unsupported.

14. *Footnote 14, Page 7 of the Intermediate Report [R. 37 and 38], Exception 15 [R. 52].*

This is an inference by the Board which is clearly unsupported by the evidence. The statement of union representatives that they have been in the practice of collecting dues and distributing papers when they were aboard dry cargo vessels under the terms and conditions of passes issued to them pursuant to contract, is immaterial and irrelevant as a basis for inferring that "Pacific Coast Shippers, who grant access" consider these matters "a proper form of aid to be given." Even if "Pacific Coast Shippers" do, it is wholly immaterial. Moreover, the inference is defective for if the Act guarantees to certified unions the right to collect dues on board so that their members may retain the benefits incident to their membership, clearly the Act also gives the same right to unions not certified but having members on board and, furthermore, it would guarantee to *employees* the right to acquire those same benefits by joining the union. To sustain the Board would be to grant to certified unions privileges not conferred by the Act and discriminate against *employees* who are not members of that particular union.

15. *Footnote 15, Pages 7-8 of the Intermediate Report* [*R. 38*], *Exception 16* [*R. 52*].

This is really an unwarranted assumption by the Board that there is some duty upon your petitioner to demonstrate some other method of settling grievances than that demanded by the unions. Here again, the Board attempts to conform the findings of fact in this case to those in the *Cities Service* case. This finding is immaterial to the issues in this case and therefore is not supported by substantial evidence.

16. *Lines 29 to 40, Page 7 of the Intermediate Report* [*R. 38*], *Exception 17* [*R. 52*].

There is not one scintilla of evidence to support this finding or conclusion and the remarks of the Board are clearly intended to throw an improper light upon your petitioner's conduct by reading into the Act the obligation on your petitioner to facilitate the convenience of the complaining unions by acceding to their demands, contrary to the best interest of the petitioner and in its opinion contrary to the best interest of its employees.

17. *Lines 42 to 45, Page 7 of the Intermediate Report [R. 38], Exception 18 [R. 52].*

This is really a conclusion based upon prior findings and conclusions, which, in turn, are not based on substantial evidence and therefore must fall.

18. *Lines 5-8, Page 8 of the Intermediate Report [R. 39, 40], Exception 19 [R. 53].*

There is no evidence to support the finding that your petitioner "does not in fact, contend that under peace time conditions it would be justified in refusing passes to the duly authorized representatives of its unlicensed deck and engine personnel for the purpose of access to its tankers * * *". Your petitioner contends and has contended throughout the entire proceeding that the Act does not require it to issue passes under any circumstances excepting only if its refusal was with the intent and purpose of accomplishing something forbidden by the Act. Your petitioner also contends that the requirement of the Act is that your petitioner bargain collectively in good faith concerning passes. This has been done and your petitioner, therefore, has not violated the Act.

19. *Lines 16-34, Page 8, and Lines 1-3, on Page 9 of the Intermediate Report [R. 40], Exception 20 [R. 53].*

There is nothing in the record to show that those persons who are permitted aboard your petitioner's vessels are not essential to such vessels. Indeed, the evidence is directly contrary. The testimony of Witness Wilder [R. 159-165] shows clearly that only persons having business essential to the operation of the tankers are permitted aboard. The statement that only union representatives have been denied access finds no support in the evidence. There is, however, evidence directly contrary on this point, for Witness Wilder testified that passes are denied to all persons [R. 127] and Witness Lamb testified to the same effect [R. 385]. The statement that it is almost the usual practice in the "shipping industry" to permit access is immaterial to the issue and ignores the fact that the tanker industry is separate and apart from the shipping industry. Tanker operators are private carriers, transporting their own merchandise between their own terminals. The dry cargo operators are common carriers, transporting merchandise for the general public between various ports of the world. The only evidence on the point is that one or two tanker operators out of the 8 or 9 tanker operators on the Pacific Coast permit access. Clearly that is directly contrary to the inference that it is the universal practice to permit access to tankers. The concluding statement to the effect that your petitioner "is practically alone in its fear of increased hazards from the presence of seamen's representatives on board vessels" is obviously intended to throw improper light on the employer's refusal to issue passes and to discredit its reasons for adopting such policy.

20. *Footnote 16, Page 9, of the Intermediate Report* [*R. 41*], *Exception 21* [*R. 53*].

The finding that the presence of union representatives on board tankers is less hazardous than others and the further statement that the armed guards afford the necessary security in wartime, are wholly without foundation in the evidence. In the first place, the evidence is directly to the contrary for the hazards are measured entirely by the time spent on board [R. 390].

The assumption of the Board that militarized guards provide the needed measure of security is without any foundation in the evidence whatsoever. The function of armed guards is to keep persons off the vessels. Clearly, if persons are on board the vessels, the presence of armed guards does not reduce the hazards. We submit that this bland statement by the Board is absurd. If guards were the answer, why then have the War Shipping Administration and the U. S. Coast Guard and the U. S. Navy and other branches of the Federal Government issued so many regulations, and security orders and undertaken so many precautionary steps. Obviously, it is an unwarranted assumption by one wholly without responsibility, who dismisses as being "without merit", the studied judgment of your petitioner who has had many years of experience in the operation of tank vessels and the handling of dangerous cargoes, and which bears the entire responsibility for the safety of the vessels, their crews and cargoes and for the carrying out of the many security orders and regulations necessary in time of war.

21. *Lines 5-17, of Page 9 of Intermediate Report* [*R. 41, 42*], *Exception 22* [*R. 53*].

Even the Trial Examiner states that your petitioner could issue any order it sees fit so long as it was not with the intent of interfering with any rights of its employees under the Act [R. 327]. There is no charge in the complaint of any such intent and no evidence was introduced concerning it. Therefore, the bald statement that your petitioner's contentions are without merit is wholly unwarranted and without any foundation whatsoever in the record. The Board states "Of utmost significance is the fact that the Navy and the Coast Guard have provided the representatives of the respondent's unlicensed deck and engine personnel with the proper identification and authority to enter restricted areas and to board tankers and vessels, including respondent's tankers, providing respondent issues its passes to the representatives." We think it is significant that the governmental authorities issue identification cards and badges which on their face show that they are not passes but are only means of identification—and it is indeed significant that they do not permit entrance into restricted areas *without the express permission of the one responsible for the safety of the premises involved.*

The Board then goes on to say that the so-called Statement of Policy of the War Shipping Administration, agreed to by the unions, has stabilized for the duration, collective bargaining contracts which contain provisions for passes for authorized representatives of seamen, thus affording access. The Statement of Policy is Board's Exhibit 7-A [R. 398], but the Board totally disregards the plain and unambiguous language in an interpretation of the Statement of Policy, which interpretation is contained in Board's Exhibit 7-B [R. 402] and provides in effect that paragraph 3 of the Statement of Policy contemplates that *no meetings may be held* on board ship which tend in any way to interfere with operations, and *whether or not they interfere with operations must be left to the judgment of the master,* for "it is thought better in view of war conditions to remedy abuses ashore rather than to have arguments and disputes aboard ship whether a given meeting 'interferes with the ship's operation.' "

22. *Footnote 18, Page 9 of the Intermediate Report [R. 42], Exception 23 [R. 53].*

The Board's finding that "visitors to piers and vessels should be limited to cases of absolute necessity" [Respondent's Exhibit 1, R. 137; Respondent's Exhibit 2, R. 138; Respondent's Exhibit 3, R. 152; Respondent's Exhibit 4, R. 156], and the finding that "the prohibition of 'crews' mass meetings, crews' committee meetings, and other similar meetings aboard ships' " contained in the Statement of Policy and the interpretation thereof [Board's Exhibit 7-A and 7-B, R. 398-403] do not apply to union representatives "having access to transact business in conformity with the provisions of the Act" begs the question.

Admittedly, if the collective bargaining agreement gives to unions certain duties and functions which require their presence on board, then those representatives will have business on board pertaining to the ship's operation, manning, etc.—but transacting union business is not ship's business—the collection of dues and distributing of union papers is strictly union business and they are visitors on board ship if they are on board for any reason except *ship's business.*

The concluding sentence in this footnote, to the effect that your petitioner has admitted that no governmental officer has ever interpreted these regulations as excluding union representatives from ship's business is correct so far as it goes, but is incomplete and very misleading. Your petitioner stipulated "we have never received instructions from any governmental organization, that is, any governmental branch that we were prohibited from issuing passes, nor have we been told that we could issue passes, nor have we been told that we could not issue passes to labor representatives or anyone else" [R. 172]. We contend that the responsibility is upon your petitioner to carry out the rules and regulations issued. If, in its opinion or the opinion of its masters, all persons should be excluded from the vessels, that ends the matter so long as that decision is not for the purpose of accomplishing something forbidden by the Act. We think that this is also the view of the War Shipping Administration. Board's Exhibit 7-B, [R. 402-403] provides specifically that whether a particular meeting on board a ship in any way interferes with operations is something which the master must judge. This evidence, therefore, is contrary to the findings of the Board.

There is a comment that should be made at this point. The Board has made a point that existing agreements were supposed to have been "frozen" and that such agreements contained pass provisions and supposedly the pass provisions were also frozen. That, however, is not the case as will be apparent from a reading of Exhibit 7-B in connection with Exhibit 7-A. The agreements were frozen *as modified by eliminating the various meetings on board ship.* These two exhibits introduced by the Board itself, taken alone, are sufficient to destroy any possible foundation in the evidence to support the Board's order.

23. *Lines 19-20, Page 9 of the Intermediate Report [R. 42], Exception 24 [R. 53-54].*

It is submitted that the only reasons in the record for refusing to issue passes are the very reasons which the Board says it does not believe to be valid. We cannot help what the Board believes concerning evidence supporting our contentions but we think that it has become very apparent by this time that the Trial Examiner and the Board believe only what they consider to be in support of the unions' demands and that they disbelieve everything that supports your petitioner's contentions or which might defeat the unions' demands, regardless of the evidence or information. In short, the Trial Examiner is prejudiced.

24. *Footnote 18, Page 9 of Intermediate Report [R. 42], Exception 25 [R. 54].*

We thoroughly agree that the wartime safety laws and duties and obligations of the master are not at variance with the rights of employees to exercise their privileges under the Act. Taken literally, this finding is in accordance with the law. However, again the Board begs the question. There is no evidence whatsoever that the privileges conferred under the Act are in any way restricted. The question is whether the duties and functions which the Board ascribes to collective bargaining representatives are conferred by the Act, and the answer to that is an emphatic "no."

25. *Lines 25-35, Page 9 of the Intermediate Report, and Lines 1-17 on Page 10 of the Intermediate Report [R. 43-44], Exception Nos. 26 and 27 [R. 54].*

These are entitled "Concluding Findings" and clearly represent a restatement in summary form of prior findings and conclusions. Just as prior findings are not supported by substantial evidence, these findings are likewise unsupported by substantial evidence and specific treatment of these summary findings would be a duplication. This whole finding may be summed up by saying that the Board finds that your petitioner's conduct violated Section 8 (1) of the Act by preventing its employees from bargaining collectively concerning grievances and by preventing their enjoyment of essential rights guaranteed by the Act.

26. *Finding of Fact No. IV on Page 10 of the Intermediate Report [R. 44], Exception 28 [R. 54].*

Finding that the conduct of your petitioner will lead to labor disputes, burdening and obstructing commerce, is based on a prior finding that your petitioner's conduct was an unfair labor practice, which we have shown is not supported by substantial evidence and clearly this finding is likewise not supported by substantial evidence.

27. *Paragraphs 1 and 2, Finding V, Entitled "The Remedy," Page 10 of the Intermediate Report [R. 44-45], Exceptions 29 and 30 [R. 54].*

This is in some respects a repetition of prior findings and it also includes what the Board conceives to be the necessary remedy. Being based on prior findings which are not based on substantial evidence, this finding is likewise not based on substantial evidence.

28. *The Last Sentence in the Third Paragraph of Finding V Entitled "The Remedy," on Page 10 of the Intermediate Report* [*R. 45*], *Exception 31* [*R. 54*].

Throughout the case, your petitioner urged that the law as established by the courts and the Board, would require your petitioner to issue passes to all unions demanding them if your petitioner is required to issue passes to the complaining unions. The Board here rejects any consideration of this contention by the simple expedient of finding that there is no jurisdictional question involved in this proceeding. Thus, the Board totally disregards uncontroverted evidence upon this point and the Board is not at liberty to disregard such evidence in the determination of this case.

29. *Conclusion of Law Numbers 3 and 4 Appearing on Page 11 of the Intermediate Report* [*R. 46*], *Exception 32* [*R. 55*].

These are erroneous conclusions of law based on findings of fact which we have shown to be unsupported by substantial evidence.

POINT IV.

The Case of Cities Service Oil Company et al., 122 Fed. (2d) 149, C. C. A. 2 (1941), Relied Upon by the Board, Is Not Controlling in This Case.

The Trial Examiner in his Intermediate Report quoted at length from the *Cities Service* case, and the Board adopted the Intermediate Report in its entirety. It is quite evident, therefore, that the Board is relying heavily upon this case as being controlling herein.

For the reasons set forth in Point I hereof the Court in the *Cities Service* case enforced an order of the Board concerning a matter beyond the power and jurisdiction of the Board. Therefore, the Court's decision in that case was erroneous in its entirety.

In the *Cities Service* case the Court expressly found that in that case there was substantial evidence to support the Board's order. In Point III hereof we have shown that the Board's order in this case is not supported by substantial evidence. Therefore, even if the *Cities Service* case were not erroneous in its entirety, it is not controlling herein.

In addition to the foregoing, the case now before this Court involves an order of the Board which goes far beyond the order as enforced in the *Cities Service* case. If that case is controlling in any respect, its limitations are likewise controlling. The Board has attempted to circumvent the restrictions in the *Cities Service* case by making finds in this case that were not made in the *Cities Service* case, but the several findings to which we have just referred, are not supported by substantial evidence. The *Cities Service* case was decided on July 25, 1941, upon facts arising long before the war and, in fact, long before the grave tanker shortage which manifested itself shortly before the war. Assuming, for the sake of argument, that the Court might have been justified in its holding under the circumstances of that case at the time the decision was rendered, there is no justification now under wartime conditions and the changed circumstances. At the time of the *Cities Service* case there was no way to settle a dispute over a term or condition of employment if the employer and the bargaining union persisted in their refusal to agree concerning a particular matter under negotiation. No doubt that situation was a vital consideration by the Court; however, that condition no longer exists. The National War Labor Board is now expressly empowered to dispose of disputes of that nature and there no longer can be any justification for the Board to assert its jurisdiction for expediency in settling such disputes, and there can be no justification for a court to enforce such an order.

Conclusion.

It is evident from the foregoing that the Board has been most arbitrary in this case. The Board has made a studied effort to enlarge upon its jurisdiction through its own fiat concerning matters heretofore held to be outside its jurisdiction and beyond its power by the several courts of the United States, including the Supreme Court of the United States and this Court.

Under the circumstances your petitioner has truly been aggrieved within the meaning of the Act and we are confident that this Honorable Court will not tolerate such arbitrary, unreasonable and capricious conduct by the Board.

Wherefore, your petitioner respectfully prays that this Court set aside the Board's order, with direction that the complaint issued by the Board be dismissed.

Respectfully submitted,

DAVID GUNTERT,
Attorney for Petitioner.

APPENDIX.

PART A.

Summary of Testimony.

Waldo Hammond Wilder, called as witness for the Board, testified substantially as follows: That he is port captain [R. 108] for Richfield Oil Corporation; that his duties consist of dispatching and inspecting vessels, maintaining crews and supplies on the six ocean going tankers operated by Richfield Oil Corporation [R. 109]; that under ordinary circumstances, these vessels are at sea for several days [R. 110] and may call at any port on the Pacific Coast [R. 111]; that Richfield Oil Corporation maintains terminals at Seattle, 2 to 2½ miles from the town proper [R. 112]; at Linnton, Oregon, 6 miles north of Portland [R. 112], at Point Richmond [R. 112] and Long Beach [R. 113]; that these vessels have docked at terminals operated by other companies [R. 111] and have docked at Oleum and Avon [R. 113]; that loading operations take from 12-48 hours [R. 113], but average 12-15 hours [R. 114]; that discharging operations take from 20-48 hours [R. 115] but vessels are in port several hours longer than the actual loading and discharging operations [R. 114, 115]; that sometimes vessels will discharge and then load at the same dock; that it is difficult to say just how long the average time in port would be [R. 114-115]; that recently, one of Richfield's tankers was in port for 56 hours [R. 124].

That vessels carry a crew of 36 to 40 [R. 116], of which about 10 are unlicensed deck personnel and 8 or 9 unlicensed engine department personnel [R. 116]; that in port, unlicensed deck personnel stand hose and tank top watch, and sometimes handle small amount of stores [R. 117]; that when available, work parties handle stores [R. 119]; that about one-third of the unlicensed deck and engine personnel (exclusive of wipers) would be required to be on board during loading and discharging operations [R. 118]; that when men are not on watch, they are free to go ashore when off duty; that sometimes when standby crews are available, the company hires them to relieve the regular crew—sometimes men do not come back for their watches and it is necessary to hire others [R. 121]; that a seaman need not get permission to go ashore if he is off watch [R. 121]; that the company prefers that the men leave the ship when not on duty because the fewer men on board, the safer the ship down to enough to move her in emergency [R. 118]; that the men do not have to be encouraged to go ashore, for, when the vessel arrives, the men off duty "just pile off" [R. 126]; that sometimes it is difficult to keep them long enough to deliver their mail [R. 126]; that practically all of the time off duty is spent ashore [R. 144]; that watches are arranged in two sets of four hours per day; that is, four hours on watch and 8 hours off watch [R. 121]; that sometimes in handling certain cargoes, the men are not fed on board, but instead are given meal allowances and they eat ashore [R. 121]; that the men are paid every 30 days but are allowed to draw money as needed, sometimes as often as two or three times a day, and there is a large turnover of men since the shipbuilding program and the bonus arrangement [R. 122]; that Richfield Oil Corporation does not issue any passes to its vessels [R. 127]; that the policy of not issuing passes is for the purpose of better safeguarding the vessels, their crews and the surrounding property [R. 127]; that when you issue passes to one organization, union trouble will result unless you issue them to all others [R. 129]; that this would increase the number of men on board the ship and increase the hazards on board ship [R. 129]; that the loading and discharging of petroleum products is a hazardous operation [R. 129]; that persons coming aboard would distract the loading officer [R. 129] and the men in their duties [R. 133]; that one going aboard would have an opportunity to commit sabotage or secure information valuable to the enemy, such as the nature of cargoes, convoy and escort vessel information, size and type of armament, etc. [R. 129-133]; that the company operates under the directions, rules and regulations of War Shipping Administration [R. 134]; that in his opinion the policy of refusing passes was in conformity with the Security Orders issued by the War Shipping Administration, because the fewer persons permitted aboard, the safer the ship [R. 135]; that no member of the War Shipping Administration has advised this witness that the Security Orders were or were not intended to refer to members of labor organizations [R. 145]; that Richfield Oil Corporation is required to abide by port regulations [R. 147] issued by the Coast Guard [R. 149]; that Richfield Oil Corporation's Marine Manager, Port Captain, Port Engineer and Port Steward, on occasion, board its vessels [R. 159]; that militarized guards are on guard at all times while in port [R. 160]; that vermin exterminators are permitted aboard when required [R. 160]; that in case of emergency, surveyors go aboard [R. 165]; that sometimes a laundryman is permitted to deliver crews' laundry [R. 161]; that when work is done on the vessel, the vessel is gas freed [R. 165] and made safe for repair operations; that when gas freed, there is no danger of explosion from the vessel's cargo; that the repair work is performed in shipyards [R. 164, 169]; that no one, including the witness, is permitted aboard without proper identification [R. 169].

That the company policy concerning passes was communicated to this witness by his superior, Mr. P. C. Lamb, Manager of the Marine Department, and the witness has been informed by his superior that the corporation issue no passes because of safety reasons [R. 171].

Harry Lundberg, Secretary- Treasurer of the Sailors' Union of the Pacific, and President of Seafarers' International Union of North America [R. 176] since October, 1938 [R. 177], called as Board's witness, testified substantially as follows: That he has been a sailor all his life [R. 177]; that he negotiates contracts and appears before congressional committees and governmental authorities [R. 178]; that contracts negotiated with dry cargo vessels are negotiated through associations; that agreements with tankers are signed individually [R. 179]; that the "Statement of Policy" signed with the War Shipping Administration "froze" existing contracts for the duration of the war [R. 179, 325]; that in his opinion, grievances under contracts are every-day occurrences [R. 180]; that he has passes to 470 vessels on the Pacific Coast under agreements with various shipowners [R. 181]; that only Richfield Oil Corporation, General Petroleum Corporation and Standard Oil Company do not give them passes; that Associated Oil Company does give them passes under contract dated November 18, 1942 [R. 181]; that Hillcone Steamship Company granted passes in January, 1943 [R. 181]; that the shore delegate that boards vessels is called a patrolman [R. 182]; that witness was a patrolman for 9 months in Seattle [R. 183]; that when he went aboard a vessel, he went to the ship's delegate who was a member of the crew to ascertain if there was any trouble [R. 183]; that if there was a dispute and it could not be settled on board, it was referred to the Port Committee [R. 184]; that he checked, himself, to see if complaints were legitimate and if not, nothing was done about them [R. 185]; that the shore delegate also collected dues; that the collection of dues by shore delegates or patrolmen is the most feasible method of collecting dues as it is important that the men keep their dues paid up to enjoy the benefits incident to membership [R. 185]; that the unions maintain offices in Honolulu, San Pedro, San Francisco, Portland, Seattle and Vancouver, B. C. [R. 186], and also at Point Richmond on San Francisco Bay [R. 187], and holds regular meetings each Monday night [R. 186]; that tanker personnel seldom attend meetings because they are in port only a limited time and have other things to do [R. 188]; that to adequately settle grievances, it is necessary for the union representative to go aboard ship and that he knows of no case yet when any steamship company handles them otherwise [R. 188]; that some companies often ask union representatives to come on board; that it was not possible to settle disputes except by going aboard ships because (1) the men wanted them settled on the ship before it leaves, (2) the necessity to check up on the dispute, and (3) if the man takes it up without the backing of the union delegate he will get fired [R. 190]; that the patrolman's qualifications require him to be a citizen and a *bona fide* seaman of three years' experience [R. 191]; that the patrolmen are trained by this witness in labor relations [R. 191]; that Board's Exhibit 2, rejected, is a contract with an association of some 20 steamship companies operating some 380 dry cargo vessels [R. 257]; that this agreement contains no pass provisions [R. 255] but the companies issued passes, through verbal arrangement, which are valid until revoked [R. 259]; that when on board these vessels the witness has seen them loading all kinds of war materials and troops [R. 260]; that Board's Exhibit 3 is a contract with an association of dry cargo vessel operators, and contains a pass provision [R. 278]; that Board's Exhibit 4, a contract with the Tide Water Associated Oil Company, contains a pass provision [R. 290]; that the Hillcone Steamship Company granted passes in 1943 on a verbal arrangement; such passes are subject to revocation [R. 181-182]; that he and the patrolmen had Navy identification badges and Coast Guard identification cards [R. 328]; that in addition to these documents, it was necessary to have the shipowners' pass to board vessels [R. 329-330]; that Richfield Oil Corporation, General Petroleum Corporation and Standard Oil Company do not issue passes; that Richfield Oil Corporation, prior to January 15, 1942, did issue passes, for San Pedro only [R. 333].

That Board's Exhibit 7-B refers to weekly meetings previously held on board ship but discontinued when the Statement of Principles was agreed upon [R. 411]; that such meetings were against the policy of his union [R. 411].

William Gries, a seaman by trade and for the past nine months a union patrolman with headquarters at San Pedro, California [R. 365], called as a witness by the Board, testified substantially as follows: That he is an organizer for the complaining unions [R. 365]; that his office is 7 or 8 miles from Richfield's Long Beach dock [R. 366]; that he settles grievances and that one specific instance involved the Waterman Steamship Company; that another instance involved the Alcoa Steamship Company [R. 367]; that in both instances, the company representative called him and asked him to come down and go aboard the vessels [R. 367]; that another instance involved the allocation of crews' quarters in which the War Shipping Administration, the Navy, or somebody, could not seem to get it straight and it was necessary for him to see that the men got the quarters to which they were entitled [R. 368]; that a patrolman does not necessarily wait until he is called before going on board [R. 369]; that sometimes he knows when a ship is coming in or is called generally by the company representative [R. 369]; that if a man with a dispute is on duty when the patrolman arrives, some other man is sent to relieve him [R. 370]; that he sometimes goes aboard just for the purpose of collecting dues and when aboard the men always have something to complain about [R. 371]; that he also distributes union trade papers [R. 371]; that he is generally on board a ship from one to two hours but if there is a dispute it might take longer [R. 372]; that one dispute he recalls involved Richfield Oil Corporation [R. 373]; that he settled about 90% of the grievances presented to him by going on board the vessels [R. 376]; that in October of 1942, the witness requested passes from Richfield and several times since then [R. 378]; that there were three meetings in November, three in December, and some in the first week in January, but that the company would not agree to issue passes subject to any stated conditions [R. 378-379]; on cross-examination the witness stated that he had the opportunity to, but did not solicit membership when on board ship [R. 379-380].

P. C. Lamb, Manager of the Marine Department of Richfield Oil Corporation, present at the request of the Trial Examiner, testified substantially as follows: That he issued orders abolishing passes to Captain Wilder [R. 383], who previously testified; that passes had not been issued by Richfield Oil Corporation since termination of the contract with the complaining unions [R. 384]; that he had instructed Captain Wilder that it was the company's policy not to issue passes to anyone [R. 385]; that the policy was formulated prior to Security Orders Nos. 1 and 2 of the War Shipping Administration [R. 386] and before the issuance of regulations by the Port Captain of the Los Angeles-Long Beach Harbor Area [R. 387]; that the policy was established primarily because of the war and the demands made by other unions [R. 388]; that repeatedly, representatives of unions with which Richfield did not have contracts had requested passes [R. 388-389]; that even in normal times the safety of the vessel is the important consideration and the primary objection to passes [R. 390]; that hazardous conditions are aggravated in wartime [R. 390]; that the presence of the union representatives on board is not more objectionable than others—the hazard depends on the time spent aboard the vessel [R. 390]; that the policy was adopted primarily upon the judgment of the company for the safety of the vessel and to reduce hazards [R. 390].

PART B.

Summary of Documentary Evidence Introduced.

During the course of the oral testimony a number of exhibits were introduced. A brief summary of these exhibits follows:

Board's Exhibit No. 1-A to 1-I, inclusive [R. 1-16].

These are the formal papers, including pleadings.

Board's Exhibit No. 2 (rejected) [R. 192-249].

This is the complaining unions' contract with certain dry cargo vessel operators, dated November 4, 1941. This agreement does not contain a pass provision. Grievance procedure is contained in Section 11 thereof [R. 196], and provides that port committees shall be set up with equal representation by the employer and the unions, to investigate and adjudicate all grievances and disputes and prevent violations of the contract. The committees shall meet within 24 hours upon request of either party. If the port committee fails to agree, the matter is referred to a referee whose decisions shall be final and binding. The detailed method of appointing the referee is contained in this section of the contract.

Board's Exhibit No. 3 [R. 262-283].

This is the complaining unions' contract with certain dry cargo vessel operators known as the Shipowners' Association of the Pacific Coast, dated October 27, 1941. Section 3 under "Conditions of Employment" provides [R. 278]:

> "3. Authorized representatives of the Union shall be allowed to visit members of the Union aboard ship at any time."

Detailed grievance procedure is set forth under section entitled "Port Committees and Labor Relations" [R. 280], and provides that port committees shall be set up with equal representation by an employer and the union. If a particular port committee is deadlocked, the matter is referred to the port committee at San Francisco and if an agreement is not reached within 48 hours the matter is referred to the Conciliation Service of the U. S. Department of Labor. If the Conciliation Service cannot bring about settlement within 48 hours, a referee shall be appointed by the Conciliation Service or by the Secretary of Labor and the decision of the referee shall be final and binding. The condition concerning which the dispute arose shall prevail until settlement is reached.

Board's Exhibit No. 4 [R. 285-323].

This is the complaining unions' contract with Tide Water Associated Oil Company dated November 18, 1942. Section 10, under "General Rules" [R. 290], reads as follows:

> "Section 10. Passes: Company shall distribute passes to authorized representatives of the Union who may board Company's vessels in ports for the purpose of transacting Union business. The Union agrees that it will comply with all rules and regulations at the place of entry. Such passes will be issued only while insurance satisfactory to the Company is held by the Union. The Union agrees that its representatives shall in no way interfere with or retard vessel operations. Any pass issued is subject to revocation."

Detailed grievance procedure is set forth under Sections 3 and 4 [R. 287]. Full text of the grievance procedure is set forth below for the reason that it is the grievance procedure previously agreed upon by your petitioner and the complaining unions (prior to filing of charges) and it is the grievance procedure that will appear in the contract between these parties when the entire agreement is approved by the War Labor Board.

Grievance Procedure in Board's Exhibit No. 4 [R. 287-288].

"Section 3. Union Delegates Aboard Ship: Company agrees to recognize one employee designated by the Union on each vessel to act as a delegate and representative of the Union.

Section 4. Grievance Procedure: For the purpose of adjusting complaints and grievances any employee shall endeavor to adjust the matter either in person or through the Union delegate according to the following procedure:

a. The employee's complaint shall be presented to the Captain or his delegated representative. If a satisfactory adjustment is not reached immediate notification shall be given to the Captain or his delegated representative of intent to carry the grievance to the second step of the grievance procedure; then,

b. The complaint, in writing with full explanation and argument, shall be then presented to the Company's shore representative and representatives of the Union; if satisfaction shall not be had thereby within twenty-four hours after presentation; then

c. The matter shall be referred to an arbitration committee consisting of one member chosen by the Union, one member appointed by the Company and a third member selected by these two; then

d. If Union and Company representatives cannot agree on selection of a third member within twenty-four hours, the third member shall be selected by the presiding judge of the Ninth Circuit Court of Appeals. The decision of this committee shall be final and binding."

Board's Exhibit No. 5 [R. 335-338].

This is a letter dated January 18, 1943, addressed to the complaining unions, in answer to their letter dated January 7, 1943, setting forth your petitioner's reasons for not agreeing to a preferential hiring clause and a clause providing for passes. This letter, introduced by the Board, shows clearly that the employer had been negotiating with the complaining unions, had reached substantial agreement with the unions, and was willing to continue negotiations and to reduce the agreement to writing.

Board's Exhibit No. 6 [R. 355].

This is a letter dated January 6, 1943, from the Regional Director advising your petitioner of the filing of charges by the complaining unions (the answer to this letter is Respondent's Exhibit No. 6 [R. 358-364]) in which your petitioner described in detail its reasons for refusing to issue passes.

Board's Exhibit No. 7-A [R. 398-401].

This is the so-called "Statement of Policy" which the complaining unions contend "froze" existing contracts, and which your petitioner contends prevents meetings on board ship against the operator's wishes.

Board's Exhibit No. 7-B [R. 402-403].

This is an interpretation by the War Shipping Administration of the provisions in the Statement of Policy concerning meetings held on board ship.

Board's Exhibit 8 [R. 407].

This is a photostatic copy of Mr. Lundeberg's Coast Guard identification card.

Board's Exhibit No. 9 [R. 410].

This is a photostatic copy of Mr. Lundeberg's "pass" issued by the U. S. Navy.

Respondent's Exhibit No. 1 [R. 137-138].

This is the WSA's Security Order No. 1 issued to your petitioner, as one of the War Shipping Administration's agents, directing full compliance with Security Orders and requiring immediate improvement in the methods of handling information concerning vessel movements, etc.

Respondent's Exhibit No. 2 [R. 138-144].

This is the War Shipping Administration's Security Order No. 2 issued by the WSA to your petitioner as one of its agents giving instructions concerning the security of vessels including the following:

> "10. Visitors. Visitors to piers and vessels should be limited to cases of absolute necessity."

Respondent's Exhibit No. 3 [R. 152].

This is an excerpt from war regulations for tank vessels in the Los Angeles-Long Beach Sea Area (issued by the U. S. Coast Guard), which reads, in part, as follows:

> "7. No person shall be admitted to a tankship except upon establishing a reasonable necessity therefor. * * *"
>
> "11. An identification is not a pass or license to go on board. Anyone whose presence on board the vessel or the dock appears inimical to the war effort, shall be excluded from the premises, despite possession of valid identification."

Respondent's Exhibit No. 4 [R. 156].

This is an excerpt from war regulations for the protection of waterfront petroleum terminals—Los Angeles-Long Beach Harbors (issued by the U. S. Coast Guard). These regulations in part require that owners or operators of waterfront oil terminals shall safeguard their premises and that the regulations are issued to, among other things,—

> "(a) Prevent access of persons to the terminals who do not exhibit the authorized credentials and who do not have necessity for entering."

Respondent's Exhibit Nos. 5-A to 5-E, inclusive [R. 344-354].

This is an exchange of correspondence between your petitioner and the Regional Director of the Board, in 1942, concerning a charge by the National Maritime Union that your petitioner refused to issue passes to that union. Upon a showing by your petitioner that it did not discriminate concerning passes but refused them to all persons alike, the Regional Director refused to issue a complaint and the Board upheld his decision. [See Exhibit 5-A, R. 344.]

Respondent's Exhibit No. 6 [R. 358].

This exhibit has been referred to in connection with Board's Exhibit No. 6. It sets forth your petitioner's reasons for refusing to issue passes and refers the Board to its decision in a similar charge filed by the National Maritime Union. [See Respondent's Exhibits 5-A to 5-E, inclusive.]

PART C.

The Board's order directs your petitioner to:

"1. Cease and desist from:

(a) Refusing to grant passes to representatives of the Sailors Union of the Pacific, a division of Seafarers' International Union of North America, and Seafarers' International Engine Division, a division of Seafarers' International Union of North America, in order that such representatives may go aboard the respondent's vessels for the purposes of collective bargaining, for the discussion and presentation of grievances, and for other mutual aid and protection of the employees represented by these Unions, including the collection of dues and distribution of trade papers to union members, provided, however, that the respondent is not required to issue passes for the solicitation of membership;

(b) Engaging in like or related acts or conduct interfering with, restraining, or coercing its employees in the exercise of the right of self-organization, to form, join, or assist labor organizations, to bargain collectively through representatives of their own choosing, and to engage in concerted activities for the purposes of collective bargaining or other mutual aid or protection as guaranteed in Section 7 of the Act.

2. Take the following affirmative action which will effectuate the policies of the Act:

(a) Grant passes to the duly authorized representatives of the Sailors Union of the Pacific, a division of Seafarers'

International Union of North America, and Seafarers' International Engine Division, a division of Seafarers' International Union of North America, to go aboard its vessels for the purposes of collective bargaining, for the discussion and presentation of grievances, and for other mutual aid and protection of the employees represented by the Unions, including the collection of dues and distribution of trade papers to union members, provided, however, that the respondent is not required to issue passes for the solicitation of membership;

(b) Post immediately in conspicuous places on its vessels, for a period of at least sixty (60) consecutive days from the date of posting, notices to the unlicensed deck and engine personnel, stating: (1) that the respondent will not engage in the conduct from which it is ordered to cease and desist in paragraphs 1 (a) and (b); (2) that the respondent will take the affirmative action set forth in paragraph 2 (a) hereof;

(c) Notify the Regional Director for the Twenty-first Region in writing within ten (10) days from the date of this Order what steps the respondent has taken to comply herewith."

PART D.

National Labor Relations Act.

WAGNER-CONNERY LABOR ACT

Act of July 5, 1935, c. 372, 49 Stat. 449. U. S. Code, Title 29, Sections 151-166.

(14,061)

An Act

To diminish the causes of labor disputes burdening or obstructing interstate and foreign commerce, to create a National Labor Relations Board, and for other purposes.

Be it enacted by the Senate and House of Representatives of the United States of America in Congress Assembled,

* * * * * * * * *

Sec. 7. *Rights of Employees.* Employees shall have the right to self-organization, to form, join, or assist labor organizations, to bargain collectively through representatives of their own choosing, and to engage in concerted activities, for the purpose of collective bargaining or other mutual aid or protection.

Sec. 8. *Unfair labor practices.* It shall be an unfair labor practice for an employer—

(1) To interfere with, restrain, or coerce employees in the exercise of the rights guaranteed in section 7.

(2) To dominate or interfere with the formation or administration of any labor organization or contribute financial or other support to it: Provided, that subject to

rules and regulations made and published by the Board pursuant to section 6 (a), an employer shall not be prohibited from permitting employees to confer with him during working hours without loss of time or pay.

(3) By discrimination in regard to hire or tenure of employment or any term or condition of employment to encourage or discourage membership in any labor organization: Provided, That nothing in this Act, or in the National Industry Recovery Act (U. S. C., Supp. VII, title 15, secs. 701-712), as amended from time to time, or in any code or agreement approved or prescribed thereunder, or in any other statute of the United States, shall preclude an employer from making an agreement with a labor organization (not established, maintained, or assisted by any action defined in this Act as an unfair labor practice) to require as a condition of employment membership therein, if such labor organization is the representative of the employees as provided in section 9(a), in the appropriate collective bargaining unit covered by such agreement when made.

(4) To discharge or otherwise discriminate against an employee because he has filed charges or given testimony under this Act.

(5) To refuse to bargain collectively with the representatives of his employees, subject to the provisions of Section 9(a).

Sec. 9(a) *Representatives and elections.* Representatives designated or selected for the purposes of collective bargaining by the majority of the employees in a unit appropriate for such purposes, shall be the exclusive representatives of all the employees in such unit for the purposes of collective bargaining in respect to rates of pay, wages, hours of employment, or other conditions of employment: Provided, That any individual employee or a group of employees shall have the right at any time to present grievances to their employer.

* * * * * * * * *

Sec. 10. *Prevention of unfair labor practices.* (a) The Board is empowered, as hereinafter provided, to prevent any person from engaging in any unfair labor practice (listed in section 8) affecting commerce. This power shall be exclusive, and shall not be affected by any other means of adjustment or prevention that has been or may be established by agreement, code, law, or otherwise.

(b) Whenever it is charged that any person has engaged in or is engaging in any such unfair labor practice, the Board, or any agent or agency designated by the Board for such purposes, shall have power to issue and cause to be served upon such person a complaint stating the charges in that respect, and containing a notice of hearing before the Board or a member thereof, or before a designated agent or agency, at a place therein fixed, not less than five days after the serving of said complaint. Any such complaint may be amended by the member, agent, or agency conducting the hearing or the Board in its discretion at any time prior to the issuancy of an order based thereon. The person so complained of shall have the right to file an answer to the original or amended complaint and to appear in person or otherwise and give testimony at the place and time fixed in the complaint. In the discretion of the member, agent or agency conducting the hearing or the Board, any other person may be allowed to intervene in the said proceeding and to present testimony. In any such proceeding the rules of evidence prevailing in courts of law or equity shall not be controlling.

(c) The testimony taken by such member, agent or agency or the Board shall be reduced to writing and filed with the Board. Thereafter, in its discretion, the Board upon notice may take further testimony or hear argument. If upon all the testimony taken the Board shall be of the opinion that any person named in the complaint has engaged in or is engaging in any such unfair labor practice, then the Board shall state its findings of fact and shall issue and cause to be served on such person an order requiring such person to cease and desist from such unfair labor practice, and to take such affirmative action, including reinstatement of employees with or without back pay, as will effectuate the policies of this Act. Such order may further require such person to make reports from time to time showing the extent to which it has complied with the order. If upon all the testimony taken the Board shall be of the opinion that no person named in the complaint has engaged in or is engaging in any such unfair labor practice, then the Board shall state its findings of fact and shall issue an order dismissing the said complaint.

(d) Until a transcript of the record in a case shall have been filed in a court, as hereinafter provided, the Board may at any time, upon reasonable notice and in such manner as it shall deem proper, modify or set aside, in whole or in part, any finding or order made or issued by it.

(e) The Board shall have power to petition any circuit court of appeals of the United States (including the Court of Appeals of the District of Columbia), or if all the circuit courts of appeals to which application may be made are on vacation, any district court of the United States (including the Supreme Court of the District of Columbia), within any circuit or district, respectively, wherein the unfair labor practice in question occurred or wherein such person resides or transacts business, for the enforcement of such order and for appropriate temporary relief or restraining order, and shall certify and file in the court a transcript of the entire record in the proceeding, including the pleadings and testimony upon which such order was entered and the findings and order of the Board. Upon such filing, the court shall cause notice thereof to be served upon such person, and thereupon shall have jurisdiction of the proceeding and of the question determined therein, and shall have power to grant such temporary relief or restraining order as it deems just and proper, and to make and enter upon the pleadings, testimony and proceedings set forth in such transcript a decree enforcing, modifying, and enforcing as so modified, or setting aside in whole or in part the order of the Board. No objection that has not been urged before the Board, its member, agent or agency, shall be considered by the court, unless the failure or neglect to urge such objection shall be excused because of extraordinary circumstances. The findings of the Board as to the facts, if supported by evidence, shall be conclusive. If either party shall apply to the court for leave to adduce additional evidence and shall show to the satisfaction of the court that such additional evidence is material and that there were reasonable grounds for the failure to adduce such evidence in the hearing before the Board, its member, agent, or agency, the court may order such additional evidence to be taken before the Board, its member, agent, or agency, and to be made a part of the transcript. The Board may modify its findings as to the facts, or make new findings, by reason of additional evidence so taken and filed, and it shall file such modified or new findings, which, if supported by evidence, shall be conclusive, and shall file its recommendations, if any, for the modification or setting aside of its original order. The jurisdiction of the court shall be exclusive and its judgment and decree shall be final, except that the same shall be subject to review by the appropriate circuit court of appeals if application was made to the district court as hereinabove provided, and by the Supreme Court of the United States upon writ of certiorari or certification as provided in sections 239 and 240 of the Judicial Code, as amended (U. S. C., title 28, secs. 346 and 347).

(f) Any person aggrieved by a final order of the Board granting or denying in whole or in part the relief sought may obtain a review of such order in any circuit court of appeals of the United States in the circuit wherein the unfair labor practice in question was alleged to have been engaged in or wherein such person resides or transacts business, or in the Court of Appeals of the District of Columbia, by filing in such court a written petition praying that the order of the Board be modified or set aside. A copy of such petition shall be forthwith served upon the Board, and thereupon the aggrieved party shall file in the court a transcript of the entire record in the proceeding, certified by the Board, including the pleading and testimony upon which the order complained of was entered and the findings and order of the Board. Upon such filing, the court shall proceed in the same manner as in the case of an application by the Board under subsection (e), and shall have the same exclusive jurisdiction to grant to the Board such temporary relief or restraining order as it deems just and proper, and in like manner to make and enter a decree enforcing, modifying, and enforcing as so modified, or setting aside in whole or in part the order of the Board; and the findings of the Board as to the facts, if supported by evidence, shall in like manner be conclusive.

(g) The commencement of proceedings under subsection (e) or (f) of this section shall not, unless specifically ordered by the court, operate as a stay of the Board's order.

(h) When granting appropriate temporary relief or a restraining order, or making and entering a decree enforcing, modifying, and enforcing as so modified or setting aside in whole or in part an order of the Board, as provided in this section, the jurisdiction of courts sitting in equity shall not be limited by the Act entitled "An Act to amend the Judicial Code and to define and limit the jurisdiction of courts sitting in equity, and for other purposes," approved March 23, 1932 (U. S. C., Supp. VII, title 29, secs. 101-115).

(i) Petitions filed under this Act shall be heard expeditiously, and if possible within ten days after they have been docketed.

INDEX

AUTHORITIES CITED

In the United States Circuit Court of Appeals for the Ninth Circuit

No. 10437

Richfield Oil Corporation, petitioner

v.

National Labor Relations Board, respondent

ON PETITION TO REVIEW AND SET ASIDE AND ON REQUEST FOR ENFORCEMENT OF AN ORDER OF THE NATIONAL LABOR RELATIONS BOARD

BRIEF FOR THE NATIONAL LABOR RELATIONS BOARD

JURISDICTION

This case is before the Court upon petition of Richfield Oil Corporation to review and set aside an order of the National Labor Relations Board issued against petitioner pursuant to Section 10 (c) of the National Labor Relations Act (49 Stat. 449, U. S. C., 1940 ed., Title 29, Sec. 151, *et seq.*) In its answer to the petition, the Board has requested that its order be enforced (R. 90–95). The jurisdiction of this Court is based upon Section 10 (e) and (f) of the Act; petitioner, a Delaware corporation, has its principal place of business at Los Angeles, California, and transacts business within this judicial circuit.[1]

[1] The pertinent provisions of the Act are set forth in the Appendix, *infra*, pp. 33–34.

STATEMENT OF THE CASE

Upon the usual proceedings under Section 10 of the Act, detailed in the Intermediate Report of the Trial Examiner (R. 24–27), the Board issued its decision,[2] setting forth its findings of fact, conclusions of law, and order (R. 59–63; 49 N. L. R. B., No. 86), which may be briefly summarized as follows:

1. *Nature of petitioner's business.*—Petitioner is engaged in producing, refining, marketing, and transporting petroleum and petroleum products. The employees to whom this proceeding relates are seamen whom petitioner employs in the operation of its ocean-going oil tankers, which ply among the Pacific Coast ports and offshore (R. 105–106). No question of jurisdiction is presented; petitioner concedes that it is subject to the Act (R. 105; 16, Par. I–III Answer to the Complaint).

2. *The unfair labor practices.*—The Board found that, although the Unions[3] are the certified, exclusive bargaining representatives of the unlicensed personnel in the deck and engine-room departments of petitioner's tankers, petitioner has refused and is refusing to allow their representatives to board its vessels while the vessels are in port for the purpose of conferring

---

[2] With minor additions, the Board's findings and conclusions were the same as those of the Trial Examiner who conducted the hearing. Accordingly, in its decision, the Board adopted, without restating, the findings and conclusions of its Examiner, and noted the additional findings it desired to make (R. 60).

[3] Sailors Union of the Pacific, a division of Seafarers' International Union of North America, and Seafarers' International Union of North America, both affiliated with the American Federation of Labor (R. 100).

with the seamen whom the Unions represent, of negotiating with the ships' officers concerning their grievances and of performing other services in their behalf; petitioner, by this conduct, has interfered and is interfering with its employees' exercise of their right to engage in concerted activity for the purposes of collective bargaining or other mutual aid or protection, in violation of Section 8 (1) of the Act (R. 37–38, 43–44).

3. *The Board's order.*—The Board directed petitioner to allow representatives of the Unions to board its vessels so that they may investigate and present grievances in behalf of the employees whom the Unions represent, collect union dues, and distribute the Unions' newspaper among the union members (R. 62). The order explicitly declares, however, that petitioner need not allow the union representatives to solicit membership on board its vessels (*ibid.*).

SUMMARY OF ARGUMENT

I. By refusing to allow representatives of the certified unions to board its vessels, petitioner has interfered and is interfering with the exercise by its employees of the rights guaranteed in Section 7 of the Act, in violation of Section 8 (1) of the Act.

II. The Board's order is valid.

ARGUMENT

Point I

By refusing to allow representatives of the certified unions to board its vessels, petitioner has interfered and is interfering with the exercise by its employees of the rights guaranteed in Section 7 of the Act, in violation of Section 8 (1) of the Act

Concededly, petitioner has refused and is refusing to allow representatives of the Unions, which are statutory bargaining agents of its employees, to board its vessels for the purpose of conferring with the employees whom the Unions represent in regard to grievances and performing other services for the Union members (R. 333–334, 335, Bd. Exh. 5; Pet. Brief in Support of Exceptions to Int. Report, pp. 1–2).[4] The only issue in this proceeding is whether, in the circumstances of this case, the Board could properly find, as it did (R. 43–44), that petitioner's refusal to allow representatives of the Unions to board its vessels constitutes interference with the right of its employees "to engage in concerted activities, for the purpose of collective bargaining or other mutual aid or protection" (Section 7 of the Act), in violation of Section 8 (1) of the Act.

---

[4] The refusal of petitioner to permit representatives of the Unions to board its vessels dates from February 15, 1942, when collective agreements between the Unions and petitioner, which had accorded the Unions such access, expired (R. 333, 386–387).

It is undisputed that when the refusal first occurred the Unions were, and that they still are, the exclusive bargaining agents of the unlicensed personnel in the deck and engine-room departments of petitioner's tankers (R. 343–344); on September 23, 1942, the Board certified them as such bargaining agents (R. 343–344).

In concluding that the denial of access to the union epresentatives by petitioner was in derogation of the tatutory rights of petitioner's employees, the Board ointed out (R. 43):

> that [petitioner's] unlicensed deck and engine personnel are in port for a short time with very little time ashore; that tanker terminals are usually located in port areas inaccessible to union headquarters; that collective bargaining procedures for the settlement of grievances, which do not involve access are in a practical sense unworkable, and do not afford the [petitioner's] unlicensed deck and engine personnel the opportunity to bargain collectively concerning their grievances; that the refusal of [petitioner] to issue passes to the duly authorized representatives of its unlicensed deck and engine personnel for the purpose of access, prevents these seamen from receiving aid, advice, and information through their duly chosen representatives; that procedure which involves access for these purposes is prevalent today, and has long been in use in the West Coast shipping industry; that with access these representatives may investigate the nature of, assess the value of, and properly present grievances on behalf of these seamen and give to them the aid, advice and information essential for mutual protection; that without access, the [petitioner's] unlicensed deck and engine personnel would be denied the benefits of essential rights, conferred upon them by the Act, providing for collective bargaining and other mutual aid through their duly chosen representatives.

563806—43——2

A review of the salient features of the evidence demonstrates that these findings are supported by substantial evidence.

Petitioner's seamen cannot enjoy the benefits of collective bargaining, especially as regards the adjustment of their grievances, unless their union representatives are permitted to confer with them and with petitioner's officers aboard ship

Conditions of employment in the shipping industry place seamen in a singularly insecure and isolated position insofar as the enjoyment of their right to collective bargaining is concerned.[5] Petitioner's employees are in no different position in this respect from other seamen. Petitioner's tankers are in port between voyages for comparatively short periods of time, usually for no longer than from 16 to 24 hours (R. 188, 114–115, 124–125). About one-third of the unlicensed personnel in the deck and engine-room departments must stand watch at all times while their vessel is in port (R.

---

[5] The working conditions of seamen which make for such insecurity have been summed up by the Maritime Labor Board as follows:

"Unlike other workers, when a seaman sells his labor he virtually sells himself, temporarily. Of necessity he lives on the ship. There is no possibility of changing his place of work or his occupation, whether or not conditions are satisfactory, until he reaches a safe port. While he is at sea, and to a less extent ashore, the seaman is restricted in matters which other workers consider definitely personal, such as food, clothing, living quarters, associates, and recreation. . . . Hours of work are irregular if not long, and there is little provision for recreation in off time. Aboard ship the seaman's working life is strictly disciplined; while on shore, lacking in general stabilizing home ties, he has little opportunity for normal participation in the social life of any place." *Report of the Maritime Labor Board to the President and the Congress*, March 1, 1940, page 26.

See also, *Encyclopaedia of the Social Sciences*, Vol. 13, p. 613; R. W. Wissman, *The Maritime Industry* (New York: Cornell Maritime Press, 1942), p. 3.

117–118); each man's watch lasts 4 hours with 8 hours off-duty between watches (R. 121). Since all members of the crew in these departments must, in turn, stand watch, they cannot all go ashore at the same time. Moreover, members of the crew not required to stand watch are frequently ordered to remain on board the vessel to perform other work, such as painting and loading stores (R. 117, 119–121, 123–124). In addition to time consumed in the performance of work duties, petitioner's seamen must spend a good deal of the time their vessel is in port aboard ship because the vessel is their home ashore as well as at sea (R. 121–122).[6] Consequently, even during their brief intervals in port, the seamen are able to spend only a few hours ashore. Their extremely limited free time ashore is, of course, subject to many calls, such as personal business, visits with their families and friends, and recreational pursuits (R. 127, 188). For these reasons, petitioner's seamen have little opportunity when ashore to get in touch with their union representatives.[7] Their difficulty in this respect is enhanced, moreover, by the fact that union headquarters are often inaccessible and distant from the

[6] While in port, the seamen sleep and eat aboard their ship; before going ashore, they ordinarily bathe, change their clothes, secure an advance of salary from the captain, and, at times, sign new shipping articles (R. 121–122).

[7] In discussing the rulings of the National Labor Relations Board as to passes, the Maritime Labor Board has pointed out:

"In considering these rulings, it must be appreciated that seamen who belong to a labor union are usually obliged by the nature of their work to remain out of contact with union headquarters for weeks or months on end, and that many of their grievances refer to living or working conditions that cannot be fully understood except by inspection of the vessel concerned. To provide for

points where petitioner's tankers dock (R. 110–113, 186–188, 365–367).[8]

Since, in the case of seamen, the employment relationship comprehends not only wages, hours, and working conditions but touches as well vital personal matters, such as food, clothing, and living quarters, it is evident that no aspect of collective bargaining is of greater concern to seamen than the prompt adjustment of their grievances.[9] An effective grievance

---

frequent contacts aboard the vessel between union representatives and crew is thus essential to the effective functioning of a labor union representing seafaring workers." (*Report of the Maritime Labor Board to the President and to the Congress*, March 1, 1940, p. 130.)

The record in the present case affords a concrete example of the practical unworkability of a grievance procedure which does not afford access; see R. 373–376.

[8] Since union headquarters must serve seamen from many ships which dock at widely separated points in the large ports touched by petitioner's tankers, such headquarters cannot, necessarily, be located conveniently near all the docking points of such ships.

[9] Contrary to the view which petitioner advanced in argument before the Board, the negotiation of a collective agreement is not the whole of the bargaining process. As the Third Circuit, sitting *en banc*, has pointed out:

"The right of collective bargaining is, however, necessarily a continuing right. Collective agreements ordinarily, as in this case, run for definitely limited periods of time. Negotiations for their renewal must take place periodically and may commence, at least preliminarily, shortly after the signing of the preceding contract. Furthermore it may at any time become desirable or indeed necessary to bargain collectively for the modification of an existing collective agreement which has proved in practice to be in some respects unfair or unworkable or for the adjustment of complaints or alleged violations of such an agreement. Collective bargaining is thus seen to be a continuing and developing process by which, as the law now recognizes, the relationship between employer and employee is to be molded and the terms and conditions of employment progressively modified along lines which are mu-

machinery is no less important to shipowners as a means of maintaining peaceable labor relations.[10] In

tually satisfactory to all concerned. It is not a detached or isolated procedure which, once reflected in a written agreement, becomes a final and permanent result. Section 7, as we have seen, guarantees to employees the right to organize and engage in concerted activities for the purpose of collective bargaining. This right must necessarily continue so long as the prospect of future bargaining remains. It will thus be seen that the act guarantees to employees the continuous right to maintain labor organizations for the purpose of collective bargaining, after the signing of a particular collective bargaining agreement as well as before." *N. L. R. B.* v. *Newark Morning Ledger Co.*, 120 F. (2d) 266, 267 (C. C. A. 3), cert. denied, 314 U. S. 693. See, also, *N. L. R. B.* v. *Sands Mfg. Co.*, 306 U. S. 332, 342; *Rapid Roller Co.* v. *N. L. R. B.*, 126 F. (2d) 452, 459 (C. C. A. 7), cert. denied 317 U. S. 650.

The foregoing judicial explanation of the bargaining process accords with the understanding of all labor economists whose views are known to us. See, e. g., Carroll R. Daugherty, *Labor Problems in American Industry* (5th ed., New York: Houghton Mifflin Co., 1941):

"Collective bargaining is the process whereby representatives of a union meet with an employer * * * to fix the terms of employment for a certain period of time. But it includes more than the creation of an agreement. There is more to it than the negotiations lasting a week or so. It involves also the *enforcement* and *interpretation* of the agreement throughout the months of its duration [p. 450].

* * * * *

"The interpretation of the various detailed terms of the employment contract is one of the most important parts of collective bargaining" [p. 452].

See also R. W. Wissman, *The Maritime Industry* (New York: Cornell Maritime Press, 1942), pp. 73–74; Clinton S. Golden and Harold J. Ruttenberg, *The Dynamics of Industrial Democracy* (New York: Harper Bros., 1942), p. 43; The Twentieth Century Fund, *How Collective Bargaining Works* (New York: The Twentieth Century Fund, 1942), pp. 51, 244, 314, 360, 362, 418, 566, 596, 644, 652, 736, 801, 858, 934–940.

[10] "The mere existence of collective agreements, therefore, while representing a step toward industrial peace, is not of itself a guarantee against labor stoppages * * *. It is also inevitable that

response to this need, an informal procedure for the adjustment of grievances has developed in the shipping industry. Under this procedure, which was described at the hearing (R. 180–186, 190–191, 258–324, 325–328, 332–333, 367–372, 278, Bd. Exh. 3, clause 3; R. 290, Bd. Exh. 4, Section 10), a representative of the accredited union, referred to as a "patrolman" or a "shore delegate," boards the vessel when it arrives in port and confers with the "ship's delegate," a member of the crew selected by the union to report grievances or other violations of the collective agreement.[11] The ship's delegate relates to the "patrolman" whatever grievances may exist; the "patrolman" then investigates the merits of the grievances by conferring with members of the crew, and, if a grievance concerns physical conditions aboard ship, by inspecting the conditions about which complaint is being made.[12] If the investigation of the grievance

---

under the manifold circumstances of day-to-day operations, misunderstandings and controversies arise. In case such differences are not effectively adjusted, they tend to culminate in the use of economic weapons and force which destroy the orderly relationships established by collective agreements. The maintenance of industrial stability, therefore, requires that proper procedure be followed for the adjustment of disputes which happen to arise during the life of an agreement * * *." R. W. Wissman, *op. cit.*, p. 74.

[11] A "patrolman" must be a citizen of the United States at the time of his appointment, and must have had at least 3 years' experience as a seaman prior to his appointment, under the Unions' regulations (R. 191).

[12] Whenever the "patrolman" finds it necessary in conducting such an investigation to confer with a member of the crew standing watch, he has another seaman of like qualifications temporarily relieve the man on duty, in order to prevent a disruption of the ship's routine (R. 370).

by the "patrolman" reveals that it is lacking in merit, that is the end of the matter. If, on the other hand, the patrolman believes that there is merit in the grievance, he endeavors to adjust the complaint through direct negotiation with the ship's officers (R. 180–185, 367–370).[13] Only if this informal procedure fails to bring about a settlement of the dispute, is resort had to the cumbersome, formal grievance ma-

---

[13] The informal procedure just described is observed throughout the Pacific Coast. The witness Lundeberg testified that his union has "passes to board 470 ships on the Pacific Coast" (R.181), and that only 2 shipowners in the coastal area, other than petitioner, have not given his union passes (*ibid.*). Indeed, in describing the grievance procedure observed generally throughout the entire maritime industry a recent study states:

"Most maritime agreements contain rules of procedure to be followed when disputes arise while they are in force * * *. The first step in the settlement of the dispute is the presentation of the complaint to his immediate superior. The latter appeals to the head of the department in which the employee involved is employed. An appeal is then made to the master. If the complaint cannot be settled to the mutual satisfaction of the employee and of the department head, or of the master, the decision of the latter is binding until the vessel arrives at the port where the "shipping articles" terminate. *The complaint is then referred to the shore delegate. In case the shore delegate* (*who goes aboard ship*) is not able to adjust the grievance in question, he refers it to the shore representative of the company concerned. If these two cannot agree either, the matter is submitted to the major officials of both the union and the company, or to the employers' association. If the deadlock persists, nevertheless, the dispute is referred to the Port Committee." R. W. Wissman, *The Maritime Industry*, pp. 74–75. [Italics supplied.]

See also: *Report of the Maritime Labor Board to the President and to the Congress*, March 1, 1940, pp. 189–192; *Hearing Before the Committee on Merchant Marine and Fisheries, House of Representatives, 75th Congress, 1st Session, on H. R. 5193*, May 26, 1937, p. 73; *Maritime Labor Grows Up, Frank M. Kleiler, Survey Graphic*, January 1939, p. 19.

chinery of the collective agreement (R. 180–181).[14] The efficiency of the informal method of adjusting grievances aboard ship is borne out by the testimony of the witness Gries, a "patrolman," that about 90 percent of the grievances which he has handled have been settled in this manner (R. 376–377). It is clear, therefore, as the Board found (R. 37–38, note 15), that as a practical matter petitioner's seamen cannot enjoy their collective bargaining rights with respect to grievances, if their union representatives are deprived of the right to board petitioner's vessels.[15]

---

[14] It is pointed out in the *Report of the Maritime Labor Board* (pp. 191–192), previously mentioned, that the formal machinery for the adjustment of grievances in maritime agreements is not frequently resorted to because a more expeditious settlement of grievances is possible through informal negotiation. One reason for this, as the *Report* explains, is that the first port at which a ship arrives after a dispute has arisen may be one in which no joint committee for the settlement of disputes is maintained. Thus, the *Report* states (p. 191, n. 17) that of 192 disputes occurring in harbors (as distinct from those occurring at sea) during a stated period, about 30 percent arose in ports other than those in which joint port committees for the adjustment of grievances existed. The *Report* continues (p. 192):

"Thus, the port committees [established under the customary grievance machinery in maritime contracts] are designed to function only after several other steps have been taken. The wide dispersion and physical mobility of the working force in this phase of the industry probably make formal consideration of disputes by a joint committee impractical in their first stages.

"These inherent factors do not entirely account for the comparatively limited use now being made of the port committee system, however. Both parties admit a preference for the direct method of adjustment and, apparently by tacit agreement, have developed the practice of convening the committees only when all other efforts have failed."

[15] As is hereinafter noted (p. 30), the Second Circuit, in *N. L. R. B.* v. *Cities Service Oil Co.*, 122 F. (2d) 149, decided the question

It is therefore apparent that, if the maritime employer could grant or deny access to his vessels to accredited union representatives at pleasure, he would be in a strategic position to hinder union activity among his seamen. Deprived of such access unions would be denied the opportunity to serve their members effectively in the area of collective bargaining most vital to them. Furthermore, the barriers to contact ashore between the union and its members, inherent in the nature of the industry, would make it virtually impossible for seamen to participate in union affairs, were they denied access to their union representatives aboard ship. An employer bent on discouraging union membership would not be slow to take advantage of such a power to insulate his employees from union representatives.[16]

here involved in accordance with the Board's position. In sustaining the Board, the Court pointed out (at p. 151):

"Ships, and particularly these oil tankers, which ordinarily remain in port for a day only, afford less opportunity for investigation of labor conditions than do factories where the employees go home every afternoon and have the evenings at their disposal. There is no cessation of work at the end of each day for seamen on a tanker. A large number of them are on watch, others are loading or discharging cargo; their hours for work and shore leave are different and, in the short time the vessel is in port, it is impossible for Union representatives to assemble the unlicensed personnel either on shore or on shipboard to discuss grievances or investigate conditions. The Union must have the members of the crew readily accessible in order to work to any real advantage and the complaints frequently relate to conditions on and even of the vessel itself."

[16] The Board not infrequently encounters such situations, the most familiar of which arises where the employer maintains a "company town" and takes advantage of his role as landlord to exclude union organizers. *Matter of Harlan Fuel Company and*

563806—43——3

It is clear from the foregoing, that by departing from its former practice of granting passes to the Unions' representatives—a practice which, as has been shown (*supra*, pp. 9–12), is generally prevalent in the industry—petitioner is depriving its employees of the only way in which they can effectively exercise their rights under the Act.

Petitioner's alleged reasons for excluding union representatives from its vessels are without substance

1. *The contention that war-time regulations of the Captain of the Port and of the War Shipping Administration require petitioner to discontinue granting*

United Mine Workers of America, District 19, 8 N. L. R. B. 25, 31–32; *Matter of Weyerhaeuser Timber Co.*, 31 N. L. R. B. 258; cf. *Matter of Commonwealth Telephone Company and Theodore R. Siplon et al.*, 13 N. L. R. B. 317, 322, 325. In *N. L. R. B.* v. *West Kentucky Coal Company*, 116 F. (2d) 816 (C. C. A. 6) the Court enforced a Board order designed to remedy such an unfair labor practice by requiring the employer to cease and desist from "denying to its employees who reside in houses owned by the respondent the right to have any persons call at their homes for the purpose of consulting, conferring or advising with, talking to, meeting, or assisting, the respondent's employees or any of them, in regard to the rights of said employees under the Act * * *." See *Matter of West Kentucky Coal Company and United Mine Workers of America, District No. 23*, 10 N. L. R. B. 88, 105–107, 133.

The principle applied in these decisions is that, "Inconvenience, or even some dislocation of property rights, may be necessary in order to safeguard the right to collective bargaining." *N. L. R. B.* v. *Cities Service Oil Co.*, 122 F. (2d) 149, 152 (C. C. A. 2). That familiar doctrine was recently applied in *N. L. R. B.* v. *The Denver Tent & Awning Co.*, decided October 25, 1943, 13 L. R. R. 284 (C. C. A. 10), in which the employer's promulgation of a plant rule prohibiting union discussion in its plant, in terms broad enough to ban such activity even at times when employees were not working, was held to violate the Act. See also *N. L. R. B.* v. *Wm. Davies Co.*, 135 F. (2d) 179 (C. C. A. 7), cert. denied 64 S. Ct. 82.

passes to the Unions is contrary to the evidence.[17]—The regulations to which petitioner refers (R. 137–157, Resp. Exhs. 1, 2, 3, and 4) merely instruct shipowners to bar visitors from piers and vessels if their visit is unnecessary. But, as petitioner conceded (R. 172–173), no agency of the Government has ever construed these regulations as requiring shipowners to deny passes to union representatives (R. 42, footnote 17; 145–146, 172–173). Indeed, the Navy and the Coast Guard—the very Agencies charged with safeguarding our piers, docks, and shipping—have provided representatives of the Unions, including "patrolmen," with identification badges authorizing them to enter piers and docks for the purpose of boarding ships on union business (R. 328–331, 405–411, Bd. Exhs. 8 and 9). At times, indeed, the Navy has itself requested union agents to board ships for that purpose (R. 260). Nor can petitioner justify its stand by the policy of the War Shipping Administration. For the War Shipping Administration issued a "Statement of Policy" on May 4, 1942, designed to stabilize collective-bargaining relations in the maritime industry by requiring all union contracts then existing to be kept in force for the duration of the War (R. 324–326, 396–401, Bd. Exh. 7–A). Many such contracts have an explicit undertaking by the employer to grant union representatives passes to board his vessels (Bd. Exh. No. 4, § 10; Bd. Exh. No. 3, p. 12, I. 3; R. 290, 278, 180–185, 258–326, 398, Bd. Exh. No. 7–A, R. 332–333). Clearly, therefore, there is no basis in fact for

[17] The Captain of the Port is an officer of the United States Coast Guard (R. 133, 149).

petitioner's assertion that the War Shipping Administration desires it to exclude union agents from its vessels.[18] The evidence, in short, demonstrates, as the Board found, that no Government regulation sanctions petitioner's refusal to allow union representatives aboard its vessels.[19]

2. *The contention that access should be denied union agents in order to minimize the hazards of accident and sabotage is without merit.*—There is not a scintilla of evidence for petitioner's assertion that the presence of union representatives aboard ship has increased these hazards. The Board pointed out, moreover, that petitioner "has not seen fit to exclude laundry agents, extra-work parties, not members of the crew. and in most instances [casual labor] 'picked up' [in the port area]" (R. 40; 119, 159–161); further, that "the record does not indicate that any individuals formerly permitted access have been denied that right except the Unions' representatives" (R. 40). And, as has been noted (*supra,* pp. 14–16), the agencies of the Government charged with responsiblity for the safety of our shipping have not excluded union repre-

[18] It should be noted that there is nothing in the Board's order that would compel petitioner to allow the crew to hold union meetings aboard ship in violation of war-time regulations. Petitioner's statement (Pet. Br., p. 53) that such meetings are contrary to instructions of the War Shipping Administration, even if correct, is therefore beside the point.

[19] In appraising petitioner's sincerity in this regard, it should be noted that petitioner had assumed the position that it would deny union representatives access to its vessels *before* the regulations upon which it professes to rely were promulgated (R. 385–388). Obviously, therefore, petitioner could not have relied upon the regulations when it adopted that position.

sentatives from piers, dock, and ships. Moreover, as the Board has said (R. 40), "it is the almost universal practice of the shipping industry on the West Coast to grant access to the duly authorized representatives of their seamen, whether or not such right is provided for in collective bargaining contracts" (pp. 9–12, note 14, *supra*).[20] In view of these facts, the Board was fully justified in finding that to compel petitioner to allow representatives of the Unions to board its vessels would not "require any conduct which is in derogation of [war-time safety regulations], or which would endanger the safety of the [petitioner's] vessels, or adversely affect discipline on board these vessels" (R. 60–61). Since petitioner has attempted to justify its conduct by war-time conditions, it should be added that to compel petitioner to grant passes will promote, not hinder, our war effort because the expeditious settlement of grievances which might provoke serious labor strife is possible only through negotiation aboard ship between the Unions' representatives and the ship's officers.[21]

---

[20] That right has been granted, it should be noted, even when ships have been taking on troops, or loading aircraft, ammunition, and torpedoes (R. 259–260, 323–325).

[21] The assertion that petitioner would be compelled by the Board's order to allow contending unions to wage membership campaigns aboard its vessels in order to escape a charge of discrimination is patently unfounded: The Board's order expressly provides that petitioner need not allow representatives of the Unions to solicit membership aboard its tankers (R. 61). Hence there would be no discrimination if petitioner refused to issue passes to a competing union for a purpose denied by the Board's order to the Unions.

3. *The contention that other reasonable methods may be employed by the Unions in bargaining concerning grievances is not well founded.*—Petitioner, ignoring the evidence previously summarized, contended before the Board that the presence aboard ship of the Unions' "patrolmen" is unnecessary for the prompt disposition of grievances. In making this assertion, petitioner stressed the role of the ship's delegate, an ordinary seaman, in attempting to settle grievances with the ship's officers, and suggested that if the seamen were dissatisfied with the outcome of a grievance in any case, they could take up their grievance with the Unions' "patrolmen" when they went ashore.

Petitioner's stress upon the role of the ship's delegate is a significant reflection of its attitude toward bargaining with the Unions. If the seamen had to rely upon the ship's delegate alone for the settlement of grievances, they would be deprived of the very thing the Act was intended to give them—the right to have their collective-bargaining agent represent them in the bargaining process. The denial of that right in the settlement of grievances would deprive the seamen of skilled negotiators whose independence is not compromised by dependence upon the shipowner for their livelihood.[22]

[22] In the maritime industry especially, the ordinary employee is in no position to bargain vigorously on his own behalf (R. 190–191). As the Maritime Labor Board, in discussing the insecure position of the individual seaman, has pointed out:

"Almost his entire life represents a departure from the normal way of living. Legally the seaman is restricted. Once he signs shipping articles he becomes a member of a group apart whose

The suggestion that the seamen could relate their grievances to the "patrolman" when they went on shore, and that the "patrolman" could negotiate a settlement of the grievances with petitioner's shore officials is notable for the extreme hardship it would cause the Unions and is unworkable because of employment conditions in the industry. As has been noted, a system of rotating watches and other work assignments while their vessel is in port makes it necessary for members of the crew to go ashore at different times (*supra*, pp. 6–7). Consequently, in order to confer with the seamen individually as they came ashore concerning a grievance, the "patrolman" would be compelled to remain on the dock for long periods of time. Such a practice would also deprive the "patrolman" of an opportunity to assess the merits of a grievance by inspecting the parts

---

rights and duties are closely circumscribed by a special code of laws. Economically he is insecure; his right to industrial self-government is often unrecognized and his collective bargaining challenged." [*Report of the Maritime Labor Board*, March 1940, at p. 26.] See also D. Yoder, *Labor Economics and Labor Problems*, 2nd ed. (1939: McGraw-Hill Book Co., Inc., New York), p. 497.

The Second Circuit, in the *Cities Service* case (*infra*, p. 30) expressly recognized the necessity for having the unions' "patrolmen" represent the seamen in adjusting grievances, saying (page 151):

"It may be true that many, or even most, grievances are settled on the ship by the ship's committee without the intervention of the Union, but one of the prime objects of the Union is to afford the seamen advisors and negotiators who are not continually under the eye of the master and inclined through fear of untoward consequences to defer to his demands. Its advice as to major differences would naturally be needed and in many cases it cannot advise the personnel wisely without visiting the ship and seeing the conditions under which work is done and of which criticism is made."

of the ship having relation to the dispute. Moreover the "patrolman's" inability to adjust a grievance with the ship's officers aboard ship would preclude resort to the employer's agents most familiar with the subject matter of the controversy. In the absence of a satisfactory means of investigating grievances, the Unions would be forced to present for adjustment through the cumbersome, formal machinery of the contract all grievances having surface validity, in order to safeguard the rights of their men. This would, of course, result in a great waste of time to no good purpose, and what is more important from the point of view of the seamen, would result in protracted delay in the disposition of their grievances.[23] In summarizing the reasons which establish how utterly unworkable are the grievance procedures which petitioner suggests, the opinion of the Court in the *Cities Service* case (page 30 *infra*) states (page 151):

[23] A grievance procedure which fails to settle grievances promptly is worse than useless—"A grievance long delayed in settlement is likely to be a grievance substantially lost." Slichter, *Union Policies and Industrial Management* (The Brookings Institution, Washington, D. C., 1941), p. 444; Daugherty, *Labor Problems in American Industry* (Houghton-Mifflin Co., New York, 1938), pp. 452–453; Bundy, *Collective Bargaining* (National Foremen's Institute, Inc., New York & Chicago, 1937), p. 20; Tead and Metcalf, *Personnel Administration* (McGraw-Hill Book Co., Inc., New York, 1933), pp. 225–230; Watkins and Dodd, *The Management of Labor Relations* (McGraw-Hill Book Co., Inc., New York, 1938), p. 695; Yoder, *Labor Economics and Labor Problems* (McGraw-Hill Book Co., Inc., New York, 1933), p. 588. This observation applies with particular force to seamen, whose grievances frequently relate to such things as unsatisfactory food and improper living conditions.

Respondents suggest that the so-called ship's committee consisting of three members of the crew chosen by the seamen can present complaints to the ship's officers and if the grievances are not settled thus, can report in person or mail statements to the Union of matters in dispute which the Union may then take up with the respondent's shore officials. But negotiations conducted in such a way would be slow and the men would lack the advantage of having their bargaining agent promptly acquainted with grievances by the seamen themselves and ready at once to negotiate with the shore officials. Moreover, so far as possible the men themselves should have the privilege of airing their individual complaints to their representatives, just as do employees whose work is on land. The suggestion that the Union representatives can be stationed on the dock, there investigate complaints by meeting members of the crew as they come off the ship and after thus learning the facts from seamen can then bargain with respondent's shore officials, is subject to the objection that the dock is manifestly no place for an adequate discussion of labor grievances. Even if, despite the inconvenience, the men were able to visit Union headquarters for such discussion of their grievances, they would not have the presence and backing of experienced bargaining representatives when presenting their claims to the ships' officers. Nor under such restrictions can there be adequate discussion by the delegate with the ships' officers of matters requiring explanation.

Summation: petitioner has violated and is violating Section 8 (1) of the Act

Through the passage of the Act, Congress sought to protect commerce by "encouraging practices fundamental to the friendly adjustment of industrial disputes * * * and by restoring equality of bargaining power between employers and employees" (Section 1 of the Act). To achieve this purpose, Congress expressly declared that it is the policy of the United States to eliminate obstructions to commerce flowing from industrial strife "by encouraging the practice and procedure of collective bargaining" (Section 1 of the Act). To make this policy effective, Section 7 of the Act guarantees employees the right "to bargain collectively through representatives of their own choosing," and Section 8 (1) enjoins employer interference with the free exercise of that right. In the Merchant Marine Act of 1936, as amended, Congress explicitly affirmed that the National Labor Relations Act should apply to maritime employees.[24]

In laying upon employers the obligation to bargain collectively with the accredited representatives of their employees, Congress could not set out in detail every aspect of the obligation it imposed. Instead, Congress used the familiar technique of enacting a broad, general command, and creating an expert administrative body to determine, in particular cases, subject to appropriate judicial review, the fair implications of that command. It would seem to be axiomatic that in discharging that responsibility the Board and the

[24] Section 1002 of the Merchant Marine Act of 1936, as amended in 1938 (52 Stat. 965, 46 U. S. C. A., Sec. 1252).

reviewing courts should, as the Second Circuit has said, effectuate the recognized legislative objectives of the Act by construing the right of employees to bargain collectively, and the correlative obligation of employers to refrain from interfering with the exercise of that right, in such a way as to comprehend "whatever is reasonably appropriate to protect it" (*Art Metals Const. Co.* v. *N. L. R. B.,* 110 F. (2d) 148, 150).[25] Cf. *H. J. Heinz Co.* v. *N. L. R. B.*, 311 U. S. 514, 523–525; *Warner* v. *Goltra,* 293 U. S. 155, 156, 158. So construed, the Act clearly condemns petitioner's refusal to allow representatives of the Unions to board its vessels as unwarranted interference with its employees' right to self-organization and collective bargaining, especially as regards grievances. Indeed, the findings of the Board, previously set out, p. 5, *supra,* demonstrate that petitioner's conduct seriously impairs "the bargaining process" and tends "to frustrate the aim of the statute to se-

[25] In recognition of this well-established canon of statutory interpretation the courts have held, for example, (1) that an employer must as an implicit aspect of his bargaining obligation be willing to enter into a signed contract with the accredited representative of his employees, once terms have been reached, notwithstanding that the Act does not impose such an obligation upon him in so many words (*H. J. Heinz Co.* v. *N. L. R. B.*, 311 U. S. 514); (2) that he must cooperate to a reasonable extent with the accredited bargaining agent in facilitating the bargaining process; hence, must make his representatives available for bargaining conferences at reasonable times and places (*N. L. R. B.* v. *P. Lorillard Co.*, 117 F. (2d) 921, 924 (C. C. A. 6), aff'd on this point, 314 U. S. 512); and (3) that he must be "sincere" in his bargaining negotiations with his employees' representative (*N. L. R. B.* v. *Biles-Coleman Lumber Co.*, 98 F. (2d) 18, 22 (C. C. A. 9).

cure industrial peace through collective bargaining." *H. J. Heinz Co.* v. *N. L. R. B.*, 311 U. S. 514, 524, 526.[26]

The fallacy in petitioner's contention that the adjustment of grievances is not part of the collective-bargaining procedure which the Act protects

The basic fallacy that runs through petitioner's entire argument is the mistaken notion that the adjustment of individual grievances is not part of the practice and procedure of collective bargaining protected by the Act. From this basic misconception, petitioner argues that *until* a collective contract has been negotiated, the statutory bargaining agent has no role to play in the adjustment of individual grievances which the employer is bound to respect (Pet. Br. pp. 21–22), and that *after* a collective agreement has been executed the only rights which an accredited union may assert under the Act, so far as grievances are concerned, are those defined in the agreement itself

[26] It may be conceded, as petitioner argued before the Board, that the matter of passes is, in some respects, an appropriate subject for bargaining. But it by no means follows, as petitioner seems to think, that petitioner is not for that reason obligated under the Act to issue passes *for certain purposes* essential to the carrying on of the collective-bargaining process. The fallacy in petitioner's assumption is exposed by the *Heinz* case (311 U. S. 514). Although a union may in the course of negotiations with an employer *agree* that the terms of a contract should not be reduced to writing—and, in this sense, the matter of a written or an oral contract is an appropriate bargaining subject—yet the Supreme Court has held that the Act compels the employer to sign a contract, once terms are agreed upon, if the accredited union makes that request. In short, it is for the Board and the courts to determine the scope of the employer's statutory obligations even though the accredited representative of the employees may in bargaining accept less than its due.

(*ibid.*) Thus, the net result of petitioner's thesis is that so far as the Act is concerned, an accredited union would have no right to adjust individual grievances either for its members, or for non-members in the appropriate bargaining unit desiring its services. Petitioner cites no authority, either legal or otherwise which, when correctly understood, supports this astounding proposition.[27] This was indeed, the very proposition that was rejected in the *Newark Morning Ledger* case (note 9, pages 8–9, *supra*).

Petitioner's thesis loses sight of the explicit declaration in Section 1 of the Act that Congress intended to encourage and protect self-organization by employees, not only "for the purpose of negotiating the terms and conditions of their employment," but for the much broader purpose, as well, of encouraging employees to utilize their collective economic strength for their "mutual aid" and "protection." The terms of Section 7 of the Act, which define the rights that the Act confers upon employees, are broadly phrased so as to effectuate this policy. In conformity with this clear expression of Congressional intent, the courts have repeatedly held that an accredited bargaining agent has the statutory right not only of negotiating a collective agreement with the employer, but has, as well, the equally important right of adjusting individual grievances both before and after a collective agreement has been entered into. Illustrative of the employer's duty to

[27] We hereinafter point out that the decisions of this Court and of the National War Labor Board relied on by petitioner cannot possibly be read as supporting this thesis (*infra*, pp. 28–30).

treat with the statutory bargaining agent concerning grievances arising *after* a collective agreement has been signed is the *Newark Morning Ledger* case, previously mentioned (note 9, pages 8–9, *supra*). This continuing employer obligation was held by the Supreme Court to encompass, moreover, not merely a duty to interpret and apply the collective agreement in adjusting grievances, but also a continuing duty to bargain in good faith with the union in regard to proposals for modification of the contract. *N. L. R. B.* v. *The Sands Manufacturing Co.,* 306 U. S. 332, 342. An illustration of the employer's statutory obligation to negotiate with the accredited union for the adjustment of grievances arising *prior* to the consummation of a collective agreement is afforded by *N. L. R. B.* v. *W. C. Bachelder,* 120 F. (2d) 574, 577–578 (C. C. A. 7), cert. denied 314 U. S. 647. In the *Bachelder* case, the accredited union requested the employer to reinstate some of its members who had previously been laid off. Contending that the question of reinstating these men was not one that the Act compelled him to discuss with the Union,[28] the employer refused to negotiate with it concerning their reinstatement. The Court, as did the Board, held that the employer had failed in his statutory bargaining obligation, resting its conclusion in large part on the employer's stand respecting the reinstatement question.

The error in petitioner's conception of the collective-bargaining process is further demonstrated by

[28] In taking this position the employer said that, "negotiation contemplates an agreement for future activities but does not contemplate a settlement of past grievances" (120 F. (2d) at 577).

a group of Supreme Court decisions, of which *National Licorice Co.* v. *N. L. R. B.,* 309 U. S. 350, is illustrative. At a time when it had no union contract, the employer in the *National Licorice* case entered into individual employment contracts with its workers, barring, among other things, the employees' right to invoke the assistance of a union in seeking to obtain the redress of grievances that might arise from their dismissal.[29] The Supreme Court's denunciation of these individual contracts rested squarely upon the Court's recognition that, aside from any collective agreement, employees have a statutory right to invoke the aid of a union in adjusting grievances with their employer. Indeed, the guaranty of the statute concerning the right of employees to act in concert through a union in regard to grievances is not even limited to grievances touching their employment. In *N. L. R. B.* v. *Peter Cailler Kohler Swiss Chocolates Co.,* 130 F. (2d) 503 (C. C. A. 2), for example, the question was presented as to whether the Act protected an employee who instigated the adoption by his union of a resolution condemning his employer for certain action the employer had taken relating to a controversy between rival milk-producers' associations. The employer discharged the employee for having instigated the adoption of such a resolution, contending

[29] In condemning this contractual surrender of employees' rights under the Act, the Supreme Court pointed out: "The effect of this clause was to discourage, if not forbid any presentation of the discharged employee's grievances to appellant through a labor organization or his chosen representatives, or in any way except personally" (309 U. S. at 360).

that the publication of the resolution in the newspapers was detrimental to its business, and that the Act did not protect employee concerted action unrelated to the employment relationship itself. In rejecting this unduly narrow view of the Act, Judge Learned Hand, writing for a unanimous Court, declared:

> When all the other workmen in a shop make common cause with a fellow workman over his separate grievance, and go out on strike in his support, they engage in a "concerted activity" for "mutual aid or protection," although the aggrieved workman is the only one of them who has any immediate stake in the outcome. The rest know that by their action each one of them assures himself, in case his turn ever comes, of the support of the one whom they are all then helping; and the solidarity so established is "mutual aid" in the most literal sense, as nobody doubts. So too of those engaging in a "sympathetic strike," or secondary boycott; the immediate quarrel does not itself concern them, but by extending the number of those who will make the enemy of one the enemy of all, the power of each is vastly increased (130 F. (2d) at 505).

In short, petitioner's assertion that the adjustment of individual grievances is not part of the practice and procedure of collective bargaining protected by the Act is contrary to the terms of the statute, contrary to its declared purpose, and is foreclosed by controlling judicial decisions.

In support of its erroneous argument, petitioner relies chiefly on *N. L. R. B.* v. *North American Avia-*

tion, Inc., 136 F. (2d) 898 (C. C. A. 9), and on a decision of the National War Labor Board (Pet. Br., pp. 23, 25). The *North American* case is clearly inapposite, for the only issue there was whether or not an individual employee *who did not wish to be represented by the union* would have the right, by virtue of the proviso to Section 9 (a) of the Act, to adjust his grievance through direct negotiation with his employer instead of through the grievance machinery provided for in the collective agreement. This Court held that the proviso to Section 9 (a) gave the employee that right. It did not hold that the employer may lawfully deny the accredited union access to his employees in circumstances such that the denial effectively prevents employees who desire to be represented by their union from enjoying their statutory rights. Nor did this Court hold that the employer can refuse to treat with the accredited union concerning individual grievances of employees *who desire to be represented by their union.* Rightly understood, therefore, this Court's decision in the *North American* case in no way conflicts with the settled doctrine that employees have the right under the Act to be represented by the accredited union in pressing their grievances if they so desire whether or not a collective contract exists, and that their employer is under a correlative obligation to negotiate with their representative for the adjustment of their grievances. It is difficult to understand why petitioner should rely upon the National War Labor Board for support of its position since that Board has squarely ruled, pending this Court's action in the instant case, that petitioner should grant passes to the Unions; this action of the National War Labor Board is based, moreover, on its finding that "No legitimate reasons were set forth by counsel for Richfield Oil Corporation why there should not be some reasonable provision for the issuance of passes to union representatives * * *."[30]

In conclusion, we respectfully refer this Court to the opinion of the Court in *N. L. R. B.* v. *Cities Service Oil Co.,* 122 F. (2d) 149 (C. C. A. 2), which, in sustaining the Board, lucidly states some of the considerations that underlie the Board's interpretation of the Act, and exposes the error in certain of the contentions on which petitioner relies.

Point II

The Board's order is valid

The cease and desist provisions of the Board's order, including paragraph 1 (b),[31] are of established validity, as is the requirement for the posting of appropriate notices.

In the *Cities Service* case, in speaking of the right of the shore delegate to solicit membership and collect dues aboard ship, the Court said, "Such activities were not shown by the Board to have been required 'for the purpose of collective bargaining or other mutual aid or protection' even if they are guaranteed

---

[30] For the convenience of the Court, we set forth in the appendix to this brief pertinent extracts from the opinion of the National War Labor Board, pp. 34–36, *infra.*

[31] "Having found the acts which constitute the unfair labor practice the Board is free to restrain the practice and other like or related unlawful acts" (*N. L. R. B.* v. *Express Publishing Co.*, 312 U. S. 426, 436).

under Section 7 under some circumstances" (122 F. (2d), at p. 152). In the present case, however, the evidence previously summarized demonstrates, as the Board found (R. 37–38, 43, 60), that conditions of employment in the maritime industry make it extremely difficult, if not impossible, for seamen to attend union meetings or visit union headquarters, except at sporadic intervals. For this reason they cannot pay union dues on time or keep abreast of union affairs if their union representatives are deprived of access to them aboard ship (*supra*, pp. 6–8, and note 15).[32] During war-time it is of the utmost importance to the men that they be afforded an opportunity to pay their union dues on time since, as the Board pointed out (R. 37–38), delinquency in that respect jeopardizes shipwreck and other insurance benefits provided them by the Unions (R. 185–186, 371). In the light of these facts, the Board found that petitioner's seamen could not fully enjoy their right to bargain collectively or to engage in concerted activities for their mutual aid and protection if they were denied the right to pay union dues and receive their union newspaper aboard ship (R. 60). These adequately supported findings establish the propriety of the direction in the Board's order which assures those rights to petitioner's seamen.[33]

[32] The record shows that the Pacific Coast Shippers who grant access to their vessels—comprising virtually the entire industry in that coastal area (R. 181–182; 258–324)—permit the union representatives to collect dues and distribute the union newspaper aboard their vessels (R. 185–186, 370–371).

[33] In the *Cities Service* case, unlike the present case, the Board found it unnecessary to prescribe the restrictions governing the

CONCLUSION

It is respectfully submitted that the Board's findings are supported by substantial evidence, that its order is valid, and that a decree should issue denying the petition to review and enforcing the Board's order, as prayed in the answer to the petition to review.

ROBERT B. WATTS,
General Counsel,
HOWARD LICHTENSTEIN,
Assistant General Counsel,
ROMAN BECK,
ISADORE GREENBERG,
Attorneys,
National Labor Relations Board.

DECEMBER 1943.

---

use of the passes which the Company was ordered to issue, since, as the Board pointed out, the bargaining negotiations revealed "that neither the principle of the issuance of passes nor the method of effectuating the principle was in question at the time of the breakdown of negotiations" (25 N. L. R. B. 36, 55). Accordingly, in the *Cities Service* case, the Board directed the Company to issue passes to the union representatives for the purpose of enabling them to meet with the seamen aboard the Company's vessels, but left the question of the number of passes and their use to be determined by the parties themselves (*id.*, p. 57).

In the present case, however, petitioner has uncompromisingly refused to grant the Unions passes for any purpose. Hence, the Board deemed it advisable itself to prescribe the *minimal* scope of the license it ordered petitioner to grant, in order to avoid future controversy on the point.

APPENDIX

The pertinent provisions of the National Labor Reations Act (Stat. 449; 29 U. S. C., 1940 ed., Sec. 151 t seq.) are as follows:

FINDINGS AND POLICY

* * * * *

It is hereby declared to be the policy of the United States to eliminate the causes of certain substantial obstructions to the free flow of commerce and to mitigate and eliminate these obstructions when they have occurred by encouraging the practice and procedure of collective bargaining and by protecting the exercise by workers of full freedom of association, self-organization, and designation of representatives of their own choosing, for the purpose of negotiating the terms and conditions of their employment or other mutual aid or protection.

* * * * *

SEC. 7. Employees shall have the right to self-organization, to form, join, or assist labor organizations, to bargain collectively through representatives of their own choosing, and to engage in concerted activities, for the purpose of collective bargaining or other mutual aid or protection.

SEC. 8. It shall be an unfair labor practice for an employer—

(1) To interfere with, restrain, or coerce employees in the exercise of the rights guaranteed in section 7.

* * *

Excerpts From Decision of National War Labor Board

In re General Petroleum Corporation (Los Angeles, Calif.) and *Seafarers' International Union of North America, Sailors' Union of the Pacific* (AFL) and *Seafarers' International Union of North America, Pacific District, Engine and Stewards Division* (AFL), Case No. 111-315-C; and *Richfield Oil Corporation* (Los Angeles, Calif.) and *Seafarers' International Union of North America, Sailors' Union of the Pacific* (AFL), and *Seafarers' International Union of North America, Pacific District, Engine Division* (AFL), Case No. 111-316-C, Nov. 1, 1943.

* * * * *

Passes.—The petitioning companies have failed to persuade the Board that the Regional Board's directive order on the issue of passes should be set aside. The Richfield Oil Company has argued that this Board has no jurisdiction to issue a directive order on the question of passes on the ground that this question is before the Circuit Court of Appeals. The National Board agrees with the Regional Board that the issue which is now before the court is not the same as the issue before this Board. The issue in the Circuit Court of Appeals, as pointed out by the Regional Board, is whether the companies have violated the National Labor Relations Act.

* * * * *

No legitimate reasons were set forth by counsel for Richfield Oil Corporation why there should not be some reasonable provision for the issuance of passes to union representatives. It was clear from the testimony and evidence submitted by the union that it is common practice for union officials to be granted passes for certain legitimate union activities. In fact the union's representative not only showed to the division of the Board passes issued by various shipping companies, both dry cargo and tanker operators, but a pass issued by the 12th Naval District entitling him to board any Navy ship with Navy cargo on board.

The Board is convinced that there is no reason why the Richfield Oil Corporation should not be required to cooperate with the union in the same manner as other operators, including the General Petroleum Corporation. In fact it is clear that if the union proportion requirement of the Regional Board's order is to be effective and workable it will be necessary that the union officials be given the privileges contained in the Regional Board's order. The Board agrees with the union's contention that the subject of passes is closely related and, in fact, a necessary part of any union-security provision.

*   *   *   *   *

The uncompromising attitude taken by the Richfield Oil Corporation satisfies the Board that it must see to it that the Regional Board's order is fully complied with. [War Labor Reports, Vol. 12, No. 1—November 10, 1943, pp. 7–19, Published by The Bureau of National Affairs, Inc., Washington, D. C.]

IN THE

United States Circuit Court of Appeals

FOR THE NINTH CIRCUIT

RICHFIELD OIL CORPORATION,

Petitioner,

vs.

NATIONAL LABOR RELATIONS BOARD,

Respondent.

On Petition to Review and Set Aside and on Request for Enforcement of an Order of the National Labor Relations Board.

REPLY BRIEF FOR THE RICHFIELD OIL CORPORATION.

DAVID GUNTERT,
555 South Flower Street, Los Angeles,
Attorney for Petitioner.

Parker & Baird Company, Law Printers, Los Angeles

TOPICAL INDEX.

TABLE OF AUTHORITIES CITED.

Cases. PAGE

IN THE

United States Circuit Court of Appeals

FOR THE NINTH CIRCUIT

RICHFIELD OIL CORPORATION,

Petitioner,

vs.

NATIONAL LABOR RELATIONS BOARD,

Respondent.

On Petition to Review and Set Aside and on Request for Enforcement of an Order of the National Labor Relations Board.

REPLY BRIEF FOR THE RICHFIELD OIL CORPORATION.

In its brief, the Board contends that anything which it or the unions consider necessary for the fullest enjoyment of union benefits must, by implication, be guaranteed by the Act. This reply brief is submitted to present petitioner's argument as to certain matters which we think

re further discussion in the light of the Board's brief n this connection we make the following points:

Petitioner is asking this court to decide only questions of law and not questions of fact as the Board seems to think.

The Board's brief distorts petitioner's contentions and throws an improper light upon petitioner's position.

The judicial authorities cited by the Board, when properly construed, actually support petitioner's position.

If the Board's position is sustained, there can be no collective bargaining concerning grievances.

Our contention that the Board disregards judicial interpretation of the Act is confirmed by a new case.

ARGUMENT.

Point I.

This court has not been asked to determine whether it is a fact:

1. That seamen have waged a long and bitter struggle to better their conditions, as recited in the *Encyclopaedia of the Social Sciences,* Vol. 13, p. 613; *Report of the Maritime Labor Board to the President and the Congress, March 1, 1940,* p. 26; *R. W. Wissman, The Maritime Industry,* p. 3 (cited in the footnote on page 6 of the Board's brief).

2. That the grievance procedure is an important contract provision, as recited in *R. W. Wissman, The Maritime Industry.* pp. 73-74; *Clinton S. Gilden and Harold J. Ruttenberg, The Dynamics of Industrial Democracy,* p. 43; The Twentieth Century Fund, *How Collective Bargaining Works* (cited in the footnote on page 9 of the Board's brief).

3. That some or a majority of shipowners have the particular grievance procedure described by the Board, as suggested in *Report of the Maritime Labor Board to the President and to the Congress, March 1, 1940,* pp. 189-192; *R. W. Wissman, The Maritime Industry,* pp. 74-75; *Hearing Before the Committee on Merchant Marine and Fisheries, House of Representatives, 75th Congress, 1st Session.* on *H. R. 5193,* p. 73; *Maritime Labor Grows Up, Frank M. Kleiler; Survey Graphic,* January, 1939, p. 19 (cited in the footnote on page 11 of the Board's brief).

4. That it is inconvenient for seamen to take an active part in union affairs as described in *N. L. R. B. v.*

Cities Service Oil Co., 122 F. (2d) 149 (cited in the footnote on page 12 of the Board's brief).

On the contrary, this court is being asked to decide the questions of law discussed in petitioner's main brief, the basic question being whether, as a matter of law, an employer that has not been charged with discrimination, failure to bargain, or any improper motive or intent, violates Section 8(1) of the Act, when, during contract negotiations carried on in good faith with certified bargaining agents of its employees, that employer refuses to accede to the bargaining agents' demand that the contract include a particular provision under which union representatives would be given free access to that employer's vessels.

Point II.

The Board's assertion that your petitioner contends that the adjustment of grievances is not a part of the practice and procedure of collective bargaining protected by the Act is a misstatement, for throughout the entire proceeding before the Board and before this court, your petitioner has contended that the grievance procedure is properly a subject of collective bargaining and that the Board has interfered with that collective bargaining by dictating just what procedure shall take place in the settlement of individual grievances. The fallacy of the Board's argument becomes apparent by the most cursory examination of the record. The grievance procedure contained in the Associated Oil Company contract (pp. 11-12 of Appendix to Petitioner's main brief) is the grievance procedure which the parties had tentatively agreed upon before this proceeding was instituted and is the grievance procedure which is now incorporated in the signed contract between the parties. That grievance procedure specifically provides for the participation in the handling of individual grievances by the certified bargaining representatives of the employees.

Not only has the Board repeatedly distorted your petitioner's contention but it has made a studied effort to cast upon your petitioner's conduct an improper light which, we are convinced, can have but one purpose—the creation in the court's mind of an impression that your petitioner is a vicious employer bent upon destroying rights created by the Act and using every conceivable means to frustrate enjoyment by its employees of such rights. For example, on page 18 of its brief, the Board states that:

> "Petitioner's stress upon the role of the ship's delegate is a significant reflection of its attitude toward bargaining with the Unions."

On page 13 of its brief, the Board asserts that the denial of passes would put your petitioner in a strategic position to hinder union activity and insinuates that your petitioner would not be slow to take advantage of that power. The Board then cites a number of cases in its footnote having to do with employers who had excluded union representatives from "company towns." It is significant that in each one of the cases cited the Board's complaint alleged discrimination and a failure to bargain and found such violations upon substantial evidence, and in this connection found that those employers had been resorting to every conceivable means of frustrating legitimate union activity.

On page 23 of its brief, the Board asserts that your petitioner's conduct tends to frustrate the aim of the statute.

Such assertions, in view of the fact that your petitioner has not been charged with any such conduct and the fact that there is not one scintilla of evidence in the record from which any such conduct can be inferred (to say nothing of its long-established fair labor policy and peaceful relations with organized employees, including the labor organizations involved in this case), forces us to conclude that the Board recognizes the invalidity of its order and is attempting to becloud the issue.

Point III.

The Board cites a number of judicial authorities in support of several propositions. As a matter of fact, when these authorities are properly construed, they support your petitioner's contentions. This will be obvious from an examination of the cases and we review them briefly as follows:

1. Each of the several cases cited in footnote 16 on pages 13-14 of the Board's brief involved findings, supported by substantial evidence, of a long record of antilabor activity with the intent and purpose of destroying employers' rights conferred by the Act. In the case now before the court, your petitioner has not been charged with any such intent or purpose and no evidence thereof was introduced.

In *N. L. R. B. v. The Denver Tent & Awning Co.*, 13 L. R. R. 284, C. C. A. 10, October 25, 1943, the court did not find the rule adopted by the employer to be an unfair labor practice because the rule interfered with union activity but because *there was evidence that the rule was merely a device to restrict or impede employees in the exercise of their rights of self-organization.* In other words, the improper intent and purpose was there, but it is missing in the case now before the court.

In the *Midland Steel Products Co.* 113 F. (2d) 800, case, cited in the *Denver Tent & Awning* case, the court specifically held that if the rule was reasonable *and not for an ulterior purpose, it did not violate the Act* even though it did prevent union activity.

In *N. L. R. B. v. William Davies Co.*, 135 F. (2d) 179 (C. C. A. 7), the court upheld a rule excluding solicitation of membership on company premises.

2. On page 23 of the Board's brief it cites the *H. J. Heinz Co.* case, 311 U. S. 514; the *P. Lorillard Co.* case, 117 F. (2d) 921, 924 (C. C. A. 6), and the *Biles-Coleman Lumber Co.* case, 98 F. (2d) 18, 22 (C. C. A. 9), upon the propositions that the employer must:

(a) Sign a contract embodying the provisions of his agreement reached, even though the Act does not expressly impose such an obligation on him;

(b) Cooperate to a reasonable extent with the accredited bargaining agent in facilitating the bargaining process; hence, must make his representatives available for bargaining conferences at reasonable times and places; and

(c) Be sincere in his bargaining negotiations.

Not one of these cases is relevant or material to the issue in this case. The agreement between the complaining unions and petitioner has been reduced to writing and signed; your petitioner has at all times facilitated the bargaining process and has furnished reasonable times and places for conferences; and it has been most sincere in its negotiations. The grievance procedure adopted requires *immediate* satisfaction or reference to the shore representatives of the employer and the union, where satisfaction must be given *within 24 hours.*

Petitioner's cooperation and sincerity of purpose has not been confined to the writing of the original agreement, but is the general policy and practice of your petitioner. Furthermore, the complaint has not alleged and the Board has not found any failure to bargain in good faith with sincere purpose.

3. Carrying this proposition a step further, the Board, on page 23 of its brief, cites the *Art Metals Const. Co.* case, 110 F. (2d) 148 (C. C. A. 2), on the proposition that because the Board has the power to order an employer to enter into a written agreement embodying the matters agreed upon when the Act does not specifically require a written agreement, that therefore the Board also has power to require an employer to embody in that contract provisions not specifically required by the Act. If this is the law, then there is no such thing as collective bargaining. We submit that this case is authority for your petitioner's position. Note what the court said on page 150:

> *"The freedom reserved to the employer is freedom to refuse concessions in working conditions to his employees, and to exact concessions from them; it is not the freedom, once they have in fact agreed upon those conditions, to compromise the value of the whole proceeding, and probably make it nugatory."* (Emphasis ours.)

4. *Warner v. Goltra,* 293 U. S. 155, 156, 158, is cited on page 23 of the Board's brief, upon the proposition that the Board has power to do what was reasonably contemplated by the Act. It should be noted that in the *Warner*

case the court was construing a particular word in the statute. In the case now before the court, we are not finding fault with the language of the Act but with the Board's action in interfering with the undisputed right of employees and the duty of employers to bargain collectively.

5. On page 8 and page 25 of the Board's brief, the Board distorts petitioner's position and then cites *N. L. R. B. v. Newark Morning Ledger Co.,* 120 F. (2d) 262, 266, 267 (C. C. A. 3), cert. denied 314 U. S. 693, as rejecting said distorted position. Petitioner's contention before the Board and now before this court is that the method of settling grievances is the subject matter of collective bargaining and that when the parties have agreed upon the procedure, that procedure governs. The court in that case did not hold that the settling of grievances was part of the collective bargaining process, but that the rights conferred by the Act continued after the execution of the contract.

The Board also cited in support of this proposition *N. L. R. B. v. Sands Mfg. Co.,* 306 U. S. 332, 342. We cannot see where the Board gets any help there for the court said on page 342:

> "The legislative history of the Act goes far to indicate that the purpose of the statute was to compel employers to bargain collectively with their employees *to the end that employement contracts binding on both parties should be made.* But we assume that the Act imposes upon the employer the further obligation to meet and bargain with his employees' representatives respecting proposed changes of an existing contract and also to discuss with them its true interpretation, *if there is any doubt as to its meaning."* (Emphasis ours.)

6. In *National Licorice Co. v. N. L. R. B.*, 309 U. S. 350, cited by the Board on page 27 of its brief, the employer had entered into individual contracts with his employees requiring them to renunciate several of the rights conferred upon them by the Act. In this connection the court said that the clause in the particular contract, discouraged, if not forbade, any presentation of grievances through a labor organization or chosen representatives of the employees. In the case now before the court the parties have agreed upon a procedure in which the employee can take his grievances up in the first instance through a representative of a labor organization and throughout the entire grievance procedure the labor organization plays a major part.

7. The citation on pages 23 and 24 of *H. J. Heinz Co. v. N. L. R. B.*, 311 U. S. 514, 524, 526, purporting to expose the fallacy of petitioner's argument can give the Board little comfort for it actually is very good authority in support of our contention. Note that the court, after considering the House Committee's recommendations, state that it has long been recognized that the signing of an agreement was the *final step* in the bargaining procedure. The court unequivocally held that Congress intends that employers shall be free to bargain concerning important contract provisions, saying:

> "the freedom of the employer to refuse to make an agreement relates to its terms in matters of substance."

That is exactly petitioner's position, for even the Board will agree that the grievance procedure is a matter of substance and it follows that Congress did not intend that the *Board* should take it upon itself to dictate what specific grievance procedure should be incorporated in a written agreement any more than it gave to the certified unions the power to say how grievances shall be settled. Moreover, Congress did not intend that the Board should have the authority to nullify a grievance procedure agreed upon by the employer and bargaining agents by prescribing still another method conflicting therewith.

8. *N. L. R. B. v. W. C. Bachelder,* 120 F. (2d) 574 (C. C. A. 7), cert. denied, 314 U. S. 647, holds that the Act contemplates that there is a duty on both sides to enter into discussion with an open and fair mind

> "and a sincere purpose to find a basis of agreement touching wages and hours and conditions of labor, and if found to embody it in a contract as specific as possible, which shall stand as a mutual guaranty of conduct, and as a guide for the adjustment of grievances."

This holding is not contrary to petitioner's position and it is not even material for there is no question of a failure to bargain in the case now before the court.

9. We think that the Board's view of the decision of this court in the *N. L. R. B. v. North American Aviation* case, 136 F. (2d) 898 (C. C. A. 9), referred to on pages 28 and 29 of the Board's brief, is a significant example of the Board's amazing versatility in adopting changed positions as expediency might demand. In that case, the Board reasoned that collective bargaining agents are exclusive bargaining agents; that grievances are proper subjects of collective bargaining; therefore, such agents have the exclusive right under the Act to settle individual grievances and that any other method afforded by the employer is an interference with the right of employees to have their chosen representatives bargain for them concerning grievances.

Now it was the Board's fallacious reasoning and not the statute that created that alleged right. In that case, the statute contained an express prohibition. In the case now before the court the Board's fallacious reasoning has again created the same alleged right. It is true in this case that the Act does not have an express prohibition concerning the results which the Board seeks to accomplish by its reasoning, but the Act, as construed by the courts, provides that an employer is not required to agree to a particular term or condition of employment. This, we think, is just as effective a limitation upon the Board's asserted power as an express prohibition in the statute and it will be observed that in both cases the Board has applied exactly the same reasoning up to the point of creating an alleged right. In the *North American* case the Board held that the granting of another grievance procedure interfered with that right and was therefore an unfair labor practice. In this case, the Board reasons that the refusal to issue passes interferes with that same alleged right and is therefore an unfair labor practice.

Clearly, if the Board is not deterred by a limitation upon its power expressed in the statute, the Board cannot be expected to be deterred by a limitation arrived at through judicial interpretation of the statute.

10. Under Point II of the Board's argument, on page 30 of the Board's brief, the Board simply asserts that it considers its order not to be too broad, and cites *N. L. R. B. v. Express Publishing Co.*, 312 U. S. 426, 436. Obviously, the Board is not seriously contending this point, and the authorities (including the *Express Publishing Co.* case) cited in petitioner's main brief clearly established that the Board's order is too broad.

Point IV.

If the Board's position is sustained, there is no such thing as collective bargaining concerning grievances, for regardless of what procedure might be formally incorporated in the contract, the unions would still have the right to ignore that procedure and establish a different procedure (for the Board says that they have this right), thereby making the negotiations concerning the procedure to be incorporated in the contract an idle act and a waste of time.

We submit that the purpose of the Act was to encourage collective bargaining to reduce the obstructions to interstate commerce resulting from disputes. It seems obvious that if the parties, as the law contemplated, can mutually agree upon a procedure to be followed, that the parties in all probability will follow that procedure in good faith, with the result that grievances will be satisfactorily settled, thereby reducing the amount of strife between the parties. The Supreme Court recognized this principle when it held on page 45 in the *Jones & Laughlin Steel Co.* case, 301 U. S. 1:

> "The theory of the Act is that free opportunity for negotiation with accredited representatives of employees is likely to promote industrial peace and may bring about the adjustments and agreements which the Act in itself does not attempt to compel."

We think the Circuit Courts, including this Circuit, are in accord. Note what the Sixth Circuit Court said in *N. L. R. B. v. P. Lorillard Co.,* 117 F. (2d) 921, beginning on page 923:

> "The Board is not authorized, by statute or court decision, to shape or control the course of the nego-

tiations between employer and employee, so long as the employer bargains collectively, in accordance with the statute. * * * Collective bargaining requires negotiations by the employer with representatives of the employees, chosen by themselves, freely and without coercion, *and has no reference to the terms of the agreement offered so long as the parties negotiate in good faith with the view of reaching an agreement.*" (Emphasis ours.)

We think it equally obvious that if, on the other hand, the employer and employees are deprived of the right to bargain concerning how grievances shall be settled, the Board in denying that right, is actually frustrating the purpose of the Act.

Although the Board's order in this case is alleged to be primarily for the purpose of guaranteeing free collective bargaining concerning the settlement of grievances, the Board also asserts that so-called "access" is necessary to full enjoyment of the mutual aid and protection provisions of the Act, more specifically, the right to have dues collected on board ship and to have union papers distributed on board ship. In taking this position the Board is actually granting new, novel and special privileges to certified unions and discriminating against minority groups among the employees, for the Board has denounced as being without merit the contention of your petitioner that if these privileges are granted to the certified unions the same privileges must be granted to other unions. Other discrimination also is apparent, for the Board has emphatically stated that the collection of dues on board ship *by shore representatives of the union* is necessary for employees to enjoy the benefits of union membership, but the Board has, with equal emphasis, stated that the employer need not permit access for the solicitation of membership. Thus the Board is discriminating against employees who wish to acquire the benefits of membership by joining a union, in favor of those who wish to acquire the benefits of union membership through the payment of delinquent dues and regaining good standing.

Point V.

Since petitioner's main brief was filed the Circuit Court of Appeals for the Second Circuit has rendered its decision in *N. L. R. B. v. Standard Oil Co.* case, No. 7, November 1, 1943, 13 L. R. R. 314, wherein that court:

1. Recognized that its prior interpretations of the *Express Publishing Co.* case have been incorrect, and that the jurisdiction of the Board to enter cease and desist orders is limited "to those unfair labor practices of which the employer had been found guilty." Thus, the Second Circuit now recognizes the invalidity of blanket cease and desist orders, but it did not have the courage to overrule its prior decisions;

2. Recognized that "the Board uniformly incorporates the (blanket) clause in its order." Thus the Second Circuit has come to realize that the Board has not been deterred from its singleminded purpose of administering the Act just as it sees fit, regardless of limitations upon its power contained in the Act either expressly or by judicial interpretation thereof, leaving the employer in the position of having to accede to the unlawful orders of the Board, or taking the time and spending the money necessary to invoke the protection of the Court. The result of this is that many unlawful orders go unchallenged, for many employers do not or cannot appeal them.

Summary.

Reduced to its simplest terms the Board's contention in this case is that it is necessary, in the Board's opinion, that shore representatives of the complaining unions be given free access to your petitioner's vessels so that your petitioner's employees may more effectively enjoy the benefits of the Act; and that, therefore, the Board may require access under its broad power to effectuate the policy of the Act, even though there is no express provision in the Act to cover. In this connection, on pages 22 and 23 of its brief, the Board in effect asserts that Congress granted to the Board the power to take whatever action the Board, in its judgment, considers will "effectuate the recognized legislative objectives of the Act."

Admittedly the Board has broad power, but even such broad power has its limitations. *Southern Steamship Co. v. N. L. R. B.*, 316 U. S. 31, 46; 86 L. Ed. 1246. The Board is not the "guardian or ruler" over employees of your petitioner. *Humble Oil & Ref. Co. v. N. L. R. B.* (C. C. A. 5), 113 Fed. (2d) 85, 88; and the Board cannot "substitute its own ideas of discipline and management for those of the employer." *N. L. R. B. v. Williamson-Dickie Mfg. Co.*, 130 Fed. (2d) 260, 267.

We submit that if the Board has the power to dictate the terms and conditions of employment so far as they concern the settlement of grievances, unquestionably one of the most important clauses in a contract, the Board also has the power to dictate the wages, hours and other conditions of employment, for the Board, bent on sustaining the cause it championed when acting in the role of accuser, would have no trouble conjuring up reasons why, in its opinion, the working of employees during certain hours would interfere with their participation in union activities or that a low wage paid for certain work would interfere with a worker's right to acquire the benefits incident to union membership because that low wage prevented him from paying the initiation fee and dues necessary to full enjoyment of the benefits conferred by the Act.

Conclusion.

Other contentions made by the Board in its brief, we submit, are patently fallacious or fully discussed in our main brief and require no discussion here.

Respectfully submitted,

David Guntert,
Attorney for Petitioner.

December 28, 1943.

TOPICAL INDEX.

PAGE

TABLE OF AUTHORITIES CITED.

Cases. PAGE

Statutes.

No. 10487.

IN THE

United States Circuit Court of Appeals

FOR THE NINTH CIRCUIT

THE PENFIELD COMPANY OF CALIFORNIA, a Corporation,
Appellant,

vs.

SECURITIES AND EXCHANGE COMMISSION,
Appellee.

OPENING BRIEF ON APPEAL.

This is an appeal by the defendant and appellant Penfield Company of California, a corporation, from an order granting an application for subpoena *duces tecum* to the applicant, Securities and Exchange Commission, through its attorneys, who applied to the District Court of the United States for a rule to show cause against the appellant why it should not produce the following before the Securities and Exchange Commission:

> "All books, records, documents, contracts, agreements, checks, bank statements, correspondence files and all other papers and memoranda in which have been entered a record of the transactions and business of The Penfield Company of California from the date of its incorporation to the date of this subpoena, including in particular, twenty items."

The order of the Securities and Exchange Commission alleged as follows:

"The Commission, having considered the aforesaid report by members of the staff, and for the purpose of (1) determining whether the persons named in the caption of this Order have violated or are about to violate the provisions of Sections 5(a) and 17(a) of the Securities Act of 1933; and (2) aiding in the enforcement of said Acts; deems it necessary and appropriate that an investigation be made to determine whether said persons have engaged in the acts and practices set forth in paragraph II hereof or any acts or practices of similar purport or object."

In a supplemental order of the Securities and Exchange Commission the Commission alleges as follows:

"The Commission, having considered the aforesaid report by members of its staff, and for the purpose of (1) determining whether the companies and persons named in the caption hereof have violated or are about to violate the provisions of Sections 5(a) and 17(a) of the Securities Act of 1933; and (2) aiding in the enforcement of said Act; deems it necessary and appropriate that an investigation be made to determine whether the said companies and persons, or any of them, have engaged in the acts and practices set forth in paragraph III hereof, or any acts or practices of similar purport.

"It Is Ordered, pursuant to Section 20(a) of the Securities Act of 1933 that the order and supplemental order directing an investigation mentioned in paragraph I hereof be and it hereby is supplemented and amended to include for determination the matters set forth in paragraph V hereof.

"It Is Further Ordered, pursuant to the provisions of Section 19(b) of the Securities Act of 1933 that for the purpose of such investigation, William Green, C. J. Odenweller, Jr., Charles E. Greaney, Hiram C. McDade and Harold O. Schroeder, and each of them, is hereby designated an officer of the Commission and empowered to administer oaths and affirmations, subpoena witnesses, compel their attendance, take evidence, and require the production of any books, papers, correspondence, memoranda or other records deemed relevant or material to the inquiry, and to perform all other duties in connection therewith as authorized by law."

Subsequent to the issuance of these orders of the Commission a subpoena *duces tecum* was issued [Exhibit C, R. 15] directing A. W. Young, Secretary-Treasurer of The Penfield Company of California, *et al.*, 8900 West Beverly, Beverly Hills, Calif., to appear and produce twenty items set forth in the subpoena.

These items were:

1. Minute Book.
2. All stock certificate stub books and cancelled certificates of common and preferred stock.
3. Alphabetical list of stockholders and addresses (if not shown on stub books indicated in Item No. 2 above).
4. General Ledger.
5. Cash Book.
6. General journal.

7. Records reflecting the sale of whiskey and/or whiskey warehouse receipts by the corporation.

8. Records relating to the sale of bottling contracts of Bourbon Sales Corporation, Louisville, Kentucky, by the corporation.

9. Records relating to the sale of bottling contracts of The Penfield Company of California, by the corporation.

10. Correspondence files, including letters received from and copies of letters sent to, all stockholders of The Penfield Company of California.

11. Correspondence files containing letters received from, and copies of letters sent to, all persons to whom bottling contracts of Bourbon Sales connection with the sale o fstock of The Penfornia were sold.

12. All cancelled checks of the corporation.

13. Copies of confirmations or advices delivered in connections with the sale of stock of The Penfield Company of California or the sale of bottling contracts of Bourbon Sales Corporation, or The Penfield Company of California.

14. All original journal entries or journal vouchers supporting entries appearing in the general journal or cash book.

15. Copies of all prospectuses, sales material, sales letters, material in salesmen's kits or similar documents used in connection with the solicitation and sale of stock in The Penfield Company of California.

16. Copies of all prospectuses, sales material, sales letters, material in salesman's kits or similar documents used in connection with the sale of bottling contracts of Bourbon Sales Corporation or The Penfield Company of California.

17. Purchase invoices or records supporting the acquisition of whiskey, whiskey warehouse receipts or bottling contracts by The Penfield Company of California from private individuals for cash or in exchange for stock, bottling contracts or other securities.

18. Purchase invoices or records supporting the acquisition of whiskey or whiskey warehouse receipts from distillers, whiskey warehouse receipts brokers or other persons or companies engaged in the whiskey business.

19. Sales invoices or records supporting the disposition of whiskey, whiskey warehouse receipts or bottling contracts procured from investors.

20. Employment or other records showing names of all employees, salesmen or other personnel with last known addresses.

Upon objections to their production the application was made to the District Court of the United States, h ch, after hearing, granted the order and stayed the execution of the appeal herein.

Appellant assigns the following errors in the record:

I.

THE DISTRICT COURT ERRED IN HOLDING THAT THE SECURITIES AND EXCHANGE COMMISSION HAD JURISDICTION TO ISSUE ITS ORDER REQUIRING APPELLANT TO PRODUCE FOR EXAMINATION BY THE COMMISSION OR ITS REPRESENTATIVES "ALL BOOKS, RECORDS, DOCUMENTS, CONTRACTS, AGREEMENTS, CHECKS, BANK STATEMENTS, CORRESPONDENCE FILES, AND ALL OTHER PAPERS AND MEMORANDA" WHICH WERE LISTED AS ITEMS ONE TO TWENTY.

(a) The District Court erred in holding that the orders of the Commission which formed the basis of the application had complied with the statutes sufficiently to give them jurisdiction;

(b) The District Court erred in holding that each of the twenty items was within the scope and jurisdiction of the Securities Act giving the Commission power to investigate them.

II.

THE DISTRICT COURT ERRED IN HOLDING THAT THE INVESTIGATION WAS NOT A GENERAL, ROVING INQUIRY, VIOLATIVE OF THE FOURTH AMENDMENT TO THE CONSTITUTION OF THE UNITED STATES, AND THAT IT DID NOT CONSTITUTE AN UNREASONABLE SEARCH AND SEIZURE OF THE PRIVATE PAPERS AND DOCUMENTS OF APPELLANT.

III.

THE DISTRICT COURT ERRED IN HOLDING THAT THE PROVISIONS OF SECTION 19(b) OF THE SECURITIES ACT OF 1933 AS AMENDED AND SUPPLEMENTED BY THE PROVISIONS OF SECTION 22(b) OF SAID ACT, INHERENTLY AND AS CONSTRUED AND APPLIED IN THIS CASE, ARE NOT INVALID AND UNCONSTITUTIONAL BECAUSE THEY DELEGATE JUDICIAL POWERS TO THE SECURITIES AND EXCHANGE COMMISSION IN VIOLATION OF ARTICLE III OF THE CONSTITUTION OF THE UNITED STATES, AND DEPRIVE THE DISTRICT COURT OF JUDICIAL FUNCTIONS AS TO WHAT MATTERS ARE OR ARE NOT RELEVANT OR MATERIAL TO THE INQUIRY.

IV.

THE DISTRICT COURT ERRED IN HOLDING THAT TRANSACTIONS IN DISTILLERS' WHISKEY WAREHOUSE RECEIPTS WERE TRANSACTIONS WITHIN THE MEANING OF SECTION 2(1) OF THE SECURITIES ACT AS AMENDED IN 1933.

V.

THE DISTRICT COURT ERRED IN HOLDING THAT BOTTLING CONTRACTS OF THE BOURBON SALES CORPORATION OR THE PENFIELD COMPANY OF CALIFORNIA WERE TRANSACTIONS IN SECURITIES, AS DEFINED IN SECTION 2(1) OF THE SECURITIES ACT OF 1933, AND THEREFORE CONFERRED JURISDICTION UPON THE SECURITIES AND EXCHANGE COMMISSION.

ARGUMENT.

I.

The District Court Erred in Holding That the Securities and Exchange Commission Had Jurisdiction to Issue Its Order Requiring Appellant to Produce for Examination by the Commission or Its Representatives "All Books, Records, Documents, Contracts, Agreements, Checks, Bank Statements, Correspondence Files, and All Other Papers and Memoranda" Which Were Listed as Items One to Twenty.

(a) The District Court Erred in Holding That the Orders of the Commission Which Formed the Basis of the Application Had Complied With the Statutes Sufficiently to Give Them Jurisdiction.

The authority for the Securities and Exchange Commission to secure a subpoena *duces tecum* is contained in Sections 19(b) and 22(b), which provide as follows:

Section 19(b) of the Act empowers the Securities and Exchange Commission to invade the privacy of citizens by making all investigations which, *in the opinion of the Commission,* are necessary and proper for the enforcement of the Act, and empowers the Commission or officers designated by it to administer oaths and affirmations, subpoena witnesses, take evidence, and require the production of any books, papers or other documents which the Commission deems relevant or material to the inquiry.

Section 22(b) of the Act provides for the issuance by the District Courts of orders to compel obedience to subpoenas issued by the Commission under the powers granted in Section 19(b) of the Act.

Assuming that the section provisions are constitutional and that Congress intended that they would comply with the provisions of the Fourth Amendment to the Constitution, which provides that "no warrants shall issue but upon probable cause, supported by oath or affirmation, and particularly describing the places to be searched, and the persons or things to be seized," the order of the Commission specifies none of the things sought by a subpoena *duces tecum.*

Nor did the proceedings before the Commission, nor any of their orders, declare that, "in the opinion of the Commission (these things) are necessary and proper for the enforcement of this title." Neither does the application to the court, nor the orders of the Commission directing the investigation, assert that the Commission "deems the particular documents and papers relevant or material to the inquiry."

Assuming that the particular section is constitutional, all statutes must be read together. The provisions for subpoenas *duces tecum* are contained in Title 28, Section 647, which provides as follows:

> "When either party in such suit applies to any judge of a United States court in such district or Territory for a subpoena commanding the witness, therein to be named, to appear and testify before said commissioner, at the time and place to be stated in the subpoena, and to bring with him and produce to such commissioner any paper or writing or written instrument or book or other document, supposed to be in the possession or power of such witness, and to be described in the subpoena, such judge, on being satisfied by the affidavit of the person applying, or otherwise, that there is reason to believe that such

paper, writing, written instrument, book, or other document is in the possession or power of the witness, and that the same, if produced would be competent and material evidence for the party applying therefor, may order the clerk of said court to issue such subpoena accordingly. And if the witness, after being served with such subpoena, fails to produce to the commissioner, at the time and place stated in the subpoena, any such paper, writing, written instrument, book, or other document, being in his possession or power, and described in the subpoena, and such failure is proved to the satisfaction of said judge, he may proceed to enforce obedience to said process of subpoena, or punish the disobedience in like manner as any court of the United States may proceed in case of disobedience to like process issued by such court. When any such paper, writing, written instrument, book, or other document is produced to such commissioner, he shall, at the cost of the party requiring the same, cause to be made a correct copy thereof, or of so much thereof as shall be required by either of the parties."

It will be noted that in order to secure a subpoena *duces tecum* such application for the subpoena must describe in the subpoena the papers, writings, books or other documents supposed to be in the possession or power of such witness, and it must be presented to a judge, who must be satisfied by the affidavit of the person applying, or otherwise, that there is reason to believe that such papers, writings, books or other documents are in the possession or power of the witness, and that the same, if produced, would be competent and material evidence for the party applying therefor.

It cannot be conceived that the Congress, in passing the Securities and Exchange Act, authorizing the issuance of a subpoena *duces tecum* in a proper case, intended that the subpoena *duces tecum* should be issued on any other conditions for the Commission than those provided for trial courts, and it did not give the Commission authority beyond or different than it gave to any person applying to a court for a subpoena *duces tecum.* Had it done any less than this it would have conflicted with the Fourth Amendment to the Constitution of the United States.

In *Grau v. United States,* 287 U. S. 124, 129, 77 L. Ed. 212, 214, the Supreme Court of the United States held that a warrant is void for failure to observe the statutory requirement that it state the particular grounds or probable cause for issuance, and for the further reason that it is based on affidavits which do not set forth the facts tending to establish the grounds of the application or probable cause for believing that they exist. The court held that the affidavits in that case were insufficient as they unduly narrowed the guaranties of the Fourth Amendment, in consonance with which the statute was passed. Those guaranties are thereby liberally construed to prevent impairment of the protection extended. (*Boyd v. United States,* 116 U. S. 616, 635, 29 L. Ed. 746, 751; *Gouled v. United States,* 255 U. S. 298, 65 L. Ed. 647, 650; *Go-Bart Imp. Co. v. United States,* 282 U. S. 344, 357, 75 L. Ed. 374, 382.)

As stated in the *Grau* case further, "Congress intended, in adopting Section 25 of Title 2 of the National Prohibition Act, to preserve, not to encroach upon, the citizen's right to be immune from unreasonable searches and seizures, and we should so construe the legislation as to effect that purpose."

Tested by the provisions of the Constitution and the statute before a valid subpoena *duces tecum* could be issued by the Securities and Exchange Commission it was necessary to be presented by the Commission a list of the things supposed to be in the possession or power of such witness, and thereupon it was necessary for the Commission to make a finding that, in its opinion, these books and papers were necessary for the proper enforcement of the title, and that the Commission deemed these articles relative or material to the inquiry.

No such request was made, apparently, of the Commission, and no finding was made by the Commission that it deemed these books and records necessary and proper for the enforcement of this title. [R. 2, 8, 12.]

At this point, for the sake of argument, if Congress could constitutionally delegate this judicial function to the Securities and Exchange Commission—to find what was necessary and proper for the enforcement of this title, then the Commission would have to have presented to it, in order to comport with the Fourth Amendment, an affidavit setting forth the articles sought and the reasons for seeking them. The documents and things sought would have to be described with particularity.

The statutory provision either must be as broad as the constitutional guaranty which it seeks to avoid, or else the statute itself is unconstitutional. The situation is comparable to that in *Counselman v. Hitchcock,* 142 U. S. 547, 35 L. Ed. 1110, wherein the immunity provisions of the Fifth Amendment were sought to be met by provisions granting to those who testified immunity from prosecution. Because the statute was not as broad as the constitutional guaranty, the Supreme Court held the statute unconstitutional.

(b) The District Court Erred in Holding That Each of the Twenty Items Was Within the Scope and Jurisdiction of the Securities Act Giving the Commission Power to Investigate Them.

The district Court erred in holding that each of the twenty items which the subpoena, issued by an employee of the Securities and Exchange Commission, sought to get, was within the scope and jurisdiction of the Securities Act, giving the Commission power to investigate them.

It was error for the District Court to grant the application of the Commission and to issue its order requiring appellant to produce for examination by the Commission or its representatives "All books, records, documents, contracts, agreements, checks, bank statement, correspondence files and all other papers and memoranda in which have been entered a record of the transactions and business of The Penfield Company of California from the date of its incorporation to the date of this subpoena, including in particular, the following:" followed by items numbered 1 to 20 inclusive of said Order, for the following reasons:

Item 1—Minute Book,—contains confidential information concerning the business and affairs of appellant not relating to transactions in securities as defined in Section 2(1) of the Securities Act of 1933, as amended, except as to the issuance and sale of the original 500 shares at the price of $1.00 per share to three persons named in the permit issued by the State Corporation Commissioner of California dated April 5, 1939, as shown by affidavits and answer of appellant, and of Franklin Black and A. W. Young, its President and Secretary-Treasurer, and M. Leland Stanford, Certified Public Accountant, filed in said proceeding, and such issuance and sale, not being a public offering of securities, was exempt from the registration requirements of Section 5(a) of the Securities Act under the exemption provisions of Section 4(1) of said Act. In any event any examination of such Minute Book should have been restricted to the issuance and sale of securities and should not have allowed the examination or inspection of any other portions or parts of such Minute Book, and certainly not the entire Minute Book, relating to many matters not in any way related to the issuance and sale of securities over which the Commission has any jurisdiction under the provisions of said Act.

Items 2 and 3—All stock certificate stub books and cancelled certificates of common and preferred stock; and alphabetical list of stockholders and addresses (if not shown on stub books indicated on Item No. 2 above)—since the affidavits and answer of appellant and of its officers showed that the only transactions recorded in such records were transfers by individual owners and holders of stock certificates for common stock of appellant out of the original issue of 500 shares and such transactions were not within the jurisdiction of the Commission and, therefore, it is not entitled to examine or inspect the records of appellant concerning or relating to same.

Items 4, 5 and 6—General Ledger, Cash Book, and General Journal—since these records relate to transactions other than transactions in securities, except the one transaction concerning the original issuance and sale of 500 shares at the price of $1.00 per share, and, therefore, the Commission has no jurisdiction over or right to examine or inspect any entries in such books relating to transactions not in securities as defined in Section 2(1) of the Securities Act of 1933, as amended.

Item 7—Records reflecting the sale of whiskey, and/or whiskey warehouse receipts by the corporation—since these transactions were not transactions in securities as defined in Section 2(1) of the Act and the Commission, therefore, has no jurisdiction to examine or inspect any records of appellant relating to or concerning such transactions.

Item 8—Records relating to the sale of bottling contracts of Bourbon Sales Corporation, Louisville, Kentucky, by the corporation—since these transactions were not transactions in securities as defined in Section 2(1) of the Act, and the Commission, therefore, has no jurisdiction to examine or inspect any records of appellant relating to or concerning such transactions.

Item 9—Records relating to the sale of bottling contracts of The Penfield Company of California, by the corporation—for the same reason as above stated in reference to Item No. 8.

Item 10—Correspondence files, including letters received from and copies of letters sent to, all stockholders of The Penfield Company of California—since the issuance and sale of its stock by appellant was not within the jurisdiction of the Commission, and therefore it had no right or authority to examine or inspect correspondence files or letters relating to or concerning same.

Item 11—Correspondence files containing letters received from, and copies of letters sent to, all persons to whom bottling contracts of Bourbon Sales Corporation or The Penfield Company of California were sold—since this correspondence relates to and concerns transactions which were not transactions in securities as defined in Section 2(1) of the Securities Act of 1933, as amended, and, therefore, the Commission has no right, authority or jurisdiction to demand the examination or inspection thereof.

Item 12—All cancelled checks of the corporation—since the only cancelled checks which the Commission has any right, authority or jurisdiction to examine or inspect, as provided in the Act, are those relating to or concerning sales by the appellant in securities as defined in Section 2(1) of the Act, and such examination should have been restricted and confined to cancelled checks relating to such transactions in securities and no other transactions whatever.

Item 13—Copies of confirmations or advices delivered in connection with the sale of stock of The Penfield Company of California or the sale of bottling contracts of Bourbon Sales Corporation, or The Penfield Company of California—since the only sale of stock by appellant was exempt from the registration provisions of the Act, and the transactions in bottling contracts were not transactions in securities as defined in Section 2(1) of the Act, and, therefore, the Commission has no authority, right or jurisdiction to examine or inspect any records of appellant relating to or concerning same.

Item 14—All original journal entries or journal vouchers supporting entries appearing in the general journal or cash book,—since the only entries to which the Commission has jurisdiction or authority to investigate or to examine and inspect the records of appellant are those relating to transactions in securities as defined in Section 2(1) of the Act, and the Order of this District Court should have been restricted and confined to such entries relating to or concerning such transactions and should not have been broad enough to cover any other entries in such books.

Item 15—Copies of all prospectuses, sales material, sales letters, material in salesmen's kits or similar documents used in connection with the solicitation and sale of stock in The Penfield Company of California—since the only sale of stock by appellant, as hereinbefore stated, and as shown by the affidavits and answers in the record in the District Court, was the original issuance and sale of 500 shares which was exempt from the provisions of the Securities Act of 1933, as amended, and the affidavits and answers filed in the proceeding in the District Court showed that there were no such documents as described in this item.

Item 16—Copies of all prospectuses, sales material, sales letters, material in salesmen's kits or similar documents used in connection with the sale of bottling contracts of Bourbon Sales Corporation or The Penfield Company of California—since such material, if any, relates to transactions not in securities as defined in Section 2(1) of the Act, and, therefore, the Commission has no jurisdiction, right or authority to examine or inspect any records of appellant relating to or concerning such transactions.

Item 17—Purchase invoices or records supporting the acquisition of whiskey, whiskey warehouse receipts of bottling contracts by The Penfield Company of California from private individuals for cash or in exchange for stock, bottling contracts or other securities—since transactions in the acquisition of whiskey, whiskey warehouse receipts or bottling contracts by appellant were not transactions in securities and, therefore, not within the jurisdiction of the Commission to investigate or to examine or inspect the records of appellant relating to or concerning same, and the evidence in the record shows conclusively that the appellant never issued any stock "or other securities" as defined in Section 2(1) of the Act for whiskey, whiskey warehouse receipts or bottling contracts.

Item 18—Purchase invoices or records supporting the acquisition of whiskey or whiskey warehouse receipts from distillers, whiskey warehouse receipts brokers or other persons or companies engaged in the whiskey business—since such transactions were merchandising transactions and not transactions in securities as defined in Section 2(1) of the Act, and therefore, the Commission is without jurisdiction over such transactions and has no right under the Act to examine or inspect any records of appellant relating to or concerning same.

Item 19—Sales invoices or records supporting the disposition of whiskey, whiskey warehouse receipts or bottling contracts procured from investors—for the reason that such transactions were not transactions in securities as defined in Section 2(1) of the Act, and, therefore, the Commission is without jurisdiction or authority to examine or inspect records of appellant relating to or concerning same.

Item 20—Employment or other records showing names of all employees, salesmen or other personnel with last known addresses—since such records have no materiality or relevance to transactions in securities as defined in Section 2(1) of the Act, but relate to other business and affairs and transactions of appellant over which the Commission has no jurisdiction and, therefore, has no right to examine such records.

The record shows that many of these things were not within the scope or sphere of the Securities and Exchange Act. The taking of them constituted an unreasonable search and seizure. (*Jones v. Securities and Exchange Commission,* 298 U. S. 1, 80 L. Ed. 1015; *Hale v. Henkel,* 201 U. S. 43, 55 L. Ed. 873; *Federal Trade Commission v. American Tobacco Co.,* 264 U. S. 298; *Boyd v. United States,* 116 U. S. 616, 29 L. Ed. 746; *Interstate Com. Commission v. Brimson,* 154 U. S. 447.)

The measure of power is the mode prescribed in the statute.

Head v. Providence Insurance Co., 2 Cranch. 156;
Zottman v. S. F., 20 Cal. 102;
Michelson v. Painter, 35 Cal. 705;
Peo. v. Gunn, 85 Cal. 238, 248.

II.

The District Court Erred in Holding That the Investigation Was Not a General, Roving Inquiry, Violative of the Fourth Amendment to the Constitution of the United States, and That It Did Not Constitute an Unreasonable Search and Seizure of the Private Papers and Documents of Appellant.

The scope of the Securities and Exchange Commission's investigation was not confined to any particular alleged violation, nor was it based on any specific complaint. In its first hearing the Commission simply set out that members of the staff had reported that from May 10, 1939 to the date of the application the persons named in the order "sold and delivered to members of the public certain securities, namely, contracts for the bottling of whiskey issued by the Bourbon Sales Corporation." It did not set forth anywhere in either Exhibit A or Exhibit B, how all of its books, correspondence, records and memoranda could aid in this inquiry. The orders were "a general roving inquiry, violative of the Fourth Amendment to the Constitution of the United States." (*Jones v. Securities and Exchange Com.*, 298 U. S. 1, 80 L. Ed. 1015.

In *Hale v. Henkel*, 201 U. S. 76, 50 L. Ed. 666, the court said:

> "We are also of opinion that an order for the production of books and papers may constitute an unreasonable search and seizure within the 4th Amendment. While a search ordinarily implies a quest by an officer of the law, and a seizure contemplates a forcible dispossession of the owner, still, as was held

in the Boyd Case, the substance of the offense is the compulsory production of private papers whether under a search warrant or a subpoena *duces tecum,* against which the person, be he individual or corporation, is entitled to protection. Applying the test of reasonableness to the present case, we think the subpoena *duces tecum* is far too sweeping in its terms to be regarded as reasonable. It does not require the production of a single contract, or of contracts with a particular corporation, or a limited number of documents, but all understandings, contracts, or correspondence between the MacAndrews & Forbes Company, and no less than six different companies, as well as all reports made and accounts rendered by such companies from the date of the organization of the MacAndrews & Forbes Company, as well as all letters received by that company since its organization from more than a dozen different companies, situated in seven different states in the Union."

In *Silverthorne Lumber Co. v. United States,* 251 U. S. 391-393, 64 L. Ed. 321, 322, Mr. Justice Holmes said:

> "It reduces the 4th Amendment to a form of words. (232 U. S. 393). The essence of a provision forbidding the acquisition of evidence in a certain way is that not merely evidence so acquired shall not be used before the court, but that it shall not be used at all. . . . In Linn v. United States, 163 C. C. A. 470, 251 Fed. 476, 480, it was thought that a different rule applied to a corporation, on the ground that it was not privileged from producing its books and papers. But the rights of a corporation against unlawful search and seizure are to be protected even if the same result might have been achieved in a lawful way."

In *Jones v. Securities and Exchange Com.*, 298 U. S. 23-27, 80 L. Ed. 1025-1027, the court said:

"The action of the commission finds no support in right principle or in law. It is wholly unreasonable and arbitrary. It violates the cardinal precept upon which the constitutional safeguards of personal liberty ultimately rest—that this shall be a government of laws—because to the precise extent that the mere will of an official or an official body is permitted to take the place of allowable official discretion or to supplant the standing law as a rule of human conduct, the government ceases to be one of laws and becomes an autocracy. Against the threat of such a contingency the courts have always been vigilant, and, if they are to perform their constitutional duties in the future, must never cease to be vigilant, to detect and turn aside the danger at its beginning. The admonition of Mr. Justice Bradley in Boyd v. United States, 116 U. S. 616, 625, 29 L. Ed. 746, 752, 6 S. Ct. 520, should never be forgotten: 'It may be that it is the obnoxious thing in its mildest and least repulsive form; but illegitimate and unconstitutional practices get their first footing in that way, namely, by silent approaches and slight deviations from legal modes of porcedure. . . . It is the duty of courts to be watchful for the constitutional rights of the citizen, and against any stealthy encroachment thereon. Their motto would be *obsta principiis.*'

"Arbitrary power and the rule of the Constitution cannot both exist. They are antagonistic and incompatible forces; and one or the other must of necessity perish whenever they are brought into conflict. To borrow the words of Mr. Justice Day—'there is no place in our constitutional system for the exercise of arbitrary power.' Garfield v. United States, 211 U.

S. 249, 262, 53 L. Ed. 167, 174, 29 S. Ct. 62. To escape assumptions of such power on the part of the three primary departments of the government, is not enough. Our institutions must be kept free from the appropriation of unauthorized power by lesser agencies as well. And if the various administrative bureaus and commissions, necessarily called and being called into existence by the increasing complexities of our modern business and political affairs, are permitted gradually to extend their powers by encroachments—even petty encroachments—upon the fundamental rights, privileges and immunities of the people, we shall in the end, while avoiding the fatal consequences of a supreme autocracy, become submerged by a multitude of minor invasions of personal rights, less destructive but no less violative of constitutional guaranties.

"*Third.* The proceeding for a stop order having thus disappeared, manifestly it cannot serve as a basis for the order of the district court compelling petitioner to appear, give testimony, and produce his private books and papers for inspection by the commission. But the commission contends that the order may rest upon the general power to conduct investigations which it says is conferred by sec. 19(b). The difficulty with that is that the investigation was undertaken for the declared and sole purpose of determining whether a stop order should issue. The first action taken by the commission was on May 20th, four days before the registration was to become effective under the statute. The commission then, after averring that upon reasonable grounds it believed the registration statement was false in material facts, directed that stop-order proceedings be instituted against the statement. It never has averred or directed anything else. This action was followed by a notice containing like results of a more detailed character, and calling upon the registrant to appear and show cause why a stop order should not be issued suspending the effectiveness of the statement. It was upon this direction and notice that all subsequent proceedings were had and upon which they must stand or fall. We do not interpret the order of the district court, the substance of which has already been stated, as resting upon a different view.

"Nothing appears in any of the proceedings taken by the commission to warrant the suggestion that the investigation was undertaken or would be carried on for any other purpose or to any different end than that specifically named. An official inquisition to compel disclosures of fact is not an end, but a means to an end; and it is a mere truism to say that the end must be a legitimate one to justify the means. The citizen, when interrogated about his private affairs, has a right before answering to know why the inquiry is made; and if the purpose disclosed is not a legitimate one, he may not be compelled to answer. Since here the only disclosed purpose for which the investigation was undertaken had ceased to be legitimate when the registrant rightfully withdrew his statement, the power of the commission to proceed with the inquiry necessarily came to an end. Dissociated from the only ground upon which the inquiry had been based, and no other being specified, further pursuit of the inquiry, obviously, would become what Mr. Justice Holmes characterized as 'a fishing expedition . . . for the chance that something discreditable might turn up' (Ellis v. Interstate Commerce Commission, 237 U. S. 434, 445, 59 L. ed. 1036, 1041, 35 S. Ct. 645)—an undertaking which uniformly has met with judicial condemnation. Re Pacific R. Commission (C. C.) 12 Sawy. 559, 32

F. 241, 250; Kilbourn v. Thompson, 103 U. S. 168, 190, 192, 193, 195, 196, 26 L. ed. 377, 386-389; Boyd v. United States, 116 U. S. 616, 29 L. ed. 746, 6 S. Ct. 520; Harriman v. Interstate Commerce Commission, 211 U. S. 407, 419, 53 L. ed. 253, 263, 29 S. Ct. 115; Federal Trade Commission v. American Tobacco Co., 264 U. S. 298, 305-307, 68 L. ed. 696, 700, 701, 44 S. Ct. 326, 32 A. L. R. 786.

"Re Pacific R. Commission involved the power of a Congressional commission to investigate the private affairs, books and papers of officers and employees of certain corporations indebted to the government. That commission called before it the president of one of these corporations, required the production of private books and papers for inspection, and submitted interrogatories which the witness declined to answer. Acting under the statute, the commission sought a peremptory order from the circuit court to compel the witness to answer the interrogatories. The court, consisting of Mr. Justice Field, Circuit Judge Sawyer, and District Judge Sabin, denied the motion of the district attorney for the order and discharged the rule to show cause. Opinions were rendered seriatim, the principal one by Justice Field. The authority of the commission was definitely denied. That decision has frequently been cited and approved by the court. Judge Sawyer, in the course of his opinion (at p. 263), after observing that a bill in equity seeking a discovery upon general, loose and vague allegations is styled 'a fishing bill', and will, at once, be dismissed on that ground (Story, Eq. Pl. sec. 325), said: 'A general, roving, offensive, inquisitorial, compulsory investigation, conducted by a commission without any allegations, upon no fixed principles, and governed by no rules of law, or of evidence, and no restrictions except its own will, or caprice, is unknown to our constitution and laws; and such an inquisition would be destructive of the rights of the citizen, and an intolerable tyranny. Let the power once be established, and there is no knowing where the practice under it would end.'

"The fear that some malefactor may go unwhipped of justice weighs as nothing against this just and strong condemnation of a practice so odious. And, indeed, the fear itself has little of substance upon which to rest. The federal courts are open to the government; and the grand jury abides as the appropriate constitutional medium for the preliminary investigation of crime and the presentment of the accused for trial.

"The philosophy that constitutional limitations and legal restraints upon official action may be brushed aside upon the plea that good, perchance, may follow, finds no countenance in the American system of government. An investigation not based upon specified grounds is quite as objectionable as a search warrant not based upon specific statements of fact. Such an investigation, or such a search, is unlawful in its inception and cannot be made lawful by what it may bring, or by what it actually succeeds in bringing, to light. Cf. Byars v. United States, 273 U. S. 28, 29, 71 L. ed. 520, 522, 47 S. Ct. 248, and cases cited. If the action here of the commission be upheld, it follows that production and inspection may be enforced not only of books and private papers of the guilty, but those of the innocent as well, notwithstanding the proceeding for 'registration, so far as the power of the commission is concerned, has been brought to an end by the complete and legal withdrawal of the registration statement.

"Exercise of 'such a power would be more pernicious to the innocent than useful to the public;' and approval of it must be denied, if there were no other reason for denial, because, like an unlawful search for evidence, it falls upon the innocent as well as upon the guilty and unjustly confounds the two. Entick v. Carrington, 19 How. St. Tr. 1030, 1074—followed by this court in Boyd v. United States, 116 U. S. 616, 629, 630, 29 L. ed. 746, 747, 751, 6 S. Ct. 522. No one can read these two great opinions, and the opinions in the Pacific R. Commission Case, from which the foregoing quotation is made, without perceiving how closely allied in principle are the three protective rights of the individual—that against compulsory self-accusation, that against unlawful searches and seizures, and that against unlawful inquisitorial investigations. They were among those intolerable abuses of the Star Chamber, which brought that institution to an end at the hands of the Long Parliament in 1640. Even the shortest step in the direction of curtailing one of these rights must be halted *in limine,* lest it serve as a precedent for further advances in the same direction, or for wrongful invasions of the others."

III.

The District Court Erred in Holding That the Provisions of Section 19(b) of the Securities Act of 1933 as Amended and Supplemented by the Provisions of Section 22(b) of Said Act, Inherently and as Construed and Applied in This Case, Are Not Invalid and Unconstitutional Because They Delegate Judicial Powers to the Securities and Exchange Commission in Violation of Article III of the Constitution of the United States, and Deprive the District Court of Judicial Functions as to What Matters Are or Are Not Relevant or Material to the Inquiry.

In the case of *Pacific Railway Commission v. Stanford,* 32 Fed. Rep. 241, approved in *Interstate Commerce Com. v. Brimson,* 154 U. S. 447, and *Innes v. Securities and Exchange Commission,* 80 L. Ed. 1015. We are quoting at length from the report of the case, but before reading it, we respectfully request this Court to note certain outstanding points of similarity between the statute construed in that case and the sections of the Securities Act of 1933 which we contend are invalid for the same reason that the Court in the above case declared the statute to be unconstitutional. Portions of the opinion deemed by counsel to be particularly important have been italicized. Following are excerpts from the syllabus prepared by the court:

> "1. The Pacific Railway Commission is not a judicial body, and possesses no judicial powers under the act of Congress of March 3, 1887, creating it, and can determine no rights of the government, or of the corporations whose affairs it is appointed to investigate.

"2. Congress cannot compel the production of private books and papers of citizens for its inspection, except in the course of judicial proceedings, or in suits instituted for that purpose, and then only upon averments that its rights in some way depend upon evidence therein contained.

"3. Congress cannot empower a commission to investigate the private affairs, books and papers of the officers and employees of corporation indebted to the government, as to their relations to other companies with which such corporations have had dealings, except so far as such officers and employees are willing to submit same for inspection; and the investigation of the Pacific Railway Commission into the affairs of officers and employees of the Pacific Railway Companies under the act of March 3, 1887, is limited to that extent.

* * * * * * * * *

"7. The judicial department is independent of the legislative, in the federal government, and Congress cannot make the courts its instruments in conducting mere legislative investigations.

* * * * * * * * *

"9. The Central Pacific Railroad Company is a state corporation, not subject to federal control, any further than a natural person similarly situated would be.

* * * * * * * * *

"12. The United States, as a creditor, cannot institute a compulsory investigation into the private affairs of the Central Pacific Railroad Company, or require it to exhibit its books and papers for inspection in any other way, or to any greater extent, than would be lawful in the case of private creditors and debtors."

The statement of facts (p. 243) contains the following:

> "It is difficult to express in general terms the extent to which the commissioners are required to go in their inquisition into the business and affairs of the aided companies; or to which they may not go into other business and affairs of the directors, officers, and employees. The act itself must be read to form any conception of the all-pervading character of the scrutiny it exacts of them. And it provides that the commissioners, or either of them, shall have the power 'to require the attendance and testimony of witnesses, and the production of all books, papers, contracts, agreements, and documents relating to the matter under investigation, and to administer oaths; *and to that end may invoke the aid of any court of the United States in requiring the attendance of witnesses, and the production of books, papers and documents.'* *And it declares that 'any of the circuit or district courts of the United States* within the jurisdiction of which such inquiry is carried on, *may,* in case of contumacy or refusal to obey a subpoena issued to any person, *issue an order requiring any such person to appear before said commissioners, or either of them, as the case may be, and produce books and papers, if so ordered, and give evidence touching the matter in question; and any failure to obey such order of the court may be punished by such court as a contempt thereof.'* And also that *'the claim that any such testimony or evidence may tend to incriminate the person giving such evidence, shall not excuse such witness from testifying, but such evidence or testimony shall not be used against such person in the trial of any criminal proceeding.'* " (Italics supplied.)

The statement of facts in the above also contains the following (p. 242):

"This is an application of the Pacific Railway Commission, created under the Act of Congress of March 3, 1887, 'Authorizing an investigation of the books, accounts, and methods of railroads which have received aid from the United States, and for other purposes,' for an order requiring a witness to answer certain interrogations propounded to him. That act authorizes the president to appoint three commissioners to examine the books, papers and methods of all railroad companies which have received aid in bonds from the government, and in terms invests them with power to make a searching investigation into the working and financial management, business, and affairs of the aided companies; and also to ascertain and report 'whether any of the directors, officers or employees of said companies, respectively, have been or are now, directly or indirectly, interested, and to what amount or extent, in any other railroad, steamship, telegraph, express, mining, construction, or other business company or corporation, and with which any agreements, undertakings or leases have been made or entered into; what amounts of money or credit have been loaned by any of said companies to any person or corporation; what amounts of money or credit have been or are now borrowed by any of said companies, giving names of lenders and the purposes for which said sums have been or are now required; what amounts of money or other valuable consideration, such as stocks, bonds, passes, and so forth, have been expended or paid out by said companies, whether for lawful or unlawful purposes, but for which sufficient and detailed vouchers have not been given or filed with the records of said company; and, further,

> to inquire and report whether said companies, or either of them, or their officers or agents, have paid any money or other valuable consideration, or done any other act or thing, for the purpose of influencing legislation.' "

The Commission found vouchers showing total payments of $733,725.68 to Leland Stanford, President of the Central Pacific Railroad, between November 9, 1870 and December 21, 1880, as reimbursement for moneys expended by him, general expenses and legal services in behalf of the company. One voucher in question was for $171,781.89. Mr. Stanford, when under examination, was asked: "Was any part of the $171,000 paid for the purpose of influencing legislation?"

On advice of counsel, the witness refused to answer and the Commission applied to the federal court for an order compelling him to answer this and other questions of a similar nature. The witness did state that he could not remember the items that went to make up the total amount of the voucher.

Field, Circuit Justice, after filing the statement of facts, delivered the opinion of the court in which he stated, among other things:

> "In resisting the motion, counsel of the respondent have not confined themselves to a discussion of the propriety and necessity of the interrogatories, and the sufficiency of the answers given by him; but they have assailed the validity of the act creating the commission, so far as it authorizes an examination into the private affairs of the directors, officers and employees of the Central Pacific Railroad Co., and confers the right to invoke the power of the federal courts in aid of the general investigation directed. Impressed with

the gravity of the questions presented, we have given them all the consideration in our power.

"The Pacific Railway Commission, created under the act of Congress of March 3, 1887, is not a judicial body; it possesses no judicial powers; it can determine no rights of the government, or of the companies whose affairs it investigates. Those rights will remain the subject of judicial inquiry and determination as fully as though the commission had never been created; and in such inquiry its report to the president of its action will not be even admissible as evidence of any of the matters investigated. It is a mere board of inquiry, directed to obtain information upon certain matters, and report the result of its investigations to the president, who is to lay the same before Congress. In the progress of its investigations, and in furtherance of them, it is in terms authorized to invoke the aid of the courts in the United States, in requiring the attendance of witnesses, and the production of books, papers, and documents. And the act provides that the circuit or district court of the United States, within the jurisdiction of which the inquiry of the commission is had, in case of contumacy or refusal of any person to obey a subpoena to him, may issue an order requiring such person to appear before the commissioners, and produce books and papers, and give evidence touching the matters in question.

* * * * * * * * *

"* * * And in addition to the usual inquiries usually accompanying the taking of a census, there is no doubt that Congress may authorize a commission to obtain information upon any subject, which, in its judgment, it may be important to possess. It may inquire into the extent of the productions of the country of every kind, natural and artificial, and seek information as to the habits, business, and even amusements of the people. *But in its inquiries it is controlled by the same guards against the invasion of private rights which limit the investigations of private parties into similar matters. In the pursuit of knowledge it cannot compel the production of the private books and papers of the citizen for its inspection, except in the progress of judicial proceedings, or in suits instituted for that purpose, and in both cases only upon averment that its rights are in some way dependent for enforcement upon the evidence those books and papers contain.* (Italics supplied.)

"Of all the rights of the citizen, few are of greater importance or more essential to his peace and happiness than the right of personal security, and that involves, not merely protection of his person from assault, but exemption of his private affairs, books and papers from the inspection and scrutiny of others. Without the enjoyment of this right, all other rights would lose half their value. The law provides for the compulsory production, in the progress of judicial proceedings, or by direct suit for that purpose, of such documents as affect the interest of others, and, in certain cases, for the seizure of criminating papers necessary for the prosecution of offenders against public justice, and only in one of the these ways can they be obtained, and their contents made known, against the will of the owners." (Italics supplied.)

"In the recent case of *Boyd v. United States,* 116 U. S. 616, the Supreme Court held that a provision of a law of Congress, which authorized a court of the United States, in revenue cases, on motion of the government attorney, to require the defendant or claimant to produce in court his private books, invoices and papers, or that the allegations of the attorney respecting them should be taken as confessed, was unconstitutional and void as applied to suits for penalties or to establish a forfeiture of the parties' goods. The court, speaking by Mr. Justice Bradley, said:

> "'Any compulsory discovery by extorting the party's oath, or compelling the production of his private books and papers, to convict him of crime or to forfeit his property, is contrary to the principles of a free government. It is abhorrent to the instincts of an Englishman; it is abhorrent to the instincts of an American. It may suit the purposes of despotic power; but it cannot abide the pure atmosphere of political liberty and personal freedom.'"

"The language thus used had reference, it is true, to the compulsory production of papers as a foundation for criminal proceedings, *but it is applicable to any such production of the private books and papers of a party otherwise than in the course of judicial proceedings, or a direct suit for that purpose. It is the forcible intrusion into, and compulsory exposure of, one's private affairs and papers, without judicial proceedings, which is contrary to the principles of a free government, and is abhorrent to the instincts of Englishmen and Americans."* (Italics supplied.)

* * * * * * * * *

"Compulsory process to produce such papers, not in a judicial proceeding, but before a commissioner of inquiry, is as subversive of 'all the comforts of society' as their seizure under the general warrant condemned in that case. (*Entick v. Carrington,* 19 How. State Tr. 1029.) The principles laid down in the opinion

of Lord Camden, [in *Entick v. Carrington*] said the Supreme Court of the United States, *'affect the very essence of constitutional liberty and security. They reach further than the concrete form of the case then before the court with its adventitious circumstances; they apply to all invasions on the part of the government, and its employees, of the sanctity of man's home and the privacies of life.'* " (Italics supplied.)

"In *Kilbourn v. Thompson,* 103 U. S. 168, we have a decision of the Supreme Court of the United States *that neither house of Congress has the power to make inquiries into the private affairs of the citizen; that is to compel exposure of such* affairs. * * *" (Italics supplied.)

After discussing the decision in *Kilbourn v. Thompson,* which that the resolution of Congress authorizing the speaker to appoint a committee to inquire into a so-called "real estate pool" was invalid as an attempt to delegate or exercise judicial power which by the Constitution is reserved to the judiciary, the court continued (p. 253):

"This case will stand for all time as a bulwark against the invasion of the right of the citizen to protection in his private affairs against the unlimited scrutiny of investigation by a congressional committee. The courts are open to the United States as they are to the private citizen, and both can there secure, by regular proceedings, ample protection of all rights and interests which are entitled to protection under a government of a written constitution and laws."

"The act of Congress not only authorizes a searching investigation into the methods, affairs, and business of the Central Pacific R. R. Co., but it makes it the duty of the railway commission to inquire into, ascertain, and report whether any of the directors, officers or employees of that company have been, or are now, directly or indirectly interested, and to what extent, in any railroad, steamship, telegraph, express, mining, construction, *or other business company or corporation, and with which any agreements, undertakings, or leases have been made or entered into.* There are over 100 officers, principal and minor, of the Central Pacific R. R. Co. and nearly 5000 employees. It is not unreasonable to suppose that a large portion of these have some interest as stockholders or otherwise, with some other company or corporation with which the railway company may have an agreement of some kind, and it would be difficult to state the extent to which the explorations of the commission into the private affairs of these persons may not go if the mandate of the act be fully carried out. But in accordance with the principles declared in the case of *Kilbourn v. Thompson,* and the equally important doctrines announced in *Boyd v. United States,* the commission is limited in its inquiries as to the interest of these directors, officers and employees in any other business, company or corporation, *to such matters as these persons may choose to dissolve. They cannot be compelled to open these books, and expose such other business to the inspection and examination of the commission.* They were not prohibited from engaging in any other lawful business because of their interest in and connection with the Central Pacific R. R. Co., and that other business might as well be the construction and management of other railroads as the planting of vines, or the raising of fruit, in which some of these directors and officers and employees have been in fact engaged. And they are entitled to the same protection and exemption from inquisitorial investigation into such business as any other citizens engaged in such business. (Italics supplied.)

"Be that as it may, the federal courts cannot, upon that concession, aid the commission in ascertaining how the moneys were expended. *Those courts cannot become the instruments of the commission in furthering its investigation. Their power, its nature and extent, is defined by the Constitution.* The government established by that instrument is one of delegated powers, supreme in its prescribed sphere, but without authority beyond it. No department of it can exercise any powers not specifically enumerated or necessarily implied in those enumerated. * * * Any legislation of Congress beyond the limits of the powers delegated is an invasion of the rights reserved to the states or *to the people,* and is necessarily void. (Italics supplied.)

* * * * * * * * *

"*The judicial power of the United States is therefore* vested [by the Constitution] in the courts, and can only be exercised by them in the cases and controveries enumerated, and in petition for units of *habeas corpus. In no other proceedings can that power be invoked, and it is not competent for Congress to require its exercise in any other way.* Any act providing for such exercise could be a direct invasion of the rights reserved to the states or to the people; and it would be the duty of the courts to declare it null and void. Story says, in his commentaries on the Constitution, that 'the functions of the judges of the courts of the United States are strictly and exclusively judicial. They cannot, therefore, be called upon to advise the president in any executive measures, or to give extrajudicial interpretations of the law, or to act as commissioners in cases of pensions or other like proceedings.'" Section 1777. (Italics supplied.)

* * * * * * * * *

The court, on p. 257, continued:

"The act of Congress creating the railway commission in terms provides, as already stated, that it may invoke the aid of any circuit or district court to require the attendance of witnesses, and the production of books, papers, and documents relating to the subject of inquiry; and empowers the court, in case of contumacy or refusal of persons to obey subpoenas to them, to issue orders requiring them to appear before the commissioners, or either of them, and produce the books, and papers ordered, and give evidence touching the matters in question, and to punish disobedience to its orders; *and does not appear to leave any discretion in the matter with the court.* It would seem as *though Congress intended that the court should make the orders upon the mere request of the commissioners, without regard to the nature of the inquiry. It is difficult to believe that it could have intended that the court should thus be the mere executor of the commissioners' will. And yet, if the commissioners are not bound, as they have asserted, by any rules of evidence in their investigations, and may receive hearsay, ex parte statements, and information of every character that may be brought to their attention, and the court is to aid them in this manner of investigation, there can be no room for the exercise of judgment as to the propriety of the questions asked, and the court if left merely to direct that the pleasure of the commissioners in the line of their inquiries be carried out.* But if it was expected that the court, when its aid is invoked, should examine the subject of the inquiries to see their character, so as to be able to determine the propriety and pertinency of the questions, and the propriety and necessity of producing the books, papers, and documents asked for before the commission, then it would be called upon to exercise advisory functions in an administrative or political proceeding, or to exercise judicial power. If the former, they cannot be invested in the court; if the latter, the power can only be exercised in the cases or controversies enumerated in the constitution, or in cases of *habeas corpus*. (Italics supplied.)

"*The provision of the act authorizing the courts to aid in the investigation in the manner indicated must therefore be adjudged void. The federal courts, under the Constitution, cannot be made the aids to any investigation by a commission or committee into the affairs of anyone. If rights are to be protected or wrongs redressed by any investigation, it must be conducted by regular proceedings in the courts of justice in cases authorized by the Constitution.*" (Italics supplied.)

At page 259 the court concluded:

"The conclusion we have thus reached disposes of the petition of the railway commissioners, and renders it unnecessary to consider whether the interrogatories propounded were proper in themselves, or were sufficiently met by the answers given by Mr. Stanford, or whether any of them were open to objections for the assumptions they made, or the imputations they implied. *It is enough that the federal courts cannot be made the instruments to aid the commissioners in their investigations.* It also renders it unnecessary to make any comment upon the extraordinary position taken by them according to the statement of the respondent, to which we have referred, that they [commisisoners] did not regard themselves bound in their examination by the ordinary rules of evidence, but would receive hearsay and *ex parte* statements, surmises, and information of every character that might be called to their attention. *It cannot be that the courts of the United States can be used in furtherance of investigations in which all rules of evidence may be thus disregarded.*" (Italics supplied.)

The decision in the above case could not have been more in point or more applicable to the constitutional question here considered had the court actually been considering Section 19(b) and 22(b) of the present Securities Act. Some of the points of similarity in the statute construed in the above case and the sections, the constitutionality of which is questioned in this procedure, are the following:

The Act of March 3, 1887, created the Pacific Railway Commission as an administrative agency of the government, just as the Securities Act of 1933 created the Securities & Exchange Commission as such an administrative agency. The 1887 statute provided that the commissioners, or either of them, shall have the power "to require the attendance and testimony of witnesses, and the production of all books, papers, contracts, agreements, and documents relating to the matter under investigation, and to administer oaths"; while Section 19(b) of this statute grants the same powers to this Commission, except that it goes very much farther because in the former statute the Act provided that the documents, the production of which could be required by the Pacific Railway Commission, must meet the requirement of *"relating to the matter under investigation."*

That language meant that it must be shown to the satisfaction of the Court in a proceeding to enforce the Commission's subpoena for documents, that such documents met with the usual requirements as to their materiality and relevancy to the subject matter of the inquiry, which question the Court, when asked to enforce such production, had opportunity to pass upon.

This statute in Section 19(b) goes farther than the statute there considered by providing that "for the purpose of all investigations *which, in the opinion of the Commission,* are necessary and proper for the enforcement of this title, any member of the Commission or any officer or officers designated by it are empowered to administer oaths and affirmations, subpoena witnesses, take evidence, and require the production of any books, papers, or other documents *which the Commission deems relevant or material to the inquiry.*"

In the *Pacific Railway Commission* case, by its wording the Act under consideration restricted the production of books, papers and documents the production of which might be demanded by the Commission, aided if necessary by the Order of the Court, to those *"relating to the matter under investigation."* There was no unlimited delegation of power or authorization to that Commission to make any investigation which *"in its opinion"* was necessary and proper for the enforcement of its Act, or to require the production of books, papers and records which the Commission (not the Court) "deemed relevant or material to the inquiry."

In the 1887 Act, it was provided:

> "Any of the Circuit or District Courts of the United States within the jurisdiction of which such

inquiry is carried on, MAY, in case of contumacy or refusal to obey a subpoena issued to any person, issue an order requiring any such person to appear before said commissioners, or either of them, as the case may be, and produce books and papers, if so ordered, and give evidence touching the matter in question; and any failure to obey such Order of the Court may be punished by such court as a contempt thereof."

Section 22(b) of the Securities Act of 1933 provides:

> "In case of contumacy or refusal to obey a subpoena issued to any person, any of the said United States courts, within the jurisdiction of which said person guilty of contumacy or refusal to obey is found or resides, upon application by the Commission, MAY issue to such person an order requiring such person to appear before the Commission, or one of its examiners designated by it, there to produce documentary evidence if so ordered, or there to give evidence touching the matter in question; and any failure to obey such order of the court may be punished by said court as a contempt thereof."

The word "may" has been capitalized and underscored in both of the above quotations for the purpose of emphasizing the importance of that particular word in both Acts.

It was contended in the *Pacific Railway Commission* case, and undoubtedly will be contended by the Commission in this case, that the word "may" leaves sufficient leeway for the exercise of their judicial discretion and judicial power and authority by the United States courts, to consider and pass upon any application of the Commission according to the established rules of judicial procedure.

But the Court's attention is respectfully invited to the quotation from page 257 of the Report, in which the District Court in the above case said that such wording "does not appear to leave any discretion in the matter with the court"; and that:

> "It would seem as though Congress intended that the court should make the orders upon the mere request of the commissioners, without regard to the nature of the inquiry. It is difficult to believe that it could have intended that the court should thus be the mere executor of the commissioners' will, and yet if the commissioners are not bound, as they have asserted, by any rules of evidence in their investigations, and may receive hearsay, *ex parte* statements, and information of every character that may be brought to their attention, and the court is to aid them in this manner of investigation, there can be no room for the exercise of judgment as to the propriety of the questions asked, and the court, if left merely to direct that the pleasure of the commissioners in the line of their inquiries be carried out."

Every word of the court which was applied to the 1887 statute, is equally and as completely applicable if applied to the Securities Act of 1933, and the use of the word "may" in both cases emphasizes the importance of this comparison.

In the present proceeding the Commission has strenuously contended before the Court below that under the provisions of Section 19(b) of its Act as supplemented by Section 22(b), all that the Commission was required to do in its application for an Order directing compliance with its subpoena *duces tecum,* was to assert that in its opinion the investigation was proper and necessary for the enforcement of the Act, and that the documents demanded in its subpoena were deemed to be relevant and material to the inquiry. The Commission itself did not so find. But if it had it would still be unconstitutional.

In support of Respondent's contention that the constitutionality of Act is not saved by the provisions of Section 22(c) of the Securities Act providing in substance that no person shall be excused from attending and testifying or from producing books, papers, contracts, agreements or other documents before the Commission on the ground of self-incrimination, or subjection to the penalty of forfeiture, and further providing that no individual shall be prosecuted or subjected to any penalty or forfeiture for, or on account of, any transaction, matter, or thing concerning which he is compelled, after having claimed his privilege against self-incrimination, to testify or produce evidence, documentary or otherwise, since a provision in similar language and effect was also included in the provision in the Act of March 3, 1887 declared to be unconstitutional, the provision in that Act being:

> "The claim that any such testimony or evidence may tend to incriminate the person giving such evidence, shall not excuse such witness from testifying, but such evidence or testimony shall not be used against such person in the trial of any criminal procedure."

In *Interstate Commerce Commission v. Brimson* (1893), 154 U. S. 447, Mr. Justice Harlan said, at pages 478-479:

> "We do not overlook these *constitutional limitations* which, for the protection of personal rights, most necessarily attend all investigations conducted under the authority of Congress. *Neither branch of the*

legislative department, still less any administrative body, established by Congress, possesses or can be invested with, a general power of making inquiry into the private affairs of a citizen. Kilbourn v. Thompson, 103 U. S. 188, 190. We said in *Boyd v. United States,* 116 U. S. 616, 630,—and it cannot be too often repeated—that the principles that embody the essence of constitutional liberty and security forbid all invasions on the part of the government and its employees of the sanctity of a man's home and the privacy of his life. As said by Mr. Justice Field in *In re Pacific Railway Commission,* 32 Fed. Rep. 241, 250, '*of all the rights of the citizen, few are of greater importance or more essential to his peace and happiness than the right of personal security, and that involves, not merely protection of his person from assault, but exemption of his private affairs, books, and papers from the inspection and scrutiny of others. Without the enjoyment of this right, all others would lose half* their value.'" (Italics supplied.)

Thus, by repeating the learned declaration of fundamental constitutional rights of citizens, and the consequent constitutional limitations on Congress in investing power in administrative agencies and commissions to invade the private rights, papers and records of citizens, the United States Supreme Court in the above case so emphatically stamped its aproval upon the decision of Judge Field in the *Pacific Railway Commission* case, that this Court, in considering that decision may well give it the same weight that it would have given if the decision had been originally expressed by, or affirmed on appeal by, the Supreme Court, and counsel respectfully asks that such weight be given that decision in ruling upon the question here presented.

Later in the *Brimson* case, *supra,* the Supreme Court referred to the amendment of the Interstate Commerce Act (27 Stat. 443, C. 83) which provided that no person should be excused from appearing, testifying, producing his books and records, etc., and granting immunity for the testimony or evidence thus compelled, but the court remarked that "that act was not in force when this case was determined below." However, in the *Pacific Railway Commission* case the statute under consideration did have such an immunity provision, the same in effect as now appears in Section 22(c) of the Securities Act, so that such right of immunity was considered, but did not change the result in that case.

Kilbourn v. Thompson (1880), 103 U. S. 168, was a case where a witness refused to answer certain questions put to him as a witness by the House of Representatives concerning the business of a real estate partnership of which he was a member, and to produce certain books and papers in relation thereto. The witness by order of the House was imprisoned for 45 days and brought suit against the Sergeant-at-arms who imprisoned him, and the members of the committee where he was adjudged in contempt.

The Court, by Mr. Justice Miller, said:

> "No general power of inflicting punishment by the Congress of the United States is found in that instrument (Constitution). It contains in the provision that 'no person shall be deprived of life, liberty or property, without due process of law,' the strongest implication against punishment by order of the legislative body. It has repeatedly been decided by this court, and by others of the highest authority, that this means a trial in which the rights of the

party shall be decided by a tribunal appointed by law, which tribunal is to be governed by rules of law previously established. An act of Congress which proposed to adjudge a man guilty of a crime and inflict the punishment, would be conceded by all thinking men to be unauthorized by anything in the Constitution. . . ."

"Whether this power of punishment in either house by fine or imprisonment goes beyond this or not, we are sure that no person can be punished for contumacy as a witness before either house, *unless his testimony is required in a matter into which the House has jurisdiction to inquire, and we feel equally sure that neither of these bodies possess the general power of making inquiry into the private affairs of the citizen.* (Italics supplied.)

* * * * * * * * *

"In looking to the preamble and resolution under which the committee acted, before which Kilbourn refused to testify, we are of opinion that the House of Representatives *not only exceeded the limit of its own authority, but assumed a power which could* only be properly exercised by another branch of the government, because it was in its nature clearly judicial." (Italics supplied.)

"The Constitution declares that the judicial power of the United States shall be vested in one Supreme Court, and in such inferior courts as the Congress may from time to time ordain and establish. If what we have said of the division of the powers of the government among the three departments be sound, this is equivalent to a declaration that no judicial power is vested in the Congress or either branch of it, save in the cases specifically enumerated to which we have referred. (Referring to punishment of its own members, etc.) If the investigation which the committee was directed to make was judicial in its character, and could only be properly and successfully made by a court of justice, and if it related to a matter wherein relief or redress could only be had by a judicial proceeding, we do not, after that has been said, deem it necessary to discuss the proposition that the power attempted to be exercised was one confided by the Constitution to the judicial and not the legislative department of the government. We think it equally clear that the power asserted is judicial and not legislative.

* * * * * * * * *

"We are of opinion, for these reasons, that the resolution of the House of Representatives authorizing the investigation was in excess of the power conferred on that body by the Constitution; that the committee, therefore, had no lawful authority to require Kilbourn to testify as a witness beyond what he voluntarily chose to tell; that the orders and resolutions of the House, and the warrant of the Speaker, under which Kilbourn was imprisoned, are, in like manner, void for want of jurisdiction in that body, and that his imprisonment was without lawful authority."

In *Boyd v. United States,* 116 U. S. 616 (1885), the court, in its opinion delivered by Mr. Justice Bradley, after reviewing the English and American law, said, among other things (pp. 631-632):

"The court of chancery had for generations been weighing and balancing the rules to be observed in granting discovery on bills filed for that purpose, in the endeavor to fix upon such as would best secure the ends of justice. To go beyond the point to which that Court had gone may well have been thought hazardous. Now it is elementary knowledge, that one cardinal rule of the court of chancery is never to decree a discovery which might tend to convict the party of a crime, or to forfeit his property. *And any compulsory discovery by extorting the party's oath, or compelling the production of his private books and papers, to convict him of crime, or to forfeit his property, is contrary to the principles of a free government.* It is abhorrent to the instincts of an Englishman; it is abhorrent to the instincts of an American. *It may suit the purposes of despotic power; but it cannot abide the pure atmosphere of political liberty and personal freedom."* (Italics supplied.)

"We have already noticed the intimate relation between the two amendments. They throw great light on each other. For the 'unreasonable searches and seizures' condemned in the Fourth Amendment are almost always made for the purpose of compelling a man to give evidence against himself, which in criminal cases is condemned in the Fifth Amendment; and compelling a man 'in a criminal case to be a witness against himself,' which is condemned in the Fifth Amendment, throws light on what is an 'unreasonable search and seizure' within the meaning of the Fourth Amendment. *And we have been unable to perceive that the seizure of a man's private books and papers to be used as evidence against him is substantially different from compelling him to be a witness against himself.* We think it is within the clear intent and meaning of those terms. We are also clearly of the opinion that proceedings instituted for the purpose of declaring a forfeiture of a man's property by reason of offenses committed by him, though they may be civil in form, are in their nature criminal . . ." (Italics supplied.)

The conclusion of the court, however, was that the statute in question did not violate the Fourth Amendment, the court saying:

> "I cannot conceive how a statute aptly framed to require the production of evidence *in a suit* by mere service of notice on the party, who has the evidence in his possession, can be held to authorize an unreasonable search or seizure, when no seizure is authorized or permitted by the statute." (Italics supplied.)

NOTE: In the above statute, however, the books were required to be produced in court in a suit duly instituted and the court could pass upon the relevancy or admissibility of anything offered as evidence by the Government, which is not true under the provisions of the Securities Act of 1933, which provides in Sections 19(b) and 22(b) for the books, papers and records to be delivered to the Commission and for no restriction upon their examination, once in possession, by reason of the materiality or relevancy of any information therein contained which might be held inadmissible if the documents were to be produced in court, where objections of counsel on these points could be offered and ruled on by the court.

In *Aetna Life Insurance Co. v. Haworth* (1936), 300 U. S. 239, Chief Justice Hughes cited the *Pacific Railway Commission Case* with approval, saying on page 239:

> "First, The Constitution limits the exercise of the judicial power to 'cases' and 'controversies.' The

> term 'controversies,' if distinguishable at all from 'cases' is so that it is less comprehensive than the latter, and includes only suits of a civil nature."

Per Mr. Justice Field in *In Re Pacific Railway Commission,* 32 Fed. 241, 255, citing *Chisholm v. Georgia,* 2 Dall. 419, 431, 432.

The *Pacific Railway Commission* decision was also cited in connection with above excerpt from Chief Justice Hughes opinion in *Smith v. Blackwell* (D. C. D. N. J. 1937), 18 F. Supp. 450, 453; in *In Re Andrews Tax Liability* (D. C. D. Md. 1937), 15 F. Supp. 804, 808; in *United States v. Hoffman* (D. C. S. D. N. Y. 1938), 24 F. Supp. 847, 849.

In *Attorney General v. Brissenden,* 271 Mass. 172 it was said by Chief Justice Rugg:

> "In conducting any investigation, whether by a committee of its members, or through other agency, the General Court is bound to observe all provisions of the Constitution designed to protect the individual in the enjoyment of life, liberty and property, and from inquisitions into private affairs."

In *Annenberg v. Roberts,* 333 Pa. 214, decided by the Supreme Court of that state (1938), the court after quoting the above excerpt from the opinion of Chief Justice Rugg of the Massachusetts Supreme Court added (p. 214):

> "While the act under consideration in the present case seems to recognize this fundamental principle, since it authorizes the issue only of such subpoenas as require answers to questions *'touching matters properly being inquired into by the Commission'* and the compulsary production only of such books, papers,

records and documents as relate *'to the subject of inquiry,'* we are in accord with the observations made by the court below as to the irrelevance of information called for in the subpoenas issued to these plaintiffs; it follows that there is a constitutional lack of power in the Commission to demand it." (Italics supplied.)

"The subpoenas show on their face that they contemplate an unreasonable search and seizure. They violate the principle which we announced in *American Car & Foundry Co. v. Alexandria Water Co.*, 221 Pa. 529, where we held that a subpoena duces tecum could not properly be issued to bring in a mass of books and papers in order that there might be a search through them to gather evidence. We, therefore, are of opinion that the subpoenas as issued commanding plaintiffs to produce before the Commission the things therein set forth are void, in that they do not show that the demands are germane to the inquiry authorized by the Governor's call. . . ."

"We cannot agree with the conclusions of the court below that these proceedings have been prematurely brought and that the time for the plaintiffs to raise their objections to the subpoena is when questions are propounded to them or documents demanded at the hearing. Under our system of constitutional government it has become established that equity will restrain public officials from acting pursuant to legislation found to be unconstitutional and that relief will be granted on the application of one whose rights are injuriously affected; the cases on this subject are numerous.

"The important question is, where and how may a person served with a demand such as appears in the record, assert the right? The parties from whom an alleged demand for documents has been made 'are not required' as we said in *Brown v. Brancato*, 321 Pa. 54, 61, to test the alleged right of such person by forcibly resisting his unlawful efforts to seize the books and records of their administration. or, for defiance of the committee's subpoenas, by subsequently justifying their resistance in proceedings for contempt or in habeas corpus (cf. *Ex Parte Caldwell*, 61 N. Va. 49, 55 S. E. 910; *McGrain v. Dougherty*, 273 U. S. 135) *or by suffering themselves to be indicted* (cf. *Com. v. Costello*, 21 D. R. 232). Equity has jurisdiction to restrain if the committee is without lawful authority in the premises (citing Pa. cases) * * *."

And at page 215, the court continued:

"A difference is to be noted between an unlawful demand contained in a subpoena duces tecum in cases pending in court (as in *American Car & Foundry Co. v. Alexandria Water Co., supra*), and a demand made by a nonjudicial body. In court parties and witnesses may, by appropriate application made in the proceedings have their rights determined and preserved, *but proceedings before a nonjudicial body are in a different class. Parties aggrieved in such proceedings must also have opportunity for judicial hearing if their rights are to be determined and preserved. Here, as before stated, the demands for the production of documents show on their face that they violate plaintiff's constitutional rights; this being so, plaintiffs are entitled now to challenge them and to have them abated and set aside, which is accordingly done.*" (Italics supplied.)

In *Crowell v. Benson* (1932), 285 U. S. 22, at page 56, the Supreme Court, in discussing the extent to which findings of a Commission may be made binding on the courts, remarked:

> "In relation to these basic facts, the question is not the ordinary one as to the propriety of provision for administrative determinations. Nor have we simply the question of due process in relation to notice and hearing. *It is rather a question of the appropriate maintenance of the Federal judicial power in requiring the observance of constitutional restriction.* It is the question whether the Congress may substitute for constitutional courts, in which the judicial power of the United States is vested, an administrative agency—in this instance a single deputy commissioner—for the final determination of the existence of the facts upon which the enforcement of the constitutional rights of the citizen depend. *The recognition of the utility and convenience of administrative agencies for the investigation and finding of facts within their proper province, and support of their authorized action, does not require the conclusion that there is no limitation of their use, and that the Congress could completely oust the courts of all determinations of fact by vesting the authority to make them with finality in its own instrumentalities or in the Executive Department. That would be to sap the judicial power as it exists under the Federal Constitution, and to establish a government of bureaucratic character alien to our system, wherever fundamental rights depend, as not infrequently they do depend, upon the facts, and finality as to facts becomes in effect finality in law.*" (Italics supplied.)

The same principle of unlawful delegation of power applies whether it be "judicial" or "legislative" power, and the following decisions on unlawful delegation of legislative powers are pertinent in considering the question now before this Court.

IV.

The District Court Erred in Holding That Transactions in Distillers' Whiskey Warehouse Receipts Were Transactions Within the Meaning of Section 2(1) of the Securities Act as Amended in 1933.

A warehouse receipt represents the property described therein, and a transfer of the same is a symbolic delivery of the goods called for by the receipt and passes title to the goods as effectually as if an actual delivery were made. (Civ. Code, sec. 1858b; *A. Widemann Co. v. Digges,* 21 Cal. App. 342, 131 Pac. 882; *Cavallaro v. Texas etc. Ry. Co.,* 110 Cal. 348, 42 Pac. 918, 52 Am. St. Rep. 94; *Garoutte v. Williamson,* 108 Cal. 135, 41 Pac. 35; *Bishop v. Fulkerth,* 68 Cal. 607, 10 Pac. 122; *Davis v. Russell,* 52 Cal. 611, 28 Am. Rep. 647.) Thus, by the issuance or transfer of a warehouse receipt for whiskey held in bond in Kentucky, there is in fact a sale and a constructive delivery within the state of California of a commodity, although at the time of the sale it is and may forever remain elsewhere, and as between the vendor and the vendee there is no distinction between the solicitation of orders for the whiskey and the solicitation of orders for warehouse receipts representing the same.

V.

The District Court Erred in Holding That Bottling Contracts of the Bourbon Sales Corporation or The Penfield Company of California Were Transactions in Securities as Defined in Section 2(1) of the Securities Act of 1933 and Therefore Conferred Jurisdiction Upon the Securities and Exchange Commission.

These contracts were contracts to bottle whiskey and pay the tax on it. They were not contracts for a security, but for the performance of certain work and labor in connection with the bottling of whiskey. Many wholesalers, retailers, large corporations, hotels, etc., daily send warehouse receipts owned by them to licensed bottlers with instructions to the bottlers to "tax pay" the whiskey, bottle and label it and ship it to them through the regular channels of bottler to a licensed wholesaler, wholesaler to licensed retailer, retailer to the original owner, etc., as the case may require. The bottler bills the wholesaler for the taxes and other charges he has paid, plus his cost of bottling. The wholesaler bills the retailer for the same charges, plus his handling fee, and the retailer does likewise.

There is nothing in the transaction, therefore, that makes it a security within the meaning of the Securities Act.

A security does not extend to ordinary commercial contracts, nor does it include interest income from the lending of money or the profits which one might make from his own efforts as the result of any ordinary commercial contract. (*Lewis v. Creasey Corp.*, 198 Ky. 407, 248 S. W. 1046.)

Conclusion.

It is therefore respectfully submitted that the District Court erred in authorizing and approving an order issuing the *subpoena duces tecum* and compelling the appellant and its representatives to produce in court all of the matters and things therein set forth; that at no time did the Commission ever establish jurisdiction by an appropriate order; that at no time did the Commission ever, by any order, declare that in its opinion or judgment the matters and things thereafter sought by one of its agents to be secured were relevant or material to the inquiry; in its opinion that such declaration is a necessary statutory foundation before any subpoena can be issued or sought; that the representatives of the Commission were about to embark upon and are embarking upon a general, roving, inquisitorial expedition, specifically forbidden by the Fourth and Fifth Amendments to the Constitution of the United States; that the statute, if given the construction placed upon it by the District Court, inherently and as construed and applied, would be unconstitutional, in violation of the Fourth and Fifth Amendments and Article III of the Constitution of the United States; that the Commission was without jurisdiction in any event to subpoena the various matters therein sought, as they, the matters allegedly the object of investigation, were not and are not securities within the meaning of the Securities and Exchange Act.

Wherefore, for each and all of these reasons appellant prays that the judgment of the District Court be reversed.

Respectfully submitted,

Morris Lavine,

Attorney for Appellant.

IN THE

United States Circuit Court of Appeals

FOR THE NINTH CIRCUIT

THE PENFIELD COMPANY OF CALIFORNIA, a corporation, *Appellant*,

v.

SECURITIES AND EXCHANGE COMMISSION, *Appellee*.

No. 10487

BRIEF FOR APPELLEE

ROGER S. FOSTER,
Solicitor.

MILTON V. FREEMAN,
Assistant Solicitor.

LOUIS LOSS,
Special Counsel.

SECURITIES & EXCHANGE COMMISSION,
18th and Locust Streets,
Philadelphia 3, Pa.

CHARLES J. ODENWELLER, JR.,
Regional Administrator.

SECURITIES & EXCHANGE COMMISSION,
1370 Ontario Street,
Cleveland 13, Ohio.

CONTENTS

CITATIONS

Cases: Page

CITATIONS—*Continued*

CITATIONS—*Continued*

CITATIONS—*Continued*

CITATIONS—*Continued*

CITATIONS—*Continued*

Constitution, Statutes and Rules:

Miscellaneous:

IN THE

UNITED STATES CIRCUIT COURT OF APPEALS

FOR THE NINTH CIRCUIT

THE PENFIELD COMPANY OF CALIFORNIA, a corporation, *Appellant*,

v.

SECURITIES AND EXCHANGE COMMISSION, *Appellee.*

No. 10487

Brief for Appellee

STATEMENT OF JURISDICTION

This is an appeal from a final order and decree entered by the District Court for the Southern District of California, Central Division, on June 1, 1943 (R. 313-17), pursuant to Section 22(b) of the Securities Act of 1933 (15 U. S. C. § 77v(b)).[1] That order directed the appellant to comply with a subpœna *duces tecum* of the Commission requiring it to appear before an officer of the Commission and to produce certain of its corporate books, papers and documents (R. 15-18).

---

[1] "In case of contumacy or refusal to obey a subpena issued to any person, any of the said United States courts, within the jurisdiction of which said person guilty of contumacy or refusal to obey is found or resides, upon application by the Commission may issue to such person an order requiring such person to appear before the Commission, or one of its examiners designated by it, there to produce documentary evidence if so ordered, or there to give evidence touching the matter in question; and any failure to obey such order of the court may be punished by said court as a contempt thereof."

STATUTE INVOLVED

In general, the Securities Act of 1933 affords protection to the investing public by requiring publicity of the material facts and circumstances bearing on the value of securities which are publicly offered through the mails or in interstate commerce.[2] Dissemination of information is achieved by the requirement that a "registration statement" describing the securities and the issuer be filed with the Securities and Exchange Commission, and by the further requirement that a "prospectus" summarizing the information contained in the registration statement be furnished to each person to whom the securities are offered. These requirements are found in Section 5 of the Act (15 U. S. C. § 77e). Section 17(a) (15 U. S. C. § 77q(a)) prohibits fraudulent sales of securities through the mails or in interstate commerce.

The Commission does not pass on the merits or value of any security (§ 23, 15 U. S. C. § 77w). Its function is to enforce the registration and anti-fraud requirements of the Act in order that the investing public may be afforded accurate and adequate information on the basis of which each investor may form his own judgment as to the merits of the securities offered to him.

Other sections of the Act make provision for the administration and enforcement of the substantive provisions of Sections 5 and 17(a). Thus the subpœna presently sought to be enforced was issued pursuant to Section 19(b) (15 U. S. C. § 77s(b))[3] in the course of an investigation insti-

---

[2] The Securities Act was last before this Court in *National Supply Co.* v. *Leland Stanford Junior University*, 134 F. (2d) 689 (1943), *cert. denied*, 88 L. Ed. (Adv. Op.) 43 (1943), and *Merger Mines Corp.* v. *Grismer*, 137 F. (2d) 335 (1943), *cert. denied*, 88 L. Ed. (Adv. Op.) 155 (1943). In both those cases the Commission filed briefs as *amicus curiæ*.

[3] "For the purpose of all investigations which, in the opinion of the Commission, are necessary and proper for the enforcement of this title, any member of the Commission or any

tuted by the Commission under Section 20(a) (15 U. S. C. § 77t(a)).[4] On the basis of the information obtained through such investigations, the Commission is authorized by Section 20(b) (15 U. S. C. § 77t(b)) to institute actions in the District Courts to enjoin existing or threatened violations of the Act, and to place the facts it has obtained before the Attorney-General for criminal prosecution.

---

officer or officers designated by it are empowered to administer oaths and affirmations, subpena witnesses, take evidence, and require the production of any books, papers, or other documents which the Commission deems relevant or material to the inquiry. Such attendance of witnesses and the production of such documentary evidence may be required from any place in the United States or any Territory at any designated place of hearing."

[4] "Whenever it shall appear to the Commission, either upon complaint or otherwise, that the provisions of this title, or of any rule or regulation prescribed under authority thereof, have been or are about to be violated, it may, in its discretion, either require or permit such person to file with it a statement in writing, under oath, or otherwise, as to all the facts and circumstances concerning the subject matter which it believes to be in the public interest to investigate, and may investigate such facts."

FACTS

On May 14, 1942, the Commission issued an order under Section 20(a) directing an investigation to determine whether a Kentucky corporation called Bourbon Sales Corporation, together with several individuals, had violated Sections 5 and 17(a) of the Act in the sale of securities consisting of contracts for the bottling of whiskey (R. 8-11).[5] On October 15, 1942, the District Court for the Western District of Kentucky directed Bourbon Sales Corporation, in a proceeding similar to the case at bar, to comply with a subpœna of the Commission very like the subpœna directed against the present appellant. *S. E. C.* v. *Bourbon Sales Corp.*, 47 F. Supp. 70.[6]

The enforcement of that subpœna disclosed information which led the Commission into its present inquiry. It was discovered that the appellant here had for some time been acting as agent for Bourbon Sales Corporation in selling bottling contracts through the mails to persons to whom that company or the appellant had previously sold whiskey warehouse receipts (R. 160, 190-91, 201-03), and that it had subsequently sold its own bottling contracts through the mails in exchange for such receipts (R. 340, 342, affidavits of Andrew C. Elder, Viola M. Eldridge, A. W. Hudson, Mrs. Johnnie McKaskle, Peter P. Valley). While investigating this phase of the appellant's activities, the Commission learned also for the first time that *stock* of the appellant

---

[5] One of the respondents in that order was The Penfield Company, an Ohio corporation. It is not to be confused with The Penfield Company of California, the appellant here, which is a California corporation (R. 26).

[6] After holding that enforcement of the Commission's subpœna did not require a holding that the whiskey bottling contracts were securities within the meaning of Section 2(1) of the Act (15 U. S. C. § 77b(1)), the Court went on to decide that they were securities in the nature of investment contracts or certificates of interest or participation in a profit-sharing agreement within the meaning of that section. No appeal was taken in that case.

was being sold to the public through the mails in exchange for bottling contracts previously issued by either the appellant or Bourbon Sales Corporation (R. 204). On April 8, 1943, therefore, the Commission supplemented its original order of investigation to name the present appellant and A. W. Young, its secretary-treasurer, and to cover the sale of the appellant's stock by the persons named in the supplemental order (R. 12-15). Accordingly, the Commission is now proceeding to investigate whether the appellant and other specified persons have violated Sections 5 and 17(a) of the Securities Act in selling both stock and whiskey bottling contracts without registration and by means of untrue statements of material facts.

On April 9, 1943, the subpœna here involved (R. 15-18) was directed to the appellant and Young by C. J. Odenweller, Jr., Regional Administrator of the Commission's Cleveland Regional Office and one of the undersigned attorneys, who was designated in the Commission's orders authorizing the investigation as one of the officers empowered "to administer oaths and affirmations, subpœna witnesses, compel their attendance, take evidence, and require the production of any books, papers, correspondence, memoranda or other records deemed relevant or material to the inquiry" (R. 11, 15). The subpœna required the production of 20 specified items of the appellant's books, papers and documents covering the four-year period from May 1, 1939, to the date of the subpœna (R. 16-18).

When the appellant failed to comply with this subpœna, the Commission filed with the court below its application for enforcement under Section 22(b) of the Securities Act (R. 2-19), alleging that at the time of the entry of its orders of investigation it "had reasonable grounds to believe that Bourbon Sales Corporation and The Penfield Company of California had violated and [were] about to violate the provisions of Sections 5(a) and 17(a) of the said Act, as more fully appears in the said orders" (R. 4). After the appellant had filed an answer together with two supporting affidavits (R. 26-125), a hearing was held and the court stated that "there should be some showing of relevancy, that is, that there is something about to be done or a probability of the violation of the Securities Law that is in the nature of a criminal violation for a Grand Jury investigation" (R. 127-28). Mr. Odenweller thereupon filed a statement concerning the materiality and relevancy of the items called for in the two subpœnas (R. 128-56), together with 19 supporting affidavits (R. 156-217). It appears from these affidavits that persons who had previously been sold whiskey warehouse receipts by either Bourbon Sales Corporation or the appellant were induced to turn over those receipts to the appellant in exchange for bottling contracts or stock; that the bottling contracts were offered or sold through the mails on the representation that the only way the receipt-holders could receive a profit would be by virtue of the skill of Bourbon Sales Corporation or the appellant and their ability to bottle and sell the whiskey with minimum expense and at the highest price; and that the stock was sold through the mails by means of literature which omitted to state its true book value and contained misrepresentations concerning the profit possibilities of the appellant (R. 160, 162, 190-93, 201-04, 340, 342, affidavits of Andrew C. Elder, Viola M. Eldridge, A. W. Hudson, Mrs. Johnnie McKaskle, Peter P. Valley).

After the filing of a supplemental answer and counter-affidavits by the appellant (R. 218-302), a further hearing was held (R. 304-10) and the court granted the Commission's application for enforcement of the subpœna (R. 331), incorporating in its final order and decree the twenty items which the subpœna specifies (R. 314-16). The court delivered no oral or written opinion specifying the grounds upon which the subpœna was enforced or ruling upon the appellant's several objections.

QUESTIONS PRESENTED

This brief seeks to establish the following propositions:

I. The Securities Act of 1933 authorizes the enforcement of the subpœna without a determination that the appellant has used the mails or an instrumentality of interstate commerce in the sale of a security; the only showing required of the Commission is that the evidence sought by the subpœna is not plainly irrelevant to any lawful purpose of the Commission in the discharge of its duties under the Act.

II. In any event there are reasonable grounds to believe that the appellant has used the mails and has done so in the sale of a "security."

III. The subpœna is valid in form and content: (A) the Act does not require the Commission to make a formal finding that in its opinion the evidence required is necessary for proper enforcement of the Act and relevant or material to the Commission's investigation, and (B) the evidence required is in fact relevant to the investigation.

IV. The subpœna is not unduly broad or burdensome and does not involve an unconstitutional search and seizure within the meaning of the Fourth Amendment.

V. The investigatory provisions of the Act do not involve an unconstitutional delegation of judicial power to the Commission.

ARGUMENT

I.

THE ACT AUTHORIZES THE ENFORCEMENT OF THE SUBPŒNA WITHOUT A DETERMINATION THAT THE APPELLANT HAS USED THE MAILS OR AN INSTRUMENTALITY OF INTERSTATE COMMERCE IN THE SALE OF A SECURITY.

The proposition that an administrative agency need not allege and prove its jurisdiction in seeking enforcement of a subpœna was established by the Supreme Court in *Endicott-Johnson Corporation* v. *Perkins*, 317 U. S. 501 (1943). In that case the Court held that the Secretary of Labor, in an investigation under the Walsh-Healey Public Contracts Act, was entitled to the enforcement of a subpœna upon a showing merely that the evidence sought was "not plainly incompetent or irrelevant to any lawful purpose of the Secretary in the discharge of her duties under the Act" (317 U. S. at 509). The Supreme Court held further that the District Court was not "authorized to decide the question of coverage itself" and "had no authority to control her [the Secretary's] procedure or to condition enforcement of her subpœnas upon her first reaching and announcing a decision on some of the issues in her administrative proceeding" (*ibid.*). One of these issues to be decided by the Secretary rather than the District Court, the Supreme Court held, was whether the respondent's employees were covered by the Act—that is, whether they were employed in plants which were subject to the Secretary's jurisdiction under the statute.[7] In other words, the Secre-

---

[7] The Walsh-Healey Act requires that contracts with the Government for the manufacture or furnishing of materials in any amount exceeding $10,000 shall provide for certain minimum wages and maximum hours (41 U. S. C. §§ 35-45). The respondent opposed the enforcement of the subpœnas, insofar as they called for records concerning employees in plants of the respondent which manufactured articles that ultimately went into the finished product, on the ground that those plants were not within the coverage of the Act.

tary having issued a subpœna which was not "plainly incompetent or irrelevant," she was entitled to its enforcement without proving that the respondent's employees were in fact covered by the statute. A contrary ruling, the Supreme Court said,

> would require the Secretary, in order to get evidence of violation, either to allege she had decided the issue of coverage before the hearing or to sever the issues for separate hearing and decision. The former would be of dubious propriety, and the latter of doubtful practicality. The Secretary is given no power to investigate mere coverage, as such, or to make findings thereon except as incident to trial of the issue of violation (317 U. S. at 508).

It is the Commission's position that, if the Commission be substituted for the Secretary and the questions of use of the mails and sale of a "security" be substituted for the question whether a particular plant is covered by the Walsh-Healey Act, the *Endicott-Johnson* case governs the case at bar.

The *Endicott-Johnson* case has been deemed controlling by the First, Second and Fifth Circuits on the question of the necessity of proving interstate commerce under the Fair Labor Standards Act, whose provisions with respect to the enforcement of subpœnas are very similar to Section 22(b) of the Securities Act.[8] The First and Second Circuits,

---

[8] We here set out in parallel columns Section 22(b) of the Securities Act and the pertinent portion of Section 9 of the Federal Trade Commission Act (15 U. S. C. § 49), which is made applicable to the Administrator of the Wage and Hour Division of the Department of Labor by Section 9 of the Fair Labor Standards Act (29 U. S. C. § 209):

Section 22(b)

"In case of contumacy or refusal to obey a subpena issued to any person, any of the said United States courts, within the jurisdiction of which said

(Continued on next page)

Section 9

"Any of the district courts of the United States within the jurisdiction of which such inquiry is carried on may, in case of contumacy or refusal

(Continued on next page)

in affirming enforcement orders under that statute, have simply acted *per curiam* on the authority of the *Endicott-Johnson* case. *Martin Typewriter Co.* v. *Walling*, 135 F. (2d) 918 (C. C. A. 1, 1943); *Application of Holland*, 44 F. Supp. 601 (S. D. N. Y. 1942), *affirmed, Walling* v. *Standard Dredging Corp.*, 132 F. (2d) 322 (C. C. A. 2, 1943), *cert. denied*, 319 U. S. 761 (1943); see also *Walling* v. *American Rolbal Corp.*, 135 F. (2d) 1003 (C. C. A. 2, 1943). The court in the *Martin Typewriter* case quoted the following language from the District Court's opinion:

> This is an application to enforce a subpœna in what appears on its face to be an authorized and orderly investigation, and I do not feel justified in turning it into a lawsuit to decide a question which must be decided by the administrator in the course of his investigation, and which, if decided wrong, can be corrected later in a proceeding to enforce the orders of the administrator. (48 F. Supp. 751, 752.)

And the Fifth Circuit has stated:

> Convenience in most cases dictates that both "coverage" and "violations" be enquired about in a single investigation. It has just been decided, and we accordingly hold that in such investigations the investigating authority has generally the right to look first into either

Section 22(b)—Continued

person guilty of contumacy or refusal to obey is found or resides, upon application by the Commission may issue to such person an order requiring such person to appear before the Commission, or one of its examiners designated by it, there to produce documentary evidence if so ordered, or there to give evidence touching the matter in question; and any failure to obey such order of the court may be punished by said court as a contempt thereof."

Section 9—Continued

to obey a subpœna issued to any corporation or other person, issue an order requiring such corporation or other person to appear before the commission, or to produce documentary evidence if so ordered, or to give evidence touching the matter in question; and any failure to obey such order of the court may be punished by such court as a contempt thereof."

question, or into both concurrently. *Endicott-Johnson Corp.* vs. *Perkins*, 317 U. S. 501.

Mississippi Road Supply Co. v. *Walling*, 136 F. (2d) 391, 393-94 (C. C. A. 5, 1943), *cert. denied.* 88 L. Ed. (Adv. Op.) 32 (1943).[9]

Likewise, with one exception, all of the Circuit Courts of Appeals which had had occasion to consider the question prior to the Supreme Court's decision in the *Endicott-Johnson* case had reached the same result under several different statutes.[10] Only the Sixth Circuit Court of Appeals had taken the opposite view, *General Tobacco and Grocery Company* v. *Fleming*, 125 F. (2d) 596 (1942), and it is the Commission's position that that case must be deemed overruled by the Supreme Court's affirmance of the Second Circuit Court's opinion in the *Endicott-Johnson* case. Although the *General Tobacco and Grocery* case is not mentioned in the Supreme Court's opinion, certiorari was

[9] The District Court for the District of New Jersey has held that the Supreme Court's holding in the *Endicott-Johnson* case must be limited to the Walsh-Healey Act, which the Supreme Court referred to as "not an Act of general applicability to industry" (317 U. S. at 507). *Application of Walling*, 49 F. Supp. 659 (D. N. J. 1943). An appeal in this case is now pending. *Walling* v. *News Printing Co., Inc.* (C. C. A. 3, No. 8443). We believe, however, that the *Endicott-Johnson* case is not limited by that language. It was not so treated in Mr. Justice Murphy's dissenting opinion or in the cases cited above under the Fair Labor Standards Act.

[10] *President* v. *Skeen*, 118 F. (2d) 58 (C. C. A. 5, 1941); *National Labor Relations Board* v. *Barrett Co.*, 120 F. (2d) 583 (C. C. A. 7, 1941); see also *Fleming* v. *Montgomery Ward & Co.*, 114 F. (2d) 384 (C. C. A. 7, 1940), *cert. denied*, 311 U. S. 690 (1940); *Cudahy Packing Co.* v. *Fleming*, 122 F. (2d) 1005, 1009 (C. C. A. 8, 1941), *reversed on other grounds, Cudahy Packing Co.* v. *Holland*, 315 U. S. 785 (1942); *United States* v. *Clyde S. S. Co.*, 36 F. (2d) 691 (C. C. A. 2, 1929), *cert. denied*, 281 U. S. 744 (1930); *Cudahy Packing Co. of Louisiana, Ltd.* v. *Fleming*, 119 F. (2d) 209 (C. C. A. 5, 1941), *reversed on other grounds, Cudahy Packing Co. of Louisiana, Ltd.* v. *Holland*, 315 U. S. 357 (1942); *National Mediation Board* v. *Virginian Ry. Co.*, unreported, Pike and Fischer, Admin. Law, 44g.31-4 (E. D. Va., June 6, 1941).

granted because of a probable conflict between the Second and Sixth Circuits, and (as the Circuit Court of Appeals decisions subsequent to the *Endicott-Johnson* case indicate) the two cases are indistinguishable notwithstanding the fact that the *Endicott-Johnson* case involved the Walsh-Healey Public Contracts Act and the *General Tobacco and Grocery Case* involved the Fair Labor Standards Act.[11]

In any event, even if the *Endicott-Johnson* decision itself be limited to the statute there involved despite the several cases we have mentioned, we submit that the same reasoning underlying the holding that a subpœna of the Secretary of Labor under the Walsh-Healey Act is enforceable without proof of coverage leads with equally compelling force to the conclusion that a subpœna of the Commission under the Securities Act is enforceable without proof of use of the mails or the existence of a "security." The philosophy of the *Endicott-Johnson* doctrine is exhaustively expounded in Judge Frank's opinion for the Second Circuit Court of Appeals which the Supreme Court affirmed. *Per-*

---

[11] See also the following District Court cases in which the doctrine of the *Endicott-Johnson* case was applied to the enforcement of subpœnas under the Fair Labor Standards Act, both before and after the Supreme Court's decision in that case: *Fleming* v. *G & C Novelty Shoppe, Inc.,* 35 F. Supp. 829 (N. D. Ill. 1940); *Fleming* v. *Lowell Sun Co.,* 36 F. Supp. 320 (D. Mass. 1940), *reversed on other grounds, Lowell Sun Co.* v. *Fleming,* 120 F. (2d) 213 (C. C. A. 1, 1941), *affirmed,* 315 U. S. 784 (1942); *Fleming* v. *Howard A. Davidson Lumber Co.,* 3 Wage Hour Rep. 526 (E. D. Mich., Nov. 25, 1940); *Fleming* v. *Minnesota Mines, Inc.,* 4 Wage Hour Rep. 563 (D. Colo., July 18, 1941), *reversed on other grounds, Minnesota Mines, Inc.* v. *Holland,* 126 F. (2d) 824 (C. C. A. 10, 1942); *Application of Walling,* 50 F. Supp. 560 (S. D. N. Y. 1943); *Walling* v. *Belikoff,* 3 F. R. D. 92 (S. D. N. Y. 1943). Aside from the *News Printing Company* case, *supra* note 9, which is presently pending on appeal in the Third Circuit, the only District Court case to the contrary which remains unreversed is *Fleming* v. *Bank of America National Trust & Savings Association,* 5 Wage Hour Rep. 242 (N. D. Cal. 1942). That case was decided before the *Endicott-Johnson* case and no appeal was taken by the Wage and Hour Administrator.

kins v. *Endicott-Johnson Corp.*, 128 F. (2d) 208 (1942).[12] Essentially that philosophy is rooted in three well-known doctrines:

(1) The first of these is that, as in the case of a grand jury investigation, the scope of an administrative investigation is "not to be limited narrowly by questions of propriety or forecasts of the probable result of the investigation, or by doubts whether any particular individual will be found properly subject to an accusation of crime. As has been said before, the identity of the offender, and the precise nature of the offense, if there be one, normally are developed at the conclusion of the grand jury's labors, not at the beginning." *Consolidated Mines of California* v. *S. E. C.*, 97 F. (2d) 704, 708 (C. C. A. 9, 1938), quoting from *Blair* v. *United States*, 250 U. S. 273, 282 (1919).[13] This analogy between administrative investigations and grand jury proceedings has been made repeatedly by both this Court and others. *Woolley* v. *United States*, 97 F. (2d) 258, 262 (C. C. A. 9, 1938); *In re S. E. C.*, 84 F. (2d) 316, 318 (C. C. A. 2, 1936); *Endicott-Johnson* case, 128 F. (2d) at 214; *President* v. *Skeen*, 118 F. (2d) 58, 59 (C. C. A. 5, 1941); *S. E. C.* v. *Bourbon Sales Corp.*, 47 F. Supp. 70, 73 (W. D. Ky. 1942).

---

[12] Citations to particular portions of Judge Frank's opinion will be referred to herein as "the *Endicott-Johnson* case, 128 F. (2d) at ——."

[13] It was at least intimated in *Howat* v. *Kansas*, 258 U. S. 181, 186 (1922), that the doctrine of the *Blair* case—that a grand jury witness cannot resist a contempt citation for failure to respond to a subpœna by attacking the jurisdiction of the grand jury or the court over the subject matter of the inquiry—is applicable also to administrative proceedings. See the *Endicott-Johnson* case, 128 F. (2d) at 213, n. 10.

Cf. also *Fenton* v. *Walling*, 139 F. (2d) 608 (C. C. A. 9, 1943), where this Court held that, in a civil contempt proceeding under Rule 37(b) of the Rules of Civil Procedure for failure to produce records pursuant to Rule 34 in injunctive proceedings under the Fair Labor Standards Act, the respondents could not raise the defense that their company had no employees engaged in interstate commerce.

Basically, therefore, the *Endicott-Johnson* doctrine is a particularization of this Court's position in the *Consolidated Mines* case, *supra*, 97 F. (2d) at 707:

> It appears to be the view of appellants that virtually conclusive evidence of a violation of the act must be in the possession of the Commission before an investigation can be ordered. If this were so there would be no point in conducting an investigation. The very purpose of the inquiry authorized by § 20(a), 15 U. S. C. A. § 77t(a), is to investigate the accuracy of information in the possession of the Commission tending to show a violation, and to aid the Commission in determining whether the facts justify injunction proceedings or the placing of the matter before the Attorney General for the institution of criminal prosecution.

An inquiry under Section 20(a) of the Securities Act necessarily has two purposes—to determine whether there is jurisdiction through use of the mails or an instrumentality of interstate commerce, and to determine whether a substantive violation of the Act has been committed by selling securities without registration or in violation of the anti-fraud provisions. As the Supreme Court pointed out in the *Endicott-Johnson* case, therefore, jurisdiction or coverage is as much an element of the administrative investigation as is any other factor. If a subpœna could be successfully resisted at the very threshhold of an investigation, the agency's statutory functions of investigation and enforcement could be effectively blocked. If the Commission were in a position to prove use of the mails and the sale of a "security" before proceeding with its investigation, there might well be no need for a subpœna at all, because the Commission would then have enough evidence to proceed, without further investigation, to institute an action for an injunction or to recommend criminal prosecution to the Attorney General.

(2) The second basis of the *Endicott-Johnson* philosophy is the policy against premature interference with the administrative process. All that is involved here is an investigation. Although it may result in the bringing of injunctive or criminal proceedings, it may likewise result in no

action whatever. The appellant will have its day in court in the event that an injunctive action is brought or an indictment is returned in due course by a grand jury. In any such action the Commission or the Government will have to establish through competent evidence the use by the appellant of the mails or some instrumentality of interstate commerce, as well as the sale by it of a security and every other element of the statutory offenses created by Sections 5 and 17(a) of the Act. To require such proof before giving the Commission a chance to investigate would put a premium upon the perpetration of fraud and severely handicap effectice enforcement of the Act. The case at bar is an example of the prolongation of litigation which occurs when respondents in an administrative investigation are permitted to litigate in a subpœna enforcement proceeding questions which go to the principal case. The subpœna in this case was issued on April 9, 1943 (R. 16). The court's order enforcing it was entered on June 1 (R. 316). This appeal is to be argued on March 31, 1944, and, by the time the Court's decision comes down, probably more than a year will have elapsed since the issuance of the subpœna. This postponement of the investigatory process is particularly serious in view of the fact that the statute of limitations on criminal prosecutions under Section 24 of the Act (15 U. S. C. § 77x) is three years (18 U. S. C. § 582) and there is no specific provision of law for tolling the statute pending the enforcement of a subpœna. "To be effective, judicial administration must not be leaden-footed." *Cobbledick* v. *United States*, 309 U. S. 323, 325 (1940).[14]

[14] The Congressional intention that the work of the Commission should not be subject to great delay in enforcing subpœnas is evident from the fact that Section 22(b) of the Securities Act calls for an "application" rather than a complaint and an "order" rather than a judgment—language which has been held to indicate that an application to enforce a subpœna is a summary proceeding to which the Rules of Civil Procedure do not apply: *Goodyear Tire & Rubber Co.* v. *National Labor Relations Board*, 122 F. (2d) 450 (C. C. A. 6, 1941); *Cudahy Packing Co.* v. *National Labor Relations Board*, 117

These considerations underlie the Supreme Court's holdings that a claim of lack of jurisdiction in the administrative agency is no ground for obtaining judicial review of an interlocutory order,[15] or an injunction against the continuation of the hearing or investigation.[16] If the same allegation of lack of jurisdiction could be litigated by resisting an administrative subpœna, the result sought unsuccessfully to be attained by interlocutory review or injunctive proceedings could be accomplished by indirection. In that event, as the Circuit Court of Appeals pointed out in the *Endicott-Johnson* case, 128 F. (2d) at 219, the defendants "would have discovered a way of 'running around the end' when blocked at the center." That the Supreme Court intended no such loophole in its earlier rulings is evident from its affirmance of that case. See also *Mississippi Road Supply Co.* v. *Walling*, 136 F. (2d) 391, 393 (C. C. A. 5, 1943), *cert. denied*, 88 L. Ed. (Adv. Op.) 32 (1943).

(3) The third basic doctrine underlying the *Endicott-Johnson* philosophy is the "presumption of legality [which] supports the official acts of public officers." *United States* v. *Chemical Foundation, Inc.*, 272 U. S. 1, 14 (1926). As the Supreme Court stated in that case (at 14-15), "in the absence of clear evidence to the contrary, courts presume that [public officers] have properly discharged their official

---

F. (2d) 692 (C. C. A. 10, 1941); see also *Endicott-Johnson* case, 128 F. (2d) at 226-27; *S. E. C.* v. *Clayton*, unreported, 1 S. E. C. Jud. Dec. 670 (D. D. C., March 16, 1939). This Court assumed in *Martin* v. *Chandis Securities Co.*, 128 F. (2d) 731, 734 (1942), that the Rules of Civil Procedure apply to the enforcement of a subpœna issued by an Internal Revenue agent, but in that case the agent contended that the rules applied and the question was not considered on the basis of an argument as to their inapplicability, as in the cases above.

[15] *Federal Power Commission* v. *Metropolitan Edison Co.*, 304 U. S. 375 (1938); *Guaranty Underwriters, Inc.*, v. *S. E. C.*, 131 F. (2d) 370 (C. C. A. 5, 1942).

[16] *Myers* v. *Bethlehem Shipbuilding Corp.*, 303 U. S. 41 (1938); *Johnson* v. *McNeill*, —— Fla. ——, 10 So. (2d) 143 (1942).

duties." See also *Mississippi Road Supply Co.* v. *Walling,* 136 F. (2d) 391, 394 (C. C. A. 5, 1943), *cert. denied,* 88 L. Ed. (Adv. Op.) 32 (1943), where the court stated, in applying the Supreme Court's decision in the *Endicott-Johnson* case to the enforcement of a subpœna under the Fair Labor Standards Act:

> If on the face of things a lawful inquiry is in progress, the court ought to assist it, assuming that the inquiring body will confine itself to its lawful functions. *Bradley Lumber Co.* vs. *N. L. R. B.,* 5 Cir., 84 Fed. (2d) 97. The burden indeed of showing that the inquiry is unlawful is upon him who is called on to show cause why a subpœna should not be obeyed. The presumption of regularity of the proceedings of public officers so places the burden, unless on the face of the proceedings they are unlawful or oppressive.

The *Endicott-Johnson* case by no means limits the court which enforces an administrative subpœna to a "routine ministerial function" as the appellant contends (R. 65). As the Supreme Court stated in *Myers* v. *Bethlehem Shipbuilding Corporation,* 303 U. S. 41, 49 (1938), "to such an application [for enforcement of a subpœna], appropriate defence may be made." Thus, an application to enforce a subpœna may properly be resisted on the ground that a privilege of a witness, such as that against self-incrimination, would be violated;[17] or that the subpœna is unduly vague or unreasonably burdensome and hence involves a "fishing expedition;"[18] or that the subpœna was not issued by the person solely vested with that power;[19] or that the hearing is not of the kind authorized by the statute;[20] or, of course,

---

[17] *Boyd* v. *United States,* 116 U. S. 616 (1886).

[18] *Hale* v. *Henkel,* 201 U. S. 43 (1906); *Ellis* v. *Interstate Commerce Commission,* 237 U. S. 434 (1915); *Federal Trade Commission* v. *American Tobacco Co.,* 264 U. S. 298 (1924).

[19] *Cudahy Packing Co.* v. *Holland,* 315 U. S. 357 (1942).

[20] *Harriman* v. *Interstate Commerce Commission,* 211 U. S. 407 (1908); *Ellis* v. *Interstate Commerce Commission,* 237 U. S. 434 (1915); *Jones* v. *S. E. C.,* 298 U. S. 1 (1936); see also *Endicott-Johnson* case, 128 F. (2d) at 215, 219.

that it is plain on the pleadings that the evidence sought to be obtained by the subpœna is not germane to any lawful inquiry of the administrative agency.

It is clear, however, that it is no defense to say that the administrative agency has not affirmatively shown that there would be jurisdiction to sustain an ultimate action to enjoin or punish a violation of the particular statute under which the investigation is proceeding.

II

In Any Event There Are Reasonable Grounds to Believe that the Appellant Has Used the Mails and Has Done So in the Sale of a "Security."

The Eighth Circuit Court of Appeals, in a subpœna enforcement proceeding arising under the Fair Labor Standards Act after the Supreme Court's decision in the *Endicott-Johnson* case, has applied a burden midway between the *Endicott-Johnson* rule (that a subpœna should be enforced upon a showing merely that the evidence is "not plainly incompetent or irrelevant") and the burden previously announced by the Sixth Circuit in *General Tobacco and Grocery Company* v. *Fleming*, 125 F. (2d) 526 (1942) (that proof of interstate commerce is required). *Walling* v. *Benson*, 137 F. (2d) 501 (C. C. A. 8, 1943), *cert. denied*, 88 L. Ed. (Adv. Op.) 119 (1943).[21] We think this test is

---

[21] In *Consolidated Mines of California* v. *S. E. C.*, 97 F. (2d) 704, 706 (C. C. A. 9, 1938), this Court stated that it sufficiently appeared from the application and showing made in support of it "that the Commission was in possession of information affording reasonable grounds for the belief" that the respondent had violated the Securities Act. The question was not raised in that case whether any lesser burden would suffice, however, and the case was decided several years before the *Endicott-Johnson* case.

In *S. E. C.* v. *Bourbon Sales Corporation*, 47 F. Supp. 70 (W. D. Ky. 1942), which, as we have seen, arose out of the same investigation here involved, the court indicated that the Commission would have to show both jurisdiction and reasonable grounds for the belief that a violation had occurred or was

improper for the reasons stated in Part I above.[22] In any event, however, we believe that under any test we have established both that the appellant has used the mails and that it has sold a "security." *A fortiori*, we think we have shown that there are "reasonable grounds" for believing that the appellant has done so.

As to use of the mails, there is evidence in the record of mailings both in selling bottling contracts (R. 160, 203, 340, 342, affidavits of Andrew C. Elder, Viola M. Eldridge, A. W. Hudson, Mrs. Johnnie McKaskle, Peter P. Valley) and in selling stock (R. 204). As to the presence of a "security,"[23] we have shown that the appellant's stock

---

threatened; but that case was decided before the *Endicott-Johnson* case and the court was, of course, bound by the holding of the Sixth Circuit in *General Tobacco and Grocery Company* v. *Fleming, supra* page 11. In fact, the District Court held in the *Bourbon Sales* case that it was not necessary to establish that the instruments under consideration were securities; and, since the *General Tobacco and Grocery* case, we believe, is no longer good law in view of the Supreme Court's decision in the *Endicott-Johnson* case, the same rationale followed by the court in the *Bourbon Sales* case as to the lack of necessity of proving the presence of a "security" would seem to apply equally to the lack of necessity of proving any use of the mails or an instrumentality of interstate commerce.

The only remaining case of which we know on this point is *S. E. C.* v. *Tung Corporation of America,* 32 F. Supp. 371 (N. D. Ill. 1940). Insofar as that case holds that the Commission in enforcing a subpœna must show reasonable grounds to believe that the respondents have been selling securities and using the mails or some instrumentality of interstate commerce, we believe it was incorrectly decided. *Cf.*, in that circuit, *Fleming* v. *Montgomery Ward & Co.,* 114 F. (2d) 384 (C. C. A. 7, 1940), *cert. denied,* 311 U. S. 690 (1940). No appeal was taken in the *Tung* case because the court did enforce the subpœna on the ground that the Commission had shown the existence of a "security."

[22] *Cf. Fleming* v. *Montgomery Ward & Co.,* 114 F. (2d) 384 (C. C. A. 7, 1940), *cert. denied,* 311 U. S. 690 (1940).

[23] As we have noted above (notes 6 and 21), it was held in the *Bourbon Sales* case, even though that court was bound at the time by the strict test of the Sixth Circuit as to the necessity of proving interstate commerce, that the Commission did not have to prove the existence of a "security" in order to obtain enforcement of its subpœna.

has been sold to the public through the mails.[24] Therefore, we are entitled under any test to enforcement of those items of the subpœna relating to sales of stock, without even demonstrating that the bottling contracts issued by both the appellant and Bourbon Sales Corporation are themselves securities.

We shall show, however, that the ruling of the District Court in the *Bourbon Sales* case that these same bottling contracts are securities was clearly correct. We express no opinion on the question whether or not the whiskey warehouse receipts for which the bottling contracts were exchanged are securities. That is a question which, if it becomes relevant, can best be decided in the light of facts to be elicited in the investigation. The appellant contends that the court erred in failing to rule that they were not securities (R. 319; Br., p. 56), but the Commission's case is not based on the assumption that they are, and we have not thus far contended that whiskey warehouse receipts *per se* are securities. Our contention is that the whiskey bottling contracts which were offered or sold to holders of those receipts, upon the representation that the appellant or Bourbon Sales Corporation would take care of all the details surrounding the taking of the whiskey out of bond and bottling and selling it and would see that the investor got a profit, are clearly securities within the definition of the term in the Act and the interpretation of that definition in a long line of cases.

---

[24] The appellant contends that it has issued only 500 shares of its capital stock; that that transaction was exempted from the registration provisions of Section 5 by Section 4(1) (15 U. S. C. § 77d(1)) as "not involving any public offering"; and that subsequent transfers of individually owned shares were exempted by the same section as "Transactions by any person other than an issuer, underwriter or dealer" (R. 27-28; Br., pp. 13-14). Even if this be assumed to be true, the Section 4(1) exemptions do not apply to the anti-fraud provisions of Section 17(a), which are likewise involved in this investigation. The Commission's supplemental order is directed at sales of the appellant's stock not alone by the appellant but also by the persons named in the order (R. 12-14).

In Section 2(1) of the Act (15 U. S. C. §77b(1)) Congress, following the pattern set by many state blue sky laws, did not restrict its definition of the term "security" to such orthodox forms as stocks, bonds, debentures or notes. Rather it provided a broad and flexible definition designed to extend the registration and anti-fraud provisions of the Act to the variegated schemes conceived by those who would circumvent the law. Under Section 2(1):

> The term "security" means any note, stock, treasury stock, bond, debenture, evidence of indebtedness, *certificate of interest or participation in any profit-sharing agreement,* collateral-trust certificate, preorganization certificate or subscription, transferable share, *investment contract,* voting-trust certificate, certificate of deposit for a security, fractional undivided interest in oil, gas, or other mineral rights, or, in general, *any interest or instrument commonly known as a "security,"* or any certificate of interest or participation in, temporary or interim certificate for, receipt for, guarantee of, or warrant or right to subscribe to or purchase, any of the foregoing. (Italics supplied.)

The term "investment contract" particularly, which appears in thirty of the state acts,[25] has been construed in a long line of cases, both federal and state, as affording the investing public a full measure of protection, whether the transaction takes one of the more normal forms of a security or whether instead the promoter clothes it with the appearance of a transaction in some species of real or personal property. By emphasizing substance rather than form,[26]

---

[25] The state statutes are collected in 132 CCH Stocks and Bonds Law Service. Although we shall confine our discussion to proving that the whiskey bottling contracts are investment contracts, we believe they are also certificates of interest or participation in a profit-sharing agreement and interests or instruments commonly known as a "security."

[26] *S. E. C.* v. *Crude Oil Corporation of America,* 93 F. (2d) 844, 846 (C. C. A. 7, 1937); *S. E. C.* v. *Universal Service Association,* 106 F. (2d) 232, 237 (C. C. A. 7, 1939), *cert. denied,* 308 U. S. 622 (1940); see also *S. E. C.* v. *Wickham,* 12 F. Supp. 245, 247 (D. Minn. 1935); *S. E. C.* v. *Tung Corporation of*

the courts have construed the term to include any transaction where "the purchasers [look] entirely to the efforts of the promoters to make their investment a profitable one." *Atherton* v. *United States*, 128 F. (2d) 463, 465 (C. C. A. 9, 1942); *S. E. C.* v. *Universal Service Association*, 106 F. (2d) 232, 237 (C. C. A. 7, 1939), *cert. denied*, 308 U. S. 622 (1940).[27]

In short, whenever an interest in what is in substance a business enterprise is offered to persons who are led to expect that they will earn a profit through the efforts of the seller or some person other than themselves, it is immaterial that their shares in the enterprise may not take the customary form of stock or bond ownership. When those conditions are present, the substance controls the form, and a sale of a "security" in the nature of an "investment contract" occurs. Under this approach, a large variety of schemes purporting to involve a "sale" or "lease" of some

---

America, 32 F. Supp. 371, 374 (N. D. Ill. 1940); *S. E. C.* v. *Payne*, 35 F. Supp. 873, 877 (S. D. N. Y. 1940); *S. E. C.* v. *Bailey*, 41 F. Supp. 647, 650 (S. D. Fla. 1941); *United States* v. *Monjar*, 47 F. Supp. 421, 426 (D. Del. 1942), *appeal pending; People* v. *White*, 124 Cal. App. 548, 555, 12 P. (2d) 1078, 1081 (1932); *Prohaska* v. *Hemmer-Miller Development Co.*, 256 Ill. App. 331 (1930); *Kerst* v. *Nelson*, 171 Minn. 191, 195, 213 N. W. 904, 905 (1927); *Klatt* v. *Guaranteed Bond Co.*, 213 Wis. 12, 21, 250 N. W. 825, 829 (1933).

[27] This is substantially the formula which appears in almost all the "investment contract" cases. See *S. E. C.* v. *Wickham*, 12 F. Supp. 245, 248 (D. Minn. 1935); *S. E. C.* v. *Timetrust, Inc.*, 28 F. Supp. 34, 39 (N. D. Cal. 1939); *S. E. C.* v. *Pyne*, 33 F. Supp. 988 (D. Mass. 1940); *S. E. C.* v. *Payne*, 35 F. Supp. 873, 878 (S. D. N. Y. 1940); *S. E. C.* v. *Bailey*, 41 F. Supp. 647, 650 (S. D. Fla. 1941); *S. E. C.* v. *Bourbon Sales Corp.*, 47 F. Supp. 70, 72-73 (W. D. Ky. 1942); *State* v. *Gopher Tire & Rubber Co.*, 146 Minn. 52, 56, 177 N. W. 937, 938 (1920); *Moore* v. *Stella*, 52 Cal. App. (2d) 766, 778, 127 P. (2d) 300, 306 (1942); *Domestic & Foreign Petroleum Co.* v. *Long*, 4 Cal. (2d) 547, 555-556, 51 P. (2d) 73, 76 (1935); *Prohaska* v. *Hemmer-Miller Development Co.*, 256 Ill. App. 331 (1930); *Lewis* v. *Creasey Corp.*, 198 Ky. 409, 413-414, 248 S. W. 1046, 1048 (1923); *State* v. *Heath*, 199 N. C. 135, 139, 153 S. E. 855, 857 (1930); Note (1936) 36 Col. L. Rev. 683.

form of tangible property, and comprehending an arrangement by which the seller retains possession and control of the subject of the "sale" or "lease" with a view to earning a profit for the nominal owners or lessees, has been held to involve a sale of a security.[28] That the present case involves a

---

[28] Under the Securities Act of 1933 the term "investment contract" has been held to cover purported sales of:

Oil leaseholds: *S. E. C.* v. *C. M. Joiner Leasing Corp.*, 320 U. S. 344 (1943); *Atherton* v. *United States*, 128 F. (2d) 463 (C. C. A. 9, 1942).

Instruments denominated "bill of sale and delivery contract for—barrels of crude oil": *S. E. C.* v. *Crude Oil Corporation of America*, 93 F. (2d) 844 (C. C. A. 7, 1937).

Land for the development of tung trees: *S. E. C.* v. *Tung Corporation of America*, 32 F. Supp. 371 (N. D. Ill. 1940); *S. E. C.* v. *Bailey*, 41 F. Supp. 647 (S. D. Fla. 1941).

Silver foxes: *S. E. C.* v. *Payne*, 35 F. Supp. 873 (S. D. N. Y. 1940).

Chinchillas: *Hollywood State Bank* v. *Wilde*, unreported, Cal. Super. Ct. for Los Angeles (No. 478,973, Aug. 11, 1943) (civil action under both Securities Act and state blue sky law).

Conditional bills of sale for oyster half-shells to be planted on oyster bottom acreage: *S. E. C.* v. *Cultivated Oyster Farms Corp.*, unreported, 1 S. E. C. Jud. Dec. 672, CCH Fed. Sec. Law Serv., par. 90,121 (S. D. Fla., No. 350, March 22, 1939).

Undivided interests in specified fishing boats: *S. E. C.* v. *Pyne*, 33 F. Supp. 988 (D. Mass. 1940).

Under state blue sky laws the term "investment contract" has similarly been held to include purported sales of:

Muskrats: *State* v. *Robbins*, 185 Minn. 202, 240 N. W. 456 (1932).

Rabbits: *Stevens* v. *Liberty Packing Corp.*, 111 N. J. Eq. 61, 161 Atl. 193 (1932); *cf. Commonwealth* v. *Sofield*, 38 Dauphin County Rep. (Pa.) 233 (1933) ("certificate in or under a profit-sharing or participating agreement").

Chinchillas: *Hollywood State Bank* v. *Wilde*, *supra*, this note.

Land to be cultivated as a vineyard by a third party: *Kerst* v. *Nelson*, 171 Minn. 191, 213 N. W. 904 (1927).

Land to be developed by the vendee as a fig orchard: *State* v. *Agey*, 171 N. C. 831, 88 S. E. 726 (1916). (The North Carolina Blue Sky Law did not include the term "investment contract," but the defendant was held to be an "investment company" within the meaning of the statute.)

(Continued on next page)

purported *purchase* of whiskey represented by warehouse receipts previously sold seems irrelevant to the reasoning of these cases.

This line of cases has recently had its culmination in the first Supreme Court decision on the definition of the term "security" in the Securities Act of 1933. *S. E. C.* v. *C. M. Joiner Leasing Corp.*, 320 U. S. 344 (1943). The defendant acquired oil and gas leases on a 3,000-acre tract in Texas. The leases were acquired from a drilling contractor, and the principal consideration which the company gave the contractor for his leases was a contract to drill a test well. In order to finance the drilling, the company resold leases on small parcels of the acreage to the public in widely scattered parts of the country. The leases were in the form of the usual Texas oil and gas lease, with no collateral agreements of any kind in writing, but the sales literature assured prospective customers that the company was engaged in the drilling of a test well that would prove the entire tract.

The Supreme Court stated that, if the offers had omitted the economic inducement of the promised exploration well, the purchasers would have had no alternative except to test their own leases at a cost of $5,000 or more per well. In that event they would have been buying merely interests in real estate, as both lower courts had held. But the defendants, the Supreme Court stated (320 U. S. at 348), were "offered no such dismal prospect." The undertaking to drill a test well was "the thread on which everybody's beads were strung" *(ibid.)*. Without it none of the leases had any value. Therefore, the Court stated (at 349), "the purchaser was paying both for a lease and for a development project," and it "is clear that an economic interest in this well-drilling

---

(Continued)

Farm land to be paid for with the proceeds of crops planted by the vendor: *Prohaska* v. *Hemmer-Miller Development Co.*, 256 Ill. App. 331 (1930).

Option contracts for the sale of land: *State* v. *Evans*, 154 Minn. 95, 191 N. W. 425 (1922); *Vercellini v. U. S. I. Realty Co.*, 158 Minn. 72, 196 N. W. 672 (1924); *Webster* v. *U. S. I. Realty Co.*, 170 Minn. 360, 212 N. W. 806 (1927).

undertaking was what brought into being the instruments that defendants were selling and gave to the instruments most of their value and all of their lure." Hence the leases were "dealt in under terms or courses of dealing which established their character in commerce as 'investment contracts,' or as 'any interest or instrument commonly known as a "security" ' " (320 U. S. at 351).

The Supreme Court rejected also the argument that the offerings were beyond the scope of the Securities Act because the leases and assignments conveyed under Texas law interests in real estate. As to this the Supreme Court stated (320 U. S. at 352-53):

> In applying acts of this general purpose, the courts have not been guided by the nature of the assets back of a particular document or offering. The test rather is what character the instrument is given in commerce by the terms of the offer, the plan of distribution, and the economic inducements held out to the prospect. In the enforcement of an act such as this it is not inappropriate that promoters' offerings be judged as being what they were represented to be.

This Court had previously come to the same conclusion in a criminal case under the Securities Act involving very similar facts. *Atherton* v. *United States*, 138 F. (2d) 463 (1942). In that case the Court stated (at 465):

> It is made clear in the indictment and in the proof that the purchasers looked entirely to the efforts of the promoters to make their investment a profitable one. The small leased acreage acquired by the individual purchaser was not itself susceptible of economic development, nor was the purchase made with the idea of independent exploitation. The leases were sold at prices ranging from $50 to $200 per acre upon the promise and representation that the proceeds of the sale would be used for bringing a well into production on the drill site, thus proving the productivity of the whole area under lease. It was proposed that when the well was completed the entire acreage, including the area selected as the drilling site, would be sold as one

unit, and that each purchaser of an assignment would receive a proportionate share of the purchase price. Clearly, the investor acquired more than a mere lease.[29]

The present case presents a clearer picture of a security than either the *Joiner* or the *Atherton* case.

In the first place, whereas the sale of a security in those cases had to be spelled out of the collateral representations exclusively, here the bottling contracts themselves contain agreements by the appellant or Bourbon Sales Corporation to bottle the whiskey represented by the whiskey warehouse receipts turned in for the bottling contracts, to sell the bottled whiskey and to pay to the contract-holders the proceeds less all expenses and a commisison of 10% of the gross sales price per case (R. 86, 88-89). This is aside from the fact that receipt-holders were influenced to accept bottling contracts in exchange for their receipts on the representations that that was the only way they could get their money back (R. 191-92, 202); that Bourbon Sales Corporation was "a large concern * * * formed to conduct business of this nature and was in the position to protect [their] interest and market the whiskey under an established trade name which would boost the price and make a better profit" (R. 202); that the appellant was in a "better position to know when [their] whiskey might age and be bottled and * * * would take the risk of loss" (R. 203); and that they would get "about double the amount [they] would by a sale of the bulk whiskey" (R. 203).[30] These contract provisions and

[29] Although the *Atherton* case was not cited in the Supreme Court's opinion in the *Joiner* case, the Commission's petition for certiorari in the latter case contended that there was a conflict between the *Atherton* case and the Fifth Circuit Court's opinion in the *Joiner* case.

[30] There is also evidence that representations that the appellant would arrange to bottle and sell the whiskey after four years of aging were made at the time the warehouse receipts were sold (R. 157). This indicates that the warehouse receipts were coupled with the bottling contracts in a scheme which as a whole involved the sale of a "security." We believe, however, that the sales of bottling contracts themselves in-

representations, as well as the fact that the contract-holders, being ordinary investors and not liquor dealers, would not have the facilities or the necessary federal and state liquor licenses (R. 96, 166) to take the whiskey out of bond and dispose of it, make it clear that they must look "entirely to the efforts of the promoters to make their investment a profitable one." *Atherton* v. *United States,* 128 F. (2d) 463, 465 (C. C. A. 9, 1942).

In the second place, the present case is stronger than the *Joiner* and *Atherton* cases also because it was represented here that there would be a pooling of the whiskey purchased by the appellant for bottling (R. 159-60). In other words, the scheme apparently did not envisage any rigid segregation of the whiskey sold to the company by each contract-holder, but contemplated that each holder, instead of obtaining the proceeds from the sale of the identical whiskey turned over by him, would actually get no more than a right to share in the avails of a mass of whiskey processed by the company. Although the cases we have cited demonstrate that this element of pooling is not essential to an "investment contract," it furnishes additional evidence of a common enterprise when it is present.

It follows under all the circumstances that the entire scheme involves in substance a speculative investment in a common enterprise necessarily contemplating complete reliance by the investor upon the appellant's efforts. Hence, (aside from the sales of its stock) the appellant has been selling securities both as agent for Bourbon Sales Corporation and as principal in the sale of its own bottling contracts.

We repeat, however, that, although we believe we have shown that the appellant has been selling securities through the use of the mails and certainly that there are "reason-

---

volved sales of securities, and that it is not a necessary element of a "security" that any particular representations were made at the time of the sale of the receipts—or even that the receipts were sold by the same company which sold the bottling contracts or by any affiliated or related company.

able grounds" for believing so, it is exceptional that we have been able to do so here before the conclusion of the investigation; and we respectfully submit that the order below should be affirmed on the basis of the doctrine of the *Endicott-Johnson* case and the other authorities and arguments we have assembled in Part I above. The very nature of the security involved in the sale of bottling contracts here, as well as the security involved in the *Joiner* and *Atherton* cases and the many others cited above (note 28), demonstrates how impracticable it would be to require the Commission to prove that what appears to be a transaction in tangible property is actually a sale of a security before it has had an opportunity to investigate the collateral representations and circumstances surrounding the transaction.

III

The Subpœna Is Valid in Form and Content.

A. *The Act Does Not Require the Commission to Make a Formal Finding that in Its Opinion the Evidence Required Is Necessary for the Proper Enforcement of the Act and Relevant or Material to the Commission's Inquiry.*

The appellant argues that the orders of the Commission which formed the basis of the application to enforce the subpœna in this case do not comply with Section 19(b) of the Act in that they do not specify any of the things sought by the subpœna and do not declare that "in the opinion of the Commission (these things) are necessary and proper for the enforcement of this title" and that the Commission "deems the particular documents and papers relevant or material to the inquiry" (Appellant's Br., p. 9).[31]

[31] We note in passing that the appellant's designation of points upon which it intends to rely on this appeal (R. 318-27) does not include this point, as required by paragraph 6 of Rule 19 of the Rules of Practice of this Court.

The short answer is that the Commission may delegate to its examining officer the authority to determine what matters are material to the inquiry, and that this Court has so held. In *Woolley* v. *United States*, 97 F. (2d) 258, 262 (1938), a case in which a conviction of perjury for giving false testimony in an investigation by this Commission was affirmed, this Court held:

> It is contended that the commission alone, under the provisions of the act, has authority to determine what matters are material to an inquiry, and that this authority cannot be delegated to the examining officer. The argument is based on the provisions of § 19(b), heretofore quoted [note 3, *supra*]. There is nothing in the language of the section to justify the argument. To adopt such interpretation would be to emasculate the provision relating to the appointment of examining officers, and require all proceedings to be conducted by the commission itself.[32]

As a matter of fact, there is an additional reason for so holding in the case at bar. Before deciding to file an application to enforce the subpœna, the Commission did obviously determine that the evidence required was both necessary and relevant. Thus, the Commission's application to enforce the subpœna alleges that the appellant has sold "certain securities, namely, contracts for the bottling of whiskey * * * and common stock" (R. 3), and that "All the books, records, documents, etc., described in the said subpœna duces tecum * * * were at the time of the issuance of the subpœna duces tecum and are now deemed by the Commission to be relevant and material to this inquiry" (R. 5). In addition, the application alleges that "At the time of the entry of the said orders [for investigation] the Applicant had reasonable grounds to believe that Bourbon

---

[32] Of course, since the procedure is governed by Section 19(b) of the Securities Act, the provisions of 28 U. S. C. § 647, cited by the appellant, have no application; they have to do solely with subpœnas to testify before a commissioner under a *dedimus potestatem*.

Sales Corporation and The Penfield Company of California had violated and [were] about to violate the provisions of Sections 5(a) and 17(a) of the said Act, as more fully appears in the said orders" (R. 4).

The appellant's contention that our position on this point violates the Fourth Amendment can be adequately answered by reference to the authorities cited below in Part IV of this brief.

B. *The Evidence Required Is in Fact Relevant to the Investigation.*

Section 19(b) of the Act authorizes the Commission or a designated officer to require the production of any books, papers or other documents "which the Commission deems relevant or material to the inquiry." As we have argued in Part I of this brief, it is our position that the only showing necessary is that the evidence specified in the subpœna is "not plainly incompetent or irrelevant to any lawful purpose" of the Commission. This showing has certainly been met and more; for the record demonstrates affirmatively that the evidence sought is relevant to a lawful inquiry—namely, a determination whether there have been violations of Sections 5 and 17(a) of the Act in the sale through the mails or in interstate commerce of securities of the appellant (both stock and bottling contracts), as well as bottling contracts of Bourbon Sales Corporation.

We do not deem it necessary to discuss extensively each of the twenty items specified in the subpœna (R. 16-18). The subpœna was carefully drafted along the lines of many similar subpœnas which have been issued by officers of the Commission in the day-to-day administration of the Act, and a glance at the twenty items should demonstrate that the records and files enumerated are essential to a determination whether a "security" has been sold and whether misrepresentations have in fact been made. Items 1, 4, 5, 6 and 14 specify the corporate books which we have found essential as a starting point for any investigation under Sections 5 and 17(a) of the Securities Act—the minute book, general ledger, cash book, general journal and supporting journal entries. Those books are apt to indicate the general scheme of financing giving rise to the suspected violations, the receipts from the sale of securities, the company's financial position, and whether it will be able to carry out the commitments made in the sale of its securities. Items 2, 3, 10, 13 and 15 specify the stock books, stockholders' lists, correspondence files with stockholders, confirmations delivered in connection with sales of stock, and sales literature used in the sale of stock. All of these can be easily furnished and are obviously vital to an examination of the question whether Sections 5 and 17(a) have been violated by any of the persons named in the orders for investigation. Items 8, 9, 11, 13 and 16 specify similar records—and for a similar reason—with respect to the sale of bottling contracts of the appellant and Bourbon Sales Corporation. Items 7, 12, 17, 18 and 19 require records reflecting the sale of whiskey or whiskey warehouse receipts by the appellant, its cancelled checks, and purchase and sales invoices supporting the acquisition or disposition of whiskey or whiskey warehouse receipts or bottling contracts. This information is specified, of course, not because the Commission is concerned with the purchase or sale of whiskey or whiskey warehouse receipts as such, but because it is necessary in order to determine whether bottling contracts have been sold in violation of the Act; it may well throw light on the volume of bottling contracts sold, on the payments made to contract-holders upon the sale of their whiskey, and on the question whether in general there has been a scheme to defraud. Finally, Item 20 requires the company's employment records, which are needed in order to permit an examination to be made of the company's salesmen and other personnel.

The subpœna enforced in this same investigation by the District Court for the Western District of Kentucky in

S. E. C. v. *Bourbon Sales Corporation*, 47 F. Supp. 70 (1942), was very similar to the subpœna in the case at bar. Moreover, as we have already noted, this Court has stated that the scope of the Commission's investigations, like those of a grand jury, are "not to be limited narrowly by questions of propriety or forecasts of the probable result of the investigation." *Consolidated Mines of California* v. *S. E. C.*, 97 F. (2d) 704, 708 (1938). Along the same lines, this Court has stated also, in *Woolley* v. *United States*, 97 F. (2d) 258, 262 (1938), a perjury case arising out of an investigation by this Commission, that "The test of materiality is whether the false testimony has a natural tendency to influence the fact-finding agency in its investigation." That the evidence specified in the subpœna here may be expected to have such a "natural tendency" can hardly be gainsaid. If that criterion will support a conviction for perjury, surely it will support an order enforcing a subpœna issued in an investigation before any charges have even been preferred.[33]

IV

The Subpœna Does Not Involve a Violation of the Fourth Amendment.

The appellant argues that the court below erred in holding that the investigation was not a general, roving inquiry constituting an unreasonable search and seizure of

---

[33] See also *Walling* v. *American Rolbal Corp.*, 135 F. (2d) 1003, 1005 (C. C. A. 2, 1943), where the court stated, in affirming an order which enforced a subpœna issued under the Fair Labor Standards Act:

> In this instance the petition alleges violations of the Act which it is clearly the duty of the administrator to investigate. It may be that the refused records will not bear directly upon that subject but we cannot say they won't or that they won't supply needed information for use in checking other facts and records. As the administrator has not been shown to have abused his discretion in the selection of the records to be inspected we agree that the order below was without error.

its private papers and documents in violation of the Fourth Amendment (Br., pp. 20-27). We disagree.

All that the Fourth Amendment requires is that the demand be reasonably specific and limited to documents relevant to the inquiry. *Wilson* v. *United States,* 221 U. S. 361, 376 (1911); *Baltimore & Ohio Railroad Co.* v. *Interstate Commerce Commission,* 221 U. S. 612, 622 (1911); *Consolidated Mines of California* v. *S. E. C.*, 97 F. (2d) 704, 708 (C. C. A. 9, 1938); *McMann* v. *S. E. C.*, 87 F. (2d) 377, 379 (C. C. A. 2, 1937), *cert. denied,* 301 U. S. 684 (1937); *Newfield* v. *Ryan,* 91 F. (2d) 700, 702-3 (C. C. A. 5, 1937), *cert. denied,* 302 U. S. 729 (1937); *Cudahy Packing Co.* v. *Fleming,* 122 F. (2d) 1005, 1009 (C. C. A. 8, 1941), *reversed on other grounds, Cudahy Packing Co.* v. *Holland,* 315 U. S. 785 (1942); *Lowell Sun Co.* v. *Fleming,* 120 F. (2d) 213 (C. C. A. 1, 1941), *affirmed per curiam, Holland* v. *Lowell Sun Co.*, 315 U. S. 784 (1942). Our discussion above in Part III-B (pages 30-31) shows that this test is clearly met by the subpœna in the case at bar.

This case certainly does not present the type of "fishing expedition" condemned in the cases cited by the appellant or the cases enumerated in Part I of this brief (notes 17-20). Specifically, it is not at all like *Jones* v. *S. E. C.*, 298 U. S. 1 (1936), on which the appellant strongly relies; in that case the subpœna was not enforced because a majority of the Supreme Court held that the withdrawal of the registration statement being investigated had deprived the Commission of any authority to conduct an investigation for the purpose of determining whether a stop order should issue suspending the statement's effectiveness. Nor is the case of *Boyd* v. *United States,* 116 U. S. 616 (1886), of any assistance here, because that case holds simply that a subpœna is bad under the Fourth and Fifth Amendments where it violates the privilege against self-incrimination—a privilege which does not extend to a corporation.[34] The other

[34] *Wilson* v. *United States,* 221 U. S. 361 (1911); *Essgee Co. of China* v. *United States,* 262 U. S. 151 (1923). We do not understand that any privilege against self-incrimination is being argued here.

cases relied upon by the appellant are cases where the subpœna sought to be enforced was clearly too broad.[35]

V

The Investigatory Provisions of the Act Do Not Involve an Unconstitutional Delegation of Judicial Power.

The appellant contends that the court below erred in holding that the provisions of Sections 19(b) and 22(b) of the Act do not involve an invalid delegation of judicial powers to the Commission in violation of Article III of the Constitution (Br., pp. 28-55).

It is at least open to doubt whether the question of the statute's constitutionality can be raised by way of defense to an application to enforce a subpœna. See the *Endicott-Johnson case,* 128 F. (2d) at 213; *cf. Howat* v. *Kansas,* 258 U. S. 181, 185-86 (1922). The point need not be pressed here, however, in view of the fact that the constitutionality of the Securities Act is no longer open to question. *Coplin* v. *United States,* 88 F. (2d) 652, 656-57 (C. C. A. 9, 1937), *cert. denied,* 301 U. S. 703 (1937), and cases there cited; *Newfield v. Ryan,* 91 F. (2d) 700 (C. C. A. 5, 1937), *cert. denied,* 302 U. S. 729 (1937); *S. E. C.* v. *Crude Oil Corporation of America,* 93 F. (2d) 844 (C. C. A. 7, 1937). With particular reference to the delegation argument, see *McMann* v. *Engel,* 16 F. Supp. 446 (S. D. N. Y. 1936), *affirmed, McMann* v. *S. E. C.*, 87 F. (2d) 377 (C. C. A. 2, 1937), *cert. denied,* 301 U. S. 684 (1937); *S. E. C.* v. *Jones,* 79 F. (2d) 617 (C. C. A. 2, 1935), *reversed on other grounds, Jones* v. *S. E. C.*, 298 U. S. 1 (1936).

The appellant relies very strongly on an opinion written by Circuit Judge Field (as he then was) in 1887. *In Re Pacific Railway Commission,* 32 Fed. 241 (C. C. N. D. Cal.).

---

[35] Insofar as the basis of the appellant's argument of a violation of the Fourth Amendment is not the breadth of the subpœna but the fact that it was issued by an administrative agency rather than a court, see Part V below.

Judge Field there held (at 258) that the provision of a statute of 1887 authorizing the courts to enforce subpœnas issued by the Pacific Railway Commission, which had been created to investigate certain matters with respect to railroads receiving aid from the United States, involved an invalid delegation of judicial power. But that is no longer the law and has not been for fifty years. To cite now the holding of that case is to ignore fifty years of development in the field of judicial administration, including this Court's holding in *Consolidated Mines of California* v. *S. E. C.*, 97 F. (2d) 704 (1938). As long ago as 1894 the Supreme Court refused to sustain a similar attack against the provision of the Interstate Commerce Act comparable to Section 19(b) of the Securities Act. *Interstate Commerce Commission* v. *Brimson*, 154 U. S. 447 (1894). The Court there held (at 474), in language equally applicable to federal regulation in the securities field:

> An adjudication that Congress could not establish an administrative body with authority to investigate the subject of interstate commerce and with power to call witnesses before it, and to require the production of books, documents, and papers relating to that subject, would go far toward defeating the object for which the people of the United States placed commerce among the States under national control. All must recognize the fact that the full information necessary as a basis of intelligent legislation by Congress from time to time upon the subject of interstate commerce cannot be obtained, nor can the rules established for the regulation of such commerce be efficiently enforced, otherwise than through the instrumentality of an administrative body, representing the whole country, always watchful of the general interests, and charged with the duty not only of obtaining the required information, but of compelling by all lawful methods obedience to such rules.

The appellant observes that courts have recently cited Judge Field's statement that "of all the rights of the citizen, few are of greater importance or more essential to his peace and happiness than the right of personal security, and that involves, not merely protection of his person from assault, but exemption of his private affairs, books, and papers from the inspection and scrutiny of others" (32 Fed. at 250). No citizen of a democracy—least of all an agency of the Government whose members and officers are sworn to uphold the Constitution—can have any wish to quarrel with those sentiments. However, the right to be protected against unreasonable searches and seizures is adequately guaranteed by the Fourth Amendment; as the Supreme Court held in the *Brimson* case, there is no additional requirement that the subpœna be issued by a court rather than an administrative agency. The fact that Judge Field's ringing phrases as to the sanctity of the right against unreasonable search have been recently cited does not, of course, serve to revive the holding of the *Pacific Railway Commission* case. *Cf.* the *Endicott-Johnson* case, 128 F. (2d) at 218. Indeed, that language of Judge Field's was quoted by the Supreme Court in the *Brimson* case, the very case in which it refused to follow Judge Field's holding (154 U. S. at 479).

As the Second Circuit Court of Appeals has stated, in applying the *Brimson* case to this Commission, "Thus for years a procedure like that authorized for the Commission has been used by another government administrative body without question as to its validity." *In re S. E. C.*, 84 F. (2d) 316, 318 (1936). Again, when the *Endicott-Johnson* case reached the Supreme Court, the Court concluded its opinion with the statement (317 U. S. at 510):

> The subpœna power delegated by the statute as here exercised is so clearly within the limits of Congressional authority that it is not necessary to discuss the constitutional questions urged by the petitioner, and on the record before us the cases on which it relies are inapplicable and do not require consideration.[36]

---

[36] The brief filed by Endicott-Johnson in the Supreme Court argued (1) that denial to the court enforcing the Secretary's subpœna of the power to determine coverage violated the Fourth Amendment, and (2) that the decision of the Circuit Court of Appeals violated Article III of the Constitution.

CONCLUSION

The order of the District Court should be affirmed.

Respectfully submitted,

ROGER S. FOSTER,
Solicitor.

MILTON V. FREEMAN,
Assistant Solicitor.

LOUIS LOSS,
Special Counsel.

SECURITIES AND EXCHANGE COMMISSION,
18th and Locust Streets,
Philadelphia 3, Pa.

CHARLES J. ODENWELLER, JR.,
Regional Administrator.

SECURITIES AND EXCHANGE COMMISSION,
1370 Ontario Street,
Cleveland 13, Ohio.

No. 10488

United States
Circuit Court of Appeals
For the Ninth Circuit.

GEORGE ROBERT GUTMAN,
Appellant,

vs.

UNITED STATES OF AMERICA,
Appellee.

Transcript of Record

Upon Appeal from the District Court of the United States for the Northern District of California, Southern Division

No. 10488

United States
Circuit Court of Appeals
For the Ninth Circuit.

GEORGE ROBERT GUTMAN,

Appellant,

vs.

UNITED STATES OF AMERICA,

Appellee.

Transcript of Record

Upon Appeal from the District Court of the United States for the Northern District of California, Southern Division

Rotary Colorprint, 590 Folsom St., San Francisco

INDEX

[Clerk's Note: When deemed likely to be of an important nature, errors or doubtful matters appearing in the original certified record are printed literally in italic; and, likewise, cancelled matter appearing in the original certified record is printed and cancelled herein accordingly. When possible, an omission from the text is indicated by printing in italic the two words between which the omission seems to occur.]

Index Page

Index **Page**

Index **Page**

United States of America.

Index **Page**

Index Page

NAMES AND ADDRESSES OF ATTORNEYS.

MR. CLARENCE E. RUST,

537 San Pablo Avenue,
Oakland, California.

Attorney for Defendant and Appellant.

MR. FRANK J. HENNESSY,

United States Attorney,
Northern District of California.

MR. JOSEPH KARESH,

Assistant United States Attorney,
Northern District of California.
Post Office Building,
San Francisco, California.

Attorneys for Plaintiff and Appellee.

In the Southern Division of the United States District Court for the Northern Division of California.

INDICTMENT

(Section 11, Selective Service Training and Service Act of 1940, As Amended, 50 USCA, Section 311).

In the March 1943 term of said Division of said District Court the Grand Jurors thereof on their oaths present:

That

GEORGE ROBERT GUTMAN,

(whose full and true name is, other than hereinabove stated, to said Grand Jurors unknown, hereinafter called "said defendant"), being a male citizen between the ages of eighteen and forty-five years, residing in the United States and under the duty to present himself for and submit to registration under the provisions of the "Selective Training and Service Act of 1940, As Amended", and thereafter to comply with the rules and regulations of said Act, As Amended, and having in pursuance of said Act, As Amended, and the rules and regulations made pursuant thereto, become a registrant of Local Board No. 86 of the Selective Service System, in the City and County of San Francisco, California, which said Local Board No. 86 was duly appointed and acting for the area of which the said defendant is a registrant, did, on or about the 14th day of May, 1943, at the City and County of San Francisco, in the Southern Division of the Northern District of California, and withint the jurisdiction of this Court, knowingly and feloniously fail and neglect to perform such duty, in that he, the said defendant, did then and there knowingly and feloniously fail and neglect to comply with the order of his said Local [1*] Board No. 86, which had theretofore classified him in Class I-A, to report for induction into the Land or Naval Forces of the United States, as provided in the said Selective Training and Service Act of 1940, As Amended, and the rules and regulations made pursuant thereto.

FRANK J. HENNESSY
United States Attorney.

Approved as to form:
R. B. McM.

[Endorsed]: Presented in Open Court and Ordered Filed May, 27 1943. Walter B. Maling, Clerk. By J. P. Welsh, Deputy Clerk. [2]

*Page numbering appearing at foot of page of original certified Transcript of Record.

District Court of the United States
Northern District of California
Southern Division

At a Stated Term of the Southern Division of the United States District Court for the Northern District of California, held at the Court Room thereof, in the City and County of San Francisco, on Thursday the 10th day of June, in the year of our Lord one thousand nine hundred and forty-three.

Present: The Honorable Michael J. Roche, District Judge.

[Title of Cause.]

No. 28001-R.

DEFENDANT'S PLEA OF NOT GUILTY ENTERED

This case came on regularly this day for entry of the plea of the defendant, George Robert Gutman. The defendant was present with Wm. Shea, Esq., his Attorney. Joseph Karesh, Esq., Assistant United States Attorney, was present for and on behalf of the United States.

The defendant was called to plead and thereupon said defendant entered a plea of "Not Guilty" to the Indictment filed herein against him, which said plea was ordered entered.

After hearing the Attorneys, it is ordered that the trial of this case be and the same is hereby set for June 17, 1943. (Jury) [3]

In the Southern Division of the United States District Court For the Northern District of California. First Division.

No. 28001-R

THE UNITED STATES OF AMERICA

vs.

GEORGE ROBERT GUTMAN

VERDICT

We, the Jury, find as to the defendant at the bar as follows: Guilty as charged.

R. M. FRAIZER
Foreman.

[Endorsed]: Filed June 18, 1943. [4]

District Court of the United States
Northern District of California
Southern Division

At a Stated Term of the Southern Division of the United States District Court for the Northern District of California, held at the Court Room thereof, in the City and County of San Francisco, on Saturday the 19th day of June, in the year of our Lord one thousand nine hundred and forty-three.

Present: The Honorable Michael J. Roche, District Judge.

No. 28001-R.

UNITED STATES OF AMERICA,

vs.

GEORGE ROBERT GUTMAN.

JUDGMENT AND SENTENCE

This case came on regularly this day for the pronouncing of judgment upon the defendant, George Robert Gutman. The defendant was present in the custody of the United States Marshal and with Wm. Shea, Esq., his Attorney. Joseph Karesh, Esq., Assistant United States Attorney, was present for and on behalf of the United States.

The defendant was called for judgment and after hearing the Attorneys and the defendant, Mr. Shea offered a certain exhibit which was marked Defendant's Exhibit "E" for identification; and thereupon, said defendant having been now asked whether he has anything to say why judgment should not be pronounced against him, and no sufficient cause to the contrary being shown or appearing to the Court,

It Is By The Court

Ordered and Adjudged that the defendant George Robert Gutman, for the offense of which he stands convicted on the verdict of the jury of guilty of the offense charged in the [5] Indictment filed herein against him, be and he is hereby committed to the custody of the Attorney General or his authorized representative for imprisonment for the period of Three (3) Years.

Ordered that a judgment be entered herein accordingly.

It Is Further Ordered that the Clerk of this Court deliver a certified copy of the judgment and commitment to the United States Marshal or other qualified officer and that the same shall serve as the commitment herein.

The Court recommends commitment to a U. S. Penitentiary. [6]

[Title of Court and Cause.]

NOTICE OF APPEAL.

Name and address of appellant

George Robert Gutman, 1892 Fell Street, San Francisco, California.

Name and address of appellant's attorney

Clarence E. Rust, 5837 San Pablo Ave., Oakland, California.

Offense: Wilful failure and refusal to report for induction in violation of act of Congress approved September 16, 1940 and known as "Selective Training and Service Act of 1940, as amended, Section 11, (50 U.S.C.A. 311).

Date of judgment

June 19, 1943.

Brief description of judgment or sentence

The defendant was sentenced by the above entitled Court to a total of three years imprisonment.

Name of prison where now confined, if not on bail San Francisco County Jail.

I, the above named appellant, hereby appeal to the Circuit Court of Appeals for the Ninth Circuit from the judgment above-mentioned on the grounds set forth below.

(Signed) GEORGE ROBERT GUTMAN
Appellant.

Dated June 23, 1943. [7]

GROUNDS OF APPEAL:

1—The insufficiency of the evidence as a matter of law to sustain the jury's verdict that the defendant was guilty of the offense charged.

2—The error of the court in denying defendant's motion for a directed verdict of not guilty on the ground of the insufficiency of the evidence to sustain a conviction as a matter of law, made at the conclusion of the testimony offered on behalf of the United States.

3—The error of the court in denying defendant's motion for a directed verdict of not guilty on the ground of the insufficiency of the evidence to sustain a conviction as a matter of law, made at the conclusion of all the testimony.

4—The error of the trial court in failing and refusing to give certain proposed instructions to the jury requested by defendant.

5—The error of the trial court in giving certain instructions to the jury, and particularly to Government's proposed instruction 3, 4, 5 and 6.

Dated: June 23, 1943.

CLARENCE E. RUST
Attorney for appellant.

Receipt of a copy of foregoing Notice of Appeal and Grounds of Appeal, admitted this 23rd day of June, 1943.

FRANK J. HENNESSY
United States Attorney
By T. SOLOMON

[Endorsed]: Filed June 23, 1943. [8]

[Title of District Court and Cause.]

BILL OF EXCEPTIONS

Be It Remembered: That the Grand Jury of the United States, in and for the Northern District of California, Southern Division, for the March, 1943 term of said Division, returned and there was filed in the Court, its indictment against the defendant and appellant in the above-entitled cause charging him with violation of the Selective Training and Service Act of 1940 (50 U.S.C.A. 311); that thereafter said defendant appeared in said Court and was duly arraigned upon said indictment and entered his plea of not guilty to the charge therein contained:

That thereafter and on June 17, 1943, the said cause came on regularly for and proceeded to trial before a jury in the above entitled Court, Hon. Michael J. Roche, United States District Judge, presiding, the United States being represented by Frank J. Hennessy, United States Attorney and Joseph Karesh, Assistant United States Attorney, and defendant being personally present in Court and represented by William Shea, his attorney; and thereupon the following proceedings were had:

MRS. PAULINE HEGBERG

called as a witness on behalf of the United States, and being [9] duly sworn, testified as follows:

I am chief clerk of Selective Service Board Number 86, San Francisco, California, and have the custody of the records of this Board and have charge of the correspondence. The defendant, George Robert Gutman is a registrant with this Board.

(The registration card of defendant was here identified by the witness and said card was admitted in evidence and marked U. S. Exhibit No. 1)

2. PLACE OF RESIDENCE (Print)

1892 Fell St. San Francisco . Ca

(Number and street) (Town, township, village, or city) (County) (State)

[THE PLACE OF RESIDENCE GIVEN ON THE LINE ABOVE WILL DETERMINE LOCAL BO JURISDICTION; LINE 2 OF REGISTRATION CERTIFICATE WILL BE IDENTICAL]

3. MAILING ADDRESS

Same

address if other than ce indicated on line 2. If same insert word same)

4. TELEPHONE

Skylin 3431

(Exchange mber)

5. AGE I

Mch. 924

(Mo.) (Yr.)

7. NAME AND

Lyda (

9. PLACE OF EMPLOYMENT OR BUSINESS

117 Adams St. Brook

(Number and street or R. F. D. number)

I AFFIRM THAT I HAVE VERIFIED ABOVE ANSWERS AND THAT THEY ARE TRUE.

D. S. S. Form 1 (Revised 6-1-42) (over)

Signed George F. Gutman

(Registrant's signature)

REGISTRAR'S REPORT

DESCRIPTION OF REGISTRANT

RACE		HEIGHT (Approx.)	WEIGHT (Approx.)	COMPLEXION	
White		6'5"	175	Sallow	
		EYES	HAIR	Light	
Negro		Blue	Blonde	Ruddy	
		Gray	Red	Dark	
Oriental		Hazel	Brown	Freckled	
		Brown	Black	Light brown	
Indian		Black	Gray	Dark brown	
			Bald	Black	
Filipino					

U. S. DIST. CT. N. D. CAL. No. 1-52212

Other obvious physical characteristics that will aid in identification

Scar between eyes

Nat. Cert. No.

I certify that my answers are true; that the person registered has read or has had read to him his own answers; that I have witnessed his signature or mark and that all of his answers of which I have knowledge are true, except as follows:

WALTER F. KEHLING, CLERK

BY [signature] DEPUTY CLERK

Signed W. R. Bent (Signature of registrar)

Registrar for Local Board (Number) (City or county) (State)

Local Board No. 86 91

Date of registration JUL . . 1942 086

1444 Haight Street

I hereby certify that thi is a true c

inal registration card D. S. Form 1

ca
be
M
si
F
J
a
a
th

c
a

b
t
o
F

(Testimony of Mrs. Pauline Hegberg.)

The registrant, defendant here, filed a selective service questionnaire, DSS Form 40, with the Board.

(The questionnaire was here identified by the witness and said questionnaire was admitted in evidence and marked U. S. Exhibit No. 2)

U. S. EXHIBIT No. 2

Selective Service Questionnaire

Order No. M 11866.

Date of mailing September 1, 1942.

[Stamp of Local Board]: Local Board No. 86—91 075 086. Sep 1, 1942. 1444 Haight Street, San Francisco, California.

Name: (First) George (Middle) Robert (Last) Gutman.

Address (Number and street or R. F. D. route) 1892 Fell Street, (City or Town) San Francisco (County) S. F. (State) California.

Notice to Registrant

You are required by the Selective Service Regulations to fill out this Questionnaire truthfully and to return it to this local board on or before the date shown below. Willful failure to do so is punishable by fine and imprisonment.

This Questionnaire Must Be Returned on or Before September 11, 1942.

P. PAUL VLAUTIN,
Member of Local Board.

(Testimony of Mrs. Pauline Hegberg.)

U. S. Exhibit No. 2—(Continued.)

(The above items are to be filled in by the local board before the Questionnaire is mailed to the registrant.)

Instructions

This Questionnaire is intended to furnish the local board with information to enable it to classify you. You will receive notice from your local board of your classification.

Oaths required in the Questionnaire may be administered by any civil officer authorized to administer oaths generally, any commissioned officer of the land or naval forces assigned for duty with the Selective Service System, any member or clerk of a local board or board of appeal, any government appeal agent or associate government appeal agent, any member or associate member of an advisory board for registrants, any postmaster, acting postmaster or assistant postmaster.

Advisory boards for registrants are organized to assist registrants in completing their Questionnaires. No charge will be made for this service. Information as to the location of a member of the advisory board for registrants who will assist in completing this form may be obtained from the local board office. If there is no advisory board member available, you must nevertheless complete your Questionnaire.

If the registrant is an inmate of an institution and is unable to complete the Questionnaire, the executive head of the institution shall communicate these facts immediately to the local board.

(Testimony of Mrs. Pauline Hegberg.)

U. S. Exhibit No. 2—(Continued.)

1. Make no alterations in the printed matter in this Questionnaire.

2. All spaces in this Questionnaire that apply to registrants must be filled in with the proper words.

3. If you furnish additional information or affidavits with your Questionnaire, attach the same securely to it.

4. If you are already in the active military or naval service, obtain a certificate to that effect from your commanding officer and attach same to your Questionnaire.

5. After this Questionnaire has been returned, report to your local board at once any change of address or any new fact which may affect your classification.

· Statements in this Questionnaire marked (Confidential) are for information only of the officials duly authorized under the regulations.

Use Ink or Typewriter in Filling Out This Form

D. S. S. Form 40

(Revised Jan. 12, 1942)

[Stamped]: Local Board No. 86—San Francisco County—91 075 086. Sep 11 1942. 1444 Haight Street, San Francisco, California. (1)

Statements of the Registrant

Series I.—Identification

Instructions.—Every registrant shall fill in all statements in this series.

(Testimony of Mrs. Pauline Hegberg.)

U. S. Exhibit No. 2—(Continued.)

1. My name is (print) (First name) George (Middle name) Robert (Last name) Gutman.

2. In addition to the name given above, I have also been known by the name or names of (If none, write "None") none.

3. My residence now is (Number and street or R. F. D. route) 1892 Fell Street, (Town—[City, town, or village]) San Francisco, (County) San Francisco, (State) California.

4. My telephone number now is (Town) San Francisco, (Exchange) SKyline (Number) 3431. (If you have no phone, write "None").

5. My Social Security number is (If none, write "None") none.

6. I was 18 years of age on my last birthday.

Series II.—Physical Condition (Confidential)

Instructions.—Every registrant shall fill in all statements in this series.

1. To the best of my knowledge, I (have, have no) have no physical or mental defects or diseases. If so, they are (List defects or diseases here).

2. I (am, am not) am not an inmate of an institution. If so, its name is (Name of hospital, prison, or other institution) and it is located at (Give address).

Series III.—Education

Instructions.—Every registrant shall fill in all statements in this series.

1. I have completed (Number) 6 years of elementary school and (Number) 4 years of high school.

(Testimony of Mrs. Pauline Hegberg.)

U. S. Exhibit No. 2—(Continued.)

2. I have had the following schooling other than elementary and high school (if none, write "None"):

Name of Vocational School, College, or University None.

Course of study (blank).

Length of Time Attended (blank).

3. I (can, cannot) can read and write the English language.

Series IV.—Present Occupation or Activity

Instructions.—Every registrant shall fill in No. 1 of this series; every registrant now at work shall fill in No. 2; every registrant now unemployed shall answer No. 3; and every registrant who is now a student, whether or not he also has a job, shall fill in No. 4.

1. (Put an X in one box) I am now [X] working at the job described under No. 2 below. [ ] unemployed for the reasons and under the circumstances described in my answer to No. 3 below. [ ] a student pursuing the course of study described under No. 4 below.

2. (a) The job I am now working at is (give full title, for example: Construction draftsman, turret-lathe operator, stationary engineer, farm laborer, prosecuting attorney, physics teacher, policeman, marriage-license clerk, etc.): Minister of the Gospel.

(b) I do the following kind of work in my present job (be specific—give a brief statement of your

(Testimony of Mrs. Pauline Hegberg.)

U. S. Exhibit No. 2—(Continued.)

duties): Conduct Bible studies and also organize new churches.

(c) I have had 3 years experience in this kind of work.

√ (d) My average (weekly, monthly, annual) monthly earnings in my present job are √ $20.00. (Confidential). (2)

Series IV.—Present Occupation or Activity.—Continued

(e) In my present job, I am—(Put an X in one box)

☐ a regular or permanent employee, working for salary, wages, commission, or other compensation; I √ have worked 3 years in my present job, and expect to continue indefinitely in it.

☐ a temporary or occasional employee; I expect that my present job will end about (Date).

☐ an apprentice under a written or oral agreement with my employer, which expires (Date).

☐ an independent worker, working on my own account, not hired by anyone, and not hiring any help.

☐ working for my father or for the head of my family, but receiving no pay.

☐ an employer or proprietor hiring........................ paid workers.

(f) I (am, am not) am not now employed in national defense work.

(g) My employer is: (Name of organization or proprietor, not foreman or supervisor) Watchtower

(Testimony of Mrs. Pauline Hegberg.)

U. S. Exhibit No. 2—(Continued.)

Bible and Tract Society, (Address of place of employment—street or R. F. D. route, city, and State) 117 Adams Street, Brooklyn, New York, whose business is (For example: Farm, airplane engine factory, retail food store, W. P. A.) Publishers for Jehovah's witnesses.

(h) Other business or work in which I am now engaged is (If none, write "None") none.

Instructions.—If your employer believes that you are a necessary man in a necessary occupation, it is his duty to fill out Form 42A requesting your deferment. You may also attach to this page any further statement by yourself which you think the local board should consider in determining your classification. Such statement will then become a part of the Questionnaire.

3. If you are not now working, attach to this page a statement (a) giving the reasons for your unemployment, when it began, and when you expect to be able to resume your work, and (b) supplying substantially the same information regarding your last job as is required in Items 2 (a) to 2 (f) above.

4. (a) (If a student) I am majoring in........ ....preparing for (Occupation or profession)..at (Name and address of school or college) ....

(b) I expect to complete this training on (Date).

(c) I (do, do not) intend to take an exami-

(Testimony of Mrs. Pauline Hegberg.)

U. S. Exhibit No. 2—(Continued.)

nation for license in (Profession). Date of examination..................................

Instructions.—A student who believes that he should be placed in Class II because preparing for a necessary occupation should see that the head of his school files with the local board the necessary supporting evidence.

Series V.—Agricultural Occupations

Instructions.—Every registrant who works on a farm shall fill in this series, in addition to filling in Series IV and VI.

1. I work on or operate a farm as—(Put an X in the correct box)

☐ sole owner of the farm. ☐ joint owner with (Name) (Address)

☐ hired manager ☐ cash tenant or renter ☐ standing rent tenant ☐ share cropper ☐ share tenant.

My agreement (if any) expires (Month) (Day) (Year).

☐ wage hand (hired man). ☐ unpaid family worker.

2. I have been engaged in farm work for .... years.

3. I (do, do not) live on the farm with which I am connected.

4. I (am, am not) actually and personally re-

(Testimony of Mrs. Pauline Hegberg.)

U. S. Exhibit No. 2—(Continued.)

sponsible for the operation of the farm on which I work.

5. The principal crops and livestock of the farm I operate or work on are:

Name of Crops (blank).

Acres Devoted to Each (blank).

Kinds of Livestock (blank).

Number of Each Now on Farm (blank).

6. The number of people who work on this farm is (Number) of whom (Number) are hired hands.

7. Other facts which I consider necessary to present fairly the farming or farm work I have described and my connection with it as a ground for classification are (if none, write "None") (blank).

(3)

Series VI.—Occupational Experience, Qualifications, and Preferences

Instructions.—Every registrant shall fill in items 1, 2, and 3 in this series. Include in item 1 any formal apprenticeship served. Items 4 and 5 are optional and are designed to aid the Reemployment Division in restoring you to civilian employment after completion of military service.

1. I have also worked at the following occupations other than my present job, during the past 5 years: (If none, write "None.")

Occupation (Give full title, for example, turret-lathe operator, farmer, etc.) Student.

Kind of Work Done (Be specific—give a brief statement of your duties) (blank).

(Testimony of Mrs. Pauline Hegberg.)

U. S. Exhibit No. 2—(Continued.)

Years Worked From— 1932 To— 1939.

2. My usual occupation, or the occupation for which I am best fitted, is Minister of the Gospel.

3. I (am, am not) am not licensed in a trade or profession; if so, I am licensed as (blank). (For example: Marine pilot, physician, aviator, stationary engineer) (blank).

4. I have worked in the following State or States during the past 2 years Calif., Utah, Kansas, Missouri, Ohio, Mich.

5. I prefer the following kind of work: Present occupation.

I (would, would not) would not consider accepting a job which would require me to move away from my present home.

Series VII.—Family Status and Dependents (Confidential except as to names and addresses of claimed dependants).

Instructions.—Every registrant shall fill in the statements numbered 1 and 2 in this series.

1. I am (Put an X in the correct box)

[X] single.
[ ] widower.
[ ] divorced.
[ ] married;

I (do, do not) live with my wife; if not, her address is..; we were married at (Place) on (Date).

2. (a) I have (Number) children under 18 years of age.

(Testimony of Mrs. Pauline Hegberg.)

U. S. Exhibit No. 2—(Continued.)

(b) Of these children (Number) live with me in my home.

Instructions.—Every registrant who lives in a family group and contributes to the support of that group shall fill in statement No. 3. "Family group" as used in this statement means two or more persons related by blood, marriage, or adoption, who live together and who pool all or a substantial part of their individual incomes for their joint support. (Such a group may not always include everyone who lives in the same house or eats at the same table. For example, when a registrant and his wife and children share a house with other relatives but do not share the income of those other relatives, the family group to be listed here would include only the registrant and his wife and children.)

The information here given is intended to describe only the economic situation of the family group as it now exists and is not intended to suggest that by altering their present domestic arrangements, present dependents of the registrant might obtain support from other persons who are not now supporting them.

3. (a) The following is a list of all members of the family group in which I live (list yourself first):

Name (Name of registrant) George Robert Gutman.

Sex Male

Age last birthday 18.

(Testimony of Mrs. Pauline Hegberg.)

U. S. Exhibit No. 2—(Continued.)

Relationship to me Self.

Date I began to contribute to this person's support. (If not contributing, write "N. C."). x x x x x

Amount this person earned by work during past 12 months $240.00.

Lyda Gutman (Mother). Female. 52. Mother. N. C. $240.00.

(b) I contributed $.......................... during the last 12 months to the support of the above-listed family group.

(c) In addition to the earnings shown in table 3 (a), only the only the following other income was received by members of this family group during the past 12 months. (State the nature and source of every item of income whether in cash or other things of value. Include income from property, relief payments, and contributions from persons outside this group. Give name, address, relationship. and age of each person outside the family group making such (4) contributions:..................................

Instructions.—Every registrant who contributes to the support of one or more persons who are not members of the family group listed above shall fill in statement No. 4.

4. (a) The following persons who are not members of the family group listed above depend wholly or partly for support on what I earn by my work in my business, occupation, or employment; they had no other sources of income during the past 12 months, except as stated below:

[Blank form not filled in.]

(Testimony of Mrs. Pauline Hegberg.)

U. S. Exhibit No. 2—(Continued.)

· (b) Of the amounts contributed by me to dependents listed in 4 (a) only (If none, write None") $........................contributed to .... (Name of dependent) was in payment for my own board and lodging.

(c) The sources of the "other income" shown in the last column of the table just above were as follows: (Give name of dependent and state whether income was earned or contributed; if contributed, give name of dependent and name and address of person or agency contributing.)................

(d) The income I earned from my work in my business, occupation, or employment during the past 12 months was $........................

(e) My income from all other sources during the past 12 months was $.....................

Instructions.—Every registrant who fills in either statement No. 3 or No. 4 shall also fill in the statements numbered 5 through 9 in this series.

5. If any of my dependents (except my wife) are over 18 years of age, the reasons why they are dependent are as follows (list each person by name):

6. The following is a description of all property, real and personal, owned by (or held in trust for) either myself or my dependents (do not include clothing, personal effects, household furnishings, or automobile; indicate which of such property is your home):

Name of Person None.

Kind of Property (blank).

(Testimony of Mrs. Pauline Hegberg.)

U. S. Exhibit No. 2—(Continued.)

Value After Deducting Encumbrances $................

Net Income From This Property Past 12 Months (If none, write "None") (blank).

7. I (do, do not) do rent the house or apartment in which I live; if so, the monthly rent now is $2.50.

8. I have contracted to purchase the following property (if none, write "None"):

Kind of Property None.

Date of Contract (blank).

Balance Now Outstanding (blank).

Monthly Payments (blank).

9. Other facts which I consider necessary to present fairly my own status and that of my dependents as a basis for my proper classification are (if none, write "None"): None.

Instructions:—With respect to any dependent (other than the registrant's own wife or child) whose support the registrant has assumed, the registrant shall furnish to the local board an affidavit of the person for whom dependency is claimed (or from the person's guardian if he is incompetent), explaining why and under what circumstances the registrant assumed such person's support. Copies of Form 40-A for this purpose may be obtained from the local board. If the dependent lives at a distance, do not delay return of the Questionnaire pending receipt of the affidavit; forward the affidavit as soon as received and it will then become a part of this Questionnaire. (5)

(Testimony of Mrs. Pauline Hegberg.)

U. S. Exhibit No. 2—(Continued.)

Series VIII.—Minister, or Student Preparing for the Ministry

Instructions.—Every registrant who is a minister or a student preparing for the ministry shall fill in the statements in this series that apply to him.

1. (a) I (am, am not) am a minister of religion.

(b) I (do, do not) do customarily serve as a minister.

(c) I have been a minister of the (Name of sect or denomination) Jehovah's witnesses since (Month, day, year) August 1, 1939.

(d) I (have, have not) have been formally ordained. If so, my ordination was performed on (Month, day, year) June 25, 1939, by (Ecclesiastical official performing the ordination) Watchtower Bible & Tract Soc. at (City and State) Los Angeles, California.

2. (a) I (am, am not) am not a student preparing for the ministry in a theological or divinity school.

(b) I am attending the (Name of theological or divinity school), which was established (before, after) September 16, 1939, and is located at (Place).

Series IX.—Citizenship

Instructions.—Every registrant shall fill in the statements numbered 1, 2, 3, and 4 in this series.

1. I was born at (Town) Bakersfield, (State) California, (Country) U. S. A.

(Testimony of Mrs. Pauline Hegberg.)

U. S. Exhibit No. 2—(Continued.)

2. I was born on (Month) March (Day) 15, (Year) 1924.

3. My race is:

☒ White;
☐ Negro;
☐ Oriental;
☐ Indian;
☐ Filipino;
Other (specify) ....

4. I (am, am not) am a citizen of the United States.

Instructions:—Every registrant who is not a citizen of the United States shall fill in the statements numbered 5, 6, 7, and 8.

5. I (am, was last) a citizen or subject of (Name of country). My Alien Registration No. is (If none, write "None").

6. My permanent residence has been in the United States since (Month) (Day) (Year).

7. I (have, have not) filed a declaration of intention to become a citizen of the United States (first papers). Declaration filed at (Place) on (Month) (Day) (Year) under No.................................

8. I (have, have not) filed a petition for naturalization (second papers). Petition filed at (Place), on (Month) (Day) (Year).

Series X.—Conscientious Objection to War

Instructions.—Any registrant who, by reason of religious training and belief, is conscientiously opposed to participation in war in any form shall sign the statement below requesting a Special Form

(Testimony of Mrs. Pauline Hegberg.)

U. S. Exhibit No. 2—(Continued.)

for Conscientious Objector (Form 47) from the local board which must be completed and returned to the local board for consideration.

By reason of religious training and belief I am conscientiously opposed to war in any form and for this reason request that the local board furnish me a Special Form for Conscientious Objector (Form 47) which I am to complete and return to the local board.

....

(Signature)

Series XI.—Court Record (Confidential)

Instructions.—Every registrant shall fill in statement No. 1.

1. I (have, have not) have not been convicted of a crime, other than minor traffic violations.

Instructions.—Every registrant who has ever been convicted of a crime, other than minor traffic violations, shall fill in statement No. 2, listing all convictions. (6)

2. The record of my convictions is as follows:

Offense None.

Date (Month, Day, Year) (blank).

Court (Name and location) (blank).

Sentence (blank).

3. I (am, am not) am not now being retained in the custody of a court of criminal jurisdiction, or other civil authority.

(Testimony of Mrs. Pauline Hegberg.)

U. S. Exhibit No. 2—(Continued.)

Series XII.—Military Service (Confidential)

Instructions.—Every registrant who now is or has been a member of the armed forces of the United States shall fill in the statements in this series. (Use a separate line for each term of service.)

My military service has been as follows:

Arm of Service (Army, Navy, National Guard, etc.) None.

Date of Entry Into Service (Month, Day, Year) (blank).

Still in Service (Yes, No) (blank).

Date of Discharge (Month, Day, Year) (blank).

Type of Discharge (Honorable, Dishonorable, Bad Conduct, Not Honorable, Undesirable, or Other —Specify) (blank).

Series XIII.—Present Members of Armed Forces, Certain Officials, Etc.

Instructions.—Every registrant who is a member of one or more of the groups named in this series shall check the appropriate item or items, and shall supply any further information called for under the item or items checked.

I am at present:

1. ☐ A commissioned officer, warrant officer, pay clerk, or enlisted man of the Regular Army, the Navy, the Marine Corps, the Coast Guard, the Coast and Geodetic Survey, the Public Health Service, the federally recognized active National Guard, the Officers' Reserve Corps, the Regular Army Reserve, the Enlisted Reserve Corps, the Naval Re-

(Testimony of Mrs. Pauline Hegberg.)

U. S. Exhibit No. 2—(Continued.)

serve, the Marine Corps Reserve, or the Coast Guard Reserve; my rank or commission is.................. in the (Name of service).

2. ☐ A cadet, United States Military Academy; midshipman, United States Naval Academy; cadet, United States Coast Guard Academy; man who has been accepted for admittance (commencing with the academic year next succeeding such acceptance) to the United States Military Academy as cadet, to the United States Naval Academy as midshipman, or to the United States Coast Guard Academy as cadet, and whose acceptance is still in effect; cadet of the advanced course, senior division, Reserve Officers' Training Corps or Naval Reserve Officers' Training Corps; I am (A cadet, midshipman, or accepted for admittance) in (Name of corps, academy, etc.).

3. ☐ The Governor of a State or Territory, a member of a legislative body of the United States or of a State or Territory, a judge of a court of record of the United States or of a State or Territory or the District of Columbia; my office is:............

....

Registrant's Statement Regarding Classification

Instructions.—It is optional with registrant whether or not he fills in this statement, and failure to answer shall not constitute a waiver of claim to deferred or other status. The local board is charged by law to determine the classification of the registrant on the basis of the facts before it, which should

(Testimony of Mrs. Pauline Hegberg.)

U. S. Exhibit No. 2—(Continued.)

be taken fully into consideration regardless of whether or not this statement is filled in.

In view of the facts set forth in this Questionnaire it is my opinion that my classification should be Class 4-D.

The registrant may write in the space below or attach to this page any statement which he believes should be brought to the attention of the local board in determining his classification.

I am appending to this page a statement of fact and Scripture that I believe should be brought to the attention of the Board in determining my classification.

Registrant's Affidavit

Instructions.—1. Every registrant shall make the registrant's affidavit. 2. If the registrant cannot read, the questions and his answers thereto shall be read to him by the officer who administers the oath.

State of California,
County of San Francisco—ss.

I, George Robert Gutman, do solemnly swear (or affirm) that I am the registrant named and described in the foregoing statements in this Questionnaire; that I have read (or have (7) had read to me) the statements made by and about me, and that each and every such statement is true and complete to the best of my knowledge, information, and

(Testimony of Mrs. Pauline Hegberg.)

U. S. Exhibit No. 2—(Continued.)

belief. The statements made by me in the foregoing (are, are not) are not in my own handwriting.

Registrant sign here ☞

GEORGE ROBERT GUTMAN.

(Signature or mark of registrant)

Subscribed and sworn to before me this 10th day of September, 1942.

[Seal] RUTH H. COSGROVE.

(Signature of officer)

Notary Public in and for the City and County of San Francisco, State of California.

My Commission expires ....

(Designation of officer)

If another person has assisted the registrant in filling out this Questionnaire, such person shall sign the following statement:

I have assisted the registrant herein named in preparation of this Questionnaire because (For example—Registrant unable to read and write English, etc.)

....

(Signature of Advisor)

Instructions.—Registrant shall write nothing below this line when filling out the Questionnaire.

Minute of Action on Request for Extension of Time for Filing Claim or Proof

The application of..

to have time for filing claim or proof extended to ...., 19........ is (granted, refused) for the

(Testimony of Mrs. Pauline Hegberg.)

U. S. Exhibit No. 2—(Continued.)

reason that ....

....

(Date)

....

Member.

Minute of Action by Local Board No...................., County ...., State..........................

The local board classifies the registrant in Class 1, Subdivision ...., by the following vote: Yes 3, No......... (Date) 11/23/42.

GEO. GILLIN,

Member.

Appeal to Board of Appeal

I hereby appeal to the board of appeal from the determination of the local board.

(Date) Dec. 21, 1942. (Signature of person appealing) George R. Gutman. (Relationship to registrant, i. e., parent, employer, appeal agent, etc.) (blank).

Minute of Action by Board of Appeal No............., County...................., State.

The board of appeal classifies the registrant in Class 1, Subdivision A, by the vollowing vote: Yes 3, No 0, 2 absent.

(Date) Feb. 10, 1943.

FRED WASS,

Chairman, Appeal Bd. 8.

Member.

(Testimony of Mrs. Pauline Hegberg.)

U. S. Exhibit No. 2—(Continued.)

Appeal to President

I hereby appeal to the President from the determination of the board of appeal.

(Date) blank. (Signature of person appealing) blank. (Relationship to registrant, i. e., parent, employer, appeal agent, etc.) blank.

Minutes of Other Actions

Dates 12/10/42 Class I A to reg P. Paul Vlautin.

2-24-43 Class I A to reg (dec. of Appeal Bd.) P. V.

4-22-43 Class I A to reg (dec. of President) Geo. B. Gillin. (8)

[Endorsed]: Filed 6/17/43.

The defendant also filed with the Board a letter in which he asked for a IV-D classification.

(The letter was here identified by the witness and said letter was admitted in evidence and marked U. S. Exhibit No. 3)

(Testimony of Mrs. Pauline Hegberg.)

U. S. EXHIBIT NO. 3

George R. Gutman
1892 Fell Street
San Francisco, Calif.

Local Draft Board No. 86
1444 Haight Street
San Francisco, Calif.

Gentlemen:

My reason for asking for Class IV-D in my questionnaire is set out below:

I am an ordained minister and being such, I devote all my time to preaching the gospel. I am, of course ordained first by the Almighty God "whose name alone is JEHOVAH". (Psalms 83:18) I am ordained also by The Watchtower Bible and Tract Society who are the publishers for Jehovah's witnesses. This second ordination is to comply with the laws of the Nation. I obtain my authority to preach this gospel from the Bible and is given by the Lord himself as recorded at Isaiah 61:1, 2.

> "The Spirit of the Lord GOD is upon me; because the Lord hath anointed me to preach good tidings unto the meek; he hath sent me to bind up the brokenhearted, to proclaim liberty to the captives, and the opening of the prison to them that are bound;"
>
> "To proclaim the acceptable year of the LORD, and the day of vengeance of our God; to comfort all that mourn;"

(Testimony of Mrs. Pauline Hegberg.)
Isaiah 43:10-12.

> "Ye are my witnesses, saith the LORD, and my servant whom I have chosen: . . . Therefore ye are my witnesses, saith the LORD, (JEHOVAH) that I am God."

Also at Ezekiel 3:16-21 and also Ezekiel 33:1-9 it is brought out by the Lord that if we warn not the people and they die in their iniquity then their blood is upon our shoulders for failing to tell them of this gospel. Further emphasizing the absolute necessity of preaching to the people, Paul, at 1 Corinthians 9:16 states:

> "For though I preach the gospel, I have nothing to glory of: for necessity is laid upon me; yea, woe is unto me, if I preach not the gospel!"

Also it is clearly shown at 1 Timothy 1:2; 2:7 and 2 Timothy 1:11 that "I am appointed (ordained) a preacher, and a apostle and a teacher unto the gentiles (Nations)." This being my commission, I could not forsake the Army of Jesus Christ for the Army of any earthly nation as that would necessarily be treason to my obligations in His services. I am as stated by Paul, at 2 Timothy 2:3, 4 a "soldier of Jesus Christ."

> "Thou therefore endure hardness, as a good soldier of Jesus Christ"

> "No man that warreth entangleth himself with the affairs of this life; that he may please him who hath chosen him to be a soldier."

(Testimony of Mrs. Pauline Hegberg.)

I am, as stated at 1 Peter 2:21 commanded to follow in the footsteps of Jesus.

> "For even hereunto were ye called: because Christ also suffered for us, leaving us an example, that ye should follow his steps."

We have a record in the following scriptures that Jesus and the apostles were continually going about from village to village preaching and showing the glad tidings of the Kingdom of God. Luke 8:1; Matthew 9:35; Matthew 10:7, 12-14; Mark 13:10; Acts 5:42; Acts 20:20. These scriptures show very forcefully that it is the obligation of every true Christian to do as Jesus did and preach this gospel. The THEOCRACY concerning which we are preaching is not to be set up by any man, group of men, or human organization, neither will it be run by any man but by the Lord JEHOVAH through his son Jesus Christ. Jesus at Matthew 6:10 instructed his faithful followers to pray for the establishment of that righteous government. At Hebrews 11th Chapter is recorded a list of some of the men who will rule as the earthly princes or governors of that THEOCRACY. Those who are now represen*tion* the THEOCRATIC GOVERNMENT are known as JEHOVAH'S witnesses, and truly they are witnesses to His name and Kingdom. The THEOCRATIC Ambassadors, of which I am proud to be one, are not of this world even as the THEOCRACY has no part with the affairs of this world. John 18:36, 37 states in part:

(Testimony of Mrs. Pauline Hegberg.)

". . . . My Kingdom is not of this world: if my kingdom were of this world, then would my servants fight, that I should not be delivered to the Jews: but now is my kingdom not from hence."

"Pilate therefore said unto him, Art thou a king then? Jesus answered, Thou sayest that I am a king. To this end was I born, and for this cause came I unto the world that I should bear witness unto the truth. . . ."

John 17:14-18

"I have given them thy word; and the world hath hated them, because they are not of the world, even as I am not of the world."

"They are not of the world even as I am not of the world."

"As thou hath sent me into the world, even so have I also sent them into the world."

John 15:18, 19

"If the world hate you, ye know that it hated me before it hated you."

"If ye were of the world, the world would love his own: But because ye are not of the world, but I have chosen you out of the world, therefor the world hateth you."

John 8:23; Luke 12:30-32; and 1 John 4:17 all prove the above statement that neither Jesus, his kingdom or his followers are of this world, but rather sent into this world for the purpose of being a witness for his name, therefore the followers of Christ cannot

(Testimony of Mrs. Pauline Hegberg.)

sidestep his obligation to preach this gospel unto all nations for a witness. Matthew 24:14.

One might ask, "Well then, are you as a follower of Jesus against one government and for another earthly government?" The correct answer is, emphatically NO. A Christian's position must be one of strict neutrality in any quarrels between the nations. Philippians 3:18-20 according to the Weymouth translation shows our citizenship is in heaven.

Philippians 3: 18-20

> "For there are many whom I have often described to you, and I now even with tears describe them, as being enemies to *to* the Cross of Christ."
>
> "Their end is destruction, their bellies are their God, their glory is in their shame, and their minds are devoted to earthly things."
>
> "We, however, are free citizens of Heaven, and we are waiting with longing expectation for the coming from Heaven of a Savior, the Lord Jesus Christ."

Therefore I must be loyal to my Citizenship in Heaven in preference to any earthly government. One could not at the same time be a servant of God and the Devil. Satan is now the invisible god or prince of this present world.

Matthew 6:24

> "No can can serve two masters: for either he will hate the one, and love the other; or else he

(Testimony of Mrs. Pauline Hegberg.)

will hold to the one, and despise the other. Ye cannot serve God and mammon."

Also Luke 16:13

"No man can serve two masters: for either he will hate the one, and love the other; or else he will hold to the one, and despise the other. Ye cannot serve God and mammon."

The following scriptures show if we are friends of the world then we enemies of God. Galatians 1:10

"For do I now persuade men, or Go? or do I seek to please men? for if I yet pleased men, I should not be the servant of Christ."

James 4:4

"Ye adulterers and adulteresses, know ye not that the friendship of the world is enmity with God? Whosoever therefore will be a friend of the world is the enemy of God."

1 John 2:15

"Love not the world, neither the things that are in the world. If any man love the world, the love of the Father is not in him."

The following scriptures give evidence of the rulership of Satan over this world;

2 Corinthians 4:4

"In whom the god of this world hath blinded the minds of them which believe not, lest the light of the glorious gospel of Christ, who is the image of God, should shine unto them."

(Testimony of Mrs. Pauline Hegberg.)

John 12:31

> "Now is the judgment of this world: Now shall the prince of this world be cast out."

John 14:30

> "Hereafter I will not talk much with you: For the prince of this world cometh, and hath nothing in me."

"Our weapons are not carnal, but as stated in 2 Corinthians 10:3-5 and also at Ephesians 6:12 (Weymouth trans.) are mighty to the pulling down of strongholds."

My neutrality was foreshadowed in Abraham's day as he was neutral when the invaders overran the country of sodom and Gomorrah in which he was domiciled. When the invaders took Lot captive Abraham pursued them and brought Lot back, not because Lot was a fellow countryman but because Lot was a fellow servant of the most High. Abraham was not a pacifist, even as I am not. When a fellow servant of Jehovah was in danger, Abraham was willing to risk his life to rescue him. Hebrews 11:9, 10 proves he was a stranger in the earth looking for a city or government whose builder and maker is God. It is further written of him in Hebrews 11:12, 13 (Diaglott Trans.) that he confessed that he was a stranger in the land, ". . . .But not they long for a better, that is, a heavenly (country. . . ." Vs. 14, 15.

The question might be asked, "But would you take such a stand with the alternative of punishment and

(Testimony of Mrs. Pauline Hegberg.)

possible death? The scriptures at Acts 5:29; Acts 4:19; Matthew 5:10-12 Matthew 10:17-19, 21-23, 28, 39 Matthew 16:25, 26; Matthew 23:33, 34; Matthew 24:9, 13 Mark 8:35, Mark 13:9, 13; Luke 12:4, 5; John 15:18-21, 25; John 1714 2 Cor. 12; 10; 2 Corinthians 4:8, 9 very conclusively show that it is much better to suffer death at the hands of the Devil's crowd that to suffer everlasting death as punishment for disobeying the Lord JEHOVAH'S commandments.

In considering the above scriptures as well as my service record I sincerely hope you will arrive at a just and honorable decision for which you may have any cause to apoligize before God.

Respectfully Yours,
GEORGE ROBERT GUTMAN
George Robert Gutman

[Endorsed]: Filed 6/17/43.

On November 23, 1942, the Board placed the defendant in classification I-A. On December 10, 1942, a classification card showing this I-A was mailed to defendant—Form 57. Thereafter he demanded a personal appearance before the Board and the same was had. Defendant submitted a series of letters to the effect that he was entitled to a ministerial exemption.

(One of the letters was here identified by the witness and same was admitted in evidence and marked U. S. Exhibit No. 4)

(Testimony of Mrs. Pauline Hegberg.)

U. S. EXHIBIT NO. 4

[Pencil Note]: Mail Reg. # .32711

San Francisco, California
November 20, 1942

[Stamped]: Local Board No. 86—San Francisco County.—91 075 086. Nov. 23, 1942. 1444 Haight Street, San Francisco, California.

Local Draft Board No. 86
1444 Haight Street
San Francisco, Calif.

Gentlemen:
I am writing in regard to submiting further evidence to my file to further support my claim for Class IV-D.

This further evidence consists of a copy of Consolation magazine of July 9, 1941. This magazine has a copy of a letter from Brig. Gen. Lewis B. Hershey to Mr. Hayden Coveington, who is the attorney for Jehovah's Witnesses. It also contains the opinion of Gen. Hershey regarding Jehovah's Witnesses and their classification. You will note that Gen Hershey says that those of Jehovah's Witnesses who devote all their time to preaching the Gospel and who are known as "pioneers" are entitled to Classification as Ordained Ministers.

As I brought out in both my questionnaires, I have been engaged in the Pioneer Service for the past 39 months, starting in August of 1939. The reason that my name does not appear on the list in Consolation is

(Testimony of Mrs. Pauline Hegberg.)
that at the time of compiling that list I was not old enough. My name has been submitted to National Headquarters for addition to the Certified Official list, as I notified you in a previous statement.

I have recently received information from H. C. Covinton to the effect that National Headquarters has just revised its policy with respect to the addition of names to the certified official list and there will be no more names added, but otherwise the present arrangement will remain in effect, namely that those possessing the usual qualifications and holding credentials proving their FULL TIME PIONEER status (such as Ordination Certificates, which you have in my file) will be given the same consideration as ministers of "other religious organizations" and the fact that the name of a pioneer does not appear on the list will not be grounds for denying the pioneer Class IV-D

It might also be well to note that since May 1, 1942 I have been what is designated as a "Special Pioneer Publisher" who have a higher minimum of hours devoted to Preaching namely 175 rather than the Pioneer 150.

Hoping that you will consider the above evidence in determining my correct Classification, I remain

Respectfully yours,

GEORGE R. GUTMAN

[Endorsed]: Filed 6-17-43.

(Testimony of Mrs. Pauline Hegberg.)

On December 17, 1942, the Board received another letter from defendant requesting reconsideration and IV-D classification for himself.

(The letter was here identified by the witness and same was admitted in evidence and marked U. S. Exhibit No. 5)

U. S. EXHIBIT NO. 5

[Stamped]: Local Board No. 86—San Francisco County.—91 075 086. Dec. 17, 1942. 1444 Haight Street, San Francisco, California.

San Francisco, Calif.
December 15, 1942

Local Draft Board No. 86
1444 Haight Street
San Francisco, California

Gentlemen:

I have received my Notice of Classification, and I notice that I have not been classified properly.

The purpose of this letter is to request a personal appearance before the Local Board so that this mistake may be cleared up. I would suggest that you check over the items in my file which include an Ordination Letter which should substantiate my claim for that of an Ordained Minister, Class IV-D.

Thanking you in advance for your consideration in this matter, I remain

Respectfully yours,
GEORGE ROBERT GUTMAN
George Robert Gutman

[Endorsed]: Filed 6-17-43.

(Testimony of Mrs. Pauline Hegberg.)

On December 20, 1942, defendant took an appeal to the Appeal Board; he filed a letter with the local Board on that date.

(The letter was here identified by the witness and same was admitted in evidence and marked U. S. Exhibit No. 6)

U. S. EXHIBIT NO. 6

[Stamped]: Local Board No. 86—San Francisco County.—91 075 086. Dec. 17, 1942. 1444 Haight Street, San Francisco, California.

San Francisco, California
December 20, 1942

Local Draft Board No. 86
1444 Haight Street
San Francisco, California

Gentlemen:

I would like to appeal my classification from that of 1-A to that of IV-D.

I have been incorrectly classified by the Local Board in Class 1-A. The reason I say incorrectly classified is because I am an Ordained Minister of Jehovah's witnesses and have been for the past 3½ years. I started in the Ministry on August 8, 1939 when I was formally recognized and appointed as a pioneer minister. I have filed with the Local Board a photostatic copy of my Ordination Letter to bear this out. I was raised in the organization of Jehovah's witnesses, My parents being also Ministers of Jehovah's witnesses. When I reached the age of 15, I began to realize the importance to me, of becoming a Min-

(Testimony of Mrs. Pauline Hegberg.)

ister and helping others to know and to realize who the True and Only God is and what are His purposes toward humankind. I was immersed in July 1939 and and then made my consecration to do the will of Jehovah God. Following shortly thereafter on August 1, 1939, I went into the fulltime pioneer minister service, receiving my aknowledgement on August 8, 1939.

In View of the fact that I was not subject to the draft at the time that the certified official list was released, my name was not included thereon, as National Headquarters asked that those who were registered, or subject to draft only, be supplied. As soon as I registered my name was filed by the Watchtower Bible and Tract Society with National Headquarters, but in view of change of policy at that time being drawn up by National Headquarters (which policy has now been put into effect and notice thereof being mailed to State Directors of Selective Service by National Headquarters) National Headquarters did not act on such new list of June registrants, including listing of my name. In view of new policy of National Headquarters not to add the name of any registrants, to the certified official list of Jehovah's witnesses, but those who have factual proof of their being full-time pioneer ministers of Jehovah's witnesses should receive full and fair consideration by the Local Board and the same recognition given ministers of all religious organizations. I am entitled to such recognition and classification in IV-D. I would like at this time to refer you again to the

(Testimony of Mrs. Pauline Hegberg.)

letter of General Hershey as of June 12, 1940, a copy of which I have filed with you, which states that Pioneers are entitled to classification of Ordained Ministers the same as Ministers of other religious organizations. This further supports my claim for classification of IV-D.

The above evidence definitely proves beyond any reasonable doubt that I am rightfully entitled to classification as an Ordained Minister, therefore in closing I hope that you will correct your error in this matter, therefore, I remain,

Respectfully,

GEORGE ROBERT GUTMAN

George Robert Gutman

[Endorsed]: Filed 6-12-43.

Thereafter the entire file was sent to the Appeal Board [10] through the State Director of Selective Service. A letter of transmittal was sent with the file.

(The letter of transmittal was here identified by the witness and same was admitted in evidence and marked U. S. Exhibit No. 7.)

(Testimony of Mrs. Pauline Hegberg.)

U. S. EXHIBIT NO. 7

Appeal Board

[Stamped]: Local Board No. 86, San Francisco County.—91 075 086. Dec. 21, 1942. 1444 Haight Street, San Francisco, California.

State Director of
Selective Service System,
Plaza Building,
Sacramento, California.

Dear Sir: Subject: George Robert Gutman. Order No. 11866

We are enclosing the entire file for the above named registrant who wishes to appeal his classification from 1-A to that of IV-D.

Yours very truly,
LOCAL BOARD NO. 86
GEORGE B. GILLIN
George B. Gillin, Chairman.

Encl.

[Endorsed]: Filed 6-17-43.

The State Director wrote the appeal Board to the effect that the defendant's name was not on the list of certified members of Jehovah's Witnesses. This letter of the Director was in turn transmitted to the local Board. It was dated February 3, 1943.

(The letter was here identified by the witness and same was admitted in evidence and marked U. S. Exhibit No. 8.)

(Testimony of Mrs. Pauline Hegberg.)

U. S. EXHIBIT NO. 8

[Cut]

State of California
Director of Selective Service
Plaza Building, Sacramento

In Replying Refer
to Subject Below:

February 1, 1943

Appeal Board No. 8
606-08 Mills Building
San Francisco, California

Subject: George Robert Gutman, #11866,
L. B. No. 86, 17-14

Gentlemen:

We acknowledge receipt of your letter of January 22nd, enclosing the file of the above named registrant and requesting information as to whether his name appears on the certified list of members of Jehovah's Witnesses.

Please be advised that the registrant's name is not listed in the official list.

Very truly yours,
K. H. LEITCH
K. H. Leitch
State Director of Selective Service

[Endorsed]: Filed 6-17-43.

(Testimony of Mrs. Pauline Hegberg.)

On February 10, 1943, the Board of Appeals classified the defendant as I-A. After the file was returned to the local Board I sent defendant a notice of the Appeal Board's action—on February 24, 1943. Thereafter defendant was sent a notice to report for induction on March 17, 1943.

(The notice of induction was here identified by the witness and same was admitted in evidence and marked U. S. Exhibit No. 9.)

U. S. EXHIBIT NO. 9

App. not Req.

[Pencil Note]: held up at request of Sacto.

Prepare in Duplicate

Local Board No. 86 91
San Francisco County 075
Mar 4 1943 086
1444 Haight Street
San Francisco, California
(Local Board Date Stamp With Code)

[Cut]

March 4, 1943
(Date of mailing)

ORDER TO REPORT FOR INDUCTION

The President of the United States,

To (First name) George (Middle name) Robert (Last name) Gutman

Order No. 11866

GREETING:

Having submitted yourself to a local board com-

(Testimony of Mrs. Pauline Hegberg.)

posed of your neighbors for the purpose of determining your availability for training and service in the armed forces of the United States, you are hereby notified that you have now been selected for training and service in the (Army, Navy, Marine Corps) Land or Naval

You will, therefore, report to the local board named above at (Place of reporting) Induction Station #1, 428 Market Street, S. F. Calif at (Hour of reporting) 7:30 a. m., on the 17th day of March, 1943

This local board will furnish transportation to an induction station of the service for which you have been selected. You will there be examined, and, if accepted for training and service, you will then be inducted ~~into the stated branch of the service.~~

Persons reporting to the induction station in some instances may be rejected for physical or other reasons. It is well to keep this in mind in arranging your affairs, to prevent any undue hardship if you are rejected at the induction station. If you are employed, you should advise your employer of this notice and of the possibility that you may not be accepted at the induction station. Your employer can then be prepared to replace you if you are accepted, or to continue your employment if you are rejected.

Willful failure to report promptly to this local board at the hour and on the day named in this notice is a violation of the Selective Training and

(Testimony of Mrs. Pauline Hegberg.)

Service Act of 1940, as amended, and subjects the violator to fine and imprisonment.

If you are so far removed from your own local board that reporting in compliance with this order will be a serious hardship and you desire to report to a local board in the area of which you are now located, go immediately to that local board and make written request for transfer of your delivery for induction, taking this order with you.

GEO. B. GILLIN

Member or clerk of the local board.

[Endorsed]: Filed 6-17-43.

Thereafter the Board received a notice to stay the induction and forward the file to State Headquarters, which was done. On March 16, 1943, a letter was written by the local Board to the State Headquarters transmitting the file for reference to National Headquarters.

(The letter of transmittal was here identified by the witness and same was admitted in evidence and marked U. S. Exhibit No. 10.)

(Testimony of Mrs. Pauline Hegberg.)

U. S. EXHIBIT NO. 10

[Written in ink]: March 16, 1943

Colonel K. H. Leitch,
State Director of
Selective Service System,
Plaza Building,
Sacramento, California.

Dear Sir:

Subject: George Robert Gutman, Order No. 11866

In accordance with telephone conversation had with your office on this date with reference to the Induction of the above named registrant, we are enclosing his file for your immediate attention. We have withheld all papers which are necessary for his induction on March 17, 1943.

Yours very truly,

LOCAL BOARD NO. 86.
GEORGE B. GILLIN,
George B. Gillin
Chairman.

Encl.

[Endorsed]: Filed 6-17-43.

Thereafter the Board received a letter from National Headquarters transmitted with a letter from State Headquarters, indicating the decision of National Headquarters.

(Testimony of Mrs. Pauline Hegberg.)

(The two letters were here identified by the witness and same were admitted in evidence and marked as one exhibit, namely, U. S. Exhibit No. 11.)

U. S. EXHIBIT NO. 11

National Headquarters
Selective Service System
21st Street and C Street, N. W.
Washington, D. C.
April 9, 1943

In Replying Address
The Director of Selective Service
and Refer to No.
3-4.9-220

State Director of Selective Service
Plaza Building
Sacramento, California

Subject: George Robert Gutman
Order No. 11866
Local Board No. 86
San Francisco County
San Francisco, California

Dear Colonel Leitch:

We acknowledge receipt of your letter of March 20, 1943, regarding the above-named registrant.

(Testimony of Mrs. Pauline Hegberg.)

No further action in this case is contemplated by this headquarters.

For The Director,
SIMON P. DUNKLE
Lt. Colonel, Infantry
Camp Operations Division

[Cut]

State of California
Director of Selective Service
Plaza Building, Sacramento
April 16, 1943

In Replying Refer
to Subject Below:

Selective Service Headquarters
Local Board No. 86
1444 Haight Street
San Francisco, California

Subject: George Robert Gutman, 9a-15
Order No. 11866

Gentlemen:

We return herewith the cover sheet of the above named registrant together with a copy of a letter from National Headquarters which is self-explanatory.

(Testimony of Mrs. Pauline Hegberg.)

This registrant may now be processed in the usual manner.

Very truly yours,

K. H. LEITCH

K. H. Leitch

State Director of Selective Service

Enclosures

[Endorsed]: Filed 6-17-43.

Thereafter on May 1, 1943 the defendant was sent a notice to report for induction on May 14, 1943.

(The notice to report for Induction was here identified [11] by the witness and same was admitted in evidence and marked U. S. Exhibit No. 12.)

(Testimony of Mrs. Pauline Hegberg.)

U. S. EXHIBIT NO. 12

App. not Req.

Prepare in Duplicate

Local Board No. 86 91
San Francisco County 075
May 1 1943 086
1444 Haight Street
San Francisco, California
(Local Board Date Stamp With Code)

[Cut]

May 1 1943
(Date of mailing)

ORDER TO REPORT FOR INDUCTION

The President of the United States,

To (First name) George (Middle name) Robert (Last name) Gutman

Order No. 11866

GREETING:

Having submitted yourself to a local board composed of your neighbors for the purpose of determining your availability for training and service in the armed forces of the United States, you are hereby notified that you have now been selected for training and service in the (Army, Navy, Marine Corps) Land or Naval

You will, therefore, report to the local board named above at (Place of reporting) Induction Station #1, 428 Market St., S. F. Calif. at (Hour of reporting) 8:00 A. m., on the 14 day of May, 1943

(Testimony of Mrs. Pauline Hegberg.)

This local board will furnish transportation to an induction station of the service for which you have been selected. You will there be examined, and, if accepted for training and service, you will then be inducted ~~into the stated branch of the service~~.

Persons reporting to the induction station in some instances may be rejected for physical or other reasons. It is well to keep this in mind in arranging your affairs, to prevent any undue hardship if you are rejected at the induction station. If you are employed, you should advise your employer of this notice and of the possibility that you may not be accepted at the induction station. Your employer can then be prepared to replace you if you are accepted, or to continue your employment if you are rejected.

Willful failure to report promptly to this local board at the hour and on the day named in this notice is a violation of the Selective Training and Service Act of 1940, as amended, and subjects the violator to fine and imprisonment.

If you are so far removed from your own local board that reporting in compliance with this order will be a serious hardship and you desire to report to a local board in the area of which you are now located, go immediately to that local board and

(Testimony of Mrs. Pauline Hegberg.)

make written request for transfer of your delivery for induction, taking this order with you.

GEO. B. GILLIN

Member or clerk of the local board.

[Endorsed]: Filed 6-17-43.

Defendant did not report for induction on said date, and he was thereafter sent a notice of delinquency.

(The notice of delinquency was here identified by the witness and same was admitted in evidence and marked U. S. Exhibit No. 13.)

U. S. EXHIBIT NO. 13

App. not Req.

NOTICE OF DELINQUENCY

[Cut]

Local Board No. 86 91

San Francisco County 075

May 15 1943 086

1444 Haight Street

San Francisco, Calif.

Local Board Date Stamp With Code)

May 15, 1943

(Date)

To	George	Robert	Gutman
	(First)	(Middle)	(Last)

Order No. 11866

Dear Sir:

According to information in possession of this

(Testimony of Mrs. Pauline Hegberg.)

local board, you have failed to perform the duty, or duties, imposed upon you under the selective service law as specified below.

☐ To present yourself, for and submit to, registration.

x x (Specify other) Failure to report to Induction Station as instructed,

You are therefore directed to report, by mail, telegraph, or in person, at your own expense, to this local board, on or before (Hour) 1:00 PM., on the 20th day of May, 1943.

Failure to report on or before the day and hour specified is an offense punishable by fine or imprisonment, or both.

GEO. B. GILLIN

Member or Clerk of the Local Board.

This form shall be made out in quadruplicate. The local board shall send the original to the suspected delinquent at his last-known address and one copy to the State Director of Selective Service. The date of mailing shall be noted on another copy, which shall be filed. The local board shall post a copy in a conspicuous place for public inspection, and, whenever practicable, shall give the information the widest possible publicity.

[Endorsed]: Filed 6-17-43.

(Testimony of Mrs. Pauline Hegberg.)

Thereafter and on May 20, 1943, the Board received a letter from defendant in response to the notice of delinquency.

(The letter was here identified by the witness and same was admitted in evidence and marked U. S. Exhibit No. 14.)

U. S. EXHIBIT NO. 14

George Robert Gutman
1892 Fell Street
San Francisco, Calif.
May 18, 1943

[Stamped]: Local Board No. 86 91
San Francisco County 075
May 20 1943 086

1444 Haight Street
San Francisco, Calif.

Local Board No. 86
1444 Haight Street
San Francisco, Calif.

Gentlemen:

I have received my Notice of Delinquency as on D.S.S. Form 281, and in compliance with the request made therein, I am using this method to answer. You have notified me that I am suspected of not reporting for induction into the United States Army as I was ordered to do by the local board.

I guess that there is really very little doubt in your

(Testimony of Mrs. Pauline Hegberg.)

minds or in mine as to whether or not I reported for induction. You know what I am and realize that being an Ordained Minister of an organized and recognized religious organization, I am in no-wise required to respond to any such order from a group of men (?) that seek to take the law into their own hands. You know as well as I that at the present time, my case is pending before National Headquarters for an appeal to the President. Of course realizing this you would naturally rush my Induction as fast as possible so as to get me in the Army before the President has a chance to act. Such action is, however, only typical of local board No. 86.

I have filed with local board #86 an abundance of evidence proving beyond all possible doubt that I am an Ordained Minister and have been recognized as such since August 1, 1939. Also filed with you were five affadavits from men who have known me for the past three years and more, showing that they do recognize me as a Minister and have for the past three and one half years. This evidence, aside from my scriptural ordination at Isaiah 61:1,2; Isaiah 43:10-12 and 2 Corinthians 9:16 was sufficient to warrent my classification as a Minister. Also submitted to you were copies of Opinions rendered by Brig. Gen. Lewis B. Hershey regarding the classification of JEHOVAH'S Witnesses. These Opinions you have entirely ignored in making your erroneously incorrect decision in my case. The latest of these

(Testimony of Mrs. Pauline Hegberg.)

Opinions states that the local board is obligated to investigate the standing of the person in question amoung others of JEHOVAH'S Witnesses. This is very true in the case of servants in the various companies of JEHOVAH'S Witnesses, such as Company Servant, Asst. Company Servant, Back-call Servant, Sound Servant (which I am) Advertising Servant (which I am(. You have failed utterly to make any effort at all to investigate my standing amoung others of the Organization. You haven't even lived up to your own law (which you claim to put so much faith in) much less the perfect and just law of JEHOVAH your God.

I hope that the above answers to your charges will suffice to help you to understand my course of action, why I have taken it and just how far I am willing to go in obeying the laws of imperfect and unjust man. Therefore I remain

Fighting for the NEW WORLD,
GEORGE ROBERT GUTMAN
George Robert Gutman
Order Number 11866

[Endorsed]: Filed 6-17-43.

Cross-Examination

By Mr. Shea:

The hearing of defendant before the Board was not less than five minutes long.

GEORGE B. GILLIN

a witness called on behalf of the United States, being duly sworn, testified as follows:

I am chairman of Selective Service Local Board 86, San Francisco, California. The other board members are Mr. Moscowitz and Mr. P. Paul Vlautin, Sr. We receive no compensation for our service on the Board. I participated in the classification of defendant. He was classified as I-A, unanimously. Defendant made several personal appearances before the Board. All members of the Board were present at the hearings.

Cross-Examination

By Mr. Shea:

I met defendant prior to considering his classification. He came up to the Board with another registrant, Mr. Fiedler, also a Jehovah's Witness. A discussion of Mr. Fiedler's classification was involved. I had a scuffle with defendant, as a result of which I filed a complaint against him in Municipal Court and he was convicted. Defendant came in several times and talked to [12] the Board and presented evidence to place in the file in reference to his claim for IV-D classification. We entertained him as long as he cared to be entertained. He was not forced out of the hearing room at any time. We examined defendant's purported certificate or ordination at the hearing. He was given the courtesy of the Board at all times, and when he wanted to leave we closed the file. We accepted all evidence he cared to present. We told him that

(Testimony of George B. Gillin.)
since he had no confidence in the Board he could appeal his case and have outside people handle the problem.

Redirect Examination

To elaborate further about the "scuffle". A Mr. Fiedler had come to the Board about his claim to being a minister and defendant had come with him. Since hearings are confidential, defendant was not admitted to the hearing but stayed in the outer room. I noticed that defendant was eavesdropping at the door. Mrs. Hegberg went out and tried to get him away from the door and she told me that she had asked him several times to get away from the door, but he refused. I then went out. I made a remark to a couple of shipyard workers who asked for their hearings because they had to go to work, that I was having a discussion with a gentleman who was trying to use the Bible to evade the draft. Defendant jumped up and said: "What is wrong with the Bible". I said: "There is nothing wrong with the Bible; I am a firm believer in it." So with that he came after me and I went after him. I am certainly not picking on a six-foot, 195 pound boy unless I am trying to protect myself.

MAURICE MOSKOWITZ

a witness called on behalf of the United States, being duly sworn, testified as follows: I was present at the defendant's hearing on December 21,

(Testimony of Maurice Moskowitz.)

1942. Defendant stated to Mr. Gillin: "I have something I want to place in my file and also to appeal my case." Mr. Gillin handed him the questionnaire, which he signed as his appeal. Defendant was exceptionally brief; had little to say. I do not think it lasted more than five minutes. No harsh words. [13]

P. PAUL VLAUTIN, SR.

a witness called on behalf of the United States, being duly sworn, testified as follows: I am a member of Draft Board 86 and was present on night of December 21, 1942, when defendant appeared befor the Board. I do not believe that Mr. Gillin said anything offensive to defendant. I participated in the classification of defendant as I-A. The decision was unanimous.

THOMAS E. O'BRIEN

a witness called on behalf of the United States, being duly sworn, testified as follows: I am a special agent for the Federal Bureau of Investigation. I know the defendant. I had a conversation with defendant on May 22, 1943 relative to an alleged Selective Service violation. He was not in custody. He stated that he had received an order to report for induction and that he had not reported. He also stated that he had received his I-A classification card; that he had appealed this classification;

(Testimony of Thomas E. O'Brien.)

that on the appeal the classification had been affirmed and that he had been notified of the action of the Appeal Board; that he then appealed to the President; that this appeal was denied. He said that he was not willing to go to a conscientious objectors' camp or to the army for combatant service or noncombatant service. He handed me a typed statement.

(The statement was here identified by the witness and same was admitted in evidence and marked U. S. Exhibit No. 15)

U. S. EXHIBIT NO. 15

TO WHOM IT MAY CONCERN

I, George Robert Gutman do hereby affirm that the statements made below are my own and that I am in entire agreement with them. I have made them of my own free will without any compulsion, and have affixed my signature to them each as being correct.

I was born at Bakersfield California on March 15, 1924. In 1939 I made my consecration to serve Jehovah and to act as a witness for him. Thereafter, on August 1, 1939, I became a Pioneer-Minister of Jehovah's Witnesses. I have been steadily engaged in this Ministerial work since, devoting at least 150 active hours in carrying the message of God's Kingdom by Christ Jesus, that is 150 hours each month. I have been Ordained by the Watchtower Bible and Tract Society, and have received from them a Letter of Ordination showing that

(Testimony of Thomas E. O'Brien.)

they, as a recognized cristian Organization, do consider me a Mininster. Of course I have my scriptural ordination as well, authorizing me to do this work as set forth at Isaiah 61:1,2; Isaiah 43:10-12; 1 Corinthians 9:16 and many others.

The reason I have taken the course of action that I have I have set out below to the best of my ability that all may know that my reasons are all based entirely on the Bible. Having devoted my life to the service of the Great God Almighty, I am required to do certain things by His written Law, bound together and called the Holy Scriptures. From this source of information we find that we are commanded to do the will of God as set forth in the following scriptures, Isaiah 61:1,2, "The Spirit of the Lord God is upon me; because the Lord hath annointed me to preach good tidings unto the meek; he hath sent me to bind up the broken-hearted, to proclaim liberty to the captives, and the opening of the prison to them that are bound;

"To proclaim the acceptable year of the Lord; and the day of vengeance of our God; to comfort all that mourn;"

Isaiah 43: 10-12, "Ye are my witnesses, saith the Lord, and my servant whom I have chosen. . . . . therefore ye are my witnesses, saith the Lord, (Jehovah) that I am God."

Ezekiel 3:16-21 and Ezekiel 33:1-9, bring out that if we have a knowledge of the Scriptures and keep it to ourselves and do not carry this knowledge to others that they might know and understand the

Truth of God's Word, then if they die in their iniquity, their blood is upon our shoulders, while if we do warn them and they continue on in their wicked course, then their blood is upon their own heads, and they shall suffer for it and no one else. Further emphasizing the great necessity of preaching to the people,

GEORGE ROBERT GUTMAN

2

The apostle Paul, at 1 Corinthians 9:16 states; "For though I preach the gospel, I have nothing to glory of: for necessity is laid upon me; yea, woe is unto me, if I preach not the gospel!" One might think that this was fine for Paul, but it doesn't apply to anyone today. On this Paul further states at 1 Corinthians 10:11, "Now all these things happened unto them for ensamples: and they are written for our admonition, upon whom the ends of the world are come."

I have already enlisted in the Army, not in the Army of the United States or any other earthly government, but in the Army of Jehovah God, and I have received my commission in that Army and therefore of course, I could not do anything that would result in treason to the Government that I am representing, The Theocracy. I have, of course, the scriptures to back me up in this stand, says 2 Timothy 2:3,4 "Thou therefore endure hardness, as a good soldier of Jesus Christ.

"No man that warreth entangleth himself with the affairs of this life; that he may please him who hath chosen him to be a soldier."

(Testimony of Thomas E. O'Brien.)

The Theocracy, which I am representing is not to be set up or run by any man or group of men, or human organization, but it will be directed by the hand of Jehovah through His King Christ Jesus. Jesus, at Matthew 6:10 instructed his faithful followers to pray for the establishment of that righteous government. At Hebrews the 11th chapter is recorded a list of some of the men who will rule as the earthly princes or governors of that Theocracy. That long hoped for government of righteousness is now here and those who have the priviledge of representing it are in this land today known as Jehovah's Witnesses, and truly they are witnesses to the name and majesty of the Great God Jehovah. As for the word "Theocracy" it does not appear in this form in the Bible, but is derived from the two words "theos" and "kratos" meaning God and dominion. Therefore the name Theocracy would mean God's Dominion, and who of us today, would not desire a government over which God's dominion ruled supreme.

The Scriptures show us very plainly that we should obey all of the laws of the Nation in which we are domociled as long as they do not conflict with God's Law, which of course will be obeyed in preference to the law of any earthly Nation, regardless of the results to the one thus acting. Acts 4:19 states, "But Peter and John answered and said unto them, Whether it be right in the sight of God to hearken unto you more than unto God, judge ye." Also Acts 5:29 "Then Peter and the other apostles

(Testimony of Thomas E. O'Brien.)

answered and said, We ought to obey God rather than men".

GEORGE ROBERT GUTMAN

3

The question may be asked, "But should this stand be taken if heavy punishment is threatened or imposed?" The answer from the Bible is a very strong Yes. This proven by many scriptures cited below showing that it is much better to have the disfavor of men and even to endure their punishment that they may heap upon you for doing God's will than to give in to the whims of selfish men and suffer eternal destruction at the hand of God. The scriptures supporting this are as follows Matthew 5:10-12; 10:17-19, 21-23, 28, 39; 16:25, 26; 23:33, 34; 24:9, 13; Mark 8:35; 13:9, 13; Luke 12:4, 5; John 15:18-21, 25; 17:14; 2 Corinthians 12:10; 4:8, 9.

I have tried in the preceding pages to present clearly the reasons for my actions rgarding the Selective Service Regulations, and I hope that you may be able to see that it is not a case of what I want to do, but because of the oaths that I have taken before God, It is a case of what I have to do, with no alternative whatsoever.

GEORGE ROBERT GUTMAN

[Endorsed]: Filed 6-17-43.

I think that defendant said he was not a conscientious objector. I don't know whether this defendant has any other occupation except that I have

(Testimony of Thomas E. O'Brien.)

seen him riding around town on two or three occasions driving a motorcycle on which is stated some occupation. I don't know whether he is working or not. It was a delivery motorcycle. I have seen him riding around within the last three months.

Here the United States Rested.

EXCEPTION NO. 1

Thereupon said defendant, through his attorney, William Shea, moved the Court for a directed verdict of not guilty on the grounds that the evidence was insufficient as a matter of law to sustain a conviction, which motion being denied, the [14] defendant then and there duly entered an exception to the ruling of the Court.

VERNE G. REUSCH

a witness called on behalf of defendant, being duly sworn, testified as follows:

I am one of Jehovah's Witnesses recognized by the Watchtower Bible and Tract Society. I have been such for twelve years. I am company servant for the San Francisco Company. I have known the defendant about a year. He was appointed by the Society to the San Francisco area. He is a "special pioneer", which is the ultimate group in the Society. His work would consist of arranging and conducting Bible classes, generally counseling, aiding and advising other company publishers and

(Testimony of Verne G. Reusch.)
the company publisher looks to the "special pioneer" for advice in scriptural matters. We hold services comparable to what are known as religious services in other religions, which consist in delivering Bible Lectures, etc., in which a man qualified for that job would act as chairman. I have seen defendant act as chairman at such services. There are only a few "special pioneers" in relation to the bulk of membership, made up of company publishers.

Cross-Examination

I have no reason to doubt that defendant became a minister at the age of 15 years. Every member of Jehovah's Witnesses is not a minister. I think we had one boy, 12 years old, who was a minister. He had been raised in the knowledge of the truth and had put in 150 hours in the proclamation of the kingdom message. The defendant is a minister recognized by the Society as *will* as by reason of direct appointment. And regardless of whether or not he was a pioneer, if engaged in the same type of work, he would still be a minister.

I consider that Board 86 acted unfairly in classifying defendant and that the Board of Appeals also acted unfairly in de- [15] nying his appeal. If the National Director's Office reviewed the case, it acted unfairly in not giving the proper classification.

C. D. EASTER

a witness called on behalf of defendant, being duly sworn, testified as follows:

I have been a member of Jehovah's Witnesses since 1918 I am assistant company servant of the Golden Gate company. I am a pioneer; outside of my pioneer work, I work about two days a week. The rest of the time I devote to the Society. I have known defendant for about 12 months; he operates through the Golden Gate company. He is a special pioneer.

Cross-Examination

There are about 75 members in the Golden Gate company. The youngest member is about 7 years old. He is not recognized by the Society as a minister. I would recognize him as a minister if he desired to preach. Samuel was 7 when he took care of the temple; Jeremiah was only 12 when he was instructed to preach the destruction of Jerusalem; Jesus preached in the temple at 12.

I believe that defendant might well have considered it treason against Almighty God, for him to go into the army. Having consecrated himself to the "kingdom" if he violates that consecration he would be guilty of treason against God. For Jehovah's Witnesses to go into the army, even as chaplains, would not be fulfilling their theocratic obligations to the Most High God.

GEORGE ROBERT GUTMAN

the defendant, was then called as a witness in his own behalf and being duly sworn, testified as follows:

I am the defendant. I am 19 years old. My mother is a Jehovah's Witness; has been for about 25 years. My father is dead; he was also a Jehovah's Witness. I have been engaged in the work of the Society for about 4 years, in full time service. The minimum hours for a general pioneer is 150 hours or approximate 5 hours [16] a day to presenting and preaching the gospel to the people. I have been a special pioneer since May 1, 1942.

(Here the witness identified a purported Certificate of Ordination and same was admitted in evidence and marked Defendant's Exhibit B)

(Testimony of George Robert Gutman.)

DEFENDANT'S EXHIBIT B

Offices:	Phone
Administration	Triangle 5-1474
124 Columbia Heights	Cable
Publishing	Watchtower
117 Adams Street	Brooklyn

Watchtower
(imprint)
Bible and Tract Society
Incorporated
'This Kingdom Gospel Must Be Preached'
Publishing . 117 Adams Street . Brooklyn, N. Y.

[Stamped]:

Local Board No. 86	91
San Francisco County	075
Dec. 21 1942	086

1444 Haight Street
San Francisco, California

Sept. 8, 1942

To Whom It May Concern:

This is to certify that George Robert Gutman, one of Jehovah's witnesses, has been associated with the Watchtower Bible and Tract Society, Inc., according to our records, since July 1939.

He was baptized in July 1939, and was appointed direct representative of this organization to perform missionary and evangelistic service in organizing and establishing churches and generally preaching the Gospel of the Kingdom of God in definitely assigned territory on August 8, 1939.

(Testimony of George Robert Gutman.)

Mr. Gutman's entire time is devoted to missionary work. He has declared himself to be a follower of Christ Jesus and wholly consecrated to do the will of Almighty God. He has taken a course of study in the Bible and Bible helps prescribed by this Society and has shown himself apt to preach and teach "this Gospel of the Kingdom".—Matthew 24:14.

He has the Scriptural ordination to preach "this Gospel of the Kingdom". (Isaiah 61:1, 2; Isaiah 52:7) He is, therefore, declared by this Society a duly ordained minister of the Gospel and is authorized to represent this Society and preach "this Gospel of the Kingdom", proclaiming the name of Jehovah God and Christ Jesus, His King.

WATCHTOWER B. & T. SOCIETY, INC.
T. J. SULLIVAN
Superintendent of Evangelists

Subscribed and sworn to before me this 8th day of Sept. 1942.

(Seal) WILLIAM K. JACKSON
Notary Public Kings County Kings Co. Clks. No. 73, Reg. 3005 Commission expires March 30, 1943
(Cut)

Jehovah's Kingdom Message Available in Books, Magazines and Phonograph Records

[Endorsed]: Filed 6-17-43.

(Testimony of George Robert Gutman.)

My first assignment to work for the Society was in August, 1939. I was sent to Paso Robles, California, where I worked for about a month. My work there was mainly in organizing Bible studies. I had no secular work. From there I was assigned to San Luis Obispo, where I remained about a month and from there I was assigned to Madera. All assignments come from the head office of the Society in Brooklyn, New York. From Madera I was assigned to Kettleman City, California. I also worked for the Society in Utah, Wyoming, Kansas and in Indianapolis, St. Louis and Detroit.

My work as a special pioneer consists of my devoting primarily at least 175 hours to preaching the gospel, each month.

(Here the witness identified certain affidavits and same were admitted in evidence and marked Defendant's Exhibit A)

(Testimony of George Robert Gutman.)

DEFENDANT'S EXHIBIT A

1892 Fell Street
(Copy) San Francisco, Calif.
February 27, 1943

[Stamped]: Local Board No. 86 91
San Francisco County 075
Mar 1 1943 086

1444 Haight Stret
San Francisco, California

State Director of Selective Service
Plaza Building,
Sacramento, California

Dear Sir:

I have just been notified by my local board that my classification of I-A has been approved by the appeal board.

The purpose of this letter is to repuest you to take an appeal in my behalf as is required by Section 628.1 of the Selective Service Regulations allowing appeals when "necessary to avoid an injustice". I am asking you to take an appeal in my behalf in view of the fact that I have been a Pioneer-Minister of Jehovah's Witnesses since August 8, 1939, proof of which I have submitted to local and appeal boards and this they have entirely ignored and have classified me with the entirely wrong classification.

I am enclosing with this letter a copy of the letter that I gave to the local board requesting an appeal be taken. I ask you to read this and take

(Testimony of George Robert Gutman.)

Defendant's Exhibit A—(Continued).

the only proper action, that of taking an appeal to National Headquarters.

I would also like to request at this time that you instruct the local board to withhold all action on my case pending review by the State Director.

I would greatly appreciate hearing from you immediately on this matter.

Respectfully,

GEORGE ROBERT GUTMAN
George Robert Gutman
Order No. 11866

[Endorsed]: Filed 6-17-43.

(Testimony of George Robert Gutman.)

Defendant's Exhibit A—(Continued).

[Stamped]: Local Board No. 86 91
San Francisco County 075
Mar 1 1943 086
1444 Haight Street
San Francisco, California

1892 Fell Street
San Francisco, Calif.
February 27, 1943

Local Board No. 86
1444 Haight Street
San Francisco, Calif.

Gentlemen:

I have received my Notice of Classification as on DSS Form 57. As the error you made in my original classification was not rectified by the appeal board, I find it necessary to take an appeal to National Headquarters.

Enclosed herewith is a true duplicate copy of the letter that I have sent to the State Director in Sacramento requesting an appeal in my behalf.

I would like to request you, as I have the State Director to withhold all action on my case pending review by the State Director.

Thanking you for your consideration in this matter, I remain

Respectfully,

GEORGE R. GUTMAN
George Robert Gutman
Order No. 11866

(Testimony of George Robert Gutman.)

Defendant's Exhibit A—(Continued).

PS. I am also enclosing at this time various affidavits from other Ministers of Jehovah's Witnesses at the various places I have been assigned to Ministerial Duties.

Burbank, Calif.
P. O. Box 172

[Stamped]: Local Board No. 86 91
San Francisco County 075
Mar 1 1943 086
1444 Haight Street
San Francisco, California

State of California
County of Los Angeles—ss.

I, Ernest L. Wasson, special representative of the Witchtower Bible and Tract Society, assigned to the Burbank Company of Jehovah's witnesses, do hereby swear and affirm:

That I have known George Robert Gutman for the past three years, and know him to be a regularly Ordained Minister of Jehovah's witnesses:

That I have worked with Mr. Gutman in preaching the Gospel of God's Kingdom, and know that he faithfully performed all his obligations as a Minister.

Witness my hand this 10th day of Feb. 1943.

ERNEST L. WASSON
Pioneer Company Servant of Burbank Company of Jehovah's witnesses.

(Testimony of George Robert Gutman.)

Defendant's Exhibit A—(Continued).

Subscribed and sworn to before me this 10th day of Feb. 1943

[Seal] SALLY H. SIMPSON
Notary Public

My Commission Expires June 2, 1946.

[Stamped]: Local Board No. 86 91
San Francisco County 075
Mar 1 1943 086
1444 Haight Street
San Francisco, California

TO WHOM IT MAY CONCERN

I, Emil Jensen, have known George Robert Gutman for the past three years and over and have had many dealings with him as a Minister of the Gospel. I first became acquainted with Mr. Gutman when he was sent by Jehovah's Witnesses to the Pasa Robles Company of Jehovah's Witnesses to perform Ministerial Duties in conjunction with the Pasa Robles Company of Jehovah's Witnesses. While working with our Church here Mr. Gutman performed his obligations as a Minister. He was engaged full time in preaching the Gospel, conducting Bible Studies among the people in this vicinity, and otherwise living up to his covenant obligations. I also had chance to show that while he was working with the Armona Calif., Company he had the responsibilities of two servants in that Company.

(Testimony of George Robert Gutman.)

Defendant's Exhibit A—(Continued).

I hereby subscribe to the above statements as being true without any reservation.

EMIL JENSEN
Emil Jensen
Company Servant of Pasa Robles Company of Jehovah's Witnesses.

Subscribed and Sworn to before me this 9th day of Feb., 1943.

[Seal] DAISY B. CLIFFORD,
Notary Public in and for the County of San Luis Obispo, State of California.

[Stamped]: Local Board No. 86 91
San Francisco County 075
Mar 1 1943 086
1444 Haight Street
San Francisco, California

TO WHOM IT MAY CONCERN

I, John Pendrak, do know George Robert Gutman. I have known Mr. Gutman for the past two years and over and do know him to be an Ordained Minister of Jehovah's Witnesses. I first became acquainted with Mr. Gutman when he was sent by the Watchtower Bible and Tract Society or Jehovah's Witnesses to work with the Park City, Utah, Company of Jehovah's Witnesses in the performance of his Ministerial duties. Mr. Gutman who at that time was working with his mother was in charge of Wasatch County and had much to do

(Testimony of George Robert Gutman.)

Defendant's Exhibit A—(Continued).

with helping to build up the Church there. He also performed Ministerial duties in and around Park City, there working in conjunction with the Company of which I am and was the Company Servant. While I have known Mr. Gutman he has always carried out his obligations as a Minister.

I do subscribe to the above statements as being the truth without exception.

JOHN PENDRAK

Company Servant of Park City Company of Jehovah's Witnesses.

Subscribed and sworn to before me this 9th day of February A. D. 1943.

[Seal] JEROME PAXTON

At Park City, Utah Notary Public

My Commission Expires March 4, 1944.

[Stamped]: Local Board No. 86 91
San Francisco County 075
Mar 1 1943 086
1444 Haight Street
San Francisco, California

TO WHOM IT MAY CONCERN

I, Cyril C. Northum, have known George Robert Gutman two years now, and I know him to be a full time Minister of the Gospel. I first became acquainted with Mr. Gutman when he was sent by

(Testimony of George Robert Gutman.)

Defendant's Exhibit A—(Continued).

the Watchtower Bible and Tract Society to perform Ministerial services in conjunction with the Armona, Calif., Company of Jehovah's Witnesses. He is a special representative of Jehovah's Witnesses serving with such Christian Organization as an Ordained Minister. While Mr. Gutman was in the Armona Company, he served as Stockeeper and Territory Servant in addition to his regular work he had as Minister, such as conducting Bible studies with the people as well as conducting Bible Meetings in the Kingdom Hall.

I do hereby swear that the above statements are the whole truth and that without any exceptions.

CYRIL C. NORTHUM
Cyril C. Northum
Company Servant of the Armona Company of J. W.

Subscribed and sworn to before me this 8th day of February 1943.

[Seal] F. R. HIGHT
Notary Public

[Stamped]: Local Board No. 86 91
San Francisco County 075
Mar 1 1943 086
1444 Haight Street
San Francisco, California

State of California,
County of Fresno—ss.

David Davidian, being first duly sworn, deposes and says:

(Testimony of George Robert Gutman.)

Defendant's Exhibit A—(Continued).

That he is now, and for more than thirty-three years has been, a resident of the City of Fresno, County of Fresno, California. That during the past thirty-three years he has been an active minister and worker as one of Jehovah's witnesses, and has had opportunity to know and come in contact with many other witnesses in the San Joaquin Valley. That he has served many of Jehovah's witnesses by giving Bible lectures and by such service has been acquainted with them. Also has met and knows many of them through association in conventions held in the State of California and also local conventions in San Joaquin Valley. That affiant has known for many years Mrs. Gutman, and knows that for more than twenty years she has been a minister of the gospel and actively engaged in preaching as one of Jehovah's witnesses. That this affiant has met her many times in conventions at Los Angeles, and other assemblies held at Fresno and Bakersfield. That affiant also knows George Robert Gutman, son of said Mrs. Gutman, and while affiant has not been associated regularly with the group where said George regularly met with Jehovah's witnesses, affiant has met him in Fresno, several times, also at assemblies held in San Joaquin Valley, and knows that said George Robert Gutman was always an active minister of the gospel. That affiant's daughter, Beulah Davidian, also a minister of the gospel, served at Hanford, California during the year 1942, and through her this

(Testimony of George Robert Gutman.)

Defendant's Exhibit A—(Continued).

affiant was informed many times that said George Robert Gutman was one of the active ministers at Armona, California.

That during the time said George Robert Gutman was serving as a minister for the congregation of Jehovah's witnesses at Armona, California, he made some trps to Fresno in connection with matters connected with literature. That thereafter, this affiant was informed that said George Robert Gutman had become a pioneer, giving full time to that service of preaching the Gospel. That when he became a pioneer, affiant with his mother were assigned to Sanger, California, and then re-assigned to San Francisco, where he is now performing his duties as minister of the Gospel.

That said George Robert Gutman is known by Jehovah's Witnesses to be a young man of good moral character, good student, and a good minister of the gospel, and fully capable of performing such work.

That this affiant now is in charge of the congregational Bible Study, 1033 Fulton St. Fresno, and is also Advertising servant of said congregation.

DAVID DAVIDIAN

Subscribed and sworn to before me this 8th day of February, 1943.

[Seal] JULIUS HANSEN

Notary Public, in and for said County and State.

[Endorsed]: Filed 6-17-43.

(Testimony of George Robert Gutman.)

In the past three months, I have devoted a total of 13 days to secular work in order to secure funds to fix our car and about two years ago, I worked at secular employment for some two months, but during all this time, I continued to perform my work for the society.

I claimed exemption as a minister from the outset. I filed papers in support of my claim, and when I received a I-A classification I demanded a hearing by the Board. The hearing was set for about December 21, 1942 and I went before the Board. The hearing did not last more than five minutes. Mr. Gillin made a statement to the effect that I had asked for a hearing and desired to know what it was for. I told him I had received an incorrect classification of I-A; I had made application for IV-D and had evidence I desired to present and would like to discuss with him on my classification as IV-D. He asked me if I wanted to take an appeal. **[17]**

I stated that I would like to discuss the matter with him further before seeing if an appeal were necessary, at which time he again asked if I wanted to appeal, and I said, "Yes, I do". And he shoved the questionnaire over and said: "Sign this, then" and he left. The evidence I had in letter form and I wanted to read it to Mr. Gillin; that evidence was not considered by him at any time during my hearing. As I left, I handed it to him and told him to put it in the file. This hearing was after my prior encounter with Mr. Gillin in connection

(Testimony of George Robert Gutman.)

with the Fiedler case. In that matter, I had gone with Fiedler to the same Board, at his request, to help him carry a record and phonograph. We waited at the Board for quite a while and then I went to make a phone call. When I came back Fiedler had gone in for his hearing before the Board.

(Here the Court adjourned until 9 o'clock a. m. Friday, June 18, 1943, and thereafter, and at said time the following proceedings were had)

GEORGE ROBERT GUTMAN

the defendant, recalled to the stand.

Direct Examination (Resumed)

Mr. Gillin came out of the hearing room in which Fielder was and as he opened the door I heard him say: "Young man, if you get that attitude you are going down the stairs damn' fast." He was standing with his hand on Fielder's shoulder. Gillin came on out into the waiting room and said: "Some guy in there pulled the Bible on me, trying to evade the draft". I asked him what was wrong with the Bible. He turned on me and asked if I was with the *buy* inside and I said that I was. He then told me to get the hell out of there. I started to get up and he grabbed me by the sleeve and tore if off. He called the police and had me arrested for disturbing the peace. He signed the

(Testimony of George Robert Gutman.)

complaint against me. All of this took place before I came up for classification before this same Board, with Mr. Gillin as chairman. [18]

I had exactly one hearing before the Board; that was December 21. The Board fixed the date of this hearing and mailed me a card. When I went to the hearing I was asked nothing about my work; I was asked one question as to whether I wanted to appeal. I was asked nothing concerning my relationship to other Jehovah's Witnesses, nor whether my functions corresponded to those of ministers in other religious groups. Mr. Gillin's attitude was very nice, but very abrupt, asking only the one question as to whether I wanted to appeal.

The Court: What do you mean by a special pioneer?

A. A special pioneer has a higher minimum of hours than a general pioneer. You must have been a general pioneer for at least one year.

My name was not on the list of certified ministers of Jehovah's Witnesses because at the time the original list was compiled I was not old enough to be subject to the draft. The Watchtower Bible and Tract Society furnished me an affidavit showing the reason why I was not on the list.

(Here the affidavit was identified by the witness and was admitted in evidence and marked Defendant's Exhibit C)

(Testimony of George Robert Gutman.)

DEFENDANT'S EXHIBIT C

Offices:	Phone
Administration	Triangle 5-1474
124 Columbia Heights	Cable
Publishing	Watchtower
117 Adams Street	Brooklyn

WATCHTOWER
Bible and Tract Society
Incorporated

'This Kingdom Gospel Must Be Preached'
Publishing - 117 Adams Street - Brooklyn, N. Y.
LSA June 14, 1943

To Whom It May Concern:

This is to certify that George Robert Gutman is and has been a pioneer minister of this Society since August 8, 1939, having been associated with this Society all his life, his mother also having been a pioneer minister since Mr. Gutman was two years old.

In June 1941 there was filed with the Selective Service System a list of pioneer ministers who were at that time subject to draft requirements. The name of Mr. Gutman was not included in said list because at that time he was not of registration age, and subject to draft requirements. He was at such time, June 1941, a pioneer minister in good standing with this Society, fully meeting the requirements of said ministers.

As soon as he registered, his name was submitted

(Testimony of George Robert Gutman.)

to National Headquarters of Selective Service System for addition to the certified list, however, before action could be taken in this respect, National Headquarters amended its policy with respect to adding names to the list, as is clearly set forth in Opinion No. 14 (Amended) November 2, 1942, paragraph 3.

Mr. Gutman is at present serving as a pioneer minister of Jehovah's witnesses and has been continuously so serving, as above stated, since August 8, 1939.

WATCHTOWER B. & T. SOCIETY, INC.
T. J. SULLIVAN
Superintendent of Evangelists

[Kings County Seal]

Subscribed and sworn to before me this 14th day of June 1943:

[Seal] WILLIAM K. JACKSON

Notary Public Kings County Kings Co. Clk's No. 119 Reg. No. 62-J-5. Commission Expires March 30, 1945

Jehovah's Kingdom Message Available in Books, Magazines and Phonograph Records

(Testimony of George Robert Gutman.)

No. 5300

State of New York,
County of Kings—ss.

I, Francis J. Sinnott, Clerk of the County of Kings, and also Clerk of the Supreme Court for the said County, the same being a Court of Record, having a seal, Do Hereby Certify, That William K. Jackson whose name is subscribed to the deposition or certificate of the proof or acknowledgments of the annexed instrument, and thereon written, was, at the time of taking such, deposition, or proof and acknowledgment, a Notary Public in and for such County, duly commissioned and sworn, and authorized by the laws of said State, to take depositions and to administer oaths to be used in any Court of said State and for general purposes; and also to take acknowledgments and proofs of deeds, of conveyances for land, tenements or hereditaments in said State of New York. And further, that I am were acquainted with the handwriting of such Notary Public, or have compared the signature of such officer with that deposited in my office by him, and verily believe that the signature to said deposition or certificate of proof or acknowledgment is genuine.

In Witness Whereof, I have hereunto set my hand and affixed the seal of the said Court and County this 15 day of June 1943.

FRANCIS J. SINNOTT
Clerk

[Kings County Seal]

[Endorsed]: Filed 6-18-43.

(Testimony of George Robert Gutman.)

I refused to report for induction because I considered the action of the Board entirely arbitrary in classifying me. I did not feel that I had received a fair classification, and myself being a minister, I was in no wise required to report for induction.

Cross-Examination

I think the Board acted unfairly because I have a letter of ordination, which is as much or more as ministers of the Catholic, Protestant and Jewish faith have, proving that I am a minister. The Watchtower Society issues ordination letters only to full time ministers.

The appeal board has never seen me. I claim it gave me a [19] wrong classification. I did not claim the Board was prejudiced; just a wrong classification. I do not consider National Headquarters of Selective Service prejudiced against me, because National Headquarters gave the Board rules to determine my classification, which, if they had been lived up to, would not have resulted in the error of classification.

National Headquarters refused to interfere. I guess they decided that the Board and the Appeal Board acted fairly; but National Headquarters was wrong because they gave me the wrong classification. The National Director had no evidence to show whether Local Board had followed out instructions to determine my standing among Jehovah's Witnesses. They all classified me improperly; I would say they are prejudiced.

(Testimony of George Robert Gutman.)

One month after I was baptized in the Society, I became a pioneer, but I have been a Jehovah's Witness all my life. I have studied since I was old enough to study. I became a minister in 1939 at the age of fifteen. Between 1939 and the present time I have worked for the Gastart Studios in Hollywood. I worked for them for a period of two months. It was about two years ago. I don't remember the exact date. Then I recently worked for a period of 12 or 13 days for the Sterling Engraving Company, driving a delivery motor.

The society does not pay me; it gives me certain expense money, anywhere from two dollars a month to twenty-five dollars a month. I get contributions from those interested in the work.

I believe that it would be treason to theocracy to enter the army, because I have made a covenant with my God, that I have enlisted in the army of Christ. Being a soldier of Christ—if one is a soldier of the United States, if he joins the army of Britain, although an ally, he is considered a deserter and will be prosecuted. As a soldier in the army of Christ, I have obligations to fulfill. If I were to give up those and take up arms [20] in the army of the United States, I could not fulfill those obligations that I have taken before the Great God Almighty.

I am not a conscientious objector. I am engaged in a war right now, between God Almighty and the Adversary, Satan, the Devil. The scripture shows it is one of the most decisive wars on the face of this earth. I am not willing to go into the Army

(Testimony of George Robert Gutman.)

of the United States. I am not willing to drive an ambulance in the Army of the United States. I am unwilling to go into a non-combatant corps and help the sick in the army.

MRS. PAULINE HEGBERG

a witness called on behalf of defendant, previously sworn, testified as follows:

Defendant brought in the correspondence and it was put in the file. Nothing in the file transmitted to the Appeal Board showed the altercation between Mr. Gillin and defendant.

(Here is a copy of Opinion 14 of the Director of Selective Service was admitted in evidence and marked Defendant's Exhibit D.)

DEFENDANT'S EXHIBIT D
VOL. III OPINION NO. 14 (AMENDED)

NATIONAL HEADQUARTERS
SELECTIVE SERVICE SYSTEM

Subject: Ministerial Status of Jehovah's Witnesses

Facts:

Jehovah's Witnesses claim exemption from training and service and classification in Class IV-D as duly ordained ministers of religion under section 5 (d), Selective Training and Service Act of 1940, as amended, and section 622.44, Selective Service

(Testimony of Mrs. Pauline Hegberg.)

Regulations, Second Edition, which read as follows:

Section 5 (d):

"Regular or duly ordained ministers of religion, and students who are preparing for the ministry in theological or divinity schools recognized as such for more than one year prior to the date of enactment of this Act, shall be exempt from training and service (but not from registration) under this Act."

Section 622.44:

"Class IV-D: Minister of religion or divinity student. (a) In Class IV-D shall be placed any registrant who is a regular or duly ordained minister of religion or who is a student preparing for the ministry in a theological or divinity school which has been recognized as such for more than 1 year prior to the date of enactment of the Selective Training and Service Act (September 16, 1940).

"(b) A 'regular minister of religion' is a man who customarily preaches and teaches the principles of religion of a recognized church, religious sect, or religious organization of which he is a member, without having been formally ordained as a minister of religion; and who is recognized by such church, sect, or organization as a minister.

"(c) A 'duly ordained minister of religion' is a man who has been ordained in accordance with the ceremonial ritual or discipline of a recognized church, religious sect, or religious organization, to

(Testimony of Mrs. Pauline Hegberg.)

teach and preach its doctrines and to administer its rites and ceremonies in public worship; and who customarily performs those duties."

Question.—May Jehovah's Witnesses be placed in Class IV-D as regular or duly ordained ministers of religion exempt from training and service?

Answer:

1. The Watchtower Bible and Tract Society, Inc., is incorporated under the laws of the State of New York for charitable, religious, and scientific purposes. The unincorporated body of persons known as Jehovah's Witnesses hold in common certain religious tenets and beliefs and recognize as their terrestrial governing organization the Watchtower Bible and Tract Society, Inc. By their adherence to the organization of this religious corporation, the unincorporated body of Jehovah's Witnesses are considered to constitute a recognized religious sect.

2. The unusual character of organization of Jehovah's Witnesses renders comparisons with recognized churches and religious organizations difficult. Certain members of Jehovah's Witnesses, by reason of the time which they devote, the dedication of their lives which they have made, the attitude of other Jehovah's Witnesses toward them, and the record kept of them and their work, are in a position where they may be recognized as having a standing in relation to the organization and the other members of Jehovah's Witnesses similar to

(Testimony of Mrs. Pauline Hegberg.)

that occupied by regular or duly ordained ministers of other religions.

3. Members of the Bethel Family are those members of Jehovah's Witnesses who devote their full time and effort to the manufacture and production of books, pamphlets, and supplies for the religious benefit of Jehovah's Witnesses, the purpose of which is to present the beliefs of Jehovah's Witnesses and to convert others. For their religious services, the members of this group receive their subsistence and lodging and in addition a very modest monthly allowance. This group of individuals consist of the office and factory workers at 117 Adams Street, Brooklyn, New York, and workers in the executive offices at 124 Columbia Heights, Brooklyn, New York, and at the Farms. Pioneers of Jehovah's Witnesses are those members of Jehovah's Witnesses who devote all or substantially all of their time to the work of teaching the tenets of their religion and in the converting of others to their belief. A certified official list of members of the Bethel Family and pioneers is being transmitted to the State Directors of Selective Service by National Headquarters of the Selective Service System simultaneously with the release of this amended Opinion. The members of the Bethel Family and pioneers whose names appear upon such certified official list come within the purview of section 5 (d) of the Selective Training and Service Act of 1940, as amended, and they may be classified in Class IV-D. The status of members of the

(Testimony of Mrs. Pauline Hegberg.)

Bethel Family and pioneers whose names do not appear upon such certified official list shall be determined under the provisions of paragraph 5 of this opinion.

4. The original paragraph 4 has been consolidated with paragraph 3 of this amended Opinion.

5. The members of Jehovah's Witnesses, known by the various names of members of the Bethel Family, pioneers, regional servants, zone servants, company servants, sound servants, advertising servants, and back-call servants, devote their time and efforts in varying degrees to the dissemination of the tenets and beliefs of Jehovah's Witnesses. The deference paid to these individuals by other members of Jehovah's Witnesses also varies in a great degree. It is impossible to make a general determination with respect to these persons as to their relationship to Jehovah's Witnesses. Whether or not they stand in the same relationship as regular or duly ordained ministers in other religions must be determined in each individual case by the local board, based upon whether or not they devote their lives in the furtherance of the beliefs of Jehovah's Witnesses, whether or not they perform functions which are normally performed by regular or duly ordained ministers of other religions, and, finally, whether or not they are regarded by other Jehovah's Witnesses in the same manner in which regular or duly ordained ministers of other religions are ordinarily regarded.

6. In the case of Jehovah's Witnesses, as in

(Testimony of Mrs. Pauline Hegberg.)

the case of all other registrants who claim exemption as regular or duly ordained ministers, the local board shall place in the registrant's file a record of all facts entering into its determination for the reason that it is legally necessary that the record show the basis of the local board's decision.

LEWIS B. HERSHEY,
Director

[Endorsed]: Filed 6-18-43.

Redirect Examination

The entire file of defendant went to National Headquarters, and the entire file went to the Appeal Board.

Whereupon the defendant rested his case.

DEFENDANT'S EXHIBIT E

SELECTIVE SERVICE REGULATION
(2nd edition)
PART 625—APPEARANCE BEFORE LOCAL BOARD
(18,625)

Sec.
625.1 Opportunity to appear in person.
625.2 Appearance before local board.
625.3 Induction stayed.

(18,625.01)

625.1 Opportunity to appear in person. (a) Every registrant, after his classification is determined by the local board (except a classification which is itself determined upon an appearance before the local board under the provisions of this part), shall have an opportunity to appear in person before the member or members of the local board designated for the purpose if he files a written request therefor within 10 days after the local board has mailed a Notice of Classification (Form 57) to him. Such 10-day period may not be extended, except when the local board finds that the registrant was unable to file such request within such period because of circumstances over which he had no control.

(b) No person other than the registrant may request an opportunity to appear in person before the local board.

(c) If the written request of the registrant to appear in person is filed with the local board within the 10-day period or if it is filed after such 10-day period and the local board finds that the registrant was unable to file such request within such period because of circumstances over which he had no control, the local board shall enter upon the Classification Record (Form 100) the date on which the request was received and the date and time fixed for the registrant to appear and shall promptly mail to the registrant a notice of the time and place fixed for such appearance.

(d) If such a written request of a registrant for an opportunity to appear in person is received after the 10-day period following the mailing of a Notice of Classification (Form 57) to the registrant, the local board, unless it specifically finds that the registrant was unable to file such a request within such period because of circumstances over which he had no control, should advise the registrant, by letter, that the time on which he is permitted to file such a request has expired, and a copy of such letter should be placed in the registrant's file. Under such circumstances, no other record of the disposition of the registrant's request need be made.

(18,625.02)

625.2 Appearance before local board. (a) At the time and place fixed by the local board, the registrant may appear in person before the member or members of the local board designated for the purpose. The fact that he does appear shall be entered in the proper place on the Classification Record (Form 100). If the registrant does not speak English adequately, he may appear with a person to act as interpreter for him. No registrant may be represented before the local board by an attorney.

(b) At any such appearance, the registrant may discuss his classification, may point out the class or classes in which he thinks he should have been placed, and may direct attention to any information in his file which he believes the local board has overlooked or to which he believes it has not given sufficient weight. The registrant may present such further information as he believes will assist the local board in determining his proper classification. Such information shall be in writing or, if oral, shall be summarized in writing and, in either event, shall be placed in the registrant's file. The information furnished should be as concise as possible under the circumstances. The member or members of the local board before whom the registrant appears may impose such limitations upon the time which the registrant may have for his appearance as they deem necessary.

(c) After the registrant has appeared before the member or members of the local board designated for the purpose, the local board shall consider the new information which it receives and shall again classify the registrant in the same manner as if he had never before been classified, provided that if he has been physically examined by the examining physician, the Report of Physical Examination and Induction (Form 221) already in his file shall be used in case his physical or mental condition must be determined in order to complete his classification.

(d) After the registrant has appeared before the member or members of the local board designated for the purpose, the local board, as soon as practicable after it again classifies the registrant, shall mail notice thereof on the Notice of Classification (Form 57) to the registrant and on Classification Advice (Form 59) to the persons entitled to receive such notice or advice on an original classification under the provisions of section 623.61. ((d) as amended January 31, 1942, and November 16, 1942.)

(e) Each such classification shall be followed by the same right or appeal as in the case of an original classification.

625.3 Induction stayed. A registrant shall not be inducted during the period afforded him to appear in person before a member or members of his local board, and if the registrant requests a personal appearance, he shall not be inducted until 10 days after the Notice of Classification (Form 57) is mailed to him by the local board, as provided in paragraph (d) of section 625.2 (Added April 3, 1943, Federal Register (8 F.R.4292) April 6, 1943.)

Approved December 18, 1941; effective February 1, 1942.

[Endorsed]: Filed 6-17-43.

EXCEPTION NO. 2

The defendant, through his attorney, William Shea, moved the Court for a directed verdict of not guilty on the grounds that the evidence was insufficient as a matter of law to sustain a conviction, which motion being denied, the defendant then and there duly entered an exception to the ruling of the Court.

EXCEPTION NO. 3

And thereupon defendant renewed his motion, made at the con- [21] clusion of the government's case in chief, for a directed verdict of not guilty on the grounds that the evidence was insufficient as a matter of law to sustain a conviction, which motion being denied, the defendant then and there duly entered an exception to the ruling of the Court.

Whereupon both the United States and the defendant rested their case. Thereupon both sides argued the case to the jury, at the conclusion of which argument, the Court instruct*ion* the jury as follows: [22]

The Court: Ladies and Gentlemen of the Jury: It now becomes the duty of the court to instruct the jury on the law of this case. It is the duty of the jury to apply the law thus given to the facts before them.

The jury are the sole judges of the facts. It is the duty of the jury to give uniform consideration to all the instructions which will be given, to consider all parts of them together and to accept such instructions as a correct statement of the law involved.

The indictment in this case charges that George Robert Gutman being a male citizen between the ages of eighteen and forty-five years, residing in the United States, and under the duty to present himself for and submit to registration under the provisions of the Selective Training and Service Act of 1940, as amended, and thereafter to comply with the rules and regulations of said Act, as amended, and having in pursuance of said Act, as amended, and the rules and regulations made pursuant thereto, become a registrant of Local Board 86 of the Selective Service System in the City and County of San Francisco, California, which said Local Board Number 86 was duly appointed and acting for the area in which said defendant was a registrant, did, on or about the 14th day of May, 1943, at the City and County of San Francisco, in the Southern Division of the Northern District of California, and within the jurisdiction of this Court, knowingly and feloniously fail and neglect to perform such duty, in that he, the said defendant, did then and there knowlingly and feloniously fail and neglect to comply with the order of said Local Board Number 86, which had theretofore classified him in Class I-A, to report for induction into the land and naval forces of the United States, as provided in said Selective Training and Service Act of 1940, as amended, and the rules and regulations made pursuant thereto. [23]

The pertinent portion of Section 11 of the Selective Training and Service Act of 1940, as amended, under which the defendant in this case is charged in the indictment, states that any person who in any manner shall knowingly fail and neglect to perform any duty required of him under this Act or rules and regulations made pursuant to this Act shall upon conviction be punished as provided in the Act.

(U. S. proposed instruction No. 3):

"I instruct you that in Class I-A shall be placed every registrant who is found available for general military service, and such registrant shall be liable for induction into the armed forces of the United States".

(U. S. proposed instruction No. 4):

"I instruct you that the Local Boards, under rules and regulations prescribed by the President, shall have power, within their respective jurisdictions, to hear and determine, subject to the right of appeal to Appeal Boards therein authorized, all questions of claims with respect to inclusion for or exemption or deferment from training and service under the Selective Training and Service Act of 1940, as amended, of all individuals within the jurisdiction of such Local Board. The decision of such Local Board shall be final except where an appeal is authorized in accordance with such rules and regulations as the President may prescribe".

(U. S. proposed instruction No. 5):

"I instruct you that each Board of Appeal shall have jurisdiction to review any decision concerning classification of the registrant by any Local Board in the area of the Board of Appeals, provided such an appeal has been filed with the Local Board. Such appeal must be taken within 10 days after the date when the Local Board mails to the registrant notice of Classification, Form 57, and the decision of the Board of Appeal shall be final unless modified or reversed by the President". [24]

I instruct you that whether a Selective Service

registrant is a minister of religion presents a question of fact which from its very nature is committed by the Act to the determination of the competent Local Draft Board, and if an appeal is taken, to the determination of the proper Appeal Board.

(U. S. proposed instruction No. 6):

"You as jurors are not to decide whether the defendant is or is not a minister of religion. What you are to determine is whether the defendant after classification intentionally ignored the Draft Board's orders to report for induction."

I instruct you that if you find beyond a reasonable doubt and to a moral certainty that on or about the 14th day of May, 1943, the defendant was under a duty to comply with the order of the Local Draft Board Number 86, the Selective Service Board with which he was registered and by which Board he had theretofore been classified in Class 1-A, to report for induction into the army of the United States, at San Francisco, California, as provided in said Selective Training and Service Act of 1940, as amended, and that he at that time and place as aforesaid knowingly failed and neglected to perform such duty, then you shall find the defendant guilty as charged.

In every crime there must be a union or joint operation of act and intent; for a conviction both elements must be proved to a moral certainty and beyond a reasonable doubt. Such intent is merely the purpose or willingness to commit such act. It does not require knowledge that such act is a violation of law. However, a person must be presumed to intend to do that which he voluntarily and willfully in fact does do, and must also be presumed to intend the natural and probable usualy consequences of his own act. Every person charged with a crime is presumed to be innocent and this presumption has the effect of evidence and continues to operate on his behalf until it is overcome by competent evidence. [25] It is not necessary for the defendant to prove his innocence. The burden rests upon the prosecution to establish every element of the crime charged, to a moral certainty and beyond a reasonable doubt.

A reasonable doubt is a doubt resting upon the judgment and reason of him who concientiously entertains it from the evidence in the case. It is a doubt based upon reason. By such a doubt is not meant merely every possible or fanciful conjecture that may be suggested or imagined. Reasonable doubt is that state of the case which, after an entire comparison and consideration of the evidence in the case, leaves the minds of the jurors in that condition that they cannot say they feel an abiding conviction to a moral certainty of the truth of the charge. Reasonable doubt is not mere imaginary or possible doubt, but fair doubt based upon reason and common sense and growing out of the testimony in the case.

In judging of the evidence, you are to give it a reasonable and fair construction, and you are not authorized, because of any feeling, sympathy or bias, to apply any strained construction or one that is unreasonable in order to justify a certain verdict, when, were it not for such feeling or bias, you would reach a contrary conclusion; and whenever, after careful consideration of all the evidence, your minds are in that state where a conclusion of innocence is indicated equally with a conclusion of guilt, or there is reasonable doubt as to whether or not the evidence is so balanced, the conclusion of innocence must be adopted.

The jury are the sole and exclusive judges of the effect and value of the evidence addressed to them, and of the credibility of the witnesses who have testified in the case. The character of the witnesses as shown by the evidence should be taken into consideration for the purpose of determining their credibility and the facts as to whether they have spoken the truth; and the jury [26] may scrutinize not only the manner of witnesses while on the stand, their relation to the case, if any, but also their degree of intelligence.

A witness is presumed to speak the truth. This presumption however, may be repelled by the manner in which he testifies, his interest in the case, if any, or his motives for testifying falsely, if any, or his bias or his prejudice, if any, against one or more of the parties, by the character of his testimony, or by evidence affecting his character for truth, honesty and integrity, or by contradictory evidence.

It is the duty of the jury to give uniform consideration to all of the instructions which will be given, and to consider all of them together.

The Court charges the jury that if you find and

believe from the evidence that the defendant, on or about the 6th day of July, 1942, was duly registered by the Selective Service Board Number 86 of the City and County of San Francisco, California, and that he thereafter duly filed his questionnaire and that he was thereafter classified in Class I-A by said Board and that he was thereafter allowed to appeal to the Board of Appeals, and further find that the Board of Appeals affirmed his classification in Class I-A and if you further find that he was then notified of his classification by the Local Board, and that thereafter he was duly notified by said Local Board Number 86 to report for induction into the service on or about the 14th day of May, 1943, and further find that the defendant thereafter knowingly, wilfully, unlawfully and feloniously failed and refused to report for service in obedience to said order of said Local Board, then you are instructed that you must find the defendant guilty as charged in the charge set out in the indictment; and if you do not so find, then you should acquit the defendant.

In determining what your verdict shall be, you are to consider [27] only the evidence before you. Any testimony as to which objection was sustained, and any testimony which was ordered stricken out, must be wholly left out of account and disregarded.

The verdict of the jury should represent the opinion of each individual juror. It by no means follows that the opinions may not be changed in the jury room. The very object of the jury system is to secure unanimity by comparison of views and by arguments among the jurors themselves in the jury room. There is nothing particularly different in the way the jury is to consider the proof in a criminal case from that by which men give their attention to any question depending upon evidence presented to them. You are to consider evidence only for the purpose for which admitted, in the light of your knowledge of the natural tendencies and propensities of human beings, and resolve the facts according to deliberate and cautious judgment; and while remembering that the defendant is entitled to any reasonable doubt remaining in your minds, remember as well that if no such doubt remains the government is entitled to a verdict.

Jurors are expected to agree upon a verdict when they can conscientiously do so, and are expected to consult with one another in the jury room; and any juror should not hesitate to abandon his own view when convinced it is erroneous. Your verdict must be unanimous.

When you retire to the jury room, you will select one of your number as foreman, and he will sign your verdict for you when it has been agreed upon, and will represent you as your foreman in the further conduct of this case in Court. The clerk has made out a form of verdict in blank and after the jury determines what their verdict shall be, it shall be filled in and signed by the foreman. The jury may retire.

EXCEPTION NO. 4

Thereupon and prior to the retirement of the jury, the defendant objec*tion* to U. S. instruction number 3 as given, which objection being overruled, defendant then and there entered an exception. [28]

EXCEPTION NO. 5

Thereupon and prior to the retirement of the jury, the defendant objected to U. S. instruction number 4 as given, which objection being overruled, defendant then and there entered an exception.

EXCEPTION NO. 6

Thereupon and prior to the retirement of the jury, the defendant objected to U. S. instruction number 5 as given, which objection being overruled, defendant then and there entered an exception.

EXCEPTION NO. 7

Thereupon and prior to the retirement of the jury, the defendant objected to U. S. instruction number 6 as given, which objection being overruled, defendant then and there entered an exception.

At the commencement of the trial, the defendant had duly submitted to the Court, the following proposed instructions:

Defendant's Proposed Instruction No. 1:

"If you find that the defendant is a regular minister of religion in the Society of Jehovah's Witnesses, or if you have reasonable doubt as to whether the defendant was a regular minister in the Society of Jehovah's Witnesses, then you must acquit the defendant.

"The foregoing instruction is based upon the authority of Section 5 (d) of the Selective Training and Service Act of 1940"

Defendant Proposed Instruction No. 2:

"If you find or have reasonable doubt as to whether the draft board acted arbitrarily and capriciously and failed to accord the defendant a hearing upon his application for deferment as a regular minister of religion in accordance with Section 625.2 of the Selective Service Regulations (2nd edition) then you should acquit the defendant.

"Based on Johnson v. U. S. 126 F. (2nd) 242, etc."

[29]

Defendant's Proposed Instruction No. 3:

"If you find or have reasonable doubt as to whether the draft board failed to consider or investigate in the manner required by Opinion No. 14 of the National Director of Selective Service whether the defendant stood in his relationship to the members of the Society of Jehovah's Witnesses in the same relationship as a regular minister of other religions, then you should acquit the defendant.

"Foregoing Based on Section 5 (g) of the Selective Training and Service Act of 1940; Opinion No. 14 of the National Director of Selective Service."

EXCEPTION NO. 8

At the conclusion of the Court's instruction to the jury and prior to the retirement of the jury, the defendant requested the Court to give to the jury defendant's proposed instruction number 1, which request being denied, defendant then and there entered an exception.

EXCEPTION NO. 9

Thereupon the defendant requested the Court to give to the jury defendant's proposed instruction number 2, which request being denied, defendant then and there entered an exception.

EXCEPTION NO. 10

Thereupon the defendant requested the Court to give to the jury defendant's proposed instruction number 3, which request being denied, defendant then and there entered an exception.

The matter was thereupon submitted to the jury, which retired for consideration and deliberation thereon and after deliberation thereon said jury returned to the courtroom with a verdict of guilty as charged.

The jury was thereupon excused and the matter continued at defendant's request until June 19, 1943.

Thereafter and on said date the Court proceeded to the [30] passing of judgment upon the defendant and on said date the Court imposed judgment and sentence as follows: That the defendant be confined to the penitentiary for a period of three years, the penitentiary to be designated by the Attorney General.

That the above Bill of Exceptions contain all of the evidence, oral and documentary, and all of the proceedings relating to the trial, conviction, motions and judgment and sentence and all the instructions to the jury, and said defendant and appellant hereby presents the same as his Bill of Exceptions and asks that the same be allowed, signed and sealed and made a part of the record in this cause.

Dated: San Francisco, California.
July 20, 1943.

CLARENCE E. RUST
Attorney for defendant and appellant

Receipt of a copy of the foregoing Bill of Exceptions admitted this 20th day of July, 1943

FRANK J. HENNESSY
United States Attorney
JOSEPH KARESH
Assistant U. S. Attorney [31]

[Title of District Court and Cause.]

STIPULATION RE BILL OF EXCEPTIONS

It is hereby stipulated and agreed by and between the respective parties hereto that the foregoing Bill of Exceptions on behalf of the above named defendant and appellant, George Robert Gutman, upon appeal herein to the Circuit Court of Appeals in and for the Ninth Circuit, has been duly presented within the time allowed by law, and the rules and orders of this Court, duly and regularly made in this behalf, and the same is in proper form and conforms to the truth, and that it may be settled, allowed, signed and authenticated by this Court as the true Bill of Exceptions herein, on behalf of said defendant and appellant, and that it may be made a part of the record in this cause.

Dated: San Francisco, California,
August 5, 1943.

FRANK J. HENNESSY
United States Attorney
JOSEPH KARESH
Assistant United States Attorney
Attorneys for plaintiff and appellee
CLARENCE E. RUST
Attorney for defendant and appellant. [32]

[Title of District Court and Cause.]

ORDER SETTLING AND ALLOWING BILL OF EXCEPTIONS AND MAKING SAME PART OF THE RECORD

The foregoing Bill of Exceptions, duly proposed by the above named appellant, George Robert Gutman, and duly agreed upon by the respective parties hereto, having been duly presented to the Court within the time allowed and required by law and by the rules and orders of this Court, duly and regularly made in that behalf, is hereby settled, allowed, signed and authenticated as in proper form and as conforming to the truth and is the true Bill of Exceptions herein and is hereby made a part of the record in this cause.

Dated: San Francisco, Calif.
August 5th, 1943.

MICHAEL J. ROCHE
United States District Judge.
[33]

[Title of District Court and Cause.]

STIPULATION RE EXHIBITS

It is hereby stipulated and agreed by and between the attorneys for the United States and for defendant and appellant that all exhibits introduced in evidence, upon the trial of the above entitled cause now in custody of the Clerk of the Court, shall be made a part of, and be deemed to be included as a part of the foregoing Bill of Exceptions with the same effect in all respects as if incorporated in said Bill of Exceptions; that all of said exhibits be transmitted by the Clerk of this Court to the Circuit Court of Appeals for the Ninth Circuit as a portion of the record on appeal to be used in the Circuit Court of Appeals and subject to such orders as may be made in the Circuit Court of Appeals relative to the printing of the same or portions thereof.

Dated: San Francisco, California.
August 5, 1943.

FRANK J. HENNESSY
United States Attorney
JOSEPH KARESH
Assistant United States Attorney, Attorneys for plaintiff and appellee.
CLARENCE E. RUST
Attorney for defendant and appellant. [34]

ORDER FOR TRANSFER OF ORIGINAL EXHIBITS TO CIRCUIT COURT OF APPEALS

Upon reading the foregoing stipulation, and it appearing to the Court that an appeal having been taken in this cause to the Circuit Court of Appeals for the Ninth Circuit, and good cause appearing therefor,

It Is Ordered that the foregoing exhibits be transmitted by the Clerk of this Court to the Circuit Court of Appeals for the Ninth Circuit pursuant to and in accordance with the terms of the foregoing stipulation relative to said exhibits.

Dated: San Francisco, California.
August 5th, 1943.

MICHAEL J. ROCHE
United States District Judge.

Lodged 7-20-43

[Endorsed]: Filed Aug. 5, 1943 [35]

[Title of District Court and Cause.]

ASSIGNMENTS OF ERROR

George Robert Gutman, the defendant in the above entitled action and plaintiff on appeal herein, having appealed to the United States Circuit Court of Appeals in and for the Ninth Circuit from the judgment and sentence entered in the above entitled cause against him and said defendant having given notice of appeal as provided by law, now makes and files the following assignments of error herein, upon which he will rely for a reversal of said judgment and sentence upon appeal, and which errors and each of them are to the great detriment, injury and prejudice of said defendant and in violation of the rights conferred upon him by law and the defendant says that in the recorded proceedings of the above entitled cause upon the hearing and determination thereof, in the Southern Division of the United States District Court for the Northern District of California there is manifest error, in this:

I.

That the court erred in denying the motion of defendant for a directed verdict of acquittal on the ground that the evidence was insufficient as a matter of law to sustain a conviction, made [36] at the conclusion of the testimony on behalf of the United States in chief, and to which ruling of the Court the defendant duly and regularly excepted.

II.

That the Court erred in denying the motion of defendant for a directed verdict of acquittal on the ground that the evidence was insufficient as a matter of law to sustain a conviction, made at the conclusion of all the testimony and evidence in the case, and to which ruling of the Court the defendant duly and regularly excepted.

III.

That the Court erred in overruling defendant's objection to the following instruction of the Court to the jury, which objection was made immediately upon the completion of the Court's instructions to the jury and prior to the jury's retirement. and to the overruling of which objection, the defendant duly and regularly excepted:

"I instruct you that in Class I-A shall be placed every registrant who is found available for general military service, and such registrant shall be liable for induction into the armed forces of the United States."

IV.

That the Court erred in overruling defendant's objection to the following instruction of the Court to the jury, which objection was made immediately upon the completion of the Court's instructions to the jury and prior to the jury's retirement, and to the overruling of which objection, the defendant duly and regularly excepted:

"I instruct you that the Local Boards, under rules and regulations prescribed by the President.

shall have power, within their respective jurisdictions, to hear and determine, subject to the right of appeal to Appeal Boards therein authorized, all ques- [37] tions of claims with respect to inclusion for or exemption for deferment from training and service under the Selective Training and Service Act of 1940, as amended, of all individuals within the jurisdiction of such Local Board. The decision of such Local Board shall be final except where an appeal is authorized in accordance with such rules and regulations as the President may prescribe."

V.

That the Court erred in overruling defendant's objection to the following instruction of the Court to the jury, which objection was made immediately upon the completion of the Court's instructions to the jury and prior to the jury's retirement, and to the overruling of which objection, the defendant duly and regularly excepted.

"I instruct you that each Board of Appeals shall have jurisdiction to review any decision concerning classification of the registrant by any Local Board in the area of the Board of Appeals, provided such an appeal has been filed with the Local Board. Such appeal must be taken within 10 days after the date when the Local Board mails to the registrant notice of Classification, Form 57, and the decision of the Board of Appeals shall be final unless modified or reversed by the President".

VI.

That the Court erred in overruling defendant's objection to the following instruction of the Court to the jury, which objection was made immediately upon the completion of the Court's instructions to the jury and prior to the jury's retirement, and to the overruling of which objection, the defendant duly and regularly excepted:

"You as jurors are not to decide whether the defendant is or is not a minister of religion. What you are to determine is whether the defendant after classification intentionally ignored the Draft [38] Board's orders to report for induction".

VII.

That the Court erred in refusing defendant's request to give defendant's proposed instruction number 1 to the jury, and to the refusal of which the defendant duly and regularly excepted, and which proposed instruction read as follows:

"If you find that the defendant is a regular minister of religion in the Society of Jehovah's Witnesses, or if you have reasonable doubt as to whether the defendant was a regular minister in the Society of Jehovah's Witnesses, then you must acquit the defendant."

VIII.

That the Court erred in refusing defendant's request to give defendant's proposed instruction number 2 to the jury, and to the refusal of which the defendant duly and regularly excepted and which proposed instruction read as follows:

"If you find or have reasonable doubt as to whether the draft board acted arbitrarily and capriciously and failed to accord the defendant a hearing upon his application for deferment as a regular minister of religion in accordance with Section 625.2 of the Selective Service Regulations (2nd edition) then you should acquit the defendant".

IX.

That the Court erred in refusing defendant's request to give defendant's proposed instruction number 3 to the jury and to the refusal of which the defendant duly and regularly excepted, and which proposed instruction read as follows:

"If you find or have reasonable doubt as to whether the draft board failed to consider or investigate in the manner required by Opinion No. 14 of the National Director of Selective Service whether the defendant stood in his relationship to the members of the Society of Jehovah's Witnesses in the same relationship as a [39] regular minister of other religions, then you should acquit the defendant".

Dated: August 2, 1943.

CLARENCE E. RUST
Attorney for appellant

Receipt of a copy of above Assignments of Error admitted this this 5th day of August, 1943.

FRANK J. HENNESSY
United States Attorney
JOSEPH KARESH
Assistant U. S. Attorney
Attorneys for appellee.

[Endorsed]: Filed Aug. 5, 1943. [40]

[Title of Court and Cause.]

PRAECIPE

To the Clerk of the District Court of the United States for the Northern District of California:

Please prepare transcript on appeal in this cause and include therein the following:

1 Indictment

2 Minutes of June 10, 1943, showing plea of "Not Guilty"

3 Minutes of June 19, 1943, showing judgment and sentence

4 Notice of Appeal

6 Bill of Exceptions

7 Assignments of error.

Dated: August 17, 1943

CLARENCE E. RUST
Attorney for defendant and appellant.

Receipt of a copy of above admitted this 17th day of August, 1943.

FRANK J. HENNESSY
U. S. Attorney, for appellee
Per T. S.

[Endorsed] Filed Aug. 17, 1943. [41]

District Court of the United States
Northern District of California

CERTIFICATE OF CLERK TO TRANSCRIPT OF RECORD ON APPEAL

I, C. W. Calbreath, Clerk of the District Court of the United States, for the Northern District of California, do hereby certify that the foregoing 41 pages, numbered from 1 to 41, inclusive, contain a full, true, and correct transcript of the records and proceedings in the case of The United States of America vs. George Robert Gutman No. 28001 R, as the same now remain on file and of record in my office.

I further certify that the cost of preparing and certifying the foregoing transcript of record on appeal is the sum of $3.65 and that the said amount has been paid to me by the Attorney for the appellant herein.

In Witness Whereof, I have hereunto set my hand and affixed the seal of said District Court at San Francisco, California, this 3rd day of November, A. D. 1943.

[Seal] C. W. CALBREATH,
Clerk

M. E. VANBUREN,
Deputy Clerk [42]

[Endorsed]: No. 10488. United States Circuit Court of Appeals for the Ninth Circuit. George Robert Gutman, appellant, vs. United States of America, Appellee. Transcript of Record. Upon Appeal from the District Court of the United States for the Northern District of California Southern Division.

Filed November 12, 1943.

PAUL P. O'BRIEN

Clerk of the United States Circuit Court of Appeals for the Ninth Circuit.

In the United States Circuit Court of Appeals for the Ninth Judicial Circuit.

No. 10,488

GEORGE ROBERT GUTMAN,

Appellant,

vs.

UNITED STATES OF AMERICA,

Appellee.

STATEMENT OF POINTS AND DESIGNATION OF PARTS OF RECORD TO BE PRINTED

I, George Robert Gutman, defendant and appellant in the above-entitled action, hereby files herewith the following statement of the points upon which he intends to rely upon this appeal and herewith designates the part of the record which he thinks necessary for the consideration thereof.

STATEMENT OF POINTS UPON WHICH HE INTENDS TO RELY

All of the points as set forth in appellant's Assignments of Error appearing in the transcript of record herein, which Assignments of Error are hereby adopted as the points upon which appellant intends to rely on this appeal.

PARTS OF RECORD NECESSARY FOR CONSIDERATION OF APPEAL

Appellant designates the entire record filed in this Court as necessary for a proper consideration of the appeal and designates the entire transcript as necessary to be printed.

Dated: November 18, 1943.

CLARENCE E. RUST
Attorney for appellant

Receipt of copy of above admitted this 18th day of Nov., 1943.

FRANK J. HENNESSY
U. S. Atty.

[Endorsed]: Filed Nov. 18, 1943. Paul P. O'Brien, Clerk.

No. 10,488

IN THE

United States Circuit Court of Appeals

For the Ninth Circuit

GEORGE ROBERT GUTMAN,
Appellant,

vs.

UNITED STATES OF AMERICA,
Appellee.

APPELLANT'S OPENING BRIEF.

CLARENCE E. RUST,
5837 San Pablo Avenue, Oakland, California,
Attorney for Appellant.

PERNAU-WALSH PRINTING CO., SAN FRANCISCO

Subject Index

Table of Authorities Cited

Cases

Codes and Statutes

IN THE

United States Circuit Court of Appeals

For the Ninth Circuit

GEORGE ROBERT GUTMAN,
Appellant,

vs.

UNITED STATES OF AMERICA,
Appellee.

APPELLANT'S OPENING BRIEF.

JURISDICTION.

The trial Court had jurisdiction under an indictment charging violation of the following section:

50 USCA 311.

This Court has jurisdiction under Section 128 (a) of the Judicial Code as amended by Act of February 15, 1925. (28 USCA 225.)

STATEMENT OF THE CASE.

George Robert Gutman, the appellant, was indicted by the Grand Jury for the Northern District of California, Southern Division, in the March 1943 term.

The indictment charged appellant with a violation of the "Selective Training and Service Act of 1940, as Amended'' 50 USCA 311, in that he failed to report for induction into the Land or Naval Forces of the United States. (Tr. pp. 2-3.)

To the indictment in question the appealing defendant entered a plea of not guilty. (Tr. p. 4.)

The appellant was found guilty by a jury of the charge contained in the indictment. (Tr. p. 5.)

The appellant was sentenced by the trial Court to imprisonment in a U. S. Penitentiary for a period of three years. (Tr. pp. 6-7.)

At the conclusion of the government's case in chief, appellant moved the Court for an instructed verdict of not guilty on the grounds that the evidence was insufficient as a matter of law to sustain a conviction, which motion was denied and to which denial an exception was taken. (Tr. p. 74.)

At the conclusion of defendant's case and of all the testimony, appellant renewed his motion for an instructed verdict of not guilty on the ground that the evidence was insufficient as a matter of law to sustain a conviction, which motion was denied and to which denial an exception was taken. (Tr. pp. 108-9.)

At the close of the evidence and after argument of counsel the Court charged the jury, that in Class I-A shall be placed every registrant who is found available for general military service, that the decision of the local draft board in classifying registrant is final except where an appeal is authorized and that in the event of such appeal to the Appeal Board that the decision of the Appeal Board is final, that the jury was not to decide whether or not registrant, the appellant, is or is not a minister, that such decision rested entirely with the local draft board and the Board of Appeal, that the only question which the jury was to determine was as to whether appellant ignored the draft board's orders to report for induction. (Tr. pp. 111-112.) Appellant duly objected and excepted to the said charge to the jury. (Tr. p. 117.)

The appellant duly requested the Court to charge the jury that if the jury found that appellant was a regular minister of religion that it should acquit the defendant (appellant), that if the draft board in classifying appellant acted arbitrarily and capriciously and failed to accord him a hearing upon his application for exemption as a minister, then the jury should acquit the defendant (appellant), that if the jury found that the draft board had not investigated appellant's claim as a minister in the manner required by Opinion 14 of the National Director of Selective Service, then it should acquit the appellant. (Tr. pp. 117-119.) That upon the Court's refusal to give said instructions, appellant duly excepted. (Tr. pp. 118-119.)

After the verdict and sentence as herein stated, the appellant duly filed a notice of appeal accompanied by the grounds relied upon. (Tr. pp. 7-9.) There was timely settled and allowed by the Court the Bill of Exceptions. (Tr. pp. 121-122.) And the assignment of errors was duly filed within the time set by the trial Court. (Tr. pp. 124-129.)

SUMMARY OF THE EVIDENCE.

Appellant testified that he was a minister of a Christian Society, known as "Jehovah's Witnesses"; that he had been engaged in full time service as a minister for about four years; that he had been a "Special Pioneer" since May 1, 1942; that his first assignment to work for the Society was in August, 1939, when he was sent to Paso Robles, California, where he organized Bible studies and he did no secular work; that he subsequently worked as a minister in various communities in California and in Utah, Wyoming, Kansas and various other states; that his work as "Special Pioneer" consisted in devoting at least 175 hours per month to the preaching of the gospel. (Tr. pp. 77-80.)

A purported Certificate of Ordination was admitted in evidence marked Defendant's Exhibit B and so far as pertinent hereto, reads as follows:

> "Watchtower Bible and Tract Society.
> 117 Adams Street,
> Brooklyn, New York. Sept. 8, 1942.
>
> To Whom it May Concern: This is to certify that George Robert Gutman, one of Jehovah's Witnesses, has been associated with the Watchtower Bible and Tract Society, Inc., according to our records, since July 1939. He was baptized in July 1939, and was appointed direct representative of this organization to perform missionary and evangelistic service in organizing and establishing churches and generally preaching the Gospel of the Kingdom of God in definitely assigned territory on August 8, 1939.

> Mr. Gutman's entire time is devoted to missionary work.
>
> He has the Scriptural ordination to preach 'this Gospel of the Kingdom'. He is therefore, declared by this Society a duly ordained minister of the Gospel and is authorized to represent this Society and preach 'this Gospel of the Kingdom'.
>
> Watchtower B. & T. Society, Inc.,
> T. J. Sullivan,
> Superintendent of Evangelists."
>
> (Tr. pp. 78-79.)

Verne G. Reusch testified that appellant was a "Special Pioneer" in the Society of Jehovah's Witnesses; that this term refers to the ultimate group in the Society; that they hold services comparable to what are known as religious services in other religions; that appellant is recognized in the Society as a minister; that he considered that the draft board acted unfairly in classifying appellant. (Tr. pp. 74-75.)

C. D. Easter testified that appellant was a "Special Pioneer" in the Society of Jehovah's Witnesses; that he believed that appellant might well have considered it treason to Almighty God, for him to go into the army; that having consecrated himself to the "kingdom" for him to violate that consecration would make him guilty of treason to God. (Tr. p. 76.)

The appellant filed the usual draft questionnaire with his local draft board, on September 11, 1942, in which he asserted his claim as a minister and stated that he believed he should have a classification of 4-D.

(Tr. pp. 13-33.) On November 23, 1942 the local board placed appellant in the classification I-A. Thereafter and on December 10, 1942 the board notified appellant of this classification. (Tr. p. 43.) At the time of filing his questionnaire, appellant had also filed with the board a lengthy statement supporting his claim as a minister. (Tr. p. 35.) And in which he set forth in detail the evidence in support of his claim. (Tr. pp. 36-43.) On November 23, 1942, appellant wrote a letter to the board in which he again emphasizes his claim and calls the board's attention to Consolation Magazine of July 9, 1941, which he sends to the board, and which magazine contained a copy of the opinion of General Hershey concerning classification of members of Jehovah's Witnesses. Appellant also states in his letter the reason why his name did not appear on the certified official list of pioneer ministers of Jehovah's Witnesses, namely, that he was not old enough to be on it as originally issued and that before his name could be added National Headquarter's of Selective Service had discontinued the practice of adding names and made the question of determining who is a minister, a question of fact to be decided in each case. (Tr. pp. 44-45.)

Within 10 days of the notice from the local board that appellant had been classified as I-A and on December 17, 1942, appellant wrote a letter to the local board requesting a personal hearing before the board and calling the board's attention to a certificate of ordination which he had filed in support of his claim. (Tr. p. 46.)

On December 21, 1942 appellant's purported hearing was had before the local board and same lasted "not less than five minutes". (Tr. p. 65.) The chairman of the local board, Mr. Gillin, testified, that the board considered his ordination certificate and all the other evidence that he had presented. He also testified that prior to this hearing he had a "scuffle" with appellant in the office of the draft board and that he had thereafter and on the basis of this "scuffle" secured the arrest and conviction of appellant in the Municipal Court. (Tr. pp. 66-67.) Appellant testified in reference to this purported hearing that the hearing "did not last more than five minutes"; that he told Mr. Gillin that he came for a hearing and wished to discuss his classification; that Mr. Gillin replied by merely asking appellant if he wanted to appeal; that the board asked him nothing about his work; nothing concerning his claim as a minister or his relationship to Jehovah's Witnesses. (Tr. pp. 91-93.) Appellant further informed the board that he had certain other evidence which he wished to present, but the answer of the board was the same: Do you want to appeal? (Tr. p. 91.)

On December 21, 1942, appellant filed an appeal from the decision of the local board to the board of appeals. (Tr. p. 34.) And at the same time addressed a letter to the local board in support of his appeal, in which he again set forth his claim to classification as a minister. (Tr. pp. 47-49.) On February 10, 1943 the appeal board affirmed the appeal. (Tr. p. 34.) Thereafter appellant wrote letters to both the State

Headquarters and the National Headquarters of Selective Service, seeking recognition of his claim and therewith submitting additional affidavits in support of same. (Tr. pp. 81-90.)

Appellant received no affirmative results from his appeal to State and National Headquarters and thereafter was ordered to report for induction into the armed forces, with which order he did not comply. That thereafter he was sent a notice of delinquency, to which he replied that he could not report as he was an ordained minister of the gospel. (Tr. pp. 61-65.)

There was also admitted in evidence at the trial as Defendant's Exhibit D, Opinion No. 14 as Amended, of the National Director of Selective Service. (Tr. pp. 99-104.)

SPECIFICATION OF ERRORS RELIED UPON.

The Court erred in denying the motion of defendant for a directed verdict of acquittal on the ground that the evidence was insufficient as a matter of law to sustain a conviction, made at the conclusion of the testimony on behalf of the United States and renewed at the conclusion of all the evidence. (Assignments of Error I and II, Tr. pp. 124 and 125.)

The Court erred in giving to the jury, over defendant's objection, an instruction that "In Class I-A shall be placed every registrant who is found available for general military service, and such registrant shall be liable for induction into the armed forces of the United States". (Assignment of Error III, Tr. p. 125.)

The Court erred in giving to the jury, over defendant's objection, the following instruction: "I instruct you that the local boards, under rules and regulations prescribed by the President shall have power, within their respective jurisdictions to hear and determine, subject to the right to appeal to appeal boards therein authorized all questions of claims with respect to inclusion for or exemption for deferment from training and service under the Selective Training and Service Act of 1940, as amended, of all individuals within the jurisdiction of such local board. The decision of such local board shall be final except where an appeal is authorized in accordance with such rules and regulations as the President may prescribe." (Assignment of Error IV, Tr. pp. 125 and 126.)

The Court erred in giving to the jury, over defendant's objection, the following instruction: "I instruct you that each board of appeals shall have jurisdiction to review any decision concerning classification of the registrant by any local board in the area of the board of appeals, provided such an appeal has been filed with the local board. Such appeal must be taken within 10 days after the date when the local board mails to the registrant notice of classification, and the decision of the board of appeals shall be final unless modified or reversed by the President." (Assignment of Error V, Tr. p. 126.)

The Court erred in giving to the jury, over defendant's objection, an instruction that "You as jurors are not to decide whether the defendant is or is not a minister of religion. What you are to determine is whether the defendant after classification intentionally ignored the draft board's orders to report for induction". (Assignment of Error VI, Tr. p. 127.)

The Court erred in refusing to give to the jury an instruction that "If you find that the defendant is a regular minister of religion in the Society of Jehovah's Witnesses, or if you have reasonable doubt as to whether the defendant was a regular minister in the Society of Jehovah's Witnesses, then you must acquit the defendant". (Assignment of Error VII, Tr. p. 127.)

The Court erred in refusing to give to the jury an instruction that "If you find or have reasonable doubt as to whether the draft board acted arbitrarily and capriciously and failed to accord the defendant a hearing upon his application for deferment as a regular minister of religion in accordance with Section 625.2 of the Selective Service Regulations then you should acquit the defendant". (Assignment of Error VIII, Tr. pp. 127 and 128.)

The Court erred in refusing to give to the jury an instruction that "If you find or have reasonable doubt as to whether the draft board failed to consider or investigate in the manner required by Opinion No. 14 of the National Director of Selective Service whether the defendant stood in his relationship to the members of the Society of Jehovah's Witnesses in the same relationship as a regular minister of other religions, then you should acquit the defendant". (Assignment IX, Tr. p. 128.)

ARGUMENT.

I. THE COURT ERRED IN DENYING THE MOTION OF DEFENDANT FOR A DIRECTED VERDICT OF ACQUITTAL ON THE GROUND THAT THE EVIDENCE WAS INSUFFICIENT AS A MATTER OF LAW TO SUSTAIN A CONVICTION. (Assignments of Error I and II, Tr. pp. 124 and 125.)

The assignments of error contained in assignments I and II may be treated under one heading since they both relate to the sufficiency of the evidence to sustain the conviction.

The evidence is wholly insufficient to sustain a conviction for the reason that the undisputed evidence showed that appellant is in fact a minister and that the draft board acted arbitrarily and capriciously in classifying him as I-A and that this action of the board and its failure to follow the prescribed procedure under the draft regulations resulted in its failure to acquire the jurisdiction or power to make an effectual order of induction.

The Selective Training and Service Act of 1940, Section 5 (d) (50 USCA Appendix 305 d) provides that: "Regular or duly ordained ministers of religions * * * shall be exempt from training and service (but not from registration) under this Act". Section 622.44 of the Selective Service Regulations provides for placing all ministers in Class IV-D.

It is to be noted that such persons are not to be *deferred* but are to be *exempted.* Once it is established that the person falls within the exempted class, he is then not subject to the orders of the draft board.

Wise v. Withers, 3 Cranch 331. Case involved a justice of the peace. Under the then militia act a justice of the peace was exempt from enforced enrollment. For failure to submit to induction he was arrested, fined and his goods seized by a court martial. He subsequently sued the army officers for trespass. Said Chief Justice Marshall:

> "It follows from this opinion that a court martial has no jurisdiction over a Justice of the Peace as a militiaman; he could never be legally enrolled; and it is a principle that a decision of such a tribunal in a case clearly without the jurisdiction cannot protect the officers who executed it. The Court and the officers are all trespassers."

In *Angelus v. Sullivan,* 246 Fed. 54 (Circuit Court, 2nd Circuit), involving the Draft Act of 1917, the Court apparently approved this language of counsel, after citing the above case of *Wise v. Withers*:

> "No difference in principle between the two cases exists, namely, that the person attempted to be drafted is not subject to the Draft Act; and therefore nothing which is done with respect to him is valid."

The task of determining in the first instance, who is exempt, rests with the draft board. (Although there is certainly room for argument that the statute making a minister exempt is so absolute in its terms that a registrant might establish the fact of his ministry in any suitable proceedings and without waiting for a decision by the board.) But the draft board does not have arbitrary power and cannot act arbitrarily or capriciously; nor without evidence nor in opposition to the evidence; nor can it decline to hear the person seeking the exemption.

In the *Angelus* case, supra, the Court said:

> "We think a decision of the Board is final only where the board has proceeded in due form and where the party involved is given a fair opportunity to be heard and to present his evidence. But if an opportunity to be heard should be denied, there can be no doubt as to the right of the aggrieved party to come into the courts for the protection of his rights."

To the same effect see, *Boitano v. District Board,* 250 Fed. 812, and *U. S. v. Kinkead,* 250 Fed. 692.

In *Johnson v. United States,* 126 Fed. (2d) 243 (8th Circuit), the Court in referring to the draft board, said:

> "But classifications by such agencies must, under the powers given them by Congress, be honestly made, and a classification made in the teeth of all the substantial evidence before such agency is not honest but arbitrary. Courts can prevent arbitrary action of such agencies from being effective."

In the present case it is fully established that the appellant is in fact a minister; that he has been such for a period of about four years, his ministry even antedating the Draft Act; that he works full time at his ministry and has no other employment; that he was ordained by the Watchtower Bible and Tract Society of New York as a direct missionary representative of them on August 8, 1939; that this organization is recognized by national headquarters of selective service as a religious institution; all of these facts appellant established beyond cavil before the draft board; there was no opposing evidence. By all the rules of evidence and fair play, appellant was entitled to be classified as a minister (IV-D), instead he was classified as I-A and thus made subject to induction into the armed forces. The board thus acted arbitrarily and capriciously and in the teeth of all the evidence and by so doing lost its jurisdiction to make the order of induction.

Not only did appellant prove his claim by ample evidence in the first instance, but, after the local board had arbitrarily rejected all his proof and had classified him, capriciously, in Class I-A, he pursued his administrative remedy by demanding a personal hearing before the local board, pursuant to Regulation 625.1, which provides that "Every registrant * * * shall have an opportunity to appear in person * * *" Rule or Regulation 625.2 provides that at such hearing the registrant may discuss his classification, may point out the class in which he thinks he ought to be classified, may direct the board's attention to particular evidence and may present such further evidence as he deems suitable.

As concerns this hearing, what does the evidence show? Simply this: That appellant appeared before the board with some additional evidence which he sought to read and also informed the board that he wished to discuss his classification. These things he had an unquestioned right to do; but the board replied through its chairman, with the inane and irrelevant question: Do you want to appeal? And it should be recalled that it was this same chairman, the spokesman for the board, who had previously had a physical encounter with the appellant and who had caused the arrest of the appellant. The whole alleged hearing consumed about five minutes. It is obvious that this alleged hearing was no hearing in contemplation of law, but was simply a farce. And this failure to accord appellant a hearing in conformity with the regulations was a failure to accord him due process of law, which in turn prevented the board from ever acquiring the jurisdiction to issue an order of induction. And its order of induction thereafter issued was void and could give no basis for an indictment.

Where the regulations provide for a personal hearing, such hearing is a part of due process.

St. Joseph Stockyards Co. v. U. S., 298 U. S. 38;

Yamatoya v. Fisher, 189 U. S. 86;

U. S. v. John Gilbert Laier, decided November 8, 1943 by St. Sure, District Judge, Northern District of California, No. 28036-S.

Quoting from the last mentioned case by Judge St. Sure:

> "Admittedly, the local board failed to comply with these provisions, and the effect of such failure would seem to be that the registrant was not classified at all, nor could he legally be inducted, at the time it made its order. In issuing its order, the board acted entirely outside its jurisdiction and without any legal authority."

To the same effect see *Olm v. Perkins,* 79 Fed. (2d) 533.

In still another respect there was a failure of the board to follow the regulations set up to govern its action in determining appellant's status as a minister. It failed to follow Opinion 14 of Selective Service (see pages 99 to 104 of transcript for full text of this regulation) in that the board made no effort to determine the relationship between appellant and other members of Jehovah's Witnesses nor whether such other members regarded him as a minister and when appellant appeared for his hearing the board made no effort to ascertain such facts. Yet these things are required specifically by this regulation. The failure to follow such regulation was fatal to the classification. See *Olm v. Perkins,* supra.

From the foregoing appellant submits that the evidence was insufficient to support a conviction and that his motion for a directed verdict of acquittal should have been granted.

II. THE COURT ERRED IN GIVING TO THE JURY, OVER DEFENDANT'S OBJECTION, AN INSTRUCTION THAT "IN CLASS I-A SHALL BE PLACED EVERY REGISTRANT WHO IS FOUND AVAILABLE FOR GENERAL MILITARY SERVICE, AND SUCH REGISTRANT SHALL BE LIABLE FOR INDUCTION INTO THE ARMED FORCES OF THE UNITED STATES". (Assignment of Error III, Tr. p. 125.)

THE COURT ERRED IN GIVING TO THE JURY, OVER DEFENDANT'S OBJECTION, THE FOLLOWING INSTRUCTION: "I INSTRUCT YOU THAT THE LOCAL BOARDS, UNDER RULES AND REGULATIONS PRESCRIBED BY THE PRESIDENT SHALL HAVE POWER, WITHIN THEIR RESPECTIVE JURISDICTIONS TO HEAR AND DETERMINE, SUBJECT TO THE RIGHT TO APPEAL TO APPEAL BOARDS THEREIN AUTHORIZED ALL QUESTIONS OF CLAIMS WITH RESPECT TO INCLUSION FOR OR EXEMPTION FOR DEFERMENT FROM TRAINING AND SERVICE UNDER THE SELECTIVE TRAINING AND SERVICE ACT OF 1940, AS AMENDED, OF ALL INDIVIDUALS WITHIN THE JURISDICTION OF SUCH LOCAL BOARD. THE DECISION OF SUCH LOCAL BOARD SHALL BE FINAL EXCEPT WHERE AN APPEAL IS AUTHORIZED IN ACCORDANCE WITH SUCH RULES AND REGULATIONS AS THE PRESIDENT MAY PRESCRIBE". (Assignment of Error IV, Tr. pp. 125 and 126.)

THE COURT ERRED IN GIVING TO THE JURY, OVER DEFENDANT'S OBJECTION, THE FOLLOWING INSTRUCTION: "I INSTRUCT YOU THAT EACH BOARD OF APPEALS SHALL HAVE JURISDICTION TO REVIEW ANY DECISION CONCERNING CLASSIFICATION OF THE REGISTRANT BY ANY LOCAL BOARD IN THE AREA OF THE BOARD OF APPEALS, PROVIDED SUCH AN APPEAL HAS BEEN FILED WITH THE LOCAL BOARD. SUCH APPEAL MUST BE TAKEN WITHIN 10 DAYS AFTER THE DATE WHEN THE LOCAL BOARD MAILS TO THE REGISTRANT NOTICE OF CLASSIFICATION, AND THE DECISION OF THE BOARD OF APPEALS SHALL BE FINAL UNLESS MODIFIED OR REVERSED BY THE PRESIDENT". (Assignment of Error V, Tr. p. 126.)

THE COURT ERRED IN REFUSING TO GIVE TO THE JURY AN INSTRUCTION THAT: "IF YOU FIND OR HAVE REA-

SONABLE DOUBT AS TO WHETHER THE DRAFT BOARD ACTED ARBITRARILY AND CAPRICIOUSLY AND FAILED TO ACCORD THE DEFENDANT A HEARING UPON HIS APPLICATION FOR DEFERMENT AS A REGULAR MINISTER OF RELIGION IN ACCORDANCE WITH SECTION 625.2 OF THE SELECTIVE SERVICE REGULATIONS THEN YOU SHOULD ACQUIT THE DEFENDANT". (Assignment of Error VIII, Tr. pp. 127 and 128.)

These assignments III, IV, V and VIII are so related and intertwined that it seems proper to consider them together.

The evidence showed that uncontradicted proof had been submitted to the draft board establishing the claim of appellant that he was a minister of religion; the evidence further showed that the draft board had ignored all of this evidence and in the teeth of it had classified appellant in Class I-A. There was thus substantial evidence before the jury tending to prove arbitrary and capricious action on the part of the draft board, which action would in law vitiate the board's decision. There was also before the jury substantial evidence tending to show that the draft board had failed to accord appellant the personal hearing provided for by the regulations, and which failure resulted in a failure of due process.

Assignment VIII was intended to instruct the jury on both these vital questions of arbitrary action and the failure to accord a hearing and ought to have been given. The effect of the failure to give this instruction, taken in connection with the instructions referred to in assignments III, IV and V, was to take entirely from the jury the whole question of arbitrary and capricious action on the part of the board and the further question of the failure of due process by reason of the failure to accord a personal hearing.

Angelus v. Sullivan, supra;
Johnson v. United States, supra;
Yamatoya v. Fisher, supra;
U. S. v. John Gilbert Laier, supra.

III. THE COURT ERRED IN GIVING TO THE JURY, OVER DEFENDANT'S OBJECTION, AN INSTRUCTION THAT: "YOU AS JURORS ARE NOT TO DECIDE WHETHER THE DEFENDANT IS OR IS NOT A MINISTER OF RELIGION. WHAT YOU ARE TO DETERMINE IS WHETHER THE DEFENDANT AFTER CLASSIFICATION INTENTIONALLY IGNORED THE DRAFT BOARD'S ORDER TO REPORT FOR INDUCTION". (Assignment of Error VI, Tr. p. 127.)

THE COURT ERRED IN REFUSING TO GIVE TO THE JURY AN INSTRUCTION THAT IF THE JURY FOUND THAT DEFENDANT WAS A REGULAR MINISTER OF RELIGION THEN IT SHOULD ACQUIT THE DEFENDANT. (Assignment of Error VII, Tr. p. 127.)

Both of these assignments relate to the question of the exemption of ministers from service in the armed forces. Under Section 5 (d) of the Selective Training and Service Act of 1940, regular or duly ordained ministers are exempt from training and service. Being so exempt, the draft board was without authority to order a minister to report for induction into the armed forces, and the question, therefore, of whether appellant was or was not a minister should have been submitted to the jury.

This question should also have gone to the jury on the basis of appellant's claim that the draft board had proceeded against him in an arbitrary and capricious manner in denying his claim as a minister. Before the jury could decide whether the board's action was arbitrary and capricious it would have to decide of necessity that the appellant was in fact a minister. The instruction covered in assignment VI should therefore not have been given and the proposed instruction covered by assignment VII should have been given.

IV. THE COURT ERRED IN REFUSING TO GIVE TO THE JURY AN INSTRUCTION THAT IF THE JURY FOUND THAT THE DRAFT BOARD FAILED TO COMPLY WITH OPINION 14 OF THE NATIONAL DIRECTOR OF SELECTIVE SERVICE, IN CLASSIFYING DEFENDANT, THEN IT SHOULD ACQUIT THE DEFENDANT. (Assignment of Error IX, Tr. p. 128.)

This opinion is a regulation of the Selective Service System made especially applicable to Jehovah's Witnesses. Such regulations have the force of law. *Olm v. Perkins,* supra. And a failure to follow such regulation by the administrative agency results in an unfair hearing, which will be nullified by the Court. See *Olm v. Perkins,* supra.

This opinion reads, in part, as follows:

> 1. The Watchtower Bible and Tract Society, Inc., is incorporated under the laws of the State of New York for charitable, religious and scientific purposes. The unincorporated body of persons known as Jehovah's Witnesses hold in common certain religious tenets and beliefs and recognizes as their terrestrial governing organization the Watchtower Bible and Tract Society, Inc.

By their adherence to the organization of this religious corporation, the unincorporated body of Jehovah's Witnesses are considered to constitute a recognized religious sect.

3. * * * Pioneers of Jehovah's Witnesses are those members of Jehovah's Witnesses who devote all or substantially all of their time to the work of teaching the tenets of their religion and in the converting of others to their belief. A certified official list of members of the Bethel Family and Pioneers is being transmitted to the State Directors of Selective Service by National Headquarters of the Selective Service System simultaneously with the release of this amended Opinion. The members of the Bethel Family and pioneers whose names appear upon such certified official list come within the purview of section 5 (d) of the Selective Training and Service Act of 1940, as amended and they may be classified in Class IV-D. The status of members of the Bethel family and pioneers whose names do not appear upon such certified official list shall be determined under the provisions of paragraph 5 of this Opinion.

5. The members of Jehovah's Witnesses, known by the various names of members of the Bethel Family, pioneers, regional servants, sound servants, advertising servants, and back-call servants, devote their time and efforts in varying degrees to the dissemination of the tenets and beliefs of Jehovah's Witnesses. The deference paid to these individuals by other members of Jehovah's Witnesses also varies in a great degree. It is impossible to make a general determination with respect to these persons as to their relationship to Jehovah's Witnesses. Whether or not they stand

in the same relationship as regular or duly ordained ministers in other religions must be determined in each individual case by the local board, based upon whether or not they devote their lives in the furtherance of the beliefs of Jehovah's Witnesses, whether or not they perform functions which are normally performed by regular or duly ordained ministers of other religions, and finally, whether or not they are regarded by other Jehovah's Witnesses in the same manner in which regular or duly ordained ministers of other religions are ordinarily regarded.

6. In the case of Jehovah's Witnesses, as in the case of all other registrants who claim exemption as regular or duly ordained ministers, the local board shall place in the registrant's file a record of all facts entering into its determination for the reason that it is legally necessary that the record show the basis of the local board's decision.

The evidence showed that the draft board made no attempt to follow this regulation. It made no attempt to determine whether or not appellant was regarded by other Jehovah's Witnesses in the same manner in which regular or ordained ministers of other religions are ordinarily regarded. Appellant had submitted his ordination certificate and a long statement in support of his claim. (Tr. pp. 46, 66-67, 35.) Finally he came before the board for a personal hearing, at which time it would be assumed that the board would attempt to ascertain the facts in accordance with this Opinion 14. Instead no question whatever is asked appellant as to his relationship with other Jehovah's Witnesses, but he is merely asked as to whether or not he wished to appeal. (Tr. pp. 91-93.)

In view of this state of the record, appellant was entitled to have submitted to the jury the question as to whether or not the board had complied with the regulation and that if the jury found that it had not, then appellant was entitled to an acquittal. *Olm v. Perkins,* supra.

CONCLUSION.

It is respectfully submitted that by reason of the errors herein set forth, the conviction of the appellant should be reversed.

Dated, Oakland, California,
January 14, 1944.

Respectfully submitted,
Clarence E. Rust,
Attorney for Appellant.

No. 10,488

IN THE

United States Circuit Court of Appeals

For the Ninth Circuit

George Robert Gutman, *Appellant,* vs. United States of America, *Appellee.*	}

BRIEF FOR APPELLEE.

Frank J. Hennessy,
United States Attorney,

R. B. McMillan,
Assistant United States Attorney,

Joseph Karesh,
Assistant United States Attorney,
Post Office Building, San Francisco,
Attorneys for Appellee.

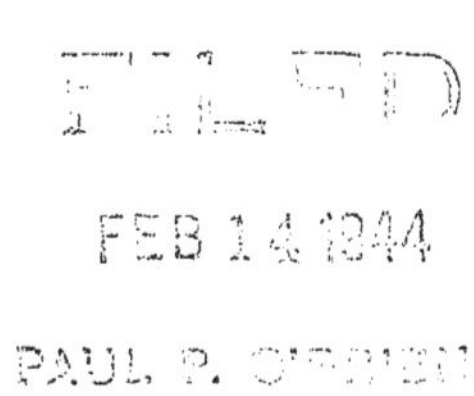

Pernau-Walsh Printing Co., San Francisco

Subject Index

Table of Authorities Cited

Cases

Statutes

No. 10,488

IN THE

United States Circuit Court of Appeals

For the Ninth Circuit

George Robert Gutman,
Appellant,

vs.

United States of America,
Appellee.

BRIEF FOR APPELLEE.

STATEMENT OF THE CASE.

The facts set forth by the appellant relative to the pleadings in this case are correctly stated.

The following is a brief statement of the essential facts disclosed from the evidence introduced at the trial:

The appellant, born March 15, 1924, registered for Selective Service with Local Board No. 86, San Francisco, California, on July 6, 1942. (T. p. 11.) He filed his questionnaire with his said Local Board on September 11, 1942. In his questionnaire he stated that he had been a minister of Jehovah's Witnesses since August 1, 1939 (T. p. 27) and claimed exemption from service in the armed forces on the grounds of such ministry. (T. p. 32.) The Local Board rejected his claim and on November 23, 1942 unanimously classified him in Class I-A and thereafter on December 10, 1942 mailed him a notice of such classification. (T. p. 43.) The appellant's name did not appear on the certified list of Jehovah's Witnesses. (T. pp. 45 and 51.) The appellant wrote a letter to the Board on December 17, 1942 requesting a personal hearing and such hearing was granted and held on December 21, 1942 before the entire Board membership. (T. pp. 65, 66 and 68.) After the hearing the Board notified the appellant that their decision was unchanged. On December 21, 1942 the appellant filed an appeal from the decision of the Local Board to the Board of Appeal. (T. p. 34.) On February 10, 1943 the Appeal Board unanimously affirmed the decision of the Local Board and the appellant was notified of such action. (T. p. 34.) Thereafter appellant wrote letters to both the State Headquarters and the National Headquarters of Selective Service seeking recognition of his claim for exemption (T. pp. 81 through 90) but after a review of the matter, both State and National headquarters refused to take affirmative action on behalf of the said appellant. (T. p. 57.) On May 1, 1943 the Local Board mailed to appellant an order to report for induction into the armed forces of the United States at San Francisco, California, on the 14th day of May, 1943. (T. p. 59.) Appellant did not comply with this order. (T. p. 61.) Appellant admitted the receipt of the order to report for induction. (T. p. 68.) The appellant was sent a notice of delinquency on May 15, 1943, to which he replied that he could not report because he was an ordained minister of the gospel. (T. pp. 61 through 65.) Appellant also stated that he was unwilling to be inducted for non-combatant military service or to go to a camp for conscientious objectors. (T. p. 69.) It was because of this failure to comply with the order of induction that he was indicted for a violation of the Selective Training and Service Act of 1940, as Amended. (50 USCA, Section 311.)

THE ISSUE.

All of the appellant's assignments of error raise but a single issue, which we believe may be fairly and correctly stated as follows:

May a defendant who has been indicted for his failure to report for induction into the armed forces of the United States, defend such failure in a criminal prosecution by collaterally attacking the Board's administrative acts?

POSITION OF THE GOVERNMENT.

The answer to the above stated question is: "No".

ARGUMENT.

The issue above stated is precisely the one considered by the Supreme Court of the United States in the case of

> *Falbo v. The United States of America,* decided January 3, 1944, (No. 73, October term 1943),

in which the said Court affirmed the conviction of the appellant. In its decision the Supreme Court said:

> "The narrow question therefore presented by this case is whether Congress has authorized judicial review of the propriety of a board's classification in a criminal prosecution for willful violation of an order directing a registrant to report for the last step in the selective process. We think it has not."

To the same effect see also:

United States v. Bowles, 131 F. (2d) 818, (CCA-3), affirmed on another ground, 319 U.S. 333;

United States v. Grieme, 128 F. (2d) 811 (CCA-3);

Fletcher v. United States, 129 F. (2d) 262 (CCA-5);

United States v. Kauten, 133 F. (2d) 703 (CCA-2);

United States v. Mroz, 136 F. (2d) 221 (CCA-7).

On authority of the decision of the Supreme Court of the United States in the *Falbo* case appellee rests his case.

Counsel for the appellant makes no mention of the *Falbo* case in his opening brief dated January 14, 1944. Certainly he can not deny its relevancy in the case at bar. It therefore can reasonably be assumed that his brief must have been in the hands of the printer before appellant learned of the decision in the *Falbo* case.

In closing, the appellee calls attention to the case of *United States v. John Gilbert Laier* (decided November 8, 1943 by St. Sure, District Judge, Northern District of California), cited by the appellant in his brief, on pages 15 and 19, and on which the said appellant places great reliance. The *Laier* case and the case at bar may be distinguished because in the *Laier* case the defendant was refused a personal hearing, while in the case of the appellant, such a hearing was accorded him, and there is nothing in the record to show that the hearing was a "farce", as the appellant describes it in his brief, because, as the board members testified (and there is no reason why they should not be believed), the appellant did have a full and fair hearing.

Assuming, however, for the sake of argument, and for the sake of argument alone, since the facts do not justify the conclusion that the appellant's hearing was, as he described it, a "farce", or let us even go further and assume that, as in the *Laier* case, there was an outright refusal to grant a personal appearance, it is nevertheless the contention of the appellee that the decision of the Supreme Court in the *Falbo* case is authority for the proposition that such a defense may not be properly raised in a prosecution for violation of the Selective Training and Service Act of 1940.

CONCLUSION.

Accordingly we respectfully submit that the judgment of the District Court was correct and it should be affirmed.

Dated, San Francisco,
February 14, 1944.

Frank J. Hennessy,
United States Attorney,
R. B. McMillan,
Assistant United States Attorney,
Joseph Karesh,
Assistant United States Attorney,
Attorneys for Appellee.

United States
Circuit Court of Appeals
For the Ninth Circuit.

B. H. PRENTICE,

Appellant,

vs.

L. BOTELER, Trustee in Bankruptcy of the Estate of DR. W. J. ROSS COMPANY, a Corporation, Bankrupt,

Appellee.

Transcript of Record

Upon Appeal from the District Court of the United States for the Southern District of California, Central Division

Rotary Colorprint, 590 Folsom St., San Francisco

No. 10497

United States
Circuit Court of Appeals
For the Ninth Circuit.

B. H. PRENTICE,

Appellant,

vs.

L. BOTELER, Trustee in Bankruptcy of the Estate of DR. W. J. ROSS COMPANY, a Corporation, Bankrupt,

Appellee.

Transcript of Record

Upon Appeal from the District Court of the United States for the Southern District of California, Central Division

Rotary Colorprint, 590 Folsom St., San Francisco

INDEX

[Clerk's Note: When deemed likely to be of an important nature, errors or doubtful matters appearing in the original certified record are printed literally in italic; and, likewise, cancelled matter appearing in the original certified record is printed and cancelled herein accordingly. When possible, an omission from the text is indicated by printing in italic the two words between which the omission seems to occur.]

Index Page

Index Page

NAMES AND ADDRESSES OF ATTORNEYS:

For Appellant:

B. H. PRENTICE, in pro per

4705 Firestone Blvd.
South Gate, Calif.

For Appellee:

CRAIG & WELLER
THOMAS S. TOBIN

817 Board of Trade Building
111 West Seventh Street
Los Angeles, Calif. [1*]

*** Page numbering appearing at foot of page of original certified Transcript of Record.**

In the District Court of the United States for the Southern District of California, Central Division

In Bankruptcy No. 40689-B

In the matter of

DR. W. J. ROSS CO.,
a corporation,

Debtor.

ORIGINAL PETITION IN PROCEEDINGS UNDER CHAPTER XI

To the Honorable Judges of the District Court of the United States, for the Southern District of California, Central Division:

The petition of Dr. W. J. Ross Co., a corporation, having its principal place of business at Los Alamitos, in the County of Orange, State of California, engaged in the business of manufacture and sale of dog food, soap, fertilizer, and in the rendering and sale of tallow, respectfully represents:

I.

Your petitioner has had its principal place of business in the City of Los Alamitos, Orange County, California, within the above jurisdictional district for a period of more than eight years last preceeding the filing of this petition, and in this jurisdictional district for more than eighteen years.

II.

No bankruptcy proceeding initiated by a petition by or against your petitioner is pending.

III.

Your petitioner is unable to pay its debts as they mature and proposes the following arrangement with its unsecured debtors:

1. Debtor to remain in possession of the assets and to operate the business of the debtor, subject to supervision of the Court, pending the confirmation of the arrangement hereinafter [2] proposed, or until further order of the Court.

2. The debtor shall conduct the business in such a manner as will accomplish the best results for all interested parties;

3. Principal assets of this debtor consist of material and supplies, machinery, tools and equipment for the purpose of manufacturing prepared dog food, soap, fertilizer, and other products of a kindred nature. In addition thereto the debtor is possessed of four certain boats equipped and suitable for the purpose of taking and rendering of various kinds of fish, including whale and shark. That said boats are of the reasonable value of Forty-five Thousand ($45,000.00) Dollars, or more. That one of said boats, commonly known as the Lottie Bennett, is subject to wharf, dock and repair charges of approximately Twelve Thousand ($12,000.00) Dollars. In addition thereto the debtor has a valuable lease on the premises occupied by it and upon which it has installed various and sundry machinery, tools and equipment.

That the liabilities are approximately as follows:

Accounts payable Sixty Thousand ($60,000.00) Dollars; notes and contracts payable, Seven Thousand Eight Hundred Seventy Dollars and Eighty-three Cents ($7,870.83); payroll and taxes approximately $2,858.41.

Your petitioner has a very valuable good will; which is capable of producing in excess of Three Hundred Fifty Thousand ($350,000.00) Dollars, or more, gross business during any one year. That by reason of certain unforeseen catastrophies, and more especially by reason of the economic conditions existing for a period of several months, and the uncertain conditions now in force and effect as a result of war conditions, and effecting businesses such as is operated by the petitioner, the business of your petitioner has suffered greatly with the result that it has been unable to pay its debts as they mature. Your petitioner feels that if a reasonable extension is granted to it by its creditors, all of its [3] creditors will eventually be paid in full and the petitioner will maintain its valuable good will and preserve the interest and investment of its stockholders.

That your petitioner proposes that the business of the debtor be operated by the debtor and under the supervision of a receiver and a creditors committee and that from the gross proceeds the debtor's obligations be paid in the following order of priority:

(a) The necessary expenses in the operation of the business;

(b) The actual necessary costs of administration of the debtor estate as fixed by the Court, including the fees of the attorney for the debtor, the fees of the receiver and disbursing agent, the fees of any counsel who will be engaged by the receiver, and the necessary amount to be expended for filing and indemnity fees;

(c) All claims and taxes entitled to priority pursuant to the provisions of Section 64(a) 4 of the Bankruptcy Act; and

(d) The claims of general unsecured creditors.

It is proposed under the above plan to pay all of the general unsecured creditors in full over a period of twenty-four months with the understanding that creditors will receive not less than 5% (five percent) per month on their claims, the first payment to commence four months after the confirmation of the plan. It is further proposed that upon the confirmation of the plan fresh operating capital in such amounts as may be necessary will be put into the business in order to maintain it.

4. That it is contemplated that the Court will retain jurisdiction for all purposes until the arrangement has been fully carried out as herein above set forth.

5. Upon the completion of the entire arrangement and the satisfaction of all creditors these proceedings shall thereupon be terminated and the debtor shall then be entitled to manage its affairs. [4]

IV.

That your petitioner is unable to file its Schedules "A" and "B" at this time as set forth in the affidavit filed herewith praying for ten days time in which to file its Schedules "A" and "B" and your petitioner upon the granting of the relief prayed for therein will file its Schedules "A" and "B" within the time allowed by the Court.

V.

The statement attached hereto, marked "Exhibit A", and verified by your petitioner's oath, contains a full and true statement of all its executory contracts as required by the provisions of the Bankruptcy Act.

VI.

That attached hereto and marked Exhibit "B", verified by your petitioner's oath, is a list of creditors of the debtor which said list is, however, subject to amendment in the schedules hereinafter to be filed.

VII.

That attached hereto and made a part hereof, and marked Exhibit "C", is a resolution of the Board of Directors of the debtor corporation authorizing the filing of these proceedings.

Wherefore your petitioner prays that proceedings may be had upon this petition in accordance with the provisions of Chapter XI of the Act of Congress relating to bankruptcy, and that a receiver be appointed to act as a custodian of the assets of the debtor corporation pending the confirmation of this arrangement and for the purpose of supervising the operation of the business by the debtor corporation.

[Seal] DR. W. J. ROSS CO.,
a corporation
By DR. W. J. ROSS
President
CHARLES H. VEALE
Attorney for Petitioner [5]

(Duly Verified May 21, 1942, by W. J. Ross.)

[Endorsed]: Filed May 23, 1942. [6]

[Title of District Court and Cause.]

APPROVAL OF DEBTOR'S PETITION AND ORDER OF REFERENCE UNDER SECTION 322 OF THE BANKRUPTCY ACT

At Los Angeles, in said District, on May 23, 1942, before the said Court the petition of Dr. W. J. Ross Co., a corporation, that it desires to obtain relief under Section 322 of the Bankruptcy Act, and within the true intent and meaning of all of the Acts of Congress relating to bankruptcy, having been heard and duly considered, the said petition is hereby approved accordingly.

It is thereupon ordered that said matter be referred to Ben E. Tarver, Esq., one of the referees in bankruptcy of this Court, to take such further proceedings therein as are required by said Acts; and that the said Dr. W. J. Ross Co., a corporation shall attend before said referee on June 1, 1942, and at such times as said referee shall designate, at his office in Santa Ana, California, and shall submit to such orders as may be made by said referee or by this Court relating to said matter.

Witness, the Honorable Paul J. McCormick, Judge of said Court, and the seal thereof, at Los Angeles, in said District, on May 23, 1942.

[Seal] R. S. ZIMMERMAN, Clerk
By E. M. ENSTROM, JR.
Deputy Clerk

[Endorsed]: Filed June 17, 1942. [8]

[Title of District Court and Cause.]

Schedule B. Statement of All Property of Bankrupt

Schedule B-1.

Real Estate

Location and Description of all Real Estate owned by Debtor, or held by him, whether under deed, lease or contract. — Incumbrances, thereon, if any, and dates thereof.—Statement of particulars relating thereto.	Etimated value of Debtor's Interest Dollars Cents
3.75 acres, more or less, of land situated on Firestone Boulevard in the City of Southgate.... (Subject to encumbrance of $1,500.00 representing balance of purchase price)	$ 5,734.09
Total	$ 5,734.09

DR. W. J. ROSS, Petitioner

[Endorsed]: Filed June 17, 1942. [9]

[Title of District Court and Cause.]

ORDER OF ADJUDICATION

At Santa Ana, in said District, on June 17, 1942;

The said Bankrupt having filed, on the 23rd day of May, 1942, its Original Petition in Proceedings under Sec. 322 of Chapter XI of the Bankruptcy Act, setting forth, among other things, that it was unable to pay its debts as they mature, and praying that proceedings might be had upon said Petition in accordance with the provisions of Chapter XI of the Bankruptcy Act relating to bankruptcy, and the Honorable Paul J. McCormick, a Judge of the above entitled Court in and for the Southern District of California, having made and filed his Order on the 23rd day of May, 1942, approving said petition and referring said bankruptcy matter to the undersigned Referee, etc., and to take such further proceedings therein as required by said Act; and

Said Bankrupt having on the 17th day of June, 1942, filed herein its withdrawal of plan of arrangement and its consent to adjudication, and admitting in writing its inability to pay its debts and its willingness to be adjudged a bankrupt; and

Said Petition and said withdrawal of plan of arrangement and consent to be adjudicated a bankrupt having been heard and duly considered, and there being no objection thereto,

It Is Adjudged that the said Dr. W. J. Ross Co., a corporation, the said petitioner, is a bankrupt under the Act of Congress relating to bankruptcy, and hereby direct that bankruptcy herein be proceeded with pursuant to the provisions of said Act.

Dated: June 17, 1942.

BEN E. TARVER
Referee in Bankruptcy.

[Endorsed]: Filed June 20, 1942. [11]

[Title of District Court and Cause.]

BOND OF TRUSTEE

Know all Men by these Presents,

That we L. Boteler of Los Angeles, California, as Principal and the Saint Paul-Mercury Indemnity Company of Saint Paul, a corporation duly incorporated under the laws of the State of Delaware, and authorized to act as surety under the Act of Congress approved August 13, 1894, whose principal office is located in Saint Paul, State of Minnesota, as Surety, are held and firmly bound unto the United States of America in the sum of Fifty Thousand and No/100 Dollars ($50,000.00) in lawful money of the United States, to be paid to the said United States, for which payment, well and truly to be made, we bind ourselves and our heirs, executors, administrators, successors and assigns, jointly and severally by these presents.

Signed and Sealed this 7th day of July A. D. 1942.

The Condition of This Obligation Is Such, That whereas the above named L. Boteler was, on the 6th day of July A. D. 1942, appointed Trustee in the case pending in bankruptcy in the said Court, wherein Dr. W. J. Ross Company, a corporation is the Bankrupt, and he, the said L. Boteler has accepted said trust with all the duties and obligations pertaining thereto.

Now, Therefore, if the said L. Boteler, Trustee as aforesaid, shall obey such orders as said Court may make in relation to said trust, and shall faithfully and truly account for all the moneys, assets and effects of the estate of the said Bankrupt which shall come into his hands and possession, and shall in all respects faithfully perform all his official duties as said Trustee, then this obligation to be void; otherwise to remain in full force and virtue.

Signature Illegible (Seal)

Signed, sealed and delivered in the presence of

Examined and recommended for approval as provided in Rule 28.

SAINT PAUL - MERCURY INDEMNITY COMPANY OF SAINT PAUL
By ARTHUR D. BOND
Its Attorney-in-fact.
FRANK C. WELLER
Attorneys.

Approved this 8th day of July A. D. 1942.

BEN E. TARVER
District Judge

Acknowledgement of Attorney-in-Fact.

State of California.
County of Los Angeles—ss.:

On this 7th day of July 1942, before me, a Notary Public, within and for the said County and State, personally appeared Arthur D. Bond, known to me to be the person whose name is subscribed to the within instrument as the Attorney-in-Fact of and for the Saint Paul-Mercury Indemnity Company, Saint Paul, Minnesota, a corporation created, organized and existing under and by virtue of the laws of the State of Delaware, and acknowledged to me that he subscribed the name of the Saint Paul-Mercury Indemnity Company thereto as Surety, and his own name as Attorney-in-Fact.

PAUL W. ROSTER JR.
Notary Public.

My Commission Expires July 26, 1945.

[Endorsed]: Filed July 9, 1942. [13]

[Title of District Court and Cause.]

REFEREE'S CERTIFICATE ON REVIEW

To the Hon. C. E. Beaumont, District Judge:

I, Ben E. Tarver, Referee in Bankruptcy, in charge of this proceeding, do hereby certify:

That in the course of such proceedings, an Order Confirming a Sale of real property, a copy of which is annexed to the petition hereinafter referred to, was made and entered on the 16th day of March, 1943:

That on the 29th day of March, 1943, Burr H. Prentice, doing business under the fictitious name of "Smileage Company, Ltd.", a would-be purchaser or bidder for said real property in such proceeding, feeling aggrieved thereat, filed a petition for a review, which was granted;

That the error complained of by the petitioner is that petitioner claims to be the highest bidder for the property described in said order confirming sale of real property first hereinabove referred to, at the time when said return of sale by the Trustee to the Baruch Corporation was before the Referee for confirmation, and that the Referee erred in not accepting his bid of $2325.00 and confirming the sale to him for said amount.

That a summary of the evidence on which such Order was based is as follows:

That at the hour of 10 o'clock on the 10th day of March, 1943 the hereinafter Referee called for hearing the petition of the Trustee to hear said Return of Sale of said property, and that there were present the following persons: Mr. Baruch, representing the successful bidder, to-wit: The Baruch Corporation; Mr. Burr H. Prentice and Mr. Clemens, representing the Smileage Company, Ltd.;

That at said time and place the Referee announced that he had before him for attention the Trustee's Return of Sale of a parcel of land for $2250.00 and his Petition for its confirmation; that he would not take the time or trouble to [15] read the Return of Sale and Petition in full, unless requested so to do by someone then and there present, but would merely read the description of the property, or enough of it to identify it as the parcel of land that was up for confirmation or sale. There being no request for the reading of the whole Return of Sale and Petition for Confirmation, the Referee merely read the description of the land before him for sale, and after doing so one of the men from the Smileage Company, Ltd. said that was the same property; whereupon the Referee asked for higher bids on the property set forth in the Return of Sale, but said that he would not consider any bid that was not at least 10% higher than the $2250.00 bid by the purchaser named in the Return of Sale;

That while the Referee asked for higher bids, as stated, he did not announce or state that he would sell the property at auction or that he would auction the sale; whereupon the person present who said he represented the Smileage Company, Ltd., said he would bid $2300.00 for that company, and a little later he raised it to $2325.00 and tendered a socalled check or company voucher for more than 10% of said last mentioned sum, to-wit: $233.00. The Referee did not retain said document herein referred to as a check or voucher, and did not clearly determine its character as it was so crudely made out, and when he asked the bidder if he wanted to leave it with the Referee, he said "No" and accepted it back again;

That when the Referee asked him if it was a certified check he said "No. Would you accept it if it was?" The Referee replied that he would not unless it was at least 10% greater in amount than the $2250.00 bid by the purchased named in said Return of Sale.

That the said sum of $2325.00 bid on behalf of said Smileage Company, Ltd. was the highest sum there bid.

Mr. Prentice, the petitioner, at about this stage of the proceedings, said there was nothing in the Bankruptcy Act that provided that the Referee should not accept any bid that was not an amount at least 10% greater than the amount bid by the purchaser in the Return of Sale. The Referee replied that neither did he understand there was any such provision in the Bankruptcy Act, but, notwithstanding, he thought it was manifestly unfair to have a purchaser at a [16] private sale bind himself in writing to pay $2250.00 for a parcel of land and then when the sale was up for confirmation before the Referee, for the Referee to accept a bid less than an increase of 10%.

At some stage of the proceedings the Referee, in the presence of those present as hereinbefore stated, rang up Mr. L. Boteler, the Trustee, in Los Angeles, and said to him that he, the Referee, was rejecting bids of $2300.00 and $2325.00 for the property in question as they were not in an amount 10% greater than the price set forth in the Return of Sale as being bid by the purchaser named therein —the Baruch Corporation, and that he did not think that any sum less than that should be accepted, and asked the Trustee if he had any different idea. The Trustee replied that he had not and agreed with the Referee, and whereupon the Referee turned to those present and said he would stand by his ruling and refuse to accept the said bid of $2325.00 and that he would confirm the sale fo the Baruch Corporation for $2250.00, unless a bid was made that was 10% higher than that sum.

That the Referee does not subscribe to the Los Angeles Daily Journal, in which the Trustee advertised, placing therein an ad stating that bids would be received for said property at the office of the undersigned Referee, on March 10, at the hour of 10 o'clock a.m. and did not have before him a copy of said ad; that while he had hastily read the ad in a copy of the said Journal in the Orange County Law Library at the Court House in Santa Ana, he did not remember all of the terms thereof, but he did not understand from said ad in said Journal that the said sale to be held before the Referee was an ordinary auction for the property in question. That he did not request said ad to be published, and had not read it before it was published, nor had he ordered any publication of said sale.

The Referee's recollection is that he also called Mr. Boteler, the Trustee, over the phone and asked him about the title, etc. and whether or not a certificate of title would be given, and about the taxes, and that the Referee having already announced that the property would be sold free and clear of incumbrances, thereupon confirmed the sale of said real property to the Baruch Corporation.

That no full stenographic report was taken or kept, either by the Referee or his Clerk, of everything done at the time said Return of Sale was up for [17] confirmation but the above is the substance of what was said and done at said time, to the best of the recollection of the undersigned Referee; that his Clerk kept notes for the Record Book, a copy of which will be found among the papers sent up to the Court for its information;

That the said Order Confirming the Sale of the real property in question was entered on the 16th day of March, 1943 and at the same time was signed, filed and stamped with the appropriate filing mark in the office of the Referee; that on the 29th day of March, 1943, and not before, the Referee received through the United States postoffice at Santa Ana, and signed for as registered mail, the Petition to Review above mentioned, in an envelope marked at Los Angeles postoffice, as there received, on the 26th day of March, 1943, and post marked by the postoffice at Santa Ana as having been received on the 27th of March, 1943. Said envelope is included in the records of this review and referred to herein as in the hereinafter numbered paragraph 5.

That the Referee was informed by the Clerk at the Registry window at the postoffice at Santa Ana that the envelope enclosing said Petition for Review was received at the Santa Ana postoffice at 9 o'clock A. M. of March 27, 1943, and although addressed to the undersigned Referee at his office in the Otis Building, the notice of the arrival of said Petition for Review was placed in the postoffice box of the Referee.

I desire to add to the statement of what took place: That Mr. Baruch, who was present and represented the purchaser named in the Return of Sale, stated that he had spent $75.00 for surveying the property in question, on the faith of having his purchase confirmed, and also that he had spent other amounts making a total of about $125.00.

That a young lady representative of Mr. Prentice, the petitioner, was in the Referee's office on the 16th day of March and spent several hours in copying the record of the proceedings of the sale and the confirmation thereof, of the property in question, to the Baruch Corporation, the bidder or purchaser named in said Return of Sale, and my clerk, at her request, laid before her all of the orders and papers filed in and about the sale of this property to the Baruch Corporation; that said Order Confirming Sale then bore the filing marks of the [18] Referee's office, showing that it was filed on the 16th day of March, 1943 in that office; that five or six days later Mr. Prentice, the petitioner, himself was in the Referee's office and spent about an hour copying some of the record in regard to said sale and confirmation, at which time he was presented with the record, including said Order Confirming the Sale to the Baruch Corporation.

That the question presented in this review is: Did the Referee herein err in refusing to accept a bid for the real property described in said Return of Sale for a sum that was not at least 10% greater than the sum of $2250.00, the sum set forth in said Return of Sale as the amount bid by the purchaser named therein, and in the absence of a higher bid than the sum of $2325.00, in confirming the sale set forth in said Return of Sale?

I hand you up herewith, for the information of the Judge, copies of the following papers:

1. The Record Book or minutes of the proceedings;

2. The original Petition on which the certificate is granted, with a copy of the Order Confirming the Sale to Baruch Corporation for $2250.00 attached thereto;

3. The Order authorizing the Trustee to sell the property;

4. The Return of Sale and Petition for its Confirmation;

5. The original envelope in which the Petition for Review was mailed by the petitioner at Los Angeles to the Referee at Santa Ana, with the Referee's notation made thereon at the time it was received, bearing the Los Angeles post marks of the date it was deposited in the postoffice in that city and the date when the said petition was received at the Santa Ana postoffice;

6. Original Points and Authorities of Petitioner to Review Order, accompanying said Petition.

Dated: April 13, 1943.

Respectfully submitted,

BEN E. TARVER

Referee in Bankruptcy.

[Endorsed]: Filed Apr. 15, 1943. [19]

[Title of District Court and Cause.]

ORDER OF SALE OF REAL PROPERTY

The Trustee herein, L. Boteler, having filed his petition for authority to sell the hereinafter described real estate and the same coming on for hearing this 20th day of July, 1942 after due notice to creditors as required by law, and said petition having been heard and duly considered, on motion of Craig & Weller, counsel for said Trustee, no adverse interests appearing thereat,

It Is Ordered That the Trustee herein be, and he is hereby authorized and directed to sell, at private sale or at public auction, to the highest and best bidder or bidders therefor, the real property described in said petition, situated in the City of Southgate, County of Los Angeles, State of California, as follows:

That part of Lot "A" of Tract No. 486 as per Map recorded in Book 15 pages 30 and 31 of Maps in the Office of the County Recorder described as follows:

> Beginning at the Northeasterly corner of said Lot "A" thence north 82° 45′ west along the northerly line of said Lot, 263.63 feet to the northeasterly corner of the land described in the deed to Southern California Edison Company, recorded in Book 8429 page 270 of Official Records of said County; thence south 34° 46′ 40″ west along the southeasterly line of the land described in said deed [20] 717.7 feet, more or less, to a point in the southerly line of said

Lot "A"; thence south 82° 34′ 40″ east along said southerly line 247.08 feet to the southeasterly corner of said Lot "A" thence northerly along the southeasterly line of said lot to the point of beginning. Except that portion thereof, if any, now included within the boundaries of Andrews & Massachia Land in Ranchio Santa Gertrudes as per map recorded in Book 12 pages 138 and 139 of maps in the office of the County Recorder.

Subject to a deed of trust dated October 1, 1940, wherein Title Guarantee & Trust Company, a California corporation, is Trustee and Lydia Bushell, a married woman, is beneficiary.

any sale of said real property is to be made subject to the confirmation of this Court.

Dated: July 20th, 1942

(Signed) BEN E. TARVER

[Endorsed]: Filed Apr. 15, 1943. [21]

[Title of District Court and Cause.]

RETURN OF SALE OF REAL PROPERTY

The Trustee herein, L. Boteler, respectfully represents to this Court that under and pursuant to an Order of Sale heretofore made and entered herein, he has sold to the Baruch Corporation, a California Corporation, for the sum of $2250.00 lawful money of the United States, the following described real property belonging to this estate, to-wit:

That part of Lot "A" of Tract No. 486 in the City of Southgate, County of Los Angeles, State of California, as per Map recorded in Book 15, pages 30 and 31 of Maps in the Office of the County Recorder of said county, described as follows:

Beginning at the Northeasterly corner of said Lot "A" thence north 82° 45′ West along the Northerly line of said Lot, 263.63 feet to the Northeasterly corner of the land described in the deed to Southern California Edison Company, recorded in Book 8429, Page 270 of Official Records of said County; thence South 34° 46′ 40″ West along the Southeasterly line of the land described in said deed 717.7 feet, more or less, to a point in the Southerly line of said Lot "A"; thence South 82° 34′ 40″ East along said Southerly line 247.08 feet to the Southeasterly corner of the said Lot "A", thence Northerly along the Southeasterly line of said Lot to the point of beginning. Except that portion thereof, if any, now included within the boundaries of Andrews & Mussachia Land in Ranchio Santa Gertrudes as per map recorded in Book 12, Pages 138 and 139 of maps in the office of the County Recorder or said county. And subject to a right of way for main San Antonio Ditch crossing said land also a right of way for irrigation ditch along the north line of the property herein described from the main ditch to Perry Road, as reserved in deed recorded in Book 2832 Page 57 of Deeds. [22]

That said purchaser has deposited its check with your Trustee in the sum of $225.00 as evidence of good faith, the balance of the purchase price to be paid in full after confirmation of sale by this Court and upon completion of escrow with the Title Insurance & Trust Company.

Your Trustee respectfully represents that said purchaser was the highest and best bidder for said property; that said sum is the highest and best bid received therefor and that the same constitutes the full value of the right, title and interest in this estate in and to said property, and your petitioner herein believes that it is to the best interest of this estate that said sale be confirmed.

Wherefore your Trustee prays that a meeting of creditors be called and that a hearing in connection therewith be had in open Court as soon as may be on this Return of Sale, and that a ten-day notice thereof be sent to creditors forthwith, and this Court's order be thereupon made and entered herein, if no objections are then made thereto, approving and confirming the sale hereinabove described, and that your Trustee be authorized and directed to deliver over said property to said purchaser upon receipt of the purchase price therefor.

(signed) L. BOTELER
Trustee

State of California
County of Los Angeles—ss.

L. Boteler being by me first duly sworn, deposes

and says: that he is the Trustee in the above entitled action; that he has heard read the foregoing Return of Sale of Real Property and knows the contents thereof; and that the same is true of his own knowledge, except the matters which are herein stated upon information or belief, and as to those matters that he believes it to be true.

(signed) L. BOTELER

Subscribed and Sworn to before me [23] this 25 day of February A. D. 1943

[Seal] (Signed) M. M. JENKS

Notary Public in and for the County of Los Angeles, State of California

[Endorsed]: Filed Apr. 15, 1943. [24]

[Title of District Court and Cause.]

REFEREE'S RECORD OF PROCEEDINGS

3-10 at 10 A. M. held sale of real property, lot on Manchester Ave. Mr. Baruch, of the Baruch Corporation, who had bid $2250.00 for the lot, was present; also B. H. Prentice and Mr. Clemens, representing The Smileage Co., Ltd. who raised the bid to $2300.00 for the Company and later made a personal bid of $2325.00, and tendered a check, or Company voucher, for $233.00, as a deposit, which the Referee did not accept as he insisted that the former bid be increased by 10%, The Referee confirmed the sale to the Baruch Corporation. The meeting adjourned.

3-16. Filed Order Confirming Sale of Real Property

[Endorsed]: Filed Apr. 15, 1943 [25]

[Title of District Court and Cause.]

PETITION TO REVIEW REFEREE'S ORDER

To Ben E. Tar*b*er, Esq. Referee in Bankruptcy

Your petitioner respectfully states that he is operating under a fictitious name, to wit "Smileage Company". That he has *heretofor* complied with section 2466 and 2468 of the C.C.P. State of California.

Furthermore your petitioner respectfully shows:

That on the 10th day of March, 1943, at the hour of 10:00 A. M. he was present in the court room of the Hon. Ben E. Tar*b*er, Referee in Bankruptcy in the City of Santa Ana, California.

That in the course of the proceeding before the Honorable Court at the said time and place an order, a copy of which is hereto attached, marked Exhibit "A", was made and entered in the above entitled cause.

That such order was erroneous in that it denied to your petitioner, as the highest bidder, his right to purchase that certain real property more fully described in "Exhibit A" hereto attached.

Wherefor, your petitioner, feeling aggrieved, because of such order, prays that the same may be reviewed, as provided in the Bankruptcy Act of

1898 and the amendments thereto, and the general orders of the Court.

Dated March 25, 1943

BURR H. PRENTICE

Petitioner [26]

[Endorsed]: Filed 3-29-43.

EXHIBIT "A"

In the District Court of the United States, Southern District of California, Central Division

In Bankruptcy No. 40689B

In the Matter of

DR. W. J. ROSS CO., a Corporation,

Bankrupt

ORDER CONFIRMING SALE OF REAL PROPERTY

The trustee in bankruptcy herein, L. Boteler, having heretofore filed his petition for an order authorizing him to sell certain real property belonging to this bankrupt estate, as hereinafter described at private sale or at public auction as the trustee deemed suited to obtain the highest and best bid *therefor,* and a meeting of creditors of the above bankrupt having been called before the undersigned Referee in Bankruptcy at his Court Room in the City of Santa Ana, County of Orange, State of California, on the 20th day of July, 1942, of which said meeting all the creditors of the above named bankrupt were given more than ten days notice as required by law, and there being no objection to the granting of said petition, and the Referee having made and entered his order of sale of real property, and after the conclusion of said meeting, authorizing and directing the trustee to sell at private sale or public auction, to the highest and best bidders *therefor,* the real property hereinafter described, and the trustee having endeavored to dispose of said real property subsequent to the entry of said order, and having finally negotiated a private sale to the Baruch Corporation, a California corporation, for the sum of $2250.00, lawful money of the United States, and having accepted a deposit in the sum of $225.00 as evidence of good faith on the part of the purchaser, subject to confirmation of the sale by this Court, and upon completion of the escrow with the Title Insurance and Trust Company, and after which the balance of the purchase price was to be paid, and the trustee having made his return of sale to the undersigned Referee in Bankruptcy, in writing, recommending confirmation thereof, and having reported [27] to the Court in said return of sale that said purchase price constituted the full value of the right, title and interest of the bankrupt estate in and to said real property, and said return having duly come on for confirmation before the undersigned Referee in Bankruptcy on March 10, 1943, at the hour of 10 o'clock, A. M., on said date, and there having appeared at said hearing on confirmation thereof, one Prentice who made an offer to raise the purchase price reported by the trustee, in the sum of $50.00, tendering a check on a San

Diego Bank, and the Referee having asked the trustee for his recommendations with regard to said $50.00 additional offer, and the trustee having recommended that any additional offers made at the time of confirmation of said sale should be at least ten per centum of the agreed sale price which had been submitted for confirmation, and the said Prentice having declined in open court to advance said proffered bid to ten per centum above the purchase price reported by the trustee, and the Referee feeling that it would be unjust and inequitable to the purchaser who had negotiated with the trustee to purchase said real property at a full and fair purchase price, to permit a bidder to raise the bid for an inadequate amount at the time of the confirmation of said sale, and the Referee having considered said matter, and being fully advised in the premises,

Finds that the purchase price of $2250.00 negotiated by the trustee with the Baruch Corporation, a California corporation, is a fair purchase price offered and accepted in good faith, and should be confirmed, and that any further bids or offers made at the time of the confirmation thereof in a sum less than ten per centum above said purchase price of $2250.00, should be rejected.

In Consideration of the foregoing, and on motion of Messrs. Craig & Weller, attorneys for the Trustee, Thomas S. Tobin of counsel, it is

Ordered that the sale of real property belonging to this bankrupt estate and situated in the City of South Gate, County of Los Angeles, State of California, described as:

That part of Lot "A" of Tract No. 486 as per Map recorded in Book 15, pages 30 and 31 of Maps in the Office of the [28] County Recorder, described as follows:

> Beginning at the Northeasterly corner of said Lot "A" thence north 82° 45′ West along the Northerly line of said Lot, 263.63 feet to the Northeasterly corner of the land described in the deed to Southern California Edison Company, recorded in Book 8429, page 270 of Official Records of said County; thence South 34° 46′ 40″ West along the Southeasterly line of the land described in said deed 717.7 feet, more or less, to a point in the Southerly line of said Lot "A"; thence South 82° 34′ 40″ East along said Southerly line 247.08 feet to the Southeasterly corner of said lot "A", thence Northerly along the Southeasterly line of said Lot to the point of beginning. Except that portion thereof, if any, now included within the boundaries of Andrews & Massachia Land in Ranchio Santa Gertrudes as per map recorded in Book 12, Pages 138 and 139 of maps in the office of the County Recorder.
>
> Subject to a Deed of Trust dated October 1, 1940, wherein Title Guarantee and Trust Company, a California corporation, is Trustee and Lydia Bushnell, a married woman, is beneficiary.

made by the trustee herein to the Baruch Corporation, a California corporation, for the sum of $2250.00, lawful money of the United States and returned to this court, be, and the same hereby is confirmed.

It Is Further Ordered that the trustee be, and he hereby is authorized to complete said sale.

Done at Santa Ana, in the Southern District of California this 16th day of March, 1943.

BEN E. TARVER
Refere in Bankruptcy

Filed 3/16/43 [29]

AFFIDAVIT OF MAILING

State of California
County of Los Angeles—ss.

M. Quinn, being first duly sworn, says: That affiant is a citizen of the United States and a resident of the County of Los Angeles, that affiant is over the age of eighteen years and is not a party to the within and above entitled action; that affiant's residence address is 9212 Hunt Street, South Gate, California. That on the 26th day of March, A. D. 1943, affiant served the within Petition to Review Referee's Order on the following interested parties in said action by placing a true copy thereof in envelopes addressed to

Craig & Weller, Thomas S. Tobin, Attorneys for L. Boteler, Trustee, at their business address at 817 Board of Trade Building, 111 West Seventh Street, Los Angeles, California, and

Julius Mackson, Counsel for Baruch Co., at the business address Commercial Exchange Building, 416 W. Eighth Street, Los Angeles,

and by then sealing said envelopes and depositing the same, with postage thereon fully prepaid, in the United States Post Office at Los Angeles, California. That there is delivery service by United States mail at the places so addressed and/or there is a regular communication by mail between the place of mailing and the places so addressed.

M. QUINN

Subscribed and Sworn to Before Me This 26th day of March, 1943.

N. FISHER

Notary Public in and for the County of Los Angeles, State of California.

My Commission Expires Sept. 11th 1946

[Endorsed]: Filed Apr. 15, 1943. [30]

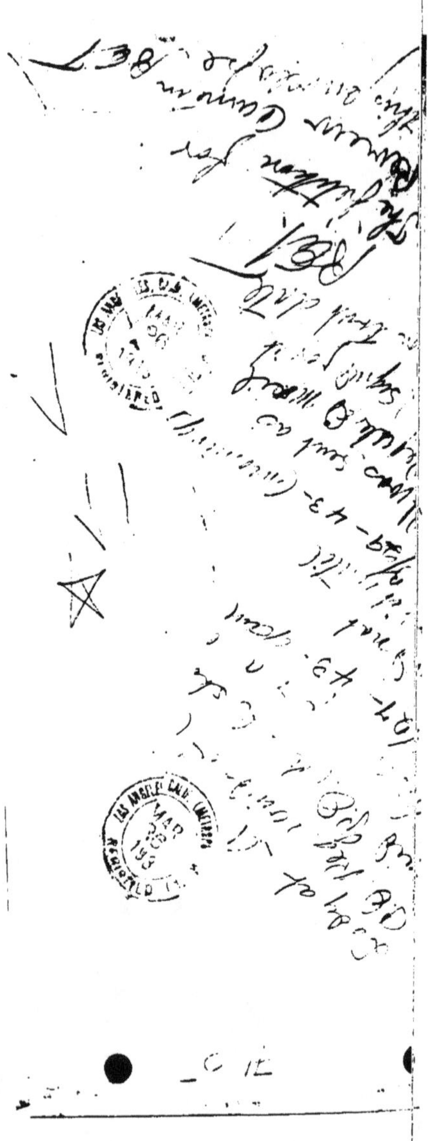

OF PET

FIRMIN

After revi
cause there a
the facts.

The Order
recites that
bid of Earn
Dollars. (P.
of Real Prop
ment as set
ceedings":

"—Mr. B
had bid $22
B. H. Prenti
Smileage Co
for the Com
of $2325.00,
voucher, for
10-15, Refere

This consi
Dollars over
accepted as
ceived theref
of Sale of R

In conn
Three Hund
petitioner
Hundred Th

[Title of District Court and Cause.]

POINTS AND AUTHORITIES IN SUPPORT OF PETITION TO REVIEW ORDER CONFIRMING SALE OF REAL PROPERTY

After reviewing the file in the above entitled cause there appears to be some disagreement as to the facts.

The Order Confirming Sale of Real Property recites that petitioner made an offer to raise the bid of Baruch Co. in the sum of Fifty ($50.00) Dollars. (Pg. 2, Line 7, Order Confirming Sale of Real Property). Contradicting this is the statement as set forth in "Referee's Record of Proceedings":

"——Mr. Baruch of the Baruch Corporation, who had bid $2250.00 for the lot, was present; also B. H. Prentice and Mr. Clemens, representing the Smileage Co., Ltd., who raised the bid to $2300.00 for the Company and later made a personal bid of $2325.00, and tendered a check, or Company voucher, for $233.00 as a deposit" *ect.* Pg. 1, Lines 10-15, Referee's Record of Proceedings).

This constitutes a raise of Seventy-Five ($75.00) Dollars over the bid of Baruch Co., which bid was accepted as being "the highest and best bid received therefor" (Pg. 2, Lines 7-8, Trustee's Return of Sale of Real Property).

In connection with this bid of Two Thousand Three Hundred Twenty Five ($2325.00) Dollars, petitioner tendered a check in the amount of Two Hundred Thirty-three ($233.00) being ten per cent of his bid and even went so far as to offer a cash deposit if the Court felt there was any question of the sufficiency of the check tendered. This is the check which the Court returned to petitioner after declining to accept the increased bid.

The sale of the property described in the Order Confirming Sale, if a [33] sale was in fact held, was not fairly and impartially conducted. Being the highest bidder for the property in open court, petitioner was discriminated against without justification and if the order under review is allowed to stand it will constitute an arbitrary abuse of discretion upon the Referee's part.

"The high bidders, however, have a standing which permits them to appear and urge the acceptance of their bids and the confirmation of the sale. They were brought to the sale by the confirmation of the Court, and having done what the Court asked them to do, they now have a right to ask the Court to approve their acts".

Jacobson vs. Larkey 245 Fed. 541.

"Acceptance of lesser of two comparable bids for property offered for sale by Trustee in Bankruptcy is an abuse of discretion calling for revision". Kimmel v Crocker 72 Fed. (2nd) 599 (Sy*la*bus).

"It would clearly be an abuse of discretion to accept the lesser of two comparable bids". Kimmel v Crocker Supra.

In the case of Jacobson v Larkey (Supra) the Court denied a motion to set aside a sale made to the high bidder wherein the only grounds put forward by the petitioner therein was that if the property were again offered for sale a higher price would be bid for it. This is a different situation than is presented in the present petition wherein this petitioner was the highest bidder at the sale. However, the Court's remarks are so pertinent that we quote:

"After much experience in scrutinizing bidding at judicial sales, courts now uniformly hold that the mere offer to pay more than the price bid is not a substantial ground for setting aside a sale, recognizing that nothing will more certainly tend to discourage and prevent bidding than a judicial determination that the highest bidder may be deprived of the advantage of his accepted bid by an offer of another person subsequently made to bid higher at resale".

There was no showing, nor is there any evidence or other circumstance [34] before the Referee or the Trustee, which would indicate that petitioner was not qualified in all respects as a bidder for the property and perfectly able to fully comply with the terms of the proposed sale and to consummate the purchase of the property. The only excuse why petitioner's higher bid was not accepted according to the record is that the "trustee recommended" that no raise or increase over the amount which he had been privately offered ($2250.00) would be entertained unless the higher offer was at least in a sum equal to ten percent more than the private bid. (Pg. 2, Lines 10-12, Order Confirming Sale of Real Property, and Pg. 1, Line 16, Referee's Record of Proceedings.)

We fail to find any authority in the Bankruptcy Act itself, or in the rules of the court relating to sales of bankrupt property, justifying a recommendation by anyone to the effect that a bid shall not be considered unless it is an increase of ten percent over the amount previously offered. Neither is there authority which would bar an increased bid if it is not in such an increased sum.

The advance bid of petitioner being Seventy Five ($75.00) Dollars more than the bid of Baruch Corporation represented a clear profit to the Bankrupt Estate of just Seventy Five ($75.00) Dollars. For the Trustee or the Referee to insist on an upset bid of Two Thousand Four Hundred Seventy Five ($2475.00) Dollars was unjust and erroneous. To do so was to permit the Baruch Co. to take the property for Two Thousand Two Hundred Fifty ($2250.00) Dollars while this petitioner would have to pay Two Thousand Four Hundred Seventy Five ($2475.00) Dollars for the same property.

Such a proposition is manifestly so unfair that it should not be necessary that petitioner cite any authorities on the point. However, the following citation is so apt to this present situation that it is quoted:

"When the property was offered for sale by the trustee all persons who, in good faith, and with a capacity to comply with the proposed terms, were present at the time and place, were entitled to make offers or bids, and the ones proposing to pay the largest and highest sum was entitled to have his bid or offer [35] accepted upon complying with the terms of sale, and reported to the court for confirmation, or such other orders in the cause as to the court should seem proper and in accordance with the interests of the parties, or the estate, and the course and practice of the court".

"It follows *therefor* that the referee had no right to impose upon Heard, as a condition precedent to opening the bidding that he make an "upset bid" of $78000. The effect of this order was that Williams & Schmulbach were entitled to take the property at $75500 unless Heard would pay $78000 altho he stood ready, willing, and able to comply with his bid of $75,525. This was manifestly unjust and therefore erroneous". In re Williams-Coal City House Furnishings Company vs. Hogue 197 Fed. 1.

In the instance now before the court there would have been no extra cost imposed on the Bankrupt Estate had the sale of the property been confirmed to petitioner. However, the courts have *heretofor* clearly set forth their views on the subject of obtaining the maximum return.

"Haag bid $12000—"an offer to bid $13000 was filed with the exception to the confirmation of the sale to Haag." (It actually sold for $13500——)

"Nevertheless the advance bid (of $13000) was sufficiently substantial in amount to insure against increased costs and present a reasonable possibility of securing for the creditors the protection of whose interest is the chief purpose of bankruptcy proceedings, the real value of the bankrupt's property". In re Wolke Lead Battery Co. 294 Fed. 511.

"in a bankruptcy proceeding the chief purpose is to protect the interest of the creditors". Colter et al Blieden et al In re Morgan Est. 104 F (2nd) 34.

"The confirmation of this sale should only have been made after a fair hearing and upon proof justifying the conclusion that the [36] properties were being sold for all that could reasonably be obtained for them, that the trustee had acted freely and fairly in making the sale, and that it was for the best interest of all concerned that the same should be consummated". Curin v Nourse 66 Fed. (2nd) 137.

There is ample authority to sustain petitioner's position that the Order Confirming the Sale of the Real Property involved herein must be set aside and the offer of petitioner to buy the property for the sum of Two Thousand Three Hundred Twenty Five ($2325.00) Dollars should be accepted and the sale of the same confirmed to him.

Petitioner was present at the time and place noticed for the sale; he made the highest bid; it was made in good faith and he had the capacity and ability to comply with the terms of sale; he tendered a check for ten percent of the amount of his offer and when objection to the form of the tender was made by the representative of the low bidder he offered to post at that time the amount of the check in currency and, in fairness and under the authorities, he was entitled to have his higher offer accepted and the sale of the property confirmed to him.

Respectfully submitted
BURR H. PRENTICE
Petitioner

Jacobson v Larkey, 245 Fed. 541
Kimmel v Crocker 72 Fed. 599
Coal City House Furnishings Co. v Hogue 197 Fed. 1
Wolke Lead Battery Co. 294 Fed. 511
Colter et al Blieden et al In Re Morgan Est. 104 Fed. (2nd) 34
Curin vs. Nourse 66 Fed. (2nd) 137

[Endorsed]: Filed Apr. 15, 1943. [37]

[Title of District Court and Cause.]

PETITIONER'S STATEMENT OF FACTS IN LIEU OF REPORTER'S TRANSCRIPT

To Ben E. Tarber, Esq. Referee in Bankruptcy and To the above District Court:

Upon the petition for review in bankruptcy proceedings from an order of Referee Ben E. Tarber confirming the sale of certain real property to Baruch Company, a corporation, the following facts are presented by the petitioner.

(1) The bankrupt is a corporation organized under the laws of the State of California to carry on the business of Packing dog food, rendering and soap making.

(2) Among the assets of the bankrupt was a certain parcel of real property located in the City of South Gate, County of Los Angeles, State of California, being a portion of Tract #486 and having an area of 3.44 more or less acres.

(3) That on or about July 20, 1942, an order was made as follows:

In the District Court of the United States for the Southern District of California, Central Division

In Bankruptcy No. 40689-B

In the Matter of

DR. W. J. ROSS CO., a Corporation,

Bankrupt

ORDER OF SALE OF REAL PROPERTY [38]

The Trustee herein, L. Boteler, having filed his petition for authority to sell the hereinafter described real estate and the same coming on for hearing this 20 day of July, 1942 after due notice to creditors as required by law, and said petition having been heard and duly considered, on motion of Craig & Weller, counsel for said Trustee, no adverse interests appearing thereat,

It Is Ordered that the Trustee herein be, and he is hereby authorized and directed to sell, at private sale or at public auction, to the highest and best bidder or bidders therefor, the real property described in said petition, situated in the city of South Gate, County of Los Angeles, State of California, as follows:

That part of Lot "A" of Tract No. 486 as per Map recorded in Book 15 pages 30 and 31 of Maps in the Office of the County Recorder described as follows:

Beginning at the Northeasterly corner of said Lot "A" thence north 82° 45′ west along the northerly line of said lot, 263.63 feet to the north-easterly corner of the land described in the deed to Southern California Edison Company, recorded in Book 8429, page 270 of Official Records of said County; thence south 34° 46′ 40″ west along the southeasterly line of the land described in said deed 717.7 feet, more or less to a point in the southerly line of said Lot "A"; thence south 82° 34′ 40″ east along said southerly line 247.08 feet to the southeasterly corner of said Lot "A" thence northerly along the southeasterly line of said lot to the point of beginning. Except that portion thereof, if any, now included within the boundaries of Andrews & Massachia Land in Ranchio Santa Gertrudes as per map recorded in Book 12 pages 138 and 139 of maps in the Office of the County Recorder.

Subject to a deed of trust dated October 1, 1940, wherein [39] Title Guarantee & Trust Company, a California corporation, is Trustee and Lydia Bushnell, a married woman, is beneficiary. Any sale of said property is to be made subject to the confirmation of this Court.

Dated: July 20th 1942

BEN E. TARVER

(4) That the said sale was advertised in the Los Angeles Daily Journal, a newspaper of general circulation, and that the said advertisement was in words and figures as follows:

Today's Assignees' Sales

Dr. W. J. Ross Co., Bankrupt—Real estate approximately 3.44 acres on Manchester Boulevard, about one mile east of Atlantic Boulevard consisting of Part of Lot "A" of Tract 486 in the City of South Gate, County of Los Angeles, as per map recorded in Book 15, Pages 30 and 31 of Maps in the office of the County Recorder as per metes and bounds description, free and clear, subject to reservations, rights of way and easements of records. Sale Wednesday, March 10, 1943, at 10 o'clock, Court Room Ben E. Tarver, Otis Building, Santa Ana, California, L. Boteler, Trustee, TRinity 1231.

(60240 Mar 5-10

That your petitioner was present in your court room on the 10th day of March, 1943, from the hour of 9:45 A. M. to the hour of 10:25 A. M. and during that time the following transpired:

The Court announced that he was going to sell at auction the piece of real property advertised in the paper.

The Court read a brief description of the property to be sold and then asked if that was sufficient description or would anyone wish to have the entire description read. Your petitioner requested that a portion of the *meets* and bounds description be read "So that we may know for sure we are bidding on the piece of property we have in mind". Whereupon the Court did [40] read a portion of the meets and bounds description of the piece of property to be sold. Whereupon your petitioner remarked "Thats all right we are both talking about the same piece of property".

A Mr. Clemens who was present asked as to the zone the property was in and the Court stated he did not know what zone the property was in. Mr. Clemens then asked the Court what easements were reserved in the deed and the Court read aloud from the file calling attention to the easements. Mr. Clemens then asked the Court if the property was free and clear of all encumbrances and the Court stated that it was.

Your petitioner then asked if the taxes on the property would be prorated to date of recordation of deed. The Court stated he would telephone Mr. Boteler and find out. The Court did telephone and apparently did contact Mr. Boteler and after some conversation stated that taxes would be prorated from the 2nd of March, 1943, to the date of sale.

Your petitioner further asked the Court if the Trustee would provide a Certificate of Title to the property and the Court discussed this (apparently with Mr. Boteler) on the telephone and then the Court stated that the Trustee would provide a Certificate of Title from the Title Insurance and Trust Company showing the property free and clear.

At this stage of the proceedings the Court stated that a deposit of 10% of the bid would be required and that he had a bid of Twenty Two Hundred Fifty ($2250.00) Dollars with a deposit of Two Hundred Twenty Five ($225.00) Dollars. Mr. Clemens then bid Twenty Three Hundred ($2300.00) Dollars whereupon the Court stated the Trustee did not want to accept any bids for less than ten percent more than the one bid of Twenty Two Hundred Fifty ($2250.00) Dollars previously had.

A gentleman whose name the petitioner does not know was present in the courtroom during all of the proceedings and at this stage in the proceedings he stated that it was not fair, that "They" had done all the preliminary work on "this" and now somebody from L. A. walks in and overbids them. Your petitioner asked this gentleman if he represents the party who made the first bid of Twenty Two Hundred Fifty ($2250.00) Dollars and he replied that [41] he did. Whereupon your petitioner stated that this was, he understood, a sale at auction of a piece of property to the highest bidder. Whereupon the Court stated he would again telephone Mr. Boteler. While the Court's secretary was getting the telephone connection through your petitioner bid Twenty Three Hundred Twenty Five ($2325.00) Dollars and at that time your petitioner tendered a check drawn on a bank at Bell, California, in the amount of Two Hundred Thirty Three and no/100 ($233.00) Dollars made payable to "L. Boteler Trustee in Bankruptcy W. J. Ross Co. Bankrupt #40689B Central Division" and endorsed on the voucher attached thereto "In payment of deposit on bid auction $2325.00 bid", stating to the Court that this check was tendered as the 10% deposit the Court had previously stated would be required.

The gentleman who claimed to represent the first bidder again protested accepting any bid other than his *principle's* bid. Whereupon the Court asked this gentleman if he would raise his bid and was informed that he would not.

After again talking on the phone apparently with Mr. Boteler the Court stated he would not accept any other bid of an amount less than Twenty Four Hundred Seventy Five ($2475.00) Dollars and that "they" came down here from "L A" and bid as little as Five ($5.00) Dollars over and expect to get a sale confirmed.

The gentleman who stated he represented the first bidder asked the Court if the check your petitioner had tendered was certified and the Court stated it was not. Your petitioner then asked this gentleman if the check his *principle* had tendered with their bid was certified and he stated it was not and he assumed it had been cashed already and that made it better than your petitioner's check. Your petitioner then stated to the Court that if there was any question of the sufficiency of the check then tendered that if the Court would consider the petitioner's bid that this petitioner would at that time post a cash deposit in lieu of the check tendered.

Whereupon the Court stated that he would not award the property to this petitioner even if there was a 10% cash deposit posted unless this petitioner's bid was at least Twenty Four Hundred Seventy Five ($2475.00) Dollars. This [42] amount your petitioner declined to bid, calling attention to the fact that this was a public auction sale of the property and that there had been no mention at the time the terms of sale were announced of any minimum bid that would be acceptable to the Court. Whereupon this petitioner protested the Court's refusal to accept your petitioner's bid of Twenty Three Hundred Twenty Five ($2325.00) Dollars calling attention to the fact that the acceptance of it would result in Seventy Five ($75.00) Dollars more in cash being realized for the benefit of the estate.

Whereupon the Court handed to this petitioner the check for Two Hundred Thirty Three ($233.00) dollars above mentioned and announced the property sold to Baruch Company, incorporated in State of California, for Twenty Two Hundred Fifty

($2250.00) Dollars, whereupon your petitioner stated that he protested the said sale.

Respectfully submitted
BURR H. PRENTICE
Petitioner

Dated March 1943
Approved

....
Referee in Bankruptcy

[Endorsed]: Filed Apr. 15, 1943. [43]

[Title of District Court and Cause.]

DEPOSIT TO GUARANTEE TO ESTATE BETTER PRICE FOR THE SALE OF CERTAIN REAL PROPERTY

To Ben E. Tar*b*er, Referee: L. Boteler, Trustee; and To The Above District Court:

Undersigned, B. H. PRENTICE, hereby deposits with you a certified check in the sum of Two Hundred Thirty-three ($233.00) Dollars, being ten percent of an offer in the sum of Two Thousand Three Hundred Twenty-five ($2325.00) Dollars which undersigned makes for the purchase of the following described real property of the above bankrupt estate, to-wit:

All of the real property belonging to this bankrupt estate and situated in the City of South Gate, County of Los Angeles, State of California, described as:

That part of Lot "A" of Tract No. 486 as per Map recorded in Book 15, pages 30 and 31 of Maps in the Office of the County Recorder, described as follows:

Beginning at the Northeasterly corner of said Lot "A" thence north 82° 45′ West along the Northerly line of said Lot, 263.63 feet to the Northeasterly corner of the land described in the deed to Southern California Edison Company, recorded in Book 8429, Page 270 of Official Records of said County; thence South 34° 46′ 40″ West along the Southeasterly line of the land described in said deed 717.7 feet, more or less, to a point in the Southerly line of said Lot "A"; thence South 82° 34′ 40″ East along said Southerly line 247.08 feet to the Southeasterly corner of said Lot "A", thence Northerly along the Southeasterly line of said Lot to the point of beginning. Except that portion thereof, if any, now included within the boundaries of Andrews & Massachia Land in Ranchio Santa Gertrudes as per [44] map recorded in Book 12, Pages 138 and 139 of Maps in the office of the County Recorder.

This deposit is a guarantee to the estate, the Trustee thereof, the Referee, and to the Court, that the Undersigned will purchase said property for the foregoing sum if the Court grants petitioner's prayer to confirm the sale of the above described real property to the undersigned.

BURR H. PRENTICE.

CALIFORNIA BANK MONEY ORDER

No. 454870

B. H. Prentice Bell, Cal., Mar 29 '43

Purchaser

Pay to the Order of L. Boteler, Trustee in Bankruptcy & Ben E. Tarber, Referee in Bankruptcy $233.00

California Bank $233 and 00 cts

Bell Office — 90 - 1051
California Bank
4476 East Gage Avenue
Bell, California

L. A. Wenzel
Authorized Officer

Money Order Receipt
No. 454870
Detach and Retain
Mar 29 '43
Date Purchased
$233.00
Amount
California Bank
Memo. [45]

[Endorsed]: Filed Apr. 15, 1943.

State of California
County of Los Angeles—ss.

AFFIDAVIT OF MAILING

M. Quinn, being first duly sworn, says:

That affiant is a citizen of the United States and a resident of the County of Los Angeles, is over the age of eighteen years, and is not a party to the within entitled action; that affiants residence address is 9212 Hunt Ave., South Gate, Calif., that on the 30th day of March 1943, affiant served the within

1. Points and Authorities in support of Petition to Review Order confirming Sale of Real Estate.
2. Deposit to Guarantee to Estate Better Price for the Sale of Certain Real Property.
3. Petitioners Statement of Facts in Lieu of Reporters Transcript.
4. Copy of Sale of Real Property.
5. Copy of Referees Record of Proceedings.

on the following interested parties in said action by placing true copies thereof in envelopes addressed to, Craig and Weller, Thomas S. Tobin, Attorneys for L. Boteler, Trustee, at their *buisness* address at 817 Board of Trade Bldg., 111 West 7th St., Los Angeles Calif., and to Julius Mackson, Counsel for Baruch Company at his *buisness* address at Commercial Exchange Bldg. 416 West Eighth St., Los Angeles, Calif. and by then sealing said envelopes and depositing the same, with postage thereon fully prepaid, in the United States Postoffice at South Gate Calif. That there is a delivery service by United States mail at the places so addressed and/or there is a regular communication by mail between the place of mailing and the places so addressed.

M. QUINN

Subscribed and sworn to before me this 30th day of March, 1943

(Seal) N. FISHER

Notary Public in and for the County of Los Angeles, State of Califronia

My Commission Expires Sept 11th 1946

[Endorsed]: Filed Apr. 15, 1943. [46]

[Title of District Court and Cause.]

NOTICE OF MOTION TO AMEND REFEREE'S CERTIFICATE ON REVIEW

To the Honorable Campbell E. Beaumont, Judge of the United States District Court and to the Honorable Ben E. Tarver, Referee in Bankruptcy and to Craig and Weller, Thomas S. Tobin, Counsel for L. Boteler, Trustee and to Julius Mackson, Counsel for Baruch Corporation, you and each of you will please take notice.

That on the 3rd day of May, 1943 Burr H. Prentice, the petitioner herein, intends to and will move the above entitled court to amend the Referee's Certificate on Review as follows:

That on the Referee's Certificate on Review, Page 1 Line 27 there be inserted between the words "property" and the word "and" the following: "and to offer for sale to the highest and best bidder then present the said property".

Page 1 Line 28, to delete the words "the successful bidder" substituting in lieu thereof the words "one of the bidders". That Line 29 be deleted in its entirety, substituting therefor "Burr H. Prentice, representing the Smileage Company and Mr. Clements".

Page 2 Line 8, that the word "but" be eliminated and that there be inserted between the words "sale" and the word [47] "said" the following, "That Mr. Clements thereupon bid Twenty Three Hundred Dollars ($2300.00) for the property. Thereupon the Referee".

Page 2 eliminate Lines 11, 12, 13, 14, and 15 substituting therefor the following "That the Referee asked for higher bids stating that he was going to sell the property at auction and Mr. Clements bid Twenty Three Hundred Dollars ($2300.00) as stated, and the Referee then having stated he would not consider any bid that was not at least 10% higher than the Twenty Two Hundred Fifty Dollars ($2250.00) bid. Mr. Prentice then bid Twenty Three Hundred Twenty Five Dollars ($2325.00) and tendered a check and voucher for".

Page 2 Line 16 eliminate the word "did". Eliminate all of Lines 17, 18, 19 and 20 substituting therefor the following, "stated that he would not accept Mr. Prentice's bid and after having handed the check and voucher to his secretary with instructions that all the information thereon be copied, the Referee returned the check and voucher to Mr.

Prentice with the statement that he would not accept it''.

Page 2 Line 24 the following be added, ''That Mr. Baruch stated that 'they' had spent considerable time and money in putting this deal over and he wished to object to any other bids being received''.

Such petition will be based on the attached affidavits of T. H. Clements and Burr H. Prentice, and the records and files of said cause.

Respectfully submitted
BURR H. PRENTICE
Petitioner. [48]

State of California
County of Los Angeles—ss.

C. L. Jones being first duly sworn, says: That affiant is a citizen of the United States and a resident of the County of Los Angeles that affiant is over the age of eighteen years and is not a party to the within and above entitled action: that affiant's business address is 4705 Firestone Blvd., South Gate Calif. That on the 29th day of April A. D., 1943, affiant served the within Notice of Motion to ammend Referees Certificate on Review on the Attorneys in said action *in said action* by placing a true copy thereof in an envelope addressed to Julius Mackson and to Craig and Weller, Thomas S. Tobin at the business address of said attorneys, as follows: Julius Mackson, Commercial Bldg. 416 Eighth St., Los Angeles Calif. and to Craig and Weller, Thomas S. Tobin, 817 Board of Trade Bldg., 111 West Seventh St., Los Angeles, Calif. and by then sealing said envelope and depositing the same with postage thereon fully prepaid, in the United State Post Office at South Gate Calif. That there is delivery service by United States mail at the place so addressed................there is regular communication by mail between the place of mailing and the place so addressed.

C. L. JONES

Subscribed and Sworn to before me this 29th day of April, 1943.

[Seal] N. FISHER

Notary Public in and for said County and State.

My Commission Expires Sept. 11th 1946. [49]

[Title of District Court and Cause.]

AFFIDAVIT OF T. H. CLEMENTS

T. H. Clements, being duly sworn, deposes and says:—That he was present in the office of the Honorable Ben E. Tarver on March 10, 1943 from about 9:40 A. M. to about 10:25 A. M. That at this time this affiant definitely states that he is not now nor has he at any previous time ever been a representative of, or had any connection with, the Smileage Company or the Smileage Company, Ltd., or any partnership or firm having any similar name.

That this affiant upon entering the office of the Honorable Ben E. Tarver at 9:40 A. M. immediately noticed on the large table adjacent to which he seated himself a signed confirmation of the sale to the Baruch Corporation having a consideration of Twenty Two Hundred Fifty Dollars ($2250.00) of the property which was advertised to be sold at 10:00 A. M. that day. At about 10:00 A. M. the Referee entered the room and asked, "Are you gentlemen here in connection with the sale of [50] real estate to be held this morning"? To which both this affiant and Mr. Pentice both replied that they were. The Referee then stated he was going to sell the property in question at auction. He then immediately declared a ten minute recess saying he had to go downstairs on some business. In a few minutes he returned and at that time he said, "Gentlemen, I am now offering this property on Firestone Boulevard for sale. I have a written offer of Twenty Two Hundred Fifty Dollars ($2250.00) for the property. Are you gentlemen familiar with the property?" Mr. Prentice, one of the three bidders present, then asked that the Referee read the legal description of the said property. The Referee read a portion of the *meets* and bounds description and Mr. Prentice said that is O.K. that is the property I have in mind. This affiant then inquired if the property was free and clear, and to what date the taxes would be prorated to, and what zone the property was in, and what right of way reservations were included in the title. The Referee then placed a long distance call for a Mr. Boteler at Los Angeles and after some conversation on the phone said the property would be sold free and clear, that he did not know about the zoning, the taxes would be prorated to date of deed and that there was a reservation for an irrigation ditch across the front of the property. The Referee then said, "Are there any bids?" This affiant then said, "I will bid Twenty Three Hundred Dollars ($2300.00)." The Referee said, "I will not accept your bid as it is not 10% more than the offered bid I now have." This affiant then said, "I understood this was an auction in which the property would go to the highest bidder." The Referee then said, "I make a practice in this court to entertain only 10% advances on bids. I do not like the habit of fellows coming down from Los Angeles and raising bids Five Dollars ($5.00) and upsetting a deal already practically *consumated.*" At this point Mr. Prentice said, "I bid Twenty Three Hundred Twenty Five Dollars [51] ($2325.00) and here is a check for 10% of the bid." And he handed the Court a check for $233.00. The Referee said he would call Mr. Boteler and see how he feels about this raise of the bid, which he did, and after having established a connection on the phone with Mr. Boteler the Referee stated on the phone what had transpired and that he had declined to accept less than a 10% increase. After completing the phone conversation he stated that Mr. Boteler agreed with him and he would decline to accept any other bid for less than Twenty Four Hundred Seventy-Five Dollars ($2475.00) At this time this affiant remonstrated to the court the imposing of special terms of sale such as a 10% minimum bid raise after bids have been made. At this point a gentleman who was there spoke up and told the court that "they" had been to quite a lot of expense in looking up this deal and he did not think any other bids should be entertained. At this time the Referee then asked this man, who this affiant presumes was Mr. Baruch, if he cared to raise his bid, and he was told he did not. The court then asked Mr. Prentice if he cared to raise his bid, and Mr. Prentice replied, "I am the high bidder." And the court said I am not accepting your bid and here is your check back. Mr. Prentice asked that his bid be noted in the minutes. Whereupon the Referee handed the Two Hundred Thirty Three Dollar ($233.00) check to his secretary and instructed her to make a record of it. The presumed representative of the Baruch Corp. inquired if the check Mr. Prentice had tendered was certified. Mr. Prentice said, "No. Was the check you tendered with your bid certified?" And the answer was, "No, but I presume it has already been cashed so that makes it better than your check." Mr. Prentice then said, "If anyone don't think that check is good and the court will consider my bid I will at this time put up currency in lieu of the check you have there." The Referee said, "I won't accept your cash on that bid as I am not accepting [52] the bid." The court then asked if there were any other bids, and this affiant did not make any further bids, it being the opinion of this affiant that this was a rigged sale and no one other than the Baruch Corporation was going to get the property regardless of what happened. Immediately after leaving the court room both Mr.

Prentice and this affiant made copious notes of what had there transpired, to which notes this affiant has repeatedly referred in preparing this affidavit and the statements made in this affidavit conform to the information as set forth in the said notes.

T. H. CLEMENTS

Subscribed and Sworn to Before Me This 28th Day of April, 1943.

[Seal] ROBERTA A. GAYLORD

Notary Public in and for the County of Los Angeles, State of California.

My Commission Expires April 28, 1946. [53]

[Title of District Court and Cause.]

AFFIDAVIT OF BURR H. PRENTICE IN SUPPORT OF PETITION TO AMEND REFEREE'S CERTIFICATE ON REVIEW

Burr H. Prentice, being first duly sworn, deposes and says:— That to the best of his knowledge and belief that the statements as set forth on "Petitioners Statement of Facts in Lieu of Reporters Transcript" *heretofor* filed in the above mentioned cause, beginning on Page 3 Line 23 and continuing to Page 6 Line 13 are true and correct.

BURR H. PRENTICE

Subscribed and Sworn to Before Me This 29th Day of April, 1943.

N. FISHER

Notary Public in and for the County of Los Angeles, State of California.

My Commission Expires Sept. 11th 1946.

[Endorsed]: Filed Apr. 30, 1943. [54]

[Title of District Court and Cause.]

NOTICE OF HEARING OF PETITION FOR REVIEW

To Burr H. Prentice, Petitioner on Review:

You Will Please Take Notice that the undersigned Attorneys for the Trustee will bring on for hearing before Honorable Campbell E. Beaumont, United States District Judge, or such Judge as may be calling his Calendar, the Petition for Review of the Order of Referee Ben E. Tarver made and entered March 16, 1943, on Monday, May 3, 1943 at the hour of 10 o'clock, A. M., on said date or as soon thereafter as counsel can be heard.

Dated: April 21, 1943.

CRAIG & WELLER,

By THOMAS S. TOBIN

Attorneys for Trustee

[Endorsed]: Filed Apr. 22, 1943. [55]

[Title of District Court and Cause.]

ORDER DISMISSING PETITION FOR REVIEW AND AFFIRMING ORDER OF REFEREE

Ben E. Tarver, Referee in Bankruptcy in charge of this proceeding having made and entered an Order on March 16, 1943 confirming the sale of real property situated in the City of Southgate, County of Los Angeles, State of California, and described as follows:

That part of Lot "A" of Tract No. 486, as per Map recorded in Book 15, Pages 30 and 31 of Maps in the office of the County Recorder, described as:

Beginning at the Northeasterly corner of said Lot "A" thence North 82° 45′ West along the Northerly line of said Lot, 263.63 feet to the Northeasterly corner of the land described in the deed to Southern California Edison Company, recorded in Book 8429, Page 270 of Official Records of said County; thence [56] South 34° 46′ 40″ West along the Southeasterly line of the land described in said deed 717.7 feet, more or less, to a point in the Southerly line of said Lot "A"; thence South 82° 34′ 40″ East along said Southerly line 247.08 feet to the Southeasterly corner of said Lot "A"; thence Northerly along the Southeasterly line of said Lot to the point of beginning. Except that portion thereof, if any, now included within the boundaries of Andrew & Massachia Land in Ranchio Santa Gertrudes as per Map recorded in Book 12, Pages 138 and 139 of Maps in the office of the County Recorder.

Subject to a Deed of Trust dated October 1, 1940, wherein Title Guarantee & Trust Company, a California corporation, is Trustee and Lydia Bushnell, a married woman, is beneficiary,

to the Baruch Corporation, a California corporation, after a private sale thereof had been negotiated, and a petition for review of said order having been filed by Burr H. Prentice, doing business under the fictitious name of Smileage Co., Ltd., seeking to have said Order reversed and annulled, and the Referee having made his Certificate on Review and filed the same herein, together with certain Exhibits, and said Petition for Review having been noticed for hearing on May 3, 1943, at the hour of 10 o'clock, A. M., on said date before the undersigned Judge of the above court, and the petitioner on review, Burr H. Prentice, having filed a motion to amend the Referee's Certificate on Review, and said matter having duly come on for hearing pursuant to said notice, and the trustee appearing by his Attorneys, Messrs. Craig & Weller, Thomas S. Tobin of counsel, and Burr H. Prentice, petitioner on review, appearing in propria persona, and both parties having announced [57] their readiness to argue and submit the matter, and said matter having been duly argued by counsel, and the Court being fully advised in the premises,

Finds that prior to the entry of the Order complained of the trustee, pursuant to an Order authorizing the sale of the real property, negotiated a private sale to the Baruch Corporation for the sum of $2250.00 and returned the same to the Referee for confirmation; that the trustee caused to be placed in the Los Angeles Daily Journal, an announcement of the same, which announcement, however, did not state that any sale was to be had of said real property at public auction, nor did the Referee cause such a notice to be inserted in the Daily Journal.

The Court further finds that at the time of the hearing on confirmation of said private sale the Referee announced that no bids would be accepted for less than ten per cent above the sum of $2250.00 for which the sale of the real property had been negotiated to the Baruch Corporation. That notwithstanding said announcement petitioner on review offered to raise the purchaser's bid by a sum not in excess of $75.00, or the sum of $2325.00.

The Court finds that the Referee declined to accept said bid and confirmed the sale to the Baruch Corporation for the sum of $2250.00.

The Court finds that according to the Referee's certificate it was stated at the hearing by one Baruch representing the successful bidder that the Baruch Corporation, relying on said private sale and the confirmation thereof, in good faith, spent a total of about $125.00 in surveying the property in question and other expenses, and the Referee found that it would be manifestly unfair, in view of said expenditures, to refuse to confirm said private sale, unless a substantial increase in bid of at least ten per cent be made at the time of the confirmation thereof.

The Court finds that the Petition for Review was filed on March 29, 1943, more than ten days after the entry of the Order complained of, and that said petitioner on review and his agent [58] knew on the 16th day of March, 1943, that said Order had been entered.

The Court concludes that the confirmation of said sale of real property and the rejection of the bid at the time of confirmation by a third person of less than ten per cent of the original purchase price was, under the circumstances, under the sound judicial discretion of the Referee.

The Court further concludes that this Petition for Review was not filed within the time prescribed by §38-c of the National Bankruptcy Act, and that no extension of time to file said petition for review was obtained.

In Consideration of the foregoing, and on motion of Messrs. Craig & Weller, Attorneys for the Trustee, Thomas S. Tobin of counsel, it is

Ordered that the Petition for Review filed herein by Burr H. Prestice be, and the same hereby is dismissed, and that the Order of Referee Ben E. Tarver entered on March 16, 1943 confirming the sale of the foregoing described real property to the Baruch Corporation for the sum of $2250.00 be, and the same hereby is affirmed.

Done at Los Angeles, in the Southern District of California, this 7th day of May, 1943.

....

United States Distict Judge.

Disapproved as to form under Rule 8.

B. H. PRENTICE

Petitioner on Review.

Objection noted on attached document. [59]

[Endorsed]: Lodged May 17, 1943.

[Title of District Court and Cause.]

OBJECTIONS TO "ORDER DISMISSING PETITION FOR REVIEW AND AFFIRMING ORDER OF REFEREE" AS PROPOSED BY COUNSEL FOR TRUSTEE

To the Honorable Paul J. McCormick, Senior Judge of the United States District Court and to Craig and Weller and Thomas S. Tobin, Counsel for L. Boteler and to Julius Mackson, Counsel for Baruch Corporation,

You and Each of You Will Please Take Notice,

That Burr H. Prentice, the petitioner herein, disapproves of the form of the "Order Dismissing Petition for Review and Affirming Order of Referee" as prepared by Counsel for the Trustee, in the following particulars, to-wit:

Objects to the word "Ltd." being included in Line 21 Page 2 and moves that the same be deleted.

Objects to Lines 23 to Line 29 inclusive on Page 3 and moves that the same be deleted on the grounds that there was no evidence before the Court to substantiate the statement therein [60] contained.

Objects to the paragraph Lines 7 to 10 inclusive on Page 4 and moves that the following be substituted therefor,

"The Court finds that the Petitioner did not file a petition for review within ten days of the date of filing of the Order Confirming Sale by the Referee and finds that the Petitioner moved for and obtained an order of the above entitled Court whereby the time to file such Petition for Review was extended to March 29th, 1943. Furthermore that there was ample justification as well as ample authority for the granting of such extension of time. Furthermore that the said Petition to Review was filed with the Referee prior to March 29, 1943."

Objects to the paragraph contained within Lines 14 to 19 inclusive on Page 4 and moves to substitute therefor the following,

"Ordered that the action of Referee Ben E. Tarver in confirming sale of the foregoing described property to the Baruch Corporation for the sum of $2250.00 be, and the same is hereby affirmed."

Respectfully submitted,

BURR H. PRENTICE,

Petitioner in pro per. [61]

State of California,
County of Los Angeles—ss:

M. Quinn, being first duly sworn, says: That affiant is a citizen of the United States and a resident of the County of Los Angeles, that affiant is over the age of eighteen years and is not a party to the within and above entitled action: that affiant's residence is 9212 Hunt Ave., South Gate, Calif. That on the 8th day of May, A. D., 1943, affiant served the within Objections to Order Dismissing Petition for Review and affirming order of Referee as proposed by counsel for trustee on the defendants in said action, by placing true copies thereof in envelopes addressed to their attorneys at the business addresses of said attorneys as follows: Craig and Weller and Thomas S. Tobin, 817 Board of Trade Bldg., 111 W. 7th St., Los Angeles; and Julius Mackson, Commercial Exchange Bldg., 416 W. 8th Street, Los Angeles, California, and by then sealing said envelopes and depositing the same, with postage thereon fully prepaid, in the United States Post Office at South Gate, California. That there is delivery service by United States mail at the place so addressed and/or there is a regular communication by mail between the place of mailing and the place so addressed.

M. QUINN.

Subscribed and Sworn to before me this 8th day of May, 1943.

[Seal] N. FISHER,

Notary Public in and for said County and State.

[Endorsed]: Lodged May 17, 1943. [62]

In the District Court of the United States, Southern District of California, Central Division.

In Bankruptcy No. 40,689-B

In the Matter of

DR. W. J. ROSS COMPANY, a Corporation, Bankrupt.

ORDER CONFIRMING ORDER OF REFEREE

Ben E. Tarver, Referee in Bankruptcy in charge of this proceeding, having made and entered an Order on March 16, 1943 confirming the sale of real property situated in the City of South Gate, County of Los Angeles, State of California, and described as follows:

That part of Lot "A" of Tract No. 486, as per Map recorded in Book 15, Pages 30 and 31, of Maps in the office of the County Recorder, described as:

Beginning at the Northeasterly corner of said Lot "A" thence North 82°45′ West along the Northerly line of said Lot, 263.63 feet to the Northeasterly corner of the land described in the deed to Southern California Edison Company, recorded in Book 8429, Page 270 of Official [63] Records of said County; thence South 34° 46′ 40″ West along the Southeasterly line of the land described in said deed 717.7 feet, more or less, to a point in the southerly line of said Lot "A"; thence South 82° 34′ 40" East along said Southerly line 247.08 feet to the Southeasterly corner of said lot "A"; thence Northerly along the Southeasterly line of said Lot to the point of beginning. Except that portion thereof, if any, now included within the boundaries of Andrew & Massachia Land in Rancho Santa Gertrudes as per Map recorded in Book 12, Pages 138 and 139 of Maps in the office of the County Recorder.

Subject to a Deed of Trust dated October 1, 1940, wherein Title Guarantee & Trust Company, a California corporation, is Trustee and Lydia Bushnell, a married woman, is beneficiary,

to the Baruch Corporation, a California corporation, after a private sale thereof had been negotiated, and a petition for review of said Order having been filed by Burr H. Prentice, doing business under the fictitious name of Smileage Co., Ltd., asking to have said Order reversed and annulled, and the Referee having made his Certificate on Review and filed the same herein, together with certain Exhibits, and said Petition for Review having been noticed for hearing on May 3, 1943, at the hour of 10 o'clock A. M., on said date before the undersigned Judge of the above Court, and the petitioner on review, Burr H. Prentice, having filed a motion to amend the Referee's Certificate on Review, and said matter having duly come on for hearing pursuant to said notice, and the Trustee appearing by his Attorneys, Messrs. Craig & Weller, Thomas S. Tobin of counsel, and Burr H. Prentice, petitioner on review, [64] appearing in propria personam, and both parties having anounced their readiness to argue and submit the matter, and said matter having been duly argued by counsel, and the Court being fully advised in the premises;

Finds that prior to the entry of the Order complained of the Trustee, pursuant to an Order authorizing the sale of the real property, negotiated a private sale to the Baruch Corporation for the sum of $2250.00 and returned the same to the Referee for confirmation; that the Trustee caused to be placed in the Los Angeles Daily Journal, an announcement of the same, which announcement, however, did not state that any sale was to be had of said real property at public auction, nor did the Referee cause such a notice to be inserted in the Daily Journal.

The Court further finds that at the time of the hearing on confirmation of said private sale the Referee announced that no bids would be accepted for less than ten percent above the sum of $2250.00 for which the sale of the real property had been negotiated to the Baruch Corporation. That notwithstanding said announcement petitioner on review offered to raise the purchaser's bid by a sum not in excess of $75.00 or the sum of $2325.00.

The Court finds that the Referee declined to accept said bid and confirmed the sale to the Baruch Corporation for the sum of $2250.00.

The Court finds that according to the Referee's Certificate, it was stated at the hearing by one, Baruch, representing the successful bidder, that the Baruch Corporation, relying on said private sale and the confirmation thereof, in good faith spent a total of about $125.00 in surveying the property in question and other expenses, and the Referee found that it would be manifestly unfair in view of said expenditures to refuse to confirm said private sale unless a substantial increase in the bid of at least ten (10%) per cent be made at the time of the confirmation thereof. [65]

The Court finds that the Petition for Review was filed on March 29, 1943, more than ten days after the entry of the Order complained of, and that said petitioner on review and his agent knew on the 16th day of March, 1943, that said Order had been entered.

The Court concludes that the confirmation of said sale of real property and the rejection of the bid at the time of confirmation by a third person of less than ten percent of the original purchase price was, under the circumstances, under the sound judicial discretion of the Referee.

The Court further concludes that this Petition for Review was not filed within the time prescribed by Section 39-c of the National Bankruptcy Act, and that on April 24, 1943 the undersigned Judge of the above named Court made an Order extending petitioner's time to review to March 31, 1943 without prejudice to the assertion by any party of any applicable rights and that said Petition for Review was filed prior to March 31, 1943.

In Consideration of the foregoing, and on motion of Messrs. Craig & Miller, Attorneys for the Trustee, Thomas S. Tobin of counsel, it is

Ordered that the Order of Referee Ben E. Tarver entered on March 16, 1943 confirming the sale of the foregoing described real property to the Baruch Corporation for the sum of $2,250.00 be, and the same hereby is confirmed.

Done at Los Angeles, in the Southern District of California, this 13th day of May, 1943.

PAUL J. McCORMICK,
United States District Judge.

Judgment entered May 13, 1943; Docketed May 13, 1943, Book 3, Page 338; Edmund L. Smith, Clerk, by B. B. Hansen, Deputy. Notation made in Bankruptcy Docket on May 13, 1943, pursuant to Rule 79(a), Civil Rules of Procedure; Edmund L. Smith, Clerk, U. S. District Court, Southern District of California, by B. B. Hansen, Deputy.

[Endorsed]: Filed May 13, 1943. [66]

[Title of District Court and Cause.]

NOTICE OF ENTRY OF ORDER

To: Burr H. Prentice, 4705 Firestone Boulevard, Southgate, California.

Please Take Notice that on the 13th day of May, 1943, Hon. Paul J. McCormick, United States District Judge, made and entered an Order Confirming Order of Referee Ben E. Tarver, dated June 16, 1943, on review. A full, true and correct copy is hereto attached and herein served upon you.

Dated: May 13, 1943.

CRAIG and WELLER,
By THOMAS S. TOBIN.

[Endorsed]: Filed Jul 19, 1943. [67]

[Title of District Court and Cause.]

AFFIDAVIT OF MAILING

State of California,
County of Los Angeles—ss:

M. Criscione, being first duly sworn, on oath, deposes and says: That she is a citizen of the United States over the age of eighteen years and not a party to the above-entitled matter, or interested therein.

That on the 13th day of May, 1943, she deposited a copy of Notice of Entry of Order in an envelope addressed to the following, to wit:

Mr. Burr H. Prentice
4705 Firestone Boulevard
Southgate, California

And after carefully sealing said envelope so containing said copy as aforesaid, and after affixing thereon the postage required by law, she deposited said envelope in the United States Post Office at Los Angeles, California; that there is a regular communication by mail from said Post Office of deposit to the place so addressed.

M. CRISCIONE.

Subscribed and Sworn to before me this 13th day of May, 1943.

OLIVE DIFFENDERFER,
Notary Public in and for the County of Los Angeles, State of California.

[Endorsed]: Filed Jul 19, 1943. [68]

[Title of District Court and Cause.]

NOTICE OF APPEAL

To L. Boteler, Trustee in Bankruptcy in the above entitled proceeding, and to Baruch Corporation, a California Corporation, and to their attorney, Julius Mackson, and to the Clerk of the above entitled Court:

B. H. Prentice, the petitioner in the matter of that certain Petition to Review Referee's Order in connection with the Referee's confirmation of sale under date of March 16, 1943 of certain real property situated in the City of South Gate, County of Los Angeles, State of California, feeling aggrieved by the Order of Referee Ben E. Tarver entered March 16, 1943, confirming the sale of certain real property and by the findings decrees and orders of the Honorable Paul J. McCormick, United States District Judge, made and entered respectively on the seventh and thirteenth days of May, 1943, in connection with Petition to Review Referee's Order, does hereby appeal to the United States Circuit Court of Appeals for the Ninth Circuit, pursuant to Rule 73, subdivision (a) and (b) of the Federal Rules of Civil Procedure.

Your petitioner prays that the proper record on appeal, as provided in Rule 75 of the Federal Rules of Civil Procedure be docketed, and that this [69] appeal be heard and determined as provided by law.

Dated this 11th day of June, 1943.

B. H. PRENTICE,
Petitioner in Propria Persona.

Names and Addresses of Attorneys

For Appellant:

B. H. Prentice, in Propria Persona
4705 Firestone Blvd.
South Gate, California

For Appellee:

Messrs. Craig and Weller, Thomas S. Tobin, Esquires,
817 Board of Trade Building
117 West 7th Street
Los Angeles, California

Julius Mackson, Esquire,
416 West 8th Street
Los Angeles, California

6-12-43 Mailed copies to above named attorneys for appellee.—TH.

[Endorsed]: Filed June 12, 1943. [70]

[Title of District Court and Cause.]

COST BOND ON APPEAL

Royal Indemnity Company.
[Insignia]
Head Office: New York
A New York Corporation.
A Stock Company
Bond No. S 197597

Whereas, B. H. Prentice, as Principal, has taken or is about to take an appeal to the United States Circuit Court of Appeals for the Ninth Circuit from an Order of Referee Ben E. Tarver entered the 16th day of March, 1943, and from the findings decrees and orders of the Honorable Paul J. McCormick, United States District Judge, made and entered respectively on the 7th and 13th days of May, 1943, in above cause.

Now, Therefore, in consideration of the premises and of such appeal, the Royal Indemnity Company, a corporation organized under the laws of the State of New York, and licensed to transact a general surety business in the State of California, as Surety, does hereby undertake and acknowledge itself bound in the sum of Two Hundred Fifty and no/100 Dollars ($250.00), that the above named appellants will prosecute their said appeal to effect and answer all damages and costs which may adjudge against them if they fail to make good their appeal.

In Witness Whereof, said Royal Indemnity Company has caused this obligation *to signed* by its

Attorney-in-Fact at Los Angeles, California, and its corporate seal *to hereinto* affixed, this 12th day of June, 1943.

ROYAL INDEMNITY COMPANY,
By E. L. COLE,
Attorney-in-Fact

[Illegible] mined and recommended for approval as Provided in Rule 13,

HAROLD L. WATT
Attorney

[Illegible] ereby approve the foregoing bond this ....day of June, 1943

....
United States District Judge.

[Illegible] e premium for this bond is $10.00 per annum.

State of California,
County of Los Angeles,—ss.

On this 12th day of June in the year 1943, before me, S. P. Gage, a Notary Public in and for the County and State aforesaid, personally appeared E. L. Cole known to be to be the person whose name is subscribed to the within instrument and known to me to be the Attorney-in-Fact of Royal Indemnity Company and acknowledged to me that he subscribed the name of the said Company thereto as principal, and his own name as Attorney-in-Fact.

S. P. GAGE
Notary Public in and for said County and State.
My commission expires July 1, 1945.

[Endorsed]: Filed June 12, 1943. [71]

[Title of District Court and Cause.]

APPELLANT'S STATEMENT OF POINTS

Pursuant to the Rules of Practice of the Court this Appellant B. H. Prentice does herein present the points upon which he relies in his appeal.

I.

It was error and an abuse of discretion for the Court to confirm the sale of the subject real property to the Baruch Company when Prentice at the time of the sale offered Seventy Five ($75.00) Dollars more for the property all other conditions of the two offers being equal.

II.

It was error for the Court to consider the statement made at the sale by the representative of the Baruch Company that they had spent about One Hundred Twenty-five Dollars anticipating that the sale of the property would be confirmed to them.

III.

It was an abuse of discretion for the Court to demand after the sale had commenced and the bid of Baruch and the bid of Clements had been received to then demand that Prentice would have to bid an amount equal to [72] 10% more than the Baruch bid.

IV.

It was an abuse of discretion for the Court to demand that Prentice bid a minimum of Twenty Four Hundred Seventy Five ($2475.00) Dollars.

V.

It was an abuse of discretion for the Court to refuse to consider the Prentice bid on the grounds that it was not in a sum equal to 10% more than the Baruch bid.

VI.

It was error and an abuse of discretion for the District Court to consider the statement contained in the Referee's Record to the effect that the Baruch Company representative claimed to have spent about One Hundred Twenty Five Dollars surveying the property *ect.*

VII.

It was error and an abuse of discretion for the District Court to confirm the order of Referee Ben E. Tarver entered on March 16, 1943, confirming the sale of the subject property to the Baruch Company.

Respectfully submitted
B. H. PRENTICE
Appellant in Propria Persona

[Endorsed]: Filed Jun 25, 1943. [73]

[Title of District Court and Cause.]

DESIGNATION OF CONTENTS OF RECORD ON APPEAL

To The Clerk of the Above Entitled Court:

Pursuant to the rules of practice of the Court, this appellant, B. H. Prentice, does hereby designate the following documents, orders, judgments and records, in the proceedings to be contained in the record on appeal in the above entitled cause, said documents being as follows:

1. Order of Sale of Real Property—Dated July 20, 1942 and referring to "That part of Lot 'A' of Tract #486, etc."

2. Return of Sale of Real Property—Including affidavit of L. Boteler attached thereto,—Filed 2/26/43.

3. Petition to Review Referee's Order—Including Exhibit "A" thereto attached.

4. Affidavit of Mailing Petition to Review Referee's Order.

5. Petitioner's Statement of Facts in Lieu of Reporter's Transcript.

6. Excerpt from Referee's Record of Proceedings commencing at the date line 3/10/43 to and including 3/16/43. [74]

7. Petitioner's Points and Authorities in support of Petition to Review Order Confirming Sale of Real Property.

8. Petitioner's Deposit to Guarantee to Estate Better Price for the Sale of Certain Real Property together with a photostat of Cashier's Check attached thereto.

9. Affidavit of Mailing.

(1) Points and Authorities in Support of Petition to Review Order Confirming Sale of Real Estate,

(2) Deposit to Guarantee to Estate Better Price for the Sale of Certain Real Property,

(3) Petitioner's Statement of Facts in Lieu of Reporter's Transcript.

(4) Copy of Sale of Real Property.

(5) Copy of Referee's Record of Proceedings.

10. Referee's Certificate on Review.

11. Notice of Motion to Amend Referee's Certificate on Review including Affidavit of T. H. Clements and Affidavit of Burr H. Prentice in Support of Petition to Amend Referee's Certificate on Review attached thereto.

12. Affidavit of Mailing Notice of Motion to Amend Referee's Certificate on Review.

13. Notice of Hearing of Petition for Review dated April 21, 1943.

14. Order Dismissing Petition for Review and Affirming Order of Referee Done at Los Angeles the 7th day of May, 1943.

15. Objections to "Order Dismissing Petition for Review and Affirming Order *or* Referee as Proposed by Counsel for Trustee."

16. Affidavit of Mailing objection to "Order Dismissing Petition for Review and Affirming Order of Referee" as Proposed by Counsel for Trustee.

17. Order Confirming Order of Referee Done at Los Angeles the 13th day of May, 1943.

18. Notice of Entry of Order.

19. Affidavit of Mailing Notice of Entry of Order.

20. Notice of Appeal—Dated June 11, 1943.

21. Names and Addresses of Attorneys. [75]

22. Appellant's Proposed Statement of the

Points on Which He Intends to Rely on the Appeal.

23. Designation of Contents of Record on Appeal.

24. Affidavit of Mailing:

(1) Appellant's Proposed Statement on the Points on Which He Intends to Rely on Appeal.

(2) Designation of Contents of Record on Appeal.

25. Certificate of Clerk.

Dated this 21st day of June, 1943.

B. H. PRENTICE,
Appellant
In Propria Persona.

[Endorsed]: Filed Jun 25, 1943. [76]

AFFIDAVIT OF MAILING

State of California,
County of Los Angeles,—ss.

M. Quinn, being first duly sworn, says: That affiant is a citizen of the United States and a resident of the County of Los Angeles, that affiant is over the age of eighteen years and is not a party to the within and above entitled action; that affiant's residence address is 9212 Hunt Ave. South Gate, Calif. That on the 29 day of June, 1943, affiant served the within Designation of Contents of Record on Appeal and Appellant's Statement of Points on Counsels for interested parties to-wit: Craig & Weller and Thomas S. Tobin Counsel for

L. Boteler, Trustee, at their office address at 817 Board of Trade Bldg., 111 W. 7th St. Los Angeles, and on Julius Mackson, Counsel for Baruch Company at his office address Commercial Exchange Bldg., 416 W. 8th St. Los Angeles, by placing true copies of the two above described documents in envelopes addressed to the several attorneys *at* above set forth at the office addresses as above set forth and by then sealing said envelopes and depositing the same, with postage thereon fully prepaid, in the United States Post Office at South Gate, California, and that there is delivery service by United States mail at the places so addressed and/or there is a regular communication by mail between the place of mailing and the places so addressed.

M. QUINN,

Subscribed and Sworn to before me this 24th day of June, 1943.

[Seal] N. FISHER

Notary Public in and for said County and State.

My Commission Expires Sept. 11th, 1946.

[Endorsed]: Filed Jun 25, 1943. [77]

[Title of District Court and Cause.]

COUNTER DESIGNATION OF PARTS OF RECORD ON APPEAL

The Appellant not having designated portions of the record on appeal sufficient to affirmatively show the jurisdiction of the court, and the qualification of the trustee, the undersigned Appellee hereby designates and requests that the following parts of the record be incorporated and printed in the record on appeal:

1. Original Petition in proceedings under Chapter XI;

2. Approval of Debtor's Petition and Order of Reference under Section 322 of the Bankruptcy Act;

3. Bankrupt's Schedule B(1)—Real Estate;

4. Order of Adjudication;

5. Trustee's Bond and approval endorsed thereon;

6. Appeal Bond;

7. This Counter Designation and Affidavit of Service by Mail of same.

Dated: At Los Angeles, in the Southern District of California [78] this 25th day of June, 1943.

CRAIG & WELLER
By THOMAS S. TOBIN
and
THOMAS S. TOBIN
Attorneys for Appellee L. Boteler, Trustee in Bankruptcy.

[Endorsed]: Filed June 26, 1943. [79]

[Title of District Court and Cause.]

CERTIFICATE OF CLERK

I, Edmund L. Smith, Clerk of the District Court of the United States for the Southern District of California, do hereby certify that the foregoing pages numbered from 1 to 79 inclusive contain full, true and correct copies of: Original Petition in Proceedings Under Chapter XI; Approval of Debtor's Petition and Order of Reference under Section 322 of the Bankruptcy Act; Schedule B-1; Order of Adjudication; Bond of Trustee; Referee's Certificate on Review; Order of Sale of Real Property; Return of Sale of Real Property; Referee's Order; Order Confirming Sale of Real Property; Points and Authorities in Support of Petition to Review Order Confirming Sale of Real Property; Petitioner's Statement of Facts in Lieu of Reporter's Transcript; Deposit to Guarantee to Estate Better Price for the Sale of Certain Real Property; Affidavit of Mailing; Notice of Motion to Amend Referee's Certificate on Review; Affidavit of T. H. Clements; Affidavit of Burr H. Prentice in Support of Petition to Amend Referee's Certificate on Review; Notice of Hearing of Petition for Review; Order Dismissing Petition for Review and Affirming Order of Referee (Not signed); Objections to "Order Dismissing Petition for Review and Affirming Order of Referee" as Proposed by Counsel for Trustee; Order Confirming Order of Referee; Notice of Entry of Order; Affidavit of Mailing; Notice of Appeal; Cost Bond on Appeal; Appellant's Statement of Points; Designation of Contents of Record on Appeal; and Counter-Designation of Parts of Record on Appeal which constitute the record on appeal to the United States Circuit Court of Appeals for the Ninth Circuit.

I further certify that my fees for comparing, correcting and certifying the foregoing record amount to $19.20 which sum has been paid to me by Appellant.

Witness my hand and the seal of said District Court this 19 day of July, 1943.

[Seal] EDMUND L. SMITH,
Clerk.
By THEODORE HOCKE,
Deputy Clerk.

[Endorsed]: No. 10497. United States Circuit Court of Appeals for the Ninth Circuit. B. H. Prentice, Appellant, vs. L. Boteler, Trustee in Bankruptcy of the Estate of Dr. W. J. Ross Company, a Corporation, Bankrupt, Appellee. Transcript of Record. Upon Appeal from the District Court of the United States for the Southern District of California, Central Division.

Filed July 21, 1943.

PAUL P. O'BRIEN,
Clerk of the United States Circuit Court of Appeals for the Ninth Circuit.

In the United States Circuit Court of Appeals
For the *North* Circuit

No. 10497

B. H. PRENTICE,

Appellant.

vs.

L. BOTELER, Trustee in Bankruptcy of the Estate of

DR. W. J. ROSS COMPANY, Bankrupt,

Appellee.

APPELLANTS STATEMENT OF THE POINTS ON WHICH HE INTENDS TO RELY ON THE APPEAL AND DESIGNATION OF RECORD

B. H. Prentice, the Appellant herein, hereby adopts his previous designation of the points on which he intends to rely on appeal, heretofore filed with the Clerk of the United States District Court, and certified by the Clerk of the Court, entitled

"Appellant's Statement of the Points on Which He Intends to Rely on the Appeal."

That Appellant further designates the entire certified record and transcript certified to you by the Clerk of the United States District Court as the record to be printed and to constitute the record in connection with this appeal.

Dated: July 22, 1943.

B. H. PRENTICE,
Appellant
In Propria Persona.

Received copy of the within document this 27 day of July 1942.

CRAIG & WELLER,
Attorney for Respondent L. Boteler.

JULIUS MACKSON,
Appellant
In Propria Persona.

[Endorsed]: Filed Jul 29 1943. Paul P. O'Brien, Clerk.

10497

No. ~~10997~~

In the United States Circuit Court of Appeals

For the Ninth Circuit

B. H. PRENTICE,

Appellant,

vs.

L. BOTELER, Trustee in Bankruptcy of the Estate of Dr. W. J. Ross Company, a Corporation, Bankrupt,

Appellee.

Appellant's Opening Brief

B. H. PRENTICE, in Pro per
4705 Firestone Blvd.,
South Gate, California,
For Appellant.

CRAIG & WELLER,
THOMAS S. TOBIN,
817 Board of Trade Building,
111 West 7th St.,
Los Angeles, California,
For Appellee.

TOPICAL INDEX

TABLE OF AUTHORITIES CITED

Cases

Statutes

In the United States Circuit Court of Appeals

For the Ninth Circuit

B. H. PRENTICE, *Appellant,* vs. L. BOTELER, Trustee in Bankruptcy of the Estate of Dr. W. J. Ross Company, a Corporation, Bankrupt, *Appellee,*	No. 10997

Appellant's Opening Brief

STATEMENT OF JURISDICTION

The District Court had jurisdiction over the parties by reason of the principal place of business of the Bankrupt having been for the eight years preceding the filing of the Original Petition under Chapter XI, in the County of Orange, State of California. (Original Petition, Par. I R. 2) (U. S. C. Title 28, Sec. 41, Subd. 19.)

This Court has jurisdiction by reason of Title 28, Section 225, Subdivision (a) of Federal Code Annotated (Judicial Code, Sec. 128) the orders appealed from being final orders. (See discussion and Citations p. 7 of this brief.)

STATEMENT OF THE CASE

Under Date of May 23, 1942 (R 7), Dr. W. J. Ross Company, a Corporation, filed their petition in Bankruptcy with the District Court of the United States, Southern District of California, Central Division under the provisions of Chapter XI, and prayed for relief under the provisions of Section 322, of the Bankruptcy Act (R 2). Whereupon the District Court approved the petition and referred the matter to Ben E. Tarver, Esquire, one of the Referees in Bankruptcy of the District Court. (R 7).

On June 17, 1942, the Bankrupt filed its withdrawal of plan of arrangement and consented to adjudication and admitted in writing its inability to pay its debt (R 9). Whereupon there being no objection it was adjudged the said Dr. W. J. Ross Company, a Corporation, was a Bankrupt. (R 9). Bond of Trustee was examined, recommended for approval and filed July 8, 1942. (R 10-11).

Among the assets of the Bankrupt was a parcel of real property situated in the City of South Gate, California and comprising some 3.75 Acres more or less of land (R 8) being a part of Lot "A" of Tract No. 486 as per map recorded in Book 15, pages 30 and 31 of

Maps in the office of the County Recorder (R 20). Under date of July 20, 1942 (R 21) the Referee authorized the Trustee to sell at private sale or at public auction to the highest and best bidders therefor the real property as above described (R 20) subject to confirmation of the Court (R 21). Under date of April 15, 1943 (R 24) the Trustee filed his Return of Sale of Real Property, (R 21), which set forth that he had sold the real property in question to the Baruch Corporation (R 21), that the purchaser had deposited its check in the sum of $225.00 with the Trustee as evidence of good faith, the balance of purchase price to be paid in full after confirmation of sale by this Court and upon completion of escrow with the Title Insurance and Trust Company (R 23).

Subsequently the Trustee ordered inserted in the Los Angeles Daily Journal (R 69) an advertisement which called attention to the subject Real Property Sale, setting forth that the sale would be held on Wednesday, March 10, 1943, at 10:00 o'clock A. M. in the Court room of Ben E. Tarver, Referee at Santa Ana, California (R 42) said advertisement was published in the said Los Angeles Daily Journal on March 5th and 10th, 1943 (R 42).

On March 10, 1943, at 10:00 o'clock A. M. this appellant was present (R 13) in the Court Room of the Referee. As to what transpired at that time there is some discrepancy in the record, as between the Referee's Record of Proceedings (R 24), the Referee's Certificate on Review (R 12), the Statement of Facts in Lieu of Reporter's Transcript (R 39), and the Statement of the proceedings as set forth in the Affidavit of T. H. Clements (R 54). There was no full Stenographer's report taken at the meeting (R 16) but copious notes of what transpired were made immediately after the sale by two of those present, which notes were later referred to in preparing the affidavit of Mr. Clements (R 58). Suffice it to say at this time that the Referee stated he had up for confirmation or sale the parcel of land in question, (R 14), that he had before him for his attention the Trustee's Return of Sale of a parcel of land for $2250.00, and his Petition for its confirmation (R 13). That a Mr. Clements who was present bid $2300.00 and this appellant bid $2325.00 for the real property in question (R 14). That this appellant tendered a check for $233.00, as a deposit (R 14). That this appellant's bid of $2325.00 was the highest sum there bid (R 15). That the bid of the Baruch Company was accompanied by the deposit of a check with the Trustee in the sum of $225.00 (R 23). That at some stage of the proceedings the Referee stated that he would not consider any bid unless it was at least 10% higher than the $2250.00 bid (R 14-49-56). This was an erroneous ruling.

Mr. Baruch representing the Baruch Corporation was present (R 13) and stated in substance that they had been to quite a lot of expense in looking up this deal and he did not think any other bids should be entertained (R 49-57). That he had spent $75.00 in surveying the property in question on the faith of having the purchase confirmed and also spent other amounts making a total of about $125.00 (R 18-69). This statement should never have been included in the record. Some question was raised as to appellant's check (R 14-45-57). and this appellant offered to post a cash deposit in lieu of the $233.00 check tendered (R 45-46-57). That the Referee returned the check for $233.00 to this appellant (R 14-46-57) and stated that he would not accept even a certified check from the Appellant unless it was in an amount 10% greater than the bid of $2250.00 (R 14-15). Which ruling constituted an arbitrary abuse of discretion.

That the Referee announced the property was sold to the Baruch Company (R 46) and the appellant protested the sale (R 46-47).

That on March 16, 1943 the Order confirming sale of the property in question to the Baruch Company, for $2250.00, was entered (R 17-30). That said order recited among other things that one Prentice (this Appellant) had offered a $50.00 raise above the bid had by the Trustee (R 27) but that the said $50.00 raise was refused by the Referee upon recommendation of the Trustee (R 28). The amount of the raise or advance bid by this appellant was actually $75.00 (R 69). (Bid by this appellant $2325.00 (R 14-15-44-56-69), by Baruch Company $2250.00 (R 13-14-44-55-69).) On April 24, 1943 the Honorable Paul J. McCormick, United States District Judge, made an order extending this appellant's time wherein to file Petition to Review Referee's Order to March 31, 1943 (R 70), and the said petition to review Referee's order was filed March 29, 1943 (R 26).

That a Notice of Motion to amend the Referee's Certificate on Review (R 51), together with Affidavit of Mailing (R 53-54) was filed by this Appellant on April 30, 1943 (R 59) together with the supporting affidavits of this Appellant (R 58), and T. H. Clements (R 54).

On May 3, 1943 the Petition to review Referee's Order and Motion to Amend Referee's Certificate on Review, came on for hearing before the Honorable Paul J. McCormick (R 68). Subsequently an order dismissing Petition for Review and Confirming Order of Referee (R 60) was prepared by counsel for Appellee, lodged and submitted to this Appellant who disapproved the same and filed his objections to the said order (R 64-65). Whereupon an order confirming Order of Referee (R 67) was filed May 13, 1943 (R 71). That in the order confirming Order of Referee (R 67) the Honorable Court found that "according to the Referee's Certificate, it was stated at the hearing by one, Baruch, representing the successful bidder, that the Baruch Corporation, relying on said private sale and the confirmation thereof, in good faith spent a total of about $125.00, in surveying the property and in other expense and the Referee found that it would be manifestly unfair in view of said expenditures to refuse to confirm said private sale unless a substantial increase in the bid of at least ten (10%) per cent at the time of the confirmation there" (R 70). Which ruling was erroneous and contrary to settled law.

Appellant filed Notice of Appeal on June 11, 1943 from the Order of the Referee of March 16, 1943, and from the Orders of the District Court of May 7th and 13th, 1943 (R 73-74). Appellant's Cost Bond on Appeal (R 75), was filed June 12, 1943 (R. 76).

ARGUMENT

The Orders appealed from were Judgments of the Court.

F. R. C. P. 54 (A).

They were final judgments in that they completely determined the rights of the appellant in the Lower Court.

AMSINCK & CO. INC. v. SPRINGFIELD GROCER CO., 7 Fed. (2nd) 855-859,

in which it was stated—

"A final judgment leaves no further judicial act to be performed."

The Confirmation of the Sale Was Error and Constitutes an Abuse of Discretion

It is the clear duty of the Trustee and Referee to obtain the greatest possible return to the creditors of the bankrupt estate.

CURIN v. NOURSE, 66 Fed. (2nd) 137-140;
KIMMEL v. CROCKER, 72 Fed. (2nd) 599-601.

In the case last above quoted the Court stated:

> "It would clearly be an abuse of discretion to accept the lesser of two comparable bids."

In the first case quoted above the Court stated,

> "The confirmation of this sale should only have been made after a fair hearing and upon proof justifying the conclusion that the properties were being sold for all that could reasonably be obtained for them, that the trustee had acted freely and fairly in making the sale, and that it was for the best interest of all concerned that the same should be consummated."

In the instant case the record clearly shows that the two bids were comparable. Both Baruch and Prentice were present at the sale (R 13). Baruch had tendered a written bid of $2250.00 (R 16) and posted a check for $225.00 (R 23), Prentice bid $2325.00 (R 14) and posted a check for $233.00 (R 14).

The Referee returned the Prentice check (R 14-46) and stated he would not accept it even though it was certified unless it was in an amount 10% greater than $2250.00 (the amount of the Baruch bid) (R 14-15). This would have required that Prentice have on his person and ready to produce a certified check in the amount of $2475.00 in order that his bid receive any consideration from the Referee. That the Referee intended to and did hold a sale of the property is evident from the four statements as set out in the Referee's Certificate on Review (R 12) wherein it is stated "or enough of it to identify it as the parcel of land that was up for confirmation *OR* sale." (R 14) "merely read the description of the land before him *for sale*" (R 14). "That while the Referee asked for higher bids as stated he did not announce that he would sell the property at auction or that he would auction *the sale,*" (R 14), "The Referee in the presence of those present as hereinbefore stated, rang up Mr. L. Boteler, the Trustee, in Los Angeles, and said to him that he, the Referee, was rejecting bids of $2300.00 and $2325.00 for the property in question as they were not in an amount 10% greater than the price set forth in the Return of Sale as being the bid by the purchaser named therein—the Baruch Corporation, and that he did not think that any sum less than that should be accepted," (R 15) Mr. Baruch evidently considered the possibility of other bidders purchasing the property at that time inasmuch as he protested the acceptance of more than one bid (his Principal's bid) (R 45).

If there was to be no sale other than to the Baruch Company why did the Referee ask for bids and then decline to accept them? (R 14-16). If it were unfair to the Baruch Company to accept the Prentice bid (R 69) at an advance of $75.00 over the Baruch bid would an advance bid by Prentice of $225.00 as demanded by the Referee (R 14-15) have revised the situation to where it would have been fair to the Baruch Company for the Referee to have confirmed the sale to Prentice?

That the property was not being sold for all that could reasonably be obtained for it is self evident. Prentice was present and bid $75.00 more than Baruch (R 14) and his bid was not considered (R 14-15). The Prentice offer was reasonable in that it was on the same terms as was the Baruch offer (R 14-23).

The Referee Should Not Have Considered Unsupported Statements in Making His Decision

F. R. C. P. Rule 43 (A);
C. C. P. 1867;
C. C. P. 1869.

The unsupported statement by Baruch made at the time of sale to the effect that they had expended about $125.00 in surveys, etc. (R 18) should not have been considered by the Referee in making his decision.

If the Baruch Company had prior to the date of sale spent $125.00 in surveying and other expenses in connection with their offer to purchase this property, as was stated at the sale (R 18) the statement should not have been considered by the Referee for two reasons. First, the record does not disclose that the person making the statement was sworn and therefore the testimony had no standing and secondly, if the sum so claimed was actually spent by the Baruch Company, such action did not impose a burden on the Referee to confirm the sale of the property to them. It was a matter of record that before title could pass the sale would necessarily have to be confirmed by the Court. (R 21)

If by the incurring of expense on the part of a prospective purchaser for property to be sold by the Trustee, prior to the Confirmation of Sale hearing, one gains the advantage of being awarded the property over the higher bids of other bidders it would be futile to hold sales. One would but have to make an offer to the Trustee to purchase and then expend a sum of money (in this case it was stated $125.00 or less than 5% of the bid) to be assured of Confirmation of the Sale.

It Was an Abuse of Discretion for the Referee To Demand An Upset Bid in Any Amount

For the Referee to demand that Prentice bid $2475.00 was error and abuse of discretion.

WILLIAMS—COAL CITY HOUSE FURNISHINGS CO. v. HOGUE, 197 Fed. 1.

In the case herein cited one Williams & Schmulbach bid $75,500.00 and one Herd bid $75,525.00, a raise of $25.00 on a $75,500.00 bid. The Trustee refused to accept the bid of Herd and reported to the Referee the sale of the property to Williams & Schmulbach for $75,500.00 requesting confirmation of sale. At the time set for confirmation of the sale Herd protested the confirmation and filed his petition moving that his bid of $75,525.00 be accepted. The Referee ruled that Herd must make an upset bid of $78,000.00 in order to have the property resold. Herd excepted to this order and filed a petition for Review in the District Court which was granted. The District Court reversed the order of the Referee and directed the Referee to sell the property provided Herd file a certified check for one-fourth of the amount of his bid (terms of sale as announced were one-fourth cash down). The assignee of the Williams & Schulbach bid appealed from the judgment of the District Court. In the decision of the United States Circuit Court of Appeals Fourth Circuit it is stated,

> "We entertain no doubt that Herd acquired, by his proposal to pay the sum of $75,525.00 accompanied by his readiness and ability to comply with the terms upon which bids were enacted by the Trustee, the right to have his bid reported to the Referee, and unless an advanced bid was made, or the Referee was of the opinion that the land had not brought a fair price, to have the sale confirmed to him. It is well settled that the Trustee is, in the absence of any controlling reason to the contrary, such as fraud, conceded, or probably manifest inability to comply with the terms of sale, bound to accept all bids and report the same to the Court. 17 Am. & Eng. Enc. 978. It is equally clear that the trustee had no right to demand that Herd disclose to him the names of the persons for whom he was acting. Conceding, however, *pro hoc vice* that he was entitled to do so, it was manifest that, when Herd, upon being told that his bid in a representative capacity could not be accepted, announced that he would thereafter bid for himself and upon his own responsibility was entitled to have his bid accepted."

Quoting further the Court says,

> "The effect of this order of the Referee was that Williams and Schmulbach were entitled to take the property at $75,500.00 unless Herd would pay $78,000.00, although he stood ready, willing and able to comply with his bid of $75,525.00. This was manifestly unjust and therefore erroneous." . . . "To the suggestion that by affirming the order of the judge, the estate will be subject to danger of losing the interest on the amount of the bid, the answer is manifest—this result is due to the improper course pursued by the Trustee in refusing to accept and report Herd's bid, the last and highest made."

This cited case is almost an exact parallel with the case now before this Court, Baruch bid $2250.00 (R 21). Prentice bid $2325.00 (R 14-15), a raise of $75.00 on a $2250.00 bid. The Trustee, informed by the Referee that he, the Referee, was rejecting the $2300.00 and $2325.00 bids, when asked for his opinion, concurred in such rejection (R 15-16). The Trustee and Referee agreed that an upset bid of $2475.00 must be made to be considered (R 15-16) thereby depriving Prentice of the right to purchase the property on like terms with the Baruch Company but at the offered price of $75.00 more than the Baruch offer, and depriving the creditors of $75.00.

It Was an Abuse of Discretion for the Referee To Demand an Upset Bid of $2475.00 Payable Immediately

The Referee is bound to accept the largest and highest sum bid.

> WILLIAMS—COAL CITY HOUSE FURNISHINGS COMPANY v. HOGUE, Supra;
> KIMMEL v. CROCKER, Supra.

The Referee and the Trustee Erred in Refusing To Accept All Bids Offered

The Referee and the Trustee erred and it constituted an abuse of discretion to refuse to accept the highest bid and in requiring that one bidder (Baruch) post a 10% deposit and another bidder (Prentice) deposit a certified check for 100% of his bid.

> WILLIAMS—COAL CITY HOUSE FURNISHINGS COMPANY v. HOGUE, Supra;
> WOLKE LEAD BATTERY CO., 294 Fed. 511;
> COULTER v. BLIEDEN, 104 Fed. (2nd) 29-34.

In Coulter v. Blieden the Court stated:

> "In bankruptcy the chief purpose is the protection of the interests of creditors."

The record here clearly indicates that the interests of the creditors "went by the Board" when the sale was confirmed to Baruch at $75.00 less than the Prentice bid (R 14).

In re Wolke Lead Batteries Company, the Court after reviewing the question of whether an offer to bid $13,000.00 on a property on which the highest bid previously received had been $12,000.00 was advantageous enough to the creditors to warrant the expenses of holding a resale, states:

> "The advance bid (of $13,000.00) offered by Knight was sufficiently substantial in amount to insure against increased costs and present a reasonable possibility of securing for the creditors, the protection of whose interest is the chief purpose of bankruptcy proceeding, the real value of the bankrupt's property."

In the instant case there would have been no additional expense involved save that of drawing a new confirmation of sale in favor of Prentice in lieu of the confirmation of sale to Baruch which had been drawn and signed prior to the advertised time of the sale (R 54-55).

The District Court Erred in Considering Statements Contained in the Referee's Certificate on Review

The unsupported statement of Baruch re the expenditures of $125.00 prior to confirmation of sale should not have been considered by the District Court.

F. R. C. P. Rule 43 (A);
C. C. P. 1867;
C. C. P. 1869.

Even had the statement so made been under oath and/or supported by receipts or other form of written evidence it still should have had no bearing on the decision of the Court.

The District Court Erred and It Was an Abuse of Discretion To Confirm the Order of the Referee

The order of the Referee being in error it follows that the order of the District Court sustaining the Referee was likewise in error.

CURIN v. NOURSE, 66 Fed. (2nd) 137;
COULTER v. BLIEDEN, 104 Fed. (2nd) 29-34;
KIMMEL v. CROCKER, 72 Fed. 599;
WILLIAMS—COAL CITY HOUSE FURNISHINGS CO. v. HOGUE, 197 Fed. 1;
WOLKE LEAD BATTERY CO., 294 Fed. 511.

SUMMARY

This Appellant feels that this record shows an arbitrary abuse of discretion both on the part of the Trustee, the Referee and the District Court. Appellant in all good faith journeyed to Santa Ana on the day appointed and in all good faith bid on the real property that had on two separate dates been advertised. The arbitrary action of the Trustee and Referee in refusing to consider this Appellant's bid unless it was in an amount arbitrarily fixed by the Referee was clearly error and the citations given herein will, it is believed, convince this Court that the orders complained of should be reversed and an order issue to confirm the sale to the Appellant.

There is no question raised in the record of the ability of Prentice to pay for the property. Furthermore as proof of his good faith Prentice did on April 15, 1943, deposit with the District Court a certified check in the sum of $233.00 made payable to L. Boteler, Trustee and Ben E. Tarver, Referee, as a deposit to guarantee to the Estate, the Trustee thereof, the Referee, and to the Court, that this Appellant will purchase this property if this Court grants Appellant's prayer and confirms the sale of the subject property to him (R 47-48).

Wherefore, it is respectfully submitted that in justice and equity this Court should reverse the order of the District Court and that an order should issue confirming the sale of the subject property to this Appellant.

Respectfully submitted,

B. H. PRENTICE,
In Pro Per.

AFFIDAVIT OF MAILING

STATE OF CALIFORNIA,
County of Los Angeles,—SS.

INEZ PATTERSON, being first duly sworn, says: That affiant is a citizen of the United States and a resident of the County of Los Angeles; that affiant is over the age of eighteen years and is not a party to the within and above entitled action; that affiant's residence address is 2911 Gage Ave., Huntington Park, Calif. That on the 22nd day of September, A. D., 1943, affiant served the within Appellant's Opening Brief on the Counsel for Appellee in said action, by placing 3 true copies thereof in an envelope addressed to Craig & Weller—Thomas S. Tobin at the business address of said Counsel, as follows: Craig & Weller—Thomas S. Tobin—817 Board of Trade Building, 111 West 7th St., Los Angeles, California, and by then sealing said envelope and depositing the same, with postage thereon fully prepaid, in the United States Post Office at South Gate, California. That there is delivery service by United States mail at the place so addressed, there is a regular communication by mail between the place of mailing and the place so addressed.

INEZ PATTERSON.

Subscribed and sworn to before me this
22nd day of September, 1943.
(SEAL) N. FISHER,
Notary Public in and for said
County and State.

No. 10497

IN THE

nited States Circuit Court of Appeals

FOR THE NINTH CIRCUIT

. H. PRENTICE,

Appellant,

vs.

. BOTELER, Trustee in Bankruptcy of the Estate of DR. W. J. ROSS COMPANY, a Corporation, Bankrupt,

Appellee.

APPELLEE'S BRIEF.

CRAIG & WELLER,
By THOMAS S. TOBIN,
817 Board of Trade Bldg.,
111 West Seventh Street,
Los Angeles, California,
Attorneys for Appellee.

Parker & Baird Company, Law Printers, Los Angeles.

TOPICAL INDEX.

TABLE OF AUTHORITIES CITED.

No. 10497

IN THE

United States Circuit Court of Appeals

FOR THE NINTH CIRCUIT

B. H. Prentice,

Appellant,

vs.

L. Boteler, Trustee in Bankruptcy of the Estate of Dr. W. J. Ross Company, a Corporation, Bankrupt,

Appellee.

APPELLEE'S BRIEF.

An examination of the printed Transcript of Record on appeal will disclose that this appellant has incorporated therein a great deal of unnecessary matter, whether with the idea in the event of reversal, of incorporating a lot of unnecessary costs in the cost judgment, or whether with the idea of confusing the Court on the record, we do not know. However, we wish to call the Court's attention to a great deal of irrelevant and extraneous matter, which this Appellant has caused to be printed after omitting all of the important jurisdictional foundations in his original designation, requiring us to file a counter designation of the jurisdictional portions of the record. [Tr. p. 82.]

We wish to call the Court's attention particularly to the Points and Authorities in support of Petition to Review Order Confirming Sale of Real Property [Tr. pp. 33-39], and Peitioner's Statement of Facts in Lieu of Reporter's Transcript [Tr. pp. 39-47], which the Referee refused to sign, also, the document designated as Deposit to Guarantee to Estate Better Price for the Sale of Certain Real Property, which indicates on its face that the deposit was not made until nineteen days after the sale and sixteen days after the Order of Confirmation also the Notice of Motion to Amend Referee's Certificate on Review. [Tr. pp. 51-59.] Appellant has also printed a form of Order Dismissing Petition for Review and Affirming Order of Referee and Objections attached thereto beginning at Transcript page 60 and ending at page 66, which was not signed Judge McCormick at all, the actual Order Confirming the Referee's Findings beginning at Transcript page 67 and ending at page 71. Why appellant has seen fit to load this record with so much extraneous matter is beyond our comprehension.

The Facts.

Omitting the preliminaries to the sale in question in the interests of brevity, the Trustee of this estate had in his possession a piece of real property, substantially encumbered, and of which he was anxious to dispose. Upon due and proper notice to creditors, and after a creditor's meeting, he obtained an Order on July 20, 1942, which, among other things, authorized him to sell this real property *at private sale*. [Tr. p. 20.] A period of a little over seven months elapsed before the Trustee was able to negotiate even a private sale of this property. When the opportunity finally presented itself, he was fortunate in being able to negotiate a sale with the Baruch Corporation for the sum of $2,250.00, which he represented to the Court in his Return of Sale as constituting the full value of the right, title and interest of the bankrupt estate in and to the real property in question. [Tr. p. 27.] Hearing on the confirmation of the private sale to the Baruch Company was set before Referee Ben Tarver at Santa Ana on March 10, 1943 at ten o'clock A. M. This appellant appeared at the hearing on confirmation of the sale to the Baruch Corporation together with one, T. H. Clements, attempted to raise the purchase price negotiated between the Trustee and the Baruch Corporation by the sum of Seventy Five Dollars, after the Referee had announced that no raises would be permitted of an amount less than 10% of the purchase price of $2,250.00 negotiated between the Baruch Corporation and the Trustee.

In discussing the facts behind this case, we are relying on the certificate on review prepared by the Referee himself, and not on the *ex parte* statements of appellant as to what the record should be or the affidavit of T. H. Clements, some of the statements contained therein shading the truth, to say the least.

The Referee refusing to consider any raises of the purchase price amounting to less than 10% by reason of the fact that the purchaser, the Baruch Corporation, relying on the confirmation of the Return of Sale of the Trustee for the full value of the property in question, had gone ahead and expended $75.00 for surveying the property and expended other amounts thereon making a total of $125.00 [Tr. p. 18], declined to consider the small advance of $75.00 offered by Prentice. Prentice thereupon fixed up some kind of a check or voucher, the character of which the Referee was unable to determine "as it was so crudely made out" [Tr. p. 14] and proceeded to confirm the sale to the Baruch Corporation. This was on March 10, 1943 and the formal Order confirming the sale was drawn, signed and filed on March 16, 1942. [Tr. p. 30.] After the ten days to take a review from the Referee's Order had expired this appellant tedered a cashier's check or bank money order, in the sum of $233.00, drawn on the California Bank, to the Referee, the check being made payable to both him and the Trustee. [Tr. p. 49.] On the same day, March 29, 1943, more than ten days after the entry of the Order of the Referee, appellant filed a Petition for Review. [Tr. p. 70.] On April 24, 1943, he obtained an *ex parte* order from Judge McCormick extending his time to review the Referee's Order to March 31, 1943 "without prejudice to the assertion by any party of any applicable rights." [Tr. p. 70.] On argument on review, the Order of the Referee was affirmed by the District Court, followed by this appeal.

Statutory Provisions.

Section 39c of the National Bankruptcy Act (11 U. S. C. A., Sec. 67c) reads as follows:

> "A person aggrieved by an order of a referee may, within ten days after the entry thereof or within such extended time as the court may for cause shown allow, file with the referee a petition for review of such order by a judge and serve a copy of such petition upon the adverse parties who were represented at the hearing. Such petition shall set forth the or-

der complained of and the alleged errors in respect thereto. Upon application of any party in interest, the execution or enforcement of the order complained of may be suspended by the court upon such terms as will protect the rights of all parties in interest."

Section 70f of the National Bankruptcy Act (11 U. S. C. A., Sec. 110f) in so far as material here, reads as follows:

"Real and personal property shall, when practicable, be sold subject to the approval of the court. It shall not be sold otherwise than subject to the approval of the court for less than 75 per centum of its appraised value. * * *"

Section 24a of the National Bankruptcy Act, in so far as material here, reads as follows:

"The Circuit Courts of Appeals of the United States * * * are hereby invested with appellate jurisdiction from the several courts of bankruptcy, in their respective jurisdictions in proceedings in bankruptcy, either interlocutory or final, and in controversies arising in proceedings in bankruptcy, to review, affirm, revise, or reverse, both in matters of law and in matters of fact: * * * Provided Further, That when any order, decree, or judgment involves less than $500, an appeal therefrom may be taken only upon allowance of the Appellate Court."

ARGUMENT.

Points and Authorities.

The Appellee respectfully submits that the Orders of the lower Courts should be affirmed and this appeal dismissed for the following reasons:

First: That the Petition for Review was not filed within ten days after the entry of the Referee's Order and the Order of the District Court made on April 24, 1943, almost a month after the Petition for Review had been filed, did not attempt to validate petitioner's failure to observe the statutory limitation on when a Petition for Review must be filed.

Second: That the amount involved in this appeal is the difference between the purchase price agreed to be paid by the Baruch Corporation for the property and the attempted increase of the same at the time of confirmation by this appellant in the amount of $75.00. That, therefore, this appeal is one allowable only by the Circuit Court of Appeals, as a matter of discretion.

Third: That in refusing to upset a private sale for the full value of the property negotiated by the Trustee with a good faith purchaser for a nominal increase, first at $50.00 and then at $75.00, the Referee exercised a sound judicial discretion, which should not be disturbed under the circumstances, and more so because this discretion was affirmed and approved by the District Judge.

We shall first address ourselves to the question of whether or not the Petition for Review was filed in time.

The Order of the Referee confirming the sale of real property was signed and entered by him on March 16, 1943. [Tr. p. 30.] The announcement of his intention to confirm and to make an Order accordingly, was made by the Referee in open court with appellant present at the time of the rejection of his bid. [Tr. p. 16.] Five or six days later, Mr. Prentice, the petitioner, was in the Referee's office and spent about an hour copying from the records in regard to the sale and confirmation thereof, in question here. [Tr. p. 18.] The Petition for Review was not filed until March 29, 1943, thirteen days after the entry of the Order. [Tr. p. 26; Referee's Certificate on Review, pp. 18-19.] On April 24, 1943, long after the Referee had certified the record up to the District Court [Tr. pp. 18-19], this appellant obtained an *ex parte* Order from Judge McCormick extending his time to review to March 31, 1943, "without prejudice to the assertion by any party of any applicable rights."

We respectfully submit that our right to move to dismiss this belated review had already accrued by reason of the petition not being filed until thirteen days after the entry of the Order. (Nat'l. Bankruptcy Act, Sec. 39c.)

In connection with the appeal taken to this Court, we submit that this is an appeal of a matter the allowance of which is discretionary with the Appellate Court, in view of the fact that the amount in controversy between the Appellant, the Trustee and the Baruch Corporation is represented by the difference in their bids or the sum of $75.00.

Prior to the enactment of the 1938 Bankruptcy Act, a great deal of confusion existed with regard to what form of appeals should be allowed by the Circuit Court of Appeals and what forms of appeals were allowable as a matter of right by the District Court. Controversies in bankruptcy, as such, were appealable only with certain exceptions, as a matter of discretion to be exercised by the Circuit Court of Appeals. Under Section 25a of the Bankruptcy Act, judgments allowing or refusing a debt or claim of $500.00 or over were appealable as a matter of right. The confusion existing as a result of these two sections of the Bankruptcy Act resulted in many appeals being dismissed as having been taken the wrong way, or in an excess of precaution, attorneys in doubtful cases appealed both ways; one of the two being invariably dismissed at the time the case was decided. The 1938 amendment, in an effort to do away with all of this confusion, has grouped all forms of appeal together, with one exception, that being that when any Order, Decree or Judgment involves less than $500.00, an appeal therefrom may be taken only upon allowance of the Appellate Court. To date, there has been but little construction of this new statute.

In *England v. Ducasse,* 104 Fed. (2d) 760, a Trustee in bankruptcy petitioned this Court for allowance of an appeal from an Order of the District Court, which reversed an Order of a Referee whereby a claim in the sum of $2,273.83 was allowed in the amount of $427.57, the balance being rejected. This Court held that this did not involve an amount less than $500.00, but actually involved the sum of $1846.26, being the difference between the amount claimed and the amount theretofore allowed, and that inasmuch as it involved over $500.00, the proposed appeal was not allowable by this Court. See, also, *In the Matter of Seville Court Apartments Building Corporation, Debtor,* C. C. A., 7th Cir., 134 Fed. (2d) 232, 53 Am. B. R. (N. S.) 84.

The reason for the $500.00 limitation on appeals as a matter of right is well set forth in the opinion of Judge Van Devanter in *Gray v. Grand Forks Mercantile Co.* (C. C. A., 8th Cir.), 138 Fed. 344, 14 Am. B. R. 780:

> "The purpose of the Congress in restricting the right of appeal was evidently to avoid inconvenience, delay, and expense to claimants and bankrupt estates which would be disproportionate to the amount in controversy. When read with due regard to this purpose, the restriction plainly has reference, not to the amount of the original claim, but to the amount of the allowance or rejection; that is, to the amount which will be put in controversy by the appeal. *Hilton v. Dickinson,* 108 U. S. 165; *Dows v. Johnson,* 110 U. S. 223."

We respectfully submit that the controversy here involves a difference of $75.00 in two bids for a piece of property and that the appeal is one of the type described in the foregoing authorities as involving a trifling amount.

Confirmation of a Private Sale of a Bankrupt's Property, Particularly Where the Purchase Price Constitutes 100% of its Value, Is a Matter of Judicial Discretion to be Exercised by the Referee With Which Discretion an Appellate Court Will Not Interfere Except Where it Is Evident That There Has Been a Clear Abuse Thereof.

Under Section 70f of the 1938 Bankruptcy Act (11 U. S. C. A., 110f) real and personal property belonging to a bankrupt estate shall be sold, subject to the approval of the court. It may not be sold otherwise than subject to the approval of the court for less than 75% of its appraised value. In the case at bar, the Trustee in his Return of Sale reported under oath that the purchase price constituted not—75%—*but the full value* of the right, title and interest of the bankrupt estate in the real property in question. [Tr. p. 27.] In an effort to overcome the force of this return at full value price, the appellant has printed at page 8 of the transcript a part of the schedules of the bankrupt in which it listed this property in the bankruptcy proceeding at its estimated value of $5,734.09. The Trustee, after the property had been duly appraised, found it to be actually worth $2,250.00, which the Baruch Corporation agreed to pay for it. In connection with the Debtor's valuation at $5,734.09, we must bear in mind that the bankrupt was seeking to put over a reorganization and that it was to his interest to inflate the assets as much as possible. The Court will note that in his Petition for Reorganization, Dr. Ross claimed to have machinery, supplies, equipment and boats worth $45,000.00 or more, a good will capable of producing $350,000.00 or more per year, and other very valuable assets as against approximately $69,-

000.00 of liabilities. Nevertheless, the bankrupt was found to be insolvent by the court and was adjudicated a bankrupt in spite of its inflated valuations.

It will be noted that the adjudication took place on June 17, 1942. [Tr. p. 10.] The Trustee qualified on July 8, 1942 [Tr. p. 11], and obtained his Order authorizing the sale of this real property on July 20, 1942. [Tr. pp. 20-21.] He did not obtain a purchaser even under the flexible provisions of the Order of Sale of Real Property until February 25, 1943, when he made his Return of Sale at the full value thereof to the Baruch Corporation. [Tr. pp. 21-24.] Hearing on confirmation of this 100% private sale was set for ten in the morning of March 10, 1943 before Referee Tarver at Santa Ana. Apparently, through inadvertence, the Trustee caused or permitted a notice to appear in the advertising columns of the Los Angeles Daily Journal, a legal publication of Los Angeles County, of the hearing on the sale. In the meantime, as certified by the Referee, the Baruch people had expended $125.00 in surveying and improvements on the property in question, rightfully assuming that inasmuch as they were paying 100% of its value for it, the sale would unquestionably be confirmed. This appellant for some reason beyond our comprehension, appeared at the hearing on the confirmation of the sale and attempted to upset it by making a small increase over the purchase price at which the Trustee had sold the property to the Baruch Corporation. Whether he intended to upset their purchase and hold them up for a greatly increased price, we do not know, but his conduct in connection with this matter would indicate, to our way of thinking, some sinister or ulterior motive.

In support of his alleged Statement of Facts, this appellant has presented in the Court below, an affidavit signed by one T. H. Clements, which has been brought up as a part of the record here at page 54, *et seq.* In a desperate effort to bolster up this appellant's cause, Clements has made some intemperate and, we are sorry to say, untrue statements in this affidavit. Clements states under oath that he entered Referee Tarver's office at 9:40 A. M. the day of the hearing and saw on the Referee's table *a signed confirmation of the sale to the Baruch Corporation having a consideration of $2,250.00* (italics ours). That this statement is manifestly untrue is evidenced at pages 26 to 30 of the transcript. An examination of the Order Confirming Sale of Real Property shows that it was signed on March 16, 1943 by Referee Tarver and filed the same day. Furthermore, the Order recites in the body thereof, the appearance of Prentice and his attempt to upset the sale. Manifestly, this Order could not have been prepared and signed in advance of the sale as Clements swears in his affidavit to be the fact. As a matter of fact, the Order was not prepared for several days after the sale, yet Clements swears it was signed by the Referee before the matter was called, a manifestly false statement. Clements also states in his affidavit that the Referee stated that he was going to sell the property in question at auction. The Referee in his certificate [Tr. p. 14] definitely certifies that he did not auction or state that he would sell the property at auction or that he would auction the same.

In his affidavit at page 57, Clements makes the following statement:

> "The Court then asked if there were any other bids, and this affiant did not make any further bids, it

> being the opinion of this affiant that this was a *rigged sale* and no one other than the Baruch Corporation was going to get the property regardless of what happened." (Italics ours.)

In other words, Mr. Clements accuses the Referee, an arm of the United States District Court, the Trustee, a bonded officer of the court, and the Baruch Corporation of being in a conspiracy to "rig" a sale simply because the Referee exercised his discretion in requiring that anyone seeking to upset a 100% private sale would have to raise it at least 10%. Had Mr. Prentice seen fit to make a 10% raise, the property would, no doubt, have been sold to him. Had he attempted to raise the sale price by the sum of fifty cents and his higher offer been turned down, he would still have complained.

We respectfully submit that in view of the expenditures made in good faith by the only prospective purchaser which the Trustee had been able to secure at private sale over a period of six months and the favorable reporting of that sale to the Referee by the Trustee and no objections being made by any creditors of this bankrupt, the Referee was vested with a sound discretion to require that any outsider coming in and seeking to upset the private sale negotiated and nearing completion be required to make a definite substantial raise of the purchaser's offer before the Court would entertain it.

Remington on Bankruptcy, Volume 6, Section 2565 at page 53 says:

> "In general, however, the court will be very cautious with respect to upsetting sales, for the contrary practice tends to drive honest business away from the bidding."

In *Century Motor Truck Co. v. Noyes,* cited in support of this statement, the Circuit Court of Appeals for the First Circuit in condoning the refusal to confirm a sale which was made for less than 75% of the appraised value of the property and after pointing out that in such cases, the District Court, as well as the Referee had discretion said:

> "Our decision in this case should not be taken as an approval of a general practice of upsetting sales which have taken place in the regular course of winding up a bankrupt estate. *Jacobsohn v. Larkey* (C. C. A., 3d Cir.); 245 Fed. 538; 40 Am. B. R. 563. This practice was long ago found in England to be an improvident one as it discouraged bidding at sales. *Graffam v. Burgess,* 117 U. S. 180; *White v. Wilson,* 14 Ves. 151."

In *Jacobsohn v. Larkey,* 245 Fed. 538-41; 40 Am. B. R. 563 at 566, the Circuit Court of Appeals for the Third Circuit says:

> "After much experience in scrutinizing bidding at judicial sales, courts now uniformly hold that the mere offer to pay more than the price bid is not a substantial ground for setting aside a sale, recognizing that nothing will more certainly tend to discourage and prevent bidding than a judicial determination that the highest bidder may be deprived of the advantage of his accepted bid by an offer of another person, subsequently made, to bid higher on resale. *Morrisse v. Inglis,* 46 N. J. Esq. 306, 19 Atl.

16; *In re Metallic Specialty Mfg. Co.,* 193 Fed. 300; *In re Shapiro,* 154 Fed. 673. * * *

When in a given case a price is grossly inadequate and when upon that ground confirmation should be refused, are matters within the judgment and discretion of the tribunal ordering the sale. When a trial tribunal orders a judicial sale subject to its confirmation under authority expressly requiring of it the exercise of discretion in approving or setting aside the sale (Bankruptcy Act, Sec. 70b), an appellate tribunal will not reverse its discretion by substituting its own nor will it otherwise disturb or interfere with its exercise so long as it does not amount to an abuse of discretion. *In re Shea* (C. C. A., 1st Cir.), 126 Fed. 153; 11 Am. B. R., 207."

In the *Matter of Orpheum Circuit, Inc.,* 20 Fed. Supp. 101; 30 Am. B. R., 131, the District Court said:

"The question is whether the referee's orders, on the proof before him, were correct. The entire bankruptcy proceeding having been committed to the charge of the referee, the power of this court is strictly one of review by an appellate judge. It has not the power to exercise an independent discretion in the matter. *In re Realty Foundation* (C. C. A., 2nd Cir.), 75 Fed. (2d) 286; 28 Am. B. R. (NS) 76."

Furthermore, any alleged irregularities (which, however, we do not concede here) in the sale of property in a bankruptcy proceeding are overcome by the confirmation of the sale by the Referee. See *Robertson v. Howard,* 229 U. S. 254; 30 Am. B. R., 611.

Conclusion.

The issue involved in this case is really one of public policy. Property of a bankrupt estate may be disposed of in any one of several ways, all, however, under the immediate supervision and direction of the Referee. In one case, it may be deemed expedient to permit the Trustee to operate the business and sell the stock in trade and other assets of the bankrupt at retail, over the counter to the public. This may be done under an Order of the Referee authorizing the operation and continuance of the business. In other cases, it may be deemed expedient to employ an auctioneer and conduct a piecemeal or bulk sale of the assets of the bankrupt, such piecemeal or bulk sales after the auctioneer's hammer has fallen on the highest bid, to be submitted to the Referee for confirmation. Many times such auction sales are held in the Referee's Court with the Referee or Trustee acting as auctioneer and the Referee summarily confirming each sale as the highest competitive bid is accepted. The fourth method of liquidation and one which is discretionary if an auction sale is not deemed feasible, is the method that was pursued in this case, the Referee issuing a permissive Order after due notice to creditors and with their approval, authorizing the Trustee to sell the property of the bankrupt to a purchaser at private sale, subject to confirmation by the Referee after such sale has been negotiated. In the case at bar, after six or seven months of effort, the Trustee succeeded in finding a purchaser, the Baruch Corporation, whose plant, we believe, adjoins the property in question. It negotiated with the Trustee for purchase of the property and agreed to pay the full valuation for it. Nothing more fair to creditors could be asked for—and no creditors are complaining here. This appellant apparently figured he could go over to Santa Ana on the date when the confirmation of the sale was up for hearing and after the purchaser, in good faith, had expended funds on its purchase, which it had every good reason to believe would be confirmed, as it was paying 100% of the value of the property, and by a mere fifty or seventy-five dollars raise either deprive the purchaser of the fruits of its purchase or hold it up for a higher price than that which had been in good faith negotiated with the Trustee. Realizing that public policy required that private sales, when authorized by the Bankruptcy Court, should be accorded some stability and as a test of the good faith of this appellant, the Referee at the very onset of the proceedings announced that no raises of Baruch's purchase price would be entertained unless they amounted to at least 10% more. This we submit was a fair test of the adequacy of the purchase price offered to and accepted by the Trustee. If the property was worth 10% more than the $2,250.00 offered by the Baruch Corporation and accepted by the Trustee, then the Referee would have a reason to believe that for some reason the offer and accepted purchase price was substantially inadequate. Prentice stubbornly refused to accede to the 10% terms announced by the Referee before confirmation of the sale and we believe has spent a great deal more money than the proposed 10% in dragging this inconsequential matter from the Referee's Court up to this tribunal.

If this property had been sold at public auction and the Baruch Corporation had bid $2,250.00 and its bid had been raised at public auction by this appellant and the

Referee had refused to accept the raise, a different situation might present itself. However, as certified by the Referee, he expressly announced that the proceeding was not a public auction, in other words that it was merely the confirmation of a negotiated private sale and that no raises would be considered less than 10%. This announcement, no doubt, was made in order to give creditors an opportunity, if they so desired, to raise the bid 10%, if dissatisfied therewith. It is true that this appellant seeks to belie the Referee's own official certificate on review, but we submit that his *ex parte* statements of what occurred are of no value and should not be considered by this Court.

Mr. Boteler acts as Trustee in bankruptcy in numerous cases, as appears by the records of this Court on appeals in which Mr. Boteler, as Trustee, has been a party in the past. He has an interest in maintaining the stability of judicial sales in bankruptcy, where honestly negotiated. Counsel for the Trustee in this case are likewise counsel for trustees in bankruptcy in numerous cases and we, too, have an interest in maintaining the integrity and stability of judicial sales. We respectfully submit that the confirmation of this sale made by the Referee after statutory notice to creditors, and without objection on the part of any of them, and affirmed by the District Court should stand, as being within the lower Court's sound judicial discretion with which this Court should not interfere.

Dated: September 29th, 1943.

Respectfully submitted,

Craig & Weller,

By Thomas S. Tobin,

Attorneys for Appellee.

No. 10497

In the
United States
Circuit Court of Appeals
For the Ninth Circuit

B. H. PRENTICE,
Appellant,

vs.

L. BOTELER, Trustee in Bankruptcy of the estate of DR. W. J. ROSS COMPANY, a Corporation Bankrupt,
Appellee.

Appellant's Answering Brief

B. H. PRENTICE, in Pro Per
4705 Firestone Blvd.,
South Gate, California,
For Appellant.

CRAIG & WELLER,
THOMAS S. TOBIN,
817 Board of Trade Bldg.,
111 West Seventh Street,
Los Angeles, California,
For Appellee.

TOPICAL INDEX

TABLE OF AUTHORITIES CITED

Cases

Statutes

In the
United States
Circuit Court of Appeals
For the Ninth Circuit

B. H. PRENTICE, *Appellant,* vs. L. BOTELER, Trustee in Bankruptcy of the estate of DR. W. J. ROSS COMPANY, a Corporation Bankrupt, *Appellee.*	No. 10497

Appellant's Answering Brief

In view of the misstatements by counsel for Appellee as well as the insinuations respecting the motives of this appellant as contained in appellee's brief it becomes necessary to reply not only to the legal questions involved in the instant case, but also to the personal attack made on this appellant.

Possibly certain documents not vital to the record were included in appellant's designation of the Record on Appeal. Also apparently through the ignorance of this appellant certain essential documents of a jurisdictional nature were omitted from appellant's designation of contents of Record on Appeal.

However it would seem to this appellant that this Court in order to be fully acquainted with the facts should have before it all the record having any bearing on what transpired in the lower court.

Counsel objects to the inclusion in the record of Appellant's Points and Authorities in support of Petition to review Order Confirming sale of Real Property. (T. R., 33-39). It would seem necessary if this Court is to rule on the decision of the lower court that this appellant should inform this Court as to the grounds the original motion to the District Court was based upon.

Petitioner's statement of Facts in Lieu of Reporter's Transcript was a part of the record reviewed by the District Court and by the way, nowhere in the record does this appellant find any statement to the effect that the Referee "refused to sign" the petitioner's statement as is stated in appellee's brief (Pg. 2).

The document designated "Deposit to Guarantee to Estate Better Price for the sale of Certain Real Property" is in this appellant's opinion quite properly a part of the record in that it constituted the giving of notice to the District Court that this appellant was a bona fide purchaser who actually intended to complete the purchase of the property. Appellee's counsel would have this court believe that this appellant's acts in prosecuting this appeal were governed by "some sinister or ulterior motive" (appellee's Brief, Pg. 11), and his reason for attending the sale was to "either deprive the purchaser of the fruits of its purchase or hold it up for a higher price" (appellee's brief, Pg. 17). Counsel even goes so far as to state in his brief that the plant of the Baruch Corporation, he believes, adjoins the property in question (appellee's brief, Pg. 16). This one statement by the appellee is a fair sample of how carelessly the truth of the matter is stated by appellee. As a matter of fact the only plant that is adjacent to the property in question on the north side of Firestone Blvd., is a refinery situated on a five acre parcel of real property. Both this refinery and the five acre parcel of real property are owned outright by this appellant, which fact is well known to Mr. Baruch of the Baruch Corporation.

The Notice of Motion to Amend Referee's Certificate is a necessary part of the record unless this court declines to consider any other document except the Referee's Certificate on Review when going into the question of what transpired at the sale on March 10, 1943. That this Court would do so is hardly possible in view of the statement in the Referee's Certificate to the effect that the record as prepared is to the best recollection of the Referee and that no stenographer's report was taken or kept of the proceedings (R. 16-17). This certificate is dated April 13, 1943 (R. 19) some 33 days after the sale was held. As opposed to this is the statement contained in Mr. Clements' affidavit to the effect that "Immediately after leaving the court room (of the Referee) both Mr. Prentice and this affiant (Mr. Clements) made copious notes of what had there transpired, to which notes this affiant has repeatedly referred in preparing this affidavit and the statements made in this affidavit conform to the information as set forth in the said notes" (R. 57-58).

There are so many inconsistent statements in the Referee's Certificate on Review that it certainly raises the question of which statements are correct and which are in error.

For instance the Referee states Mr. Clements represents the Smileage Co., Ltd. (R. 13). Mr. Clements under oath states "that he is not now nor has he at any previous time ever been a representative of, or had any connection with, the Smileage Company or the Smileage Co., Ltd., or any partnership or firm having a similar name" (R. 54). This is a matter of some importance which this appellant believes this Court can decide as to which of the statements are true and which error. And while we are speaking of Mr. Clements' affidavit wherein he states on oath that at 9:40 A. M. on the date of sale he "noticed on the large table adjacent to which he seated himself a signed confirmation of the sale to the Baruch Corporation having a consideration of Twenty-two Hundred Fifty ($2250.00) Dollars, of the property which was advertised to be sold at 10 A. M. that day" (R. 54-55). Appellee states that this was manifestly untrue inasmuch as the confirmation of sale was not signed until March 16, 1943 and furthermore the Order recites in the body thereof the appearance of Prentice and "his attempt to upset the sale" (appellee's brief, Pg. 12). Might it not be possible that Mr. Clements did see a signed confirmation of sale as he states and that when it became apparent that there was to be some controversy over the conduct of the sale that this confirmation of sale was laid aside and a new order drawn and signed and filed?

Counsel also objects to the printing in the record of an Order Dismissing Petition for Review and Affirming Order of Referee as prepared by Counsel for appellee and served on this appellant. This last document "which was not signed by Judge McCormick at all" (appellee's brief, pg. 2) contained among other mis-statements the following: "The Court further concludes that this Petition for Review was not filed within the time prescribed by Sec. 38-C of the National Bankruptcy Act, and that no extension of time to file said petition for review was obtained" (R. 63). Bearing in mind that this quoted paragraph was a part of appellee's document it is not surprising that Judge McCormick did not sign it and that another and very different "order Confirming Referee's Finding" was signed by Judge McCormick (R. 67-71) in lieu thereof. There was no intention or desire on the part of this appellant to "load this record." Appellant's only wish was and is to present fully and fairly the facts involved that this Court may decide the issue.

The appellee states in his brief, "However, as certified by the Referee, he expressly announced that the proceeding was not a public auction, in other words that it was merely the confirmation of a negotiated private sale and that no raise would be considered less than 10%. This announcement, no doubt, was made in order to give creditors an opportunity, if they so desired, to raise the bid 10% if dissatisfied therewith" (appellee's brief, p. 18). This is far, far from the truth and one has but to look at the Referee's Certificate on Review to learn the true facts about this particular phase of the case. The Referee's Certificate on Review has this to say, "Whereupon the Referee asked for higher bids on the property set forth in the Return of Sale but said he would not consider any bid that was not at least 10% higher than the $2250.00 bid by the purchaser named in the return of sale" (R. 14) and also speaking of who was present at the sale the Referee's Certificate on Review says: "that there were present the following persons: Mr. Baruch representing the successful bidder, to wit, the Baruch Corporation; Mr. Burr H. Prentice and Mr. Clements representing the Smileage Company, Ltd." (R. 13). This would seem to dispose of appellee's thought that the auction was for the purpose of allowing creditors to bid the property up if they so desired. There were no creditors present at the sale. While it may be immaterial this appellant has been informed by counsel for the Baruch Corporation that Mr. Baruch was not present at the sale but did have a representative there. Apparently if this be true the Referee was in error as to just who was there representing the Baruch Corporation.

THE FACTS

The order authorizing the trustee to sell the property in question was worded as follows:

> "It is ordered that the trustee herein be, and he is hereby authorized and directed to sell, at private sale or at public auction, to the highest and best bidder or bidders therefor, the real property —(and here follows the legal description of the property in question)—*any sale of said real property is to be made subject to the confirmation of this court.*" (Italics ours.)

If the Trustee did during a seven months' period actually make an honest endeavor to sell the property, it is strange that he did not contact this appellant who owns and operates the refinery adjacent to the property in question. Counsel states that the trustee "was fortunate in being able to negotiate a sale with the Baruch Corporation." (Appellee's Brief, p. 2.) Possibly so.

The Petition to review Referee's Order was mailed in Los Angeles on March 26, 1943, and was addressed to the Referee at his office address in Santa Ana (R. 32). The Referee in his Certificate on Review states that he did not receive the document until March 29th, although it was postmarked in Los Angeles March

26th (R. 32). As to why there were three days consumed in the transmission of this registered letter a distance of thirty-five miles is a mystery to this appellant. However the facts speak for themselves. When this appellant learned of this delay a motion was promptly made that the time wherein to file Petition to Review Referee's Order be extended to March 31, 1943, which motion was granted by Judge McCormick (R. 70). There is ample authority for the granting of such order.

THE DISTRICT COURT HAD AUTHORITY TO EXTEND TIME WHEREIN TO FILE PETITION TO REVIEW REFEREE'S ORDER.

Thummess v. Von Hoffman, 109 Fed. 2nd 291, at 292-293.

In the case cited the ten day period following the entry of the referee's order expired without a petition for review having been filed or an extension of time for such filing having been made—The lower court entered an order extending the time for the filing of the petition to review for five days. From the order extending the time to file the Trustee appealed. In the decision of the United States Circuit Court of Appeals, Third Circuit, it is stated:

> "The question here is simply one of legislative intent, and as to that, we are of the opinion that the court below acted within its power when, for cause shown, it extended the time for the filing of a petition for review after the expiration of the

ten days following the entry of the order of the referee."

The case here cited is an exact parallel with the case now before this Court. There was never any question raised as to the sufficiency of the motion or the affidavit supporting the same. Therefore we have simply the question of whether the District Court had authority to extend the time wherein to file.

See:

In re Albert, 122 Fed. 2nd 393-394.

In this quoted case, through an oversight, an attorney for a creditor failed to file a petition to review a referee's order within 10 days after the entry of such order. The appellant moved for an order extending the time wherein to file. The judge denied the motion. An appeal was taken and in the decision of the United States Circuit Court of Appeals, Second District, it is stated:

> "We think the statutory limitation of ten days is not a condition upon jurisdiction and that in the exercise of a sound discretion an extension may be granted though not applied for until after the time for filing a petition to review has run."

The order of the District Court refusing to grant an extension of time wherein to file the Petition to Review Referee's Order was reversed.

See:

Sec. 39, sub. C, of the Chandler Act; 11 U.S.C.A. 67

provides:

"A person aggrieved by an order of a referee may within ten days after the entry thereof, *or within such extended time as the court for cause shown allow,* (italics ours) file with the Referee a petition for review of such order by a judge. . . ."

In the instant case the time wherein to file was extended by the District Judge—No question is presented as to whether the cause shown was good or not. It is therefore presumed that it was good.

THE AMOUNT INVOLVED IS NOT LESS THAN $500.00

Gage v. Pumpelly and others, 108 U. S. 164-165.

In this quoted case a motion was made in the U. S. Circuit Court, Northern District of Illinois, to dismiss for want of jurisdiction. In the original suit there was involved a tax bill for $1120.79 and costs of suit. There was some question as to the value of the property involved. Several affidavits stated the value of the property to be less than the statutory requirements of $5000.00 and several affidavits were to the effect that the value of the property exceeded $5000.00. In the decision of the U. S. Supreme Court, Mr. Chief Justice Waite says:

> "Many of the affidavits sent up with the transcript stated distinctly that the value of the property, which is the matter in dispute, exceeds $5000.00. When an appeal has been allowed after a contest as to the value of the matter in dispute, and there is evidence in the record which sustains our jurisdiction, the appeal will not be dismissed simply because upon examination of all the affidavits we may be of the opinion that possibly the estimates acted upon below were too high. There is no such decided preponderance of the evidence in the case against jurisdiction as to make it our duty to dismiss the appeal which has been allowed —Motion denied."

In the above quoted case the original sum involved was $1120.79 plus costs. At no place in the decision of the Supreme Court is any mention made of this sum as having any bearing on the question of jurisdiction. The only question raised was, What is the value of the property?

In the instant case the question of jurisdiction does not hinge on the $50.00 or $75.00 difference between the various bids. The question is, Does the Value of the property involved exceed $500.00? The answer is unquestionably, Yes it does. The value as established by the trustee's Return of Sale of Real Property (R. 21) is $2250.00. This sum the Trustee swears is the full value of the estate's interest in the real property (R. 23). This appellant contends the value is in excess of that sum: to wit, $2325.00. In any event there can be no question but that the value exceeds $500.00.

See:

England v. Ducasse, 104 Fed. (2) 760.

In this quoted case a claim in the total sum of $2273.83 was presented and which claim was allowed by the court in the sum of $427.57. There is no question but that the difference between the two sums would be the amount involved.

In the instant case, however, there is no question of a partition of the real property. Either this appellant is entitled to be adjudged the purchaser of the entire property at the offered price of $2325.00, or he is entitled to nothing. It follows, therefore, that the amount involved is the value of the title to the real property, namely $2325.00. In all cases cited on this point by appellee the items involved in the appeal constituted monies. There was no question raised in any cited case as to the jurisdiction of this Court to decide whether the lower court erred in deciding who should have title to real property valued at in excess of $2000.00.

There seems to be some misapprehension in appellee's mind as to the sale of the property.

IT WAS ERROR FOR THE COURT TO CONFIRM THE SALE OF THE PROPERTY TO THE LOWEST OF THREE COMPARABLE BIDS.

Prentice was a bidder at the sale. At the time he bid for the property there had been no confirmation of sale to Baruch Co.—Their position was that they had submitted a written offer to buy supported by a 10% deposit. Before the sale was confirmed to them Prentice raised the bid and likewise supported his bid with a 10% deposit. This is not a situation where after confirmation of a sale Prentice attempted to have the sale upset so that he could bid more than the sale price. As the highest bidder he was entitled to purchase the property. This point was covered in Appellant's Opening Brief.

Neither is there any question raised by Appellant of the adequacy of the price.

There is no question raised as to irregularities in the lack of an appraisal or in any published notice of the sale of the property.

This appellant repeats: The sole and only question raised is "Was it an abuse of discretion for the referee to accept the lowest of three comparable bids for the property."

CONCLUSION

Appellant finds very little pertinent matter in appellee's brief. There is a great deal of space devoted to an attempt to vilify the character of both Mr. Prentice and Mr. Clements and to call this Court's attention to how very interested Mr. Boteler, Mr. Craig, Mr. Weller and Mr. Tobin are in maintaining the stability of judicial sales in bankruptcy.

Possiby this is essential to the appellee's presentation of his case. Appellant however questions its necessity.

Respectfully submitted,

B. H. PRENTICE,
In Pro Per.

CPSIA information can be obtained
at www.ICGtesting.com
Printed in the USA
BVHW060835140119
537774BV00020B/809/P

9 781527 991620